CHRISTIAN
APOLOGETICS

CHRISTIAN APOLOGETICS

An Anthology of Primary Sources

Edited by KHALDOUN A. SWEIS and CHAD V. MEISTER

ZONDERVAN ACADEMIC

ZONDERVAN ACADEMIC

Christian Apologetics
Copyright © 2012 by Khaldoun A. Sweis and Chad V. Meister

Published in Grand Rapids, Michigan, by Zondervan. Zondervan is a registered trademark of The Zondervan Corporation, L.L.C., a wholly owned subsidiary of HarperCollins Christian Publishing, Inc.

Requests for information should be addressed to customercare@harpercollins.com.

Zondervan titles may be purchased in bulk for educational, business, fundraising, or sales promotional use. For information, please email SpecialMarkets@Zondervan.com.

ISBN 978-0-310-17337-3 (softcover)
ISBN 978-0-310-58968-6 (ebook)

Library of Congress Cataloging-in-Publication Data

Christian apologetics : an anthology of primary sources / edited by Khaldoun A. Sweis
   and Chad V. Meister.
       p. cm.
   Includes bibliographical references and index.
   ISBN 978-0-310-32533-8 (hardcover)
   1. Apologetics—History—Sources. I. Sweis, Khaldoun A., 1972- II. Meister, Chad V., 1965-.
BT1109.C56 2012
239—dc23   2011045222

Copyright and permission notices are found on pages 11–12.

Any Internet addresses (websites, blogs, etc.) and telephone numbers in this book are offered as a resource. They are not intended in any way to be or imply an endorsement by Zondervan, nor does Zondervan vouch for the content of these sites and numbers for the life of this book.

Cover design: Tammy Johnson
Cover photography: Bridgeman Art Library, Sijmen Hendriks Photography
Interior design: Beth Shagene

I dedicate this book to my lovely wife, Luciana, my beautiful daughter, AnaKaterina Cosette, and my amazing son, Daniel Zacharias. – K.S.

I dedicate this book to my parents, who continue to inspire me to think critically, carefully, and clearly and to respect and learn from those with whom I disagree. – C.M.

Contents

Acknowledgments

We would first like to express our appreciation and admiration for all the great Christian theologians and philosophers who have steadfastly defended the faith throughout the centuries. We stand on the shoulders of giants. There are many more who could be included in this book, and we are grateful for their important work in advancing the kingdom of God. We would also like to thank the following apologists for their insightful comments on this project: Paul Copan, William Lane Craig, Norman Geisler, Gary Habermas, J. P. Moreland, and Richard Swinburne. Their kind assistance and valuable input have made this book a much better volume than it would have been otherwise.

Special thanks are due to Verlyn Verbrugge for his guidance and careful eye to detail and to the entire Zondervan team for first-rate work on all dimensions of this project. Also, special thanks go to Carolyn Campbell and Stefanie Segovia for their excellent editing assistance with the book and especially with the indexes. Last, but certainly not least, we are grateful to Rhonda Hogan for her valorous efforts in obtaining permissions. Finally, we are thankful to God for the privilege of advancing the apologetics discussion through the construction of this book.

Permissions

Permissions are in the order that the articles appear in the book.

All articles that are not noted below are either within fair use guidelines or are common domain.

Founder of Christianity." *Truth Journal*. Essay modified and used by the kind permission of the author.

Eugene Carpenter. "Resources for Discovering the Literary, Conceptual, and Historical Context of the OT," in the *Journal of the International Society of Christian Apologetics*, Volume 2, No. 1, 2009. Used by the kind permission of the author and the journal.

Norman Geisler. "Miracles and Modern Scientific Thought." *Truth Journal* and *LeaderU*. Online at http://www.leaderu.com/truth/1truth19.html. Used by the kind permission of the author and website manager of *LeaderU*.

Richard Swinburne. *Is There a God?* Oxford: Oxford University Press, 1996, pp. 114–129. Reprinted with permission by Oxford University Press. All rights reserved.

Thomas Aquinas. *Summa Theologica*. Second and revised edition, 1920. III, Q. 53–59. Trans. by Fathers of the English Dominican Province. Online Edition. Copyright © 2008 by Kevin Knight. Available at http://www.newadvent.org/summa/. Used by permission.

John Warwick Montgomery, ed. *Evidence for Faith*. Plano, TX: Probe Books, 1991. Used by the kind permission of the author and the publisher.

Gary R. Habermas. "Experiences of the Risen Jesus: The Foundational Historical Issue in the Early Proclamation of the Resurrection." *Dialog: A Journal of Theology*, Vol. 45; No. 3 (Fall, 2006): 288–297. Used by the kind permission of the author and publisher.

William Lane Craig. "The Bodily Resurrection of Jesus," found online at http://www.leaderu.com/offices/billcraig/docs/bodily.html. Revised by and used with the kind permission of the author.

Thomas Aquinas. *Summa Contra Gentiles*, selections from Bk II: 68, 69, 79, 82, and *Summa Theologica*, 1: Q: 75 Ar: 2, 4. Online Edition. Copyright © 2008 by Kevin Knight. Available at http://www.newadvent.org/summa/. Used by permission.

J. P. Moreland. *Scaling the Secular City*. Grand Rapids: Baker Academic, a division of Baker Publishing Group, 1987. Used by the kind permission of the author and publisher.

Augustine. *Earlier Writings*, ed. John H. S. Burleigh. © 1953. Used in North America by permission of Westminster John Knox Press. www.wjkbooks.com.

Alvin Plantinga. *God, Freedom, and Evil*. © 1989. Grand Rapids: Eerdmans. Reprinted by permission of the publisher; all rights reserved.

John Hick. "An Irenaean Theodicy," from *Encountering Evil* by Stephen T. Davis. © 2001. Westminster John Knox Press. Used by permission of Westminster John Knox Press. www.wjkbooks.com.

Peter Kreeft. From *Making Sense out of Suffering*. © 1986 by Peter Kreeft. Reprinted with permission of St. Anthony Messenger Press, 28 W. Liberty St., Cincinnati, Ohio 45202. To order copies, call 1-800-488-0488 or visit Catalog.AmericanCatholic.org.

Marilyn McCord Adams. "Horrendous Evils and the Goodness of God," *Proceedings of the Aristotelian Society*, supplementary volume 63 (1989), pp. 297–310. Reprinted by courtesy of the Editor of the Aristotelian Society: © 1989.

John Polkinghorne. "God and Science." Taken from *God Is Great, God Is Good: Why Believing in God Is Reasonable and Responsible*, edited by William Lane Craig and Chad Meister. Copyright © 2009 by William Lane Craig and Chad Meister. Used by permission of InterVarsity Press, PO Box 1400, Downers Grove, IL 60515. www.ivpress.com.

Del Ratzsch. "Design and Science. Taken from *Science and Its Limits: The Natural Sciences in Christian Perspective* by Del Ratzsch. Copyright © 2000 Del Ratzsch. Used by permission of InterVarsity Press, PO Box 1400, Downers Grove, IL 60515. www.ivpress.com.

Kurt Wise. "The Origin of Life's Major Groups." Taken from *The Creation Hypothesis: Scientific Evidence for an Intelligent Designer*, edited by J. P. Moreland. Copyright © 1994. Used by permission of InterVarsity Press, PO Box 1400, Downers Grove, IL 60515. www.ivpress.com.

The Epistle to Diognetus. Copyright © 2009 by Kevin Knight. Available at http://www.newadvent.org/fathers/0101.htm. Used by permission.

Augustine. *The City of God*. Bk 1 Ch. 35–36; Bk 15, Ch 1–6. Copyright © 2009 by Kevin Knight. Available at http://www.newadvent.org/fathers/1201.htm. Used by permission.

Francis Schaeffer. "A Christian Manifesto." Adapted from *A Christian Manifesto* by Francis Schaeffer, © 2005. Used by permission of Crossway, a publishing ministry of Good News Publishers, Wheaton, IL 60187, www.crossway.org. Adaptation by Francis Schaeffer found online at http://www.peopleforlife.org/francis.html.

Pope Benedict XVI. "Christianity Yesterday, Today, and Tomorrow." Used by Permission of Libreria Editrice Vaticana (©Libreria Editrice Vaticana).

List of Authors

Adams, Marilyn McCord (1943 –), is distinguished research professor at University of North Carolina at Chapel Hill and was the Regius Professor of Divinity at the University of Oxford.

Alston, William Payne (1921 – 2009), was professor emeritus of philosophy at Syracuse University.

Anselm of Canterbury (1033 – 1109) was a highly influential Christian philosopher and theologian of the eleventh century.

Aquinas, Thomas (1225 – 1274), has been an immensely influential philosopher and theologian in the tradition of scholasticism.

Athanasius of Alexandria (296 – 373) was bishop of Alexandria. He is also known as St. Athanasius the Great and St. Athanasius the Confessor.

Augustine, Aurelius (354 – 430), also known as St. Augustine of Hippo, was a North African bishop. He is one of the towering figures of Christian philosophy and theology whose authority and thought came to exert a profound, pervasive, and enduring influence well into the modern period.

Bahnsen, Greg L. (1948 – 1995), was an ordained minister in the Orthodox Presbyterian Church and a full-time scholar in residence for the Southern California Center for Christian Studies.

Behe, Michael J. (1952 –), is professor of biological sciences at Lehigh University in Pennsylvania.

Beilby, James K., is professor of systematic and philosophical theology at Bethel University in St. Paul, Minnesota.

Calvin, John (1509 – 1564), was an influential French theologian and Protestant Reformer, author of the *Institutes of the Christian Religion*, and father of Calvinism.

Carpenter, Eugene, is professor of Old Testament and Hebrew and scholar in residence at Bethel College, Mishawaka, Indiana.

Collins, Robin, serves as professor of philosophy at Messiah College in Grantham, Pennsylvania.

Copan, Paul, is a professor of philosophy and ethics, and the Pledger Family Chair at Palm Beach Atlantic University, Florida.

Craig, William Lane (1949 –), is research professor of philosophy at Talbot School of Theology at Biola University, California.

Descartes, René (1596 – 1650), was a French philosopher and writer. He is known as the Father of Modern Philosophy.

Epistle to Diognetus (c. second century), also known as the *Epistle of Mathetes* (which means "disciple") to Diognetus, is one of earliest examples of Christian apologetics. Diognetus was a tutor of the emperor Marcus Aurelius. The author is unknown.

France, R. T. (1938 – 2012), is a New Testament scholar and Anglican cleric. He served as Principal of Wycliffe Hall Oxford from 1989 to 1995 and as Vice-Principal of the London School of Theology.

Geisler, Norman L. (1932 –), is distinguished professor of apologetics and theology and chair of Christian apologetics at Veritas Evangelical Seminary in Murrieta, California.

Habermas, Gary (1950 –), is distinguished professor of apologetics and philosophy and chairman of the department of philosophy and theology at Liberty University in Lynchburg, Virginia.

Hick, John (1922 –), is emeritus professor of both Birmingham University, UK, and Claremont Graduate University, California. He is also a Fellow of the Institute for Advanced Research in Arts and Social Sciences, University of Birmingham, UK, and a Vice-President of the British Society for the Philosophy of Religion and of the World Congress of Faiths.

Kreeft, Peter (1937 –), is a professor of philosophy at Boston College and The King's College.

Leibniz, Gottfried Wilhelm (1646 – 1716), was a German philosopher and mathematician.

Lewis, Clive Staples (1898 – 1963), was professor of medieval and renaissance literature at Magdalene College, Oxford and Cambridge Universities.

Locke, John (1632 – 1704), was an English philosopher and physician and is regarded as one of the most influential Enlightenment thinkers.

Montgomery, John Warwick (1931 –), is distinguished research professor of philosophy and Christian thought at Patrick Henry College in Virginia and emeritus professor of law and humanities at the University of Luton (England).

Moreland, James Porter (1948 –), is distinguished professor of philosophy at Talbot School of Theology at Biola University in La Mirada, California.

Morris, Thomas V. (1952 –), is former professor of philosophy at the University of Notre Dame and founder of the Morris Institute of Human Values.

Netland, Harold, is professor of philosophy of religion and intercultural studies and the Naomi A. Fausch Chair of Missions at Trinity Evangelical Divinity School in Deerfield, Illinois.

Origen (185 – 254) was one of the most distinguished philosopher/theologians of the early church.

Paley, William (1743 – 1805), was a British Christian philosopher and apologist. He is most known for his teleological argument.

Pascal, Blaise (1623 – 1662), was a French scientist, mathematician, and philosopher.

Paul the apostle (c. 5 – 67), also referred to as the apostle Paul, Saul of Tarsus, and Saint Paul. He was one of the most influential early Christian theologians and missionaries, with his writings forming a major portion of the New Testament.

Plantinga, Alvin (1932 –), is an American analytic philosopher and emeritus John A. O'Brien Professor of Philosophy at the University of Notre Dame.

Polkinghorne, John (1930 –), was professor of mathematical physics at the University of Cambridge from 1968 to 1979 and is an Anglican priest. He served as the president of Queens' College, Cambridge, from 1988 until 1996.

Pope Benedict XVI, Joseph Aloisius Ratzinger (1927 –), is the 265th pope and the head of the Roman Catholic Church.

Ratzsch, Del, is professor and department chair of philosophy at Calvin College in Grand Rapids, Michigan.

Richard of St. Victor (d. 1173) was a prominent mystical theologian and was prior of the Augustinian Abbey of Saint Victor in Paris.

Schaeffer, Francis (1912 – 1984), was a philosopher, theologian, and pastor. He founded the L'Abri community in Switzerland.

Stein, Gordon S. (1941 – 1996), was the senior editor of *Free Inquiry* magazine, taught at the University of Rhode Island, and was director of libraries at the Center for Inquiry.

Swinburne, Richard G. (1934 –), is professor of philosophy emeritus at the University of Oxford. He is one of the most influential Christian apologists of the past century.

Teresa of Avila, Saint (1515 – 1582), also referred to as Saint Teresa of Jesus, was a prominent Spanish mystic, Roman Catholic saint, and Carmelite nun.

Wise, Kurt P. (1959 –), studied under Stephen Jay Gould at Harvard and is director of the Creation Research Center at Truett-McConnell College.

General Introduction

Since its inception nearly two thousand years ago, Christianity has faced myriad challenges from both within and without its boundaries. Indeed, those very boundaries have themselves oftentimes been at issue. While its central message — that God has sought reconciliation with sinful humanity, and that through the life, death, and resurrection of the incarnate Son of God he has made reconciliation possible such that an eternal, loving, and compassionate community with God is the end goal — has remained constant throughout history, these challenges have been ever present. Because of them, Christian apologists (from the Greek term *apologia* = a defense) arose early on to make a defense of the faith. Throughout the centuries these apologists have continued to contend for the truth of the Christian message — a message that is ultimately rooted in one man who in many ways forever altered the course of human history: Jesus of Nazareth.

We find the first apologists in the pages of the Bible itself. For example, the apostle Paul regularly engaged in apologetics as can be seen from the various references to him "reasoning," "defending," "contending," and "arguing" for the faith (e.g., Acts 17 – 19; 2 Cor. 10; Phil. 1; Titus 1). He describes an aspect of his apologetic strategy this way: "We demolish arguments and every pretension that sets itself up against the knowledge of God, and we take captive every thought to make it obedient to Christ" (2 Cor. 10:5). Peter, too, speaks about the need for apologetics in what is perhaps the most rehearsed passage in the New Testament on this subject: "Always be prepared to give an answer to everyone who asks you to give the reason for the hope that you have. But do this with gentleness and respect" (1 Peter 3:15). And Jude, the brother of Jesus, counsels this way: "Dear friends, although I was very eager to write to you about the salvation we share, I felt compelled to write and urge you to contend for the faith that was once for all entrusted to God's holy people" (Jude 3).

Century after century, Christians have found it necessary to provide a ready defense of the faith. Different times and places call for different approaches. In his introduction to *A History of Apologetics*, Fr. Avery Dulles writes:

> The goals and methods of apologetics have frequently shifted. The earliest apologists were primarily concerned with obtaining civil toleration for the Christian community — to prove that Christians were not malefactors deserving the death penalty. Gradually through the early centuries the apologies for Christianity became less defensive. Assuming the counteroffensive, they aimed to win converts from other groups. Some were addressed to pagans, others to Jews. Subsequently apologetics turned its attention to Moslems, then to atheists, agnostics, and religious indifferentists. Finally apologists came to recognize that every Christian harbors within himself a secret infidel. At this point apologetics became, to some extent, a dialogue between the believer and the unbeliever in the heart of the Christian himself. In speaking to his unregenerate self the apologist assumed — quite correctly — that he would best be able to reach others similarly situated.[1]

As Fr. Dulles suggests, the "secret infidel" within each of us needs answers and reasons to solidify and strengthen his or her own faith.

---

1. Avery Dulles, *A History of Apologetics* (San Francisco: Ignatius Press, 1971), xvi.

This book is a sampling of some of the best works written by Christian apologists throughout the centuries. While the emphasis is on Western Christianity, we have attempted to be nonsectarian in our inclusion. We were limited in what we could include for many reasons, not the least of which were space constraints. Nevertheless, we believe that this collection provides a snapshot of Christian apologetics at its best across the spectrum of time and culture. It is a book for believer and unbeliever alike. The Christian message and doctrines articulated and defended in this volume are not ones that a person need affirm by blind faith. Indeed, evidences for them have been honed, refined, and forged on the anvils of logic, reason, and history. But arguments and evidences do not

of themselves bring someone into new life in Christ. Here the work of the Holy Spirit is central, and we must be willing to surrender to his leading and his truth and his goodness if we are to truly dwell with the Lord. Arguments and evidences can be powerful forces for removing barriers to faith and for strengthening the faith of believers. But it must always be remembered that God's work in individual lives is what ultimately transforms.

This book is our offering to the advancement of the kingdom of God through the works of many of the great apologists of yesterday and today. It is our hope that it will be effective in removing obstacles hindering faith in Christ and in bolstering faith in those who already believe. To God be the glory!

PART 1

HISTORY, METHODOLOGY, AND ENGAGEMENT

Christian apologetics has a very long history. In fact, we see it initially in the New Testament writings that date to the first century AD. Indeed, apologetics has been an integral part of the Christian faith from its very inception. We begin this volume with one of the earliest Christian apologetic speeches ever recorded: the apostle Paul's Mars Hill address found in Acts 17.

The next selection is provided by John Warwick Montgomery. He sketches the history of apologetics, beginning in the Bible, working through the Patristic and Medieval periods, then into the Renaissance and Reformation, and finally into the modern period up through our own day.

Not only does Christian apologetics have a long history, but it also involves a number of different approaches. Why is this so, and what are the various approaches that have been utilized by many of the leading apologists throughout history? James Beilby delineates the major approaches and methodologies that have been used as Christians have attempted to defend the faith. In doing so, he examines five *meta-apologetic questions* that have led to the various methods and perspectives in apologetics.

Perhaps no time in history has reflected the need for interreligious apologetics as our own day. With globalization and pluralism in the West, there are many perspectives that require attention by apologists in the twenty-first century. Harold Netland guides us through this important issue. He demonstrates that even prior to the modern era, there was a long tradition of interreligious apologetics. But today, many see interreligious apologetics as inappropriate in our pluralistic culture and believe that respect and mutual understanding, rather than polemics, are most appropriate. Netland provides practical and theoretical insights into how to approach this terrain and how to engage in apologetics in our postmodern era.

Next, Norman Geisler argues for the knowability of history. Unlike some religions, Christianity is inseparably tied to historical events — most especially the life, death, and resurrection of Jesus of Nazareth. Without knowledge of such historical events, orthodox Christianity is lost. Since the knowability of history is challenged by a number of contemporary historians, it is important for the apologist to rebut this claim in order to defend the Christian faith.

In the last selection of this section, Alvin Plantinga offers some advice to Christian philosophers — advice we believe is beneficial to all Christian thinkers irrespective of their particular academic discipline. He notes that while much of the intellectual culture of our day is nontheistic, or even antitheistic, nonetheless Christian philosophy is flourishing and growing. He offers sage advice, which he sums up with three points: (1) Christian thinkers should display more independence from the rest of the intellectual world; (2) they should display more integrity; and (3) they must display more trust in the Lord. He carefully delineates each of these points.

CHAPTER 1

A First Century Apologetic: Acts 17

Saint Paul

[1]When Paul and his companions had passed through Amphipolis and Apollonia, they came to Thessalonica, where there was a Jewish synagogue. [2]As was his custom, Paul went into the synagogue, and on three Sabbath days he reasoned with them from the Scriptures, [3]explaining and proving that the Messiah had to suffer and rise from the dead. "This Jesus I am proclaiming to you is the Messiah," he said. [4]Some of the Jews were persuaded and joined Paul and Silas, as did a large number of God-fearing Greeks and quite a few prominent women.

[5]But other Jews were jealous; so they rounded up some bad characters from the marketplace, formed a mob and started a riot in the city. They rushed to Jason's house in search of Paul and Silas in order to bring them out to the crowd. [6]But when they did not find them, they dragged Jason and some other believers before the city officials, shouting: "These men who have caused trouble all over the world have now come here, [7]and Jason has welcomed them into his house. They are all defying Caesar's decrees, saying that there is another king, one called Jesus." [8]When they heard this, the crowd and the city officials were thrown into turmoil. [9]Then they made Jason and the others post bond and let them go.

[10]As soon as it was night, the believers sent Paul and Silas away to Berea. On arriving there, they went to the Jewish synagogue. [11]Now the Berean Jews were of more noble character than those in Thessalonica, for they received the message with great eagerness and examined the Scriptures every day to see if what Paul said was true. [12]As a result, many of them believed, as did also a number of prominent Greek women and many Greek men.

[13]But when the Jews in Thessalonica learned that Paul was preaching the word of God at Berea, some of them went there too, agitating the crowds and stirring them up. [14]The believers immediately sent Paul to the coast, but Silas and Timothy stayed at Berea. [15]Those who escorted Paul brought him to Athens and then left with instructions for Silas and Timothy to join him as soon as possible.

[16]While Paul was waiting for them in Athens, he was greatly distressed to see that the city was full of idols. [17]So he reasoned in the synagogue with both Jews and God-fearing Greeks, as well as in the marketplace day by day with those who happened to be there. [18]A group of Epicurean and Stoic philosophers began to debate with him. Some of them asked, "What is this babbler trying to say?" Others remarked, "He seems to be advocating foreign gods." They said this because Paul was preaching the good news about Jesus and the resurrection. [19]Then they took him and brought him to a meeting of the Areopagus, where they said to him, "May we know what this new teaching is that you are presenting? [20]You are bringing some strange ideas to our ears, and we would like to know what they mean." [21](All the Athenians and the foreigners who lived there spent their time doing nothing but talking about and listening to the latest ideas.)

[22]Paul then stood up in the meeting of the Areopagus and said: "People of Athens! I see that in every way you are very religious. [23]For as I walked around and looked carefully at your objects of worship, I even found an altar with this inscription: TO AN UNKNOWN GOD. So you are ignorant of the very thing you worship — and this is what I am going to proclaim to you.

[24]"The God who made the world and everything in it is the Lord of heaven and earth and does not live in temples built by human hands. [25]And he is not served by human hands, as if he needed anything. Rather, he himself gives everyone life and breath and everything else. [26]From one man he made all the nations, that they should inhabit the whole earth; and he marked out their appointed times in history and the boundaries of their lands. [27]God did this so that they would seek him and perhaps reach out for him and find him, though he is not far from any one of us. [28]'For in him we live and move and have our being.' As some of your own poets have said, 'We are his offspring.'

[29]"Therefore since we are God's offspring, we should not think that the divine being is like gold or silver or stone — an image made by human design and skill. [30]In the past God overlooked such ignorance, but now he commands all people everywhere to repent. [31]For he has set a day when he will judge the world with justice by the man he has appointed. He has given proof of this to everyone by raising him from the dead."

[32]When they heard about the resurrection of the dead, some of them sneered, but others said, "We want to hear you again on this subject." [33]At that, Paul left the Council. [34]Some of the people became followers of Paul and believed. Among them was Dionysius, a member of the Areopagus, also a woman named Damaris, and a number of others.

From the New International Version

CHAPTER 2

A Short History of Apologetics

John Warwick Montgomery

The history of the defence of Christian faith is coterminous with the history of Christianity itself.[1] This is the case because Christianity, unlike religions of the East, such as Buddhism and Hinduism, is non-syncretic: Christianity asserts that religious truth can ultimately be found only in Jesus Christ and Christian revelation (John 14:6, Acts 4:12). From this it follows that religious claims contradicting Christian faith cannot be true and must be opposed, and negative criticisms of the truth of the Christian position must be answered.

Covenant theology bifurcates the history of salvation, treating it in terms of Old Testament or Covenant, and New Testament. Dispensationalists prefer to divide salvation history into numerous epochs, often seven in number. We shall try to satisfy both! The major divide in the history of apologetics occurs at the time of the 18th-century so-called "Enlightenment," when secular thinkers such as Thomas Paine endeavoured to replace the "Book of Scripture" with the "Book of Nature"; subsequently, apologetics followed a very different path from that of the preceding centuries. Prior to that massive ideological divide, Christianity had occupied stage centre in Western intellectual history; afterwards, it found itself relegated to the wings.

But the expanse of apologetic history from biblical times to the 21st century can also be discussed in terms of seven epochs or styles of defence, and we shall briefly comment on each of them in turn: (1) Apologetics in the Bible itself; (2) Patristic defence of the faith; (3) Medieval apologetics; (4) Renaissance and Reformation; (5) Apologetics at the zenith of the "classical Christian era"; (6) Response to the Enlightenment in the 18th and 19th centuries; (7) Apologetics today. In our final section, we shall have opportunity to reflect on the weaknesses of the apologetic situation in today's church.

Apologetics in the Bible

Charles Finney was supposed to have downgraded apologetic argument by remarking: "Defend the Bible? How would you defend a lion? Let it out of its cage and it'll defend itself!" But, in point of fact, the Bible, unlike the Qur'an and the "holy books" of other religions, does not expect its readers to accept its revelational character simply because the text claims to be true. In the Old Testament, Elijah competes with the false prophets of Baal, and the superior miraculous demonstration by the power of the God of Israel wins the day (I Kings 18). In the Gospels, Jesus makes the truth of his entire ministry depend on a single sign — that of his resurrection from the dead (Matthew 12:39 – 40). In the Epistles, not only is Christ's physical resurrection asserted, but the Apostle is concerned

---

1. Readers interested in the history of apologetics may wish to consult: Bernard Ramm, *Varieties of Christian Apologetics* (rev. ed.; Grand Rapids, MI: Baker, 1961 [evangelical]; Joseph H. Crehan, "Apologetics," *A Catholic Dictionary of Theology*, vol. 1 (London: Thomas Nelson, 1962); Avery Dulles, *A History of Apologetics* (New York: Corpus; Philadelphia: Westminster Press, 1971) [Roman Catholic bias — as with Crehan]; L. Russ Bush (ed.), *Classical*

Readings in Christian Apologetics A.D. 100 – 1800 (Grand Rapids, MI: Zondervan, 1983) [evangelical]; William Edgar and K. Scott Oliphint (eds.), *Christian Apologetics Past and Present: A Primary Source Reader* (2 vols.; Wheaton, IL: Crossway, 2009 – 2010) [presuppositionist bias]. It should be noted that these works treat inadequately, or not at all, the 21st century scene.

as well to provide a list of eyewitnesses to the risen Christ (I Cor. 15:4 – 8).

·The biblical apologetic focuses in four areas, and these are subsequently employed throughout Christian history: *miracle, fulfilled prophecy, natural revelation,* and *personal experience* (what the philosophers term "subjective immediacy"). Three caveats: (1) natural revelation (proofs of God from nature), though present in the Bible (e.g., Ps. 19:1), is the least emphasised apologetic; (2) personal experience never "floats free": the subjective is always grounded in one or more of the objective areas of proof — generally miracle and prophecy; (3) occasionally, a "double-barreled" argument is made through *miracle* being the object of *prophecy,* as in the case of the Virgin Birth of our Lord (Isa. 7:14; Mt. 1; Lk. 1 – 2).

· Since the biblical plan of salvation centres on God's revealing himself in real history, through prophets, priests, and finally by the incarnation of his eternal Son, Jesus Christ, the biblical apologetic is essentially one of asserting and demonstrating the *factual* nature of the events recounted. The Apostle is willing to make the entire truth of the faith turn on the reality of Jesus' resurrection (I Cor. 15:17 – 20). The case for biblical truth, then, connects with the nature of Christianity as "historical religion": it is in principle falsifiable — and, in this case, verifiable — thereby removing Christianity from the analytical philosophers' category of a meaningless metaphysical claim and placing it in the realm of the empirical and the synthetic, along with historical events in general.

Patristic Apologetics

The church fathers closest to the New Testament understandably followed its apologetic lead: prophecy and miracle were their preferred arguments. The earliest of them (Irenaeus, for example) favoured the prophecies of the Old Testament fulfilled in Christ, since in his time the gospel was being proclaimed and defended "to the Jew first." Moreover, the Gnostic heretics employed pseudo-miracles (sherbet in Eucharistic wine!), but had no fulfilled prophecies to support

their views. As Christian evangelism reached a predominately Gentile audience, miracle evidence came to the fore. Eusebius of Caesarea, in his *Ecclesiastical History,* employs a testimonial argument in support of Christ's miraculous resurrection from the dead, sarcastically asking whether it would be reasonable to suppose that the Apostles, had they known that Jesus did not rise from the dead, would have lost all they had and ultimately been martyred whilst maintaining that he *had* in fact conquered death. Tertullian's oft-quoted phrase, "*Credo quia absurdum,*" rather than being an invitation to irrationality, expressed the belief that the Christian gospel was almost too good to be true — as the children in C. S. Lewis' Narnian chronicles would later discover.

The bridge between the Patristic and medieval worlds was Augustine of Hippo. He was converted from neo-Platonism to Christianity and offered an apologetic of a Platonic nature to the intellectuals of his time, convinced as they were that Plato was the summation of classical philosophy. For Plato, one must rationally (and for neo-Platonists, rationally *and* spiritually) rise from the world of phenomena to the world of ideas/ideals — of which the highest expression is the Good, the True, and the Beautiful. Augustine identified that realm with the God of the Bible. He also, in his *Confessions,* made a compelling argument from personal experience: "Thou hast made us for thyself, O God, and our hearts are restless until they rest in thee." In the 20th century, Edward John Carnell would expand on this in his axiological apologetic, *A Philosophy of the Christian Religion.*

Medieval Defense of the Faith

Theodore Abu Qurra, an Eastern theologian (9th century) set forth an apologetic parable demonstrating comprehension of the apologetic task well in advance of his time; it raises the critical question as to how one can test multiple revelation claims (in his case, Islam vs. Christianity). For Abu Qurra, one asks each religion what it says of God, what it says of sin, and what sort of remedy it offers for the human condition — thereby demonstrating the superiority of Christianity.[2]

Although a primitive form of the ontological argument for God's existence can be found in St. Augustine, St. Anselm of Canterbury provided its classic formulation in the 11th century. The argument purports to prove God's existence from the concept of God itself: God is "that than which no greater can be conceived"; he must therefore have all properties; and since *existence* is a property, God exists! The argument rests on the idealistic assumption that ideas have reality untouched by the phenomenal world (so rational idealists have been somewhat comfortable with it), but the overwhelming fallacy in the argument is simply that "existence" is not a property alongside other properties; *existence* is the name we give to something that in fact *has* properties. To determine whether a something (God?) exists, we need to investigate the empirical evidences of its/his reality. Thus the far better Christian argument is that "God was in Christ, reconciling the world unto himself" (II Cor. 5:19). This critique having been offered, it is worth noting that neo-Orthodox theologian Karl Barth (*Anselm: Fides Quaerens Intellectum*) was quite wrong that Anselm was not trying to do apologetics but was simply preaching to the converted.[3]

The most influential medieval apologist of western Christendom was its most influential theologian: Thomas Aquinas. Though probably having never met a pagan, he wrote his *Summa contra gentiles* ("Summation against the pagans"). By his time — the 13th century — Aristotle had replaced Plato as the most favoured classical philosopher, so Aquinas developed his apologetic along Aristotelian lines. He took over Aristotle's traditional proofs for God's existence, and argued that they can establish a foundation of Reason upon which Faith can operate. This stress on the Aristotelian proofs would have a tremendous influence on all subsequent Christian apologetics.

Contemporaneous with Aquinas was Ramon Lull (or Lullius), a Catalonian who is considered to be the first European missionary to the Muslims. Lull was a philosopher, but not a scholastic in the Aristotelian tradition. He developed an original "method" for the conversion of the infidel through the combining of theological and philosophical concepts and the illustrative use of rotating, interlocking disks. He now figures in the prehistory of the modern computer.[4] Lull also practiced literary apologetics by way of his apologetic novel, *Blanquerna*.

Renaissance and Reformation

By the time of the Italian Renaissance (15th – 16th centuries), the world was opening up to exploration and Plato had returned to philosophical prominence. Thus the apologists of that era directed their efforts to adventurous thinkers committed to a Platonic view of the world. Thomas More, in his *Utopia*, well illustrates this. The Utopians pray each night that "if there is a better and truer faith, may God bring it to us." More's explorers reach Utopia and present the Christian religion as that better faith. The Utopians, in seeking the Good, the True, and the Beautiful, accept the God of Christian revelation.

The Protestant Reformers were not concerned with apologetics as such; they had more than enough to do cleaning up the theology of the medieval church. But their work had much indirect value for apologetics. Thus, Luther's insistence on *sola Scriptura* and thoroughgoing christocentricity were healthy counteractives to medieval Aristotelian/Thomistic emphases.[5] And when the Roman Catholic opponents of the

---

2. See Montgomery, *Faith Founded on Fact* (Nashville, TN: Thomas Nelson, 1978), pp. 119 – 21.

3. Cf. Montgomery, *Where Is History Going?* (Minneapolis: Bethany, 1969), pp. 109 – 110.

4. See Montgomery, "Computer Origins and the Defence of the Faith," 56/3 *Perspectives on Science and Christian Faith* (September, 2004), 189 – 203.

5. In an otherwise very useful handbook, Boa and Bowman's classification of Luther as an apologetic "fideist" — and the placing of him in the same bed with Kierkegaard, Karl Barth, and Donald Bloesch — would be ludicrous if it were not so factually wide of the mark: Kenneth D. Boa and Robert M. Bowman, Jr., *Faith Has Its Reasons* (2d ed.; Milton Keynes, UK: Paternoster, 2005).

Reformation argued that the Bible is an obscure book, requiring the Roman Church to interpret it, Protestants such as Andreas Althamer produced books defending the clarity ("perspicuity") and non-contradictory nature of the teachings of Holy Scripture. Such writings are the forerunners of modern treatises that deal with and refute claims to alleged errors and contradictions in the Bible.

17th-Century Apologetics

This was the last century of "old Western man" — the last century when Christian thought dominated the intellectual landscape of the West. It was the era of "system" — Protestant systematic theology, the musical summation of the Western musical tradition in the labours of Lutheran J. S. Bach, the literary summation in Milton's *Paradise Lost*, the architectural summation in Wren's magnificent churches constructed after London's Great Fire of 1666.

As for apologetics, Hugo Grotius, the father of international law, published in 1622 his *De Veritate religionis Christianae* ("On the truth of the Christian Religion"). This seminal work was widely translated and in print until the 19th century. It sets forth a modern, historical apologetic for the soundness of Jesus' claims in the New Testament.

Even more famous and influential was the apologetic work of Blaise Pascal, a Roman Catholic but a follower of the Port Royal, Jansenist movement, which was regarded by its conservative Catholic enemies as tantamount to Protestantism — owing to its great appreciation for St. Augustine and central stress on salvation by grace through faith. Pascal's posthumously collected *Pensées* ("Thoughts") offer a powerful apologetic for the truth of biblical revelation and the saving work of Christ. His "wager" (even if Christianity were false, in accepting it you would be better off, for you would obtain the best ethic and the best human example — Jesus) was not intended as the totality of his apologetic (as his philosophical critics generally

maintain, in order to make it appear silly), but only as a device for getting the unbeliever's attention. Having been struck by the force of the wager, the unbeliever would then have powerful reason to examine the full gamut of evidence for the faith and thereby come to see that the probabilities are overwhelmingly in favour of Christian commitment.[6]

The Great Divide and Its Apologetic Aftermath

The 18th century was characterised politically by the French and American Revolutions and ideologically by Deism: the belief that one could and should dispense with the "revealed" religion of historic Christianity, contaminated by superstition (blood sacrifice, miracles, etc.) and substitute a "religion of Nature," focusing on a God of immutable natural law and morality.[7] "Enlightenment" philosophers included Immanuel Kant, who claimed that the traditional proofs of God's existence were inadequate and that only an absolute ethic could be established (the "categorical imperative"); Gotthold Ephraim Lessing, who dug his "Ditch" between absolute, philosophical truth on the one hand, and what he considered the inadequacies of history (including biblical history), on the other; and David Hume, who claimed that, owing to "uniform experience," miracles could always be rejected out of hand, since it would always be more miraculous if the witness were telling the truth than that the miracle actually happened.

These attacks were devastating and historic Christianity lost much intellectual ground as a result of them. The identification of the churches with the privileges of monarchy and the Old Régime only made matters worse. But apologists for the faith heroically entered the fray.

In the 18th century itself, William Paley (*Natural Theology*; *Evidences*) argued for the soundness of the biblical witness — both as to God's hand in nature and as to the soundness of the New Testament por-

---

6. Boa and Bowman also incorrectly classify Pascal as a "fideist"! For a proper understanding of Pascal, see the writings of Emile Cailliet; also, Montgomery, "Computer Origins ..." (*loc. cit.*).

7. Cf. Montgomery, *The Shaping of America* (Minneapolis: Bethany, 1976).

trait of Jesus[8]; and Thomas Sherlock pointed out, in his legally-orientated work, *The Tryal of the Witnesses of the Resurrection of Jesus,* that people of the 1st century were as capable as those of his own "enlightened" time to distinguish between a dead body and a live one — and that the case for Jesus' resurrection could not therefore be dismissed philosophically.[9]

.The most famous defence of faith in the 18th century was Bishop Butler's *Analogy of Religion,* which attempted to convince the Deist using his own reasoning: the Scriptural teaching, said Butler, was directly *analogous* to the work of God in nature — and since the Deist accepted the latter, he had no ground for rejecting the former. Examples: nature displays seeds falling into the ground and dying, followed by life again every spring, and Scripture presents the crucifixion followed by the resurrection; human society survives only because each person acts for others by doing work the other cannot do, and Scripture makes divine substitution the key to salvation.

· The 19th century dealt a further, perhaps even more crushing, blow to the faith. With the publication of Darwin's *Origin of Species* in 1859, even the Deist's God of Nature could be discarded: natural selection could allegedly account for all development of flora and fauna. Defenders of the faith offered two very different apologetic approaches to this incipient atheism that culminated, at the end of century, in Nietzsche's famous declaration that "God is dead."

The great Roman Catholic (former Anglican) apologist John Henry Newman doggedly fought the revelational battle on epistemological and historical grounds (*Essays on Miracles; Grammar of Assent*): he refined the notion of historical probability with his concept of the *illative sense*: when "congeries" (concatenations) of facts inexorably point to the same conclusion — as

in the testimonies to the resurrection of Christ — they raise the level of the argument to a practical certainty and cannot rationally be dismissed.

Lay philosopher and theologian Søren Kierkegaard, the father of existentialism, took an inner route: for him, "truth is subjectivity." As finite creatures, we cannot, à la Hegel and German idealistic philosophy, discover the "essence" of things; we can only experience our own "existence" — which, owing to the fall, is *Angst* and estrangement without Christ. But his successor existentialists in the 20th century (Heidegger, Sartre), left with only their own subjectivity, did not find Christ, but a valueless, atheistic world, both microcosmically and macrocosmically. By discounting the value of probability and historical reasoning to vindicate Christian revelation, Kierkegaard ended up substituting an unstable, subjective experientialism for the objectivist *hubris* of the unbelieving philosophers he opposed. Modern evangelicalism has frequently made the same mistake.

Apologetics Today

In the early decades of the 20th century, what appeared to be a powerful case against all metaphysical and religious thinking appeared on the scene. This stemmed from Ludwig Wittgenstein's *Tractatus Logico-Philosophicus* and from the so-called Vienna Circle of analytical philosophers and logical positivists. They argued that truth claims, including metaphysical and religious views, were meaningless unless they could be verified. Many theologians and most metaphysicians tried to counter this position by discounting the need for verification (a Pyrrhic victory if there ever was one!). In point of fact, as this essayist has maintained in his major work (*Tractatus Logico-Theologicus*[10]), whereas secular metaphysical systems and virtually all non-Christian

---

8. Paley's continuing relevance is evidenced by the fact that atheist Richard Dawkins makes him his foil in arguing for biological evolutionism (*The Blind Watchmaker*). Paley, incidentally, was a barrister and wrote as a lawyer with Christ as his client; he was roundly (and unfairly) criticised for doing apologetics "in the spirit of the advocate rather than of the judge" by the great classicist Benjamin Jowett: *The Interpretation of Scripture and Other Essays* (London: George Routledge and Sons, n.d.), p. 129.

9. Sherlock's *Tryal* is photolithographically reprinted in Montgomery (ed.), *Jurisprudence: A Book of Readings* (rev. ed.; Strasbourg, France: International Scholarly Publishers, 1980); available from www.ciltpp.com.

10. Montgomery, *Tractatus Logico-Theologicus* (4th ed.; Bonn, Germany: Verlag fuer Kultur und Wissenschaft, 2009), *passim.* Available from www.ciltpp.com.

religions do in fact entirely lack testability, Christian faith alone offers the solid, empirical, historical evidence of its truth by way of the case for Jesus Christ.

The 20th century and the onset of the 21st have been marked by a number of influential Christian apologists and by several apologetic schools of thought. Needless to say, the liberal churches did not carry on apologetic activity, since inherent to theological liberalism has always been an accommodating of the faith to secular ideology rather than a defending of it over against secularism (cf. liberal theologian Willard L. Sperry's "Yes, But" — The Bankruptcy of Apologetics). The Scopes evolution trial drove many American evangelicals into a radical separation from mainline intellectual life and therefore from apologetic activity: the only choice they saw was to pluck "brands from the burning" through revival campaigns and personal testimony. But even the twelve popular, paperbound volumes that introduced the term "fundamentalist" into the language (The Fundamentals, 1910) contained fine apologetic defences of historic Christianity by such notables as James Orr and B. B. Warfield.

Warfield, as a Princeton Theological Seminary professor, commanded great respect. His defence of scriptural inerrancy (The Inspiration and Authority of the Bible) had immense impact, especially in Reformed theological circles. Later, this would be blunted by the Westminster Theological Seminary theologian Cornelius Van Til, who criticised Warfield's evidential argumentation as not being sufficiently Calvinistic — since it did not insist on starting from the presupposition of the truth of the faith and God's sovereignty, above and beyond evidential considerations.

In the 1940's, Moody Bible Institute instructor and Bible commentator Wilbur M. Smith wrote his book, Therefore Stand: A Plea for a Vigorous Apologetic. Essentially a work of historical apologetics, this book had wide influence: its author could be trusted as not being a closet intellectual or one critical of the evangelical life-style. Therefore Stand remains a classic, demonstrating on every page the wide learning of the preeminent theological bibliographer of 20th century evangelicalism.

Smith would later accept a chair at the newly founded Fuller Theological Seminary. There (before Fuller gave up its inerrancy position) apologist Edward John Carnell produced exceedingly important works: An Introduction to Christian Apologetics and A Philosophy of the Christian Religion. The Introduction endeavours, without success, to combine a Van Tilian presuppositionalism with E. S. Brightman's truth test of "systematic consistency" (a true assertion must be logically consistent and must also fit the facts of the external world) — but the second part of the book contains masterful responses to a host of common objections to biblical religion: the problem of evil, evolutionary theory, anti-miraculous views, etc.

The mid – 20th century was also marked by the writings of the most influential of all English-language apologists of the time: C. S. Lewis. To apply the terminology of William James, Lewis successfully practised both "toughminded" and "tenderminded" apologetics. His broadcast talks (later combined under the title Mere Christianity) brought many to the faith in England: my Cornell professor, the late literary critic David Daiches, remarked that more had been converted through Lewis than in the British revival campaigns of Billy Graham! Miracles dealt with Hume's attempt to short-circuit historical investigation through philosophical speculation[11]; The Problem of Pain was a superb popular justification of the God of the Bible against the standard argument that an all-powerful and loving God could not exist in the face of the evils of the world. On the tenderminded front, Lewis' science-fiction trilogy (Out of the Silent Planet, Perelandra, That Hideous Strength) and his Narnian chronicles brought many who were indifferent to traditional apologetics to see the truth of the faith on the level of "deep myth."[12]

---

11. Cf. more recent — and systematic — decimations of Hume: philosopher (and non-Christian) John Earman, Hume's Abject Failure: The Argument Against Miracles (New York: Oxford University Press, 2000); and David Johnson, Hume, Holism and Miracles (Ithaca, NY: Cornell University Press, 1999).

12. Cf. Montgomery (ed.), Myth, Allegory and Gospel (Minneapolis: Bethany, 1974).

A number of "schools" of apologetics came into existence in the latter years of the 20th century and continue to influence the intellectual climate. We have mentioned above the *presuppositionalist* approach. Its major representatives have been philosopher Gordon Clark and theologian Cornelius Van Til; its epicentre is the Westminster Theological Seminary (Philadelphia) and its advocates include John Frame and the late Greg Bahnsen. Though there are important differences among these thinkers, they are all convinced that, owing to the fall of man, facts cannot be used to convince unbelievers of Christian truth; as Van Til put it: "All is yellow to the jaundiced eye." Generally (but not in every case) this presuppositionalism is combined with an ultra-Calvinist understanding of predestination.

Philosopher Alvin Plantinga's "Reformed epistemology" can be regarded as a variant of the presuppositionalist position. For Plantinga, historical argumentation is necessarily inadequate and no demonstration that Christianity is true will succeed with the unbeliever: the apologetic task cannot go beyond showing that Christian theism is a legitimate option, plausible and "warranted" — unable to be discounted epistemologically. This position has been severely critiqued for its weakness by non-presuppositionalists[13] — and by presuppositionalists of the stricter variety as well.[14] But Plantinga's *God and Other Minds* is one of the best treatments of the problem of evil, and, almost single-handedly, he has been responsible for making Christian thinking respectable in secular philosophical circles in America.[15]

Over against presuppositionalism are the *evidentialists* and the self-styled *classical apologists*. Evidentialists hold that the fall, though certainly keeping sinful man from re-entering Eden by human effort or will, did not destroy his capacity to distinguish fact from non-fact, even in the religious realm (when God calls to Adam in the garden after he has eaten the forbidden fruit, Adam can still recognise God's voice). The apologetic task consists, then, of marshalling the full panoply of factual evidence to show that Christianity is true and its rivals false. Among prominent evidentialists are the author of this article; Gary Habermas; and the many advocates of the "Intelligent Design" movement (the most important being William Dembski).

"Classical" apologists, such as Norman Geisler, R. C. Sproul, and William Lane Craig, insist that, prior to making a factual, historical case for Jesus Christ, one must establish God's existence — generally using the classical, Aristotelian proofs, or sophisticated variants on those proofs (such as Craig's favourite, the medieval, Arabic *kalam* cosmological argument). Evidentialists almost invariably take the christocentric route, focusing their apologetic on the case for Jesus Christ and especially his resurrection — and approaching issues of God's existence by way of the incarnate Christ (Jesus to Philip: "he who has seen me has seen the Father" — John 14:8 – 9).

As Edward John Carnell once remarked, "There are as many apologetics as there are facts in the world." One should therefore expect specialised apologetic approaches in particular factual areas. Intelligent Design is such an approach — focusing on scientific fact. Other examples include *literary apologetics*, as exemplified by G. K. Chesterton, the Inklings (C. S. Lewis, J. R. R. Tolkien, Charles Williams), and contemporary literary scholars such as Gene Edward Veith[16]; and *juridical* (or *legal*) *apologetics*, where the sophisticated evidential techniques of the law are applied to the collection and interpretation of evidence in behalf of the faith. Historical representatives of legal apologetics would certainly include Thomas Sherlock (*The*

---

13. E.g., Jason Colwell, "The Historical Argument for the Christian Faith: A Response to Alvin Plantinga," 53/3 *International Journal for Philosophy of Religion* (2003), 147 – 61.

14. E.g., K. Scott Oliphint, "Plantinga on Warrant," 57/2 *Westminster Theological Journal* (1995), 415 – 35, and "Epistemology and Christian Belief," 63/1 *Westminster Theological Journal* (2001), 151 – 82.

15. In England, respect for the philosophical defence of Christian faith has not needed rehabilitation; see, for example, the valuable apologetic work of Richard Swinburne.

16. See Montgomery, "Neglected Apologetic Styles: The Juridical and the Literary," *Evangelical Apologetics*, ed. Michael Bauman, David Hall, and Robert Newman (Camp Hill, PA: Christian Publications, 1996), pp. 119 – 133.

Tryal of the Witnesses of the Resurrection of Jesus) and Simon Greenleaf (*The Testimony of the Evangelists*[17]); contemporary work in the field has been carried out by the author of this article, and by others such as Craig Parton and Ross Clifford. A recent survey of the area is William P. Broughton's *The Historical Development of Legal Apologetics, with an Emphasis on the Resurrection.*[18]

And there are what might be termed non-apologetic apologists, such as Regent College's John G. Stackhouse (*Humble Apologetics: Defending the Faith Today*). Stackhouse is highly critical of the kind of decisiveness represented by the title of Josh McDowell's influential book of popular apologetics, *Evidence That Demands a Verdict*, as well as aggressive attempts to defend the faith through public debates with unbelievers (he particularly dislikes the approach of William Lane Craig). Stackhouse seems to favour a postmodernist style of non-confrontation: the building of relationships with unbelievers rather than argumentation.[19]

How effective is the contemporary Christian apologetic? In spite of fine examples, there is much room for improvement. Here are three serious difficulties, as the present essayist sees them:

> · A continuing, virtually endemic disinterest on the part of many evangelical denominations, pastors, and laymen for the kind of rigorous academic study apologetics demands — and a corresponding preference for non-intellectual, subjective religiosity ("the devotional life"), group activities within the church ("fellowship"), and church-growth activism ("megachurchism"). This may appear on the surface as spirituality, but it is just the opposite — since it leaves the seeking unbeliever without an adequate witness.

> · The self-defeating nature of presuppositional and "humble" apologetic approaches. In the Apostolic witness of the New Testament (Paul on the Areopagus, for example), the Christian starts from a common ground with the unbeliever, moving him or her to the cross of Christ. One does not argue that the non-Christian's worldview is utterly inadequate and that only by starting from the Christian presupposition can any proper knowledge be arrived at. And the Apostles certainly did not fear confrontation or insist first on establishing personal "relationships" before the case for Christianity could be made. Our modern secular world is much like the pagan world of the Apostles, and it would behove us to consider seriously their defence of the faith as the proper model for ours.

> · Overemphasis on issues of God's existence rather than on the case for incarnation. We have seen how, owing to Aquinas' baptism of the traditional Aristotelian proofs for God's existence, these proofs became central to Roman Catholic apologetics and to much of Protestant defences of the faith during and even after the 18th-century "Enlightenment." We are not questioning the underlying logic of these proofs, but we are questioning the emphasis placed upon them. Salvation does not depend on believing in God: Scripture tells us that "the devils also believe, and tremble" (James 2:19). Salvation requires coming to terms with Jesus Christ — as the only Saviour from sin, death, and the devil. Thus the Christian apologetic needs to be, root and branch, an apologetic for Jesus Christ — not a disguised exercise in the philosophy of religion.[20]

The history of apologetics is really a special case of the history of evangelism. And the more secular the modern world becomes, the more important it is. If we neglect to answer the legitimate intellectual concerns of the unbelievers of our time, we are admitting that we do not really care about their eternal destiny. Apologetics does not save; only Jesus Christ is able to do that. But apologetics can — and should — serve as a John the Baptist, making the paths straight, facilitating routes to the cross of Christ.

---

17. Reprinted in Montgomery, *The Law Above the Law* (Minneapolis: Bethany, 1975).

18. Xulon Press, 2009.

19. For an interesting critique of this approach, by Canadian judge Dallas Miller, see 4/3 *Global Journal of Classical Theology,* October, 2004: http://phc.edu/gj_1_toc_v4n3.php

20. Cf. Montgomery, "Apologetics for the Twenty-first Century," *Reasons for Faith,* ed. Norman L. Geisler and Chad V. Meister (Wheaton, IL: Crossway, 2007), pp. 41–52.

CHAPTER 3

Varieties of Apologetics

James K. Beilby

1. Why Are There So Many Differences?[1]

Even a cursory study of the history of Christian apologetics will reveal that there are many different approaches to the subject. At first blush, this might be surprising. Why is there such a vast gulf standing between the approach of Aquinas and Luther, Locke and Kierkegaard, Barth and Schleiermacher, and Van Til and Swinburne? The answer lies in the range of possible answers that might be given to a series of fundamental questions. These questions have been called *meta-apologetic questions* since they are questions about the "methods, concepts, and foundations of apologetic systems and perspectives."[2] I will briefly discuss five such questions, the first three of which are theological in nature.

What is the relationship between faith and reason? From Augustine's time to today this question has preoccupied Christian theologians and apologists who have desired to explain what is involved in the Christian's belief in and commitment to God. Do we start with faith and only then try to explain it? Or is it possible to provide reasons for Christianity and only then, on the basis of those reasons, commit oneself in faith? There is, of course, a continuum of possible answers to this question.

John Locke represents the position known as *Rationalism*, the assertion that reason is the sole arbiter of truth and that faith is unnecessary when rational arguments are present. Thomas Aquinas and John Henry Newman ably represent the tradition of *Natural Theology*, a position that places primacy on reason but reserves an important role for faith in providing certitude for those unable to formulate theistic arguments. *Reformed Theology* reverses the primacy, giving faith the principal role. Augustine and John Calvin both held that arguments for the faith are truly valuable, but only for those who have already embraced faith and have received the regenerating work of the Holy Spirit. At the opposite end of the continuum from Rationalism, the *Fideism* of Henry Dodwell and Cornelius Van Til sharply delimits the use of rational arguments in apologetics, albeit for different reasons — Dodwell because arguments do not provide the level of certainty required for faith and Van Til because sinful humans must accept the authority of Scripture before they can understand arguments for its truthfulness. Finally, between Natural and Reformed Theology is *Synergism*, a position that gives universal primacy to neither reason nor faith. In some contexts and for some people, reason will lead; in others contexts and for other people, faith. Moreover, faith is absolutely reasonable and utilizing one's reason is, in an important sense, an act of faith. While Pascal admits that the primary truths of Christianity cannot be proved by reason, he avers that it is reason that shows humanity this fact. And responding to Christ in faith, for Pascal, is the most reasonable thing a person can do.

To what extent can humans understand God's nature? Closely connected with the previous meta-apologetic question is a question concerning the extent to which human language and thought can be said to refer to God. Of course, no one holds that the

---

1. This essay is a revised version of chapter four in my *Thinking About Christian Apologetics* (Downers Grove, InterVarsity, 2011). Used with permission.

2. Mark Hanna, *Crucial Questions in Apologetics* (Grand Rapids, MI: Baker, 1981) 94.

finite human mind can *fully* comprehend God's nature — as finite beings, it is doubtful that we can fully cognize anything, much less a being like God. The debate is over the extent to which human finitude and sinfulness affects our reasoning about God.

Some even question whether humans could understand God, even if sin was not a factor. The emphasis Karl Barth places on God's being "wholly other," for example, suggests that even if the noetic effects of sin were not a problem, Barth would still be highly suspicious of using human logic to demonstrate God's existence and nature. Others have a more optimistic view, believing that the fact that God created humans to be in relationship with him entails that he would have created humans with the ability to understand certain fundamental things about his nature — his goodness, love, and existence, for example. Such a perspective opens up the possibility for meaningful understanding of God's nature and therefore potentially persuasive arguments regarding his being or existence.

What is the role of the Holy Spirit in apologetics? This question is profoundly important in theology as well as in apologetics. Some see the primary role of the Holy Spirit as preparing the heart of unbelievers for apologetic encounters, others see the Holy Spirit as directing our attention to whom we should speak, still others see the Holy Spirit as helping the unbeliever to get from believing in God to committing themselves to God. Finally, some see the Holy Spirit as causally directing the entire process and see our contribution as minimal — our goal is to present the gospel and stay out of the way of the working of the Spirit. Many who see a profound role for the Holy Spirit will demand a diminished role for apologetic arguments. But it is important to see that this is not a zero-sum game. It is possible to see the apologist as significantly involved and still hold that the Holy Spirit will determine the effectiveness of our efforts.

In addition to these three theological questions, one's apologetic method will be affected by the following two philosophical meta-apologetic questions.

• *What is the nature of truth?* Apologetics is the defense of the *truthfulness* of the Christian worldview.

But what is truth? Most Christian apologists have understood truth as a quality or property of statements (or propositions). A statement possesses the quality or property of *being true* if it accurately represents the aspect of reality it is trying to describe. The statement "My laptop's battery is depleted" is true if and only if that particular state of affairs is real. There are, of course, many nuances that need to be added, but that is the typical picture of truth, usually called *the correspondence theory of truth*. Some, however, have attempted to deny the correspondence theory and have sought to replace it with pragmatic utility (beliefs are true if they are useful), coherence (beliefs are true if they are coherent or logically fit with a larger body of beliefs or facts), or personal embodiment (beliefs are not best thought of as true or false; truth is personal, i.e., Jesus is the truth). Still others have felt obliged by what some consider the implications of postmodernism to dispense with the concept of truth completely. Of course, if one rejects truth, one must also reject the notion that views contrary to your own are wrong. In such a state, arguments for your position and against other positions are out-of-place at best (and ludicrous at worst) and apologetics ceases to be a viable enterprise.

• *What is the task of apologetics?* The answer to this question may appear obvious, but it is not. Differences in how this question is answered account for a good bit of the differences between apologetic systems. Consider three different answers. First, one might see the task of apologetics as demonstrating the rationality of Christian belief. If so, then arguments against objections to Christian belief and for its reasonability will be the primary tools of the apologist. Second, some construe the task of apologetics as demonstrating that Christian belief is true. Apologists with such an understanding will have to not only give arguments for the reasonableness of Christianity, but against other rival worldviews. Moreover, if the apologist deems arguments insufficient to demonstrate the truthfulness of Christianity, he or she may argue that the truthfulness of Christianity must be accepted or presupposed, rather than argued for. Finally, one might see the task of apologetics as demonstrating that one ought to commit one's life to Jesus Christ. If so, while arguments may be important, they will only be part of the picture. Since it is possible to accept the truth of the Christian worldview but fail to commit one's life to Christ, it will be necessary to go beyond arguments for Christianity to personal appeals or pragmatic considerations in an attempt to make the person aware of their need for Christ.

2. Different Ways of Categorizing Apologetic Systems

In the 200 years (or so) that Christians began thinking systematically about the nature and methodology of apologetics, there have been a number of attempts to categorize the different types of approaches to apologetics. For those engaged in this task it has been tempting to divide apologetic systems into precise, mutually exclusive categories. Such an approach to categorization, however, has proved to be problematic. The best approach is to allow numerous categories, acknowledging that there will be overlap between these categories.[3]

There have been a variety of ways used to talk about the differences between apologetic systems.[4] Bernard Ramm, for example, distinguishes three families of apologetic systems: (1) Systems that stress the uniqueness of the Christian experience of grace, (2) Systems that stress natural theology as the point at which apologetics begins, and (3) systems that stress revelation as the foundation upon which apologetics must be built.[5] The strengths of Ramm's approach are many. Grace, natural theology, and revelation are undoubtedly absolutely fundamental concepts for any apologetic system. Nevertheless, some have objected

that Ramm's approach is not fine-grained enough.[6] His approach does not, some claim, take into account the real and important differences within his apologetic families.

Another important taxonomy of apologetic systems has been developed by Gordon Lewis.[7] He distinguishes different apologetic systems or methods according to their religious epistemology — that is, according to their beliefs about how one acquires religious knowledge. As helpful as Lewis's taxonomy is in many respects, there are two substantial drawbacks: first, appreciating the differences between the different apologetic systems requires a fairly substantial amount of philosophical training — something that most Christians lack, even many of those interested in apologetics; second, while there are philosophical differences between, for example, Pure empiricism and Rational empiricism, it is unclear that these philosophical differences mirror substantial differences in apologetic methodology.

Despite the strengths of Ramm's and Lewis's taxonomies (and, undoubtedly, because of their weaknesses), another method of describing apologetic systems has become more commonly used. This method categorizes apologetic systems by their *primary argumentative strategy*.[8] Even here, there are differences in terminology and classification. Norman Geisler and Steve Cowan each offer five views, but their lists overlap only on three: Classical Apologetics, Evidentialist Apologetics, and Presuppositional Apologetics.[9] Kenneth Boa, on the other hand, suggests four views: Classical (with a rationalist focus), Evidentialism (with an empirical focus), Reformed (with an authoritarian approach), and Fideism (with an intuitive approach).[10]

---

3. Norman Geisler, "Apologetics, Types of," in *Baker Encyclopedia of Christian Apologetics* (Grand Rapids, MI: Baker, 1999) 41.

4. In the introduction to *Five Views on Apologetics*, Steven Cowan does a nice job of discussing the various ways the differences between apologetics systems can be conceptualized (Grand Rapids, MI: Zondervan, 2000) 9 – 15.

5. Bernard Ramm, *Types of Christian Apologetics* (Wheaton, IL: Van Kampen, 1953) 7 – 13; *Varieties of Christian Apologetics* (Grand Rapids, MI: Baker, 1961) 14 – 17.

6. For example, Steve Cowan, "Introduction," 12 – 14.

7. Gordon Lewis, *Testing Christianity's Truth Claims* (Chicago: Moody, 1976).

8. Steven B. Cowan, "Introduction," in *Five Views on Apologetics*, ed. Steven Cowan (Grand Rapids, MI: Zondervan, 2000) 14.

9. Geisler, "Apologetics, Types of" in *Baker Encyclopedia of Christian Apologetics* (Grand Rapids, MI: Baker, 1999) 41 – 44; Cowan, 15 – 20.

10. Boa, *Faith Has Its Reasons: An Integrative Approach to Defending Christianity* (Colorado Springs: NavPress, 2001) 33 – 36.

Finally, David Clark employs the same four views as Boa (with different titles), but offers a second class of views, one with a person-centered approach rather than a content-centered approach. My own taxonomy of apologetic systems is informed by the conviction that there are three broad argumentative strategies: the Evidentialist Strategy (which emphasizes rational arguments of a variety of types), the Presuppositionalist Strategy (which emphasizes the authoritative testimony of Scripture), and the Experientialist Strategy (which, not surprisingly, emphasizes experience).

3. The Evidentialist Strategy

As its name indicates, the hallmark of evidentialism is its emphasis on the value of rational arguments and evidences. The evidentialist is committed to three ideas. First, since human beings have been created as rational beings and cannot commit themselves to what they believe to be false, rational and evidential arguments for the faith are a crucial element of an apologetic for Christianity. Second, there are profound intellectual objections to the faith that require a well-reasoned, well-supported response. Third, rational and evidential arguments can be very effective in overcoming people's objections to the faith and, at times, in encouraging people to take a step of faith itself. Evidentialists commonly offer C. S. Lewis as the poster-child for the ultimate success of evidentialist apologetics. Lewis likened his conversion to the return of a prodigal "brought in kicking, struggling, resentful, and darting his eyes in every direction for a chance of escape."[11] While it is unreasonable to see Lewis's conversion as exclusively evidentially motivated, it is undoubtedly true that rational arguments played a substantial role.

Evidentialist apologetics needs to be distinguished from *Evidentialism*, a position which involves the claim that one who accepts a belief without basing it on arguments is irrational. W. K. Clifford gave this view its classic expression saying, "it is wrong, always, everywhere, and for anyone to believe anything upon insufficient evidence."[12] While all evidentialist apologists embrace the apologetic *value* of rational arguments and evidences, only some of them aver that evidences and arguments are *necessary* for rational belief in God and that one who accepts a religious belief without basing it on arguments is irrational. There are other ways of distinguishing between Evidentialists. While all Evidentialists embrace rational evidences as their primary argumentative strategy, not all use evidence in the same way. In fact, three different schools can be identified within the evidentialist family tree.[13]

Classical apologetics. So called because of its ancient pedigree, the defining characteristic of the Classical apologetic method is its "two-step" approach.[14] The classical apologist argues, first, for the existence of God and, second, that Christianity is the most reasonable form of theism. Such a two-step approach is necessary, claims the classical apologist, because it is ludicrous to argue about which God exists when it has not been established that *any* God exists. Similarly, appeals to fulfilled prophecies or miracles are ineffective apart from the assumption that a God exists to reveal prophecies or act miraculously.[15] Classical apologists typically make ample use of a wide variety of theistic arguments as well as historical evidences for the reliability of Scripture and the reality of the resurrection of Jesus Christ. Noted contemporary classical apologists include William Lane Craig, Norman Geisler, and R. C. Sproul.

Historical apologetics. While Historical apologists share the classical apologist's emphasis on rational and evidential arguments, they dispute the necessity

---

11. C. S. Lewis, *Surprised by Joy* (London: Fontana, 1959) 183.

12. W. K. Clifford, "The Ethics of Belief," in *The Ethics of Belief and Other Essays*, ed. Timothy Madigan (Amherst, NY: Prometheus, 1999) 77.

13. Some go so far as to label these as separate apologetic systems. I do not do so because I believe that it is clear that their family resemblance is far more significant than their differences.

14. Norman Geisler, "Apologetics, Types of," in *Baker Encyclopedia of Christian Apologetics* (Grand Rapids: Baker, 1999) 41 – 44; see also idem, "Classical Apologetics," 154.

15. See R. C. Sproul, John Gerstner, and Arthur Lindsley, *Classical Apologetics: A Rational Defense of the Christian Faith* (Grand Rapids, MI: Zondervan, 1984) 146.

of arguing for God's existence prior to employing historical arguments from miracles or fulfilled prophecy. According to the Historical apologist, historical evidences are sufficient to demonstrate the truthfulness of both Christianity and theism. After all, if one is persuaded of the historicity of the resurrection story, it is not at all difficult to embrace the existence of a miracle-working deity. Consequently, historical apologetics is labeled a "one-step" approach. A common historical apologetic approach is to use historical evidences to demonstrate the historicity of the New Testament, including the historicity of the miracles of Christ, especially the resurrection. Or a historical apologist might argue that the historical details of the resurrection are explicable only if a God like that described by Christianity actually exists. Contemporary historical apologists include Gary Habermas, Josh McDowell, and John Warwick Montgomery.

Cumulative case apologetics. Those preferring a cumulative case approach to apologetics share the emphasis on rational arguments and evidences held by the classical and evidentialist apologists, but insist on neither a one-step nor a two-step approach. Rather, the cumulative case method might be called a "many-step" approach because it involves piecing together a series of converging arguments and evidences that, taken together, form a hypothesis that (it is claimed) is superior in explanatory power than any of its competitors. Cumulative case arguments could be used to demonstrate the reasonableness of Christian theism taken as a whole or to explain the reasonableness of a particular Christian doctrine, such as the bodily resurrection of Jesus Christ. Contemporary cumulative case apologists include Paul Feinberg and Richard Swinburne.

4. The Presuppositionalist Strategy

Presuppositional apologetics is substantially different from the Evidentialist strategy. Typically coming from a Reformed or Calvinist theological tradition, presup-

positionalists are leery of any attempt to appeal to a "common ground" with the non-Christian — either shared concepts or premises, a shared method of arguing, or shared experiences — holding that such attempts to build on common ground with the non-Christian do not take seriously enough the corruption of all worldviews or systems of thought that do not place the Christian God and his revelation at the center. In other words, according to the presuppositionalist, the problem with the non-Christian is not a lack of good reasons, but innate sinfulness manifested as rebellion against God, a rebellion that first and foremost amounts to a refusal to acknowledge God's proper place. Consequently, the authority of Scripture and of Jesus Christ must be presupposed before sense can be made of arguments for the truthfulness of Christianity. Presuppositionalism is, therefore sometimes labeled a "no-step" apologetic approach, for there are no argumentative steps that lead directly to the conclusion of the truthfulness of Christianity.

Generally speaking, if the hallmark of evidentialism is an appeal to reasons or arguments, presuppositionalism is an appeal to authority. There are, however, differences between presuppositionalists on how that appeal to authority is articulated. Consequently, as with Evidentialism, there are a variety of Presuppositionalists.[16] The best known and most influential is the *Revelational Presuppositionalism* of Cornelius Van Til (1895 – 1987). Van Til's approach replaces standard arguments and evidences for Christianity with a *transcendental* argument designed to show that the biblical God is necessary to all claims of meaning or intelligibility. Truth, logic, meaning, and value can exist only on the presupposition that the Christian God exists. This argument is not a direct argument for Christianity, but a *reductio ad absurdum* for the non-Christian's position, an argument that demonstrates the absurd conclusions entailed by all non-Christian worldviews. Van Til's standard has been ably taken up by his students Greg Bahnsen and John Frame.

16. Here I am following the terminology of Norman Geisler, "Presuppositional Apologetics," in *The Baker Encyclopedia of Christian Apologetics*, 607.

A second variety of presuppositionalism is the *Rational Presuppositionalism* of Gordon H. Clark (1902–1985). A staunch opponent of Van Til, Clark placed a much greater value on logical arguments than Van Til. Because he remained a presuppositionalist, however, he maintained one must accept the starting points or axioms of Christianity—that "what the Bible says, God has spoken."[17] As in geometry, axioms are never deduced but are assumed without proof, but Clark asserts that one can know that Christianity is true because it alone is logically consistent and all competing worldviews or philosophies are logically inconsistent. Clark's well-known student, Carl F. H. Henry (1913–2003), also championed this brand of presuppositionalism.

5. The Experientialist Strategy

Like presuppositional apologists, experiential apologists do not rely on logical arguments or evidences, but their reasons for rejecting an exclusively rational approach are different. They do not hold that the truth of Christianity must be presupposed, but rather that it must be experienced. Consequently, while the experiential apologist does not offer outward, logical evidences for the non-Christian to believe, they do offer internal, subjective reasons. For this reason, experiential apologetics might also be termed a "one-step" approach, although this one step is experiential, not logical.

While religious experience is central to experiential apologetics, it is important to distinguish between arguments for God's existence based on religious experience and experiential apologetics. Some who make apologetic use of religious experiences are not experiential apologists. For example, Richard Swinburne (an evidentialist) has developed detailed arguments for theistic belief based on religious experience.

One type of experiential argument calls attention to the transformative powers of the Christian life. The Christian philosopher William Alston explains this eloquently:

> The final test of the Christian scheme comes from trying it out in one's own life, testing the promises the scheme tells us God has made, following the way enjoined on us by the Church and seeing whether it leads to the new life of the Spirit. Admittedly, it is not always clear exactly what this involves; it is not always clear whether we are satisfying the conditions laid down for entering the kingdom; it is not always clear where we are at a given moment in our pilgrimage, whether, for example, an apparent setback or regression is part of the master plan or a failure on our part. And then there is the inconvenient fact that not all members of the body of Christ agree as to just what is required and just how the payoff is to be construed. But with all this looseness and open texture, the fact remains that over the centuries countless Christians who have set out to follow the way have found in their lives that the promises of God have been fulfilled, that their lives have been different, not 100 percent of the time and not as quickly and dramatically as they may have wished, but unmistakenly and in the direction the tradition predicts.[18]

Another experiential argument, articulated with impressive force by Pascal, Søren Kierkegaard, and C. S. Lewis, might be called "the argument from non-religious experience." Drawing on Pascal, Lewis has given this argument its most famous expression, asserting that there is a "God-shaped hole" in the heart of every human being. Apart from God, humans flounder in their effort to find happiness and meaning in life. Only in a relationship with God can humans find joy, meaning, and purpose.

6. An Evaluation of the Traditional Apologetic Systems

From the 60s to the 80s the debate between evidentialists and presuppositionalists raged throughout the halls of evangelical colleges and seminaries. While the

---

17. Gordon H. Clark, *In Defense of Theology* (Milford, MI: Mott Media, 1984) 32–33.

18. William Alston, *Perceiving God: The Epistemology of Religious Experience* (Ithaca, NY: Cornell University Press, 1991) 304.

debate is less shrill today than it has been, it is still worthwhile to briefly consider the sorts of arguments for and against the three traditional apologetics systems. I will, however, ignore what might be called "inter-category debates" — for example, the vigorous debates between historical apologists and classical apologists and between revelational and rational presuppositionalists.

An evaluation of the evidentialist strategy. In the past, some Evidentialist apologists have held that the arguments for Christian belief were sufficient to produce certain beliefs that the central teachings of Christianity were true. Theistic arguments were, some held, "proofs" whose conclusions followed from self-evident or obviously true premises without any possibility of doubt or uncertainty. Today, however, such a position is extremely rare. Most Evidentialists accept that arguments for God's existence are such that a sufficiently motivated skeptic can resist the intended conclusion. The typical goal of Evidentialist apologetics is to argue that arguments and evidences are sufficient to demonstrate that belief in the Christian God is not only reasonable, but also more reasonable than other competing worldviews. Evidentialist apologists also rightly stress the importance of the intellectual dimension when it comes to religious beliefs.

Non-evidentialists respond in a variety of ways. First, they charge Evidentialists with over-estimating the scope of human reason. There are many beliefs that are widely held for which there is no persuasive argument — belief in other minds, the existence of the past, and that we do not exist in the Matrix. Second, many argue that Evidentialists underestimate the deleterious effects of human sin. Sin affects not just our moral beliefs, but our reasoning and especially our willingness to submit to God's authority. Moreover, non-Evidentialists are quick to point out that even if God reveals himself to his creation, it is far from obvious that God's existence would be equally obvious to all, regardless of their presuppositions or motives for seeking God. God might after all only grant knowledge of himself to those who seek with a subservient attitude. Third, non-Evidentialists argue that Evidentialists tend to over-simplify important theological matters, sometimes compromising theological integrity in order to state the evidence in its most persuasive manner. And there is always the risk that the desire to present the strongest possible evidential case for Christianity will lead those who embrace an Evidentialist approach to treat evidence in a piecemeal fashion and ignore counter-evidence. Finally, non-Evidentialists argue that there is a fundamental disconnect between the best possible results of a theistic argument and the goal of biblical faith. Suppose a theistic argument demonstrated that the probability of Christian belief was 90 percent likely. This argument would place the believer in a situation analogous to the person who hears the weatherman announce that "There is a 90 percent chance of rain this afternoon." In such a case, one might act as if it will rain (i.e., bring an umbrella), but one should not believe "It will rain." And if you did, your belief would be unjustified. Rather, one should believe "It is very *likely* it will rain."[19] And this conclusion, non-Evidentialists object, is insufficient for grounding the level of commitment that accompanies biblical faith.

An evaluation of the presuppositional strategy. Presuppositional apologetics rightly places significant emphasis on the extent to which sin affects how humans view God, his revelation, and our responsibility with respect to God's revelation. The differences between the Christian and the non-Christian do not merely amount to differences of opinion, but fundamentally different perspectives on reality. Moreover, Scripture makes clear that unbelievers do not just reject knowledge of God, they suppress knowledge of God. In a very real sense, their presuppositions blind non-Christians to the truth of Christian belief. Moreover, Presuppositionalists join Experiential apologists in arguing that mental assent to evidences for

---

19. An argument made by Alvin Plantinga in "Rationality and Public Evidence," 220–221. Plantinga makes a similar argument in *Warranted Christian Belief*, 271, n. 56.

Christianity falls far short of the sort of commitment described in the Bible as faith.

The most fundamental objection to presuppositionalism is that presuppositionalists overstate their case in a variety of respects. It is far from obvious that the unbeliever's failure to presuppose God's existence, authority, and revelation makes it impossible for them to understand truths about the physical world and even about important aspects of the spiritual world. True, they cannot fully understand everything, but they might partially understand some things. Furthermore, even if arguments and reasons are insufficient to produce biblical faith, that doesn't imply that they are irrelevant. And even if it might be theologically problematic to build a comprehensive apologetic approach solely from presuppositions already embraced by the unbeliever, that doesn't imply that apologists cannot make effective use of arguments and evidences which appeal to presuppositions *shared* by Christians and non-Christians. If such arguments can increase the plausibility of Christian belief for a person or decrease their resistance to Christian belief, then it is difficult to see why they cannot be part of an apologist's arsenal.

An evaluation of the experientialist strategy. Experientialist apologetics rightly places emphasis on the necessity of experience. The Christian faith is not an abstract set of concepts to be believed but a life to be embraced, a life that includes all of a person — head, heart, and hands, reason, emotion, and will. The Christian idea of salvation involves a transformative relationship with the creator of the universe. It is not merely about one's beliefs, for "even the demons believe" (James 2:19). Further, when asked, it is doubtful that a majority of mature Christians will say that their belief is based on argument. Rather, it is likely that their faith is based on the fact that they have experienced the risen Christ in prayer, in the liturgies and sacraments of the Church, and in Christian community.

While many apologists make use of arguments based on religious experiences, experiential apologists are unique in their argument that experiential factors alone are sufficient to ground belief in God's existence. Evidentialists will push for rational explanations that support religious experiences and presuppositionalists will object that human sinfulness affects not only our reasoning but also the interpretations of our experiences.

Those who build their apologetic approach solely on experiential factors have to overcome at least two hurdles: (1) alternative explanations of religious experience and (2) the diversity of religious experiences. While it may seem obvious to the person having the experience that they have sensed God's presence, many other interpretations are possible, ranging from the skeptical to the arcane. A person may convince themselves that they have experienced God in order to help themselves deal with the difficulties of this world (Freud) or in order to justify economic oppression (Marx) or in order to lend credence to their aspirations and desires (Foucault). Or a person might be deceived by a malevolent demon or hallucinating. Of course, none of this suggests that religious experiences cannot be genuine, only that it is possible that they are not.

A second objection to experiential approaches to apologetics comes from the diversity of religious experiences. While the lack of religious experience is not evidence against the possibility of genuine religious experiences (since absence of evidence is not evidence of absence), the presence of conflicting religious experiences does constitute a problem for experiential apologetics. While many people in many different cultures and religions claim to have "experienced God" (in some sense), their experiences range widely. The experiential apologist must explain why the experiences of God which conflict with Christianity are not valid. An inability to do so is suggestive either that no religious experience is valid, or that all are. In the former case, experiential apologetics is pointless; in the latter case, it would be difficult to call the experiences "Christian."

7. The Possibility of an Eclectic Apologetic Methodology

In the past it was often assumed that the dividing lines between apologetic systems were clear and precise.

Increasingly, however, it is acknowledged that there are no such clear lines. These three strategies are probably best described as ideal types — categories that are rarely perfectly exemplified. As conceptual tools they have substantial value, but when they are applied to individual apologists the lines that divide systems become profoundly blurred. This is because sometimes the differences between apologists represent fundamental philosophical and theological convictions and, as such, concern how apologetics *must be* practiced. Other times the differences between apologists in competing systems are merely pragmatic in nature, reflecting personally preferred styles of argumentation.[20] As such, they concern only how apologetics *might be* practiced.

To help account for the gray areas between apologetic strategies, we need a distinction. An apologist who is, for example, a presuppositionalist for fundamental theological or philosophical reasons, is a *Strict* Presuppositionalist, and one who embraces presuppositionalism for pragmatic reasons is an *Eclectic* Presuppositionalist. A Strict Presuppositionalist will reject the Evidentialist and Experientialist approaches as viable options. They will hold that there are theological or philosophical factors that make Presuppositionalism the only viable approach. The same would go for the Strict Evidentialist or the Strict Experientialist. Cornelius Van Til is undoubtedly a strict Presuppositionalist, Francis Schaeffer is not; John Locke is a Strict Evidentialist, Richard Swinburne is not; and Søren Kierkegaard is a Strict Experientialist, C. S. Lewis is not. While eclectic apologists might (and very likely will) prefer one approach over the others, they will not see their approach as the only viable one. Of course, an eclectic apologist might see one of the other approaches as severely problematic. For example, an Eclectic Evidentialist apologist might embrace aspects of Experiential apologetics, but absolutely reject Presuppositionalism. And it is possible that an apologist will embrace aspects of all three methodologies.

Therefore, much as one can produce 16 million different colors[21] just from blending the three primary colors, one can employ a chromatic metaphor to explain the dizzying diversity of approaches to apologetics in terms of the emphasis each places on these three fundamental intuitions. Just as one can produce the color magenta by 255 parts blue, 255 parts red, and 0 parts green, one might describe a particular apologetic approach as 100 parts Evidentialist, 200 parts Presuppositionalist, and 50 parts Experientialist. Some might see the rise of Eclectic apologetic methodologies as symptomatic of postmodernism. The problem with this perspective is that long before our postmodern age, Augustine, Anselm, and Pascal made use of an eclectic approach. And there are many contemporary apologists whose work is best labeled "Eclectic." I will close this essay by briefly mentioning just three.

First, Edward Carnell (1919 – 1967) was a Presuppositionalist who defended a substantial role for theological arguments and evidences. He held that "Because we know God's existence and nature in our heart, we recognize Him in his handiwork."[22] But he also sought to "build on useful points of contact between the gospel and culture."[23] These points of contact included the law of non-contradiction, values, judicial sentiment, and love. Part of the uniqueness of his apologetic approach is that he allowed it to be governed by specific situations. He said: "There is no 'official' or 'normative' approach to apologetics.... The approach is governed by the climate of the times. This means, as it were, that an apologist must play it by ear."[24]

Second, C. Stephan Evans models an eclectic approach to apologetics in his book *Why Believe? Reason and Mystery as Pointers to God*. Strongly influenced by the emphasis on personal experience and

20. William Lane Craig, "A Classical Apologist's Response," in *Five Views on Apologetics*, ed. Steven B. Cowan, 122.

21. Actually, 16,777,216.

22. Edward Carnell, *An Introduction to Christian Apologetics* (Grand Rapids: Eerdmans, 1948) 169.

23. Carnell, *The Kingdom of Love and the Pride of Life* (Grand Rapids, MI: Eerdmans, 1960) 6.

24. Carnell, *The Kingdom of Love and the Pride of Life*, 5.

mystery found in Søren Kierkegaard, he also finds a substantial role for theistic arguments. Experience and rational argument are not opposed to each other for Evans because, while human beings are certainly rational beings, rational arguments can only take one so far. Drawing upon an insight developed by both Kierkegaard and Pascal, Evans asserts that while logical arguments may convince the mind, they make little impression upon the heart. Consequently, both arguments based on our observations of the world and experiences of the mysterious can point us to God, says Evans. The case for Christianity will not be based on a single argument, but on the sum total of evidence available from each and every aspect of human experience.

Finally, Alvin Plantinga blends aspects of presuppositionalism with experientialism. Ironically, Plantinga uses highly sophisticated philosophical arguments to demonstrate that religious belief need not, and even should not, be based solely on arguments. Further, following John Calvin, Plantinga argues that God has created humans with an innate ability — called the *sensus divinitatis* — to form beliefs about God in certain circumstances — when viewing a starry sky, for example. While sin suppresses this innate ability, God's act of redemption can restore a degree of functionality of the *sensus divinitatis*. Plantinga, therefore, is opposed to Evidentialism, but he is not opposed to giving arguments for God's existence. In fact, he has developed what some feel is a successful version of the ontological argument. And while he emphasizes the essential role of Christian experiences in his work, he does not do so in a way that excludes rational thought and argument. Finally, while Plantinga believes that the essential truths of the faith cannot be proved and therefore may be, in some sense of the word, presupposed by the Christian, nothing in his work suggests that Christians cannot or should not develop arguments to support their faith. He claims only that Christians need not do so in order to be rational.

CHAPTER 4

Interreligious Apologetics

Harold Netland

Since the eighteenth century Christian apologists in the West have been concerned largely with responding to the challenges to Christian faith presented by religious agnosticism or atheism. This is understandable, given the intensity and sophistication of such critiques. Yet, with globalization and the pluralization of Western societies, secular atheism is just one of many perspectives demanding attention by apologetics in the twenty-first century. A quite different set of issues emerges from the various religious worldviews attracting attention today. Despite the growing numbers of those who are explicitly non-religious, the overwhelming majority of people today worldwide regard themselves as followers of some religious tradition. Roughly 80% of people worldwide profess some religious affiliation.[1] Resurgent religions such as Islam, Hinduism, Buddhism, Jainism and Sikhism provide comprehensive perspectives on life, the cosmos, and what is religiously ultimate that are different from — and at points incompatible with — Christianity.

While they include much more than merely doctrines, religions characteristically make far-reaching assertions about the nature of reality. Religions offer particular perspectives on what is of ultimate significance, the nature of the predicament confronting humankind, and the way to overcome this predicament and realize a much more desirable state. As Keith Yandell puts it, "A religion proposes a diagnosis of a deep, crippling spiritual disease universal to non-divine sentience and offers a cure."[2] Religions hold that realization of the desired state — whether salvation or liberation or enlightenment — depends in part upon accepting the central teachings of the religion as true and acting appropriately on them.

But the religions notoriously disagree about the nature of the religious ultimate, the diagnosis of the problem afflicting humankind, and the cure. Thus, it has traditionally been maintained that not all of the religions can be correct in their claims. Buddhists, for example, insist that there is no creator God whereas Muslims teach that the universe was created by God. Christians maintain that Jesus of Nazareth was God incarnate, fully God and fully man. Muslims deny this. Theravada Buddhists deny the ontological reality of an enduring soul, whereas Advaita Vedantin Hindus not only affirm the reality of the soul but hold that the soul is (somehow) to be identified with Brahman (whose existence Buddhists also reject). Not all of these claims can be true.[3]

Given globalization, massive migrations, and the

1. Joanne O'Brien and Martin Palmer, *The Atlas of Religion* (Berkeley: University of California Press, 2007) p. 14.

2. Keith Yandell, "How to Sink in Cognitive Quicksand: Nuancing Religious Pluralism", in Michael L. Peterson and Raymond J. VanArragon, eds. *Contemporary Debates in Philosophy of Religion* (Oxford: Balckwell, 2004) p. 191.

3. On conflicting truth claims in the religions see William A. Christian, *Oppositions of Religious Doctrines* (New York: Herder and Herder, 1972); idem, *Doctrines of Religious Communities: A Philosophical Study* (New Haven: Yale University Press, 1987). Religious pluralists, who argue that all major religions are roughly equal with respect to truth, rationality and soteriological effectiveness, try to acknowledge both that the religions make conflicting truth claims and that the religions can nevertheless be regarded as equally legitimate responses to the same ultimate divine reality. See John Hick, *An Interpretation of Religion*, 2nd ed. (New Haven: Yale University Press, 2004 1989.). For a critical assessment of religious pluralism, see Harold Netland, *Encountering Religious Pluralism* (Downers Grove, IL: InterVarsity Press, 2001).

telecommunications revolutions, people today are aware of religious diversity and disagreement as never before. Thus, Christian apologetics in the days ahead must contend with not only the critiques of atheists and radical secularists but also the sophisticated challenges from intellectuals in other religions.

Interreligious Apologetics in Premodern Times

Many today think of Christian apologetics as a modern Western response to the various challenges posed by the European Enlightenment. Many assume that while there may be a place for apologetics in the modern West (although many would dispute even this!) there is no place for it in encounters with other religions. Religions of Asia, it is said, have not been concerned with demonstrating the distinctive truth or rationality of their own views; indeed, reason plays little role in Asian religions. Interreligious apologetics is thus at best a Western, theistic concern that is not shared by Asian religious traditions.

But this common assumption is seriously misleading. First, apologetics, understood as providing reasons for one's own religious commitments and raising questions about the beliefs of religious others, is not a modern, post-Enlightenment innovation but can be traced back to the early church fathers. During the second and third centuries Christian apologists such as Justin Martyr, Claudius Apollinaris, Athenagoras, Tatian, Theophilus of Antioch, Clement of Alexandria, Tertullian and Origen, responded to critics with important defenses of Christian belief and practice. Some addressed attacks from pagan Greco-Roman thinkers; others tried to persuade Jews to accept the claims of the New Testament.[4]

Whereas during the first four centuries Christian apologists addressed issues arising from Judaism or the surrounding Greco-Roman world, by the eighth century attention turned to a new challenge — Islam. With the rapid rise of Islam in the eighth and ninth centuries, Christians in places such as Damascus and Baghdad were forced to come to grips with Islamic religious and intellectual currents and they did so by producing some incisive works in apologetics and theology. John of Damascus (d. 749), who wrote the *Fount of Knowledge*, arguably the first systematic theology, lived all his life among Muslims and even held an administrative post under the Umayyad caliphs in Damascus. The *Fount of Knowledge* was not merely a systematic compendium of orthodox teachings of the early church. It was also a "response to the commanding intellectual challenge of Islam" and was intended "to discredit the religious and intellectual claims of Islam in the eyes of inquiring Christians."[5] John of Damascus also wrote *A Dialogue Between a Saracen and a Christian*, a work explicitly devoted to apologetics in the Islamic context. Patriarch Timothy (d. 823), the patriarch of the Church of the East in Baghdad, was an accomplished apologist who debated with Muslim thinkers in the presence of the Muslim caliph al-Mahdi.[6] But perhaps the most significant early medieval apologist concerning Islam was Theodore Abu Qurrah (d. 830), a disciple of John of Damascus. Abu Qurrah wrote *God and the True Religion* in Arabic, and in it he confronts the problem of choosing among Zoroastrian religion, Samaritan religion, Judaism, Christianity, Manichaeism, and Islam — all of which claim divine revelation. He attempted to demonstrate "that Christianity presents the most plausible idea of God, exhibits the fullest understanding of man's actual religious needs, and prescribes what appear to be the most appropriate remedies."[7] Abu Qurrah also participated in a debate with Muslim scholars and the caliph al-Mamun in 829.

Early Christian thinkers from at least the second century were aware of the teachings of the Buddha,

---

4. See Robert M. Grant, *Greek Apologists of the Second Century* (Philadelphia: Westminster Press, 1988); Mark Edwards, Martin Goodman and Simon Price, eds., *Apologetics in the Roman Empire* (Oxford: Oxford University Press, 1999); and Avery Dulles, *A History of Apologetics* (Philadelphia: Westminster, 1971) chapter 2.

5. Sidney H. Griffith, *The Church in the Shadow of the Mosque: Christians and Muslims in the World of Islam* (Princeton, NJ: Princeton University Press, 2008) p. 42.

6. Ibid., pp. 45 – 48.

7. Avery Dulles, *A History of Apologetics*, p. 74.

although they seem not to have had a very clear understanding of Buddhist precepts.[8] One of the earliest accounts of a Christian engagement with Buddhism is found in the diaries of William of Rubruck, a Franciscan friar who reached the Mongol court in 1253. William gives us a fascinating look at a debate between a Buddhist and himself in 1254 before Mongke Khan, the grandson of the notorious Mongol ruler Genghis Khan. It is clear from William's account (which is our only source for the debate) that William and the Buddhist engaged in a vigorous exchange as each probed perceived weaknesses in the other's worldview. The Buddhist pressed hard on the problem of evil, an issue that Buddhists regard as devastating for monotheism. "If your God is as you say, why does he make the half of things evil?" When William insisted that all that proceeds from God is good, the Buddhist demanded, "Whence then comes evil?"[9]

In the sixteenth century the Jesuit missionary scholar Matteo Ricci (d. 1610) journeyed to the imperial court in China, and embarked upon a serious study of early Chinese religious and intellectual traditions.[10] Ricci mastered classical Chinese and became recognized as an authority on the Confucian classics. He became convinced that early Confucianism had been monotheistic and that Chinese Christians could adopt much of the Confucian terminology and conceptual categories, although he believed that Daoism and Buddhism were incompatible with Christian teachings. In 1603 Ricci published *On the True Meaning of the Lord of Heaven*, an impressive work in Christian apologetics which attempts to establish the existence of a personal creator God and thus show the inadequacy of Daoist and Buddhist conceptions of religious ultimacy.[11] Ricci had a significant impact upon the Chinese cultured elite, and a number of Confucian literati became Christians through his ministry. Thus, there is a long history of Christian apologetics with respect to other religions prior to the modern era.

Furthermore, the attempt to defend the truth of one's own religious beliefs through appeal to reason and argument, and to persuade others to accept them as well, is not unknown among Asian religious traditions. While it is true that some traditions within Hinduism, Buddhism and Daoism minimize the role of reason in favor of direct, intuitive experiences of the religious ultimate that allegedly transcend reason, many other traditions within these religions historically have made use of rigorous rational analysis in supporting religious claims. There were vigorous debates among competing schools within Hinduism or Buddhism, for example, as well as between adherents of religions such as Jainism, Hinduism, Buddhism, Daoism and Confucianism.[12] Speaking of Hinduism, for example, Richard Fox Young observes that,

[P]roponents of the great *darsanas*, philosophical views or systems, endeavored to brace their own ideas or doctrines by exposing the fallacies of others. To cite only one instance, Sankara's commentary on the Brahmasutras refuted, in turn, each of the major theories, cosmological, metaphysical, soteriological, etc., to which other Hindu thinkers, Buddhists, Jains, and materialists subscribed. Apologetics was so much a part of classical works on religion and philosophy that a text without at least an adumbration of the

8. Lawrence Sutin, *All is Change: The Two Thousand Year Journey of Buddhism to the West* (New York: Oxford University Press, 2006) p. 24.

9. Richard Fox Young, "*Deus Unus or Dei Plures Sunt*? The Function of Inclusivism in the Buddhist Defense of Mongol Folk Religion Against William of Rubruck (1254)", *Journal of Ecumenical Studies* 26, no. 1 (1989) p. 115. See also Samuel Hugh Moffett, *A History of Christianity in Asia*, vol. 1 (New York: HarperCollins, 1992) pp. 409 – 14.

10. See Andrew Ross, *A Vision Betrayed: The Jesuits in Japan and China, 1542 – 1742* (Maryknoll, NY: Orbis, 1994); Jonathan Spence,

The Memory Palace of Matteo Ricci (New York: Viking, Penguin, 1984); and Liam Matthew Brockery, *Journey to the East: The Jesuit Mission to China, 1579 – 1724* (Cambridge, MA: Harvard University Press, 2007).

11. See Matteo Ricci, *The True Meaning of the Lord of Heaven*, trans. Douglas Lancashire and Peter Hu Kuo-chen (St. Louis: Institute of Jesuit Sources, 1985).

12. For a classic statement of how representatives of Christianity, Judaism, Islam Buddhism, and Hinduism have engaged with claims of other religions with respect to truth and rationality see Ninian Smart, *A Dialogue of Religions* (London: SCM Press, 1960).

standard criticisms of its rivals would surely seem incomplete.[13]

There were rigorous debates between Hindus, Buddhists and Jains over issues such as whether there are enduring substantial souls (Hindus and Jain said yes, Buddhists denied this) or whether a creator God exists (some Hindus said yes, Jains and Buddhists denied this).[14]

The introduction of Christianity to Asian cultures was regarded by Hindus, Muslims and Buddhists as a direct threat to their teachings and ways of life. Proclamation of the Christian gospel often was met with hard-hitting intellectual responses by Hindus, Muslims and Buddhists, who attempted to demonstrate the falsity or irrationality of Christian claims.[15] Francis Xavier introduced Christianity to Japan in 1549 and in the next decades the number of Christians grew dramatically. The Jesuit missionary presence provoked a vigorous response by Japanese Buddhists, who argued that Christianity not only was unreasonable but would be harmful for the Japanese people.

One of the most interesting Japanese polemicists was Fabian (Fukansai) Fucan (d. 1621), a Buddhist monk who converted to Christianity and began preparing for the priesthood. But when it became clear that the Jesuits would not admit him into the priesthood, Fabian abandoned the Christian faith and became a sharp critic of Christianity. While with the Jesuits, Fabian had written *Myotei Mondo* [*Myotei Dialogue*], a work in Christian apologetics which defends the idea of a personal creator and tries to show the falsehood of Buddhism, Confucianism and Shinto. Having abandoned Christianity, however, Fabian wrote *Ha Daiusu* [*Deus Destroyed*], a stinging refutation of Christianity.[16] There were numerous debates between Christians and Japanese Buddhists during this time, as well as many polemical writings intended to demonstrate the falsity of Christianity and the superiority of Japanese religious traditions. Much later, when Protestant missionaries entered Japan in the nineteenth century, Buddhists launched a sharp anti-Christian campaign that criticized the idea of a personal creator, the divine inspiration of the Bible and — due to the recent influence of German religious and scientific scholarship upon Japanese education — the alleged incompatibility of the biblical account of creation with Darwinian science.[17]

During the nineteenth and twentieth centuries, with the expansion of the Christian church throughout Asia, there were many polemical exchanges between Hindus and Christians in India and Ceylon, as well as between Christians and Muslims throughout Asia. Hinduism, Buddhism and Islam all experienced a religious resurgence in the post-colonial world of the twentieth century, as leading intellectuals within the religions argued for the rejection of Christianity,

13. Richard Fox Young, *Resistant Hinduism: Sanskrit Sources on Anti-Christian Apologetics in Early Nineteenth Century India* (Vienna: Institut für Indologie der Universität Wien, 1981) p. 13.

14. For Buddhist critiques of the existence of God see Parimal G. Patil, *Against a Hindu God: Buddhist Philosophy of Religion in India* (New York: Columbia University Press, 2009); Arvind Sharma, *The Philosophy of Religion: A Buddhist Perspective* (Delhi: Oxford University Press, 1995); and Gunapala Dharmasiri, *A Buddhist Critique of the Christian Concept of God* (Antioch, CA: Golden Leaves Publishing Company, 1988). For analysis of such critiques see Paul Williams, "Aquinas Meets the Buddhists: Prolegomena to an Authentically Thomas-ist Basis for Dialogue", in *Aquinas in Dialogue: Thomas for the Twenty-First Century*, ed. Jim Fodor and Christian Bauerschmidt (Oxford: Blackwell Publishing, 2004) pp. 87 – 117; and Keith Yandell and Harold Netland, *Buddhism: A Christian Exploration and Appraisal* (Downers Grove, IL: InterVarsity Press, 2009) pp. 180 – 92.

15. See Richard Fox Young, *Resistant Hinduism: Sanskrit Sources*

on *Anti-Christian Apologetics in Early Nineteenth Century India*; R. F. Young and S. Jebanesan, *The Bible Trembled: The Hindu-Christian Controversies of Nineteenth Century Ceylon* (Vienna: Institut für Indologie der Universität Wien, 1995); Kenneth W. Jones, ed., *Religious Controversy in British India* (Albany, NY: State University of New York Press, 1992); Harold Coward, ed., *Hindu-Christian Dialogue: Perspectives and Encounters* (Maryknoll, NY: Orbis, 1989); and Paul J. Griffiths, ed., *Christianity Through Non-Christian Eyes* (Maryknoll, NY: Orbis, 1990).

16. See George Elison, *Deus Destroyed: The Image of Christianity in Early Modern Japan* (Cambridge, MA: Harvard University Press, 1973), and Monika Schrimpf, "The Pro- and Anti- Christian Writings of Fukan Fabian (1565 – 1621)", *Japanese Religions*, vol. 33 nos.1 and 2 (July 2008) 35 – 54.

17. See Notto Thelle, *Buddhism and Christianity in Japan: From Conflict to Dialogue, 1854 – 1899* (Honolulu: University of Hawaii Press, 1987) chapter 2.

which was linked to Western colonialism, and urged a return to their respective religious traditions.

Issues in Interreligious Apologetics

It is clear, then, that even prior to the modern era there has been a long tradition of interreligious apologetics, with Christians and adherents of other religions engaging in vigorous debate, each side attempting to demonstrate the intellectual superiority of its own position. Nor should this be surprising. For religious leaders have characteristically understood their religious claims to be of great significance, and those within a particular tradition are expected to accept these teachings as true and to live in accordance with the truth of such beliefs. It is accepted across the religions that counter-assertions from other traditions, which implicitly call into question one's own commitments, must be addressed and shown to be unwarranted.

But interreligious apologetics strikes many today as distasteful and inappropriate in our pluralistic world. For many today, interreligious encounters should be marked by the search for mutual understanding, respect, and common ground, objectives best achieved by interreligious dialogue and not polemics. Thus, Paul Griffiths speaks of "an underlying scholarly orthodoxy on the goals and functions of interreligious dialogue" that maintains that "understanding is the only legitimate goal; that judgment and criticism of religious beliefs and practices other than those of one's own community is always inappropriate; and that an active defense of the truth of those beliefs and practices to which one's community appears committed is always to be shunned."[18] Griffiths provides a trenchant critique of this view, arguing that in certain circumstances religious communities actually have an obligation to engage in interreligious apologetics. If representative intellectuals of a specific religious community come to believe that some or all of their own core doctrines are incompatible with some claims made by representatives of another religious community, then they have an obligation to respond to the alien religious claims by attempting to show that the alien claims are unwarranted or that one's own beliefs are not threatened by such claims.[19]

Griffiths suggests that there is both an epistemic and a moral component to this obligation.[20] Religious communities hold their own religious beliefs to be true, and thus when a particular community is confronted by other claims challenging these beliefs it has an epistemic duty to consider whether the challenge does make it improper (epistemically) for the community to continue believing as it does. Moreover, most religious traditions maintain not only that their claims are true but also that there is significant salvific value in accepting and acting on these beliefs as true. If a religious community believes that humankind suffers from a general malady (sin, ignorance), that its central religious claims are true, and that accepting and acting appropriately upon these beliefs can bring about salvation or liberation from the malady, then the community has an ethical obligation to share this good news with those outside the tradition, trying, in appropriate ways, to persuade them of the truth of the community's beliefs.

The kind of issues dealt with in interreligious apologetics will differ somewhat from the issues addressed in apologetics in contexts of religious agnosticism or atheism. Some questions will be similar. The question of God's existence and the problem of evil will be central with Buddhists and Jains as well as with secular agnostics and atheists. Questions about the deity of Jesus Christ are relevant for both atheists and Muslims, Hindus and Buddhists. Other issues are especially significant in an interreligious context. How is one to know which, if any, sacred scriptures are indeed divinely inspired? Why accept the Bible as God's Word but not the Qur'an? Many religions include miracle claims.[21] Are they all to be accepted as

18. Paul Griffiths, *An Apology for Apologetics: A Study in the Logic of Interreligious Dialogue* (Maryknoll, NY: Orbis, 1991) p. xi.

19. Ibid., p. 3.

20. Ibid., pp. 15 – 16.

21. See Kenneth L. Woodward, *The Book of Miracles: The Meaning of the Miracle Stories in Christianity, Judaism, Buddhism, Hinduism, and Islam* (New York: Touchstone, 2000). For a helpful Christian treatment of the subject see David K. Clark, "Miracles

true? If not, why should we accept the miracle claims in the Bible but not those in other religious texts? Do certain mystical states provide direct access to ultimate reality? If not, why not? How should we assess reports of religious experiences in the many religions? Are they all veridical? How do we distinguish those that are veridical from those that are not? And so on. As with Christian apologetics generally, the two most significant issues will likely be the question of God's existence and the identity of Jesus of Nazareth. If there are good reasons for believing that an eternal creator God exists, then there are good reasons for rejecting religious worldviews, such as classical Buddhism and Jainism, which include as an essential component denial of God's existence. If there are good reasons for accepting the New Testament picture of Jesus as fully God and fully man, the one Lord and Savior for all humankind, then there are good reasons for rejecting religious worldviews which deny this.

Interreligious apologetics presupposes the falsity of what is sometimes called the incommensurability thesis. The incommensurability thesis, as applied to religions, maintains that religions are such comprehensive and integrative wholes, and are so different from each other, that they can be understood only from within a particular religious system, and that any criteria for assessing religious worldviews are strictly internal to particular religious or non-religious worldviews. There are no criteria for assessing alternative religious worldviews for truth or rationality that somehow transcend the religions themselves. While one can from within a particular religious worldview understand and speak meaningfully of the "truth" of that worldview, one who is not an insider to that worldview can neither really understand it nor make responsible judgments about its truth or reasonableness. The incommensurability thesis, then, is a sophisticated form of relativism applied to religious worldviews. If true, then interreligious apologetics is impossible. Not only would it be impossible to understand another religious worldview (and how can one offer a responsible critique of what one cannot understand?) but any criteria used in assessing the truth or rationality of a religious worldview would be merely the product of one's own worldview and thus arbitrary. The issues here are complex, but suffice it to say that there are no good reasons for accepting the incommensurability thesis.[22] Understanding is not a matter of all or nothing, it is a matter of degrees. There is no reason to suppose that an adherent of one religion cannot attain a sufficiently accurate and deep understanding of another religious worldview to make responsible judgments about its truth. Nor is there any good reason to hold that there are no criteria for assessing truth or rationality that apply across religious worldviews.

Those engaging in interreligious apologetics must take necessary time to study other religious traditions carefully, making sure that they understand other religious worldviews accurately and are not simply dealing with simplistic caricatures. This will demand rigorous and extensive study, mastering the languages necessary for study of their authoritative texts as well as supplementing literature-based research with ethnographic studies of religious communities. Responsible interreligious apologetics will be fair in its treatment of other religious worldviews, willingly acknowledging what is true and good in them even as it points out what is false or otherwise problematic. The objective is not to score easy points at the expense of the other but rather to understand the other's position adequately so that one can provide compelling reasons for considering what the Scriptures say about the gospel of Jesus Christ.

Our world is marked by deep ethnic, cultural and religious tensions which too often find expres-

in the World Religions", in *In Defense of Miracles*, ed. R. Douglas Geivett and Gary Habermas (Downers Grove, IL: InterVarsity Press, 1997) pp. 199–213.

22. See Harold Netland, *Encountering Religious Pluralism*, pp. 284–307; Keith Yandell, *Christianity and Philosophy* (Grand Rapids: Eerdmans, 1984) pp. 272–285; Ninian Smart, *Reasons and Faiths: An Investigation of Religious Discourse, Christian and Non-Christian* (London: Routledge & Kegan Paul, 1958); and Eliot Deutsch, ed., *Culture and Modernity: East-West Philosophic Perspectives* (Honolulu: University of Hawaii Press,1991).

sion in acts of religious violence.[23] Sadly, Christian apologetics is often viewed as contributing to interreligious tensions. Those engaging in apologetics in contexts of religious and ethnic diversity need to be especially sensitive to potential misunderstandings and the importance of culturally appropriate means of persuasion. Interreligious encounters do not occur in a historical or cultural vacuum; both sides of the encounter bring with them the accumulated heritage of the past as well as the potential for misunderstandings in the present. Effective use of morally acceptable and culturally appropriate means of persuasion requires appreciation of the past and present realities within which the interreligious encounter takes place.

Christian apologists must be especially sensitive to the place of symbolic power within interreligious encounters. The attempt to persuade religious others that they should change their fundamental beliefs and accept core Christian claims as true can easily be perceived as an inappropriate assertion of power, especially if the Christian is associated with significant cultural, economic, political or military frameworks of power. Moreover, any activity that is manipulative or coercive, or otherwise infringes upon the dignity of the other, must be rejected. Certain historical factors make interreligious apologetics in certain contexts especially difficult. Contexts in which Christianity has been closely associated with cultural superiority, racism, or economic exploitation make interreligious apologetics particularly problematic. Christians should be especially careful about apologetics encounters with religious communities, such as Jewish and Muslim communities, which have suffered greatly in the past at the hands of Christendom. Christian apologists in interreligious contexts must be not only skilled at defending the truth of the Christian message, but they must also be winsome and gracious, serving as peacemakers and instruments of reconciliation as appropriate. But when conducted properly, Christian apologetics with respect to other religious worldviews is an essential and significant part of Christian witness and discipleship. For in the decades ahead the issue will not simply be whether to be a Christian rather than an atheist; the question will be, Given all of the religious and non-religious worldviews available, why should one become or remain a follower of Jesus Christ?

---

23. See Mark Juergensmeyer, *Global Rebellion: Religious Challenges to the Secular State, From Christian Militias to Al Qaeda* (Berkeley, CA: University of California Press, 2008).

CHAPTER 5

The Knowability of History

Norman L. Geisler

Unlike some religions, historical Christianity is inseparably tied to historical events, including the lives of Adam, Abraham, Moses, David, Jesus. These events, especially those of the life, death, and resurrection Christ, are crucial to the truth of evangelical Christianity (cf. 1 Cor. 12–15); without them, it would cease to exist. Thus, the existence and knowability of certain historical events are essential to maintaining biblical Christianity.

The knowability of history is important not only theologically but also apologetically, for the overall argument in defense of Christianity is based on the historicity of the New Testament documents [...]. Hence, since the objective knowability of history is strongly challenged by contemporary historians, it is necessary to counter this claim for the defense of Christianity.

Objections to the Objectivity of History

Many arguments have been advanced against the position that history is objectively knowable (see Craig, *NH*),[1] and several will now be examined (see Beard, "TND" in Stern, *VH*, 323–25).[2] If these disputations are valid, they make the essential historical basis of Christianity both unknowable and unverifiable. These arguments fall into six broad categories: epistemological, axiological, methodological, metaphysical, psychological, and hermeneutical.

The Epistemological Objections

Epistemology deals with how one *knows*, and relativists believe objective truth is unknowable. Since this position has earlier been examined and found wanting, the focus here will be on the historical relativists, who contend that the very conditions by which one knows history are so subjective that one cannot have an objective knowledge of it. Three main challenges are offered.

The Unobservability of History

Historical subjectivists argue that history, unlike science, is not directly observable; in other words, that the historian does not deal with past events but with statements about past events. This enables the historian to deal with facts in an imaginative way, attempting to reconstruct events he did not observe as they occurred. Historical facts, they insist, exist only within the creative mind of the historian, and historical documents do not contain facts, but are without the historian's understanding mere ink lines on the paper. Further, once the event is over it can never be fully recreated. Hence, the historian must impose meaning on his fragmentary and secondhand record (see Becker, "DWH," in Snyder, *DWH*, 131).

There are two reasons offered as to why the historian has only indirect access to the past. *First,* it is claimed that, unlike a scientist, the historian's world is composed of records and not events. This is why the

---

1. Much of the discussion here follows an excellent summary found in an unpublished master's thesis by William L. Craig, *The Nature of History* (Trinity Evangelical Divinity School, Deerfield, Ill., 1976).

2. With the kind permission of the author we have removed

Axiological, Psychological, and Hermeneutic objections and responses sections from this essay. They are addressed in the chapter from which this essay originated: Norman Geisler, *Systematic Theology*, volume 1 (Minneapolis: Bethany House), 2002.

historian must contribute a "reconstructed picture" of the past, and in this sense the past is really a product of the present.

Second, historical relativists assert that the scientist can test his view, whereas the historian cannot-experimentation is not possible with historical events. The scientist has the advantage of repeatability; he may subject his views to falsification. However, the unobservable historical event is no longer verifiable; it is part of the forever departed past. Therefore, what one believes about the past is no more than a reflection of his own imagination, a subjective construction in the minds of present historians that cannot hope to be an objective representation of what really happened.

The Fragmentary Nature of Historical Accounts

The second objection to the objectivity of history relates to its fragmentary nature. At best historians can hope for completeness of documentation, but completeness of the events themselves is never possible. Optimally, documents cover only a small fraction of the events themselves (Beard, "TND" in Stern, *VH,* 323), and from only fragmentary documents one cannot validly draw full and final conclusions.

Furthermore, the documents do not present the events, but only an interpretation of the events mediated through the one who recorded them. The best-case scenario, then, is that we have only a fragmentary record of what someone else thought happened: "What really happened would still have to be reconstructed in the mind of the historian" (Carr, *WIH,* 20). Because the documents are so fragmentary and the events so distant, objectivity becomes a will-o'-the-wisp for the historian. He not only has too few pieces of the puzzle, but the partial pictures on the few pieces he does have were merely painted from the mind of the one who passed the pieces down to us.

The Historical Conditioning of the Historian

Historical relativists insist that the historian is a product of his time, and as such he is subject to the unconscious programming of his era. It is impossible, allegedly, for the historian to stand back and view history objectively because he too is part of the historical process. Hence, historical synthesis depends on the personality of the writer as well as the social and religious milieu in which he lives (Pirenne, "WAHTD" in Meyerhoff, *P,* 97). In this sense one must study the historian before one can understand his history.

Since the historian is part of the historical process, objectivity, it is said, can never be attained. The history of one generation will be rewritten by the next, and so on; no historian can transcend his historical relativity and view the world process from the outside (Collingwood, *IH,* 248). At best there can be successive but less than final historical interpretations, each viewing history from the vantage point of its own generation of historians. Therefore, there is no such person as a neutral historian; each remains a child of his own day.

[…]

The Methodological Objections

Methodological objections relate to the procedure by which history is done. There are several methodological objections to the belief in objective history necessary to establish the truth of Christianity.

The Selective Nature of Historical Methodology

As was suggested by the epistemological objections, the historian does not have direct access to the events of the past, but merely to fragmentary interpretations of those events contained in historical documents. Now, what makes objectivity even more hopeless is the fact that the historian makes a selection from these fragmentary reports and builds his interpretation of the past events on a select number of partial reports of the past events. There are volumes in archives that most historians do not even touch (Beard, "TND" in Stern, *VH,* 324).

The actual selection among the fragmentary accounts, so the argument goes, is influenced by many subjective and relative factors, including personal prejudice, availability of materials, knowledge of the languages, personal beliefs, social conditions, and so on. Hence, the historian himself is inextricably involved with the history he writes, and what is included versus what is excluded in his interpretation will always be a matter of subjective choice. No matter how objective an historian may attempt to be, it is practically impossible for him to present what really happened. His "history" is no more than his own interpretation based on his own subjective selection of fragmentary interpretations of past and unrepeatable events.

It is argued, consequently, that the facts of history do not speak for themselves: "The facts speak only when the historian calls on them; it is he who decides to which facts to give the floor, and in what order or context" (Carr, *WIH*, 32). To summarize, when the "facts" speak, it is not the original events that are speaking but later fragmentary opinions about those events. The original facts or events have long since perished, and so, according to historical relativism, by the very nature of the endeavor the historian can never hope for objectivity.

The Need to Select and Arrange Historical Materials

Once the historian takes his fragmentary documents that he must view indirectly through the interpretation of the original source, and once he takes his selected amount of material from the available archives and begins to provide an interpretive structure to it, by the use of his own value-laden language, and within the overall worldview that he presupposes, he not only understands it from the relative vantage point of his own generation but he also must select and arrange the topic of history in accordance with his own subjective preferences. In short, the dice are loaded against objectivity before he picks up his pen. That is, in the actual writing of the fragmentary, secondhand accounts from his philosophical and personal point of view, there is a further subjective choice of arrangement of the material (Collingwood, *IH*, 285–90).

The selection and arrangement of material will be determined by personal and social factors already discussed. The final written product will be prejudiced by what is included in and what is excluded from the material. It will lack objectivity by how it is arranged and by the emphasis given to it in the overall presentation. The selection made in terms of the framework will either be narrow or broad, clear or confused. Whatever its nature, the framework is necessarily reflective of the mind of the historian (Beard, "TND" in Stern, *VH*, 150–51), and this moves one still further away from objectively knowing what really happened. It is concluded by the subjectivists, then, that the hopes of objectivity are finally dashed.

The Metaphysical (Worldview) Objections

Several metaphysical objections have been leveled against the belief in objective history. Each one is predicated, either theoretically or practically, on the premise that one's worldview colors the study of history.

The Need to Structure the Facts of History

This objection is stated along these lines: Partial knowledge of the past makes it necessary for the historian to "fill in" gaping holes out of his own imagination. As a child draws the lines between the dots on a picture, so the historian supplies the connections between events. Without the historian the dots are not numbered, nor are they arranged in an obvious man. The historian must use his imagination in order to provide continuity to the disconnected and fragmentary facts provided him.

Furthermore, the historian is not content to tell us simply *what* happened; he feels compelled to explain *why* it happened (Walsh, *PH*, 32). In this way history is made fully coherent and intelligible — good history has theme and unity, which are provided by the historian. Facts alone do not make history any more than disconnected dots make a picture, and herein, according to the subjectivist, lies the difference between chronicle and history: The former is merely the unrefined material used by the historian to construct history. Without the structure provided by the historian, the mere "stuff" of history would be meaningless.

In addition, the study of history is a study of causes. The historian wants to know *why*; he wishes to weave a web of interconnected events into a unified whole. Because of this he cannot avoid interjecting his own subjectivity into history; hence, even if there is some semblance of objectivity in chronicle, nonetheless there is no hope for objectivity in history. History is in principle nonobjective, since the very thing that makes it history (as opposed to mere chronicle) is the interpretive structure or framework given to it from the subjective vantage point of the historian. Therefore, it is concluded that the necessity of structure inevitably makes his objectivity impossible.

The Unavoidability of Worldviews

Every historian interprets the past within the overall framework of his own *Weltanschauung*, that is, his world-and-life-view. Basically, there are three different philosophies of history within which historians operate: the chaotic, the cyclical, and the linear views of history (Beard, "TND" in Stern, *VH*, 151). Which one of these the historian adopts will be a matter of faith or philosophy and not a matter of mere fact.

Unless one view or another is presupposed, no overall interpretation is possible; the *Weltanschauung* will determine whether the historian sees the events of the world as a meaningless maze (chaotic), as a series of endless repetitions (cyclical), or as moving in a purposeful way toward a goal (linear). These worldviews inevitably are both necessary and value-oriented. So, it is argued by the subjectivists, without one of these worldviews, the historian cannot interpret the events of the past. However, through a worldview objectivity becomes impossible.

Further, subjectivists insist that a worldview is not generated from the facts; facts do not speak for themselves, but gain their meaning only within the overall context of the worldview. Without the *structure* of the worldview framework, the stuff of history has no meaning. Augustine (354 – 430), for example, viewed history as a great theodicy,[3] but Hegel (1770 – 1831) saw it as an unfolding of the divine. Supposedly, then, it is not any archaeological or factual find but the religious or philosophical presuppositions that prompted each man to develop his view. Eastern philosophies of history are even more diverse, as they involve a cyclical rather than a linear pattern.

Once one admits the relativity or perspectivity of his worldview as opposed to another, the historical relativists insist that he has thereby given up all right to claim objectivity. If there are several different ways to interpret the same facts, depending on the overall perspective one takes, then there is no single objective interpretation of history.

Miracles Are by Nature Superhistorical

Even if one grants that secular history could be known objectively, there still remains the problem of the subjectivity of religious history. Some writers make a strong distinction between *Historie* and *Geschichte* (Kahler, *SCHJ*, 63): The former is empirical and objectively knowable to some degree, but the latter is spiritual and unknowable, historically speaking — as spiritual or superhistorical, there is no objective way to verify it.

Spiritual history, allegedly, has no necessary connection with the spatiotemporal continuum of empirical events. It is a myth with subjective religious significance to the believer but with no objective grounding. Like the story of George Washington and the cherry tree, *Geschichte* is a story made up of events that probably never happened, but that inspire men to some moral or religious good.

If this distinction is applied to the New Testament, then even if the life and central teachings of Jesus of Nazareth could be objectively established, there is no historical way to confirm the New Testament's miraculous dimension. Miracles do not happen as part of *Historie* and, therefore, are not subject to objective analysis; they are *Geschichte* events and as such cannot be analyzed by historical methodology.

Many theologians have accepted this distinction. Paul Tillich (1886 – 1965) claimed that it is "a disastrous distortion of the meaning of faith to identify it

---

3. Theodicy is "vindication of the justice of God, especially in ordaining or permitting natural or moral evil" (*Webster's Third New International Dictionary*).

with the belief in the historical validity of the biblical stories" (*DF,* 87). He believed, with Søren Kierkegaard, that the important thing is whether or not it evokes an appropriate religious response. With this Rudolf Bultmann and Schubert Ogden would also concur, along with much of recent theological thought.

Even those like Karl Jaspers (1883–1969), who opposed Bultmann's more radical demythologization view, accepted, nevertheless, the distinction between the spiritual and empirical dimensions of miracles (Jaspers, *MC,* 16–17). On the more conservative end of those maintaining this distinction is Ian Ramsey (d. 1972), who insisted, "It is not enough to think of the facts of the Bible as 'brute historical facts' to which the evangelists give distinctive 'interpretation.'" For Ramsey, the Bible is historical only if "'history' refers to situations as odd as those which are referred to by that of the Fourth Gospel: 'the Word became flesh.'" Ramsey concludes, "No attempt to make the language of the Bible conform to a precise, straightforward public language — whether that language be scientific of historical — has ever succeeded" (*RL,* 118–19).

According to the historical subjectivists, there is always something "more" than the empirical in every religious or miraculous situation. The purely empirical situation is "odd" and thereby evocative of a discernment that calls for a commitment of religious significant.

Miracles Are in Principle Historically Unknowable

On the basis of Ernst Troeltsch's principle of analogy (see quotation below), some historians have come to object to the possibility of ever establishing a miracle based on testimony about the past. Troeltsch (1865–1923) stated the problem this way:

On the analogy of the events known to us we seek by conjecture and sympathetic understanding to explain and reconstruct the past.... [And] since we discern the same process of phenomena in operation in the past as in the present, we see, there as here, the various historical cycles of human life influencing and

intersecting one another. (Troeltsch, "H" in Hastings, *ERE.*)

Without uniformity, so the argument goes, we could know nothing about the past, for without an analogy from the present we could know nothing about what happened previously. In accord with this principle, some have insisted, "No amount of testimony is ever permitted to establish as past reality a thing that cannot be found in present reality.... In every other case the witness may have a perfect character — all that goes for nothing" (Becker, "DWH" in Snyder, *DWH,* 12–13). In other words, unless one can identify miracles in the present, he has no experience on which to base his understanding of alleged miracles in the past.

The historian, like the scientist, must adopt a methodological skepticism toward alleged events in the past for which he has no parallel in the present — the present is the foundation of our knowledge of the past. As F. H. Bradley put it:

We have seen that history rests in the last resort upon an inference from our experience, a judgment based upon our own present state of things.... [So] when we are asked to affirm the existence in past time of events, the effects of causes which confessedly are without analogy in the world in which we live, and which we know — we are at a loss for any answer but this, that ... we are asked to build a house without a foundation .... How can we attempt this without contradicting ourselves? (Bradley, *PCH,* 100.)

[...]

A Response to Historical Relativism

Despite these many strong objections to the possibility of historical objectivity, the case is by no means closed, for there are many flaws in the historical relativists' position. First, a direct response will be offered to each objection. Then, some overall arguments against historical subjectivism will be given.

The direct responses given are in the order of the above objections.

A Response to the Epistemological Objections

Response to the Problem of the Unobservability of Historical Events

The first and most fundamental response to the historical subjectivists is to point out that whatever is meant by the "objective" knowledge of history they deny, it must be possible, since in their very denial they imply that they have it. How could they know that everyone's knowledge of history was not objective unless they had an objective knowledge of it by which they determine that these other views were not objective? One cannot know *not that* unless he knows *that*.

Further, if by "objective" the subjectivists mean absolute knowledge, then of course no human historian can be objective. On the other hand, "objective" means an *accurate and adequate*[4] presentation that people should accept, then the door is open to the possibility of objectivity.

Assuming this latter sense, it should be argued that history can be just as objective as some sciences (Block, *HC*, 50). For example, paleontology (historical geology) is considered to be an objective science, and with it physical facts and processes of the past. However, the events represented by the fossil finds are no more directly accessible or *repeatable* to the scientists than are historical events to the historian.

True, there are some differences. The fossil is a mechanically accurate imprint of the original event, and the eyewitness of history may be less precise in his report. But the historian may rejoin by pointing out that the natural processes that mar the fossil imprint parallel the potential personal filtering of events through the testimony of the eyewitness. At least it may be argued that if one can determine the integrity and reliability of the eyewitness, one cannot slam the door on the possibility of objectivity in history any more than on objectivity in geology.

The scientist might contend that he can repeat the processes of the past by present experimentation, whereas the historian cannot. But even here the situations are similar, for in this sense history too can be "repeated." Similar patterns of events, by which comparisons can be made, recur today as they occurred in the past. Limited social experiments can be performed to see if human history repeats itself, so to speak, and widespread experiments can be observed naturally in the differing conditions throughout the ongoing history of the world. In short, the historian, no less than the scientist, has the tools for determining what really happened in the past. The lack of direct access to the original facts or events does not hinder the one more than the other.

Some have suggested that there is yet a crucial difference between history and science of past events. They insist that scientific facts "speak for themselves," while historical facts do not. However, even here the analogy is close for several reasons.

If "fact" means the original event, then neither geology nor history is in possession of any facts. "Fact" must be taken by both to mean information about the original event, and in this latter sense facts do not exist merely subjectively in the mind of the historian. Facts are objective data whether anyone reads them or not.

What one does with data, that is, what meaning or interpretation he gives to them, can in no way eliminate the data. There remains for both science and history a solid core of objective facts, and the door is thereby left open for objectivity in both fields. In this way one may draw a valid distinction between propaganda and history: the former lacks sufficient basis in objective fact, but the latter does not. Indeed, without objective facts, no protest can be raised either against poor history *or* propaganda.

If history is entirely in the mind of the beholder, there is no reason one cannot decide to behold it any way he desires. In this case there would be no difference between good history and trashy propaganda.

---

4. To be more accurate, a historical presentation does not have to be either totally comprehensive or unrevisable. One can always learn more and improve a limited but accurate account.

But historians, even historical subjectivists, recognize the difference. Hence, even they assume an objective knowledge of history.

Response to the Problem of Fragmentary Accounts

The fact that accounts of history are fragmentary does not destroy historical objectivity any more than the existence of only a limited amount of fossils destroys the objectivity of geology. The fossil remains represent only a very tiny percentage of the living beings of the past; this does not hinder scientists from attempting to reconstruct an objective picture of what really happened in geological history. Scientists sometimes reconstruct a whole man on the basis of only partial skeletal remains — even a single jawbone. While this procedure is perhaps rightly suspect, nonetheless one does not need every bone in order to fill in the probable picture of the whole animal. Like a puzzle, as long as one has the key pieces he can reconstruct the rest with a measurable degree of probability. For example, by the principle of bilateral similarity one can assume that the left side of a partial skull would look like the right side that was found.

Of course, the finite reconstruction of both science and history is subject to revision. Subsequent finds may provide new facts that call for new interpretations. But at least there is an objective basis in fact for the meaning attributed to the find. Interpretations can neither create the facts nor ignore them if they wish to approach objectivity. We may conclude, then, that history need be no less objective than geology for depending on fragmentary accounts. The history of human beings is transmitted to us by partial record; scientific knowledge is also partial, and it depends on assumptions and an overall framework that may prove to be partially inadequate upon the discovery of more facts.

Whatever difficulty there may be from a strictly scientific point of view in filling in the gaps between the facts, once one has assumed a philosophical stance toward the world, the problem of objectivity in general is resolved. If there is a God, and good evidence says there is, then the overall picture is already drawn; the facts of history will merely fill in the details of its meaning. If this is a theistic universe, then the artist's framework is already known in advance; the detail and coloring will come only when all the facts of history are fit into the overall sketch known to be true to the theistic framework. In this sense, historical objectivity is most certainly possible within a given framework — such as a theistic worldview. Objectivity resides in the view that best fits all the facts into the overall system, that is, into systematic consistency.

[…]

A Response to the Methodological Objections

Every historian employs a methodology — this in itself does not demonstrate the inadequacy of his history. *The question* is *whether his methodology* is *good or bad.* In response to this objection, several dimensions of the problem need discussion.

Response to the Problem of Historical Conditioning

It is true that every historian is a product of his time; each person does occupy a relative place in the changing events of the spatio-temporal world. However, it does not follow that because the historian is a product of his time, his history is also purely a product of the time. That a person cannot avoid a relative place in history does not mean his perspective cannot attain a meaningful degree of objectivity. This criticism confuses the content knowledge and the process of attaining it (Mandelbaum, *PHK*, 94), as well as incorrectly joining the formation of a view with its verification. Where one derives a hypothesis is not essentially related to how its truth can be established.

Further, if relativity is unavoidable, then the position of the relativists is self-refuting, for either their view is historically conditioned and therefore unobjective, or else it is not relative but objective. If the latter, it thereby admits that it is possible to be objective in viewing history.

On the contrary, if the position of historical relativism is itself relative, then it cannot be taken as objectively true — it is simply a subjective opinion that has no immovable basis. In short, if it is a subjective opinion it cannot eliminate the possibility that history is objectively knowable, and if it is an objective fact about history, then objective facts can be known about history. In the first case objectivity is not eliminated, and in the second relativity is self-defeated; in either case, objectivity is possible.

Finally, the constant rewriting of history is based on the assumption that objectivity is possible: Why strive for accuracy unless it is believed that the revision is more objectively true than the previous view? Why critically analyze unless improvement toward a more accurate view is the assumed goal? Perfect objectivity may be practically unattainable within the limited resources of the historian on most if not all topics, but be this as it may, the inability to attain 100 percent objectivity is a long way from relativity. Reaching a degree of objectivity that is subject to criticism and revision is a more realistic conclusion than the relativist's arguments. There is no reason to eliminate the possibility of a sufficient degree of historical objectivity.

Response to the Problem of the Selectivity of Materials

That the historian must select his materials does not automatically make history purely subjective. Jurors make judgments "beyond reasonable doubt" without having *all* the evidence. If the historian has the relevant and crucial evidence, it will be sufficient to attain objectivity; one need not know everything in order to know something. No scientist knows all the facts, and yet objectivity is claimed for his discipline. As long as no important fact is overlooked, there is no reason to eliminate the possibility of objectivity in history any more than in science.

The selection of facts can be objective to the degree that the facts are selected and reconstructed in the context in which the events represented actually occurred. Since it is impossible for any historian to pack into his account everything available on a subject, it is important for him to select the points representative of the period of which he writes (Collingwood, *IH*, 100).

Condensation need not imply distortion; the minimum can be an objective summary of the maximum.

What is more, the evidence for the historicity of the New Testament, from which Christian apologetics draws its primary evidence, is greater than for that of any other document from the ancient world (see part 2, 26). Thus, if the events behind it cannot be known objectively, then it is impossible to know anything else from that time period.

A Response to the Metaphysical (Worldview) Objections

Admittedly, each historian has a worldview, and the events are interpreted through this grid. But this in itself does not make objectivity impossible, since there are objective ways to treat the question of worldviews.

Response to the Problem of Arranging Materials

There is no reason why the historian cannot arrange materials without distorting the past (Nagel, "LHA" in Meyerhoff, *P,* 208). Since the original construction of events is available to neither the historian nor the geologist, it is necessary to reconstruct the past on the basis of the available evidence. Yet *reconstruction* does not necessitate *revision*; selecting material may occur without neglecting significant matters. Every historian must arrange his material. The important thing is whether or not it is arranged or rearranged in accordance with the original arrangement of events as they really occurred. As long as the historian incorporated consistently and comprehensively all the significant events in accordance with the way things really were, he was being objective. It is neglecting or twisting important facts that distorts objectivity.

The historian may desire to be selective in the compass of his study; he may wish to study only the political, economic, or religious dimensions of a specific period. But such specialization does not demand total subjectivity, for one can be particular without losing the overall context in which he operates. It is one thing to focus on specifics within an overall field and quite another to totally ignore or deliberately distort the big picture in which the intensified interest is occurring.

As long as the specialist stays in touch with reality rather than reflecting the pure subjectivity of his own fancy, there is no reason why a measurable degree of objectivity cannot be maintained.

Response to the Problem of the Structuring of the Materials

Those who argue against the objectivity of history apart from an overall worldview must be granted the point, for without a worldview it makes no sense to talk about objective meaning (Popper, *PH*, 150f). Meaning is system-dependent within a given meaning, but within another system it may have a very different meaning. Without a context meaning cannot be determined, and the context is provided by the worldview and not by the bare facts themselves.

Assuming the correctness of this criticism, as we do, does not eliminate the possibility of an objective understanding of history. Rather, it points to the necessity of establishing a worldview in order to attain objectivity. This has already been done earlier in establishing the evidence for a theistic worldview. Once this is clear, the metaphysical framework for an objective view of history is in place.

Without such a metaphysical structure, one is simply arguing in a circle with regard to the assumed causal connection and the attributed importance of events. To affirm that facts have "internal arrangement" begs the question; the real question is, "How does one know the correct arrangement?" Since the facts are arrangeable in at least three different ways (chaotic, cyclical, and linear), it is logically fallacious to assume that one of these is the way the facts were actually arranged. The same set of dots can have the lines drawn in many ways.

The assumption that the historian is simply discovering (and not drawing) the lines is gratuitous. The fact is that the lines are not known to be there apart from an interpretive framework through which one views them. Therefore, the problem of the objective meaning of history cannot be resolved apart from appeal to worldview. Once the skeletal sketch is known, then one can know the objective placing (meaning) of the facts. However, apart from a structure the mere grist of history means nothing.

Without a metaphysical framework there is no way to know which events in history are the most significant and, hence, there is no way to know the true significance of these and other events in their overall context. The argument that importance is determined by which events influence the most people is inadequate for several reasons. This is a form of historical utilitarianism, and as such it is subject to the same criticisms as any utilitarian test for truth. The most does not determine the best; all that is proved by great influence is great influence, not great importance or great value. Even after most people have been influenced, one can still ask the question as to the truth or value of the event that influenced them. Significance is not determined by ultimate outcome but by overall framework. Of course, if one assumes as an overall framework that the events that influence the most people in the long run are most significant, then that utilitarian framework will indeed determine the significance of an event. But what right does one have to assume a utilitarian framework any more than a nonutilitarian one? Here again, it is a matter of justifying one's overall framework or worldview.

The argument advanced by some objectivists is that past events must be structured or they are unknowable and faulty. However, all this argument proves is that it is necessary to understand facts through some structure, otherwise it makes no sense to speak of facts. The question of which structure is correct must be determined on some basis other than the mere facts themselves. Further, even if there were an objectivity of bare facts, it would provide at best only the mere *what* of history. But objective meaning deals with the *why* of these events; this is impossible apart from a structure of meaning in which the facts may find their placement of significance. Objective meaning apart from a worldview is impossible.

Nevertheless, granted that there is justification for adopting a theistic context, the objective meaning of history becomes possible, for within the theistic context each fact of history becomes a theistic fact. Given the factual order of events and the known causal connection of events, the possibility of objective meaning surfaces. The chaotic and the cyclical frameworks are eliminated in favor of the linear, and within the linear view of events causal connections emerge as the result of their context in a theistic universe. Theism provides the sketch on which history paints the complete picture. The pigments of mere fact take on real meaning as they are blended together on the theistic sketch. In this context, objectivity means systematic consistency; that is, the most meaningful way all of the facts of history can be blended together into the whole theistic sketch is what really happened — historical facts.

Response to the Alleged Unknowability of Miracles

Even if the objectivity of history is accepted, many historians object to any history that contains miracles, which poses a further metaphysical problem for Christianity. This secular rejection of miracle-history is often based on Troeltsch's principle of analogy, and this argument turns out to be similar to Burne's objection to miracles built on the uniformity of nature. David Burne argued that no testimony about alleged miracles should be accepted if it contradicts the uniform testimony of nature; in like manner, Troeltsch would reject any particular event in the past for which there is no analogue in the uniform experience of the present.

Now, there are at least two reasons for rejecting Troeltsch's argument from analogy. *First,* as C. S. Lewis insightfully commented,

> If we admit God, must we admit Miracles? Indeed, indeed, you have no security against it. That is the bargain. Theology says to you in effect, "Admit God and with Him the risk of a few miracles, and I in return will ratify your faith in uniformity as regards the overwhelming majority of events" (Lewis, *M*, 109).

A miracle is a special act of God. If God exists, then acts of God are possible; hence, any alleged historical procedure that eliminates miracles is bogus.

Second, Troeltsch's principle begs the question in favor of a naturalistic interpretation of all historical

events — it is a methodological exclusion of the possibility of accepting the miraculous in history. The testimony for regularity in general is in no way a testimony against an unusual event in particular; the cases are different and should not be evaluated in the same way. As we demonstrated, empirical generalizations (e.g., "Men do not rise from the dead") should not be used as counter-testimony to good eyewitness accounts that in a particular case someone *did* rise from the dead. The historical evidence for any particular historical event must be assessed on its own merits, completely aside from generalizations about other events.

There is another objection to the Troeltsch analogy-type argument: It proves too much. Again, as Richard Whateley (1787 – 1863) convincingly argued, on this uniformitarian assumption not only would miracles be excluded but so would many unusual events of the past, including those surrounding Napoleon Bonaparte (1769 – 1821) (Whateley, *HDCENB*, all).

No one can deny that the probability against Napoleon's successes was great. His prodigious army was destroyed in Russia, and a few months later he led a different army in Germany that likewise was ruined at Leipzig. However, the French supplied him with yet another army sufficient to make a formidable stand in France — this was repeated five times until at last he was confined to an island. Without question, the particular events of his career were highly improbable, but there is no reason on these grounds that we should doubt the historicity of the Napoleonic adventures. History, contrary to scientific hypothesis, does not depend on the universal and repeatable; rather, it stands on the sufficiency of good testimony for particular and unrepeatable events. Were this not so, nothing could be learned from history.

It is clearly a mistake to import uniformitarian methods from scientific experimentation into historical research. Repeatability and generality are needed to establish scientific laws or general patterns (of which miracles would be particular exceptions), but what is needed to establish historical events is credible testimony that these particular events did indeed occur. So it is with miracles — it is an unjustifiable mistake in historical methodology to assume that no unusual and particular event can be believed no matter how great the evidence for it. Troeltsch's principle of analogy would destroy genuine historical thinking. The honest historian must be open to the possibility of unique and particular events of the past, whether they are miraculous or not. He must not exclude a priori the possibility of establishing events like the resurrection of Christ without a careful examination of the testimony and evidence concerning them.

It is incorrect to assume that the same principles by which *empirical* science works can be used in *forensic* science. Since the latter deals with unrepeated and unobserved events in the past, it operates on the principles *origin science,* not on those of *operation science* (see Geisler, "O, S" in *BECA,* 567f.). These principles do not eliminate, but establish, the possibility of objective knowledge of the past — whether in science or history.

Observations on the Nature of Miracles and History

In response to these analyses of the historical objectivity of miracles, it is important to make several observations.

First, surely the Christian apologist does not want to contend that miracles are a mere product of the historical process. The supernatural occurs *in* the historical process but it is not a product *of* the natural process. What makes it miraculous is the fact that what the natural process alone does not account for there must be an injection from the realm of the supernatural into the natural or else there is no miracle. This is especially true of a New Testament miracle, where the means by which God performed the miracle is unknown.

Second, in accordance with the objectivity of history just discussed, there are good reasons why the Christian should yield to the radical existential theologians on the question of the objective and historical dimensions of miracle. Again, miracles are not of the natural historical process, but do occur in it. Even Karl Barth (1886 – 1968) made a similar distinction when he wrote,

The resurrection of Christ, or his second coming ... is not a historical event; the historians may reassure themselves ... that our concern here is with the event which, though it is the only real happening in, is not a real happening of, history. (*WGWM,* 90).

But unlike many existential theologians, we must also preserve the historical context in which a miracle occurs, for without it there is no way to verify the objectivity of the miraculous. Miracles do have a historical dimension without which no objectivity of religious history is possible, and, as was argued above, historical methodology can identify this objectivity (just as surely as scientific objectivity can be established) within an accepted work of a theistic world. In short, miracles may be more than historical but they cannot be less than historical. It is only if miracles do have historical dimensions that they are both objectively meaningful and apologetically valuable.

Third, a miracle can be identified within an empirical or historical context both directly and indirectly, both objectively and subjectively. A miracle is both scientifically unusual as well as theologically and morally relevant. The first characteristic is knowable in a directly empirical way; the second is knowable only indirectly through the empirical in that it is "odd" and evocative of something more than the mere empirical data of the event. For example, a virgin birth is scientifically odd, but in the case of Christ it is represented as a sign that was used to draw attention to Him as something more than human. *The theological and moral characteristics of a miracle are not empirically objective;* in this sense they are experienced subjectively.

This does not mean, however, that there is no objective basis for the moral dimensions of a miracle. Since this is a theistic universe, morality is objectively grounded in God. Therefore, the nature and will of God are the objective grounds by which one can test whether or not the event is subjectively evocative of what is objectively in accord with what is already known of God; if not, one shouldn't believe the event is a miracle. It is axiomatic that acts of a theistic God would not be used to confirm what is not the truth of God.

To sum up, miracles happen *in* history but are not completely *of* history. Miracles, nonetheless, are historically grounded — they are more than historical but are not less than historical. There are both empirical and superempirical dimensions to supernatural events. The former are knowable in an objective way, and the latter have a subjective appeal to the believer. But even here there is an objective ground in the known truth and goodness of God by which the believer can judge whether or not the empirically odd situations that appeal to him for a response are really acts of this true and good God.

[...]

Some General Remarks Concerning the Objectivity of History

There are several general conclusions to be drawn from the foregoing analysis of the subjectivity/objectivity controversy. *First,* absolute objectivity is possible only for an infinite Mind. Finite minds must be content with systematic consistency, that is, fair but revisable attempts to reconstruct the past based on an established framework of reference that comprehensively and consistently incorporates all the facts into the overall sketch provided by the worldview. Of course, if there is good reason to believe this infinite Mind exists (and there is), and if this infinite Mind (God) has revealed Himself, then an interpretation of history from an absolute perspective is available in His Word (the Bible).

Second, even without this absolute perspective, an adequately objective, finite interpretation of history is possible, for, as was shown above, the historian can be as objective as the scientist. Neither geologists nor historians have direct access to complete data on repeatable events. Further, both must use value judgments in selecting and structuring the partial material available to them.

Third, in reality, neither the scientist nor the historian can attain objective meaning without the use of some worldview by which he understands the facts.

Bare facts cannot even be known apart from some interpretive framework; hence, the need for structure or a meaning-framework is crucial to the question of objectivity. Unless one can settle the question as to whether this is a theistic or non-theistic world on grounds independent of the mere facts themselves, there is no way to determine the objective meaning of history. If, on the other hand, there are good reasons to believe that this is a theistic universe, then objectivity in history is a possibility, for once the overall viewpoint is established, it is simply a matter of finding the view of history that is most consistent with that overall system. That is, systematic consistency is the test for objectivity in matters historical as well as scientific.

Summary and Conclusion

Some historians contend that there is no objective basis for determining the past, and that even if there were an objective basis, miracles are not a part of objective history. These arguments, however, fail. History can be as objective as science. Once again, the geologist likewise has only secondhand, fragmentary, and unrepeatable evidence viewed from his own vantage point and in terms of his own values and interpretive framework. Although it is true that interpretive frameworks are necessary for objectivity, it is not true that every worldview must be totally relative and subjective. Indeed, this argument is self-defeating, for it assumes that it is an objective statement about history that all statements about history are necessarily not objective.

As to the objection that miracle-history is not objectively verifiable, two points are important. *First,* miracles can occur *in* the historical process without being *of* that natural process. *Second,* the moral and historical dimensions of miracles are not totally subjective. They call for a subjective response, but there are objective standards of truth and goodness (in accordance with the theistic God) by which the miracle can be objectively assessed. It can be concluded, then, that the door for the objectivity of history and thus the objective historicity for miracles is open. No mere question-begging uniformitarian principle of analogy can slam the door a priori. Evidence that supports the general nature of scientific law may not be legitimately used to rule out good historical evidence for unusual but particular events of history. This kind of argument is not only invincibly naturalistic in its bias but if applied consistently it would rule out much of known and accepted secular history. The only truly honest approach is to examine carefully the evidence for an alleged event in order to determine authenticity.

Sources

Barth, Karl. *The Word of God and the Word of Man.*

Bauman, Michael, ed. *Evangelical Apologetics.*

Beard, Charles. "That Noble Dream," in Fritz Stern, *The Varieties of History.*

Becker, Carl L. "Detachment and the Writing of History," in *Detachment and the Writing of History,* Phil L. Snyder, ed.

———. "What Are Historical Facts?" in *The Philosophy of History in Our Time.*

Block, Marc. *The Historian's Craft.*

Bradley, F. H. *The Presuppositions of Critical History.*

Butterfield, Herbert. "Moral Judgments in History," in *Philosophy,* Hans Meyerhoff, ed.

Carr, E. H. *What Is History?*

Clark, Gordon. *Historiography: Secular and Religious.*

Collingwood, R. G. *The Idea of History.*

———. "The Limits of Historical Knowledge," in *Essays in the Philosophy of History,* William Debbins, ed.

Craig, William L. *The Nature of History* (unpublished master's thesis for Trinity Evangelical Divinity School, Deerfield, Ill., 1976).

Dray, W. H., ed. *Philosophy of History.*

Gardiner, Patrick, ed. *Theories of History.*

Geisler, Norman. *Christian Apologetics* (6 15).

———. "Origins, Science of," in *Baker Encyclopedia of Christian Apologetics.*

———, ed. *Why I Am a Christian.*

Grant, Michael. *Jesus: An Historian's Review of the Gospels.*

Habermas, Gary. "Philosophy of History, Historical Relativism and History as Evidence" in *Evangelical Apologetics,* Michael Bauman, et al., eds.

Harvey, Van A. *The Historian and the Believer.*

Jaspers, Karl, et al. *Myth and Christianity.*

Kahler, Martin. *The So-Called Historical Jesus.*

Lewis, C. S. *Miracles.*

Mandelbaum, Maurice. *The Problem of Historical Knowledge.*

Meyerhoff, Hans, ed. *The Philosophy of History.*

Montgomery, John W. *The Shape of the Past.*

Nagel, Ernest. "The Logic of Historical Analysis," in *Philosophy,* Hans Meyerhoff, ed.

Pirenne, Henri. "What Are Historians Trying to Do?" in *Philosophy,* Hans Meyerhoff, ed.

Plutarch. *The Lives of the Noble Grecians and Romans in Great Books of the Western World,* Robert Maynard, ed.

Popper, Karl. *The Poverty of Historicism.*

Ramsey, Ian. *Religious Language.*

Sherwin-White, A. N. *Roman Society and Roman Law in the New Testament.*

Stern, Fritz, ed. *The Varieties of History.*

Tillich, Paul. *Dynamics of Faith.*

Troeltsch, Ernst. "Historiography," in *Encyclopedia of Religion and Ethics,* James Hastings, ed.

Walsh, W. H. *Philosophy of History.*

Whateley, Richard. *Historical Doubts Concerning the Existence of Napoleon Bonaparte.*

White, Hayden. *Metahistory: The Historical Imagination in Nineteenth-Century Europe.*

CHAPTER 6

Advice to Christian Philosophers

Alvin Plantinga

I. Introduction

Christianity, these days, and in our part of the world, is on the move. There are many signs pointing in this direction: the growth of Christian schools, of the serious conservative Christian denominations, the furor over prayer in public schools, the creationism/evolution controversy, and others.

There is also powerful evidence for this contention in philosophy. Thirty or thirty-five years ago, the public temper of mainline establishment philosophy, in the English speaking world was deeply non-Christian. Few establishment philosophers were Christian; even fewer were willing to admit in public that they were, and still fewer thought of their being Christian as making a real difference to their practice as philosophers. The most popular question of philosophical theology, at that time, was not whether Christianity or theism is *true;* the question, instead, was whether it even *makes sense* to *say* that there is such a person as God. According to the logical positivism then running riot, the sentence "there is such a person as God" literally makes no sense; it is disguised nonsense; it altogether fails to express a thought or a proposition. The central question wasn't whether theism is *true;* it was whether there *is* such a thing as theism — a genuine factual claim that is either true or *false — at all.* But things have changed. There are now many more Christians and many more unabashed Christians in the professional mainstream of American philosophical life. For example, the foundation of the Society for Christian Philosophers, an organization to promote fellowship and exchange of ideas among Christian philosophers, is both an evidence and a consequence

of that fact. Founded some six years ago, it is now a thriving organization with regional meetings in every part of the country; its members are deeply involved in American professional philosophical life. So Christianity is on the move, and on the move in philosophy, as well as in other areas of intellectual life.

But even if Christianity is on the move, it has taken only a few brief steps; and it is marching through largely alien territory. For the intellectual culture of our day is for the most part profoundly nontheistic and hence non-Christian — more than that, it is antitheistic. Most of the so-called human sciences, much of the non-human sciences, most of non-scientific intellectual endeavor and even a good bit of allegedly Christian theology is animated by a spirit wholly foreign to that of Christian theism. I don't have the space here to elaborate and develop this point; but I don't have to, for it is familiar to you all. To return to philosophy: most of the major philosophy departments in America have next to nothing to offer the student intent on coming to see how to be a Christian in philosophy — how to assess and develop the bearing of Christianity on matters of current philosophical concern, and how to think about those philosophical matters of interest to the Christian community. In the typical graduate philosophy department there will be little more, along these lines, than a course in philosophy of religion in which it is suggested that the evidence for the existence of God — the classical theistic proofs, say — is at least counterbalanced by the evidence against the existence of God — the problem of evil, perhaps; and it may then be added that the wisest course, in view of such maxims as Ockham's Razor, is to dispense with the whole idea of God, at least for philosophical purposes.

My aim, in this talk, is to give some advice to philosophers who are Christians.

And although my advice is directed specifically to Christian philosophers, it is relevant to all philosophers who believe in God, whether Christian, Jewish or Muslim. I propose to give some advice to the Christian or theistic philosophical community: some advice relevant to the situation in which in fact we find ourselves. "Who are you," you say, "to give the rest of us advice?" That's a good question. I shall deal with it as one properly deals with good questions to which one doesn't know the answer: I shall ignore it. My counsel can be summed up on two connected suggestions, along with a codicil. First, Christian philosophers and Christian intellectuals generally must display more autonomy — more independence of the rest of the philosophical world. Second, Christian philosophers must display more integrity — integrity in the sense of integral wholeness, or oneness, or unity, being all of one piece. Perhaps 'integrality' would be the better word here. And necessary to these two is a third: Christian courage, or boldness, or strength, or perhaps Christian self-confidence. We Christian philosophers must display more faith, more trust in the Lord; we must put on the whole armor of God. Let me explain in a brief and preliminary way what I have in mind; then I shall go on to consider some examples in more detail.

Consider a Christian college student — from Grand Rapids, Michigan, say, or Arkadelphia, Arkansas — who decides philosophy is the subject for her. Naturally enough, she will go to graduate school to learn how to become a philosopher. Perhaps she goes to Princeton, or Berkeley, or Pittsburgh, or Arizona; it doesn't much matter which. There she learns how philosophy is presently practiced. The burning questions of the day are such topics as the new theory of reference; the realism/anti-realism controversy; the problems with probability; Quine's claims about the radical indeterminacy of translation; Rawls on justice; the causal theory of knowledge; Gettier problems; the

artificial intelligence model for the understanding of what it is to be a person; the question of the ontological status of unobservable entities in science; whether there is genuine objectivity in science or anywhere else; whether mathematics can be reduced to set theory and whether abstract entities generally — numbers, propositions, properties – can be, as we quaintly say, "dispensed with"; whether possible worlds are abstract or concrete; whether our assertions are best seen as mere moves in a language game or as attempts to state the sober truth about the world; whether the rational egoist can be shown to be irrational, and all the rest. It is then natural for her, after she gets her Ph.D., to continue to think about and work on these topics. And it is natural, furthermore, for her to work on them in the way she was taught to, thinking about them in the light of the assumptions made by her mentors and in terms of currently accepted ideas as to what a philosopher should start from or take for granted, what requires argument and defense, and what a satisfying philosophical explanation or a proper resolution to a philosophical question is like. She will be uneasy about departing widely from these topics and assumptions, feeling instinctively that any such departures are at best marginally respectable. Philosophy is a social enterprise; and our standards and assumptions — the parameters within which we practice our craft — are set by our mentors and by the great contemporary centers of philosophy.

From one point of view this is natural and proper; from another, however, it is profoundly unsatisfactory. The questions I mentioned are important and interesting. Christian philosophers, however, are the philosophers of the Christian community; and it is part of their task as *Christian* philosophers to serve the Christian community. But the Christian community has its own questions, its own concerns, its own topics for investigation, its own agenda and its own research program. Christian philosophers ought not merely take their inspiration from what's going on at Princeton or Berkeley or Harvard, attractive and scintillating as that may be; for perhaps those questions and topics are not the ones, or not the only ones, they should be thinking about as the philosophers of the Christian community. There are other philosophical topics the Christian community must work at, and other topics the Christian community must work at philosophically. And obviously, Christian philosophers are the ones who must do the philosophical work involved. If they devote their best efforts to the topics fashionable in the non-Christian philosophical world, they will neglect a crucial and central part of their task as Christian philosophers. What is needed here is more independence, more autonomy with respect to the projects and concerns of the non-theistic philosophical world.

But something else is at least as important here. Suppose the student I mentioned above goes to Harvard; she studies with Willard van Orman Quine. She finds herself attracted to Quine's programs and procedures: his radical empiricism, his allegiance to natural science, his inclination towards behaviorism, his uncompromising naturalism, and his taste for desert landscapes and ontological parsimony. It would be wholly natural for her to become totally involved in these projects and programs, to come to think of fruitful and worthwhile philosophy as substantially circumscribed by them. Of course she will note certain tensions between her Christian belief and her way of practicing philosophy; and she may then bend her efforts to putting the two together, to harmonizing them. She may devote her time and energy to seeing how one might understand or reinterpret Christian belief in such a way as to be palatable to the Quinian. One philosopher I know, embarking on just such a project, suggested that Christians should think of God as a *set* (Quine is prepared to countenance sets): the set of all true propositions, perhaps, or the set of right actions, or the union of those sets, or perhaps their Cartesian product. This is understandable; but it is also profoundly misdirected. Quine is a marvelously gifted philosopher: a subtle, original and powerful philosophical force. But his fundamental commitments, his fundamental projects and concerns, are wholly different from those of the Christian community — wholly different and, indeed, antithetical to them. And the result of attempting to graft Christian thought onto his basic view of the world will be at best an unintegral *pastiche;* at worst it will seriously compromise, or distort, or trivialize the claims of Christian theism. What is needed here is more wholeness, more integrality.

So the Christian philosopher has his own topics and projects to think about; and when he thinks about the topics of current concern in the broader philosophical world, he will think about them in his own way, which may be a *different* way. He may have to reject certain currently fashionable assumptions about the philosophic enterprise — he may have to reject widely accepted assumptions as to what are the proper starting points and procedures for philosophical endeavor. And — and this is crucially important — the Christian philosopher has a perfect right to the point of view and pre-philosophical assumptions he brings to philosophic work; the fact that these are not widely shared outside the Christian or theistic community is interesting but fundamentally irrelevant. I can best explain what I mean by way of example; so I shall descend from the level of lofty generality to specific examples.

II. Theism and Verifiability

First, the dreaded "Verifiability Criterion of Meaning." During the palmy days of logical positivism, some thirty or forty years ago, the positivists claimed that most of the sentences Christians characteristically utter — "God loves us," for example, or "God created the heavens and the earth" — don't even have the grace to be false; they are, said the positivists, literally meaningless. It is not that they express *false* propositions; they don't express any propositions at all. Like that lovely line from *Alice in Wonderland,* "T'was brillig, and the slithy toves did gyre and gymbol in the wabe," they say nothing false, but only because they say nothing at all; they are "cognitively meaningless," to use the positivist's charming phrase. The sorts of things theists and others had been saying for centuries, they said, were now shown to be without sense; we theists had all been the victims; it seems, of a cruel hoax — perpetrated, perhaps, by ambitious priests and foisted upon us by our own credulous natures.

Now if this is true, it is indeed important. How had the positivists come by this startling piece of intelligence? They inferred it from the Verifiability Criterion of Meaning, which said, roughly, that a sentence is meaningful only if either it is analytic, or its truth or falsehood can be determined by empirical or scientific investigation — by the methods of the empirical sciences. On these grounds not only theism and theology, but most of traditional metaphysics and philosophy and much else besides was declared nonsense, without any literal sense at all. Some positivists conceded that metaphysics and theology, though strictly meaningless, might still have a certain limited value. Carnap, for example, thought they might be a kind of *music*. It isn't known whether he expected theology and metaphysics to supplant Bach and Mozart, or even Wagner; I myself, however, think they could nicely supersede *rock*. Hegel could take the place of The Talking Heads; Immanuel Kant could replace The Beach Boys; and instead of The Grateful Dead we could have, say, Arthur Schopenhauer.

Positivism had a delicious air of being *avant garde* and with-it; and many philosophers found it extremely attractive. Furthermore, many who didn't endorse it nonetheless entertained it with great hospitality as at the least extremely plausible. As a consequence many philosophers — both Christians and non-Christians — saw here a real challenge and an important danger to Christianity: "The main danger to theism today," said J. J. C. Smart in 1955, "comes from people who want to say that 'God exists' and 'God does not exist' are equally absurd." In 1955 *New Essays in Philosophical Theology* appeared, a volume of essays that was to set the tone and topics for philosophy of religion for the next decade or more; and most of this volume was given over to a discussion of the impact of Verificationism on theism. Many philosophically inclined Christians were disturbed and perplexed and felt deeply threatened; could it really be true that linguistic philosophers had somehow discovered that the Christian's most cherished convictions were, in fact, just meaningless? There was a great deal of anxious hand wringing among philosophers, either themselves theists or sympathetic to theism. Some suggested, in the face of positivistic onslaught, that the thing for the Christian community to do was to fold up its tents and silently slink away, admitting that the verifiability criterion was probably true. Others conceded that strictly speaking, theism really *is* nonsense, but is *important* nonsense. Still others suggested that the sentences in question should be reinterpreted in such a way as not to give offense to the positivists; someone seriously suggested, for example, that Christians resolve, henceforth, to use the sentence "God exists" to mean "some men and women have had, and all may have, experiences called 'meeting God' "; he added that when we say "God created the world from nothing" what we should mean is "everything we call 'material' can be used in such a way that it contributes to the well-being of men." In a different context but the same spirit, Rudolph Bultmann embarked upon his program of demythologizing Christianity. Traditional supernaturalistic Christian belief, he said, is "impossible in this age of electric light and the wireless." (One can perhaps imagine an earlier village skeptic taking a similar view of, say, the tallow candle and the printing press, or perhaps the pine torch and the papyrus scroll.)

By now, of course, Verificationism has retreated into the obscurity it so richly deserves; but the moral remains. This hand wringing and those attempts to accommodate the positivist were wholly inappropriate. I realize that hindsight is clearer than foresight and I do not recount this bit of recent intellectual history in order to be critical of my elders or to claim that we are wiser than our fathers: what I want to point out is that we can *learn* something from the whole nasty incident. For Christian philosophers should have adopted a quite different attitude towards positivism and its verifiability criterion. What they should have said to the positivists is: "Your criterion is mistaken: for such statements as 'God loves us' and 'God created the heavens and the earth' are clearly meaningful; so if they aren't verifiable in your sense, then it is false that all and only statements verifiable in that sense are meaningful." What was needed here was less accommodation to current fashion and more Christian self-confidence: Christian theism is true; if Christian theism is true, then the verifiability criterion is false; so the verifiability criterion is false. Of course, if the verificationists had given cogent *arguments* for their criterion, from premises that had some legitimate claim on Christian or theistic thinkers, then perhaps there would have been a problem here for the Christian philosopher; then we would have been obliged either to agree that Christian theism is cognitively meaningless, or else revise or reject those premises. But the Verificationists never gave any cogent arguments; indeed, they seldom gave any arguments at all. Some simply trumpeted this principle as a great discovery, and when challenged, repeated it loudly and slowly; but why should *that* disturb anyone? Others proposed it as a *definition* — a definition of the term "meaningful." Now of course the positivists had a right to use this term in any way they chose; it's a free country. But how could their decision to use that term in a particular way show anything so momentous as that all those who took themselves to be believers in God were wholly deluded? If I propose to use the term 'Democrat' to mean 'unmitigated scoundrel,' would it follow that Democrats everywhere should hang their heads in shame? And my point, to repeat myself, is that Christian philosophers should have displayed more integrity, more independence, less readiness to trim their sails to the prevailing philosophical winds of doctrine, and more Christian self-confidence.

III. Theism and Theory of Knowledge

I can best approach my second example by indirection. Many philosophers have claimed to find a serious problem for theism in the existence of *evil,* or of the amount and kinds of evil we do in fact find. Many who claim to find a problem here for theists have urged the *deductive argument from evil:* they have claimed that the existence of an omnipotent, omniscient, and wholly good God is *logically incompatible* with the presence of evil in the world — a presence conceded and indeed insisted upon by Christian theists. For their part, theists have argued that there is no inconsistency here. I think the present consensus, even among those who urge some form of the argument from evil, is that the deductive form of the argument from evil is unsuccessful.

More recently, philosophers have claimed that the existence of God, while perhaps not actually *inconsistent* with the existence of the amount and kinds of evil we do in fact find, is at any rate *unlikely* or *improbable* with respect to it; that is, the probability of the existence of God with respect to the evil we find, is less than the probability, with respect to that same evidence, that there is no God — no omnipotent, omniscient and wholly good Creator. Hence the existence of God is improbable with respect to what we know. But if theistic belief *is* improbable with respect to what we know, then, so goes the claim, it is irrational or in any event intellectually second rate to accept it.

Now suppose we briefly examine this claim. The objector holds that

(1) God is the omnipotent, omniscient and wholly good creator of the world

is improbable or unlikely with respect to

(2) There are 10^{13} turps of evil

(where the *turp* is the basic unit of evil).

I've argued elsewhere[1] that enormous difficulties beset the claim that (1) is unlikely or improbable given (2). Call that response "the low road-reply." Here I want to pursue what I shall call the *high road* reply. Suppose we stipulate, for purposes of argument, that (1) *is,* in fact, improbable on (2). Let's agree that it is unlikely, given the existence of 10^{13} turps of evil, that the world has been created by a God who is perfect in power, knowledge and goodness. What is supposed to follow from that? How is that to be construed as an objection to theistic belief? How does the objector's argument go from there? It doesn't follow, of course, that theism is false. Nor does it follow that one who accepts both (1) and (2) (and let's add, recognizes that (1) is improbable

1. "The Probabilistic Argument from Evil," *Philosophical Studies,* 1979, pp. 1–53.

with respect to (2)) has an irrational system of beliefs or is in any way guilty of noetic impropriety; obviously there might be pairs of propositions A and B, such that we *know* both A and B, despite the fact that A is improbable on B. I might know, for example, both that Feike is a Frisian and 9 out of 10 Frisians can't swim, and also that Feike can swim; then I am obviously within my intellectual rights in accepting both these propositions, even though the latter is improbable with respect to the former. So even if it were a fact that (1) is improbable with respect to (2), that fact, so far, wouldn't be of much consequence. How, therefore, can this objection be developed?

Presumably what the objector means to hold is that (1) is improbable, not just on (2) but on some appropriate body of *total evidence-perhaps* all the evidence the theist has, or perhaps the body of evidence he is rationally obliged to have. The objector must be supposing that the theist has a relevant body of total evidence here, a body of evidence that includes (2); and his claim is that (1) is improbable with respect to this relevant body of total evidence. Suppose we say that T_s is the relevant body of total evidence for a given theist T; and suppose we agree that a belief is rationally acceptable for him only if it is not improbable with respect to T_s. Now what sorts of propositions are to be found in T_s? Perhaps the propositions he *knows* to be true, or perhaps the largest subset of his beliefs that he can rationally accept without evidence from other propositions, or perhaps the propositions he knows *immediately — knows*, but does not know on the basis of other propositions. However exactly we characterize this set T_s the question I mean to press is this: why can't belief in God be itself a member of T_s? Perhaps for the theist — for many theists, at any rate — belief in God is a member of T_s, in which case it obviously won't be improbable with respect to T_s. Perhaps the theist has a right to *start from* belief in God, taking that proposition to be one of the ones with probability with respect to which determines the rational propriety of *other* beliefs he holds. But if so, then the Christian *philosopher* is entirely within his rights in starting from belief in God to his philosophizing. He

has a right to take the existence of God for granted and go on from there in his philosophical work — just as other philosophers take for granted the existence of the past, say, or of other persons, or the basic claims of contemporary physics.

And this leads me to my point here. Many Christian philosophers appear to think of themselves *qua* philosophers as engaged with the atheist and agnostic philosopher in a common search for the correct philosophical position *vis-à-vis* the question whether there is such a person as God. Of course the Christian philosopher will have his own private conviction on the point; he will believe, of course, that indeed there is such a person as God. But he will think, or be inclined to think, or half inclined to think that as a *philosopher* he has no right to this position unless he is able to show that it follows from, or is probable, or justified with respect to premises accepted by all parties to the discussion — theist, agnostic and atheist alike. Furthermore, he will be half inclined to think he has no right, as a philosopher, to positions that presuppose the existence of God, if he can't show that belief to be justified in this way. What I want to urge is that the Christian philosophical community ought *not* to think of itself as engaged in this common effort to determine the probability or philosophical plausibility of belief in God. The Christian philosopher quite properly *starts from* the existence of God, and presupposes it in philosophical work, whether or not he can show it to be probable or plausible with respect to premises accepted by all philosophers, or most philosophers, or most philosophers at the great contemporary centers of philosophy.

Taking it for granted, for example, that there is such a person as God and that we are indeed within our epistemic rights (are in that sense justified) in believing that there is, the Christian epistemologist might ask what it is that confers justification here: by virtue of what is the theist justified? Perhaps there are several sensible responses. One answer he might give and try to develop is that of John Calvin (and before him, of the Augustinian, Anselmian, Bonaventurian tradition of the Middle Ages): God, said Calvin, has implanted in humankind a tendency or nisus or disposition to believe in him:

"There is within the human mind, and indeed by natural instinct, an awareness of divinity." This we take to beyond controversy. To prevent anyone from taking refuge in the pretense of ignorance, God himself has implanted in all men a certain understanding of his divine majesty.... Therefore, since from the beginning of the world there has been no region, no city, in short, no household, that could do without religion, there lies in this a tacit confession of a sense of deity inscribed in the hearts of all.[2]

Calvin's claim, then, is that God has so created us that we have by nature a strong tendency or inclination or disposition towards belief in him.

Although this disposition to believe in God has been in part smothered or suppressed by *sin,* it is nevertheless universally present. And it is triggered or actuated by widely realized conditions:

Lest anyone, then, be excluded from access to happiness, he not only sowed in men's minds that seed of religion of which we have spoken, but revealed himself and daily disclosed himself in the whole workmanship of the universe. As, a consequence, men cannot open their eyes without being compelled to see him (p. 51).

Like Kant, Calvin is especially impressed in this connection, by the marvelous compages of the starry heavens above:

Even the common folk and the most untutored, who have been taught only by the aid of the eyes, cannot be unaware of the excellence of divine art, for it reveals itself in this innumerable and yet distinct and well-ordered variety of the heavenly host (p. 52).

And now what Calvin says suggests that one who accedes to this tendency and in these circumstances accepts the belief that God has created the world — perhaps upon beholding the starry heavens, or the splendid majesty of the mountains, or the intricate, articulate beauty of a tiny flower — is quite as rational and quite as justified as one who believes that he sees a tree upon having that characteristic being-appeared-to-treely kind of experience.

No doubt this suggestion won't convince the skeptic; taken as an attempt to convince the skeptic it is circular. My point is just this: the Christian has his own questions to answer, and his own projects; these projects may not mesh with those of the skeptical or unbelieving philosopher. He has his own questions and his own starting point in investigating these questions. Of course, I don't mean to suggest that the Christian philosopher must accept Calvin's answer to the question I mentioned above; but I do say it is entirely fitting for him to give to this question an answer that presupposes precisely that of which the skeptic is skeptical — even if this skepticism is nearly unanimous in most of the prestigious philosophy departments of our day. The Christian philosopher does indeed have a responsibility to the philosophical world at large; but his fundamental responsibility is to the Christian community, and finally to God.

Again, a Christian philosopher may be interested in the relation between faith and reason, and faith and knowledge: granted that we hold some things by faith and know other things; granted that we believe that there is such a person as God and that this belief is true; do we also *know* that God exists? Do we accept this belief by faith or by reason? A theist may be inclined towards a *reliabilist* theory of knowledge; he may be inclined to think that a true belief constitutes knowledge if it is produced by a reliable belief-producing mechanism. (There are hard problems here, but suppose for now we ignore them.) If the theist thinks God has created us with the *sensus divinitatis* Calvin speaks of, he will hold that indeed there is a reliable belief-producing mechanism that produces theistic belief; he will thus hold that we *know* that God exists. One who follows Calvin here will also hold that a

---

2. *Institutes of the Christian Religion,* tr. Ford Lewis Battles (Philadelphia: The Westminister Press, 1960), Bk. I, Chap. III, pp. 43 – 44.

capacity to apprehend God's existence is as much part of our natural noetic or intellectual equipment as is the capacity to apprehend truths of logic, perceptual truths, truths about the past, and truths about other minds. Belief in the existence of God is then in the same boat as belief in truths of logic, other minds, the past, and perceptual objects; in each case God has so constructed us that in the right circumstances we acquire the belief in question. But then the belief that there is such a person as God is as much among the deliverances of our natural noetic faculties as are those other beliefs. Hence we *know* that there is such a person as God, and don't merely believe it; and it isn't by *faith* that we apprehend the existence of God, but by reason; and this whether or not any of the classical theistic arguments is successful.

Now my point is not that Christian philosophers must follow Calvin here. My point is that the Christian philosopher has a right (I should say a duty) to work at his own projects — projects set by the beliefs of the Christian community of which he is a part. The Christian philosophical community must work out the answers to *its* questions; and both the questions and the appropriate ways of working out their answers may presuppose beliefs rejected at most of the leading centers of philosophy. But the Christian is proceeding quite properly in starting from these beliefs, even if they are so rejected. He is under no obligation to confine his research projects to those pursued at those centers, or to pursue his own projects on the basis of the assumptions that prevail there.

Perhaps I can clarify what I want to say by contrasting it with a wholly different view. According to the theologian David Tracy,

> In fact the modern Christian theologian cannot ethically do other than challenge the traditional self-understanding of the theologian. He no longer sees his task as a simple defense of or even as an orthodox reinterpretation of traditional belief. Rather, he finds that his ethical commitment to the morality of scientific knowledge forces him to assume a critical posture towards his own and his tradition's beliefs.... In principle, the fundamental loyalty of the theologian *qua* theologian is to that morality of scientific knowledge which he shares with his colleagues, the philosophers, historians and social sciences. No more than they, can he allow his own — or his tradition's — beliefs to serve as warrants for his arguments. In fact, in all properly theological inquiry, the analysis should be characterized by those same ethical stances of autonomous judgment, critical judgment and properly skeptical hard-mindedness that characterizes analysis in other fields.[3]

Furthermore, this "morality of scientific knowledge insists that each inquirer start with the present methods and knowledge of the field in question, unless one has evidence of the same logical type for rejecting those methods and that knowledge," Still further, "for the new scientific morality, one's fundamental loyalty as an analyst of any and all cognitive claims is solely to those methodological procedures which the particular scientific community in question has developed" (6).

I say *caveat lector*. I'm prepared to bet that this "new scientific morality" is like the Holy Roman Empire: it is neither new nor scientific nor morally obligatory. Furthermore the "new scientific morality" looks to me to be monumentally inauspicious as a stance for a Christian theologian, modern or otherwise. Even if there were a set of methodological procedures held in common by most philosophers, historians and social scientists, or most secular philosophers, historians, and social scientists, why should a Christian theologian give ultimate allegiance to them rather than, say, to God, or to the fundamental truths of Christianity? Tracy's suggestion as to how Christian theologians should proceed seems at best wholly unpromising. Of course I am only a philosopher, not a modern theologian; no doubt I am venturing beyond my depths. So I don't presume to speak for modern theologians; but however things stand for them, the modern Christian *philosopher* has a perfect right, as a philosopher, to start from his belief in God. He has a right to assume it, take

3. *Blessed Rage for Order* (New York: Seabury Press), 1978, p. 7.

it for granted, in his philosophical work — whether or not he can convince his unbelieving colleagues either that this belief is true or that it is sanctioned by those "methodological procedures" Tracy mentions.

And the Christian philosophical community ought to get on with the philosophical questions of importance to the Christian community. It ought to get on with the project of exploring and developing the implications of Christian theism for the whole range of questions philosophers ask and answer. It ought to do this whether or not it can convince the philosophical community at large either that there really is such a person as God, or that it is rational or reasonable to believe that there is. Perhaps the Christian philosopher *can* convince the skeptic or the unbelieving philosopher that indeed there is such a person as God. Perhaps this is possible in at least some instances. In other instances, of course, it may be impossible; even if the skeptic in fact accepts premises from which theistic belief follows by argument forms he also accepts, he may, when apprised of this situation, give up those premises rather than his unbelief. (In this way it is possible to reduce someone from knowledge to ignorance by giving him an argument he sees to be valid from premises he knows to be true.)

But whether or not this is possible, the Christian philosopher has other fish to fry and other questions to think about. Of course he must listen to, understand, and learn from the broader philosophical community and he must take his place in it; but his work as a philosopher is not circumscribed by what either the skeptic or the rest of the philosophical world thinks of theism. Justifying or trying to justify theistic belief in the eyes of the broader philosophical community is not the only task of the Christian philosophical community; perhaps it isn't even among its most important tasks. Philosophy is a communal enterprise. The Christian philosopher who looks exclusively to the philosophical world at large, who thinks of himself as belonging primarily to *that* world, runs a two-fold risk. He may neglect an essential part of his task as a Christian philosopher; and he may find himself adopting principles and procedures that don't comport well

with his beliefs as a Christian. What is needed, once more, is autonomy and integrality.

IV. Theism and Persons

My third example has to do with philosophical anthropology: how should we think about 'human persons'? What sorts of things, fundamentally, *are* they? What is it to be a person, what is it to be a *human* person, and how shall we think about personhood? How, in particular, should Christians, Christian philosophers, think about these things? The first point to note is that on the Christian scheme of things, *God* is the premier person, the first and chief exemplar of personhood. God, furthermore, has created man in his own image; we men and women are image bearers of God, and the properties most important for an understanding of our personhood are properties we share with him. How we think about God, then, will have an immediate and direct bearing on how we think about humankind. Of course we learn much about ourselves from other sources — from everyday observation, from introspection and self-observation, from scientific investigation and the like. But it is also perfectly proper to start from what we know as Christians. It is not the case that rationality, or proper philosophical method, or intellectual responsibility, or the new scientific morality, or whatever, require that we start from beliefs we share with everyone else — what common sense and current science teach, e. g. — and attempt to reason to or justify those beliefs we hold as Christians. In trying to give a satisfying philosophical account of some area or phenomenon, we may properly appeal, in our account or explanation, to anything else we already rationally believe — whether it be current science or Christian doctrine.

Let me proceed again to specific examples. There is a fundamental watershed, in philosophical anthropology, between those who think of human beings as *free — free* in the libertarian sense — and those who espouse determinism. According to determinists, every human action is a consequence of initial conditions outside our control by way of causal laws that are also outside our control. Sometimes underlying this claim is a picture of the universe as a vast machine where, at any rate at the macroscopic level, all events, including human actions, are determined by previous events and causal laws. On this view every action I have in fact performed was such that it wasn't within my power to refrain from performing it; and if, on a given occasion I did *not* perform a given action, then it wasn't then within my power to perform it. If I now raise my arm, then, on the view in question, it wasn't within my power just then not to raise it. Now the Christian thinker has a stake in this controversy just by virtue of being a Christian. For she will no doubt believe that God holds us human beings responsible for much of what we do — responsible, and thus properly subject to praise or blame, approval or disapproval. But how can I be responsible for my actions, if it was never within my power to perform any action I didn't in fact perform, and never within my power to refrain from performing any I did perform? If my actions are thus determined, then I am not rightly or justly held accountable for them; but God does nothing improper or unjust, and he holds me accountable for some of my actions; hence it is not the case that all of my actions are thus determined. The Christian has an initially strong reason to reject the claim that all of our actions are causally determined — a reason much stronger than the meager and anemic arguments the determinist can muster on the other side. Of course if there *were* powerful arguments on the other side, then there might be a problem here. But there aren't; so there isn't.

Now the determinist may reply that freedom and causal determinism are, contrary to initial appearances, in fact compatible. He may argue that my being free with respect to an action I performed at a time *t,* for example, doesn't entail that it was then within my power to refrain from performing it, but only something weaker — perhaps something like *if I had chosen not to perform it, I would not have performed it.* Indeed, the clearheaded compatibilist will go further. He will maintain, not merely that freedom is *compatible* with determinism, but that freedom *requires* determinism. He will hold with Hume that the propo-

sition *S is free with respect to action A* or *S does A freely* entails that *S* is causally determined with respect to *A* — that there are causal laws and antecedent conditions that together entail either that *S* performs *A* or that *S* does not perform *A* . And he will back up this claim by insisting that if *S* is not thus determined with respect to *A*, then it's merely a matter of *chance — due,* perhaps, to quantum effects in *S' s* brain — that *S* does *A*. But if it is just a matter of chance that *S* does *A,* then either *S* doesn't really do *A* at all, or at any rate *S* is not responsible for doing *A*. If *S' s* doing *A* is just a matter of chance, then *S's* doing *A* is something that just *happens* to him; but then it is not really the case that he *performs A — at* any rate it is not the case that he is *responsible* for performing *A*. And hence freedom, in the sense that is required for responsibility, itself requires determinism.

But the Christian thinker will find this claim monumentally implausible. Presumably the determinist means to hold that what he says characterizes actions generally, not just those of human beings. He will hold that it is a *necessary* truth that if an agent isn't caused to perform an action then it is a mere matter of chance that the agent in question performs the action in question. From a Christian perspective, however, this is wholly incredible. For God performs actions, and performs free actions; and surely it is not the case that there are causal laws and antecedent conditions outside his control that determine what he does. On the contrary: God is the author of the causal laws that do in fact obtain; indeed, perhaps the best way to think of these causal laws is as records of the ways in which God ordinarily treats the beings he has created. But of course it is not simply a matter of *chance* that God does what he does — creates and upholds the world, let's say, and offers redemption and renewal to his children. So a Christian philosopher has an extremely good reason for rejecting this premise, along with the determinism and compatibilism it supports.

What is really at stake in this discussion is the notion of agent causation: the notion of a person as an ultimate source of action. According to the friends of agent causation, some events are caused, not by other events, but by substances, objects — typically personal agents. And at least since the time of David Hume, the idea of agent causation has been languishing. It is fair to say, I think, that most contemporary philosophers who work in this area either reject agent causation outright or are at the least extremely suspicious of it. They see causation as a relation among *events;* they can understand how one event can cause another event, or how events of one kind can cause events of another kind. But the idea of a *person,* say, causing an event, seems to them unintelligible, unless it can be analyzed, somehow, in terms of event causation. It is this devotion to event causation, of course, that explains the claim that if you perform an action but are not caused to do so, then you're performing that action is a matter of chance. For if I hold that all causation in ultimately event causation, then I will suppose that if you perform an action but are not caused to do so by previous events, then your performing that action isn't caused at all and is therefore a mere matter of chance. The devotee of event causation, furthermore, will perhaps argue for his position as follows. If such agents as persons cause effects that take place in the physical world — my body's moving in a certain way, for example — then these effects must ultimately be caused by volitions or *undertakings — which,* apparently, are immaterial, unphysical events. He will then claim that the idea of an immaterial event's having causal efficacy in the physical world is puzzling or dubious or worse.

But a Christian philosopher will find this argument unimpressive and this devotion to event causation uncongenial. As for the argument, the Christian already and independently believes that acts of volition have causal efficacy; he believes indeed, that the physical universe owes its very existence to just such volitional acts — God's undertaking to create it. And as for the devotion to event causation, the Christian will be, initially, at any rate, strongly inclined to reject the idea that event causation is primary and agent causation to be explained in terms of it. For he believes that God does and has done many things: he has created the world; he sustains it in being; he communicates

with his children. But it is extraordinarily hard to see how these truths can be analyzed in terms of causal relations among events. What events could possibly cause God's creating the world or his undertaking to create the world? God himself institutes or establishes the causal laws that do in fact hold; how, then, can we see all the events constituted by his actions as related to causal laws to earlier events? How could it be that propositions ascribing actions to him are to be explained in terms of event causation?

Some theistic thinkers have noted this problem and reacted by soft-pedaling God's causal activity, or by impetuously following Kant in declaring that it is of a wholly different order from that in which we engage, an order beyond our comprehension. I believe this is the wrong response. Why should a Christian philosopher join in the general obeisance to event causation? It is not as if there are cogent *arguments* here. The real force behind this claim is a certain philosophical way of looking at persons and the world; but this view has no initial plausibility from a Christian perspective and no compelling argument in its favor.

So on all these disputed points in philosophical anthropology the theist will have a strong initial predilection for resolving the dispute in one way rather than another. He will be inclined to reject compatibilism, to hold that event causation (if indeed there is such a thing) is to be explained in terms of agent causation, to reject the idea that if an event isn't caused by other events then its occurrence is a matter of chance, and to reject the idea that events in the physical world can't be caused by an agent's undertaking to do something. And my point here is this. The Christian philosopher is within his right in holding these positions, whether or not he can convince the rest of a philosophical world and whatever the current philosophical consensus is, if there is a consensus. But isn't such an appeal to God and his properties, in this philosophical context, a shameless appeal to a *deus ex machina?* Surely not. "Philosophy," as Hegel once exclaimed in a rare fit of lucidity, "is thinking things over." Philosophy is in large part a clarification, systematization, articulation, relating and deepening of pre-philosophical opinion. We come to philosophy with a range of opinions about the world and humankind and the place of the latter in the former; and in philosophy we think about these matters, systematically articulate our views, put together and relate our views on diverse topics, and deepen our views by finding unexpected interconnections and by discovering and answering unanticipated questions. Of course we may come to change our minds by virtue of philosophical endeavor; we may discover incompatibilities or other infelicities. But we come to philosophy with pre-philosophical opinions; we can do no other. And the point is: the Christian has as much right to his prephilosophical opinions as others have to theirs. He needn't try first to 'prove' them from propositions accepted by, say, the bulk of the non-Christian philosophical community; and if they are widely rejected as naive, or pre-scientific, or primitive, or unworthy of "man come of age," that is nothing whatever against them. Of course if there were genuine and substantial arguments against them from premises that have some legitimate claim on the Christian philosopher, then he would have a problem; he would have to make some kind of change somewhere. But in the absence of such arguments — and the absence of such arguments is evident — the Christian philosophical community, quite properly starts, in philosophy, from what it believes.

But this means that the Christian philosophical community need not devote all of its efforts to attempting to refute opposing claims and or to arguing for its own claims, in each case from premises accepted by the bulk of the philosophical community at large. It ought to do this, indeed, but it ought to do more. For if it does only this, it will neglect a pressing philosophical task: systematizing, deepening, clarifying Christian thought on these topics. So here again: my plea is for the Christian philosopher, the Christian philosophical community, to display, first, more independence and autonomy: we needn't take as our research projects just those projects that currently enjoy widespread popularity; we have our own questions to think about. Secondly, we must display more

integrity. We must not automatically assimilate what is current or fashionable or popular by way of philosophical opinion and procedures; for much of it comports ill with Christian ways of thinking. And finally, we must display more Christian self-confidence or courage or boldness. We have a perfect right to our pre-philosophical views: why, therefore, should we be intimidated by what the rest of the philosophical world thinks plausible or implausible?

These, then, are my examples; I could have chosen others. In ethics, for example: perhaps the chief theoretical concern, from the theistic perspective, is the question how are right and wrong, good and bad, duty, permission and obligation related to God and to his will and to his creative activity? This question doesn't arise, naturally enough, from a nontheistic perspective; and so, naturally enough, nontheist ethicists do not address it. But it is perhaps the most important question for a Christian ethicist to tackle. I have already spoken about epistemology; let me mention another example from this area. Epistemologists sometimes worry about the confluence or lack thereof of epistemic *justification,* on the one hand, and *truth,* or *reliability,* on the other. Suppose we do the best that can be expected of us, noetically speaking; suppose we do our intellectual duties and satisfy our intellectual obligations: what guarantee is there that in so doing we shall arrive at the truth? Is there even any reason for supposing that if we thus satisfy our obligations, we shall have a better chance of arriving at the truth than if we brazenly flout them? And where do these intellectual obligations come from? How does it happen that we have them? Here the theist has, if not a clear set of answers, at any rate clear suggestions towards a set of answers. Another example: creative antirealism is presently popular among philosophers; this is the view that it is human behavior — in particular, human thought and language — that is somehow responsible for the fundamental structure of the world and for the fundamental kinds of entities there are. From a theistic point of view, however, universal creative anti-realism is at best a mere impertinence, a piece of laughable bravado. For *God,* of course, owes neither his existence nor his properties to us and our ways of thinking; the truth is just the reverse. And so far as the created universe is concerned, while it indeed owes its existence and character to activity on the part of a person, that person is certainly not a *human* person.

One final example, this time from philosophy of mathematics. Many who think about *sets* and their nature are inclined to accept the following ideas. First, no set is a member of itself. Second, whereas a property has its extension contingently, a set has *its* membership essentially. This means that no set could have existed if one of its members had not, and that no set could have had fewer or different members from the ones it in fact has. It means, furthermore, that sets are contingent beings; if Ronald Reagan had not existed, then his unit set would not have existed. And thirdly, sets form a sort of iterated structure: at the first level there are sets whose members are non-sets, at the second level sets whose members are non-sets or first level sets; at the third level, sets whose members are non-sets or sets of the first two levels, and so on. Many are also inclined, with Georg Cantor, to regard sets as *collections* — *as* objects whose existence is dependent upon a certain sort of intellectual activity — a collecting or "thinking together" as Cantor put it. If sets were collections of this sort, that would explain their displaying the first three features I mentioned. But if the collecting or thinking together had to be done by *human* thinkers, or any finite thinkers, there wouldn't be nearly enough sets — not nearly as many as we think in fact there are. From a theistic point of view, the natural conclusion is that sets owe their existence to *God's* thinking things together. The natural explanation of those three features is just that sets are indeed collections, collections collected by God; they are or result from God's thinking things together. This idea may not be popular at contemporary centers of set theoretical activity; but that is neither here nor there. Christians, theists, ought to understand sets from a *Christian* and *theistic* point of view. What they believe as theists affords a resource for understanding sets not available to the non-theist; and why shouldn't they employ it? Perhaps here we *could* proceed without appealing to what we believe as theists; but why *should* we, if these beliefs are useful and explanatory? I could probably get home this evening by hopping on one leg; and conceivably I could climb Devil's Tower with my feet tied together. But why should I want to?

The Christian or theistic philosopher, therefore, has his own way of working at his craft. In some cases there are items on his agenda — pressing items — not to be found on the agenda of the non-theistic philosophical community. In others, items that are currently fashionable appear of relatively minor interest from a Christian perspective. In still others, the theist will reject common assumptions and views about how to start, how to proceed, and what constitutes a good or satisfying answer. In still others the Christian will take for granted and will start from assumptions and premises rejected by the philosophical community at large. Of course I don't mean for a moment to suggest that Christian philosophers have nothing to learn from their non-Christian and non-theist colleagues: that would be a piece of foolish arrogance, utterly belied by the facts of the matter. Nor do I mean to suggest that Christian philosophers should retreat into their own isolated enclave, having as little as possible to do with non-theistic philosophers. Of course not! Christians have much to learn and much of enormous importance to learn by way of dialogue and discussion with their non-theistic colleagues. Christian philosophers must be intimately involved in the professional life of the philosophical community at large, both because of what they can learn and because of what they can contribute. Furthermore, while Christian philosophers need not and ought not to see themselves as involved, for example, in a common effort to determine whether there is such a person as God, we are all, theist and non-theist alike, engaged in the common human project of understanding ourselves and the world in which we find ourselves. If the Christian philosophical community is doing its job properly, it will be engaged in a complicated, many-sided dialectical discussion, making its own contribution to that common human project. It must pay careful attention to other contributions; it must gain a deep understanding of them; it must learn what it can from them and it must take unbelief with profound seriousness.

All of this is true and all of this is important; but none of it runs counter to what I have been saying. Philosophy is many things. I said earlier that it is a matter of systematizing, developing and deepening one's pre-philosophical opinions. It is that; but it is also an arena for the articulation and interplay of commitments and allegiances fundamentally religious in nature; it is an expression of deep and fundamental perspectives, ways of viewing ourselves and the world and God. The Christian philosophical community, by virtue of being Christian, is committed to a broad but specific way of looking at humankind and the world and God. Among its most important and pressing projects are systematizing, deepening, exploring, articulating this perspective, and exploring its bearing on the rest of what we think and do. But then the Chris-tian philosophical community has its own agenda; it need not and should not automatically take its projects from the list of those currently in favor at the leading contemporary centers of philosophy. Furthermore, Christian philosophers must be wary about assimilating or accepting presently popular philosophical ideas and procedures; for many of these have roots that are deeply anti-Christian. And finally the Christian philosophical community has a right to its perspectives; it is under no obligation first to show that this perspective is plausible with respect to what is taken for granted by all philosophers, or most philosophers, or the leading philosophers of our day.

In sum, we who are Christians and propose to be philosophers must not rest content with being philosophers who happen, incidentally, to be Christians; we must strive to be Christian philosophers. We must therefore pursue our projects with integrity, independence, and Christian boldness.[4]

---

4. Delivered November 4, 1983, as the author's inaugural address as the John A. O'Brien Professor of Philosophy at the University of Notre Dame.

QUESTIONS AND FURTHER READINGS

Questions for Discussion

1. What are some beneficial points to be gleaned from Paul's apologetic approach on Mars Hill? What are some ways the context probably influenced this approach?

2. What other biblical passages, besides Acts 17, reflect apologetics themes? What can be learned from them?

3. What are some aspects of apologetics that have remained constant throughout history? What are some important changes that have occurred?

4. Do some research on a major Christian apologist of the first five centuries AD. What issues were being addressed? How were they being addressed?

5. Do some research on a major Christian apologist of the Medieval period. What issues were being addressed? How were they being addressed?

6. Which apologetic methodology, as described in the essay by James Beilby, do you find most appealing? Why?

7. Describe in a paragraph or so interreligious apologetics as Harold Netland explains it in his essay. What are some ways you can incorporate this in your own apologetics discussions?

8. What are some important differences between interreligious apologetics and apologetics with atheists and agnostics? What are some similarities?

9. Is history knowable? How is that question relevant to apologetics?

10. Consider one piece of advice offered by Alvin Plantinga. How might you implement this suggestion in your own life and discipline? Your ministry?

Further Readings

Boa, Kenneth D., and Robert M. Bowman Jr. (2005). *Faith Has Its Reasons: Integrative Approaches to Defending the Christian Faith*. Waynesboro, GA: Paternoster. (A comprehensive analysis of Christian apologetics systems.)

Christian, William (1972). *Oppositions of Religious Doctrines: A Study in the Logic of Dialogue among Religions*. New York: Herder and Herder.

Cowen, Steven B., ed. (2000). *Five Views on Apologetics*. Grand Rapids: Zondervan. (Covers five prominent apologetics approaches: Classical, Evidential, Presuppositional, Reformed Epistemology, and Cumulative Case.)

Dulles, Avery Cardinal (2005). *A History of Apologetics*. Revised edition. San Francisco: Ignatius Press. (A classic and brief history of the subject.)

Edgar, William, and K. Scott Oliphint (2009). *Christian Apologetics Past and Present: A Primary Source Reader*. Wheaton, IL: Crossway. (A very helpful collection of primary sources in the history of Christian apologetics.)

Frame, John M. (1994). *Apologetics to the Glory of God: An Introduction*. Phillipsburg, NJ: Presbyterian & Reformed. (An introduction to apologetics from a Reformed perspective that emphasizes the transcendental argument.)

Griffiths, Paul J. (1991). *An Apology for Apologetics: A Study in the Logic of Interreligious Dialogue*. Maryknoll, NY: Orbis.

McGrath, Alister (2009). *Heresy: A History of Defending the Faith*. New York: HarperCollins. (Examines the relations between heresy, orthodoxy, and power; filled with historical discussions on major theological issues.)

Meister, Chad, and J. B. Stump (2010). *Christian Thought: A Historical Introduction*. London and New York: Routledge. (An overview of the main theological issues in the history of Christianity, including chapters on the apologists and heresies.)

Mittelberg, Mark (2008). *Choosing Your Faith: In a World of Spiritual Options*. Carol Stream, IL: Tyndale. (Tackles the question, "How do we choose what to believe — especially in the area of faith?"; a very helpful apologetics resource.)

Nash, Ronald (1992). *Worldviews in Conflict*. Grand Rapids: Zondervan. (A clear, concise, and helpful analysis of the three basic worldviews described in this section.)

Netland, Harold (2001). *Encountering Religious Pluralism: The Challenge to Christian Faith and Mission*. Downers Grove, IL: InterVarsity Press.

Plantinga, Alvin (2000). *Warranted Christian Belief*. Oxford: Oxford University Press. (The third volume in his trilogy on warrant, this book examines warrant's role in theistic belief and examines whether we are rational and warranted in accepting Christian belief.)

Sire, James (2004). *Naming the Elephant: Worldview as a Concept*. Downers Grove, IL: InterVarsity Press. (A very helpful guide to worldview thinking.)

Smith, Huston. *The World's Religions*. New York: HarperSanFrancisco, 1991. (This classic on the world religions, which includes an emphasis on their solutions to the human condition, has now sold over two million copies.)

Stackhouse, John G. Jr. (2002). *Humble Apologetics*. Oxford: Oxford University Press. (An overview of the difficulties of engaging in Christian apologetics in a postmodern, pluralistic culture; insightfully instructs Christians on how best to present their faith to others.)

PART 2

THE EXISTENCE OF GOD

A central question in recorded human history has been whether there are reasons and evidences for the belief that God exists. Throughout the centuries there have been leading thinkers who defended the existence of God utilizing arguments — claims that have premises in support of them. This section includes a number of these arguments, both classic and contemporary, for God's existence.

The first section of this part is on the *cosmological* argument. The word *cosmological* is derived from two Greek terms: *cosmos* = world or universe, and *logos* = rational account. There are different versions of the cosmological argument, but they all begin with the claim that the universe exists and, for one reason or another, depending on the argument form, needs an explanation for its existence.

The first selection is by the medieval theologian and philosopher Thomas Aquinas (1225 – 1274) from his major work, the *Summa Theologica*. Aquinas offers five different proofs for the existence of God — what are now famously referred to as the "Five Ways." The first four proofs, which are included here, are different versions of the cosmological argument. His fifth proof is a type of teleological argument. All four of the cosmological-type arguments have a common structure: they each begin with some kind of contingent or dependent beings and then argue to a noncontingent, uncaused Being — God.

The next selection is by William Lane Craig. Also a cosmological argument, it is of a different order than those given by Aquinas. This "kalam" cosmological argument is a cutting-edge version of an argument advanced in the Middle Ages by Islamic thinkers. According to the argument, the universe began to exist at some point in the finite past. Since whatever begins to exist needs a cause, the universe itself must have a cause. Furthermore, this cause must be a personal God.

The third cosmological argument is one offered by the German rationalist Gottfried Wilhelm Leibniz (1646 – 1716). In his book *The Monadology*, Leibniz formulates his Principle of Sufficient Reason as "no fact can be real or existent, no statement true, unless there be a sufficient reason why it is so and not otherwise." From this principle he argues that there must be a sufficient reason why anything exists. He then argues that the sufficient reason cannot be in any particular thing in the universe, so there must exist a being that is necessary in its existence. This, he says, we call God.

The next type of argument we include is the *teleological*, or design, argument. Unlike cosmological arguments, which begin with the existence of the world as a foundational presupposition, design arguments focus on a specific aspect of the world: the apparent order or design contained within it. One of the most famous versions of the design argument was offered by William Paley in his early nineteenth-century book, *Natural Theology*. In this work he argues that just as we find parts ordered to achieve a certain end in machines made by human beings, so in the natural world we find similar structures. Given the similarity between the ordered patterns in a machine, such as a watch, and the ordered patterns in the natural world, we can infer a designer of the world just as reasonably as we can the machine.

The next selection is written by one of the major figures in the recent "Intelligent Design" movement, an intellectual movement that includes a scientific research program for investigating intelligent causes in the universe. In this piece Michael Behe argues that evidence in biochemistry reveals a kind of complexity, what he calls "irreducible complexity," that reflects finely calibrated chemical "machines" in living organisms. These irreducibly complex systems, he argues, lead one to conclude that life was designed by an intelligent agent.

In the next article, Robin Collins looks at recent discoveries in the realms of physics and cosmology. His focus is on the structure of the world in which living organisms are able to flourish, and he argues that the fine-tuning of the universe provides good evidence for preferring theism over naturalism.

The arguments above are all *a posteriori* in nature; that is, they include premises that are known through experience of the natural world. There is another kind of argument, however, which is *a priori* in nature; it is based on premises that can be known independently of experience of the natural world. This argument type is called the *ontological* argument (from the Greek terms *ôn, ontos* = being, and *logos* = word). In the eleventh century a Benedictine monk named Anselm devised an argument that seemed to prove, beyond any doubt, that God exists. According to this argument, God is the greatest conceivable being, "a being than which none greater can be conceived." Once we understand the meaning of this concept, we see that such a being must exist, for if it didn't exist, it would not be a being than which none greater can be conceived; it would not be the *greatest* conceivable being. Thus, understanding the very concept of God logically forces one to the conclusion that God exists.

In recent decades, with the rise of modal logic, new modal varieties of the ontological argument have emerged. One important modal version is offered by Alvin Plantinga. Put concisely, his argument can perhaps be stated this way: It is possible that God exists. But God is not a contingent being. So it is necessary that God exists. Therefore, God exists.

In addition to the traditional arguments for God's existence (cosmological, teleological, and ontological), there are also a number of more recent arguments. We have included four types: *transcendental, wager, moral,* and an argument based on *religious experience.*

Regarding the *transcendental argument* — an attempt to demonstrate the existence of

God using logical absolutes — we have included a debate on the subject between Greg Bahnsen and Gordon Stein.

In his classic *wager argument*, Blaise Pascal provides a pragmatic reason for believing in God: it is a better bet. He argues that the possible benefits of believing in God are much greater than the benefits of nonbelief. Even if the evidence for God is scant or nonexistent, the rational person will wager on God since she has the possibility of eternal gain by believing and the possibility of eternal loss by choosing not to believe.

In the next piece, on the *moral argument*, C. S. Lewis argues that there is real Right and Wrong (an objective morality), and one who denies this lives inconsistently with his or her own beliefs. People across the world know the moral law; they live by it and sometimes violate it. In the next selection, Paul Copan maintains that the supernatural is necessary to ground morality. Since objective moral values do exist, he argues, there must be a God.

Finally, we include two selections on *religious experience*. In the first, Teresa of Avila argues that her religious experiences, great favors bestowed on her, could be neither the work of the devil nor her own imaginations; they must be from God. In the next selection — the last one in this section — William Alston argues that one's experience of God plays an epistemic role with respect to beliefs about God that is analogous to the way sense perception plays an epistemic role with respect to beliefs about the physical world. When a person believes that she has experienced God, that belief is justified unless she has sufficient reasons to think the belief is false or not sufficiently indicative of the truth of the belief.

CHAPTER 7

The Classical Cosmological Argument

Thomas Aquinas

Whether God Exists

Objection 1. It seems that God does not exist; because if one of two contraries be infinite, the other would be altogether destroyed. But the word "God" means that He is infinite goodness. If, therefore, God existed, there would be no evil discoverable; but there is evil in the world. Therefore God does not exist.

Objection 2. Further, it is superfluous to suppose that what can be accounted for by a few principles has been produced by many. But it seems that everything we see in the world can be accounted for by other principles, supposing God did not exist. For all natural things can be reduced to one principle which is nature; and all voluntary things can be reduced to one principle which is human reason, or will. Therefore there is no need to suppose God's existence.

On the contrary, it is said in the person of God: "I am Who am" (Exodus 3:14).

I answer that, The existence of God can be proved in five ways.

The first and more manifest way is the argument from motion. It is certain, and evident to our senses, that in the world some things are in motion. Now whatever is in motion is put in motion by another, for nothing can be in motion except it is in potentiality to that towards which it is in motion; whereas a thing moves inasmuch as it is an act. For motion is nothing else than the reduction of something from potentiality to actuality. But nothing can be reduced from potentiality to actuality, except by something in a state of actuality. Thus that which is actually hot, as fire, makes wood, which is potentially hot, to be actually hot, and thereby moves and changes it. Now it is not possible that the same thing should be at once in actuality and potentiality in the same respect, but only in different respects. For what is actually hot cannot simultaneously be potentially hot; but it is simultaneously potentially cold. It is therefore impossible that in the same respect and in the same way a thing should be both mover and moved, i.e., that it should move itself. Therefore, whatever is in motion must be put in motion by another. If that by which it is put in motion be itself put in motion, then this also must needs be put in motion by another, and that by another again. But this cannot go on to infinity, because then there would be no first mover, and, consequently, no other mover; seeing that subsequent movers move only inasmuch as they are put in motion by the first mover; as the staff moves only because it is put in motion by the hand. Therefore it is necessary to arrive at a first mover, put in motion by no other; and this everyone understands to be God.

The second way is from the nature of the efficient cause. In the world of sense we find there is an order of efficient causes. There is no case known (neither is it, indeed, possible) in which a thing is found to be the efficient cause of itself; for so it would be prior to itself, which is impossible. Now in efficient causes it is not possible to go on to infinity, because in all efficient causes following in order, the first is the cause of the intermediate cause, and the intermediate is the cause of the ultimate cause, whether the intermediate cause be several, or only one. Now to take away the cause is to take away the effect. Therefore, if there be no first cause among efficient causes, there will be no ultimate, nor any intermediate cause. But if in efficient causes it is possible to go on to infinity, there will be no first efficient cause, neither will there be an ultimate effect, nor any intermediate efficient causes; all of which is plainly false. Therefore it is necessary to admit a first efficient cause, to which everyone gives the name of God.

The third way is taken from possibility and necessity, and runs thus. We find in nature things that are possible to be and not to be, since they are found to be generated, and to corrupt, and consequently, they are possible to be and not to be. But it is impossible for these always to exist, for that which is possible not to be at some time is not. Therefore, if everything is possible not to be, then at one time there could have been nothing in existence. Now if this were true, even now there would be nothing in existence, because that which does not exist only begins to exist by something already existing. Therefore, if at one time nothing was in existence, it would have been impossible for anything to have begun to exist; and thus even now nothing would be in existence — which is absurd. Therefore, not all beings are merely possible, but there must exist something the existence of which is necessary. But every necessary thing either has its necessity caused by another, or not. Now it is impossible to go on to infinity in necessary things which have their necessity caused by another, as has been already proved in regard to efficient causes. Therefore we cannot but postulate the existence of some being having of itself its own necessity, and not receiving it from another, but rather causing in others their necessity. This all men speak of as God.

The fourth way is taken from the gradation to be found in things. Among beings there are some more and some less good, true, noble and the like. But "more" and "less" are predicated of different things, according as they resemble in their different ways something which is the maximum, as a thing is said to be hotter according as it more nearly resembles that which is hottest; so that there is something which is

truest, something best, something noblest and, consequently, something which is uttermost being; for those things that are greatest in truth are greatest in being, as it is written in Metaph. ii. Now the maximum in any genus is the cause of all in that genus; as fire, which is the maximum heat, is the cause of all hot things. Therefore there must also be something which is to all beings the cause of their being, goodness, and every other perfection; and this we call God.

The fifth way is taken from the governance of the world. We see that things which lack intelligence, such as natural bodies, act for an end, and this is evident from their acting always, or nearly always, in the same way, so as to obtain the best result. Hence it is plain that not fortuitously, but designedly, do they achieve their end. Now whatever lacks intelligence cannot move towards an end, unless it be directed by some being endowed with knowledge and intelligence; as the arrow is shot to its mark by the archer. Therefore some intelligent being exists by whom all natural things are directed to their end; and this being we call God.

Reply to Objection 1. As Augustine says (Enchiridion xi): "Since God is the highest good, He would not allow any evil to exist in His works, unless His omnipotence and goodness were such as to bring good even out of evil." This is part of the infinite goodness of God, that He should allow evil to exist, and out of it produce good.

Reply to Objection 2. Since nature works for a determinate end under the direction of a higher agent, whatever is done by nature must needs be traced back to God, as to its first cause. So also whatever is done voluntarily must also be traced back to some higher cause other than human reason or will, since these can change or fail; for all things that are changeable and capable of defect must be traced back to an immovable and self-necessary first principle, as was shown in the body of the Article.

Summa Theologica, 1 p, Q 2, Art 3.

CHAPTER 8

The Kalam Cosmological Argument

William Lane Craig

Introduction[1]

"The first question which should rightly be asked," wrote G.W.F. Leibniz, is *"Why is there something rather than nothing?"*[2] This question does seem to possess a profound existential force, which has been felt by some of mankind's greatest thinkers. According to Aristotle, philosophy begins with a sense of wonder about the world, and the most profound question a man can ask concerns the origin of the universe.[3] In his biography of Ludwig Wittgenstein, Norman Malcolm reports that Wittgenstein said that he sometimes had a certain experience which could best be described by saying that "when I have it, *I wonder at the existence of the world*. I am then inclined to use such phrases as 'How extraordinary that anything should exist?'"[4] Similarly, one contemporary philosopher remarks, "... My mind often seems to reel under the immense significance this question has for me. That anything exists at all does seem to me a matter for the deepest awe."[5]

Why *does* something exist instead of nothing? Leibniz answered this question by arguing that something exists rather than nothing because a necessary being exists which carries within itself its reason for existence and is the sufficient reason for the existence of all contingent beings.[6]

Although Leibniz (followed by certain contemporary philosophers) regarded the non-existence of a necessary being as logically impossible, a more modest explication of necessity of existence in terms of what he calls "factual necessity" has been given by John Hick: a necessary being is an eternal, uncaused, indestructible, and incorruptible being.[7] Leibniz, of course, identified the necessary being as God. His critics, however, disputed this identification, contending that the material universe could itself be assigned the status of a necessary being. "Why," queried David Hume, "may not the material universe be the necessary existent Being, according to this pretended explanation of necessity?"[8] Typically, this has been precisely the position of the atheist. Atheists have not felt compelled to embrace the view that the universe came into being out of nothing for no reason at all; rather, they regard the universe itself as a sort of factually necessary being: the universe is eternal, uncaused, indestructible, and incorruptible. As Russell neatly put it, "... The universe is just there, and that's all."[9]

---

1. This is a revised and updated version of an earlier work published with the same title in *Truth: A Journal of Modern Thought*, Fall, 1990, 85–96. It is used with the kind permission of the author.

2. G.W. Leibniz, "The Principles of Nature and of Grace, Based on Reason," in *Leibniz Selections*, ed. Philip P. Wiener, The Modern Student's Library (New York: Charles Scribner's Sons, 1951), p. 527.

3. Aristotle *Metaphysica* Lambda. 1. 982b10–15.

4. Norman Malcolm, *Ludwig Wittgenstein: A Memoir* (London: Oxford University Press, 1958), p. 70.

5. J.J.C. Smart, "The Existence of God," *Church Quarterly Review* 156 (1955): 194.

6. G.W. Leibniz, *Theodicy: Essays on the Goodness of God, the Freedom of Man, and the Origin of Evil,* trans. E.M. Huggard (London: Routledge & Kegan Paul, 1951), p. 127; cf. idem, "Principles," p. 528.

7. John Hick, "God as Necessary Being," *Journal of Philosophy* 57 (1960): 733–34.

8. David Hume, *Dialogues concerning Natural Religion,* ed. with an Introduction by Norman Kemp Smith, Library of the Liberal Arts (Indianapolis: Bobbs-Merrill. 1947), p. 190.

9. Bertrand Russell and F.C. Copleston, "The Existence of God," in *The Existence of God,* ed. with an Introduction by John Hick, Problems of Philosophy Series (New York: Macmillan & Co., 1964), p. 175.

Does Leibniz's argument therefore leave us in a rational impasse, or might there not be some further resources available for untangling the riddle of the existence of the world? It seems to me that there are. It will be remembered that an essential property of a necessary being is eternality. If then it could be made plausible that the universe began to exist and is not therefore eternal, one would to that extent at least have shown the superiority of theism as a rational world view.

Now there is one form of the cosmological argument, much neglected today but of great historical importance, that aims precisely at the demonstration that the universe had a beginning in time.[10] Originating in the efforts of Christian theologians to refute the Greek doctrine of the eternity of matter, this argument was developed into sophisticated formulations by medieval Islamic and Jewish theologians, who in turn passed it back to the Latin West. The argument thus has a broad inter-sectarian appeal, having been defended by Muslims, Jews, and Christians both Catholic and Protestant.

This argument, which I have called the *kalam* cosmological argument, can be exhibited as follows:

1   Whatever begins to exist has a cause of its existence.

2   The universe began to exist.

2.1   Argument based on the impossibility of an actual infinite.

2.11   An actual infinite cannot exist.

2.12   An infinite temporal regress of events is an actual infinite.

2.13   Therefore, an infinite temporal regress of events cannot exist.

2.2   Argument based on the impossibility of the formation of an actual infinite by successive addition.

2.21   A collection formed by successive addition cannot be actually infinite.

2.22   The temporal series of past events is a collection formed by successive addition.

2.23   Therefore, the temporal series of past events cannot be actually infinite.

2.3   Confirmation from the Expansion of the Universe.

2.4   Confirmation from the Thermodynamic Properties of the Universe.

Therefore, the universe has a cause of its existence.

Let us examine this argument more closely.

Defense of the Kalam Cosmological Argument

Second Premise

Clearly, the crucial premise in this argument is (2), and two independent arguments are offered in support of it. Let us therefore turn first to an examination of the supporting arguments.

First Supporting Argument

In order to understand (2.1), we need to understand the difference between a potential infinite and an actual infinite. Crudely put, a potential infinite is a collection which is increasing toward infinity as a limit, but never gets there. Such a collection is really indefinite, not infinite. The sign of this sort of infinity, which is used in calculus, is ∞. An actual infinite is a collection in which the number of members really *is* infinite. The collection is not growing toward infinity; it is infinite, it is "complete." The sign of this sort of infinity, which is used in set theory to designate sets which have an infinite number of members, such as $\{1, 2, 3, \ldots\}$, is $\aleph_0$. Now (2.11) maintains, not that a potentially infinite number of things cannot exist, but that an actually infinite number of things cannot exist. For if an actually infinite number of things could exist, this would spawn all sorts of absurdities.

Perhaps the best way to bring home the truth of (2.11) is by means of an illustration. Let me use one

10. See William Lane Craig, *The Cosmological Argument from Plato to Leibniz,* Library of Philosophy and Religion (London: Macmillan, 1980), pp. 48–58, 61–76, 98–104, 128–31.

of my favorites, Hilbert's Hotel, a product of the mind of the great German mathematician, David Hilbert. Let us imagine a hotel with a finite number of rooms. Suppose, furthermore, that *all the rooms are full.* When a new guest arrives asking for a room, the proprietor apologizes, "Sorry, all the rooms are full." But now let us imagine a hotel with an infinite number of rooms and suppose once more that all the rooms are full. There is not a single vacant room throughout the entire infinite hotel. Now suppose a new guest shows up, asking for a room. "But of course!" says the proprietor, and he immediately shifts the person in room #1 into room #2, the person in room #2 into room #3, the person in room #3 into room #4 and so on, out to infinity. As a result of these room changes, room #1 now becomes vacant and the new guest gratefully checks in. But remember, before he arrived, all the rooms were full! Equally curious, according to the mathematicians, there are now no more persons in the hotel than there were before: the number is just infinite. But how can this be? The proprietor just added the new guest's name to the register and gave him his keys — how can there not be one more person in the hotel than before? But the situation becomes even stranger. For suppose an infinity of new guests show up the desk, asking for a room. "Of course, of course!" says the proprietor, and he proceeds to shift the person in room #1 into room #2, the person in room #2 into room #4, the person in room #3 into room #6, and so on out to infinity, always putting each former occupant into the room number twice his own. As a result, all the odd numbered rooms become vacant, and the infinity of new guests is easily accommodated. And yet, before they came, all the rooms were full! And again, strangely enough, the number of guests in the hotel is the same after the infinity of new guests check in as before, even though there were as many new guests as old guests. In fact, the proprietor could repeat this process *infinitely many times* and yet there would never be one single person more in the hotel than before.

But Hilbert's Hotel is even stranger than the German mathematician gave it out to be. For suppose some of the guests start to check out. Suppose the guest in room #1 departs. Is there not now one less person in the hotel? Not according to the mathematicians — but just ask the woman who makes the beds! Suppose the guests in room numbers 1, 3, 5, . . . check out. In this case an infinite number of people have left the hotel, but according to the mathematicians there are no less people in the hotel — but don't talk to that laundry woman! In fact, we could have every other guest check out of the hotel and repeat this process infinitely many times, and yet there would never be any less people in the hotel. But suppose instead the persons in room number 4, 5, 6, . . . checked out. At a single stroke the hotel would be virtually emptied, the guest register reduced to three names, and the infinite converted to finitude. And yet it would remain true that the *same number* of guests checked out this time as when the guests in room numbers 1, 3, 5, . . . checked out. Can anyone sincerely believe that such a hotel could exist in reality? These sorts of absurdities illustrate the impossibility of the existence of an actually infinite number of things.

That takes us to (2.12). The truth of this premiss seems fairly obvious. If the universe never began to exist, then prior to the present event there have existed an actually infinite number of previous events. Hence, a beginningless series of events in time entails the existence of an actually infinite number of things, namely, past events.

Given the truth of (2.11) and (2.12), the conclusion (2.13) logically follows. The series of past events must be finite and have a beginning. But since the universe is not distinct from the series of events, it follows that the universe began to exist.

At this point, we might find it profitable to consider several objections that might be raised against the argument. First let us consider objections to (2.11). Wallace Matson objects that the premiss must mean that an actually infinite number of things is *logically* impossible; but it is easy to show that such a collection is logically possible. For example, the series of negative numbers { ... – 3, – 2, – 1} is an actually infinite collection with no first member.[11] Matson's error here lies in thinking that (2.11) means to assert the *logical* impossibility of an actually infinite number of things. What the premiss expresses is the real or factual impossibility of an actual infinite. To illustrate the difference between real and logical possibility: there is no logical impossibility in something's coming to exist without a cause, but such a circumstance may well be really or metaphysically impossible. In the same way, (2.11) asserts that the absurdities entailed in the real existence of an actual infinite show that such an existence is metaphysically impossible. Hence, one could grant that in the conceptual realm of mathematics one can, given certain conventions and axioms, speak consistently about infinite sets of numbers, but this in no way implies that an actually infinite number of things is really possible. One might also note that the mathematical school of intuitionism denies that even the number series is actually infinite (they take it to be potentially infinite only), so that appeal to number series as examples of actual infinites is a moot procedure.

The late J. L. Mackie also objected to (2.11), claiming that the absurdities are resolved by noting that for infinite groups the axiom "the whole is greater than its part" does not hold, as it does for finite groups.[12] Similarly, Quentin Smith comments that once we understand that an infinite set has a proper subset which has the same number of members as the set itself, the purportedly absurd situations become "perfectly believable."[13] But to my mind, it is precisely this feature of infinite set theory which, when translated into the realm of the real, yields results which are perfectly incredible, for example, Hilbert's Hotel. Moreover, not all the absurdities stem from infinite set theory's denial of Euclid's axiom: the absurdities illustrated by guests checking out of the hotel stem from the self-contradictory results when the inverse operations of subtraction or division are performed using transfinite numbers. Here the case against an actually infinite collection of things becomes decisive.

Finally one might note the objection of Sorabji, who maintains that illustrations such as Hilbert's Hotel involve no absurdity. In order to understand what is wrong with the *kalam* argument, he asks us to envision two parallel columns beginning at the same point and stretching away into the infinite distance, one the column of past years and the other the column of past days. The sense in which the column of past days is no larger than the column of past years, says Sorabji, is that the column of days will not "stick out" beyond the far end of the other column, since neither column has a far end. Now in the case of Hilbert's Hotel there is the temptation to think that some unfortunate resident at the far end will drop off into space. But there is no far end: the line of residents will not stick out beyond the far end of the line of rooms. Once this is seen, the outcome is just an explicable — even if a surprising and exhilarating — truth about infinity.[14] Now Sorabji is certainly correct, as we have seen, that Hilbert's Hotel illustrates an explicable truth about the nature of the actual infinite. If an actually infinite number of things could exist, a Hilbert's Hotel would be possible. But Sorabji seems to fail to understand the heart of the paradox: I, for one, experience no temptation to think of people dropping off the far end of the hotel, for there is none, but I do have difficulty believing that a hotel in which all the rooms are occupied can accommodate more guests. Of course, the line of guests will not stick out beyond the line of rooms, but if all of those infinite rooms *already* have guests in them, then can moving those guests about really create empty rooms? Sorabji's own illustration of the columns of past years and days I find not a little disquieting: if we divide the columns into foot-long segments and mark one column as the years and the other as the days, then one column is as long as the other and yet

11. Wallace Matson, *The Existence of God* (Ithaca, N.Y.: Cornell University Press, 1965), pp. 58 – 60.

12. J.L. Mackie, *The Miracle of Theism* (Oxford: Clarendon Press, 1982), p. 93.

13. Quentin Smith, "Infinity and the Past," *Philosophy of Science* 54 (1987): 69.

14. Richard Sorabji, *Time, Creation and the Continuum* (Ithaca, N.Y.: Cornell University Press, 1983), pp. 213, 222 – 23.

for every foot-length segment in the column of years, 365 segments of equal length are found in the column of days! These paradoxical results can be avoided only if such actually infinite collections can exist only in the imagination, not in reality. In any case, the Hilbert's Hotel illustration is not exhausted by dealing only with the addition of new guests, for the subtraction of guests results in absurdities even more intractable. Sorabji's analysis says nothing to resolve these. Hence, it seems to me that the objections to premise (2.11) are less plausible than the premise itself.

With regard to (2.12), the most frequent objection is that the past ought to be regarded as a potential infinite only, not an actual infinite. This was Aquinas's position versus Bonaventure, and the contemporary philosopher Charles Hartshorne seems to side with Thomas on this issue.[15] Such a position is, however, untenable. The future is potentially infinite, since it does not exist; but the past is actual in a way the future is not, as evidenced by the fact that we have traces of the past in the present, but no traces of the future. Hence, if the series of past events never began to exist, there must have been an actually infinite number of past events.

The objections to either premise therefore seem to be less compelling than the premises themselves. Together they imply that the universe began to exist. Hence, I conclude that this argument furnishes good grounds for accepting the truth of premise (2) that the universe began to exist.

Second Supporting Argument

The second argument (2.2) for the beginning of the universe is based on the impossibility of forming an actual infinite by successive addition. This argument is distinct from the first in that it does not deny the possibility of the existence of an actual infinite, but the possibility of its being *formed* by successive addition.

Premiss (2.21) is the crucial step in the argument. One cannot form an actually infinite collection of things by successively adding one member after another. Since one can always add one more before arriving at infin-

ity, it is impossible to reach actual infinity. Sometimes this is called the impossibility of "counting to infinity" or "traversing the infinite." It is important to understand that this impossibility has nothing to do with the amount of time available: it belongs to the nature of infinity that it cannot be so formed.

Now someone might say that while an infinite collection cannot be formed by beginning at a point and adding members, nevertheless an infinite collection could be formed by never beginning but ending at a point, that is to say, ending at a point after having added one member after another from eternity. But this method seems even more unbelievable than the first method. If one cannot count to infinity, how can one count down from infinity? If one cannot traverse the infinite by moving in one direction, how can one traverse it by simply moving in the opposite direction?

Indeed, the idea of a beginningless series ending in the present seems to be absurd. To give just one illustration: suppose we meet a man who claims to have been counting from eternity and is now finishing: $\ldots, -3, -2, -1, 0$. We could ask, why did he not finish counting yesterday or the day before or the year before? By then an infinite time had already elapsed, so that he should already have finished by then. Thus, at no point in the infinite past could we ever find the man finishing his countdown, for by that point he should already be done! In fact, no matter how far back into the past we go, we can never find the man counting at all, for at any point we reach he will have already finished. But if at no point in the past do we find him counting, this contradicts the hypothesis that he has been counting from eternity. This illustrates the fact that the formation of an actual infinite by successive addition is equally impossible whether one proceeds to or from infinity.

Premiss (2.22) presupposes a dynamical view of time according to which events are actualized in serial fashion, one after another. The series of events is not a sort of timelessly subsisting world-line which appears successively in consciousness. Rather, becoming is

---

15. Charles Hartshorne, *Man's Vision of God and the Logic of Theism* (Chicago: Willett, Clark, & Co., 1941), p. 37.

real and essential to temporal process. Now this view of time is not without its challengers, but to consider their actions in this article would take us too far afield.[16] In this piece, we must rest content with the fact that we are arguing on common ground with our ordinary intuitions of temporal becoming and in agreement with a good number of contemporary philosophers of time and space.

Given the truth of (2.21) and (2.22), the conclusion (2.23) logically follows. If the universe did not begin to exist a finite time ago, then the present moment could never arrive. But obviously, it has arrived. Therefore, we know that the universe is finite in the past and began to exist.

Again, it would be profitable to consider various objections that have been offered against this reasoning. Against (2.21), Mackie objects that the argument illicitly assumes an infinitely distant starting point in the past and then pronounces it impossible to travel from that point to today. But there would in an infinite past be no starting point, not even an infinitely distant one. Yet from any given point in the infinite past, there is only a finite distance to the present.[17] Now it seems to me that Mackie's allegation that the argument presupposes an infinitely distant starting point is entirely groundless. The beginningless character of the series only serves to accentuate the difficulty of its being formed by successive addition. The fact that there is *no beginning at all,* not even an infinitely distant one, makes the problem more, not less, nettlesome. And the point that from any moment in the infinite past there is only a finite temporal distance to the present may be dismissed as irrelevant. The question is not how any finite portion of the temporal series can be formed, but how the whole infinite series can be formed. If Mackie thinks that because every segment of the series can be formed by successive addition therefore the whole series can be so formed, then he is simply committing the fallacy of composition.

Sorabji similarly objects that the reason it is impossible to count down from infinity is because counting involves by nature taking a starting number, which is lacking in this case. But completing an infinite lapse of years involves no starting year and is, hence, possible.[18] But this response is clearly inadequate, for, as we have seen, the years of an infinite past could be enumerated by the negative numbers, in which case a completed infinity of years would, indeed, entail a beginningless countdown from infinity. Sorabji anticipates this rebuttal, however, and claims that such a backwards countdown is possible in principle and therefore no logical barrier has been exhibited to the elapsing of an infinity of past years. Again, however, the question I am posing is not whether there is a logical contradiction in such a notion, but whether such a countdown is not metaphysically absurd. For we have seen that such a countdown should at any point already have been completed. But Sorabji is again ready with a response: to say the countdown should at any point already be over confuses counting an *infinity* of numbers with counting *all* the numbers. At any given point in the past, the eternal counter will have already counted an infinity of negative numbers, but that does not entail that he will have counted all the negative numbers. I do not think the argument makes this alleged equivocation, and this may be made clear by examining the reason why our eternal counter is supposedly able to complete a count of the negative numbers ending at zero. In order to justify the possibility of this intuitively impossible feat, the argument's opponent appeals to the so-called Principle of Correspondence used in set theory to determine whether two sets are equivalent (that is, have the same number of members) by matching the members of one set with the members of the other set and *vice versa*. On the basis of this principle the objector argues that since the counter has lived, say, an infinite number of years and since the set of past years can be put into a one-to-one

16. G.J. Whitrow defends a form of this argument which does not presuppose a dynamical view of time, by asserting that an infinite past would still have to be "lived through" by any everlasting, conscious being, even if the series of physical events subsisted timelessly (G.J. Whitrow, *The Natural Philosophy of Time*, 2d ed. [Oxford: Clarendon Press, 1980], pp. 28 – 32).

17. Mackie, *Theism*, p. 93.

18. Sorabji, *Time, Creation, and the Continuum*, pp. 219 – 22.

correspondence with the set of negative numbers, it follows that by counting one number a year an eternal counter would complete a countdown of the negative numbers by the present year. If we were to ask why the counter would not finish next year or in a hundred years, the objector would respond that prior to the present year an infinite number of years will have already elapsed, so that by the Principle of Correspondence, all the numbers should have been counted by now. But this reasoning backfires on the objector: for, as we have seen, on this account the counter should at any point in the past have already finished counting all the numbers, since a one-to-one correspondence exists between the years of the past and the negative numbers. Thus, there is no equivocation between counting an infinity of numbers and counting all the numbers. But at this point a deeper absurdity bursts in view: for suppose there were another counter who counted at a rate of one negative number per day. According to the Principle of Correspondence, which underlies infinite set theory and transfinite arithmetic, both of our eternal counters will finish their countdowns at the same moment, even though one is counting at a rate 365 times faster than the other! Can anyone believe that such scenarios can actually obtain in reality, but do not rather represent the outcome of an imaginary game being played in a purely conceptual realm according to adopted logical conventions and axioms?

As for premiss (2.22), many thinkers have objected that we need not regard the past as a beginningless infinite series with an end in the present. Popper, for example, admits that the *set* of all past events is actually infinite, but holds that the *series* of past events is potentially infinite. This may be seen by beginning in the present and numbering the events backwards, thus forming a potential infinite. Therefore, the problem of an actual infinite's being formed by successive addition does not arise.[19] Similarly, Swinburne muses that it is dubious whether a completed infinite series with no beginning but an end makes sense, but he proposes to solve the problem by beginning in the present and regressing into the past, so that the series of past events would have no end and would therefore not be a completed infinite.[20] This objection, however, clearly confuses the *mental regress* of counting with the *real progress* of the temporal series of events itself. Numbering the series from the present backwards only shows that if there are an infinite number of past events, then we can denumerate an infinite number of past events. But the problem is, how can this infinite collection of events come to be *formed* by successive addition? How we mentally conceive the series does not in any way affect the ontological character of the series itself as a series with no beginning but an end, or in other words, as an actual infinite completed by successive addition.

Once again, then, the objections to (2.21) and (2.22) seem less plausible than the premises themselves. Together they imply (2.23), or that the universe began to exist.

First Scientific Confirmation

These purely philosophical arguments for the beginning of the universe have received remarkable confirmation from discoveries in astronomy and astrophysics during this century. These confirmations might be summarized under two heads: the confirmation from the expansion of the universe and the confirmation from thermodynamic properties of the universe.

Prior to the 1920s, scientists had always assumed that the universe was stationary and eternal. Tremors of the impending earthquake that would topple this traditional cosmology were first felt in 1917, when Albert Einstein made a cosmological application of his newly discovered gravitational theory, the General Theory of Relativity (GR). To his chagrin, Einstein found that GR would not permit an eternal, static model of the universe unless he fudged the equations in order to offset the gravitational effect of matter. As

---

19. K.R. Popper, "On the Possibility of an Infinite Past: a Reply to Whitrow," *British Journal for the Philosophy of Science* 29 (1978): 47–48.

20. R.G. Swinburne, "The Beginning of the Universe," *The Aristotelian Society* 40 (1966): 131–32.

a result, Einstein's universe was balanced on a razor's edge, and the least perturbation — even the transport of matter from one part of the universe to another — would cause the universe either to implode or to expand. By taking this feature of Einstein's model seriously, the Russian mathematician Alexander Friedman and the Belgian astronomer Georges Lemaître were able to formulate independently in the 1920s solutions to his equations which predicted an expanding universe.

In 1929 the American astronomer Edwin Hubble showed that the light from distant galaxies is systematically shifted toward the red end of the spectrum. This red-shift was taken to be a Doppler effect indicating that the light sources were receding in the line of sight. Incredibly, what Hubble had discovered was the expansion of the universe predicted by Friedman and Lemaître on the basis of Einstein's GR. It was a veritable turning point in the history of science. "Of all the great predictions that science has ever made over the centuries," exclaims John Wheeler, "was there ever one greater than this, to predict, and predict correctly, and predict against all expectation a phenomenon so fantastic as the expansion of the universe?"[21]

According to the Friedman-Lemaître model, as time proceeds, the distances separating the galaxies become greater. It's important to appreciate that as a GR-based theory, the model does not describe the expansion of the material content of the universe into a pre-existing, empty space, but rather the expansion of space itself. The galaxies are conceived to be at rest with respect to space but to recede progressively from one another as space itself expands or stretches, just as buttons glued to the surface of a balloon will recede from one another as the balloon inflates. As the universe expands, it becomes less and less dense. This has the astonishing implication that as one reverses the expansion and extrapolates back in time, the universe becomes progressively denser until one arrives at a state of infinite density at some point in the finite past. This state represents a singularity at which space-time curvature, along with temperature, pressure, and density, becomes infinite. It therefore constitutes an edge or boundary to space-time itself. P. C. W. Davies comments,

> If we extrapolate this prediction to its extreme, we reach a point when all distances in the universe have shrunk to zero. An initial cosmological singularity therefore forms a past temporal extremity to the universe. We cannot continue physical reasoning, or even the concept of spacetime, through such an extremity. For this reason most cosmologists think of the initial singularity as the beginning of the universe. On this view the big bang represents the creation event; the creation not only of all the matter and energy in the universe, but also of spacetime itself.[22]

The term "Big Bang," originally a derisive expression coined by Fred Hoyle to characterize the beginning of the universe predicted by the Friedman-Lemaître model, is thus potentially misleading, since the expansion cannot be visualized from the outside (there being no "outside," just as there is no "before" with respect to the Big Bang). On such a model the universe originates *ex nihilo* in the sense that at the initial singularity it is true that *There is no earlier space-time point* or it is false that *Something existed prior to the singularity*. The standard Big Bang model thus predicts an absolute beginning of the universe. If this model is correct, then we have amazing scientific confirmation of the second premise of the *kalam* cosmological argument.

So is the model correct, or, more importantly, is it correct in predicting a beginning of the universe? We've already seen that the red-shift in the light from distant galaxies provides powerful evidence for the Big Bang. In addition, the best explanation for the abundance of certain light elements like helium in the universe is that they were formed in the hot, dense Big Bang. Finally, the discovery in 1965 of a cosmic

21. John A. Wheeler, "Beyond the Hole," in *Some Strangeness in the Proportion,* ed. Harry Woolf (Reading, Mass.: Addison-Wesley, 1980), p. 354.

22. P. C. W. Davies, "Spacetime Singularities in Cosmology," in *The Study of Time III,* ed. J. T. Fraser (Berlin: Springer Verlag, 1978), pp. 78–79.

background of microwave radiation is best explained as a vestige of the Big Bang.

Nevertheless, the standard Big Bang model will need to be modified in various ways. The model is based on Einstein's General Theory of Relativity. But Einstein's theory breaks down when space is shrunk down to sub-atomic proportions. We shall need to introduce sub-atomic physics at that point, and no one is sure how this is to be done. Moreover, the expansion of the universe is probably not constant, as in the standard model. It is probably accelerating and may have had a brief moment of super-rapid expansion in the past.

But none of these adjustments need affect the fundamental prediction of the absolute beginning of the universe. Indeed, physicists have proposed scores of alternative models over the decades since Friedman and LeMaître's work, and those that do not have an absolute beginning have been repeatedly shown to be unworkable. Put more positively, the only viable non-standard models are those that involve an absolute beginning to the universe. That beginning may or may not involve a beginning *point*. But on theories (such as Stephen Hawking's "no boundary" proposal) that do not have a point-like beginning, the past is still finite, not infinite. The universe has not existed forever according to such theories but came into existence, even if it did not do so at a certain point.

Indeed, something of a watershed appears to have been reached in 2003, when three leading cosmologists, Arvin Borde, Alan Guth, and Alexander Vilenkin, were able to prove that *any* universe which has, on average, been expanding throughout its history cannot be infinite in the past but must have a past space-time boundary.

What makes their proof so powerful is that it holds *regardless* of the physical description of the very early universe. Because we can't yet provide a physical description of the very early universe, this brief moment has been fertile ground for speculations. One scientist has compared it to the regions on ancient maps labeled "Here there be dragons!" — it can be filled with all sorts of fantasies. But the Borde-Guth-Vilenkin theorem is independent of any physical description of that moment. Their theorem implies that the quantum vacuum state out of which our universe may have evolved — which some scientific popularizers have misleadingly and inaccurately referred to as "nothing" — cannot be eternal in the past but must have had a beginning. Even if our universe is just a tiny part of a so-called "multiverse" composed of many universes, their theorem requires that the multiverse itself must have an absolute beginning. Speculative theories, such as Pre-Big Bang Inflationary scenarios, have been crafted to try to avoid the absolute beginning required by the Borde-Guth-Vilenkin theorem; but none of these theories has succeeded in restoring an eternal past. At most they just push the beginning back a step.

Vilenkin is blunt about the implications:

> It is said that an argument is what convinces reasonable men and a proof is what it takes to convince even an unreasonable man. With the proof now in place, cosmologists can no longer hide behind the possibility of a past-eternal universe. There is no escape, they have to face the problem of a cosmic beginning.[23]

We can fully expect that new theories will be proposed, attempting to avoid the universe's beginning. Such proposals are to be welcomed, and we have no reason to think that they will be any more successful than their failed predecessors. Of course, scientific results are always provisional. Nevertheless, it's pretty clear which way the evidence points. Today the proponent of the *kalam* cosmological argument stands comfortably within the scientific mainstream in holding that the universe began to exist.

Second Scientific Confirmation

As if this were not enough, there is a second scientific confirmation of the beginning of the universe based on the thermodynamic properties of various

---

23. Vilenkin, *Many Worlds in One*, p. 176.

cosmological models. According to the second law of thermodynamics, processes taking place in a closed system always tend toward a state of equilibrium. Now our interest is in what implications this has when the law is applied to the universe as a whole. For the universe is a gigantic closed system, since it is everything there is and no energy is being fed into it from without. The second law seems to imply that, given enough time, the universe will reach a state of thermodynamic equilibrium, known as the "heat death" of the universe. This death may be hot or cold, depending on whether the universe will expand forever or eventually re-contract. On the one hand, if the density of the universe is great enough to overcome the force of the expansion, then the universe will re-contract into a hot fireball. As the universe contracts, the stars burn more rapidly until they finally explode or evaporate. As the universe grows denser, the black holes begin to gobble up everything around them and begin themselves to coalesce until all the black holes finally coalesce into one gigantic black hole which is coextensive with the universe, from which it will never re-emerge. On the other hand, if the density of the universe is insufficient to halt the expansion, as seems more likely, then the galaxies will turn all their gas into stars and the stars will burn out. At 10^{30} years the universe will consist of 90% dead stars, 9% supermassive black holes, and 1% atomic matter. Elementary particle physics suggests that thereafter protons will decay into electrons and positrons, so that space will be filled with a rarefied gas so thin that the distance between an electron and a positron will be about the size of the present galaxy. At 10^{100} years some scientists believe that the black holes themselves will dissipate into radiation and elementary particles. Eventually all the matter in the dark, cold, ever-expanding universe will be reduced to an ultra-thin gas of elementary particles and radiation. Equilibrium will prevail throughout, and the entire universe will be in its final state, from which no change will occur.

Recent discoveries provide strong evidence that there is effectively a positive cosmological constant which causes the cosmic expansion to accelerate rather than decelerate. Paradoxically, since the volume of space increases exponentially, allowing greater room for further entropy production, the universe actually grows farther and farther from an equilibrium state as time proceeds. But the acceleration only hastens the cosmos's disintegration into increasingly isolated material patches no longer causally connected with similarly marooned remnants of the expanding universe. Each of these patches faces, in turn, thermodynamic extinction. Therefore, the grim future predicted on the basis of the second law remains fundamentally unaltered.

Now the question which needs to be asked is this: why, if the universe has existed forever, is it not now in a cold, dark, dilute, and lifeless state? In contrast to their nineteenth century forbears, contemporary physicists have come to question the implicit assumption that the universe is past eternal. Davies reports,

> Today, few cosmologists doubt that the universe, at least as we know it, did have an origin at a finite moment in the past. The alternative — that the universe has always existed in one form or another — runs into a rather basic paradox. The sun and stars cannot keep burning forever: sooner or later they will run out of fuel and die.
>
> The same is true of all irreversible physical processes; the stock of energy available in the universe to drive them is finite, and cannot last for eternity. This is an example of the so-called second law of thermodynamics, which, applied to the entire cosmos, predicts that it is stuck on a one-way slide of degeneration and decay towards a final state of maximum entropy, or disorder. As this final state has not yet been reached, it follows that the universe cannot have existed for an infinite time.[24]

Davies concludes, "The universe can't have existed

24. Paul Davies, "The Big Bang — and Before," The Thomas Aquinas College Lecture Series, Thomas Aquinas College, Santa Paula, Calif., March 2002.

forever. We know there must have been an absolute beginning a finite time ago."[25]

So once again the scientific evidence of thermodynamics confirms the truth of the second premise of the *kalam* cosmological argument. This evidence is especially impressive because thermodynamics is so well understood by physicists that it is practically a completed field of science. This makes it highly unlikely that these findings will be reversed.

We therefore have both philosophical argument and scientific confirmation for the beginning of the universe. On this basis I think that we are amply justified in concluding the truth of premiss (2) that the universe began to exist.

First Premiss

Premiss (1) strikes me as relatively non-controversial. It is based on the metaphysical intuition that something cannot come out of nothing. Hence, any argument for the principle is apt to be less obvious than the principle itself. Even the great skeptic David Hume admitted that he never asserted so absurd a proposition as that something might come into existence without a cause; he only denied that one could *prove* the obviously true causal principle.[26] With regard to the universe, if originally there were absolutely *nothing*—no God, no space, no time—, then how could the universe possibly come to exist? The truth of the principle *ex nihilo, nihil fit* is so obvious that I think we are justified in foregoing an elaborate defense of the argument's first premiss.

Nevertheless, some thinkers, exercised to avoid the theism implicit in this premiss within the present context, have felt driven to deny its truth. In order to avoid its theistic implications, Davies presents a scenario which, he confesses, "should not be taken too seriously," but which seems to have a powerful attraction

for Davies.[27] He has reference to a quantum theory of gravity according to which spacetime itself could spring uncaused into being out of absolutely nothing. While admitting that there is "still no satisfactory theory of quantum gravity," such a theory "would allow spacetime to be created and destroyed spontaneously and uncaused in the same way that particles are created and destroyed spontaneously and uncaused. The theory would entail a certain mathematically determined probability that, for instance, a blob of space would appear where none existed before. Thus, spacetime could pop out of nothingness as the result of a causeless quantum transition."[28]

Now in fact particle pair production furnishes no analogy for this radical *ex nihilo* becoming, as Davies seems to imply. This quantum phenomenon, even if an exception to the principle that every event has a cause, provides no analogy to something's coming into being out of nothing. Though physicists speak of this as particle pair creation and annihilation, such terms are philosophically misleading, for all that actually occurs is conversion of energy into matter or vice versa. As Davies admits, "The processes described here do not represent the creation of matter out of nothing, but the conversion of pre-existing energy into material form."[29] Hence, Davies greatly misleads his reader when he claims that "Particles ... can appear out of nowhere without specific causation" and again, "Yet the world of quantum physics routinely produces something for nothing."[30] On the contrary, the world of quantum physics *never* produces something for nothing.

In fact, quantum theory does not at all involve the sort of spontaneous becoming *ex nihilo* which Davies suggests. A quantum theory of gravity has the goal of providing a theory of gravitation based on the exchange of particles (gravitons) rather than the

25. Paul Davies, "The Big Questions: In the Beginning," ABC Science Online, interview with Phillip Adams, http://aca.mq.edu.au/pdavieshtml.

26. David Hume to John Stewart, February, 1754, in *The Letters of David Hume*, ed. J.Y.T. Greig (Oxford: Clarendon Press, 1932), 1:187.

27. Paul Davies, *God and the New Physics* (New York: Simon & Schuster, 1983), p. 214.

28. Ibid., p. 215.

29. Ibid., p. 31.

30. Ibid., pp. 215, 216.

geometry of space, which can then be brought into a Grand Unification Theory that unites all the forces of nature into a supersymmetrical state in which one fundamental force and a single kind of particle exist. But there seems to be nothing in this which suggests the possibility of spontaneous becoming *ex nihilo*.

Indeed, it is not at all clear that Davies's account is even intelligible. What can be meant, for example, by the claim that there is a mathematical probability that nothingness should spawn a region of spacetime "where none existed before?" It cannot mean that given enough time a region of spacetime would pop into existence at a certain place, since neither place nor time exist apart from spacetime. The notion of some probability of something's coming out of nothing thus seems incoherent.

I am reminded in this connection of some remarks made by A. N. Prior concerning an argument put forward by Jonathan Edwards against something's coming into existence uncaused. This would be impossible, said Edwards, because it would then be inexplicable why just any and everything cannot or does not come to exist uncaused. One cannot respond that only things of a certain nature come into existence uncaused, since prior to their existence they have no nature which could control their coming to be. Prior made a cosmological application of Edwards's reasoning by commenting on the steady state model's postulating the continuous creation of hydrogen atoms *ex nihilo*:

> It is no part of Hoyle's theory that this process is cause-less, but I want to be more definite about this, and to say that if it is causeless, then what is alleged to happen is fantastic and incredible. If it is possible for objects — objects, now, which really are objects, "substances endowed with capacities" — to start existing without a cause, then it is incredible that they should all turn out to be objects of the same sort, namely, hydrogen atoms. The peculiar nature of hydrogen atoms cannot possibly be what makes such starting-to-exist pos-

sible for them but not for objects of any other sort; for hydrogen atoms do not have this nature until they are there to have it, i.e. until their starting-to-exist has already occurred. That is Edwards's argument, in fact; and here it does seem entirely cogent....[31]

Now in the case at hand, if originally absolutely nothing existed, then why should it be spacetime that springs spontaneously out of the void, rather than, say, hydrogen atoms or even rabbits? How can one talk about the probability of any particular thing's popping into being out of nothing?

Davies on one occasion seems to answer as if the laws of physics are the controlling factor which determines what may leap uncaused into being: "But what of the laws? They have to be 'there' to start with so that the universe can come into being. Quantum physics has to exist (in some sense) so that a quantum transition can generate the cosmos in the first place."[32] Now this seems exceedingly peculiar. Davies seems to attribute to the laws of nature themselves a sort of ontological and causal status such that they constrain spontaneous becoming. But this seems clearly wrong-headed: the laws of physics do not themselves cause or constrain anything; they are simply propositional descriptions of a certain form and generality of what does happen in the universe. And the issue Edwards raises is why, if there were absolutely nothing, it would be true that any one thing rather than another should pop into being uncaused? It is futile to say it somehow belongs to the nature of spacetime to do so, for if there were absolutely nothing then there would have been no nature to determine that spacetime should spring into being.

Even more fundamentally, however, what Davies envisions is surely metaphysical nonsense. Though his scenario is cast as a scientific theory, someone ought to be bold enough to say that the Emperor is wearing no clothes. Either the necessary and sufficient conditions for the appearance of spacetime existed or not;

31. A.N. Prior, "Limited Indeterminism," in *Papers on Time and Tense* (Oxford: Clarendon Press, 1968), p.65.

32. Davies, *God*, p. 217.

if so, then it is not true that nothing existed; if not, then it would seem ontologically impossible that being should arise out of absolute non-being. To call such spontaneous springing into being out of non-being a "quantum transition" or to attribute it to "quantum gravity" explains nothing; indeed, on this account, there is no explanation. It just happens.

It seems to me, therefore, that Davies has not provided any plausible basis for denying the truth of the cosmological argument's first premiss. That whatever begins to exist has a cause would seem to be an ontologically necessary truth, one which is constantly confirmed in our experience.

A Personal Creator

Given the truth of premises (1) and (2), it logically follows that (3) the universe has a cause of its existence. In fact, I think that it can be plausibly argued that the cause of the universe must be a personal Creator. For how else could a temporal effect arise from an eternal cause? If the cause were simply a mechanically operating set of necessary and sufficient conditions existing from eternity, then why would not the effect also exist from eternity? For example, if the cause of water's being frozen is the temperature's being below zero degrees, then if the temperature were below zero degrees from eternity, then any water present would be frozen from eternity. The only way to have an eternal cause but a temporal effect would seem to be if the cause is a personal agent who freely chooses to create an effect in time. For example, a man sitting from eternity may will to stand up; hence, a temporal effect may arise from an eternally existing agent. Indeed, the agent may will from eternity to create a temporal effect, so that no change in the agent need be conceived. Thus, we are brought not merely to the first cause of the universe, but to its personal Creator.

Summary and Conclusion

In conclusion, we have seen on the basis of both philosophical argument and scientific confirmation that it is plausible that the universe began to exist. Given the intuitively obvious principle that whatever begins to exist has a cause of its existence, we have been led to conclude that the universe has a cause of its existence. On the basis of our argument, this cause would have to be uncaused, eternal, changeless, timeless, and immaterial. Moreover, it would have to be a personal agent who freely elects to create an effect in time. Therefore, on the basis of the *kalam* cosmological argument, I conclude that it is rational to believe that God exists.

CHAPTER 9

The Argument from Sufficient Reason

Gottfried Wilhelm Leibniz

28. In so far as the concatenation of their perceptions is due to the principle of memory alone, men act like the lower animals, resembling the empirical physicians, whose methods are those of mere practice without theory. Indeed, in three-fourths of our actions we are nothing but empirics. For instance, when we expect that there will be daylight tomorrow, we do so empirically, because it has always so happened until now. It is only the astronomer who thinks it on rational grounds.

29. But it is the knowledge of necessary and eternal truths that distinguishes us from the mere animals and gives us Reason and the sciences, raising us to the knowledge of ourselves and of God. And it is this in us that is called the rational soul or mind [*esprit*].

30. It is also through the knowledge of necessary truths, and through their abstract expression, that we rise to acts of reflexion, which make us think of what is called I, and observe that this or that is within us: and thus, thinking of ourselves, we think of being, of substance, of the simple and the compound, of the immaterial, and of God Himself, conceiving that what is limited in us is in Him without limits. And these acts of reflexion furnish the chief objects of our reasonings.

31. Our reasonings are grounded upon two great principles, that of contradiction, in virtue of which we judge false that which involves a contradiction, and true that which is opposed or contradictory to the false;

32. And that of sufficient reason, in virtue of which we hold that there can be no fact real or existing, no statement true, unless there be a sufficient reason, why it should be so and not otherwise, although these reasons usually cannot be known by us.

33. There are also two kinds of truths, those of reasoning and those of fact. Truths of reasoning are necessary and their opposite is impossible: truths of fact are contingent and their opposite is possible. When a truth is necessary, its reason can be found by analysis, resolving it into more simple ideas and truths, until we come to those which are primary.

34. It is thus that in Mathematics speculative Theorems and practical Canons are reduced by analysis to Definitions, Axioms and Postulates.

35. In short, there are simple ideas, of which no definition can be given; there are also axioms and postulates, in a word, primary principles, which cannot be proved, and indeed have no need of proof; and these are identical propositions, whose opposite involves an express contradiction.

36. But there must also be a sufficient reason for contingent truths or truths of fact, that is to say, for the sequence or connexion of the things which are dispersed throughout the universe of created beings, in which the analyzing into particular reasons might go on into endless detail, because of the immense variety of things in nature and the infinite division of bodies. There is an infinity of present and past forms and motions which go to make up the efficient cause of my present writing; and there is an infinity of minute tendencies and dispositions of my soul, which go to make its final cause.

37. And as all this detail again involves other prior or more detailed contingent things, each of which still needs a similar analysis to yield its reason, we are no further forward: and the sufficient or final reason must be outside of the sequence or series of particular contingent things, however infinite this series may be.

38. Thus the final reason of things must be in a necessary substance, in which the variety of particular changes exists only eminently, as in its source; and this substance we call God.

39. Now as this substance is a sufficient reason of all this variety of particulars, which are also connected together throughout; there is only one God, and this God is sufficient.

40. We may also hold that this supreme substance, which is unique, universal and necessary, nothing outside of it being independent of it — this substance, which is a pure sequence of possible being, must be illimitable and must contain as much reality as is possible.

41. Whence it follows that God is absolutely perfect; for perfection is nothing but amount of positive reality, in the strict sense, leaving out of account the limits or bounds in things which are limited. And where there are no bounds, that is to say in God, perfection is absolutely infinite.

42. It follows also that created beings derive their perfections from the influence of God, but that their imperfections come from their own nature, which is incapable of being without limits. For it is in this that they differ from God. An instance of this original imperfection of created beings may be seen in the natural inertia of bodies.

43. It is farther true that in God there is not only the source of existences but also that of essences, in so far as they are real, that is to say, the source of what is real in the possible. For the understanding of God is the region of eternal truths or of the ideas on which they depend, and without Him there would be nothing real in the possibilities of things, and not only would there be nothing in existence, but nothing would even be possible.

44. For if there is a reality in essences or possibilities, or rather in eternal truths, this reality must needs be founded in something existing and actual, and consequently in the existence of the necessary Being, in whom essence involves existence, or in whom to be possible is to be actual.

45. Thus God alone (or the necessary Being) has this prerogative that He must necessarily exist, if He is possible. And as nothing can interfere with the possibility of that which involves no limits, no negation and consequently no contradiction, this [His possibility] is sufficient of itself to make known the existence of God a priori. We have thus proved it, through the reality of eternal truths. But a little while ago we proved it also a posteriori, since there exist contingent beings, which can have their final or sufficient reason only in the necessary Being, which has the reason of its existence in itself.

CHAPTER 10

The Classical Design Argument

William Paley

State of the Argument

In crossing a heath, suppose I pitched my foot against a *stone*, and were asked how the stone came to be there; I might possibly answer, that, for any thing I knew to the contrary, it had lain there for ever: nor would it perhaps be very easy to show the absurdity of this answer. But suppose I had found a *watch* upon the ground, and it should be inquired how the watch happened to be in that place; I should hardly think of the answer which I had before given, that, for any thing I knew, the watch might have always been there. Yet why should not this answer serve for the watch as well as for the stone? Why is it not as admissible in the second case, as in the first? For this reason, and for no other, viz., that, when we come to inspect the watch, we perceive (what we could not discover in the stone) that its several parts are framed and put together for a purpose, e.g., that they are so formed and adjusted as to produce motion, and that motion so regulated as to point out the hour of the day; that, if the different parts had been differently shaped from what they are, of a different size from what they are, or placed after any other manner, or in any other order, than that in which they are placed, either no motion at all would have been carried on in the machine, or none which would have answered the use that is now served by it. To reckon up a few of the plainest of these parts, and of their offices, all tending to one result: We see a cylindrical box containing a coiled elastic spring, which, by its endeavour to relax itself, turns round the box. We next observe a flexible chain (artificially wrought for the sake of flexure), communicating the action of the spring from the box to the fusee. We then find a series of wheels, the teeth of which catch in, and apply to, each other, conducting the motion from the fusse to the balance, and from the balance to the pointer; and at the same time, by the size and shape of those wheels, so regulating that motion, as to terminate in causing an index, by an equable and measured progression, to pass over a given space in a given time. We take notice that the wheels are made of brass in order to keep them from rust; the springs of steel, no other metal being so elastic; that over the face of the watch there is placed a glass, a material employed in no other part of the work, but in the room of which, if there had been any other than a transparent substance, the hour could not be seen without opening the case. This mechanism being observed (it requires indeed an examination of the instrument, and perhaps some previous knowledge of the subject, to perceive and understand it; but being once, as we have said, observed and understood), the inference, we think, is inevitable, that the watch must have had a maker: that there must have existed, at some time, and at some place or other, an artificer or artificers who formed it for the purpose which we find it actually to answer; who comprehended its construction, and designed its use.

I. Nor would it, I apprehend, weaken the conclusion, that we had never seen a watch made; that we had never known an artist capable of making one; that we were altogether incapable of executing such a piece of workmanship ourselves, or of understanding in what manner it was performed; all this being no more than what is true of some exquisite remains of ancient art, of some lost arts, and, to the generality of mankind, of the more curious productions of modern manufacture. Does one man in a million know how oval frames are turned? Ignorance of this kind exalts our opinion of the unseen and unknown artist's skill, if he be unseen and unknown, but raises no doubt in our minds of the existence and agency of such an artist, at some former time, and in some place or other. Nor can I perceive that it varies at all the inference, whether the question arise concerning a human agent, or concerning an agent of a different species, or an agent possessing, in some respects, a different nature.

II. Neither, secondly, would it invalidate our conclusion, that the watch sometimes went wrong, or that it seldom went exactly right. The purpose of the machinery, the design, and the designer, might be evident, and in the case supposed would be evident, in whatever way we accounted for the irregularity of the movement, or whether we could account for it or not. It is not necessary that a machine be perfect, in order to show with what design it was made: still less necessary, where the only question is, whether it were made with any design at all.

III. Nor, thirdly, would it bring any uncertainty into the argument, if there were a few parts of the watch, concerning which we could not discover, or had not yet discovered, in what manner they conduced to the general effect; or even some parts, concerning which we could not ascertain, whether they conduced to that effect in any manner whatever. For, as to the first branch of the case; if by the loss, or disorder, or decay of the parts in question, the movement of the watch were found in fact to be stopped, or disturbed, or retarded, no doubt would remain in our minds as to the utility or intention of these parts, although we should be unable to investigate the manner according to which, or the connexion by which, the ultimate effect depended upon their action or assistance; and the more complex the machine, the more likely is this obscurity to arise. Then, as to the second thing supposed, namely, that there were parts which might be spared, without prejudice to the movement of the watch, and that we had proved this by experiment, — these superfluous parts, even if we were completely assured that they were such, would not vacate the

reasoning which we had instituted concerning other parts. The indication of contrivance remained, with respect to them, nearly as it was before.

IV. Nor, fourthly, would any man in his senses think the existence of the watch, with its various machinery, accounted for, by being told that it was one out of possible combinations of material forms; that whatever he had found in the place where he found the watch, must have contained some internal configuration or other; and that this configuration might be the structure now exhibited, viz., of the works of a watch, as well a different structure.

V. Nor, fifthly, would it yield his inquiry more satisfaction to be answered, that there existed in things a principle of order, which had disposed the parts of the watch into their present form and situation. He never knew a watch made by the principle of order; nor can he even form to himself an idea of what is meant by a principle of order, distinct from the intelligence of the watchmaker.

VI. Sixthly, he would be surprised to hear that the mechanism of the watch was no proof of contrivance, only a motive to induce the mind to think so:

VII. And not less surprised to be informed, that the watch in his hand was nothing more than the result of the laws of *metallic* nature. It is a perversion of language to assign any law, as the efficient, operative cause of any thing. A law presupposes an agent; for it is only the mode, according to which an agent proceeds: it implies a power; for it is the order, according to which that power acts. Without this agent, without this power, which are both distinct from itself, the *law* does nothing; is nothing. The expression, "the law of metallic nature," may sound strange and harsh to a philosophic ear; but it seems quite as justifiable as some others which are more familiar to him, such as "the law of vegetable nature," "the law of animal nature," or indeed as "the law of nature" in general, when assigned as the cause of phenomena, in exclusion of agency and power; or when it is substituted into the place of these.

VIII. Neither, lastly, would our observer be driven out of his conclusion, or from his confidence in its truth, by being told that he knew nothing at all about the matter. He knows enough for his argument: he knows the utility of the end: he knows the subserviency and adaptation of the means to the end. These points being known, his ignorance of other points, his doubts concerning other points, affect not the certainty of his reasoning. The consciousness of knowing little need not beget a distrust of that which he does know.

[…]

V. Our observer would further also reflect, that the maker of the watch before him was, in truth and reality, the maker of every watch produced from it; there being no difference (except that the latter manifests a more exquisite skill) between the making of another watch with his own hands, by the mediation of files, lathes, chisels, etc., and the disposing, fixing, and inserting of these instruments, or of others equivalent to them, in the body of the watch already made in such a manner, as to form a new watch in the course of the movements which he had given to the old one. It is only working by one set of tools, instead of another.

The conclusion of which the *first* examination of the watch, of its works, construction, and movement, suggested, was, that it must have had, for the cause and author of that construction, an artificer, who understood its mechanism, and designed its use. This conclusion is invincible. A *second* examination presents us with a new discovery. The watch is found, in the course of its movement, to produce another watch, similar to itself; and not only so, but we perceive in it a system of organization, separately calculated for that purpose. What effect would this discovery have, or ought it to have, upon our former inference? What, as hath already been said, but to increase, beyond measure, our admiration of the skill, which had been employed in the formation of such a machine? Or shall it, instead of this, all at once turn us round to an opposite conclusion, viz., that no art or skill whatever has been concerned in the business, although all other evidences of art and skill remain as they were, and this last and supreme piece of art be now added to the rest? Can this be maintained without absurdity? Yet this is atheism.

Application of the Argument

This is atheism: for every indication of contrivance, every manifestation of design, which existed in the watch, exists in the works of nature; with the difference, on the side of nature, of being greater and more, and that in a degree which exceeds all computation. I mean that the contrivances of nature surpass the contrivances of art, in the complexity, subtlety, and curiosity of the mechanism; and still more, if possible, do they go beyond them in number and variety; yet, in a multitude of cases, are not less evidently mechanical, not less evidently contrivances, not less evidently accommodated to their end, or suited to their office, than are the most perfect productions of human ingenuity....

CHAPTER 11

Evidence for Intelligent Design from Biochemistry

© Laszlo Bencze

Michael J. Behe

A Series of Eyes[1]

How do we see? In the 19th century the anatomy of the eye was known in great detail, and its sophisticated features astounded everyone who was familiar with them. Scientists of the time correctly observed that if a person were so unfortunate as to be missing one of the eye's many integrated features, such as the lens, or iris, or ocular muscles, the inevitable result would be a severe loss of vision or outright blindness. So it was concluded that the eye could only function if it were nearly intact.

Charles Darwin knew about the eye too. In the *Origin of Species*, Darwin dealt with many objections to his theory of evolution by natural selection. He discussed the problem of the eye in a section of the book appropriately entitled "Organs of extreme perfection and complication." Somehow, for evolution to be believable, Darwin had to convince the public that complex organs could be formed gradually, in a step-by-step process.

He succeeded brilliantly. Cleverly, Darwin didn't try to discover a real pathway that evolution might have used to make the eye. Instead, he pointed to modern animals with different kinds of eyes, ranging from the simple to the complex, and suggested that the evolution of the human eye might have involved similar organs as intermediates.

Here is a paraphrase of Darwin's argument. Although humans have complex camera-type eyes, many animals get by with less. Some tiny creatures have just a simple group of pigmented cells, or not much more than a light sensitive spot. That simple arrangement can hardly be said to confer vision, but it can sense light and dark, and so it meets the creature's needs. The light-sensing organ of some starfishes is somewhat more sophisticated. Their eye is located in a depressed region. This allows the animal to sense which direction the light is coming from, since the curvature of the depression blocks off light from some directions. If the curvature becomes more pronounced, the directional sense of the eye improves. But more curvature lessens the amount of light that enters the eye, decreasing its sensitivity. The sensitivity can be increased by placement of gelatinous material in the cavity to act as a lens. Some modern animals have eyes with such crude lenses. Gradual improvements in the lens could then provide an image of increasing sharpness, as the requirements of the animal's environment dictated.

Using reasoning like this, Darwin convinced many of his readers that an evolutionary pathway leads from the simplest light sensitive spot to the sophisticated camera-eye of man. But the question remains, how did vision begin? Darwin persuaded much of the world that a modern eye evolved gradually from a simpler structure, but he did not even try to explain where his starting point for the simple light-sensitive spot came from. On the contrary, Darwin dismissed the question of the eye's ultimate origin.

How a nerve comes to be sensitive to light hardly concerns us more than how life itself originated. He

---

1. Michael J. Behe is Associate Professor of Chemistry at Lehigh University in Pennsylvania and a Fellow of the Discovery Institute's Center for Renewal of Science & Culture. This article is used by the kind permission of the author. Modified March 14, 2011, from a speech delivered at Discovery Institute's God & Culture Conference in 1996.

had an excellent reason for declining the question: it was completely beyond nineteenth-century science. How the eye works; that is, what happens when a photon of light first hits the retina simply could not be answered at that time. As a matter of fact, no question about the underlying mechanisms of life could be answered. How did animal muscles cause movement? How did photosynthesis work? How was energy extracted from food? How did the body fight infection? No one knew.

To Darwin vision was a black box, but today, after the hard, cumulative work of many biochemists, we are approaching answers to the question of sight. Here is a brief overview of the biochemistry of vision. When light first strikes the retina, a photon interacts with a molecule called 11-cis-retinal, which rearranges within picoseconds to trans-retinal. The change in the shape of retinal forces a change in the shape of the protein, rhodopsin, to which the retinal is tightly bound. The protein's metamorphosis alters its behavior, making it stick to another protein called transducin. Before bumping into activated rhodopsin, transducin had tightly bound a small molecule called GDP. But when transducin interacts with activated rhodopsin, the GDP falls off and a molecule called GTP binds to transducin. (GTP is closely related to, but critically different from, GDP.)

GTP-transducin-activated rhodopsin now binds to a protein called phosphodiesterase, located in the inner membrane of the cell. When attached to activated rhodopsin and its entourage, the phosphodiesterase acquires the ability to chemically cut a molecule called cGMP (a chemical relative of both GDP and GTP). Initially there are a lot of cGMP molecules in the cell, but the phosphodiesterase lowers its concentration, like a pulled plug lowers the water level in a bathtub.

Another membrane protein that binds cGMP is called an ion channel. It acts as a gateway that regulates the number of sodium ions in the cell. Normally the ion channel allows sodium ions to flow into the cell, while a separate protein actively pumps them out again. The dual action of the ion channel and pump keeps the level of sodium ions in the cell within a narrow range. When the amount of cGMP is reduced because of cleavage by the phosphodiesterase, the ion channel closes, causing the cellular concentration of positively charged sodium ions to be reduced. This causes an imbalance of charge across the cell membrane which, finally, causes a current to be transmitted down the optic nerve to the brain. The result, when interpreted by the brain, is vision.

My explanation is just a sketchy overview of the biochemistry of vision. Ultimately, though, this is what it means to "explain" vision. This is the level of explanation for which biological science must aim. In order to truly understand a function, one must understand in detail every relevant step in the process. The relevant steps in biological processes occur ultimately at the molecular level, so a satisfactory explanation of a biological phenomenon such as vision, or digestion, or immunity must include its molecular explanation.

Now that the black box of vision has been opened it is no longer enough for an "evolutionary explanation" of that power to consider only the anatomical structures of whole eyes, as Darwin did in the nineteenth century, and as popularizers of evolution continue to do today. Each of the anatomical steps and structures that Darwin thought were so simple actually involves staggeringly complicated biochemical processes that cannot be papered over with rhetoric. Darwin's simple steps are now revealed to be huge leaps between carefully tailored machines. Thus biochemistry offers a Lilliputian challenge to Darwin. Now the black box of the cell has been opened and a Lilliputian world of staggering complexity stands revealed. It must be explained.

Irreducible Complexity

How can we decide if Darwin's theory can account for the complexity of molecular life? It turns out that Darwin himself set the standard. He acknowledged that:

> If it could be demonstrated that any complex organ existed which could not possibly have been formed by numerous, successive, slight modifications, my

theory would absolutely break down. But what type of biological system could not be formed by "numerous, successive, slight modifications"?

Well, for starters, a system that is irreducibly complex. Irreducible complexity is just a fancy phrase I use to mean a single system which is composed of several interacting parts, and where the removal of any one of the parts causes the system to cease functioning.

Let's consider an everyday example of irreducible complexity: the humble mousetrap. The mousetraps that my family uses consist of a number of parts. There are: 1) a flat wooden platform to act as a base; 2) a metal hammer, which does the actual job of crushing the little mouse; 3) a spring with extended ends to press against the platform and the hammer when the trap is charged; 4) a sensitive catch which releases when slight pressure is applied, and 5) a metal bar which connects to the catch and holds the hammer back when the trap is charged. Now you can't catch a few mice with just a platform; add a spring and catch a few more mice, add a holding bar and catch a few more. All the pieces of the mousetrap have to be in place before you catch any mice. Therefore the mousetrap is irreducibly complex.

An irreducibly complex system cannot be produced directly by numerous, successive, slight modifications of a precursor system, because any precursor to an irreducibly complex system that is missing a part is by definition nonfunctional. An irreducibly complex biological system, if there is such a thing, would be a powerful challenge to Darwinian evolution. Since natural selection can only choose systems that are already working, then if a biological system cannot be produced gradually it would have to arise as an integrated unit, in one fell swoop, for natural selection to have anything to act on.

Demonstration that a system is irreducibly complex is not a proof that there is absolutely no gradual route to its production. Although an irreducibly complex system can't be produced directly, one can't definitively rule out the possibility of an indirect, circuitous route. However, as the complexity of an interacting system increases, the likelihood of such an indirect route drops precipitously. And as the number of unexplained, irreducibly complex biological systems increases, our confidence that Darwin's criterion of failure has been met skyrockets toward the maximum that science allows.

The Cilium

Now, are any biochemical systems irreducibly complex? Yes, it turns out that many are. A good example is the cilium. Cilia are hairlike structures on the surfaces of many animal and lower plant cells that can move fluid over the cell's surface or "row" single cells through a fluid. In humans, for example, cells lining the respiratory tract each have about 200 cilia that beat in synchrony to sweep mucus towards the throat for elimination. What is the structure of a cilium? A cilium consists of bundle of fibers called an axoneme. An axoneme contains a ring of 9 double "microtubules" surrounding two central single microtubules. Each outer doublet consists of a ring of 13 filaments (subfiber A) fused to an assembly of 10 filaments (subfiber B). The filaments of the microtubules are composed of two proteins called alpha and beta tubulin. The 11 microtubules forming an axoneme are held together by three types of connectors: subfibers A are joined to the central microtubules by radial spokes; adjacent outer doublets are joined by linkers of a highly elastic protein called nexin; and the central microtubules are joined by a connecting bridge. Finally, every subfiber A bears two arms, an inner arm and an outer arm, both containing a protein called dynein.

But how does a cilium work? Experiments have shown that ciliary motion results from the chemically powered "walking" of the dynein arms on one microtubule up a second microtubule so that the two microtubules slide past each other. The protein cross-links between microtubules in a cilium to prevent neighboring microtubules from sliding past each other by more than a short distance. These cross-links, therefore, convert the dynein-induced sliding motion to a bending motion of the entire axoneme.

Now, let us consider what this implies. What

components are needed for a cilium to work? Ciliary motion certainly requires microtubules; otherwise, there would be no strands to slide. Additionally we require a motor, or else the microtubules of the cilium would lie stiff and motionless. Furthermore, we require linkers to tug on neighboring strands, converting the sliding motion into a bending motion, and preventing the structure from falling apart. All of these parts are required to perform one function: ciliary motion. Just as a mousetrap does not work unless all of its constituent parts are present, ciliary motion simply does not exist in the absence of microtubules, connectors, and motors. Therefore, we can conclude that the cilium is irreducibly complex; an enormous monkey wrench thrown into its presumed gradual, Darwinian evolution.

Blood Clotting

Now let's talk about a different biochemical system of blood clotting. Amusingly, the way in which the blood clotting system works is reminiscent of a Rube Goldberg machine.

The name of Rube Goldberg, the great cartoonist who entertained America with his silly machines, lives on in our culture, but the man himself has pretty much faded from view. Here's a typical example of his humor. In this cartoon Goldberg imagined a system where water from a drain-pipe fills a flask, causing a cork with attached needle to rise and puncture a paper cup containing beer, which sprinkles on a bird. The intoxicated bird falls onto a spring, bounces up to a platform, and pulls a string thinking it's a worm. The string triggers a cannon which frightens a dog. The dog flips over, and his rapid breathing raises and lowers a scratcher over a mosquito bite, causing no embarrassment while talking to a lady.

When you think about it for a moment you realize that the Rube Goldberg machine is irreducibly complex. It is a single system which is composed of several interacting parts, and where the removal of any one of the parts causes the system to break down. If the dog is missing the machine doesn't work; if the needle hasn't been put on the cork, the whole system is useless.

It turns out that we all have Rube Goldberg in our blood. Here's a picture of a cell trapped in a clot. The meshwork is formed from a protein called fibrin. But what controls blood clotting? Why does blood clot when you cut yourself, but not at other times when a clot would cause a stroke or heart attack? Here's a diagram of what's called the blood-clotting cascade. Let's go through just some of the reactions of clotting.

When an animal is cut a protein called Hageman factor sticks to the surface of cells near the wound. Bound Hageman factor is then cleaved by a protein called HMK to yield activated Hageman factor. Immediately the activated Hageman factor converts another protein, called prekallikrein, to its active form, kallikrein. Kallikrein helps HMK speed up the conversion of more Hageman factor to its active form. Activated Hageman factor and HMK then together transform another protein, called PTA, to its active form. Activated PTA, in turn, together with the activated form of another protein (discussed below) called convertin, switch a protein called Christmas factor to its active form. Activated Christmas factor, together with antihemophilic factor (which is itself activated by thrombin in a manner similar to that of proaccelerin), changes Stuart factor to its active form. Stuart factor, working with accelerin, converts prothrombin to thrombin. Finally thrombin cuts fibrinogen to give fibrin, which aggregates with other fibrin molecules to form the meshwork clot you saw in the last picture.

Blood clotting requires extreme precision. When a pressurized blood circulation system is punctured, a clot must form quickly or the animal will bleed to death. On the other hand, if blood congeals at the wrong time or place, then the clot may block circulation as it does in heart attacks and strokes. Furthermore, a clot has to stop bleeding all along the length of the cut, sealing it completely. Yet blood clotting must be confined to the cut or the entire blood system of the animal might solidify, killing it. Consequently, clotting requires this enormously complex system so that the clot forms only when and only where it is required. Blood clotting is the ultimate Rube Goldberg machine.

The Professional Literature

Other examples of irreducible complexity abound in the cell, including aspects of protein transport, the bacterial flagellum, electron transport, telomeres, photosynthesis, transcription regulation, and much more. Examples of irreducible complexity can be found on virtually every page of a biochemistry textbook. But if these things cannot be explained by Darwinian evolution, how has the scientific community regarded these phenomena of the past forty years? A good place to look for an answer to that question is in the *Journal of Molecular Evolution*. JME is a journal that was begun specifically to deal with the topic of how evolution occurs on the molecular level. It has high scientific standards, and is edited by prominent figures in the field. In a recent issue of JME there were published eleven articles; of these, all eleven were concerned simply with the comparison of protein or DNA sequences. A sequence comparison is an amino acid-by-amino acid comparison of two different proteins, or a nucleotide-by-nucleotide comparison of two different pieces of DNA, noting the positions at which they are identical or similar, and the places where they are not. Although useful for determining possible lines of descent, which is an interesting question in its own right, comparing sequences cannot show how a complex biochemical system achieved its function, the question that most concerns us here. By way of analogy, the instruction manuals for two different models of computer put out by the same company might have many identical words, sentences, and even paragraphs, suggesting a common ancestry (perhaps the same author wrote both manuals), but comparing the sequences of letters in the instruction manuals will never tell us if a computer can be produced step by step starting from a typewriter.

None of the papers discussed detailed models for intermediates in the development of complex biomolecular structures. In the past ten years JME has published over a thousand papers. Of these, about one hundred discussed the chemical synthesis of molecules thought to be necessary for the origin of life, about 50 proposed mathematical models to improve sequence analysis, and about 800 were analyses of sequences. There were ZERO papers discussing detailed models for intermediates in the development of complex biomolecular structures. This is not a peculiarity of JME. No papers are to be found that discuss detailed models for intermediates in the development of complex biomolecular structures in the *Proceedings of the National Academy of Science*, *Nature*, *Science*, the *Journal of Molecular Biology* or, to my knowledge, any science journal whatsoever.

"Publish or perish" is a proverb that academicians take seriously. If you do not publish your work for the rest of the community to evaluate, then you have no business in academia and, if you don't already have tenure, you will be banished. But the saying can be applied to theories as well. If a theory claims to be able to explain some phenomenon but does not generate even an attempt at an explanation, then it should be banished. Despite comparing sequences, molecular evolution has never addressed the question of how complex structures came to be. In effect, the theory of Darwinian molecular evolution has not published, and so it should perish.

Detection of Design

What's going on? Imagine a room in which a body lies crushed, flat as a pancake. A dozen detectives crawl around, examining the floor with magnifying glasses for any clue to the identity of the perpetrator. In the middle of the room next to the body stands a large, gray elephant. The detectives carefully avoid bumping into the pachyderm's legs as they crawl, and never even glance at it. Over time the detectives get frustrated with their lack of progress but resolutely press on, looking even more closely at the floor. You see, textbooks say detectives must "get their man," so they never consider elephants.

There is an elephant in the roomful of scientists who are trying to explain the development of life. The elephant is labeled "intelligent design." To a person who does not feel obliged to restrict his search to unintelligent causes, the straightforward conclusion is that many biochemical systems were designed. They were designed not by the laws of nature, not by chance and necessity. Rather, they were planned. The designer knew what the systems would look like when they were completed; the designer took steps to bring the systems about. Life on earth at its most fundamental level, in its most critical components, is the product of intelligent activity.

The conclusion of intelligent design flows naturally from the data itself, not from sacred books or sectarian beliefs. Inferring that biochemical systems were designed by an intelligent agent is a humdrum process that requires no new principles of logic or science. It comes simply from the hard work that biochemistry has done over the past forty years, combined with consideration of the way in which we reach conclusions of design every day.

What is "design"? Design is simply the purposeful arrangement of parts. The scientific question is how we detect design. This can be done in various ways, but design can most easily be inferred for mechanical objects. While walking through a junkyard you might observe separated bolts and screws and bits of plastic and glass, most scattered, some piled on top of each other, some wedged together. Suppose you saw a pile that seemed particularly compact, and when you picked up a bar sticking out of the pile, the whole pile came along with it. When you pushed on the bar it slid smoothly to one side of the pile and pulled an attached chain along with it. The chain in turn yanked a gear which turned three other gears which turned a red-and-white striped rod, spinning it like a barber pole. You quickly conclude that the pile was not a chance accumulation of junk, but was designed, was put together in that order by an intelligent agent, because you see that the components of the system interact with great specificity to do something.

It is not only artificial mechanical systems for which design can easily be concluded. Systems made entirely from natural components can also evince design. For example, suppose you are walking with a friend in the woods. All of a sudden your friend is pulled high in the air and left dangling by his foot from a vine attached to a tree branch. After cutting him down you reconstruct the trap. You see that the vine was wrapped around the tree branch, and the end pulled tightly down to the ground. It was securely anchored to the ground by a forked branch. The branch was attached to another vine, hidden by leaves so that, when the trigger-vine was disturbed, it would pull down the forked stick, releasing the spring-vine. The end of the vine formed a loop with a slipknot to grab an appendage and snap it up into the air. Even though the trap was made completely of natural materials you would quickly conclude that it was the product of intelligent design.

A Complicated World

A word of caution; intelligent design theory has to be seen in context: it does not try to explain everything. We live in a complex world where lots of different things can happen. When deciding how various rocks came to be shaped the way they are a geologist might consider a whole range of factors: rain, wind, the movement of glaciers, the activity of moss and lichens, volcanic action, nuclear explosions, asteroid impact, or the hand of a sculptor. The shape of one rock might have been determined primarily by one mechanism, the shape of another rock by another mechanism. The possibility of a meteor's impact does not mean that volcanos can be ignored; the existence of sculptors does not mean that many rocks are not shaped by weather. Similarly, evolutionary biologists have recognized that a number of factors might have affected the development of life: common descent, natural selection, migration, population size, founder effects (effects that may be due to the limited number of organisms that begin a new species), genetic drift (spread of neutral, nonselective mutations), gene flow (the incorporation of genes into a population from a separate population), linkage (occurrence of two genes on the same chromosome), meiotic drive (the preferential selection during sex cell production of one of the two copies of a gene inherited from an organism's parents), transposition (the transfer of a gene between widely separated species by non-sexual means), and much more. The fact that some biochemical systems were designed by an intelligent agent does not mean that any of the other factors are not operative, common, or important.

Curiouser and Curiouser

So as this essay concludes, we are left with what many people feel to be a strange conclusion: that life was designed by an intelligent agent. In a way, though, all of the progress of science over the last several hundred years has been a steady march toward the strange. People up until the Middle Ages lived in a natural world. The stable earth was at the center of things; the sun, moon, and stars circled endlessly to give light by day and night; the same plants and animals had been known since antiquity. Surprises were few.

Then it was proposed, absurdly, that the earth itself moved, spinning while it circled the sun. No one could feel the earth spinning; no one could see it. But spin it did. From our modern vantage it's hard to realize what an assault on the senses was perpetrated by Copernicus and Galileo; they said in effect that people could no longer rely on even the evidence of their eyes.

Things got steadily worse over the years. With the discovery of fossils it became apparent that the famil-iar animals of field and forest had not always been on earth; the world had once been inhabited by huge, alien creatures who were now gone. Sometime later Darwin shook the world by arguing that the familiar biota was derived from the bizarre, vanished life over lengths of time incomprehensible to human minds. Einstein told us that space is curved and time is relative. Modern physics says that solid objects are mostly space, that subatomic particles have no definite position, that the universe had a beginning.

Now it's the turn of the fundamental science of life, modern biochemistry, to disturb. The simplicity that was once expected to be the foundation of life has proven to be a phantom. Instead, systems of horrendous, irreducible complexity inhabit the cell. The resulting realization that life was designed by an intelligence is a shock to us in the twentieth century who have gotten used to thinking of life as the result of simple natural laws. But other centuries have had their shocks and there is no reason to suppose that we should escape them. Humanity has endured as the center of the heavens moved from the earth to beyond the sun, as the history of life expanded to encompass long-dead reptiles, as the eternal universe proved mortal. We will endure the opening of Darwin's black box.

CHAPTER 12

A Recent Fine-Tuning
Design Argument

Robin Collins

I. Introduction

The Evidence of Fine-Tuning

Suppose we went on a mission to Mars, and found a domed structure in which everything was set up just right for life to exist. The temperature, for example, was set around 70° F and the humidity was at 50 percent; moreover, there was an oxygen recycling system, an energy gathering system, and a whole system for the production of food. Put simply, the domed structure appeared to be a fully functioning biosphere. What conclusion would we draw from finding this structure? Would we draw the conclusion that it just happened to form by chance? Certainly not. Instead, we would unanimously conclude that it was designed by some intelligent being. Why would we draw this conclusion? Because an intelligent designer appears to be the only plausible explanation for the existence of the structure. That is, the only alternative explanation we can think of — that the structure was formed by some natural process — seems extremely unlikely. Of course, it is *possible* that, for example, through some volcanic eruption various metals and other compounds could have formed, and then separated out in just the right way to produce the "biosphere," but such a scenario strikes us as extraordinarily unlikely, thus making this alternative explanation unbelievable.

The universe is analogous to such a "biosphere," according to recent findings in physics. Almost everything about the basic structure of the universe — for example, the fundamental laws and parameters of physics and the initial distribution of matter and energy — is balanced on a razor's edge for life to occur. As the eminent Princeton physicist Freeman Dyson notes, "There are many ... lucky accidents in physics. Without such accidents, water could not exist as liquid, chains of carbon atoms could not form complex organic molecules, and hydrogen atoms could not form breakable bridges between molecules"[1] — in short, life as we know it would be impossible.

Scientists call this extraordinary balancing of the parameters of physics and the initial conditions of the universe the "fine-tuning of the cosmos." It has been extensively discussed by philosophers, theologians, and scientists, especially since the early 1970s, with hundreds of articles and dozens of books written on the topic. Today, it is widely regarded as offering by far the most persuasive current argument for the existence of God. For example, theoretical physicist and popular science writer Paul Davies — whose early writings were not particularly sympathetic to theism — claims that with regard to basic structure of the universe, "the impression of design is overwhelming."[2] Similarly, in response to the life-permitting fine-tuning of the nuclear resonances responsible for the oxygen and carbon synthesis in stars, the famous astrophysicist Sir Fred Hoyle declares that

> I do not believe that any scientists who examined the evidence would fail to draw the inference that the laws of nuclear physics have been deliberately designed with regard to the consequences they pro-

1. Freeman Dyson, *Disturbing the Universe* (New York: Harper and Row, 1979), 251.

2. Paul Davies, *The Cosmic Blueprint: New Discoveries in Nature's Creative Ability to Order the Universe* (New York: Simon and Schuster, 1988), 203.

duce inside stars. If this is so, then my apparently random quirks have become part of a deep-laid scheme. If not then we are back again at a monstrous sequence of accidents.[3]

A few examples of this fine-tuning are listed below:

1. If the initial explosion of the Big Bang had differed in strength by as little as one part in 10^{60}, the universe would have either quickly collapsed back on itself, or expanded too rapidly for stars to form. In either case, life would be impossible. (As John Jefferson Davis points out, an accuracy of one part in 10^{60} can be compared to firing a bullet at a one-inch target on the other side of the observable universe, twenty billion light years away, and hitting the target.)[4]

2. Calculations indicate that if the strong nuclear force, the force that binds protons and neutrons together in an atom, had been stronger or weaker by as little as five percent, life would be impossible.[5]

3. Calculations by Brandon Carter show that if gravity had been stronger or weaker by one part in 10^{40}, then life-sustaining stars like the sun could not exist. This would most likely make life impossible.[6]

4. If the neutron were not about 1.001 times the mass of the proton, all protons would have decayed into neutrons or all neutrons would have decayed into protons, and thus life would not be possible.[7]

5. If the electromagnetic force were slightly stronger or weaker, life would be impossible, for a variety of different reasons.[8]

Imaginatively, one could think of each instance of fine-tuning as a radio dial: unless all the dials are set exactly right, life would be impossible. Or, one could think of the initial conditions of the universe and the fundamental parameters of physics as a dart board that fills the whole galaxy, and the conditions necessary for life to exist as a small one-foot wide target: unless the dart hits the target, life would be impossible. The fact that the dials are perfectly set, or that the dart has hit the target, strongly suggests that someone set the dials or aimed the dart, for it seems enormously improbable that such a coincidence could have happened by chance.

Although individual calculations of fine-tuning are only approximate and could be in error, the fact that the universe is fine-tuned for life is almost beyond question because of the large number of independent instances of apparent fine-tuning. As philosopher John Leslie has pointed out, "Clues heaped upon clues can constitute weighty evidence despite doubts about each element in the pile."[9] What is controversial, however, is the degree to which the fine-tuning provides evidence for the existence of God. As impressive as the argument from fine-tuning seems to be, atheists have raised several significant objections to it. Consequently, those who are aware of these objections, or have thought of them on their own, often will find the argument unconvincing. This is not only true of atheists, but also many theists. I have known, for instance, both a committed Christian Hollywood filmmaker and a committed Christian biochemist who remained unconvinced because of certain atheist objections to the argument. This is unfortunate, particularly since the fine-tuning argument is probably the most powerful current argument for the existence of God. My goal in this chapter, therefore, is to make the fine-tuning argument as strong as possible. This will involve developing the argument in as objective and rigorous

---

3. Fred Hoyle, in *Religion and the Scientists* (1959); quoted in *The Anthropic Cosmological Principle*, ed. John Barrow and Frank Tipler (Oxford: Oxford University Press, 1986), 22.

4. See Paul Davies, *The Accidental Universe* (Cambridge: Cambridge University Press, 1982), 90–91. John Jefferson Davis, "The Design Argument, Cosmic 'Fine-tuning,' and the Anthropic Principle," *The International Journal of Philosophy of Religion* 22 (1987): 140.

5. John Leslie, *Universes* (New York: Routledge, 1989), 4, 35;

Anthropic Cosmological Principle, 322.

6. Paul Davies, *Superforce: The Search for a Grand Unified Theory of Nature* (New York: Simon and Schuster, 1984), 242.

7. Leslie, *Universes*, 39–40.

8. John Leslie, "How to Draw Conclusions from a Fine-Tuned Cosmos," in *Physics, Philosophy and Theology: A Common Quest for Understanding*, ed. Robert Russell et al. (Vatican City State: Vatican Observatory Press, 1988), 299.

9. Leslie, "How to Draw Conclusions," 300.

a way as I can, and then answering the major atheist objections to it. Before launching into this, however, I will need to make a preliminary distinction.

A Preliminary Distinction

To develop the fine-tuning argument rigorously, it is useful to distinguish between what I shall call the *atheistic single-universe hypothesis* and the *atheistic many-universes hypothesis*. According to the atheistic single-universe hypothesis, there is only one universe, and it is ultimately an inexplicable, "brute" fact that the universe exists and is fine-tuned. Many atheists, however, advocate another hypothesis, one which attempts to explain how the seemingly improbable fine-tuning of the universe could be the result of chance. We will call this hypothesis the *atheistic many-worlds hypothesis,* or *the atheistic many-universes hypothesis.* According to this hypothesis, there exists what could be imaginatively thought of as a "universe generator" that produces a very large or infinite number of universes, with each universe having a randomly selected set of initial conditions and values for the parameters of physics. Because this generator produces so many universes, just by chance it will eventually produce one that is fine-tuned for intelligent life to occur.

Plans of the Chapter

Below, we will use this distinction between the atheistic single-universe hypothesis and the atheistic many-universes hypothesis to present two separate arguments for theism based on the fine-tuning: one which argues that the fine-tuning provides strong reasons to prefer theism over the atheistic single-universe hypothesis and one which argues that we should prefer theism over the atheistic many-universes hypothesis. We will develop the argument against the atheistic single-universe hypothesis in section II below, referring to it as the *core* argument. Then we will answer objections to this core argument in section III, and

finally develop the argument for preferring theism to the atheistic many-universes hypothesis in section IV. An appendix is also included that further elaborates and justifies one of the key premises of the core argument presented in section III.

II. Core Argument Rigorously Formulated

General Principle of Reasoning Used

The Principle Explained

We will formulate the fine-tuning argument against the atheistic single-universe hypothesis in terms of what I will call the *prime principle of confirmation.* The prime principle of confirmation is a general principle of reasoning which tells us when some observation counts as evidence in favor of one hypothesis over another. *Simply put, the principle says that whenever we are considering two competing hypotheses, an observation counts as evidence in favor of the hypothesis under which the observation has the highest probability (or is the least improbable).* (Or, put slightly differently, the principle says that whenever we are considering two competing hypotheses, H_1 and H_2, an observation, O, counts as evidence in favor of H_1 over H_2 if O is more probable under H_1 than it is under H_2.) Moreover, the degree to which the evidence counts in favor of one hypothesis over another is proportional to the degree to which the observation is more probable under the one hypothesis than the other.[10] For example, the fine-tuning is much, much more probable under theism than under the atheistic single-universe hypothesis, so it counts as strong evidence for theism over this atheistic hypothesis. In the next major subsection, we will present a more formal and elaborated rendition of the fine-tuning argument in terms of the prime principle. First, however, let's look at a couple of illustrations of the principle and then present some support for it.

Additional Illustrations of the Principle

For our first illustration, suppose that I went hiking

---

10. For those familiar with the probability calculus, a precise statement of the degree to which evidence counts in favor of one hypothesis over another can be given in terms of the odds form of

Bayes' Theorem: that is, $P(H_1/E)/P(H_2/E) = [P(H_1)/P(H_2)] \times [P(E/H_1)/P(E/H_2)]$. The general version of the principle state here, however, does not require the applicability or truth of Bayes' Theorem.

in the mountains, and found underneath a certain cliff a group of rocks arranged in a formation that clearly formed the pattern "Welcome to the mountains, Robin Collins." One hypothesis is that, by chance, the rocks just happened to be arranged in that pattern — ultimately, perhaps, because of certain initial conditions of the universe. Suppose the only viable alternative hypothesis is that my brother, who was in the mountains before me, arranged the rocks in this way. Most of us would immediately take the arrangements of rocks to be strong evidence in favor of the "brother" hypothesis over the "chance" hypothesis. Why? Because it strikes us as extremely *improbable* that the rocks would be arranged that way by chance, but *not improbable* at all that my brother would place them in that configuration. Thus, by the prime principle of confirmation we would conclude that the arrangement of rocks strongly supports the "brother" hypothesis over the chance hypothesis.

Or consider another case, that of finding the defendant's fingerprints on the murder weapon. Normally, we would take such a finding as strong evidence that the defendant was guilty. Why? Because we judge that it would be *unlikely* for these fingerprints to be on the murder weapon if the defendant was innocent, but *not unlikely* if the defendant was guilty. That is, we would go through the same sort of reasoning as in the above case.

Support for the Principle

Several things can be said in favor of the prime principle of confirmation. First, many philosophers think that this principle can be derived from what is known as the *probability calculus*, the set of mathematical rules that are typically assumed to govern probability. Second, there does not appear to be any case of recognizably good reasoning that violates this principle. Finally, the principle appears to have a wide range of applicability, undergirding much of our reasoning in science and everyday life, as the examples above illustrate. Indeed, some have even claimed that a slightly more general version of this principle undergirds all scientific reasoning. Because of all these reasons in favor of the principle, we can be very confident in it.

Further Development of the Argument

To further develop the core version of the fine-tuning argument, we will summarize the argument by explicitly listing its two premises and its conclusion:

Premise 1. The existence of the fine-tuning is not improbable under theism.

Premise 2. The existence of the fine-tuning is very improbable under the atheistic single-universe hypothesis.

Conclusion: From premises (1) and (2) and the prime principle of confirmation, it follows that the fine-tuning data provide strong evidence to favor the design hypothesis over the atheistic single-universe hypothesis.

At this point, we should pause to note two features of this argument. First, the argument does not say that the fine-tuning evidence proves that the universe was designed, or even that it is likely that the universe was designed. In order to justify these sorts of claims, we would have to look at the full range of evidence both for and against the design hypothesis, something we are not doing in this chapter. Rather, the argument merely concludes that the fine-tuning strongly *supports* theism *over* the atheistic single-universe hypothesis.

In this way, the evidence of the fine-tuning argument is much like fingerprints found on the gun: although they can provide strong evidence that the defendant committed the murder, one could not conclude merely from them alone that the defendant is guilty; one would also have to look at all the other evidence offered. Perhaps, for instance, ten reliable witnesses claimed to see the defendant at a party at the time of the shooting. In this case, the fingerprints would still count as significant evidence of guilt, but this evidence would be counterbalanced by the testimony of the witnesses. Similarly the evidence of fine-tuning strongly supports theism over the atheistic single-universe hypothesis, though it does not itself show that, everything considered, theism is the most plausible explanation of the world. Nonetheless, as I argue in the conclusion of this chapter, the evidence of fine-tuning provides a much stronger and more objective argument for theism (over the atheistic single-universe hypothesis) than the strongest atheistic argument does against theism.

The second feature of the argument we should note is that, given the truth of *the prime principle of confirmation,* the conclusion of the argument follows from the premises. Specifically, if the premises of the argument are true, then we are guaranteed that the conclusion is true: that is, the argument is what philosophers call *valid*. Thus, insofar as we can show that the premises of the argument are true, we will have shown that the conclusion is true. Our next task, therefore, is to attempt to show that the premises are true, or at least that we have strong reasons to believe them.

Support for the Premises

Support for Premise (1)

Premise (1) is easy to support and fairly uncontroversial. One major argument in support of it can be simply stated as follows: *since God is an all good being, and it is good for intelligent, conscious beings to exist, it is not surprising or improbable that God would create a world that could support intelligent life.* Thus, the fine-tuning is not improbable under theism, as premise (1) asserts.

Support for Premise (2)

Upon looking at the data, many people find it very obvious that the fine-tuning is highly improbable under the atheistic single-universe hypothesis. And it is easy to see why when we think of the fine-tuning in terms of the analogies offered earlier. In the dart board analogy, for example, the initial conditions of the universe and the fundamental parameters of physics are thought of as a dart board that fills the whole galaxy, and the conditions necessary for life to exist as a small one-foot wide target. Accordingly, from this analogy it seems obvious that it would be highly improbable for the fine-tuning to occur under the atheistic single-universe hypothesis — that is, for the dart to hit the target by chance.

Typically, advocates of the fine-tuning argument are satisfied with resting the justification of premise (2), or something like it, on this sort of analogy. Many atheists and theists, however, question the legitimacy of this sort of analogy, and thus find the argument unconvincing. For these people, the appendix to this chapter offers a rigorous and objective justification of premise (2) using standard principles of probabilistic reasoning. Among other things, in the process of rigorously justifying premise (2), we effectively answer the common objection to the fine-tuning argument that because the universe is a unique, unrepeatable event, we cannot meaningfully assign a probability to its being fine-tuned.

III. Some Objections to Core Version

As powerful as the core version of the fine-tuning argument is, several major objections have been raised to it by both atheists and theists. In this section, we will consider these objections in turn.

OBJECTION 1: More Fundamental Law Objection

One criticism of the fine-tuning argument is that, as far as we know, there could be a more fundamental law under which the parameters of physics *must* have the values they do. Thus, given such a law, it is not improbable that the known parameters of physics fall within the life-permitting range.

Besides being entirely speculative, the problem with postulating such a law is that it simply moves the improbability of the fine-tuning up one level, to that of the postulated physical law itself. Under this hypothesis, what is improbable is that of all the conceivable fundamental physical laws there could be, the universe just happens to have the one that constrains the parameters of physics in a life-permitting way. Thus, trying to explain the fine-tuning by postulating this sort of fundamental law is like trying to explain why the pattern of rocks below a cliff spell "Welcome to the mountains, Robin Collins" by postulating that an earthquake occurred and that all the rocks on the cliff face were arranged in just the right configuration to fall into the pattern in question. Clearly this explanation merely transfers the improbability up one level, since now it seems enormously improbable that of all the possible configurations the rocks could be in on the cliff face, they are in the one which results in the pattern "Welcome to the mountains, Robin Collins."

A similar sort of response can be given to the claim that the fine-tuning is not improbable because it might be *logically necessary* for the parameters of physics to have life-permitting values. That is, according to this claim, the parameters of physics must have life-permitting values in the same way 2 + 2 must equal 4, or the interior angles of a triangle must add up to 180 degrees in Euclidian geometry. Like the "more fundamental law" proposal above, however, this postulate simply transfers the improbability up one level: of all the laws and parameters of physics that conceivably could have been logically necessary, it seems highly improbable that it would be those that are life-permitting.[11]

OBJECTION 2: Other Forms of Life Objection

Another objection people commonly raise to the fine-tuning argument is that as far as we know, other forms of life could exist even if the parameters of physics were different. So, it is claimed, the fine-tuning argument ends up presupposing that all forms of intelligent life must be like us. The answer to this objection is that most cases of fine-tuning do not make this presupposition. Consider, for instance, the case of the fine-tuning of the strong nuclear force. If it were slightly smaller, no atoms could exist other than hydrogen. Contrary to what one might see on *Star Trek,* an intelligent life-form cannot be composed merely of hydrogen gas: there is simply not enough stable complexity. So, in general the fine-tuning argument merely presupposes that intelligent life requires some degree of stable, reproducible organized complexity. This is certainly a very reasonable assumption.

OBJECTION 3: Anthropic Principle Objection

According to the weak version of the so-called *anthropic principle,* if the laws of nature were not fine-tuned, we would not be here to comment on the fact. Some have argued, therefore, that the fine-tuning is not really *improbable or surprising* at all under atheism, but simply follows from the fact that we exist. The response to this objection is to simply restate the argument in terms of our existence: our existence as embodied, intelligent beings is extremely unlikely under the atheistic single-universe hypothesis (since our existence requires fine-tuning), but not improbable under theism. Then, we simply apply the prime principle of confirmation to draw the conclusion that *our existence* strongly confirms theism over the atheistic single-universe hypothesis.

To further illustrate this response, consider the following "firing squad" analogy. As John Leslie points out, if fifty sharpshooters all miss me, the response "if they had not missed me I wouldn't be here to consider the fact" is not adequate. Instead, I would naturally conclude that there was some reason why they all missed, such as that they never really intended to kill me. Why would I conclude this? Because my continued existence would be very improbable under the hypothesis that they missed me by chance, but not improbable under the hypothesis that there was some reason why they missed me. Thus, by the prime principle of confirmation, my continued existence strongly confirms the latter hypothesis.[12]

---

11. Those with some training in probability theory will want to note that the kind of probability invoked here is what philosophers call *epistemic probability,* which is a measure of the rational degree of belief we should have in a proposition (see appendix, subsection iii). Since our rational degree of belief in a necessary truth can be less than 1, we can sensibly speak of it being improbable for a given law of nature to exist necessarily. For example, we can speak of an unproven mathematical hypothesis — such as Goldbach's conjecture that every even number greater than 6 is the sum of two odd primes — as being probably true or probably false given our current evidence, even though all mathematical hypotheses are either necessarily true or necessarily false.

12. Leslie, "How to Draw Conclusions," 304.

OBJECTION 4: The "Who Designed God?" Objection

Perhaps the most common objection that atheists raise to the argument from design, of which the fine-tuning argument is one instance, is that postulating the existence of God does not solve the problem of design, but merely transfers it up one level. Atheist George Smith, for example, claims that:

If the universe is wonderfully designed, surely God is even more wonderfully designed. He must, therefore, have had a designer even more wonderful than He is. If *God* did not require a designer, then there is no reason why such a relatively less wonderful thing as the universe needed one.[13]

Or, as philosopher J. J. C. Smart states the objection:

If we postulate God in addition to the created universe we increase the complexity of our hypothesis. We have all the complexity of the universe itself, and we have in addition the at least equal complexity of God. (The designer of an artifact must be at least as complex as the designed artifact).... *If the theist can show the atheist that postulating God actually reduces the complexity of one's total world view, then the atheist should be a theist.*[14]

The first response to the above atheist objection is to point out that the atheist claim that the designer of an artifact must be as complex as the artifact designed is certainly not obvious. But I do believe that their claim has some intuitive plausibility: for example, in the world we experience, organized complexity seems only to be produced by systems that already possess it, such as the human brain/mind, a factory, or an organism's biological parent.

The second, and better, response is to point out that, at most, the atheist objection only works against a version of the design argument that claims that all organized complexity needs an explanation, and that God is the best explanation of the organized complex-ity found in the world. The version of the argument I presented against the atheistic single-universe hypothesis, however, only required that the fine-tuning be more probable under theism than under the atheistic single-universe hypothesis. But this requirement is still met even if God exhibits tremendous internal complexity, far exceeding that of the universe. Thus, even if we were to grant the atheist assumption that the designer of an artifact must be as complex as the artifact, the fine-tuning would still give us strong reasons to prefer theism over the atheistic single-universe hypothesis.

To illustrate, consider the example of the "biosphere" on Mars presented at the beginning of this paper. As mentioned above, the existence of the biosphere would be much more probable under the hypothesis that intelligent life once visited Mars than under the chance hypothesis. Thus, by the prime principle of confirmation, the existence of such a "biosphere" would constitute strong evidence that intelligent, extraterrestrial life had once been on Mars, even though this alien life would most likely have to be much more complex than the "biosphere" itself.

The final response theists can give to this objection is to show that a supermind such as God would *not* require a high degree of unexplained organized complexity to create the universe. Although I have presented this response elsewhere, presenting it here is beyond the scope of this chapter.

IV. The Atheistic Many-Universes Hypothesis

The Atheistic Many-Universes Hypothesis Explained

In response to the theistic explanation of fine-tuning of the cosmos, many atheists have offered an alternative explanation, what I will call the atheistic many-universes hypothesis. (In the literature it is more commonly referred to as the *many-worlds hypothesis,*

---

13. George Smith, "The Case Against God, "reprinted in *An Anthology of Atheism and Rationalism*, ed. Gordon Stein (Buffalo: Prometheus Press, 1980), 56.

14. J.J.C. Smart, "Laws of Nature and Cosmic Coincidence," *The Philosophical Quarterly* 35 (July 1985): 275 – 76, italics added.

though I believe this name is somewhat misleading.) According to this hypothesis, there are a very large — perhaps infinite — number of universes, with the fundamental parameters of physics varying from universe to universe.[15] Of course, in the vast majority of these universes the parameters of physics would not have life-permitting values. Nonetheless, in a small proportion of universes they would, and consequently it is no longer improbable that universes such as ours exist that are fine-tuned for life to occur.

Advocates of this hypothesis offer various types of models for where these universes came from. We will present what are probably the two most popular and plausible, the so-called *vacuum fluctuation* models and the *oscillating big bang* models. According to the vacuum fluctuation models, our universe, along with these other universes, was generated by quantum fluctuations in a preexisting superspace.[16] Imaginatively, one can think of this preexisting superspace as an infinitely extending ocean full of soap, and each universe generated out of this superspace as a soap bubble which spontaneously forms on the ocean.

The other model, the oscillating big bang model, is a version of the big bang theory. According to the big bang theory, the universe came into existence in an "explosion" (that is, a "bang") somewhere between ten and fifteen billion years ago. According to the *oscillating* big bang theory, our universe will eventually collapse back in on itself (what is called the "big crunch") and then from that "big crunch" will arise another "big bang," forming a new universe, which will in turn itself collapse, and so on. According to those who use this model to attempt to explain the fine-tuning, during every cycle, the parameters of physics and the initial conditions of the universe are reset at random. Since this process of collapse, explosion, collapse, and explosion has been going on for all eternity, eventually a fine-tuned universe will occur, indeed infinitely many of them.

In the next section, we will list several reasons for rejecting the atheistic many-universes hypothesis.

Reasons for Rejecting the Atheistic Many-Universes Hypothesis

First Reason

The first reason for rejecting the atheistic many-universes hypothesis, and preferring the theistic hypothesis, is the following general rule: *everything else being equal, we should prefer hypotheses for which we have independent evidence or that are natural extrapolations from what we already know.* Let's first illustrate and support this principle, and then apply it to the case of the fine-tuning.

Most of us take the existence of dinosaur bones to count as very strong evidence that dinosaurs existed in the past. But suppose a dinosaur skeptic claimed that she could explain the bones by postulating a "dinosaur-bone-producing-field" that simply materialized the bones out of thin air. Moreover, suppose further that, to avoid objections such as that there are no known physical laws that would allow for such a mechanism, the dinosaur skeptic simply postulated that we have not yet discovered these laws or detected these fields. Surely, none of us would let this skeptical hypothesis deter us from inferring the existence of dinosaurs. Why? Because although no one has directly observed dinosaurs, we do have experience of other animals leaving behind fossilized remains, and thus the dinosaur explanation is a *natural extrapolation* from our common experience. In contrast, to explain the dinosaur bones, the dinosaur skeptic has invented a set of physical laws, and a set of mechanisms that are *not* a natural extrapolation from anything we know or experience.

In the case of the fine-tuning, we already know that minds often produce fine-tuned devices, such as Swiss watches. Postulating God — a supermind — as the explanation of the fine-tuning, therefore, is a natural

---

15. I define a "universe" as any region of space-time that is disconnected from other regions in such a way that the parameters of physics in that region could differ significantly from the other regions.

16. Quentin Smith, "World Ensemble Explanations," *Pacific Philosophical Quarterly* 67 (1986): 82.

extrapolation from what we already observe minds to do. In contrast, it is difficult to see how the atheistic many-universes hypothesis could be considered a natural extrapolation from what we observe. Moreover, unlike the atheistic many-universes hypothesis, we have some experiential evidence for the existence of God, namely religious experience. Thus, by the above principle, we should prefer the theistic explanation of the fine-tuning over the atheistic many-universes explanation, everything else being equal.

Second Reason

A second reason for rejecting the atheistic many-universes hypothesis is that the "many-universes generator" seems like it would need to be designed. For instance, in all current worked-out proposals for what this "universe generator" could be — such as the oscillating big bang and the vacuum fluctuation models explained above — the "generator" itself is governed by a complex set of physical laws that allow it to produce the universes. It stands to reason, therefore, that if these laws were slightly different the generator probably would not be able to produce any universes that could sustain life. After all, even my bread machine has to be made just right in order to work properly, and it only produces loaves of bread, not universes! Or consider a device as simple as a mousetrap: it requires that all the parts, such as the spring and hammer, be arranged just right in order to function. It is doubtful, therefore, whether the atheistic many-universe theory can entirely eliminate the problem of design the atheist faces; rather, at least to some extent, it seems simply to move the problem of design up one level.[17]

Third Reason

A third reason for rejecting the atheistic many-universes hypothesis is that the universe generator must not only select the parameters of physics at random,

but must actually randomly create or select the very laws of physics themselves. This makes this hypothesis seem even more farfetched since it is difficult to see what possible physical mechanism could select or create laws.

The reason the "many-universes generator" must randomly select the laws of physics is that, just as the right values for the parameters of physics are needed for life to occur, the right set of laws is also needed. If, for instance, certain laws of physics were missing, life would be impossible. For example, without the law of inertia, which guarantees that particles do not shoot off at high speeds, life would probably not be possible.[18] Another example is the law of gravity: if masses did not attract each other, there would be no planets or stars, and once again it seems that life would be impossible. Yet another example is the *Pauli Exclusion Principle,* the principle of quantum mechanics that says that no two fermions — such as electrons or protons — can share the same quantum state. As prominent Princeton physicist Freeman Dyson points out,[19] without this principle all electrons would collapse into the nucleus and thus atoms would be impossible.

Fourth Reason

The fourth reason for rejecting the atheistic many-universes hypothesis is that it cannot explain other features of the universe that seem to exhibit apparent design, whereas theism can. For example, many physicists, such as Albert Einstein, have observed that the basic laws of physics exhibit an extraordinary degree of beauty, elegance, harmony, and ingenuity. Nobel prize-winning physicist Steven Weinberg, for instance, devotes a whole chapter of his book *Dreams of a Final Theory*[20] explaining how the criteria of beauty and elegance are commonly used to guide physicists in formulating the right laws. Indeed, one of the most prominent theoretical physicists of this century, Paul

---

17. Moreover, the advocate of the atheistic many-universes hypothesis could not avoid this problem by hypothesizing that the many universes always existed as a "brute fact" without being produced by a universe generator. This would simply add to the problem: it would not only leave unexplained the fine-tuning or our

own universe, but would leave unexplained the existence of these other universes.

18. Leslie, *Universes,* 59.
19. Dyson, *Disturbing the Universe,* 251.
20. Chapter 6, Beautiful Theories."

Dirac, went so far as to claim that "it is more important to have beauty in one's equations than to have them fit an experiment."[21]

Now such beauty, elegance, and ingenuity make sense if the universe was designed by God. Under the atheistic many-universes hypothesis, however, there is no reason to expect the fundamental laws to be elegant or beautiful. As theoretical physicist Paul Davies writes, "If nature is so 'clever' as to exploit mechanisms that amaze us with their ingenuity, is that not persuasive evidence for the existence of intelligent design behind the universe? If the world's finest minds can unravel only with difficulty the deeper workings of nature, how could it be supposed that those workings are merely a mindless accident, a product of blind chance?"[22]

Final Reason

This brings us to the final reason for rejecting the atheistic many-universes hypothesis, which may be the most difficult to grasp: namely, neither the atheistic many-universes hypothesis (nor the atheistic single-universe hypothesis) can at present adequately account for the improbable initial arrangement of matter in the universe required by the second law of thermodynamics. To see this, note that according to the second law of thermodynamics, the entropy of the universe is constantly increasing. The standard way of understanding this entropy increase is to say that the universe is going from a state of order to disorder. We observe this entropy increase all the time around us: things, such as a child's bedroom, that start out highly organized tend to "decay" and become disorganized unless something or someone intervenes to stop it.

Now, for purposes of illustration, we could think of the universe as a scrabble-board that initially starts out in a highly ordered state in which all the letters are arranged to form words, but which keeps getting randomly shaken. Slowly, the board, like the universe, moves from a state of order to disorder. The problem for the atheist is to explain how the universe could have started out in a highly ordered state, since it is extraordinarily improbable for such states to occur by chance.[23] If, for example, one were to dump a bunch of letters at random on a scrabble-board, it would be very unlikely for most of them to form into words. At best, we would expect groups of letters to form into words in a few places on the board.

Now our question is, Could the atheistic many-universes hypothesis explain the high degree of initial order of our universe by claiming that given enough universes, eventually one will arise that is ordered and in which intelligent life occurs, and so it is no surprise that we find ourselves in an ordered universe? The problem with this explanation is that it is overwhelmingly more likely for local patches of order to form in one or two places than for the whole universe to be ordered, just as it is overwhelmingly more likely for a few words on the scrabble-board randomly to form words than for all the letters throughout the board randomly to form words. Thus, the overwhelming majority of universes in which intelligent life occurs will be ones in which the intelligent life will be surrounded by a small patch of order necessary for its existence, but in which the rest of the universe is disordered. Consequently, even under the atheistic many-universes hypothesis, it would still be enormously improbable for intelligent beings to find themselves in a universe such as ours which is highly ordered throughout.[24]

Conclusion

Even though the above criticisms do not definitively refute the atheistic many-universes hypothesis,

---

21. Paul Dirac, "The Evolution of the Physicist's Picture of Nature," *Scientific American* (May 1963): 47.

22. Davies, *Superforce*, 235–36.

23. This connection between order and probability, and the second law of thermodynamics in general, is given a precise formulation in a branch of fundamental physics called *statistical mechanics*, according to which a state of high order represents a very improbable state, and a state of disorder represents a highly probable state.

24. See Lawrence Sklar, *Physics and Chance: Philosophical Issues in the Foundation of Statistical Mechanics* (Cambridge: Cambridge University Press, 1993), chapter 8, for a review of the nontheistic explanations for the ordered arrangement of the universe and the severe difficulties they face.

they do show that it has some severe disadvantages relative to theism. This means that if atheists adopt the atheistic many-universes hypothesis to defend their position, then atheism has become much less plausible than it used to be. Modifying a turn of phrase coined by philosopher Fred Dretske: these are inflationary times, and the cost of atheism has just gone up.

V. Overall Conclusion

In the above sections I showed there are good, objective reasons for claiming that the fine-tuning provides strong evidence for theism. I first presented an argument for thinking that the fine-tuning provides strong evidence for preferring theism over the atheistic single-universe hypothesis, and then presented a variety of different reasons for rejecting the atheistic many-universes hypothesis as an explanation of the fine-tuning. In order to help one appreciate the strength of the arguments presented, I would like to end by comparing the strength of the *core* version of the argument from the fine-tuning to what is widely regarded as the strongest atheist argument against theism, the argument from evil.[25]

Typically, the atheist argument against God based on evil takes a similar form to the core version of the fine-tuning argument. Essentially, the atheist argues that the existence of the kinds of evil we find in the world is very improbable under theism, but not improbable under atheism. Thus, by the prime principle of confirmation, they conclude that the existence of evil provides strong reasons for preferring atheism over theism.

What makes this argument weak in comparison to the core version of the fine-tuning argument is that, unlike in the case of the fine-tuning, the atheist does not have a significant objective basis for claiming that the existence of the kinds of evil we find in the world is highly improbable under theism. In fact, their judgment that it is improbable seems largely to rest on a mistake in reasoning. To see this, note that in order

to show that it is improbable, atheists would have to show that it is *unlikely* that the types of evils we find in the world are necessary for any morally good, greater purpose, since if they are, then it is clearly not at all unlikely that an all-good, all-powerful being would create a world in which those evils are allowed to occur. But how could atheists show this without first surveying all possible morally good purposes such a being might have, something they have clearly not done? *Consequently, it seems at most the atheist could argue that since no one has come up with any adequate purpose yet, it is unlikely that there is such a purpose.* This argument, however, is very weak, as I will now show.

The first problem with this atheist argument is that it assumes that the various explanations people have offered for why an all-good God would create evil — such as the free will theodicy — ultimately fail. But even if we grant that these theodicies fail, the argument is still very weak. To see why, consider an analogy. Suppose someone tells me that there is a rattlesnake in my garden, and I examine a portion of the garden and do not find the snake. I would only be justified in concluding that there was probably no snake in the garden if either: i) I had searched at least half the garden; or ii) I had good reason to believe that if the snake were in the garden, it would likely be in the portion of the garden that I examined. If, for instance, I were randomly to pick some small segment of the garden to search and did not find the snake, I would be unjustified in concluding from my search that there was probably no snake in the garden. Similarly, if I were blindfolded and did not have any idea of how large the garden was (e.g., whether it was ten square feet or several square miles), I would be unjustified in concluding that it was unlikely that there was a rattlesnake in the garden, even if I had searched for hours with my rattlesnake-detecting dogs. Why? Because I would not have any idea of what percentage of the garden I had searched.

---

25. A more thorough discussion of the atheist argument from evil is presented in Daniel Howard-Snyder's chapter (pp. 76–115), and a discussion of other atheistic arguments is given in John O'Leary-Hawthorn's chapter (pp. 116–34) in *reason for Hope Within.*

As with the garden example, we have no idea of how large the realm is of possible greater purposes for evil that an all-good, omnipotent being could have. Hence we do not know what proportion of this realm we have actually searched. Indeed, considering the finitude of our own minds, we have good reason to believe that we have so far only searched a small proportion, and we do not have significant reason to believe that all the purposes God might have for allowing evil would be in the proportion we searched. Thus, we have little objective basis for saying that the existence of the types of evil we find in the world is highly improbable under theism.

From the above discussion, therefore, it is clear that the relevant probability estimates in the case of the fine-tuning are much more secure than those estimates in the probabilistic version of the atheist's argument from evil, since unlike the latter, we can provide a fairly rigorous, objective basis for them based on actual calculations of the relative range of life-permitting values for the parameters of physics. (See the appendix to this chapter for a rigorous derivation of the probability of the fine-tuning under the atheistic single-universe hypothesis.) *Thus, I conclude, the core argument for preferring theism over the probabilistic version of the atheistic single-universe hypothesis is much stronger than the atheist argument from evil.*[26]

Appendix

In this appendix, I offer a rigorous support for premise (2) of the main argument: that is, the claim that the fine-tuning is very improbable under the atheistic single-universe hypothesis. Support for premise (2) will involve three major subsections. The first subsection will be devoted to explicating the fine-tuning of gravity since we will often use this to illustrate our arguments. Then, in our second subsection, we will show how the improbability of the fine-tuning under the atheistic single-universe hypothesis can be derived from a commonly used, objective principle of probabilistic reasoning called the *principle of indifference.* Finally, in our third subsection, we will explicate what it could mean to say that the finetuning is improbable given that the universe is a unique, unrepeatable event as assumed by the atheistic single-universe hypothesis. The appendix will in effect answer the common atheist objection that theists can neither *justify* the claim that the fine-tuning is improbable under the atheistic single-universe hypothesis, nor can they provide an account of what it could possibly *mean* to say that the fine-tuning is improbable.

i. The Example of Gravity

The force of gravity is determined by Newton's law $F = Gm_1m_2/r^2$. Here G is what is known as the *gravitational constant,* and is basically a number that determines the force of gravity in any given circumstance. For instance, the gravitational attraction between the moon and the earth is given by first multiplying the mass of the moon (m_1) times the mass of the earth (m_2), and then dividing by the distance between them squared (r^2). Finally, one multiplies this result by the number G to obtain the total force. Clearly the force is directly proportional to G: for example, if G were to double, the force between the moon and the earth would double.

In the previous section, we reported that some calculations indicate that the force of gravity must be fine-tuned to one part in 10^{40} in order for life to occur. What does such fine-tuning mean? To understand it, imagine a radio dial, going from 0 to $2G_o$, where G_o represents the current value of the gravitational constant. Moreover, imagine the dial being broken up into 10^{40} — that is, ten thousand, billion, billion, billion, billion — evenly spaced tick marks. To claim that the strength of gravity must be fine-tuned to one part in 10^{40} is simply to claim that, in order for life to exist, the constant of gravity cannot vary by even one tick mark along the dial from its current value of G_o.

26. This work was made possible in part by a Discovery Institute grant for the fiscal year 1997–1998.

ii. The Principle of Indifference

In the following subsections, we will use the *principle of indifference* to justify the assertion that the fine-tuning is highly improbable under the atheistic single-universe hypothesis.

a. The Principle Stated

Applied to cases in which there is a finite number of alternatives, the principle of indifference can be formulated as the claim that we should assign the same probability to what are called *equipossible alternatives,* where two or more alternatives are said to be equipossible if we have no reason to prefer one of the alternatives over any of the others. (In another version of the principle, alternatives that are relevantly symmetrical are considered equipossible and hence the ones that should be assigned equal probability.) For instance, in the case of a standard two-sided coin, we have no more reason to think that the coin will land on heads than that it will land on tails, and so we assign them each an equal probability. Since the total probability must add up to one, this means that the coin has a 0.5 chance of landing on heads and a 0.5 chance of landing on tails. Similarly, in the case of a standard six-sided die, we have no more reason to think that it will land on one number, say a 6, than any of the other numbers, such as a 4. Thus, the principle of indifference tells us to assign each possible way of landing an equal probability—namely 1/6.

The above explication of the principle applies only when there are a finite number of alternatives, for example six sides on a die. In the case of the fine-tuning, however, the alternatives are not finite but form a continuous magnitude. The value of G, for instance, conceivably could have been any number between 0 and infinity. Now, continuous magnitudes are usually thought of in terms of ranges, areas, or volumes depending on whether or not we are considering one, two, three, or more dimensions. For example, the amount of water in an 8 oz. glass could fall anywhere within the *range* 0 oz. to 8 oz., such as 6.012345645 oz. Or, the exact position that a dart hits a dart board can fall anywhere within the *area* of the dart board. With

some qualifications to be discussed below, the principle of indifference becomes in the continuous case the principle that *when we have no reason to prefer any one value of a parameter over another, we should assign equal probabilities to equal ranges, areas, or volumes.* So, for instance, suppose one aimlessly throws a dart at a dart board. Assuming the dart hits the board, what is the probability it will hit within the bull's eye? Since the dart is thrown aimlessly, we have no more reason to believe it will hit one part of the dart board than any other part. The principle of indifference, therefore, tells us that the probability of its hitting the bull's eye is the same as the probability of hitting any other part of the dart board of equal area. This means that the probability of its hitting the bull's eye is simply the ratio of the area of the bull's eye to the rest of the dart board. So, for instance, if the bull's eye forms only 5 percent of the total area of the board, then the probability of its hitting the bull's eye will be 5 percent.

b. Application to Fine-Tuning

In the case of the fine-tuning, we have no more reason to think that the parameters of physics will fall within the life-permitting range than within any other range, given the atheistic single-universe hypothesis. Thus according to the principle of indifference, equal ranges of these parameters should be assigned equal probabilities. As in the case of the dart board mentioned in the last section, this means that the probability of the parameters of physics falling within the life-permitting range under the atheistic single-universe hypothesis is simply the ratio of the range of life-permitting values (the "area of the bull's eye") to the total *relevant* range of possible values (the "relevant area of the dart board").

Now physicists can make rough estimates of the range of *life-permitting* values for the parameters of physics, as discussed above in the case of gravity, for instance. But what is the "total *relevant* range of possible values"? At first one might think that this range is infinite, since the values of the parameters could conceivably be anything. This, however, is not correct, for although the possible range of values could be infinite, for most of these values we have no way of estimating whether they are life-permitting or not. We do not truly know, for example, what would happen if gravity were 10^{60} times stronger than its current value: as far as we know, a new form of matter might come into existence that could sustain life. Thus, as far as we know, there could be other life-permitting ranges far removed from the actual values that the parameters have. Consequently, all we can say is that the life-permitting range is very, very small *relative* to the limited range of values for which we can make estimates, a range that we will hereafter refer to as the *"illuminated"* range.

Fortunately, however, this limitation does not affect the overall argument. The reason is that, based on the principle of indifference, we can still say that it is very improbable for the values for the parameters of physics to have fallen in the life-permitting range *instead* of some other part of the "illuminated" range.[27] And this *improbability* is all that is actually needed for our main argument to work. To see this, consider an analogy. Suppose a dart landed on the bull's eye at the center of a huge dart board. Further, suppose that this bull's eye is surrounded by a very large empty, bull's-eye-free, area. Even if there were many other bull's eyes on the dart board, we would still take the fact that the dart landed on the bull's eye instead of some other part of the large empty area surrounding the bull's eye as strong evidence that it was aimed. Why? Because we would reason that *given that the dart landed in the empty area,* it was very improbable for it to land in the bull's eye by chance but not improbable if it were aimed. Thus, by the prime principle of confirmation, we could conclude that the dart landing on the bull's eye strongly confirms the hypothesis that it was aimed over the chance hypothesis.

c. The Principle Qualified

Those who are familiar with the principle of indifference, and mathematics, will recognize that one important qualification needs to be made to the above account of how to apply the principle of indifference. (Those who are not mathematically adept might want to skip this and perhaps the next paragraph.) To understand the qualification, note that the ratio of ranges used in calculating the probability is dependent on how one parameterizes, or writes, the physical laws. For example, suppose for the sake of illustration that the range of life-permitting values for the gravitational constant is 0 to G_o, and the "illuminated" range of possible values for G is 0 to $2G_o$. Then, the ratio of life-permitting values to the range of "illuminated" possible values for the gravitational constant will be ½. Suppose, however, that one writes the law of gravity in the mathematically equivalent form of $F = \sqrt{U}m_1m_2/r^2$ instead of $F=Gm_1m_2/r^2$, where $U=G^2$. (In this way of writing Newton's law, U becomes the new gravitational constant.) This means that $U_o = G_o^2$, where U_o, like G_o, represents the actual value of U in our universe. Then, the range of life-permitting values would be 0 to U_o, and the "illuminated" range of possible values would be 0 to $4U_o$ on the U scale (which is equivalent to 0 to $2G_o$ on the G scale). Hence, calculating the ratio of life-permitting values using the U scale instead of G scale yields a ratio of ¼ instead of ½. Indeed, for almost any ratio one chooses — such as one in which the life-permitting range is about the same size as the "illuminated" range — there exist mathematically equivalent forms of Newton's law that will yield that ratio. So, why choose the standard way of writing Newton's law to calculate the ratio instead of one in which the fine-tuning is not improbable at all?

The answer to this question is to require that the proportion used in calculating the probability be between *real* physical ranges, areas, or volumes, not merely mathematical representations of them. That is, the proportion given by the scale used in one's representation must directly correspond to the proportions actually existing in physical reality. As an illustration,

---

27. In the language of probability theory, this sort of probability is known as a conditional probability. In the case of G, calculations indicate that this conditional probability of the fine-tuning would be less than 10^{-40} since the life-permitting range is less than 10^{-40} of the range 0 to $2G_o$, the latter range being certainly smaller than the total "illuminated" range for G.

consider how we might calculate the probability that a meteorite will fall in New York State instead of somewhere else in the northern, contiguous United States. One way of doing this is to take a standard map of the northern, contiguous United States, measure the area covered by New York on the map (say 2 square inches) and divide it by the total area of the map (say 30 square inches). If we were to do this, we would get approximately the right answer because the proportions on a standard map directly correspond to the actual proportions of land areas in the United States.[28] On the other hand, suppose we had a map made by some lover of the East Coast in which, because of the scale used, the East Coast took up half the map. If we used the proportions of areas as represented by this map we would get the wrong answer since the scale used would not correspond to real proportions of land areas. Applied to the fine-tuning, this means that our calculations of these proportions must be done using parameters that directly correspond to physical quantities in order to yield valid probabilities. In the case of gravity, for instance, the gravitational constant G directly corresponds to the force between two unit masses a unit distance apart, whereas U does not. (Instead, U corresponds to the square of the force.) Thus, G is the correct parameter to use in calculating the probability.[29]

d. Support for Principle

Finally, although the principle of indifference has been criticized on various grounds, several powerful reasons can be offered for its soundness if it is restricted in the ways explained in the last subsec-tion. First, it has an extraordinarily wide range of applicability. As Roy Weatherford notes in his book, *Philosophical Foundations of Probability Theory*, "an astonishing number of extremely complex problems in probability theory have been solved, and usefully so, by calculations based entirely on the assumption of equiprobable alternatives [that is, the principle of indifference]."[30] Second, at least for the discrete case, the principle can be given a significant theoretical grounding in information theory, being derivable from Shannon's important and well-known measure of *information*, or *negative entropy*.[31] Finally, in certain everyday cases the principle of indifference seems the only justification we have for assigning probability. To illustrate, suppose that in the last ten minutes a factory produced the first fifty-sided die ever produced. Further suppose that every side of the die is (macroscopically) perfectly symmetrical with every other side, except for there being different numbers printed on each side. (The die we are imagining is like a fair six-sided die except that it has fifty sides instead of six.) Now, we all immediately know that upon being rolled the probability of the die coming up on any given side is one in fifty. Yet, we do not know this directly from experience with fifty-sided dice, since by hypothesis no one has yet rolled such dice to determine the relative frequency with which they come up on each side. Rather, it seems our only justification for assigning this probability is the principle of indifference: that is, given that every side of the die is relevantly macroscopically symmetrical with every other side, we have no reason to believe that the die will land on one side

---

28. I say "approximately right" because in this case the principle of indifference only applies to strips of land that are the same distance from the equator. The reason for this is that only strips of land equidistant from the equator are truly symmetrical with regard to the motion of the earth. Since the northern, contiguous United States are all about the same distance from the equator, equal land areas should be assigned approximately equal probabilities.

29. This solution will not always work since, as the well-known Bertrand Paradoxes illustrate (e.g., see Roy Weatherford, *Foundations of Probability Theory* [Boston: Routledge and Kegan Paul, 1982], 56), sometimes there are two equally good and conflicting parameters that directly correspond to a physical quantity and to which the principle of indifference applies. In these cases, at best we can say that the probability is somewhere between that given by the two conflicting parameters. This problem, however, typically does not seem to arise for most cases of fine-tuning. Also, it should be noted that the principle of indifference applies best to *classical* or *epistemic* probability, not other kinds of probability such as *relative frequency*. (See subsection iii below.)

30. Weatherford, *Probability Theory*, 35.

31. Sklar, *Physics and Chance*, 191; Bas van Fraassen, *Laws and Symmetry* (Oxford: Oxford University Press, 1989), 345.

over any other side, and thus we assign them all an equal probability of one in fifty.[32]

iii. The Meaning of Probability

In the last section we used the principle of indifference to rigorously justify the claim that the fine-tuning is highly improbable under the atheistic single-universe hypothesis. We did not explain, however, what it could *mean* to say that it is improbable, especially given that the universe is a unique, unrepeatable event. To address this issue, we shall now show how the probability invoked in the fine-tuning argument can be straightforwardly understood either as what could be called *classical probability* or as what is known as *epistemic probability*.

Classical Probability

The *classical conception of probability* defines probability in terms of the ratio of number of "favorable cases" to the total number of equipossible cases.[33] Thus, for instance, to say the probability of a die coming up "4" is one out of six is simply to say that the number of ways a die could come up "4" is one-sixth the number of equipossible ways it could come up. Extending this definition to the continuous case, classical probability can be defined in terms of the relevant ratio of ranges, areas, or volumes over which the principle of indifference applies. Thus, under this extended definition, to say that the probability of the parameters of physics falling into the life-permitting value is very improbable simply *means* that the ratio of life-permitting values to the range of possible values is very, very small. Finally, notice that this definition of probability implies the principle of indifference, and thus we can be certain that the principle of indifference holds for classical probability.

Epistemic Probability

Epistemic probability is a widely recognized type of probability that applies to claims, statements, and hypotheses — that is, what philosophers call *propositions*.[34] (A proposition is any claim, assertion, statement, or hypothesis about the world.) Roughly, the epistemic probability of a proposition can be thought of as the degree of credence — that is, degree of confidence or belief — we rationally should have in the proposition. Put differently, epistemic probability is a measure of our rational degree of belief under a condition of ignorance concerning whether a proposition is true or false. For example, when one says that the special theory of relativity is probably true, one is making a statement of epistemic probability. After all, the theory is actually either true or false. But, we do not know for sure whether it is true or false, so we say it is probably true to indicate that we should put more confidence in its being true than in its being false. It is also commonly argued that the probability of a coin toss is best understood as a case of epistemic probability. Since the side the coin will land on is determined by the laws of physics, it is argued that our assignment of probability is simply a measure of our rational expectations concerning which side the coin will land on.

Besides epistemic probability simpliciter, philosophers also speak of what is known as the *conditional* epistemic probability of one proposition on another. The conditional epistemic probability of a proposition R on another proposition S — written as $P(R/S)$ — can be defined as the degree to which the proposition S of

---

32. Of course, one could claim that our experience with items such as coins and dice teaches us that whenever two alternatives are macroscopically symmetrical, we should assign them an equal probability, unless we have a particular reason not to. All this claim implies, however, is that we have experiential justification for the principle of indifference, and thus it does not take away from our main point that in certain practical situations we must rely on the principle of indifference to justify our assignment of probability.

33. See Weatherford, *Probability Theory*, ch. 2.

34. For an in-depth discussion of epistemic probability, see Richard Swinburne, *An Introduction to Confirmation Theory* (London: Methuen, 1973); Ian Hacking, *The Emergence of Probability: A Philosophical Study of Early Ideas About Probability, Induction and Statistical Inference* (Cambridge: Cambridge University Press, 1975); and Alvin Plantinga, *Warrant and Proper Function* (Oxford: Oxford University Press, 1993), chapters 8 and 9.

itself should rationally lead us to expect that *R* is true. For example, there is a high conditional probability that it will rain today on the hypothesis that the weatherman has predicted a 100 percent chance of rain, whereas there is a low conditional probability that it will rain today on the hypothesis that the weatherman has predicted only a 2 percent chance of rain. That is, the hypothesis that the weatherman has predicted a 100 percent chance of rain today should strongly lead us to expect that it will rain, whereas the hypothesis that the weatherman has predicted a 2 percent chance should lead us to expect that it will not rain. Under the epistemic conception of probability, therefore, the statement that *the fine-tuning of the cosmos is very improbable under the atheistic single-universe hypothesis* makes perfect sense: it is to be understood as making a statement about the degree to which the atheistic single-universe hypothesis would or should, *of itself,* rationally lead us to expect the cosmic fine-tuning.[35]

Conclusion

The above discussion shows that we have at least two ways of understanding improbability invoked in our main argument: as classical probability or epistemic probability. This undercuts the common atheist objection that it is meaningless to speak of the probability of the fine-tuning under the atheistic single-universe hypothesis since under this hypothesis the universe is not a repeatable event.

---

35. It should be noted here that this rational degree of expectation should not be confused with the degree to which one should expect the parameters of physics to fall within the life-permitting range if one believed the atheistic single-universe hypothesis. For even those who believe in this atheistic hypothesis should expect the parameters of physics to be life-permitting since this follows from the fact that we are alive. Rather, the conditional epistemic probability in this case is the degree to which the atheistic single-universe hypothesis *of itself* should lead us to expect parameters of physics to be life-permitting. This means that in assessing the conditional epistemic probability in this and other similar cases, one must exclude contributions to our expectations arising from other information we have, such as that we are alive. In the case at hand, one way of doing this is by means of the following sort of thought experiment. Imagine a disembodied being with mental capacities and a knowledge of physics comparable to that of the most intelligent physicists alive today, except that the being does not know whether the parameters of physics are within the life-permitting range. Further, suppose that this disembodied being believed in the atheistic single-universe hypothesis. Then, the degree that being should rationally expect the parameters of physics to be life-permitting will be equal to our conditional epistemic probability, since its expectation is solely a result of its belief in the atheistic single-universe hypothesis, not other factors such as its awareness of its own existence.

CHAPTER 13

The Classical Ontological Argument

Anselm of Canterbury

Truly there is a God, although the fool has said in his heart, there is no God.

And so, Lord, do you, who do give understanding to faith, give me, so far as you knowest it to be profitable, to understand that you are as we believe; and that you are that which we believe. And indeed, we believe that you are a being than which nothing greater can be conceived. Or is there no such nature; since the fool has said in his heart, there is no God? (Psalms xiv. 1). But, at any rate, this very fool, when he hears of this being of which I speak — a being than which nothing greater can be conceived — understands what he hears, and what he understands is in his understanding; although he does not understand it to exist.

For, it is one thing for an object to be in the understanding, and another to understand that the object exists. When a painter first conceives of what he will afterwards perform, he has it in his understanding, but be does not yet understand it to be, because he has not yet performed it. But after he has made the painting, he both has it in his understanding, and he understands that it exists, because he has made it.

Hence, even the fool is convinced that something exists in the understanding, at least, than which nothing greater can be conceived. For, when he hears of this, he understands it. And whatever is understood exists in the understanding. And assuredly that, than which nothing greater can be conceived, cannot exist in the understanding alone. For, suppose it exists in the understanding alone: then it can be conceived to exist in reality; which is greater.

Therefore, if that, than which nothing greater can be conceived, exists in the understanding alone, the very being, than which nothing greater can be conceived, is one, than which a greater can be conceived. But obviously this is impossible. Hence, there is doubt that there exists a being, than which nothing greater can be conceived, and it exists both in the understanding and in reality.

Chapter III

God cannot be conceived not to exist. — God is that, than which nothing greater can be conceived. — That which can be conceived not to exist is not God.

And it assuredly exists so truly, that it cannot be conceived not to exist. For, it is possible to conceive of a being which cannot be conceived not to exist; and this is greater than one which can be conceived not to exist. Hence, if that, than which nothing greater can be conceived, can be conceived not to exist, it is not that, than which nothing greater can be conceived. But this is an irreconcilable contradiction. There is, then, so truly a being than which nothing greater can be conceived to exist, that it cannot even be conceived not to exist; and this being you are, O Lord, our God.

So truly, therefore, do you exist, O Lord, my God, that you cannot be conceived not to exist; and rightly. For, if a mind could conceive of a being better than you, the creature would rise above the Creator; and this is most absurd. And, indeed, whatever else there is, except you alone, can be conceived not to exist. To you alone, therefore, it belongs to exist more truly than all other beings, and hence in a higher degree than all others. For, whatever else exists does not exist so truly, and hence in a less degree it belongs to it to exist. Why, then, has the fool said in his heart, there is no

God (Psalms xiv. 1), since it is so evident, to a rational mind, that you do exist in the highest degree of all? Why, except that he is dull and a fool?

Chapter IV

How the fool has said in his heart what cannot be conceived. — A thing may be conceived in two ways: (1) when the word signifying it is conceived; (2) when the thing itself is understood. As far as the word goes, God can be conceived not to exist; in reality he cannot.

But how has the fool said in his heart what he could not conceive; or how is it that he could not conceive what he said in his heart? Since it is the same to say in the heart, and to conceive.

But, if really, nay, since really, he both conceived, because he said in his heart; and did not say in his heart, because he could not conceive; there is more than one way in which a thing is said in the heart or conceived. For, in one sense, an object is conceived, when the word signifying it is conceived; and in another, when the very entity, which the object is, is understood.

In the former sense, then, God can be conceived not to exist; but in the latter, not at all. For no one who understands what fire and water are can conceive fire to be water, in accordance with the nature of the facts themselves, although this is possible according to the words. So, then, no one who understands what God is can conceive that God does not exist; although he says these words in his heart, either without any or with some foreign, signification. For, God is that than which a greater cannot be conceived. And he, who thoroughly understands this, assuredly understands that this being so truly exists, that not even in concept can it be non-existent. Therefore, he who understands that God so exists cannot conceive that he does not exist.

I thank you, gracious Lord, I thank you; because what I formerly believed by your bounty, I now so understand by your illumination, that if I were unwilling to believe that you do exist, I should not be able not to understand this to be true.

Chapter V

God is whatever it is better to be than not to be; and he, as the only self-existent being, creates all things from nothing.

What are you, then, Lord God, than whom nothing greater can be conceived? But what are you, except that which, as the highest of all beings, alone exists through itself, and creates all other things from nothing? For, whatever is not this is less than a thing which can be conceived of. But this cannot be conceived of you. What good, therefore, does the supreme Good lack, through which every good is? Therefore, you are just, truthful, blessed, and whatever it is better to be than not to be. For it is better to be just than not just; better to be blessed than not blessed.

CHAPTER 14

A Recent Modal Ontological Argument

Alvin Plantinga

The third theistic argument I wish to discuss is the famous "ontological argument" first formulated by Anselm of Canterbury in the eleventh century. This argument for the existence of God has fascinated philosophers ever since Anselm first stated it. Few people, I should think, have been brought to belief in God by means of this argument; nor has it played much of a role in strengthening and confirming religious faith. At first sight Anselm's argument is remarkably unconvincing if not downright irritating; it looks too much like a parlor puzzle or word magic. And yet nearly every major philosopher from the time of Anselm to the present has had something to say about it; this argument has a long and illustrious line of defenders extending to the present. Indeed, the last few years have seen a remarkable hurry of interest in it among philosophers. What accounts for its fascination? Not, I think, its religious significance, although that can be underrated. Perhaps there are two reasons for it. First, many of the most knotty and difficult problems in philosophy meet in this argument: Is existence a property? Are existential propositions — propositions of the form *x exists — ever* necessarily true? Are existential propositions about what they seem to be about? Are there, in any respectable sense of "are," some objects that do not exist? If so, do they have any properties? Can they be compared with things that do exist? These issues and a hundred others arise in connection with Anselm's argument. And second, although the argument certainly looks at first sight as if it ought to be unsound, it is profoundly difficult to say what, exactly, is wrong with it. Indeed, I do not believe that any philosopher has ever given a cogent and conclusive refutation of the ontological argument in its various forms.

Anselm states his argument as follows:

> And so, Lord, do thou, who dost give understanding to faith, give me, so far as thou knowest it to be profitable, to understand that thou art as we believe; and that thou art that which we believe. And indeed, we believe that thou art a being than which nothing greater can be conceived. Or is there no such nature, since the fool hath said in his heart, there is no God?... But, at any rate, this very fool when he hears of this being of which I speak — a being than which nothing greater can be conceived — understands what he hears, and what he understands is in his understanding, although he does not understand it to exist.
>
> For, it is one thing for any object to be in the understanding, and another to understand that the object exists. When a painter first conceives of what he will afterwards perform, he has it in his understanding, but he does not yet understand it to be, because he has not yet performed it. But after he has made the painting, he both has it in his understanding, and he understands that it exists, because he has made it.
>
> Hence, even the fool is convinced that something exists in the understanding, at least, than which nothing greater can be conceived. For when he hears of this, he understands it. And whatever is understood, exists in the understanding. And assuredly that, than which nothing greater can he conceived, cannot exist in the understanding alone. For, suppose it exists in the understanding alone; then it can be conceived to exist in reality; which is greater.
>
> Therefore, if that, than which nothing greater can be conceived, exists in the understanding alone, the

very being, than which nothing greater can be conceived, is one, than which a greater can be conceived. But obviously this is impossible. Hence, there is no doubt that there exists a being, than which nothing greater can be conceived, and it exists both in the understanding and in reality.[1]

At first sight, this argument smacks of trumpery and deceit; but suppose we look at it a bit more closely. Its essentials are contained in these words:

And assuredly that, than which nothing greater can be conceived, cannot exist in the understanding alone. For suppose it exists in the understanding alone; then it can be conceived to exist in reality; which is greater.

Therefore, if that, than which nothing greater can be conceived, exists in the understanding alone, the very being, than which nothing greater can be conceived, is one, than which a greater can be conceived. But obviously this is impossible. Hence there is no doubt that there exists a being, than which nothing greater can be conceived, and it exists both in the understanding and in reality.[2]

How can we outline this argument? It is best construed, I think, as a *reductio ad absurdum* argument. In a *reductio* you prove a given proposition *p* by showing that its denial, *not p,* leads to (or more strictly, entails) a contradiction or some other kind of absurdity. Anselm's argument can be seen as an attempt to deduce an absurdity from the proposition that there is no God. If we use the term "God" as an abbreviation for Anselm's phrase "the being than which nothing greater can be conceived," then the argument seems to go approximately as follows: Suppose

(1) God exists in the understanding but not in reality.

(2) Existence in reality is greater than existence in the understanding alone. (premise)

(3) God's existence in reality is conceivable. (premise)

(4) If God did exist in reality, then He would he greater than He is. [from (1) and (2)]

(5) It is conceivable that there is a being greater than God is. [(3) and (4)]

(6) It is conceivable that there be a being greater than the being than which nothing greater can be conceived. [(5) by the definition of "God"]

But surely (6) is absurd and self-contradictory; how could we conceive of a being greater than the being than which none greater can be conceived? So we may conclude that

(7) It is false that God exists in the understanding but not in reality.

It follows that if God exists in the understanding, He also exists in reality; but clearly enough He *does* exist in the understanding, as even the fool will testify; therefore, He exists in reality as well.

Now when Anselm says that a being *exists in the understanding,* we may take him, I think, as saying that someone has *thought of* or thought about that being. When he says that something *exists in reality,* on the other hand, he means to say simply that the thing in question really does exist. And when he says that a certain state of affairs is *conceivable,* he means to say, I believe, that this state of affairs is possible in our broadly logical sense; there is a possible world in which it obtains. This means that step (3) above may be put more perspicuously as

(3′) It is possible that God exists
and step (6) as

(6′) It is possible that there be a being greater than the being than which it is not possible that there be a greater.

An interesting feature of this argument is that all of its premises are *necessarily* true if true at all. (I) is the assumption from which Anselm means to deduce a contradiction. (2) is a premise, and presumably necessarily true in Anselm's view; and (3) is the only remaining premise (the other items are consequences of preceding steps); it says of some *other* proposition *(God exists)* that it is possible. Propositions which thus ascribe a modality — possibility, necessity,

1. St. Anselm, *Proslogium,* chap. 2, in *The Ontological Argument,* ed. A. Plantinga (New York: Doubleday Anchor, 1965), pp. 3–4.

2. Ibid., p. 4.

contingency — to another proposition are themselves either necessarily true or necessarily false. So all the premises of the argument are, if true at all, necessarily true. And hence if the premises of this argument are true, then [provided that (6) is really inconsistent] a contradiction can be deduced from (I) together with necessary propositions; this means that (I) entails a contradiction and is, therefore, necessarily false.

1. Gaunilo's Objection

Gaunilo, a contemporary of Anselm's, wrote a reply which he entitled *On Behalf of the Fool*. Here is the essence of his objection.

> For example: it is said that somewhere in the ocean is an island, which, because of the difficulty, or rather the impossibility, of discovering what does not exist, is called the lost island. And they say that this island has an inestimable wealth of all manner of riches and delicacies in greater abundance than is told of the Islands of the Blest; and that having no owner or inhabitant, it is more excellent than all other countries, which are inhabited by mankind, in the abundance with which it is stored.
>
> Now if someone should tell me that there is such an island, I should easily understand his words, in which there is no difficulty. But suppose that he went on to say, as if by a logical inference: "You can no longer doubt that this island which is more excellent than all lands exists somewhere, since you have no doubt that it is in your understanding. And since it is more excellent not to be in the understanding alone, but to *exist* both in the understanding and in reality, for this reason it must exist. For if it does not exist, any land which really exists will be more excellent than it; and so the island already understood by you to be more excellent will not be more excellent."
>
> If a man should try to prove to me by such reasoning that this island truly exists, and that its existence should no longer be doubted, either I should believe that he was jesting or I know not which I ought to regard as the greater fool: myself, supposing that I

should allow this proof; or him, if he should suppose that he had established with any certainty the existence of this Island.[3]

Gaunilo was the first of many to try to discredit the ontological argument by showing that one can find similar arguments to prove the existence of all sorts of absurd things — a greatest possible island, a highest possible mountain, a greatest possible middle linebacker, a meanest possible man, and the like. But Anselm was not without a reply.[4]

He points out, first, that Gaunilo misquotes him. What is under consideration is not a being that is *in fact* greater than any other, but one such that a greater *cannot be conceived*; a being than which it's *not possible* that there be a greater. Gaunilo seems to overlook this. And thus his famous lost island argument isn't strictly parallel to Anselm's argument; his conclusion should be only that there is an island such that no other island is greater than it — which, if there are any islands at all, is a fairly innocuous conclusion.

But obviously Gaunilo's argument can be revised. Instead of speaking, as he did, of an island that is more excellent than all others, let's speak instead of an island than which a greater or more excellent cannot be conceived — an island, that is, than which it's not possible that there be a greater. Couldn't we use an argument like Anselm's to "establish" the existence of such an island, and if we could, wouldn't that show that Anselm's argument is fallacious?

2. Anselm's Reply

Not obviously. Anselm's proper reply, it seems to me, is that it's impossible that there be such an island. The idea of an island than which it's not possible that there be a greater is like the idea of a natural number than which it's not possible that there be a greater, or the idea of a line than which none more crooked is possible. There neither is nor could be a greatest possible natural number; indeed, there isn't a greatest *actual* number, let alone a greatest possible. And the same

---

3. Plantinga, *The Ontological Argument*, p. 11.   4. Ibid., pp. 11 – 27.

goes for islands. No matter how great an island is, no matter how many Nubian maidens and dancing girls adorn it, there could always be a greater one with twice as many, for example. The qualities that make for greatness in islands — number of palm trees, amount and quality of coconuts, for example — most of these qualities have no *intrinsic maximum*. That is, there is no degree of productivity or number of palm trees (or of dancing girls) such that it is impossible that an island display more of that quality. So the idea of a greatest possible island is an inconsistent or incoherent idea; it's not possible that there be such a thing. And hence the analogue of step (3) of Anselm's argument (it is possible that God exists) is not true for the perfect island argument; so that argument fails.

But doesn't Anselm's argument itself founder upon the same rock? If the idea of a greatest possible island is inconsistent, won't the same hold for the idea of a greatest possible being? Perhaps not. For what are the properties in virtue of which one being is greater, just as a being, than another? Anselm clearly has in mind such properties as wisdom, knowledge, power, and moral excellence or moral perfection. And certainly knowledge, for example, does have an intrinsic maximum: if for every proposition *p*, a being *B* knows whether or not *p* is true, then *B* has a degree of knowledge that is utterly unsurpassable. So a greatest possible being would have to have this kind of knowledge: it would have to be *omniscient*. Similarly for *power*; omnipotence is a degree of power that can't possibly be excelled. Moral perfection or moral excellence is perhaps not quite so clear; still a being could perhaps always do what is morally right, so that it would not be possible for it to be exceeded along those lines. But what about a quality like *love*? Wouldn't that be a property that makes for greatness? God, according to Christian theism, loves His children and demonstrated His love in the redemptive events of the life and death of Jesus Christ. And what about the relevant qualities here — love, or acting out of love: do they

have intrinsic maxima? The answer isn't very clear either way. Rather than pause to discuss this question, let's note simply that there may be a weak point here in Anselm's argument and move on.

3. Kant's Objection

The most famous and important objection to the ontological argument is contained in Immanuel Kant's *Critique of Pure Reason*.[5] Kant begins his criticism as follows:

> If, in an identical proposition, I reject the predicate while retaining the subject, contradiction results; and I therefore say that the former belongs necessarily to the latter. But if we reject the subject and predicate alike, there is no contradiction; for nothing is then left that can be contradicted. To posit a triangle, and yet to reject its three angles, is self-contradictory, but there is no contradiction in rejecting the triangle together with its three angles. The same holds true of the concept of an absolutely necessary being. If its existence is rejected, we reject the thing itself with all its predicates; and no question of contradiction can then arise. There is nothing outside it that would then be contradicted, since the necessity of the thing is not supposed to be derived from anything external; nor is there anything internal that would be contradicted, since in rejecting the thing itself we have at the same time rejected all its internal properties. "God is omnipotent" is a necessary judgment. The omnipotence cannot be rejected if we posit a Deity, that is, an infinite being; for the two concepts are identical. But if we say "There is no God," neither the omnipotence nor any other of its predicates is given; they are one and all rejected together with the subject, and there is therefore not the least contradiction in such a judgment.
>
> For I cannot form the least concept of a thing which, should it be rejected with all its predicates, leaves behind a contradiction!"[6]

One characteristic feature of Anselm's argument, as we have seen, is that if successful, it establishes that

---

5. Immanuel Kant, *Critique of Pure Reason,* ed. Norman Kemp Smith (New York: Macmillan Co., 1929). Some relevant passages are reprinted in Plantinga, *The Ontological Argument,* pp. 57–64.
6. Plantinga, *The Ontological Argument,* p. 59.

God exists is a *necessary* proposition. Here Kant is apparently arguing that no *existential* proposition — one that asserts the existence of something or other — is necessarily true; the reason, he says, is that no *contra-existential* (the denial of an existential) is contradictory or inconsistent. But in which of our several senses of inconsistent? What he means to say, I believe, is that no existential proposition is necessary in the broadly *logical* sense. And this claim has been popular with philosophers ever since. But why, exactly, does Kant think it's true? What is the argument? When we take a careful look at the purported reasoning, it looks pretty unimpressive; it's hard to make out an argument at all. The conclusion would apparently be this: if we deny the existence of something or other, we can't be contradicting ourselves; no existential proposition *is* necessary and no contra-existential is impossible. Why not? Well, if we say, for example, that God does not exist, then says Kant, "There is nothing outside it (i.e., God) that would then be contradicted, since the *necessity* of the thing is not supposed to be derived from anything external; nor is there anything internal that would be contradicted, *since* in rejecting the thing itself we have at the same time rejected all its internal properties."

But how is this even *relevant*? The claim is that *God does not exist* can't be necessarily false. What could be meant, in this *context*, by saying that there's nothing "outside of" God that would be contradicted if we denied His existence? What would contradict a proposition like *God does not exist* is some other proposition — God *does exist*, for example. Kant seems to think that if the proposition in question *were* necessarily false, it would have to contradict, not a proposition, but some *object* external to God — or else contradict some internal part or aspect or property of God. But this certainly looks like confusion; it is *propositions* that contradict each other; they aren't contradicted by objects or parts, aspects or properties of objects. Does he mean instead to be speaking of *propositions* about things external to God, or about his aspects or parts or properties? But clearly many such propositions do contradict *God does not exist*; an example would be *the world was created by God*. Does he mean to say that no *true* proposition contradicts *God does not exist*? No, for that would be to affirm the *nonexistence* of God, an affirmation Kant is by no means prepared to make.

So this passage is an enigma. Either Kant was confused or else he expressed himself very badly indeed. And either way we don't have any argument for the claim that contra-existential propositions can't be inconsistent. This passage seems to be no more than an elaborate and confused way of *asserting* this claim. The heart of Kant's objection to the ontological argument, however, is contained in the following passage:

"Being" is obviously not a real predicate; that is, it is not a concept of something which could be added to the concept of a thing. It is merely the positing of a thing, or of certain determinations, as existing in themselves. Logically, it is merely the copula of a judgment. The proposition "God is omnipotent" contains two concepts, each of which has its object — God and omnipotence. The small word "is" adds no new predicate, but only serves to posit the predicate in its relation to the subject. If, now, we take the subject (God) with all its predicates (among which is omnipotence), and say "God is," or "There is a God," we attach no new predicate to the concept of God, but only posit it as an object that stands in relation to my concept. The content of both must be one and the same; nothing can have been added to the concept, which expresses merely what is possible, by .my thinking its object (through the expression "it is") as given absolutely. Otherwise stated, the real contains no more than the merely possible. A hundred real thalers do not contain the least coin more than a hundred possible thalers. For as the latter signify the concept and the former the object and the positing of the concept, should the former contain more than the latter, my concept would not, in that case, express the whole object, and would not therefore be an adequate concept of it. My financial position, however, is affected very differently by a hundred real thalers than it is by the mere concept of them (that is, of the possibility). For the object, as it actually exists, is not analytically contained in my concept, but is added to my concept (which is a determination of my state) synthetically; and yet the conceived hundred thalers are not themselves in the least increased through thus acquiring existence outside my concept.

By whatever and by however many predicates we may think a thing — even if we completely determine it — we do not make the least addition to the thing when we further declare that this thing is. Otherwise it would not be exactly the same thing that exists, but something more than we had thought in the concept: and we could not, therefore, say that the object of my concept exists. If we think in a thing every feature of reality except one, the missing reality is not added by my saying that this defective thing exists.[7]

Now how, exactly is all this relevant to Anselm's argument? Perhaps Kant means to make a point that we could put by saying that it's not possible to *define things into existence*. (People sometimes suggest that the ontological argument is just such an attempt to define *God* into existence.) And this claim is somehow connected with Kant's famous but perplexing *dictum* that *being* (or existence) is not a real predicate or property. But how shall we understand Kant here? What does it mean to say that existence isn't (or *is*) a real property?

Apparently Kant thinks this is equivalent to or follows from what he puts variously as "the real *contains no more than the merely possible*"; "the *content* of both (i.e., concept and object) must be one and the same"; "being is not the concept of something that could be *added to* the concept of a thing," and so on. But what does all this mean? And how does it bear on the ontological argument? Perhaps Kant is thinking along the following lines. In defining a *concept* — *bachelor,* let's say, or *prime number* — one lists a number of properties that are *severally necessary* and *jointly sufficient* for the concept's applying to something. That *is,* the concept applies to a given thing only if that thing has each of the listed properties, and if a thing does have them all, then the concept in question applies to it. So, for example, to define the concept *bachelor* we list

such properties as *being unmarried, being male, being over the age of twenty-five,* and the like. Take any one of these properties: a thing is a bachelor only if it has it, and if a thing has all of them, then it follows that it is a bachelor.

Now suppose you have a concept C that has application *contingently* if at all. That is to say, it is not necessarily true that there are things to which *this* concept applies. The concept *bachelor* would be an example; the proposition *there are bachelors,* while *true,* is obviously not necessarily true. And suppose $P_1, P_2 \ldots, P_n$ are the properties jointly sufficient and severally necessary for something's falling under C. Then C can be defined as follows:

A thing x is an instance of C (i.e., C applies to x) if and only if x has $P_1, P_2 \ldots, P_n$.

Perhaps Kant's point is this. There is a certain kind of mistake here we may be tempted to make. Suppose $P_1 \ldots, P_n$ are the defining properties for the concept *bachelor.* We might try to define a new concept *superbachelor* by adding *existence* to $P_1 \ldots, P_n$ That is, we might say

x is a superbachelor if and only if x has $P_1, P_2 \ldots, P_n$, and x exists.

Then (as we might mistakenly suppose) just as it is a necessary truth that bachelors are unmarried, so it is a necessary truth that superbachelors exist. And in this way it looks as if we've defined superbachelors into existence.

But of course this is a mistake, and perhaps that is Kant's point. For while indeed it is a necessary truth that bachelors are unmarried, what this means is that the proposition

(8) Everything that is a bachelor is unmarried

is necessarily true. Similarly, then,

(9) Everything that is a superbachelor exists

will be necessarily true. But obviously it doesn't follow that there *are* any superbachelors. All that follows is that

(10) All the superbachelors there are exist

which is not really very startling. If it is a contingent

---

7. Ibid., pp. 61 – 62.

truth, furthermore, that there are bachelors, it will be equally contingent that there are superbachelors. We can see this by noting that the defining properties of the concept *bachelor* are included among those of *superbachelor*; it is a necessary truth, therefore, that every superbachelor is a bachelor. This means that

(11) There are some superbachelors

entails

(12) There are some bachelors.

But then if (12) is contingent, so is (11). Indeed, the concepts *bachelor* and *superbachelor* are equivalent in the following sense: it is impossible that there exists an object to which one but not the other of these two concepts applies. We've just seen that every superbachelor must be a bachelor. Conversely, however, every bachelor is a superbachelor: for every bachelor exists and every existent bachelor is a superbachelor. Now perhaps we can put Kant's point more exactly. Suppose we say that a property or predicate P is *real* only if there is some list of properties P_1 to P_n such that the result of adding P to the list does not define a concept equivalent (in the above sense) to that defined by the list. It then follows, of course, that existence is not a real property or predicate. Kant's point, then, is that one cannot *define things into existence* because *existence* is not a real property or predicate in the explained sense.[8]

4. The Irrelevance of Kant's Objection

If this is what he means, he's certainly right. But is it relevant to the ontological argument? Couldn't Anselm thank Kant for this interesting point and proceed merrily on his way? Where did he try to define God into being by adding existence to a list of properties that defined some concept? According to the great German philosopher and pessimist Arthur Schopenhauer, the ontological argument arises when "someone excogitates a conception, composed out of all sorts of predicates, among which, however, he takes care to include the predicate actuality or existence, either openly or wrapped up for decency's sake in some other predicate, such as perfection, immensity, or something of the kind." If this were Anselm's procedure — if he had simply added existence to a concept that has application contingently if at all — then indeed his argument would be subject to the Kantian criticism. But he didn't, and it isn't.

The usual criticisms of Anselm's argument, then, leave much to be desired. Of course, this doesn't mean that the argument is successful, but it does mean that we shall have to take an independent look at it. What about Anselm's argument? Is it a good one? The first thing to recognize is that the ontological argument comes in an enormous variety of versions, some of which may be much more promising than others. Instead of speaking of *the* ontological argument, we must recognize that what we have here is a whole family of related arguments. (Having said this I shall violate my own directive and continue to speak of *the* ontological argument.)

5. The Argument Restated

Let's look once again at our initial schematization of the argument. I think perhaps it is step (2)

(2) Existence in reality is greater than existence in the understanding alone

that is most puzzling here. Earlier we spoke of the properties in virtue of which one being is greater, just as a being, than another. Suppose we call them *great-making properties*. Apparently Anselm means to suggest that *existence* is a great-making property. He seems to suggest that a nonexistent being would be greater than in fact it is, if it did *exist*. But how can we make sense of that? How could there be a nonexistent being anyway? Does that so much as make sense?

Perhaps we can put this perspicuously in terms of possible worlds. You recall that an object may *exist* in some possible worlds and not others. There

8. For a more detailed and extensive discussion of this argument, see Plantinga, *God and Other Minds*, pp. 29 – 38, and A. Plantinga, "Kant's Objection to the Ontological Argument."

are possible worlds in which you and I do not exist; these worlds are impoverished, no doubt, but are not on that account impossible. Furthermore, you recall that an object can have different properties in different worlds. In the actual world Paul J. Zwier is not a good tennis player; but surely there are worlds in which he wins the Wimbledon Open. Now if a person can have different properties in different worlds, then he can have different degrees of greatness in different worlds. In the actual world Raquel Welch has impressive assets; but there is a world RW_f in which she is fifty pounds overweight and mousy. Indeed, there are worlds in which she does not so much as exist. What Anselm means to be suggesting, I think, is that Raquel Welch enjoys very little greatness in those worlds in which she does not exist. But of course this condition is not restricted to Miss Welch. What Anselm means to say, more generally, is that for any being x and worlds W and W', if x exists in W but not in W', then x's greatness in W exceeds x's greatness in W. Or, more modestly, perhaps he means to say that if a being x does not exist in a world W (and there is a world in which x does exist), then *there is at least one world* in which the greatness of x exceeds the greatness of x in W'. Suppose Raquel Welch does not exist in some world W. Anselm means to say that there is at least one possible world in which she has a degree of greatness that exceeds the degree of greatness she has in that world W. (It is plausible, indeed, to go much further and hold that she has *no greatness at all* in worlds in which she does not exist.) But now perhaps we can restate the whole argument in a way that gives us more insight into its real structure. Once more, use the term "God" to abbreviate the phrase "the being than which it is not possible that there be a greater." Now suppose

(13) God does not exist in the actual world.

Add the new version of premise (2):

(14) For any being x and world W, if x does not exist in W, then there is a world W' such that the greatness of x in W' exceeds the greatness of x in W.

Restate premise (3) in terms of possible worlds:

(15) There is a possible world in which God exists.

And continue on:

(16) If God does not exist in the actual world, then there is a world W' such that the greatness of God in W' exceeds the greatness of God in the actual world. [from (14)]

(17) So there is a world W' such that the greatness of God in W' exceeds the greatness of God in the actual world. [(13) and (16)]

(18) So there is a possible being x and a world W' such that the greatness of x in W' exceeds the greatness of God in actuality. [(17)]

(19) Hence it's possible that there be a being greater than God is. [(18)]

(20) So it's possible that there be a being greater than the being than which it's not possible that there be a greater. (19), replacing "God" by what it abbreviates.

But surely

(21) It's not possible that there be a being greater than the being than which it's not possible that there be a greater.

So (13) [with the help of premises (14) and (15)] appears to imply (20), which, according to (21), is necessarily false. Accordingly, (13) is false. So the actual world contains a being than which it's not possible that there be a greater — that is, God exists.

Now where, if anywhere, can we fault this argument? Step (13) is the hypothesis for *reductio,* the assumption to be reduced to absurdity, and is thus entirely above reproach. Steps (16) through (20) certainly look as if they follow from the items they are said to follow from. So that leaves only (14), (15), and (20). Step (14) says only that it is possible that God exists. Step (15) also certainly seems plausible: if a being doesn't even *exist* in a given world, it can't have much by way of greatness in that world. At the very least it can't have its *maximum* degree of greatness — a degree of greatness that it does not excel in any other world — in a world where it doesn't exist. And consider (20): surely it has the ring of truth. How could there be a being greater than the being than which it's not possible that there be a greater? Initially, the argument seems pretty formidable.

6. Its Fatal Flaw

But there is something puzzling about it. We can see this if we ask what sorts of things (14) is supposed to be *about*. It starts off boldly: "For any being *x* and world *W*,..." So (14) is talking about worlds and beings. It says something about each world-being pair. And (16) follows from it, because (16) asserts of *God* and *the actual world* something that according to (14) holds of every being and world. But then if (16) follows from (14), God must be a *being*. That is, (16) follows from (14) only with the help of the additional premise that God is a being. And doesn't this statement — that God is a being — imply that *there is* or *exists* a being than which it's not possible that there be a greater? But if so, the argument flagrantly begs the question; for then we can accept the inference from (14) to (16) only if we already know that the conclusion is true.

We can approach this same matter by a slightly different route. I asked earlier what sorts of things (14) was *about*; the answer was: beings and worlds. We can ask the same or nearly the same question by asking about the *range* of the *quantifiers* — "*for any being,*" "*for any world*" — in (14). What do these quantifiers range over? If we reply that they range over possible worlds and beings — actually *existing* beings — then the inference to (16) requires the additional premise that God is an actually existing being, that there *really is* a being than which it is not possible that there be a greater. Since this is supposed to be our conclusion, we can't very gracefully add it as a *premise*. So perhaps the quantifiers don't range just over actually existing beings. But what else is there? Step (18) speaks of a *possible being* — a thing that may not in fact exist, but *could* exist. Or we could put it like this. A possible being is a thing that exists in some possible world or other; a thing *x* for which there is a world *W*, such that if *W* had been actual, *x* would have existed. So (18) is really about worlds and *possible beings*. And what it says is this: take any possible being *x* and any possible world *W*. If *x* does not exist in *W*, then there is a possible world *W'* where *x* has a degree of greatness that surpasses the greatness that it has in *W*. And hence to

make the argument complete perhaps we should add the affirmation that God is a *possible being*.

But *are* there any possible beings — that is, *merely* possible beings, beings that don't in fact exist? If so, what sorts of things are they? Do they have properties? How are we to think of them? What is their status? And what reasons are there for supposing that there are any such peculiar items at all?

These are knotty problems. Must we settle them in order even to consider this argument? No. For instead of speaking of *possible beings* and the worlds in which they do or don't exist, we can speak of *properties* and the worlds in which they do or don't *have instances,* are or are not *instantiated* or *exemplified.* Instead of speaking of a possible being named by the phrase, "the being than which it's not possible that there be a greater," we may speak of the property *having an unsurpassable degree of greatness* — *that* is, *having a degree of greatness such that it's not possible that there exist a being having more.* And then we can ask whether this property is instantiated in this or other possible worlds. Later on I shall show how to restate the argument this way. For the moment please take my word for the fact that we can speak as freely as we wish about possible objects; for we can always translate ostensible talk about such things into talk about properties and the worlds in which they are or are not instantiated.

The argument speaks, therefore, of an unsurpassably great being — of a being whose greatness is not excelled by any being in any world. This being has a degree of greatness so impressive that no other being in any world has more. But here we hit the question crucial for this version of the argument. *Where* does this being have that degree of greatness? I said above that the same being may have different degrees of greatness in different worlds; in which world does the possible being in question have the degree of greatness in question? All we are really told, in being told that God is a possible being, is this: among the possible beings there is one that in some world or other has a degree of greatness that is nowhere excelled.

And this fact is fatal to this version of the argument. I said earlier that (21) has the ring of truth; a closer look (listen?) reveals that it's more of a dull thud. For it is ambiguous as between

(21′) It's not possible that there be a being whose greatness surpasses that enjoyed by the unsurpassably great being *in the worlds where its greatness is at a maximum*

and

(21″) It's not possible that there be a being whose greatness surpasses that enjoyed by the unsurpassably great being *in the actual world.*

There is an important difference between these two. The greatest possible being may have different degrees of greatness in different worlds. Step (21′) points to the worlds in which this being has its maximal greatness; and it says, quite properly, that the degree of greatness this being has in those worlds is nowhere excelled. Clearly this is so. The greatest possible being is a possible being who in some world or other has unsurpassable greatness. Unfortunately for the argument, however, (21′) does not contradict (20). Or to put it another way, what follows from (13) [together with (14) and (15)] is not the denial of (21′). If that *did* follow, then the *reductio* would be complete and the' argument successful. But what (20) says is not that there is a possible being whose greatness exceeds that enjoyed by the greatest possible being *in a world where the latter's greatness is at a maximum*; it says only that there is a possible being whose greatness exceeds that enjoyed by the greatest possible being *in the actual world* — where, for all we know, its greatness is *not* at a maximum. So if we read (21) as (21′), the *reductio* argument falls apart.

Suppose instead we read it as (21″). Then what it says is that there couldn't be a being whose greatness surpasses that enjoyed by the greatest possible being in Kronos, the actual world. So read, (21) does contradict (20). Unfortunately, however, we have no reason, so far, for thinking that (21″) is true at all, let alone

necessarily true. If, among the possible beings, there is one whose greatness *in some world or other* is absolutely maximal — such that no being in any world has a degree of greatness surpassing it — then indeed there couldn't be a being that was greater than *that*. But it doesn't follow that this being has that degree of greatness in the *actual* world. It has it *in some world or other* but not necessarily in Kronos, the actual world. And so the argument fails. If we take (21) as (21′), then it follows from the assertion that God is a possible being; but it is of no use to the argument. If we take it as (21″), on the other hand, then indeed it is useful in the argument, but we have no reason whatever to think it true. So this version of the argument fails.[9]

7. A Modal Version of the Argument

But of course there are many other versions; one of the argument's chief features is its many-sided diversity. The fact that *this* version is unsatisfactory does not show that *every* version is or must be. Professors Charles Hartshorne[10] and Norman Malcolm[11] claim to detect two quite different versions of the argument in Anselm's work. In the first of these versions *existence* is held to be a perfection or a great-making property; in the second it is *necessary existence*. But what could *that* amount to? Perhaps something like this. Consider a pair of beings A and B that both do in fact exist. And suppose that A exists in every other possible world as well — that is, if any other possible world has been actual, A would have existed. On the other hand, B exists in only some possible worlds; there are worlds W such that had any of *them* been actual, B would not have existed. Now according to the doctrine under consideration, A is so far greater than B. Of course, *on balance* it may be that A is not greater than B; I believe that the number seven, unlike Spiro Agnew, exists in every possible world; yet I should be hesitant to affirm on that account that the number seven is greater than

9. This criticism of this version essentially follows David Lewis, "Anselm and Actuality," Nous 4 (1970); 175–188. See also Plantinga, *The Nature of Necessity*, pp. 202–205.

10. Charles Hartshorne, *Man's Vision of God* (New York, Harper and Rose, 1941). Portions reprinted in Plantinga, *The*

Oncological Argument, pp. 123–135.

11. Norman Malcolm, "Anselm's Ontological Arguments," *Philosophical Review* 69 (1960); reprinted in Plantinga, *The Ontological Argument*, pp. 136–159.

Agnew. Necessary existence is just one of several great-making properties, and no doubt Agnew has more of some of these others than does the number seven. Still, all this is compatible with saying that necessary existence is a great-making property. And given this notion, we can restate the argument as follows:

(22) It is possible that there is a greatest possible being.

(23) Therefore, there is a possible being that in some world W' or other has a maximum degree of greatness — a degree of greatness that is nowhere exceeded.

(24) A being B has the maximum degree of greatness in a given possible world W only if B exists in every possible world;

(22) and (24) are the premises of this argument; and what follows is that if W had been actual, B would have existed in every possible world. That is, if W' had been actual, B's nonexistence would have been impossible. But logical possibilities and impossibilities do not vary from world to world. That is to say, if a given proposition or state of affairs is impossible in at least one possible world, then it is impossible in every possible world. There are no propositions that in fact are possible but could have been impossible; there are none that are in fact impossible but could have been possible.[12] Accordingly, B's nonexistence is impossible in every possible world; hence it is impossible in *this* world; hence B exists and exists necessarily.

8. A Flaw in the Ointment

This is an interesting argument, but it suffers from at least one annoying defect. What it shows is that if it is possible that there be a greatest possible being (if the idea of a greatest possible being is coherent) and if that idea includes necessary existence, then in fact there is a being that exists in every world and in *some* world has a degree of greatness that is nowhere

excelled. Unfortunately it doesn't follow that the being in question has the degree of greatness in question in Kronos, the actual world. For all the argument shows, this being might *exist* in the actual world but be pretty insignificant here. In some world or other it has maximal greatness; how does this occur? J. N. Findlay once offered what can only be called an ontological *disproof* of the existence of God.[13] Findlay begins by pointing out that God, if He exists, is an "adequate object of religious worship." But such a being, he says, would have to be a *necessary* being; and, he adds, this idea is incredible "for all who share a contemporary outlook." "Those who believe in necessary truths which aren't merely tautological think that such truths merely connect the *possible* instances of various characteristics with each other; they don't expect such truths to tell them whether there *will* be instances of any characteristics. This is the outcome of the whole medieval and Kantian criticism of the ontological proof.[14] I've argued above that "the whole medieval and Kantian criticism" of Anselm's argument may be taken with a grain or two of salt. And certainly most philosophers who believe that there are necessary truths, believe that *some* of them *do* tell us whether there will be instances of certain characteristics; the proposition *there are no married bachelors* is necessarily true, and it tells us that there will be no instances whatever of the characteristic *married bachelor*. Be that as it may what is presently relevant in Findlay's piece is this passage:

> Not only is it contrary to the demands and claims inherent in religious attitudes that their object should *exist* "accidentally"; it is also contrary to these demands that it should *possess its various excellences* in some merely adventitious manner. It would be quite unsatisfactory from the religious stand point, if an object merely *happened* to be wise, good, powerful, and so forth, even to a superlative degree.... And so we are led on irresistibly, by the demands inherent in

---

12. See Plantinga, "World and Essence," *Philosophical Review* 79 (October 1970): 475; and Plantinga, *The Nature of Necessity*, chap. 4, sec. 6.

13. J. N. Findlay, "Can God's Existence Be Disproved?" *Mind*

57 (1948): 176–183. Reprinted in ed., Plantinga, The *Ontological Argument*, pp. 111–122.

14. P. 119. Mr. Findlay no longer endorses this sentiment. See the preface to his *Ascent to the Absolute (1970).*

religious reverence, to hold that an adequate object of our worship must possess is various excellences *in some necessary manner*.[15]

I think there is truth in these remarks. We could put the point as follows. In determining the greatness of a being *B* in a world *W*, what counts is not merely the qualities and properties possessed by *B in W*; what *B* is like in *other* worlds is also relevant. Most of us who believe in God think of Him as a being than whom it's not possible that there be a greater. But we don't think of Him as a being who, had things been different, would have been powerless or uninformed or of dubious moral character. God doesn't *just happen* to be a greatest possible being; He couldn't have been otherwise. Perhaps we should make a distinction here between *greatness* and *excellence*. A being's excellence in a given world *W*, let us say, depends only upon the properties it has in *W*; its *greatness* in *W* depends upon these properties but also upon what it is like in other worlds. Those who are fond of the calculus might put it by saying that there is a function assigning to each being in each world a degree of excellence; and a being's *greatness* is to be computed (by someone unusually well informed) by integrating its excellence over all possible worlds. Then it is plausible to suppose that the maximal degree of greatness entails *maximal excellence in every world*. A being, then, has the maximal degree of *greatness* in a given world *W* only if it has *maximal excellence in every possible world*. But *maximal excellence* entails *omniscience, omnipotence, and moral perfection*. That is to say, a being *B* has maximal excellence in a world *W* only if *B* has omniscience, omnipotence, and moral perfection in *W* — only if *B* would have been omniscient, omnipotent, and morally perfect if *W* had been actual.

9. The Argument Restated

Given these ideas, we can restate the present version of the argument in the following more explicit way.

(25) It is possible that there be a being that has maximal greatness.

(26) So there is a possible being that in some world *W* has maximal greatness.

(27) A Being has maximal greatness in a given world only if it has maximal excellence in every world.

(28) A being has maximal excellence in a given world only if it has omniscience, omnipotence, and moral perfection in that world.

And now we no longer need the supposition that necessary existence is a perfection; for obviously a being can't be omnipotent (or for that matter omniscient or morally perfect) in a given world unless it *exists* in that world. From (25), (27), and (28) it follows that there actually exists a being that is omnipotent, omniscient, and morally perfect; this being, furthermore, exists and has these qualities in every other world as well. For (26), which follows from (25), tells us that there is a possible world *W'*, let's say, in which there exists a being with maximal greatness. That is, had *W'* been actual, there would have been a being with maximal greatness. But then according to (27) this being has maximal excellence in every world. What this means, according to (28), is that in *W* this being has omniscience, omnipotence, and moral perfection *in every world*. That is to say, if *W'* had been actual, there would have existed a being who was omniscient and omnipotent and morally perfect and who would have had these properties in every possible world. So if *W* had been actual, it would have been *impossible* that there be no omnipotent, omniscient, and morally perfect being. But while *contingent* truths vary from world to world, what is logically impossible does not. Therefore, in every possible world *W* it is impossible that there be no such being; each possible world *W* is such that if it had been actual, it would have been impossible that there be no such being. And hence it is impossible in the *actual* world (which is one of the possible worlds) that there be no omniscient, omnipotent, and morally perfect being. Hence there really does exist a being who is omniscient, omnipotent, and morally perfect and who exists and

---

15. J. N. Findlay, "Can God's Existence Be Disproved?" p. 117.

has these properties in every possible world. Accordingly these premises, (25), (27), and (28), entail that God, so thought of, exists. Indeed, if we regard (27) and (28) as consequences of a *definition* — a definition of maximal greatness — then the only premise of the argument is (25).

But now for a last objection. What about (26)? It says that there *is* a *possible being* having such and such characteristics. But what *are* possible beings? We know what *actual* beings are — the Taj Mahal, Socrates, you and I, the Grand Teton — these are among the more impressive examples of actually existing beings. But what is a *possible* being? Is there a possible mountain just like Mt. Rainier two miles directly south of the Grand Teton? If so, it is located at the same place as the Middle Teton. Does that matter? Is there another such possible mountain three miles east of the Grand Teton, where Jenny Lake is? Are there possible mountains like this all over the world? Are there also possible oceans at all the places where there are possible mountains? For any place you mention, of course, it is *possible* that there be a mountain there; does it follow that in fact *there is* a possible mountain there?

These are some questions that arise when we ask ourselves whether there are merely possible beings that don't in fact exist. And the version of the ontological argument we've been considering seems to make sense only on the assumption that there are such things. The earlier versions also depended on that assumption; consider for example, this step of the first version we considered:

(18) So there is a possible being *x* and a world *W'* such that the greatness of *x* in *W'* exceeds the greatness of God in actuality.

This possible being, you recall, was God Himself, supposed not to exist in the actual world. We can make sense of (18), therefore, only if we are prepared to grant that there are possible beings who don't in fact exist. Such beings exist in other worlds, of course; had things been appropriately different, they would have existed. But in fact they don't exist, although nonetheless there *are* such things.

I am inclined to think the supposition that there

are such things — things that are possible but don't in fact exist — is either unintelligible or necessarily false. But this doesn't mean that the present version of the ontological argument must be rejected. For we can restate the argument in a way that does not commit us to this questionable idea. Instead of speaking of *possible beings* that do or do not exist in various possible worlds, we may speak of *properties* and the worlds in which they are or are not *instantiated*. Instead of speaking of the possible fat man in the corner, noting that he doesn't exist, we may speak of the property *being a fat man in the corner*, noting that it isn't instantiated (although it could have been). Of course, the *property* in question, like the property *being a unicorn*, exists. It is a perfectly good property which exists with as much equanimity as the property of equininity, the property of being a horse. But it doesn't happen to apply to anything. That is, in *this* world it doesn't apply to anything; in other possible worlds it does.

10. The Argument Triumphant

Using this idea we can restate this last version of the ontological argument in such a way that it no longer matters whether there are any merely possible beings that do not exist. Instead of speaking of the possible being that has, in some world or other, a maximal degree of greatness, we may speak of *the property of being maximally great* or *maximal greatness*. The premise corresponding to (25) then says simply that maximal greatness is possibly instantiated, i.e., that (29) there is a possible world in which maximal greatness is instantiated. And the analogues of (27) and (28) spell out what is involved in maximal greatness:

(30) Necessarily, a being is maximally great only if it has maximal excellence in every world

and

(31) Necessarily, a being has maximal excellence in every world only if it has omniscience, omnipotence, and moral perfection in every world.

Notice that (30) and (31) do not imply that there are possible but nonexistent beings — any more than does, for example,

(32) Necessarily, a thing is a unicorn only if it has one horn.

But if (29) is true, then there is a possible world W such that if it had been actual, then there would have existed a being that was omnipotent, omniscient, and morally perfect; this being, furthermore, would have had these qualities in every possible world. So it follows that if W had been actual, it would have been *impossible* that there be no such being. That is, if W had been actual,

(33) There is no omnipotent, omniscient, and morally perfect being

would have been an impossible proposition. But if a proposition is impossible in at least one possible world, then it is impossible in every possible world; what is impossible does not vary from world to world. Accordingly (33) is impossible in the *actual* world, i.e., impossible *simpliciter. But* if it is impossible that there be no such being, then there actually exists a being that is omnipotent, omniscient, and morally perfect; this being, furthermore, has these qualities essentially and exists in every possible world.

What shall we say of this argument? It is certainly valid; given its premise, the conclusion follows. The only question of interest, it seems to me, is whether its main premise — that maximal greatness *is* possibly instantiated — is *true*. I think it *is* true; hence I think this version of the ontological argument is sound.

But here we must be careful; we must ask whether this argument is a successful piece of natural theology, whether it *proves* the existence of God. And the answer must be, I think, that it does not. An argument for God's existence may be *sound*, after all, without in any useful sense proving God's existence.[16] Since I believe in God, I think the following argument is sound:

Either God exists or 7 + 5 = 14
It is false that 7 + 5 = 14
Therefore God exists.

But obviously this isn't a *Proof*; no one who didn't already accept the conclusion, would accept the first premise. The ontological argument we've been examining isn't just like this one, of course, but it must be conceded that not everyone who understands and reflects on its central premise — that the existence of a maximally great being is *possible* — *will* accept it. Still, it is evident, I think, that there is nothing *contrary to reason* or *irrational* in accepting this premise.[17] What I claim for this argument, therefore, is that it establishes, not the *truth* of theism, but its rational acceptability. And hence it accomplishes at least one of the aims of the tradition of natural theology.

---

16. See George Mavrodes, *Belief in God* (New York: Macmillan Co., 1970), pp. 22ff.

17. For more on this see Plantinga, *The Nature of Necessity,* chap. 10, sec. 8.

CHAPTER 15

A Transcendental Argument for God's Existence

Greg Bahnsen and Gordon Stein

SEGMENT ONE

I. Opening Statement — Bahnsen

A. Introductory Remarks about the Nature of the Debate

1. Defining Terms

- The argument is for Christian theism.

It is necessary at the outset of our debate to define our terms; that is always the case.

And in particular here, I should make it clear what I mean when I use the term "God".

I want to specify that I'm arguing particularly in favor of Christian theism and for it as a unit or system of thought and not for anything like theism in general, and there are reasons for that. The various conceptions of deity found in world religions are in most cases logically incompatible, leaving no unambiguous sense to general theism — whatever that might be.

I have not found the non-Christian religions to be philosophically defensible, each of them being internally incoherent or undermining human reason and experience.

Since I am by the grace of God a Christian, I cannot, from the heart, adequately defend those religious faiths with which I disagree. My commitment is to the Triune God and the Christian world view based on God's revelation in the Old and New Testaments. So, first I am defending Christian theism.

2. What the Debate Is About

- We are debating about philosophical systems, not the people who adhere to or profess them.

Our concern is with the objective merits of the case which can be made for atheism or Christian theism, not related subjective or personal matters.

The personalities of those individuals who adhere to different systems of thought are not really relevant to the truth or falsity of the claims made by those systems. Atheists and Christians can equally be found emotional, unlearned, intolerant or rude in their approaches.

Subjective claims made about the experience of inner satisfaction or peace — claims that are made in earnest by both Christians and atheists in their literature — and promotional claims made about the superiority of Christianity or atheism.

For instance, some atheist literature suggests that greater mental health comes through the independence of the atheist outlook. These sorts of things are always subject to conflicting interpretations and explanations, being, I think, more autobiographical, rather than telling us anything for sure about the truth of the system under consideration.

The issue is not whether atheists or professing Christians have ever done anything undesirable or morally unacceptable.

One need only think respectively of the atheist involvement in the Reign of Terror in the French Revolution, and the professing Christian involvement in the Spanish Inquisition.

The question is *not* whether the adherents to these systems have lived spotless lives, but whether atheism or Christian theism as philosophical systems are objectively true. And so I'll be defending Christian theism, and I'll be defending it as a philosophical system.

B. A Concession to Stein's Area of Expertise

My last introductory remark is something to the effect that I want to concede to my opponent all issues pertaining to *The Control of Ovarian Maturation in Japanese Whales,* the subject of his doctoral dissertation in 1974 at Ohio State.

Dr. Stein is a man of intelligence, and that's not a question in this debate. I would not pretend to hold my own in a discussion with him in the empirical details of his narrow domain of specialized natural science.

However, our subject tonight is really much different, calling for intelligent reflection upon issues which are philosophical or theological in character. For some reason, Dr. Stein has, over the last decade, left his field of expertise and given his life to a campaign for atheism. Whatever his perception of the reason for that, I do not believe that it is because of any genuinely cogent philosophical case which might be made for atheism as a world view. And it is to this subject that I now turn for tonight's debate.

C. Opening Case for the Existence of God

My opening case for the existence of God will cover three areas of thought: the nature of evidence, the presuppositional conflict of world views, and the transcendental argument for God's existence.

1. The Nature of the Evidence

How should the difference of opinion between the theist and the atheist be rationally resolved? What Dr. Stein has written indicates that he, like many atheists, has not reflected adequately on this question. He writes, and I quote, "The question of the existence of God is a factual question, and should be answered in the same way as any other factual questions."

The assumption that all existence claims are questions about matters of fact, the assumption that all of these are answered in the very same way is not only over simplified and misleading, it is simply mistaken. The existence, factuality or reality of different kinds of things is not established or disconfirmed in the same way in every case.

We might ask, "Is there a box of crackers in the pantry?" And we know how we would go about answering that question. But that is a far, far cry from the way we go about answering questions determining the reality of say, barometric pressure, quasars, gravitational attraction, elasticity, radio activity, natural laws, names, grammar, numbers, the university itself that you're now at, past events, categories, future contingencies, laws of thought, political obligations, individual identity over time, causation, memories, dreams, or even love or beauty. In such cases, one does not do anything like walk to the pantry and look inside for the crackers. There are thousands of existence or factual questions, and they are not at all answered in the same way in each case.

Just think of the differences in argumentation and the types of evidences used by biologists, grammarians, physicists, mathematicians, lawyers, magicians, mechanics, merchants, and artists. It should be obvious from this that the types of evidence one looks for in existence or factual claims will be determined by the field of discussion and especially by the metaphysical nature of the entity mentioned in the claim under question.

Dr. Stein's remark that the question of the existence of God is answered in the same way as any other factual question, mistakenly reduces the theistic question to the same level as the box of crackers in the pantry, which we will hereafter call the crackers in the pantry fallacy.

2. The Presuppositional Conflict of World Views

Dr. Stein has written about the nature of evidence in the theistic debate, and what he has said points to a second philosophical error of significant proportions. In passing, we would note how unclear he is, by the way, in speaking of the evidence which must be used, describing it variously as logic, facts, or reason. Each of these terms is susceptible to a whole host of differing senses, not only in philosophy, but especially in ordinary usage, depending on who is using the terms.

I take it he wishes to judge hypotheses in the common sense — by tests of logical coherence and empirical observation. The problem arises when Dr. Stein elsewhere insists that every claim that someone makes must be treated as a hypothesis which must be tested by such evidence before accepting it. "There is to be nothing," he says, "which smacks of begging the question or circular reasoning."

This, I think, is oversimplified thinking and again misleading, what we might call the Pretended *Neutrality* fallacy. One can see this by considering the following quotation from Dr. Stein: "The use of logic or reason is the *only* valid way to examine the truth or falsity of any statement which claims to be factual."

One must eventually ask Dr. Stein, then, how he proves this statement itself. That is, how does he prove that logic or reason is the only way to prove factual statements?

He is now on the horns of a real epistemological dilemma. If he says that the statement is true by logic or reason, then he is engaging in circular reasoning; and he's begging the question which he [supposedly] forbids. If he says that the statement is proven in some other fashion, then he refutes the statement itself, that logic or reason is the only way to prove things.

Now my point is not to fault Dr. Stein's commitment to logic or reason, but to observe that it actually has the nature of a precommitment or a presupposition. It is not something that he has proven by empirical experience or logic, but it is rather that by which he proceeds to prove everything else. He is not presuppositionally neutral in his approach to factual questions and disputes. He does not avoid begging crucial questions, rather than proving them in what we might call the garden variety, ordinary way.

Now this tendency to beg crucial questions is openly exposed by Dr. Stein when the issue becomes the existence of God; because he demands that the theist present him with the evidence for the existence of God. Well, theists like myself would gladly and readily do so. There is the evidence of the created order itself testifying to the wisdom, power, plan, and glory of God. One should not miss the testimony of the solar system, the persuasion of the sea, and the amazing intricacies of the human body.

There's the evidence of history: God's deliverance of His people, the miracles on Passover night and [at] the Red Sea, the visions in Isaiah, the Shekinah Glory that filled the Temple, the Virgin Birth of Jesus, His mighty miracles, and His resurrection from the dead.

There's the evidence of Special Revelation, the wonder of the Bible as God's Word, unsurpassed in its coherence over time, in its historical accuracy and its life-renewing power.

In short, there is no shortage of empirical indicators or evidences of God's existence — from the [billions of] stars of the heavens to the 500 witnesses of Christ's resurrection. But, *Dr. Stein precludes the very possibility of any of this empirical evidence counting as proof for God's existence.* He writes, "Supernatural explanations are not allowed in science. The theist is hard put to document his claims for the existence of the supernatural if he is in effect forbidden from evoking the supernatural as a part of his explanation. Of course, this is entirely fair; as it would be begging the question to use what has to be proved as a part of the explanation."

In advance, you see, Dr. Stein is committed to disallowing any theistic interpretation of nature, history or experience. What he seems to overlook is that this is just as much begging the question on his own part as it is on the part of the theist, who appeal to such evidence. He has not at all proven by empirical observation and logic *his* precommitment to Naturalism. He has assumed it in advance, accepting and rejecting all further factual claims in terms of that controlling and unproved assumption.

Now the theist does the very same thing, don't get me wrong. When certain empirical evidences are put forth as likely disproving the existence of God, the theist regiments his commitments in terms of *his* presuppositions, as well. Just as the Naturalist would insist that Christ could not have risen from the dead, or that there is a natural explanation yet to be found of how he did rise from the dead, so the supernaturalist will insist that the alleged discrepancies in the Bible have an explanation — some yet to be found, perhaps — and that the evil of this world has a sufficient reason behind it, known at least to God. They both have their governing presuppositions by which the facts of experience are interpreted, even as *all* philosophical systems, *all* world views do.

At the most fundamental level of everyone's thinking and beliefs there are primary convictions about reality, man, the world, knowledge, truth, behavior, and such things. Convictions about which all other experience is organized, interpreted, and applied. Dr. Stein has such presuppositions, so do I, and so do all of you. And it is these presuppositions which determine what we accept by ordinary reasoning and evidence, for they are assumed in all of our reasoning — even about reasoning itself.

3. *The Transcendental Proof of God's Existence*

How should the difference of opinion between the atheist and the theist be rationally resolved? That was my opening question. We've seen two of Dr. Stein's errors regarding it: the crackers in the pantry fallacy and the pretended neutrality fallacy. In the process of discussing them we've observed that belief in the existence of God is not tested in any ordinary way like other factual claims. And the reason for that is metaphysically because of the non-natural character of God, and epistemologically, because of the presuppositional character of commitment for or against His existence.

Arguments over conflicting presuppositions *between* world views, therefore, must be resolved somewhat differently, and yet still rationally, from conflicts over factual existence claims *within* a world view or system of thought.

When we go to look at the different world views that atheists and theists have, I suggest *we can prove the existence of God from the impossibility of the contrary. The transcendental proof for God's existence is that without Him it is impossible to prove anything.* The atheist world view is irrational and cannot consistently provide the preconditions of intelligible experience, science, logic, or morality. The atheist world view cannot allow for laws of logic, the uniformity of nature, the ability for the mind to understand the world, and

moral absolutes. In that sense the atheist world view cannot account for our debate tonight.

II. Opening Statement — Stein

A. Introductory Remarks

I will grant Dr. Bahnsen his expertise on *A Conditional Resolution of the Apparent Paradox of Self-Deception*, which was his dissertation. I don't know how much more relevant that is to our discussion tonight than mine is, probably not any more. But I would also like to thank Dr. Bahnsen for showing us that he really doesn't understand too much about atheism. I will try to straighten him out.

This is an important question we're discussing. Perhaps it is the most important question in the field of religion, because if God doesn't exist, then the Bible is not the word of God, Jesus can't be the Messiah, and Christianity can't be true, as well as any other religion. So, we're dealing with an important issue here.

Now, Dr. Bahnsen repeated for me that the existence of God is a factual question. I don't think he would dispute that. I think he misinterpreted what I said, when I said we resolve factual questions in the same way. I didn't mean exactly in the same way; I meant with the use of reason, logic, and evidence. And that is what I am holding.

B. Definitions

1. Atheism

Now, first of all, let me make clear what atheism is and is not. I think this has been a very commonly misunderstood subject. Atheists do not say that they can prove there is no God. Also, an atheist is not someone who denies there is a God. Rather, an atheist says that he has examined the proofs that are offered by the theists, and finds them inadequate.

Now, if I were to say that this gentleman sitting in the front steps could fly by flapping his arms, I'd be making a kind of unusual statement. And it would be up to me or him to demonstrate that he can fly. If he can't demonstrate it, then we don't believe that he can fly. Now, if he doesn't demonstrate it right now, it doesn't mean that he can't fly; it just means that he can't fly right now. So, we do not deny that he can fly because he can't demonstrate it right now; but you see, he has not proven his case. And therefore, we do not believe that he can fly until he proves so.

And this is what the atheist says about the existence of God: He says the case is unproved not disproved. So, an atheist is really someone who is without a belief in God, or he does not believe in a God. It is not someone who denies the existence of God, or who says that one does not exist, or that he can prove that one does not exist.

2. God

Well, I think I would like to define a god, as well. I'm not so sure I like his definition. I'm not going to stick to just the Christian God, I'm going to stick to all kinds of gods. I'm going to use the definition which Father Coppleston and Bertrand Russell both agreed on in their debate. Now this is a definition that both sides agreed to, so I think it must be an adequate one, if not a great one. And this is the definition: "A supreme personal being, distinct from the world, and creator of the world."

Now before asking for proof of God's existence we need a satisfactory definition, and I think I've given one which I will find at least satisfactory. If Dr. Bahnsen doesn't agree, we can hear from him. Nothing can qualify as evidence of the existence of a god unless we have some idea of what we're searching for. That's why we need the definition.

3. The Burden of Proof

Throughout history there are eleven major kinds of evidence or proof that have been offered for God's existence. In my campus visits all kinds of other things have been offered as proof, but they all can fit under these eleven categories with some juggling. Now if these eleven proofs do not work out logically, or lead to logical self-contradictions, then we can only say that God's existence is not proven; it is unproved, not disproved, as I mentioned before.

Now if I assert that this gentleman can fly by flapping his arms, as I said, the burden of proof is on him.

Suppose I make a more complicated statement. Suppose I say that my dog can talk in complete sentences. Well, again, I'm making a kind of unusual statement, and it's up to me to offer the evidence. So, I'd better be prepared to do that, or I'd better be prepared to have people not believe what I say.

I'd like a demonstration either of this gentleman flying or of my dog talking, if I were the person being asked to make a decision before I admitted that such things were possible or existed. How easy would it be to show that this gentleman cannot fly or that my dog cannot talk in complete sentences? As I mentioned before, you get into a real problem trying to show that something cannot happen or that something does not exist.

For example, if I wanted to prove that unicorns do not exist, I could examine this room and conclude that there are no unicorns in this room, which is a small area. To prove the general nonexistence of something like unicorns, you would have to search the entire universe simultaneously. And then you could only say that no unicorns existed at the moment we searched the universe. But maybe they were there five minutes before, or if maybe we only searched the whole earth, they were on another planet at the time. There are all kinds of possibilities. So, you cannot prove that something does not exist. That's why, as I mentioned before, the definition of an atheist is not someone who thinks he has proven that God does not exist, because he cannot.

C. The Theistic Proofs

I want to quickly go over some of the eleven major proofs. They have been 900 years in the formulation, and during these 900 years, this is what people have basically come up with.

1. The First Cause (Cosmological) Argument

Everything must have a cause, therefore the universe must have a cause, and that cause was God. God was the first or uncaused cause.

Response: This leads to a real logical bind for the theist, because, if everything must have a cause, then

God must have a cause. If God had a cause, he cannot be the first or uncaused cause. If God did not have a cause, then not everything must have a cause. If not everything needs a cause, then perhaps the universe doesn't need a cause. Thus, there is a logical bind and the proof fails.

2. The Design (Teleological) Argument

The universe is wonderful and exhibits evidence of design and order. These things must have had a designer that was even more wonderful, and that designer was God.

Response: Surely if the world is wonderfully designed, and God, the designer, is more wonderfully designed, then God must have a designer even more wonderful than He is. If God didn't need a designer, than neither should the relatively less wonderful thing such as the universe have needed one. Again, there is a logical self-contradiction.

3. The Argument from Life

Life cannot originate from the random movement of atoms, and yet life exists. Therefore the existence of a God was necessary to create life.

Response: Basically, life didn't originate from the random movement of atoms, and no scientists would say so. Because there are limits of a chemical composition and physics of atoms, and they do not move in any possible way, chemicals do not combine in any possible way. That's why when you see these one billion to one kind of odds that people have set for life originating, they're all wet. They haven't considered the possibility that not every reaction can occur. So, it's possible to explain the origins of life without a god and using the principle of parsimony or Occam's Razor, I think we are left with the simpler explanation, [which is] the one without the God. I'll go into more detail on that later.

4. The Argument from Revealed Theology

The Bible says that God exists, and the Bible is the inspired word of God, therefore what it says must be true. Therefore God exists.

Response: Well, this is obviously a circular argument. It begs the question. We are trying to show whether God exists; therefore, calling the Bible the word of God is not permitted, because it assumes the existence of the very thing we are trying to prove. So, if the Bible is not the word of God, then we cannot give any real weight to the fact that it mentions that God exists. Thus, it does not become a proof. In fact, to prove God from the Bible is standing things on its head. First you must prove God, and then you may say whether God dictated it or inspired it. But you can't really use the Bible as Dr. Bahnsen seems to want to do as evidence for existence of God, per se.

5. The Argument from Miracles

The existence of miracles requires the presence of a supernatural force, or a God. Miracles do occur, and therefore there is a supernatural force or God.

Response: Again, this is begging the question; it requires that you must believe in a God first, beforehand. Then you say there are such things as miracles, which are active of a God who creates violations of his own laws. So, it is not evidence, per se. It can serve as supplementary evidence, once you have good evidence in another kind of way for the existence of a God — you can use miracles as an additional argument, but in and of itself it doesn't show the existence of a God, because it assumes that which needs to be proven.

A quote from Thomas Paine about miracles: "When you see an account is given about such a miracle, by a person who says he saw it, it raises a question in the mind that is very easily decided. Is it more probable that nature should go out of her course, or that a man could tell a lie? We have never seen in our time Nature go out of her course, but we have good reason to believe that millions of lies have been told in this same time. It is therefore at least millions to one that the reporter of a miracle tells a lie." I think those are good odds.

6. The Ontological Argument

God is, by definition, perfect. A necessary quality

of any perfect object is that it exists. If it did not exist it would not be perfect. If perfection requires existence, then God exists.

Response: There is a problem with the word *exists*. In order for something to be perfect, it must first exist. If something didn't exist, the word *perfect wouldn't* mean anything. First you must have existence, then possibly you may have perfection. So, this again is going backwards; you must first have an existing God, and then you can decide whether He's perfect. If perfection is a quality of a God, then He may be perfect, but He first must exist.

7. The Moral Argument

All people have moral values. The existence of these values cannot be explained unless they were implanted in people by a God. Therefore, God exists.

An atheist's problem: There are simpler ways to explain the origin of moral values without requiring the existence of a God to implant them into people. Besides, if moral values did come from a God, then all people should have the same moral values. They don't. People's moral values are a result of an accommodation they have made with their particular environment and have taught to their children as a survival mechanism.

8. The Wish Argument

Without the existence of a God people wouldn't have any reason to live or be good, therefore there has to be a God. Most people believe in a God, therefore there is a God.

Response: This really isn't a proof, it is just a wish. It's like saying that it would be nice to have a God (which it would), but that doesn't have anything to do with whether there is one or not.

9. The Argument from Faith

The existence of God cannot be proven by the use of reason, but only by the use of faith. The use of faith shows that there is a God, therefore God exists.

Response: Reason is a proven way to obtain factual information about the universe.

Faith has not been shown to produce true information about the universe because faith is believing something is so because you want it to be so, without adequate evidence. Therefore, faith cannot be used to prove the existence of anything.

In addition, there is the fact that faith often gives you the opposite answer to what is given by reason to the same problem. This also shows that faith does not provide valid answers.

10. The Argument from Religious Experience

Many people have claimed to have a personal experience or encounter with God, therefore God must exist.

Response: This is a difficult one to handle, because, first of all, I've never had such an experience, but I'm sure that people have absolutely honestly thought they've had such experiences. But, the *feeling* of having met God cannot be confused with the *fact* of having met God. There is a semantic confusion; and also, we cannot use our own feelings as if they were valid ways to obtain information about the world. They are feelings that we have inside of us, but we cannot demonstrate them to another person. They cannot be used as evidence. If everyone had that same experience; like if we all looked around the room and we all agreed that there is a clock over there, then we might say that the vision of a clock is a consensual one, if everyone agreed on it. Other than that, if you saw a clock and no one else did, or if only two or three people did in the room, then you have a bit of a problem.

11. Pascal's Wager

We have no way of knowing if a God exists or not, and we have no way of finding out. But you have nothing to lose by believing in a God, but on the other hand, you do have a lot to lose by not believing in a God, and it turns out later on that there is one after we're dead.

Response: This is only true if 1) You are right about a God, and 2) you have picked the right religion, because you might wind up on the Judgment Day and be right about a God, but He says, "What religion were you?" and you say, "I was a believer in Islam." And He says, "Sorry, Catholicism is the right religion. Down you go." So, in addition, you might have a God who punishes people who have lived virtuous lives. Say an atheist who has lived a virtuous life, did wonderful deeds in the world, but just does not believe in a God. If the God punishes him, you have an irrational God who is just as likely to punish the believer as the unbeliever.

III. Cross-Examination

A. Bahnsen Examines Stein

Bahnsen: Dr. Stein, do you have any sources that you can give to us, very briefly, that defines atheism as one who finds the theistic proofs inadequate rather than one who denies the existence of God?

Stein: Yes, sir. George Smith's book, which you will find for sale at the back of the room upstairs, later, called *Atheism: The Case Against God,* makes what I think is the finest book ever written on the subject which was quite explicit. I have a copy right here. I can quote you, in exact words if you like....

Bahnsen: Oh, I don't think that will be necessary. Do you have any other sources?

Stein: Do I have any other sources?

Bahnsen: Do *you* have any other sources?

Stein: Sure.

Bahnsen: What will they be?

Stein: Charles Bradlaugh, who, I will give you right now. 100 years ago Charles Bradlaugh made the comment in one of his pleas for atheism. He said....

Bahnsen: That will be fine. Dr. Stein, did you hear Dr. Bahnsen use the following argument: "The Bible says that God exists; the Bible is the inspired word of God; therefore what it says must be true; therefore God exists"?

Stein: You did not use that; you just assume that was so because you were quoting from the Bible as if it were....

Bahnsen: I didn't ask you what I assumed; I asked you if I used that argument.

Stein: No, you did not use the argument; but you used the results of the argument.

Bahnsen: Dr. Stein, you mentioned eleven basic proofs for the existence of God. Did you mention Transcendental Proof for the existence of God?

Stein: No, I didn't mention it by name. I think it is not a proof. I wouldn't call it a proof. As I understand it, the way you said it ...

Bahnsen: There's no time for rebuttal on that point. Otherwise you didn't deal with that particular one. All right, are all rational questions answered in the very same way?

Stein: No, they're not. They are answered by logical methods, though, that are the same: reason, logic, and presenting evidence and facts.

Bahnsen: I heard you use "logical binds" and "logical self-contradiction" in your speech. You did say that?

Stein: I used that phrase, yes.

Bahnsen: Do you believe there are laws of logic then?

Stein: Absolutely.

Bahnsen: Are they universal?

Stein: They are agreed upon by human beings not realizing it is just out in nature.

Bahnsen: Are they simply conventions then?

Stein: They are conventions that are self-verifying.

Bahnsen: Are they sociological laws or laws of thought?

Stein: They are laws of thought which are interpreted by man.

Bahnsen: Are they material in nature?

Stein: How could a law be material?

Bahnsen: That's the question I'm going to ask you.

Stein: I would say no.

B. Stein Examines Bahnsen

Stein: Dr. Bahnsen, would you call God material or immaterial?

Bahnsen: Immaterial.

Stein: What is something that's immaterial?

Bahnsen: Something not extended in space.

Stein: Can you give me any other example, other than God, that's immaterial?

Bahnsen: The laws of logic.

Stein: Are we putting God as an equivalent thing to the laws of logic?

Bahnsen: No, only if you think all factual questions are answered in the very same way would you even assume that by thinking that there are two immaterial things that they must be identical....

Stein: I'm not assuming that. I'm just assuming that because the laws of logic are conventions among men. Are you saying that God is a convention among men?

Bahnsen: I don't accept the claim that the laws of logic — that Christ's laws of logic — are conventional.

Stein: OK, is your God omnipotent, omniscient, and omnibenevolent?

Bahnsen: He is.

Stein: You don't find this to be a contradiction at all?

Bahnsen: I do not.

Stein: Well, we'll show, a little later, that it is. If your argument that favors the existence of God is shown to be incorrect, will you relinquish your belief in God?

Bahnsen: If my arguments are disproved?

Stein: Yes.

Bahnsen: Will I relinquish my belief in God? If there were no arguments for the existence of God, I wouldn't believe in God.

Stein: That's not quite answering the question. If someone could show you that there are no arguments, would you relinquish your belief? I'm trying to see what's the basis of your belief.

Bahnsen: You're the one who said that it's impossible to show a universal negative; no one could show that there are no arguments for the existence of God. So you can only deal with the ones I know of.

Stein: OK. If someone showed that all the ones you produced were invalid, what would be your position?

Bahnsen: Rationally speaking, if there is no basis for believing in the existence of God, I would relinquish that belief.

Stein: Is God good?

Bahnsen: Yes, He is.

Stein: How do you know that?

Bahnsen: He saved me. He created me. He made the world and made it good. He sent His Son into the world to die for my sins. Many of these evidences are quite convincing to me, but I don't use them outside of a world view in which they make sense, in which they are taken as true. If you mean if God is good in such a way — or can I give you evidence that you would accept — that would depend on what your presuppositions are.

Stein: Well, I'm asking if God says something, anything, is it right because ... anything God does is good because God is good, or does it become good just because God said it. I don't know if I said that right. I guess I did.

Bahnsen: No, I understand the problem. What God says to be good is good, because it reflects his own character. God is good and is the *standard* of goodness. That's one of the presuppositions to the Christian world view.

Stein: But isn't it indeed a presupposition which is presupposed before there is any actual data from God?

Bahnsen: Is this a question about my first opening statement?

Stein: In a sense it is, because it has to do with the whole idea of whether there are absolutes outside of God which is an important issue in this debate which may come up later.

Bahnsen: I still think we are straining at the limits of debate rules here; but I will answer your question. There are no absolutes outside of God.

Stein: So, in other words, the fact that God is good is something that God told you; and that's why you accepted it rather than moving ahead and assuming it as a presupposition which is what you said a minute ago.

Bahnsen: That's extremely simplistic. God told me *and* provided evidence of it.

Stein: But you also said it was a presupposition.

Bahnsen: That's right.

Stein: Isn't that a contradiction?

Bahnsen: Not at all. There are many things which are presupposed as well as evidenced in this world. For instance: The laws of logic.

Stein: I would disagree with that. When we talk about immaterial things are you also saying that there is such a thing, let's say, as a ghost or the soul, which are examples of immaterial things? Would you put them under immaterial?

Bahnsen: I would say that man is a living soul and has an immaterial aspect to his being, yes.

Stein: And how would you prove this?

Bahnsen: Does this have to do with the existence of God then?

Stein: Well it has to do with the existence of immaterial things.

Bahnsen: Well, if there is an immaterial Being, God, and if the Bible is His Word, then I would say that his revealing of the human nature of man in the Bible is sufficient proof. And that takes us back logically to what you're bound to say to whether God Himself does exist. That's what we're supposed to be debating.

Stein: So, you're giving me a circular argument.

Bahnsen: No, I'm telling you what the debate is about.

Stein: I know what the debate is about. I'm asking for an answer to the question. I didn't get one.

Bahnsen: I'm not debating the nature of the soul tonight, but the existence of God. Yes, I believe man has a soul.

Stein: The only reason I asked about the soul is because this is a simpler immaterial object that most will hold to.

Bahnsen: I don't believe it is similar. I mean that's *your* point.

Stein: Simpler, not similar, I said.

IV. Rebuttal—Bahnsen

We are debating the existence of God. I specified I would be speaking in order to avoid logical contradictions on one particular view of God, the Christian view of God, which I personally hold. Dr. Stein said he will not restrict himself to the Christian conception of God. That's fine, he may not. But all the time he uses anything outside the Christian conception of God will be irrelevant. In fact I would join him in refuting those other conceptions of God. The existence of God that I'm arguing tonight is the Christian one.

Secondly, when Dr. Stein defines an atheist as one who finds the theistic proofs inadequate, that is unproved but not disproved, he's engaging in some linguistic revision. He does quote for us, of course, (he said that he could and I trust that he can) two atheists who likewise define atheism in that way. But you see, that strikes me as similar to a Christian who defines his position as being true at the outset; and therefore it must be true, because it is true by definition.

He has minimized the task that is before him by simply saying, "I'm here to show the theistic proofs are inadequate." Well, you see even at that point he didn't do his job, even though that was less than he really should be doing. Because he gave us eleven basic proofs for God, attributing one to me which I didn't use, do not use, and do not assume. He mentioned eleven basic proofs, but did not deal with the ones I gave in my opening presentation. So he has not dealt yet with the argument that is before us this evening.

Dr. Stein has mentioned logical binds and logical self-contradictions. He says that he finds that the laws of logic are universal; however, they are conventional in nature. That is not at all acceptable philosophically. If the laws of logic are conventional in nature, then you might have different societies that use different laws of logic.

It might be appropriate in some societies to say, "Well, my car is in the parking lot, and it's *not* the case that my car is in the parking lot." There are laws in certain societies that have a convention that says, "Go ahead and contradict yourself." But then there are in a sense, some groups in our own society that might think that way. Thieves have a tendency to say, "This is not my wallet, but it is *not* the case that it's not my wallet." They may engage in contradictions like that, but I don't think any of us would want to accept this.

The laws of logic are not conventional or sociological. I would say the laws of logic have a transcendental necessity about them. They are universal; they are invariant, and they are not material in nature. And if they are not that, then I'd like to know, in an atheist universe, how it is possible to have laws in the first place. And secondly, how it is possible to justify those laws?

The laws of logic, you see, are abstract. As abstract entities, which is the appropriate philosophical term, not spiritual — entities that Dr. Stein is speaking of — abstract entities — that is to say, not individual (or universal in character). They are not materialistic. As universal, they are not experienced to be true. There may be experiences where the laws of logic are used, but no one has universal experience. No one has tried every possible instance of the laws of logic.

As invariant, they don't fit into what most materialists would tell us about the constantly changing nature of the world. And so, you see, we have a real problem on our hands. Dr. Stein wants to use the laws of logic tonight. I maintain that by so doing he's borrowing my world view. For you see, in the theistic world view the laws of logic make sense, because in the theistic world view there can be abstract, universal, invariant entities such as the laws of logic. Within the theistic world view you cannot contradict yourself, because to do so you're engaging in the nature of lying, and that's contrary to the character of God as we perceive it. And so, the laws of logic are something Dr. Stein is going to have to explain as an atheist or else relinquish using them.

The transcendental argument for the existence of God, then, which Dr. Stein has yet to touch, and which I don't believe he can surmount, is that without the existence of God it is impossible to prove anything. And that's because in the atheistic world you cannot justify, you cannot account for, laws in general: the laws of thought in particular, laws of nature, cannot account for human life, from the fact that it's more than electrochemical complexes in depth, and the fact that it's more than an accident. That is to say, in the atheist conception of the world, there's really no reason to debate; because in the end, as Dr. Stein has said, all these laws are conventional. All these laws are not really law-like in their nature; they're just, well, if you're an atheist and materialist, you'd have to say they're just something that happens inside the brain.

But you see, what happens inside *your* brain is not what happens inside *my* brain. Therefore, what happens inside your brain is not a law. It doesn't necessarily correspond to what happens in mine. In fact, it can't be identical with what is inside my mind or brain, because we don't have the same brain.

As the laws of logic come down to being materialistic entities, then they no longer have their law-like character. If they are only social conventions, then, of course, what we might do to limit debate is just define a new set of laws and ask for all who want the convention that says, "Atheism must be true or theism must be true, and we have the following laws that we conventionally adopt to prove it," and see who'd be satisfied.

But no one can be satisfied without a rational procedure to follow. The laws of logic cannot be avoided; the laws of logic cannot be accounted for in a Materialist universe. Therefore, the laws of logic are one of the many evidences that without God you can't prove anything at all.

V. Rebuttal — Stein

Okay, I'll now touch on the transcendental evidence for the existence of God which the only time I could really do such is in my rebuttal. But first I'd like to do one more important thing. Rather than asking what is the cause of the universe, we must first ask, "Does the universe require a causal explanation?" Rather than asking what is responsible for the design in nature, we must ask, "Does nature exhibit design?"

God is given as a solution to a metaphysical problem, but no consideration is given to whether such a problem exists in the first place. But God is not an explanation for anything. For example, if you say, if I ask you, "How did the universe come [into existence]?" and you say, "God created it," that doesn't answer the question. The question is, "*How* did God create it?" And I defy any theist to define how God created it. Basically what you're saying is that an unknowable Being is responsible for a given phenomenon which He caused through unknowable means. And that's not an explanation, but rather a concession that the phenomena is totally inexplicable.

Now, about the laws of science in an atheist world: first of all I don't think that Dr. Bahnsen understands what a scientific law is. A scientific law is an observation that is made over and over and over again. The law of gravitation: we drop objects all over the world in different situations and we always observe they fall to the earth. So eventually we make a statistical statement that objects are likely, almost 100% likely, to fall to the earth if they're not accelerating in the opposite direction. Or if a rocket doesn't fall immediately, but [it] eventually will if it doesn't escape the gravity of the earth. So these scientific laws are merely consensuses based on thousands and hundreds of thousands of observations.

The laws of logic arc also consensuses based on observations. The fact that they can predict something correctly shows they're on the right track; they're corresponding to reality in some way.

If I can plug in a formula and show exactly where a cannon ball is going to land and predict exactly where it will strike, then my mathematics is reflecting something valid about the behavior of cannon balls that are fired on this earth. Otherwise, I wouldn't have picked the exact spot. And mathematics is basically logic again used in the same way by consensus of tested things that are self verifying. I'm not explaining it as well as I could, but that's basically what I'm saying.

An atheist's universe, then, goes on the basis of the fact that matter has certain intrinsic behavior patterns. Electrons repel each other because they're both negatively charged. Protons repel each other and electrons and protons attract each other. The opposite poles of a magnet do that. It's an inherent property of matter.

That is what produces the regularity in the universe. If there were no regularity then there would be no science possible, because you couldn't predict anything. Matter wouldn't behave the same way the second time as it did the first time, or the third or the fourth. So the lack of having a God is in no way detrimental to logic and to having laws in an atheist universe.

In fact, if we had a God we could very easily have an irrational God who did things capriciously. So that if I threw a ball one time I threw it would go up and the next time down and crash right down and soar right up. That would be just as much evidence for a God as

a regularly behaving ball or object dropped. You could have a God who makes the rules and changes them from time to time, or we could have one that makes things the same or we could have a universe that just behaves that way normally.

Now, to ask what caused the universe, although we didn't get into this exact thing. I'm trying to show you that it's to ask an absurd question in the first place. To give God as the answer, first of all, I mentioned it doesn't explain anything; but secondly, before something can act as a cause it must first exist. That is, it must be a part of the universe, and the universe sets the foundation for a causal explanation, but it cannot itself require a causal explanation.

I don't know if that's clear. If I say every human being had a mother, that's a valid question. But if I ask, "who is the mother of the human race," that is a non-valid question, because the human race did not have a mother.

I can ask what was the cause of this planet exploding, but to ask what was the cause of the universe is to ask an invalid question. And to offer the answer as God is to offer an invalid answer to an invalid question.

We haven't gotten into morality. I think I'm going to leave that for the second half. If Dr. Bahnsen doesn't raise it I will. He makes an awful lot of statements that are basically feelings: he felt God enter his life; he felt this happened, he felt that Jesus was resurrected. If he were held to a historian's standard, especially the standard when a miracle is done, as David Hume said, "When a miraculous or very unlikely event such as the resurrection ...," although he didn't use that exact analogy, that exact example, "occurs, we must demand an extraordinary amount of proof."

If I say, "The sun is going to rise tomorrow," you don't need too much proof because it's been rising every day. If I say, "The sun is not going to rise tomorrow," then we need an extraordinary amount of evidence, because it's an extraordinary event. Now he has not been held up to the historian's standard to a lot of the things he's accepted from the Bible as evidence from God; and I think if he did so, he would soon see that those evidences dried up.

Now to get to the transcendental evidence, finally — the statement that if God did not exist we couldn't prove anything, and that logic and scientific laws would be invalid is *nonsense,* and I think I've demonstrated part of that.

He says that the laws of logic are the same everywhere. This is not true, although they are mostly the same. And I wonder if he ever heard of a Zen Koan, and the answer to a Zen Koan is something which is like — "what is the sound of one hand clapping" is the most famous Zen Koan — the answer to that kind of question is in a different kind of logic in a sense, or extralogical, if you want to call it that.

But I think that most logic that we accept in the Western world and most of the Eastern world is the basis of agreement on people that reflect something about the universe. The idea that transcendental evidence of the existence of God is the impossibility of the opposite, that the world view would not be rational if it were atheistic, is total nonsense; and I've demonstrated to you that it depends on the inherent properties of matter. If matter has properties that it behaves then we have order in the universe, and we have a logical, rational universe without God. The God issue is not germane if matter behaves in a regular way; and I would hold that the properties of matter, as demonstrated over and over again, are regular. It's an inherent property of matter.

So I think the transcendental evidence statement can be dismissed as mere wishful thinking coupled with misinformation about what scientific laws are and what atheists would hold. In fact most scientists are atheists — in fact science itself is atheistic. Science is not allowed to use a supernatural explanation for anything.

There's a very good reason for that. If your experiment came out one way you could say God did it. If it came out the opposite way you could say God did that. You would never make any progress in explaining anything in science. And so the agreed-upon consensus or rules of science is that naturalistic explanations only are asked for and allowed.

SEGMENT TWO

I. Opening Statement — Stein

It would be logically wrong to say that if all the proofs fail for the existence of God that one is justified in saying that there is no God. There's a logical fallacy — argumentum ad ignorantum (or something like that) that says that you accept something just because all evidence to the contrary fails.

However, we have two other factors here that we must consider. One of them is the fact that 900 years have passed since Anselm first postulated the Ontological Proof, and Thomas Aquinas in 1200 or so. So we have a long period of time in which all these proofs that are being professed failed; that's some evidence about probability — about there being a proof that someone will come up with that will succeed being pretty unlikely.

In addition, we have a number of things which I wouldn't call *proofs,* but I would call *evidence* which make the existence of God even more improbable. One of them is the problem of evil: If an all-good God exists, why is there evil in the world?

We are told that with God all things are possible. If it is possible, if all things *are* possible, it would be possible to create a world in which the vast majority of suffering which is morally pointless, such as the pain and misery of animals, the cancer and blindness of little children, the humiliations of senility and insanity are avoided.

These are apparently the inflictions of the Creator Himself, or else we have a God who isn't omnipotent. If you admit that, then you deny His goodness. If you say that He could not have done otherwise, then you deny [that] with Him all things are possible.

So the atheist can present several arguments [in] which we sort of increase the possibility that there is not a God. [But they are] not proofs, as I said. One of them would be the problem of evil. The idea is that the presence of evil is incompatible with the all good, all knowing, all powerful God as Dr. Bahnsen says he believes in.

Now he can come up with the statement that all the injustice in this world will be corrected in the next world, but that would be something [a statement] that he would make without any evidence whatsoever. It's just, again, wishful thinking.

He could also get out of this bind by saying that God is not all powerful, that some evil things are done without His permission, so to speak, in which case his statement that he believes in an omnipotent God is falsified.

He could also [use] the old argument about free will. That's basically a morass into which he may fall if he likes, but it will not do. To say that God gave man a free will, and therefore can choose between evil and good is to imply that God is unable to make a man who could examine both sides and always choose the good.

In other words, He's limited; and the only way He could do it is to let man choose it for himself, as if that would take something away from man if he could examine both sides and still have guidance within himself to always choose the good.

Now there's no obvious physical evidence of a God. If God wanted man to believe in Him ... all He'd have to do is put in an appearance, and that way anyone would believe in Him, except a fool.

Well, the Christian says this may sound logical to you but it doesn't to God. God evidently wants man to believe on faith without adequate evidence. Well, if He does, then why did He give man the power of reason? And why did He give man more reason than any other animal has?

If all the many things on the earth were created by a god, and if He is an all-loving God who made man in His own image, how do you explain the fact that He must have created the tapeworm, the malaria parasite, tetanus germs, polio, ticks, mosquitoes, cockroaches, and fleas? Now, surely, the dog is not suffering from Original Sin and needs to be infected with fleas, so that he can get to doggie heaven which will be better than his present life!

The standard answer of theists to this kind of question is that things have to be better after death. You know, we have these things on earth; it's veil of tears, so to speak. That doesn't make much sense. I mean, any God that would punish a man for what his ancestors did is not a very moral God. (We're talking about Original Sin now — Adam and Eve and the Garden of Eden.)

There are many instances on this earth in which no distinction seems to be made between the innocent and the guilty, between the Christian and the non-believer, for example, in natural disasters like an earthquake or a fire. It kills Christians; it kills babies; it kills animals; it kills non-Christians. You surely can't say that these people were punished in some way for something they did. It also demolishes churches and hospitals without distinction. Isn't this evidence that, at the very least, whatever force there is controlling these things doesn't care if people are Christians or not? Or whether they're innocent or not?

If there's only one God and He cares at all [about] how He's worshipped, why are there so many different conceptions of God and so many different religions, all claiming to be the one true religion? Does that mean they're all mistaken? Does it mean that one is correct, and all the others are mistaken?

There's an old joke about that atheist in which he said to a believer, "You now, you believe that 99 of 100 gods are false. I just go one step further and say that the 100th one is also false. I'm sure that Dr. Bahnsen — in fact he even agreed that he would help me refute any other gods but the Christian God.

If Christianity is the one true religion, why are so many people who sincerely believe in it found in the slums and organized crime? I'm not saying that all people there are Christians; I'm not saying that all people in organized crime are Christians, either. But, evidently, if Christianity led to an elevation of moral standards — which we haven't gotten into yet, but I'm going to jump the gun here a little bit — Christians would be expected to be highly moral, not less moral.

In fact studies of the religious beliefs of prisoners have shown that almost all are devout Christians. The numbers of atheists is less than one percent. These statistics were so disturbing to the people that conducted them that they stopped collecting them recently. You can't argue with the facts, though. Any system that seems to fail in its application as frequently as Christianity does is not a very good or practical system for mankind to follow.

I don't want to get into a real discussion of Christianity, except that Dr. Bahnsen insists that the Christian God and Jesus and the other evidences that come from the Christian God and the concomitants with them are true while the others are not.

What are we left with after this exercise? Well, we can see that we can't prove the existence of God by any rational or logical process — and Dr. Bahnsen has not offered us any.

We have a factual issue here. Again, as I've said, because the proofs fail, it doesn't mean that His existence is disproved; but it certainly is unproved. This does not leave us in a bleak, horrible world; there are many things that the atheist does with his life which makes this world a nice place and in order to get to the solving of the problems of this world, instead of hoping for a pie in the sky, which does not seem to be very probable.

II. Opening Statement — Bahnsen

You've heard Dr. Stein refer to the transcendental argument and try to dismiss it simply as wishful thinking. If our debate is going to degenerate to that level, then I dismiss everything he's been saying as wishful thinking and delusion, and why don't we all go home. But I know we're here to argue. We're here to argue a point, and I'm going to stay with the argument that has been proposed and see if Dr. Stein has any better answer than just to engage in name calling.

Dr. Stein proposes an atheist world view. I propose a Christian theistic world view. There are other proposals out there that may want their evening to debate as well. I'm maintaining that the proof of the Christian world view is that the denial of it leads to irrationality. That is, without the Christian God, you cannot prove anything.

As one illustration of that, although I want to get into more than that in the second speech, I have referred to the laws of logic. An atheist universe cannot account for the laws of logic. Dr. Stein, in his responding to that, spoke more about scientific law than he did about the laws of logic, and I'm going to come back to that in my rebuttal to ask about his understanding of scientific law. However, we still hear him saying that laws of logic are a matter of consensus and are just this way. That is to say, "I don't have to prove that the laws of logic exist or that they are justified. It's just this way."

Now friends, how would you like it if I would have conducted the debate in that fashion this evening? God exists because it's just that way. You just can't avoid it. You see, that's not debate, that's not argument, and it's not rational. And therefore, we have, interestingly, an illustration in our very debate tonight that atheists cannot sustain a rational approach to this question.

What are the laws of logic, Dr. Stein, and how are they justified? We'll still have to answer that question from a materialist standpoint. From a Christian standpoint, we have an answer — obviously they reflect the thinking of God. They are, if you will, a reflection of the way God thinks and expects us to think.

But if you don't take that approach and want to justify the laws of logic in some *a priori* fashion, that is apart from experience, something that he suggests when he says these things are self-verified. Then we can ask why the laws of logic are universal, unchanging, and invariant truths — why they, in fact, apply repeatedly in the realm of contingent experience.

Dr. Stein told you, "Well, we use the laws of logic because we can make accurate predictions using them." Well, as a matter of fact, that doesn't come anywhere close to discussing the vast majority of the laws of logic. That isn't the way they're proven. It's very difficult to conduct experiments of the laws of logic of that sort. They are more conceptual by nature rather than empirical or predicting certain outcomes in empirical experience. But even if you want to try to justify all of them in that way, we have to ask why is it that they apply repeatedly in a contingent realm of experience.

Why, in a world that is random, not subject to personal order, as I believe [it is] for a Christian God, why is it that the laws of logic continue to have that success-generating feature about them? Why should they be assumed to have anything to do with the realm of history? [And] why should reasoning about history or science, or empirical experience have these laws of thought imposed upon it?

Once again we have to come back to this really unacceptable idea that they are conventional. If they are conventional, then of course there ought to be just numerous approaches to scholarship everywhere, with approaches to history, to science, and so forth, because people just adopt different laws of logic. That just isn't the way scholarship proceeds, and if anyone thinks that is adequate, they just need to go to the library and read a bit more.

The laws of logic are just not treated as conventions. To say that they are merely conventions is to simply say, "I haven't got an answer." Now if you want to justify logical truths along *a posteriori* lines, that is rather than arguing that they are self-evident, but rather arguing that there is evidence for them that we can find in experience or by observation — that approach, by the way, was used by John Stuart Mill — people will say we gain confidence in the laws of logic through repeated experience, then that experience is generalized. But in some weaker moments I think Dr. Stein was trying to say that.

Of course, some of the suggested logical truths, it turns out, are so complex or so unusual that it is difficult to believe that anyone has perceived their instances in experience. But even if we restrict our attention to the other more simple laws of logic, it should be seen that if [their] truth cannot be decided independently of experience, then they actually become contingent. That is, if people cannot justify the laws of logic independent of experience, then you can only say they apply, as far as I know, to any past experience that I've had.

They are contingent; they lose their necessity, universality, and invariance. Why should a law of logic, which is verified in one domain of experience, by the way, be taken as true for unexperienced domains as well? Why should we universalize or generalize about the laws of logic — especially in a materialistic universe, not subject to the control of a personal God?

Now, it turns out, if the *a priori* and the *a posteriori* lines of justification for logical truths are unconvincing — as I'm suggesting briefly they both are — perhaps we could say they are linguistic conventions about certain symbols. Certain philosophers have suggested that the laws of logic would not be taken as inexorably dictated, but rather we impose their necessity on our language. They become, therefore, somewhat like rules of grammar, and as John Dewey pointed out so persuasively earlier in the century, laws of grammar, you see, are just culturally relative. If the laws of logic are like grammar, then the laws of logic are culturally relative, too.

Why then, are not contradictory systems deemed equally rational? If the laws of logic can be made culturally relative, then we can win the debate by simply stipulating that a law of logic that says "anybody who argues in this way has gotten a tautology on his hands, and therefore it's true."

Why are arbitrary conventions like the logical truths so useful if they're only conventional? Why are they so useful in dealing with problems in the world of experience?

We must ask whether the atheist has a rational basis for his claims. Atheists love to talk about laws of science and laws of logic. They speak as though there are certain moral absolutes from which Christians were just a few minutes ago being indicted because they didn't live up to them. But who is the atheist to tell us about laws? In a materialist universe there are no laws, much less laws of morality that anybody has to live up to.

When we consider that the lectures and essays that are written by logicians and others are not likely filled with just uninterrupted series of tautologies, we can examine those propositions which logicians are most concerned to convey. For instance, logicians will say things like, "a proposition has the opposite truth value from its negation."

Now when we look at those kinds of propositions, we have to ask the general question: what type of evidence do people have for that kind of teaching? Is it the same sort of evidence that is utilized by the biologist, by the mathematician, the lawyer, the mechanic, by your beautician? What is it that justifies a law of logic, or even believes that there is such a thing? What is a law of logic, after all?

There's no agreement on that question. If we had universal agreement, perhaps it would be silly to ask the question. It's been suggested to you that it is absurd to ask these sorts of things, although the analogy that was used by Dr. Stein about the absurdity of asking about the cause of the world is not at all relevant because that isn't what my argument is … by the way, it's not absurd to ask that question either. It may be unnecessary to ask it if you're an atheist, but certainly not absurd to ask it.

But it isn't absurd to ask the question that I'm asking about logic. You see, logicians are having a great deal of difficulty deciding on the nature of their claims. Anybody who reads in the philosophy of logic must be impressed with that today.

Some say the laws of logic are inferences comprised of judgments made up of concepts. Others say that they are arguments comprised of propositions made up of terms. Others say they are proofs comprised of sentences made up of names. Others have simply said they are electrochemical processes in the brain. In the end, what you think the laws of logic are will determine the nature of the evidence you will suggest for them.

Now in an atheist universe, what are the laws of logic? How can they be universal, abstract, invariant? And how does an atheist justify the use of them? Are they merely conventions imposed on our experience, or are they something that look like absolute truth?

Dr. Stein, tonight, has wanted to use the laws of logic. I want to suggest to you one more time that Dr. Stein, in so doing, is borrowing my world view. He's using the Christian approach to the world, so that there can be such laws of logic, scientific inference, or what have-you. But then he wants to deny the very foundation of it.

III. Cross-Examination

A. Stein Examines Bahnsen

Stein: Is mathematics either atheistic or theistic?

Bahnsen: Foundations of mathematics, yes.

Stein: Which?

Bahnsen: Theistic.

Stein: Theistic?

Bahnsen: Christian theistic.

Stein: How do you figure that?

Bahnsen: From the impossibility of the contrary. No other world view can justify the laws of mathematics or of logic, because no other world view can account for universal invariant, abstract entities such as them.

Stein: Do you think it's fair, since you pointed out that logicians themselves are in great disagreement about the nature of the laws of logic, to ask me to explain them in a way that you would find satisfactory?

Bahnsen: Yes, it's fair.

Stein: Why?

Bahnsen: Because this is a rational debate about world views. You have a naturalistic world view; I have a supernaturalistic one. I want something even beginning to be an answer of how a naturalist can justify a universal abstract entity. I haven't heard one yet.

Stein: OK. Is logic based upon mathematics?

Bahnsen: No.

Stein: Never? Not symbolic logic, for example?

Bahnsen: No.

Stein: I would disagree with you.

Bahnsen: Well, if we want to get into Russell and Whitehead and debate those issues, I'd be glad to do that, but if you ask a simple question, I can only give you a simple answer.

Stein: You said …

Bahnsen: Assume the opposite. As far as I'm concerned, as a Christian, I'm not committed one way or another to that. If you want to say mathematical laws and the permutation laws of math are the same as those used in logic, that's fine. How do you justify either one of them is my question.

Stein: Well, I would ask you a more fundamental question that is: you explained that the laws of logic reflect the thinking of God. Number one, how do you know this, and number two, what does it mean?

Bahnsen: What difficulty are you having understanding what it mean?

Stein: I don't know how you are privy to the thinking of God.

Bahnsen: He revealed Himself through the Scriptures of the Old and New Testaments.

Stein: And that explains the logic?

Bahnsen: That explains why there are universal standards of reasoning, yes.

Stein: It doesn't explain them to me. Could you explain them again?

Bahnsen: Yeah, we have Bible studies from time to time where we delve into it.

Stein: You mean you spend some time rationalizing the irreconcilable, or reconciling the irreconcilable? Like the two accounts in Genesis, the two …

Bahnsen: This is a cross-examination. If you have something other than a rhetorical question, I'll try to answer it.

Stein: Well, it's not intended as a rhetorical question, it's intended as …

Bahnsen: The previous one was rhetorical only.

Stein: Well, it was intended to show that your …

Moderator: Please limit your comments to questions.

Stein: OK. Saying that logic reflects the thinking of God is to make a non-statement. How is that an answer to anything that's relevant in this discussion?

Bahnsen: It answers the general metaphysical issue of how there can be universal, invariant, abstract entities in a particular person's world view. If you want to know the precise relationship, for instance, if somebody wants to know for instance, "how did God make a cow?" OK. The statement that God made the cow has meaning apart from my being able to explain the mechanics of God making a cow. Likewise, the statement that the laws of logic are intelligible within a Christian theistic universe has meaning because there are things which are, in fact, spiritual, immaterial, and have a universal quality, such as God's thinking, and those standards that He imposes on people.

And so again we can at least metaphysically make sense of invariant abstract entities in one universe, whereas we can't make sense of them at all in the other. We're not asking for the mechanics here, or anything precise such as resolving the relationship of logic to math. I'm simply asking a more general question. If you're an atheist, how, in the atheist universe is it possible to have an abstract, universal law?

B. Bahnsen Examines Stein

Bahnsen: Well, Dr. Stein, you made reference to David Hume and his rejection of miracles. Have you also read David Hume and his discussion of induction — or more popularly — the Uniformity of Nature?

Stein: A long time ago. I can't recall exactly what he says, but I have read David Hume.

Bahnsen: Were you convinced a long time ago that you had an answer to Hume's skepticism about induction?

Stein: I can't answer that question. I don't remember what … This was at least fifteen years ago I read this.

Bahnsen: The validity of Scientific Laws were undermined by Hume when he contended that we have no rational basis for expecting the future to be like the past — to be the types of events (so that when one event happened, it's a type of event so that when you see it happening somewhere else) you can expect the same consequence from similar causation. Hume suggested that there was no rational basis for expecting the future to be like the past, in which case Science is based simply on convention or habits of thought. Do you agree with him?

Stein: Not on this issue I don't.

Bahnsen: Do you now have an answer for David Hume?

Stein: I think he was wrong on that one thing, but I also think he was right about a lot of other things.

Bahnsen: What is the basis for the Uniformity of Nature?

Stein: The Uniformity of Nature comes from the fact that matter has certain properties which it regularly exhibits. It's a part of the nature of matter. Electrons, opposite things attract; [whereas] the same charged things repel. There are certain valences that fill up the shell of an atom, and that's as far as they can combine.

Bahnsen: Have you tested all electrons?

Stein: All the electrons that have been tested repel each other. I have not tested all of them.

Bahnsen: Have you read all the tests on electrons?

Stein: Me personally? Or can I go on the witness of experts?

Bahnsen: Have you read all the witnesses about electrons?

Stein: All it takes is one witness to say "no", and it will be on the front pages of every physics journal, and there are none. So I'd say, in effect, yes.

Bahnsen: Well, physicists have their [own] presuppositions by which they exclude contrary evidence, too.... In other words, you haven't experienced all the electrons, but you would generalize that all the electrons under certain conditions repel each other.

Stein: Just statistically, on the basis of past observation.

Bahnsen: But we don't know that it's going to be that way ten minutes after this debate then.

Stein: But we see no evidence that things have switched around, do we?

Bahnsen: Do you accept the Zen Buddhist logic that allows for koans, the different kind of logic that you referred to which is used by Zen Buddhists?

Stein: I'd use the word "extralogical"; it's outside the normal kinds of logic. It's not necessarily a different kind of logic, but it's just non-logical — accepted in place of logic.

Bahnsen: Are extralogical things absurd?

Stein: They may seem that way to us, but I would say "no, they aren't absurd in the grand scheme of things."

Bahnsen: Can claims about extra logical matters be true?

Stein: That's impossible to answer; because if we're using logic to answer if something is true or not, then extra logical things are not something in the analysis of logic.

Bahnsen: Are claims about extra logical entities allowed or disallowed in your world view?

Stein: It depends on what we're talking about. If we're talking about things like Zen Buddhism, and they confine themselves to these philosophical speculations, then yes; if you're talking about science, no.

Bahnsen: That sounds very arbitrary.

IV. Rebuttal — Stein

I would first like to make one little factual rebuttal (to) a statement that slipped by in the first speech of Dr. Bahnsen — that atheists caused the French Revolution. This is a false statement. The leader of the French Revolution was Robespierre, who was a Christian. There may have been atheists there, but that doesn't mean they caused the French Revolution. There are atheists everywhere.

We've spent a lot of time talking about logic. And yet I'd like to know why Dr. Bahnsen stresses the laws of logic so much when he has refused to apply them to the existence of God. I'm not so sure it's even falsifiable; so, therefore I don't know if it's a statement that can even be tested in any way.

He has stressed the laws of logic because he knows there is no explanation for the laws of logic that philosophers agree upon. This is a trap! I might have fallen into it, I don't know. [Yet] it's not relevant to his position. He doesn't have an answer to the laws of logic, either.

To say that they reflect the thinking of God is to make a non-statement. First of all, he doesn't know what the thinking of God is. All he knows is what has been by men to be what they thought the thinking of a god might have been many years ago — maybe, if we granted all the possible things in his favor.

It's like saying God created the universe. Unless you explain how He created it, you have not made a statement that has any intrinsic value to it. You may have made part of a statement, but I want to hear the other half. What is there in the method that God used that we can learn from? Why did God do it?

Science doesn't try to answer the question "why" … only "how." But theologians do ask the question "why" and try to answer it. I haven't heard an answer to why God did anything He supposedly did. Nor have I heard how he did it. These are the two most essentially meaningful answers to asking a question. If we don't supply these we have ducked the whole center of the issue, and it's just giving you another mumbling that doesn't go anywhere.

[I'll give you] an example: If I said, "How did that car that's parked in the parking lot — the red car — how did it get there?" And you say, "General Motors made it," that doesn't explain how the car got there.

Now if you want to go and explain that in Detroit 100 men worked a certain number of hours to make this car out of steel which they got from Youngstown, Ohio — from the smelting plant — then maybe we're getting somewhere: I mean, how it got here in existence. To say that General Motors made it is not answering the question of how the car got here. Neither is it an answer to say that God made it.

I would ask Dr. Bahnsen to explain if he thinks he knows the answer [which] none of these philosophers knows about the laws of logic … to put his answer in some kind of meaningful language. To say that the laws of logic reflect the thinking of God is to make a non-meaningful statement — not just to me, [but] to anyone.

I want to know whether God thinks rationally all the time, or whether he can be irrational. How do we know when he's being irrational? Is it possible for him to be irrational? I want to know what kind of logic God uses. Does He use the kind of logic that we can demonstrate, that we can test the same way we use the logic that we are talking about in science? If so, should it be impossible for God to contradict Himself in any way?

Can he make a stone so big he can't lift it? Is that a logical impossibility? Is God limited by that kind of a thing? Can God make a square circle? These are little logical games we play, but they have to reflect a problem that he is having with his concept of God. If God can do anything, if He's omnipotent, omniscient, and omnibenevolent, can he do those things I asked? And if He does, what kind of logic is he using? The logic of self contradiction? Until we have some answers to these questions, I don't think we have gotten very much that is meaningful from Dr. Bahnsen in the first place about any issue. He certainly hasn't applied logic to the proofs of the existence of God that have been offered by philosophers.

V. Rebuttal — Bahnsen

Dr. Stein has demonstrated, it seems to me repeatedly, in the course of tonight's debate, the claim that was made very early on in my original statement, and that's that the atheist world view cannot give an account of those things which are necessary for a rational discourse or science.

When asked about Hume and the skepticism that he generated about induction or the uniformity of nature, we don't hear an answer coming forth. I don't think there will be an answer coming forth from the atheist world view. However, Dr. Stein, who is an atheist, has said — and I think this is close to a quote — "If there were no uniformity, science would be impossible."

Exactly, Dr. Stein! If there were no uniformity, science would be impossible. So on what basis in an atheist's universe is science possible, since in an atheist's universe there is no basis for assuming that there is going to be uniformity?

For someone to say, "Well, it's been that way in all the cases in the past that we know of and therefore very probably is going to be that way in the future" is to assume, because you're using probability, that the future is going to be like the past, that is to say, is to beg the very question that's being asked you.

Now, of course, if you don't like the tough philosophical questions that are asked of you about the nature of laws of logic, how they are justified, the nature of natural law, how it is justified, and so forth, and just dismiss it as absurd questions or non-questions that no one understands and do not have meaning, seems to me is just to try to give medicine to a dead man. You see, it's to say, "I'm not going to reason about that, because I don't have an answer to it, and that's just uncomfortable." But you see, these are philosophical questions which not just Christians, by the way, but all philosophers have had to ask and face throughout the centuries.

Dr. Stein doesn't even begin to scratch the surface of giving us an answer of how an atheist world view can account for laws — laws of science, laws of logic, laws of morality. And yet he does tell us without them, science would be impossible.

As for the transcendental argument "not being logical," I mean, you can claim that, but I have yet to see Dr. Stein shows any self-contradiction on any violation of the laws of logic in it; but of course, if he were, I would ask him if that law of logic is one of the things that we are necessarily to live according to?

Are we to reason by this law, or is that just a convention? Should I say, "Well, it's your convention, but it's not mine." Or is that law of logic universal, invariant and something that must be followed if we're going to arrive at truth? If it is, I'm going to ask him how it's possible to have such a thing in his universe; how he can justify it at all. But he hasn't shown any contradiction; he has simply, again, called it illogical.

Whether it's falsifiable or not — I mean, even asking that question, I think, shows that Dr. Stein is not really aware of the philosophical nature of the question in the debate before us. No, transcendentals are not falsifiable — that's right — but they are very meaningful, the very sorts of things that philosophers deal with all the time. Look at Kant or Aristotle or other philosophers: you'll see they deal with the preconditions of experience. And since they are preconditions of experience, they are not falsifiable, and yet they are meaningful.

He says that I do not have an answer to these questions either. Well, I certainly do! It's just that he doesn't like the answer. The answer is that God created the world, and this world reflects the uniformity that He imposes on it by His governing, and our thinking is to reflect the same consistency or logical coherence that is in God's thinking.

How do we learn about those things? He revealed Himself to us. Again, these are simple answers, the sorts of things Sunday school children learn, but, you know, I've yet to find any reason not to believe them.

For Dr. Stein to say, "Well, these aren't answers," doesn't convince me at all. He says there aren't going to be answers unless I include how it took place. What is God's method, and why did he do it? Well, I don't accept those standards. I don't accept that this is a requirement for an explanation at all. And he doesn't give us a good reason except that he's not going to be satisfied or it's unhelpful to him.

He says it's a non-meaningful statement to say that the laws of logic reflect the thinking of God. He wants to know things like, "Can God be irrational?" Well, if you'd ask those questions in cross examination, I'd answer them. No, God cannot be irrational. Rationality is measured by the standard of his thinking and his revelation.

The atheist world view cannot account for the laws of logic, [and] cannot account for any universals or abstract entities, for that matter. [It] cannot account for the uniformity of nature, and therefore, [it] cannot account for the successes of science.

Nor can the atheist's universe give us universal and absolute laws of morality. And so on; three of the most important issues philosophically that men must face — logic, science, and morality — the atheist's universe is completely at odds with those things.

Well, we have one minute left, and I want to answer very quickly those few things that Dr. Stein brought up in his second presentation so that I might rebut them.

He wants to know about the problem of evil. My answer to the problem of evil is this: there is no problem of evil in an atheist's universe because there is no evil in an atheist's universe. Since there is no God, there is no absolute moral standard, and nothing is wrong. The torture of little children is not wrong in an atheist's universe. It may be painful, but it is not wrong.

It is morally wrong in a theistic universe, and therefore, there is a problem of evil of perhaps the psychological or emotional sort, but *philosophically the answer to the problem of evil is you don't have an absolute standard of good by which to measure evil in an atheist's universe.* You can only have that in a theistic universe, and therefore, the very posing of the problem presupposes my world view, rather than his own. God has a good reason for the evil that He plans or allows.

SEGMENT THREE

I. Closing Statement — Stein

Dr. Bahnsen in his last response, and, indeed, throughout his entire talk, has made a number of claims about what's possible in an atheist's universe and what is not possible in an atheist's universe. All I can say is that he has a very strange conception of an atheist universe and perhaps of the universe in general.

First of all, evil in an atheist's universe. Yes, indeed there can be evil in an atheist's universe. *Evil is*, by definition, in an atheist's universe, *that which decreases the happiness of people, the most unhappiness in people.* In other words, if we have two things that we want to make a comparative evil statement, which is more evil than another, the thing is more evil which causes more people to be unhappy.

Well, how do we know this? *We don't know this; it's a consensus, just like morality in general is a consensus.* It's a consensus reinforced by the teachings of society through its parents to children, teachers to students, the media, literature, the Bible: all these things reinforce morality through teaching and the socialization process. And also we pass laws to punish people that violate some of the more blatant [offenders in] cases that we have said are no-no's.

So the idea that there's no evil in an atheist's universe is utter hogwash. Our evil is at least a rational determinate thing. We don't say, "Well, did God make this evil?" and then have to go flipping through the Bible to see if it was covered at all. You know, there [are] a hundred volumes of commentary — at least a hundred volumes, more — called the Talmud which is the Jew's interpretation of all the places that the Old Testament didn't give them any guidance for ethical and moral issues. So, I mean, these things are not clearly spelled out in the Bible.

We have no guidance on a lot of things, as to what's evil. Is organ transplant evil? I mean, you won't find that in your Bible! So, I mean, we have standards by which we determine evil and good and in an atheistic world, the atheistic world view.

I think I've demonstrated that the regularity of matter, which is an inherent property of matter, explains the way we are able to make laws, which are generalizations in the field of science. To say that (first of all, most, many, many scientists are atheists it's been shown by studies over and over again). So to claim or, as Dr. Bahnsen claims to claim, that science doesn't give us an atheistic world view that is in conformity with science. I mean that science is not in conformity with an atheistic world view is utter nonsense! Science is in itself atheistic. It doesn't use God to explain things, and it understands that matter behaves in a regular and therefore predictable ways. And that is the way in which scientific research is done.

The same with logic; logic is a consensus, and I think it has a mathematical and linguistic basis; it has some conformity to the reality of the world. I don't know how many times we have to repeat that to get through to Dr. Bahnsen, but it doesn't seem to be.

And he seems to specialize in what we call the "thinking makes it so" school of logic, if you want to call it that. Because he says something is so, because he knows what God's thinking was, therefore it is so. The omniscient Dr. Bahnsen has answered. Well, that doesn't answer anything, if we're going to apply the tests of reason to what he says. His statements are not only irrational, they are unreasonable.

The idea that the future is going to be like the past; it's a statistical probability statement. We have never seen a future. Today is the future from yesterday. And yesterday, what is happening today was the future. We have not seen anything in that time period that we have observed, which is several hundred years, to show that the regularity of matter and its behavior is going to change. If it changes, scientific experiments will go haywire, and we'll know it right off the bat, and then we'll have to revise a lot of things. I think the chances of that happening are pretty small.

Now, let me just finish by saying that atheism is not a bleak and negative concept. It frees man, it sweeps away the theological debris that has prevented man from taking action to correct the problems of this world. We want to feed the hungry, we want to educate the illiterate, we want to clothe the naked, we want to raise the standard of living, we want to spread reason and thinking and progress and science.

These are all things which are, in and of themselves, atheistic. We don't do them because God tells us to do them, we do them because they're right; they need to be done in this world. And if we do them because they're right and they make people happy, we will be made happy ourselves by making other people happy. It's a very positive world outlook, something which I don't think Dr. Bahnsen has even mentioned, but it's certainly the other side of the coin.

I mean, what happens when you wipe away the God concept? Are you left with nothing? No, you're left with responsibility that you have to take on yourself. You are responsible for your actions, and also, you get the credit for the things that you do.

And I would rather have a realistic world view that gives up a few things that would be nice to have but just don't happen to be true, and I'd rather operate on a world view like that than I would on making wish fulfillment on things that just are not so.

II. Closing Statement — Bahnsen

As far as my rebuttal/closing statement, I need to deal first of all, perhaps in the entire time, analyzing this remark that my statements tonight have been irrational. Perhaps they have, but saying so doesn't make it so. That's something we just heard, as well. If my statements have been irrational then we need some standards of reasoning by which these statements have been shown to be irrational.

Dr. Stein has yet to explain to us even in the broad-est, simplest Sunday-school-child manner that I told you about laws of logic, laws of science and laws of morality. He hasn't even begun to scratch the surface to tell us how in his world view that there can be laws of any sort. And if there can't be laws, or standards in his world view, then he can't worry about my irrationality, my alleged irrationality.

The transcendental argument for the existence of God has not been answered by Dr. Stein. It's been evaded and made fun of, but it hasn't been answered. That's what we're here for: rational interchange. The transcendental argument says the proof of the Christian God is that without God one cannot prove anything.

Notice the argument doesn't say that atheists don't prove things, or that they don't use logic, science or laws of morality. In fact they do. *The argument is that their world view cannot account for what they are doing.* Their world view is not consistent with what they are doing; in their world view there are no laws; there are no abstract entities, universals, or prescriptions. There's just a material universe, naturalistically explained (as) the way things happen to be. That's not law-like or universal; and therefore, their world view doesn't account for logic, science or morality.

But, atheists, of course, use science and morality. In this argument atheists give continual evidence to the fact that in their heart of hearts they are not atheists. In their heart of hearts they know the God I'm talking about. This God made them, reveals Himself continually to them through the natural order, through their conscience, and through their very use of reason.

They know this God, and they suppress the truth about him. One of the ways that we know that they suppress the truth about him is because they do continue to use the laws of logic, science and morality though their world view doesn't account for them.

Dr. Stein has said that the laws of logic are merely conventional. If so, then on convention he wins tonight's debate, and on convention I win tonight's debate. And if you're satisfied with that, you didn't need to come in the first place. You expected the laws of logic to be applied as universal standards of rationality. Rationality isn't possible in a universe that just consigns them to convention.

Dr. Stein said the laws of science are law-like because of the inherent character of matter. But Dr. Stein doesn't know the inherent character of matter. Now if he were God he might reveal that to us, as I think God has revealed certain things to us about the operation of the universe. But he's not God. He doesn't even believe there is a God.

Since he hasn't experienced all the instances of matter and all the electron reactions and all the other things that scientists look at, he doesn't know the future is going to be like the past. When he says, "Well, it always has been in the past and what if it changes tomorrow, won't that make the front pages," that's not an answer. You see, we're asking *what justifies* your proceeding on the expectation that the future's going to be like the past? When they say, "Well, it's always been that way in the past," it's just to beg the question. We want to know on what basis your world view allows for this uniformity of nature and laws of science.

Thirdly, we talked about laws of morality. He said they had morality, the utilitarian standard of what brings the greatest happiness to the greatest number of people. Well that doesn't justify utilitarianism [simply] to announce it. He's announced that it's a standard. But why, in an atheistic universe, should we live by that standard? Marquis de Sade enjoyed torturing women. Now why should he give up torturing women, so that he may bring greater happiness to those women that he is torturing?

Now, I've got an answer for that. It's not one that Dr. Stein likes, and maybe [it's] not one that you like, but at least I can begin philosophically to deal with that. I have an answer — a universal absolute about morality — Dr. Stein does not. He simply has an announced, stipulated standard. And if morality can be stipulated, then of course Marquis de Sade can stipulate his own even as Dr. Stein has stipulated his own.

Why should he feed the poor? He says they want to do that. I grant that. My argument has never been that atheists are the lousiest people in the world. That's not the point. Some Christians can be pretty lousy, too.

But why is it that I can call atheists or Christians lousy when they act in the ways we're thinking of? [It's] because I have absolute standards of morality to judge. Dr. Stein does not.

Therefore, from a transcendental standpoint the atheistic view cannot account for this debate tonight; because this debate has assumed that we're going to use the laws of logic as standards of reasoning, or else we're irrational; that we're going to use laws of science; that we're going to be intelligent men; that we're going to assume induction and causation and all those things that scientists do. It's assumed in a moral sense that we're not going to be dishonest and try to lie or just try to deceive you.

If there are no laws of morality, I'd just take out a gun right now and say, "OK, Dr. Stein, make my day: is there a God or not?" You see, if he says, "Oh no, you can't murder me because there are laws of morality," of course he has made my day, because I've won the debate. That shows that the atheist's universe is not correct.

But if he says, "Oh no, there are no absolute standards; it's all by convention and stipulation," then I just pull the trigger and I win the debate anyway. Except you wouldn't expect me to win the debate in that fashion. Absolutely not. You came here expecting rational interchange. I don't think we've heard much from Dr. Stein.

I've asked him repeatedly — it's very simple, I don't want a lot of details, just begin to scratch the surface — how, in a material, naturalistic outlook on life and man, his place in the world, can you account for the laws of logic, science, and morality?

The atheist world view cannot do it, and therefore I feel justified concluding as I did in my opening presentation this evening by saying that the proof of the Christian God is the impossibility of the contrary. Without the Christian world view this debate wouldn't make sense.

The Bible tells us, "The fool has said in his heart: there is no God." Don't misunderstand that. When the Bible uses the word *fool* it is not engaging in name-calling. It's trying to describe somebody who is dense in the sense that they will not use their reason as God has given them. Someone who is rebellious and hard-hearted is the fool who says in his heart there is no God.

Paul tells us in I Corinthians, the first chapter, that God has made foolish the wisdom of this world. He calls rhetorically, "Where are the wise? Where is the debater of this age? Hasn't God made foolish the wisdom of this world?" In a sense I think what Paul is telling us, if I can amplify or read between the lines, is that the whole history of Philosophy is an argument for the existence of God. The whole history of Philosophy is an argument for the existence of God because of the impossibility of the contrary.

Someone who wants to say [something that is] contrary to what the Bible says about God let him stand up and answer these questions. Let him show that in his heart he may say there is no God; but he can't live that way. He can't reason that way.

In Romans, the first chapter, Paul says God is making himself known continually and persuasively to all men, so that men do not have an excuse for their rejection of the existence of the Christian God. That isn't to say that all men confess this God. Not all will own up to Him as their heavenly Father. Not all will submit to Him. Some continue to rebel. Some continue to devise their fools' errands and rationalizations of why they don't have to believe in Him.

That's what the Bible teaches. I didn't just come here and make this up. I didn't come here to say, "If you don't agree you're just being rebellious." That is what the Bible says.

What I want you to do tonight is to go home and consider whether there isn't something to that: Why is it that some people continue to use laws of logic, morality, science, and yet they have a world view that just clashes with that; and [yet] they just won't do anything to resolve that contradiction?

Dr. Stein tonight made reference to my doctoral dissertation on self-deception. He wondered how relevant it might be. Well, it's very relevant, because what I do in that doctoral dissertation is to show that there are some people who know the truth and yet work very hard to convince themselves that it's not true.

Now, of course, atheists think that's what Christians are doing. I recognize that and that we'd have to argue about the evidence for and against the self-deception. All I want to leave with you tonight is the fact that self-deception is a real phenomenon. It does happen to people. People can know the truth and yet work very hard to rationalize the evidence, as Paul says, "suppress the truth in unrighteousness" in order to convince themselves that there is no God.

Well, you may want to choose tonight between the Christian world view and the atheist world view. We haven't touched all the issues that you may want to look into. However, in broad strokes we have touched on a very important issue. If you're going to be a rational man, a moral man, a man of science, can you do so in an atheist universe? I say you can't.

SEGMENT FOUR

Moderator: The first question in keeping with our format this evening will be directed to Dr. Greg Bahnsen.

What solid evidence do you have to maintain that the Christian faith is the only true religion with a God? There are religions far older and more or just as widespread which millions of people consider valid. Once again, what solid evidence do you have to maintain that the Christian faith is the only true religion with a God?

Bahnsen: That's a very good and relevant question. I want to say two things just by way of preface.

One, that isn't what the subject of our debate was tonight. However, that can't just be taken for granted and its worthy of a debate. It's just that we couldn't do everything in one debate.

Secondly, you might be interested to know that in my original opening statement, I have a long paragraph dealing with that very question so that it wouldn't be thought that I was just flying over it arbitrarily, and dealing with the matter. But, when I read it back to myself and timed myself, it just turned out that I had to cut a number of things out, and so I cut that down.

What I did say, however, was that — if I can find it here — that I have not found the non-Christian religions to be philosophically defensible, each of them being internally incoherent or undermining human reason and experience.

Unless it will violate your debate format, I'll give just a couple of illustrations; it's obviously not going to cover all of them. But, for instance, Hinduism assumes that God, or *Brahman,* is the impersonal universal soul of the unchanging One of which all things are part, for instance, and because of that particular outlook Hinduism says that everything in terms of my normal experience of the world and thinking is *Maya,* or illusion, because everything in experience and thinking presupposes distinctions. But that is contrary to the most fundamental metaphysical fact, and that is that there are no distinctions — all is one. So basically, Hinduism tells me that all of my thinking, all of my reasoning, is illusion, and in so doing underlies reason.

You can take religions such as Shintoism — it's a view of *Kami* and the forces that permeate the universe — or Taoism, the ordering force in the universe and they are impersonal forces and as such are even less than human beings because they don't have volition or intelligence.

Stein: Well, Dr. Bahnsen has criticized Hinduism.

I would make the case that Hinduism is no more irrational than Christianity is, nor do I think it is anymore irrational than Islam is, nor is it anymore irrational than almost any other religion that you might name. With one exception, I'd say Buddhism is more rational than either Christianity or Hinduism. That doesn't mean I accept Buddhism either, but I just think it's more rational; at least it makes some psychological sense if nothing else.

Moderator: The next question will be directed to you, Dr. Stein. And the question reads as follows:

According to your definition and basis for evil, why was Hitler's Germany wrong or was it? Note: Jews and others were defined as non-persons, so their happiness doesn't really count. Once again, according to you definition and basis for evil, why was Hitler's Germany wrong, or was it?

Stein: Well, Germany is part of the Western European tradition; it's not deepest Africa, or some place or Mars.

They have the same Judeo-Christian background and basically the same connection with the rest of the developed world, so therefore the standards of morality that have been worked out as consensuses of that society apply to them, too.

They can't arbitrarily, Hitler can't arbitrarily, say, "Well, I'm not going by the consensuses that genocide is evil or wrong. I'm just going to change it and make it right." He has not the prerogative to do that; neither does the German society as a whole because it is still a part of a larger society, which you might call a Western society.

So, even though morality is a consensus of an entire civilization, he cannot just arbitrarily do that, so what he did is evil and wrong.

Bahnsen: Dr. Stein continues to beg the most important questions that are brought up.

He tells us that Hitler's Germany was wrong because Hitler or the German people didn't have the right to break out of the consensus of Western civilization. Why not? Why is there any moral obligation upon Hitler and the German people to live up to the past tradition of Western morality? In an atheist universe there is no answer to that question. He gives the answer, but it is totally arbitrary.

Moderator: Next question is directed to you, Dr. Bahnsen. Why is there pain and evil in the world?

Bahnsen: There are a number of answers that could be given to a question, "Why is something the way it is?"

One relevant one, but not the most ultimate answer, would be that there is pain and evil in this world because men have decided to rebel against God, their maker, and that's one of the consequences of rebelling against God.

Now somebody can say, "Well, that's not fair, God shouldn't punish people for rebelling against Him." Well, if there is a God, as I have maintained, and if he is the Christian God as revealed in Scriptures, it won't do any good to complain about that. That's the way God governs mankind and if you think you know better than God about morality, then you're in Job's position. You want to have an interview with God and you'll end up like Job. You'll put your hand over your mouth and you'll say, "I've spoken too soon. I can't contend with the Almighty."

One answer is that God has decided what would be the outcome of people who decided to rebel against Him; and if they want to be their own little gods, if they want to make their own rules of morality and live by them, then the consequences are going to be such and such, and that includes pain for animals in the created order, because in so doing man represented all of creation.

Even as the second man, Jesus Christ, represents all of creation, and the new heavens and the new earth, which I believe based on faith in the Scriptures is yet to come. In that new heavens and new earth, there will be a redeemed earth where pain and suffering have been removed.

Why is there evil ultimately? The answer is obviously because God has planned it. I believe that he governs everything that's in history. Does that mean that he caused it? No, I don't believe he compelled Adam to fall into sin.

Stein: Well, Dr. Bahnsen has given us another one of his famous non-answers. Basically, what he said is anything God does is what He does. It's a tautology, it doesn't say anything.

Now, how can someone rebel against omnipotent God? This is a logical self-contradiction. If God is omnipotent, He has the power to prevent them from rebelling against him. And assuming he doesn't like rebellion — which I think Dr. Bahnsen would concede, because man is evidently going to be punished for this in some way for his rebellion, eventually, on the Day of Judgment — if God had the power to prevent them from rebelling, then he *ought* to [have] prevented them from rebelling.

And just to say the God does what he does is not to give us an answer at all.

Moderator: The next question is directed to you, Dr. Stein. It reads:

If you haven't examined all the evidence, then is it not true that you are really an agnostic? Isn't it true that you are open to the fact that God may exist? If you haven't examined all the evidence, then isn't it true that you are an agnostic?

Stein: Well, *agnostic* is a word that is very badly used. Thomas Huxley, who invented the word, used it in an entirely different way from the way we use it today. And in fact, the way we use it today is entirely different from the way Herbert Spencer used it.

I would define an agnostic as a subtype of atheist. An atheist is someone who does not believe in a God. A theist is someone who does believe in a God. There's no middle ground. You either do or you don't.

Now an agnostic doesn't not believe in a God because of either one or two things.

Either he thinks it's impossible to know if there is one or not. That's the Spencerian, the Herbert Spencer-type agnostic that thinks there are unknowables. Or secondly, because he or she has never examined the evidence that exists and therefore has not made up his or her mind, but still at this point he does not believe in a God. Now if he examined the evidence and found it convincing, then he would move into the theist camp.

So, no, I am not an agnostic because I do think that these answers to these questions are sound; if not, maybe we do not know the answer now, but I think we can eventually know the answer so I'm not a Spencerian agnostic, and I have examined things so I'm not the other kind of agnostic. Whatever that kind is called, they don't have a name for it.

Bahnsen: It's interesting that the word *agnostic* is being used as a subclass of *atheist*. I would agree with that, but for reasons different than have been suggested.

It's also interesting, that *atheist* is being redefined.

Earlier in the debate an atheist is one who finds a theist's proofs inadequate. I said, "No, traditionally an atheist is one who denies the existence of God, or he doesn't believe in the existence of God." Now he's using the traditional definition to answer the question.

One more interesting comment about that and we'll let it go; he says, "We do believe there are answers to these problems. We have yet to find them." You see, that's the problem: atheists live by faith.

Moderator: The final set of questions are here before me. Dr. Bahnsen, the question for you reads: Why is it necessary for the abstract universal laws to be … derived from the transcendental nature of God? Why not assume the transcendental nature of logic?

Bahnsen: Somebody who wrote the question is good, in that you've studied philosophical issues.

The answer may not be meaningful to everybody in the audience, but very briefly, it is that I *do* believe in the transcendental nature of the laws of logic. However, the laws of logic do not justify themselves just because they are transcendental, that is a precondition of intelligibility. Why isn't it just "sound and fury signifying nothing"? That's a possibility too.

So the laws of logic do have a transcendental necessity about them; but it seems to me you need to have a world view in which the laws of logic are meaningful; especially when you consider such possible antinomies as the laws of logic being universal and categorizing things in that way and yet we have novelties in our experience. I mean the world of empirical observation isn't set rigidly by uniformity and by sameness, as it were. There isn't a continuity in experience in that way as there is a necessary continuity in the laws of logic.

How can the laws of logic, then, be utilized when it comes to matters of personal experience in the world? We have a contingent changing world and unchanging and variant laws of logic. How can these two be brought together? You need a world view in which the transcendental necessity of logic can make sense of the human experience. I believe Christianity provides that and I just can't find any other one that competes with it that way.

Stein: I do not have a rebuttal to that particular answer. I do have a rebuttal … to the last rebuttal if I may make that very briefly.

Dr. Bahnsen's comment that atheists believe things on faith is a false statement. We have confidence based on experience. We have confidence that things happen in a certain way, that we have learned a lot of things about the world; and therefore, we will continue to learn a lot more about the world, things that we do not know now, we will eventually have answers to. That's not faith, that's confidence based on experience. So, I think he's misusing the word faith.

Moderator: Dr. Stein, the final question is directed to you. It reads: You have said that there has been no adequate evidence put forth for God's existence. What for you personally would constitute adequate evidence for God's existence?

Stein: Well, it's very simple. I can give you two examples.

If that podium suddenly rose into the air five feet, stayed there for a minute and then dropped right down again, I would say that is evidence of a supernatural because it would violate everything we knew about the laws of physics and chemistry.

Assuming that there wasn't an engine under there or a wire attached to it, we can make those obvious exclusions. That would be evidence for a supernatural violation of the laws. We could call it a miracle right before your eyes. That would be evidence I would accept.

Any kind of a supernatural being putting it into appearance and doing miracles that could not be stage magic would also be evidence that I would accept. Those are the two simplest ways. I would also accept evidence that is logically non-contradictory, and I have not heard any yet here tonight that hasn't been offered already.

Bahnsen: Dr. Stein, I think, is really not reflecting on the true nature of atheism and human nature when he says, "All it would take is a miracle in my very presence to believe in God." History is replete with first of all things which would be apparently miracles to people.

Now, from an atheistic or naturalistic standpoint, I will grant, in terms of the hypothesis, that that's because they were ignorant of all the calls of factors and so it appeared to be miracles. But you see that didn't make everybody into a theist. In fact, the Scriptures tell us that there were instances of people who witnessed miracles, who all the more hardened their heart, and eventually crucified the Lord of glory. They saw his miracles, that didn't change their mind.

People are not made theists by miracles. People must change their world views; their hearts must be changed. They need to be converted. That's what it takes, and that's what it would take for Dr. Stein to finally believe it. If this podium rose up five feet off the ground and stayed there, Dr. Stein would eventually have in the future some naturalistic explanation because they believe things on faith, by which I mean that they believe things which they have not proven by their senses.

CHAPTER 16

The Wager

Blaise Pascal

Infinite nothing. Our soul is cast into a body, where it finds number, dimension. Thereupon it reasons, and calls this nature necessity, and can believe nothing else.

Unity joined to infinity adds nothing to it, no more than one foot to an infinite measure. The finite is annihilated in the presence of the infinite, and becomes a pure nothing. So our spirit before God, so our justice before divine justice. There is not so great a disproportion between our justice and that of God as between unity and infinity. The justice of God must be vast like His compassion. Now justice to the outcast is less vast and ought less to offend our feelings than mercy towards the elect.

We know that there is an infinite, and are ignorant of its nature. As we know it to be false that numbers are finite, it is therefore true that there is an infinity in number. But we do not know what it is. It is false that it is even, it is false that it is odd; for the addition of a unit can make no change in its nature. Yet it is a number, and every number is odd or even (this is certainly true of every finite number). So we may well know that there is a God without knowing what He is. Is there not one substantial truth, seeing there are so many things which are not the truth itself? We know then the existence and nature of the finite, because we also are finite and have extension. We know the existence of the infinite and are ignorant of its nature, because it has extension like us, but not limits like us. But we know neither the existence nor the nature of God, because He has neither extension nor limits.

But by faith we know His existence; in glory we shall know His nature. Now, I have already shown that we may well know the existence of a thing, without knowing its nature.

Let us now speak according to natural lights. If there is a God, He is infinitely incomprehensible, since, having neither parts nor limits, He has no affinity to us. We are then incapable of knowing either what He is or if He is. This being so, who will dare to undertake the decision of the question? Not we, who have no affinity to Him.

Who then will blame Christians for not being able to give a reason for their belief, since they profess a religion for which they cannot give a reason? They declare, in expounding it to the world, that it is a foolishness, *stultitiam* [I Cor. 1. 21] and then you complain that they do not prove it! If they proved it, they would not keep their word; it is in lacking proofs that they are not lacking in sense. "Yes, but although this excuses those who offer it as such and takes away from them the blame of putting it forward without reason, it does not excuse those who receive it." Let us then examine this point, and say, "God is, or He is not." But to which side shall we incline? Reason can decide nothing here. There is an infinite chaos which separated us. A game is being played at the extremity of this infinite distance where heads or tails will turn up. What will you wager? According to reason, you can do neither the one thing nor the other; according to reason, you can defend neither of the propositions.

Do not, then, reprove for error those who have made a choice; for you know nothing about it. "No, but I blame them for having made, not this choice, but a choice; for again both he who chooses heads and he who chooses tails are equally at fault, they are both in the wrong. The true course is not to wager at all."

Yes; but you must wager. It is not optional. You are embarked. Which will you choose then? Let us see.

Since you must choose, let us see which interests you least. You have two things to lose, the true and the good; and two things to stake, your reason and your will, your knowledge and your happiness; and your nature has two things to shun, error and misery. Your reason is no more shocked in choosing one rather than the other, since you must of necessity choose. This is one point settled. But your happiness? Let us weigh the gain and the loss in wagering that God is. Let us estimate these two chances. If you gain, you gain all; if you lose, you lose nothing. Wager, then, without hesitation that He is. "That is very fine. Yes, I must wager; but I may perhaps wager too much." Let us see. Since there is an equal risk of gain and of loss, if you had only to gain two lives, instead of one, you might still wager. But if there were three lives to gain, you would have to play (since you are under the necessity of playing), and you would be imprudent, when you are forced to play, not to chance your life to gain three at a game where there is an equal risk of loss and gain. But there is an eternity of life and happiness. And this being so, if there were an infinity of chances, of which one only would be for you, you would still be right in wagering one to win two, and you would act stupidly, being obliged to play, by refusing to stake one life against three at a game in which out of an infinity of chances there is one for you, if there were an infinity of an infinitely happy life to gain. But there is here an infinity of an infinitely happy life to gain, a chance of gain against a finite number of chances of loss, and what you stake is finite. It is all divided; wherever the infinite is and there is not an infinity of chances of loss against that of gain, there is no time to hesitate, you must give all. And thus, when one is forced to play, he must renounce reason to preserve his life, rather than risk it for infinite gain, as likely to happen as the loss of nothingness.

For it is no use to say it is uncertain if we will gain, and it is certain that we risk, and that the infinite distance between the *certainty* of what is staked and the *uncertainty* of what will be gained, equals the finite good which is certainly staked against the uncertain infinite. It is not so, as every player stakes a certainty to gain an uncertainty, and yet he stakes a finite certainty to gain a finite uncertainty, without transgressing against reason. There is not an infinite distance between the certainty staked and the uncertainty of the gain; that is untrue. In truth, there is an infinity between the certainty of gain and the certainty of loss. But the uncertainty of the gain is proportioned to the certainty of the stake according to the proportion of the chances of gain and loss. Hence it comes that, if there are as many risks on one side as on the other, the course is to play even; and then the certainty of the stake is equal to the uncertainty of the gain, so far is it from fact that there is an infinite distance between them. And so our proposition is of infinite force, when there is the finite to stake in a game where there are equal risks of gain and of loss, and the infinite to gain. This is demonstrable; and if men are capable of any truths, this is one.

"I confess it, I admit it. But, still, is there no means of seeing the faces of the cards?" Yes, Scripture and the rest, etc. "Yes, but I have my hands tied and my mouth closed; I am forced to wager, and am not free. I am not released, and am so made that I cannot believe. What, then, would you have me do?"

True. But at least learn your inability to believe, since reason brings you to this, and yet you cannot believe. Endeavour, then, to convince yourself, not by increase of proofs of God, but by the abatement of your passions. You would like to attain faith and do not know the way; you would like to cure yourself of unbelief and ask the remedy for it. Learn of those who have been bound like you, and who now stake all their possessions. These are people who know the way which you would follow, and who are cured of an ill of which you would be cured. Follow the way by which they began; by acting as if they believed, taking the holy water, having masses said, etc. Even this will naturally make you believe, and deaden your acuteness. "But this is what I am afraid of." And why? What have you to lose?

But to show you that this leads you there, it is this which will lessen the passions, which are your stumbling blocks.

The end of this discourse. Now, what harm will befall you in taking this side? You will be faithful, humble, grateful, generous, a sincere friend, truthful. Certainly you will not have those poisonous pleasures, glory and luxury; but will you not have others? I will tell you that you will thereby gain in this life, and that, at each step you take on this road, you will see so great certainty of gain, so much nothingness in what you risk, that you will at last recognize that you have wagered for something certain and infinite, for which you have given nothing.

"Ah! This discourse transports me, charms me," etc.

If this discourse pleases you and seems impressive, know that it is made by a man who has knelt, both before and after it, in prayer to that Being, infinite and without parts, before whom he lays all he has, for you also to lay before Him all you have for your own good and for His glory, so that strength may be given to lowliness.

CHAPTER 17

God and the Moral Law

C. S. Lewis

Everyone has heard people quarrelling. Sometimes it sounds funny and sometimes it sounds merely unpleasant; but however it sounds, I believe we can learn something very important from listening to the kind of things they say. They say things like this: 'How'd you like it if anyone did the same to you ?' – 'That's my seat, I was there first' – 'Leave him alone, he isn't doing you any harm' – 'Why should you shove in first?' – 'Give me a bit of your orange, I gave you a bit of mine' – 'Come on, you promised.' People say things like that every day, educated people as well as uneducated, and children as well as grown-ups.

Now what interests me about all these remarks is that the man who makes them is not merely saying that the other man's behaviour does not happen to please him. He is appealing to some kind of standard of behaviour which he expects the other man to know about. And the other man very seldom replies: 'To hell with your standard.' Nearly always he tries to make out that what he has been doing does not really go against the standard, or that if it does there is some special excuse. He pretends there is some special reason in this particular case why the person who took the seat first should not keep it, or that things were quite different when he was given the bit of orange, or that something has turned up which lets him off keeping his promise. It looks, in fact, very much as if both parties had in mind some kind of Law or Rule of fair play or decent behaviour or morality or whatever you like to call it, about which they really agreed. And they have. If they had not, they might, of course, fight like animals, but they could not quarrel in the human sense of the word. Quarrelling means trying to show that the other man is in the wrong. And there would

be no sense in trying to do that unless you and he had some sort of agreement as to what Right and Wrong are; just as there would be no sense in saying that a footballer had committed a foul unless there was some agreement about the rules of football.

Now this Law or Rule about Right and Wrong used to be called the Law of Nature. Nowadays, when we talk of the 'laws of nature' we usually mean things like gravitation, or heredity, or the laws of chemistry. But when the older thinkers called the Law of Right and Wrong 'the Law of Nature', they really meant the Law of Human Nature. The idea was that, just as all bodies are governed by the law of gravitation, and organisms by biological laws, so the creature called man also had his law – with this great difference, that a body could not choose whether it obeyed the law of gravitation or not, but a man could choose either to obey the Law of Human Nature or to disobey it.

We may put this in another way. Each man is at every moment subjected to several different sets of law but there is only one of these which he is free to disobey. As a body, he is subjected to gravitation and cannot disobey it; if you leave him unsupported in mid-air, he has no more choice about falling than a stone has. As an organism, he is subjected to various biological laws which he cannot disobey any more than an animal can. That is, he cannot disobey those laws which he shares with other things; but the law which is peculiar to his human nature, the law he does not share with animals or vegetables or inorganic things, is the one he can disobey if he chooses.

This law was called the Law of Nature because people thought that every one knew it by nature and did not need to be taught it. They did not mean, of

Deprestione is though by one who knows the better way to

the reverse of one who say what is or what is not

course, that you might not find an odd individual here and there who did not know it, just as you find a few people who are colour-blind or have no ear for a tune. But taking the race as a whole, they thought that the human idea of decent behaviour was obvious to every one. And I believe they were right. If they were not, then all the things we said about the war were nonsense. What was the sense in saying the enemy were in the wrong unless Right is a real thing which the Nazis at bottom knew as well as we did and ought to have practised? If they had had no notion of what we mean by right, then, though we might still have had to fight them, we could no more have blamed them for that than for the colour of their hair.

I know that some people say the idea of a Law of Nature or decent behaviour known to all men is unsound, because different civilisations and different ages have had quite different moralities.

But this is not true. There have been differences between their moralities, but these have never amounted to anything like a total difference. If anyone will take the trouble to compare the moral teaching of, say, the ancient Egyptians, Babylonians, Hindus, Chinese, Greeks and Romans, what will really strike him will be how very like they are to each other and to our own. Some of the evidence for this I have put together in the appendix of another book called *The Abolition of Man*; but for our present purpose I need only ask the reader to think what a totally different morality would mean. Think of a country where people were admired for running away in battle, or where a man felt proud of double-crossing all the people who had been kindest to him. You might just as well try to imagine a country where two and two made five. Men have differed as regards what people you ought to be unselfish to – whether it was only your own family, or your fellow countrymen, or every one. But they have always agreed that you ought not to put yourself first. Selfishness has never been admired. Men have differed as to whether you should have one wife or four. But they have always agreed that you must not simply have any woman you liked.

But the most remarkable thing is this. Whenever you find a man who says he does not believe in a real Right and Wrong, you will find the same man going back on this a moment later. He may break his promise to you, but if you try breaking one to him he will be complaining 'It's not fair' before you can say Jack Robinson. A nation may say treaties don't matter; but then next minute, they spoil their case by saying that the particular treaty they want to break was an unfair one. But if treaties do not matter, and if there is no such thing as Right and Wrong – in other words, if there is no Law of Nature – what is the difference between a fair treaty and an unfair one? Have they not let the cat out of the bag and shown that, whatever they say, they really know the Law of Nature just like anyone else?

It seems, then, we are forced to believe in a real Right and Wrong. People may be sometimes mistaken about them, just as people sometimes get their sums wrong; but they are not a matter of mere taste and opinion any more than the multiplication table. Now if we are agreed about that, I go on to my next point, which is this. None of us are really keeping the Law of Nature. If there are any exceptions among you, I apologise to them. They had much better read some other book, for nothing I am going to say concerns them. And now, turning to the ordinary human beings who are left: I hope you will not misunderstand what I am going to say. I am not preaching, and Heaven knows I do not pretend to be better than anyone else. I am only trying to call attention to a fact; the fact that this year, or this month, or, more likely, this very day, we have failed to practise ourselves the kind of behaviour we expect from other people. There may be all sorts of excuses for us. That time you were so unfair to the children was when you were very tired. That slightly shady business about the money – the one you have almost forgotten – came when you were very hard-up. And what you promised to do for old So-and-so and have never done – well, you never would have promised if you had known how frightfully busy you were going to be. And as for your behaviour to your wife (or husband) or sister (or brother) if I knew how irritating they could be, I would not wonder at it – and who the dickens am I, anyway? I am just the same.

the heart of man Genesis

That is to say, I do not succeed in keeping the Law of Nature very well, and the moment anyone tells me I am not keeping it, there starts up in my mind a string of excuses as long as your arm. The question at the moment is not whether they are good excuses. The point is that they are one more proof of how deeply, whether we like it or not, we believe in the Law of Nature. If we do not believe in decent behaviour, why should we be so anxious to make excuses for not having behaved decently? The truth is, we believe in decency so much – we feel the Rule of Law pressing on us so – that we cannot bear to face the fact that we are breaking it, and consequently we try to shift the responsibility. For you notice that it is only for our bad behaviour that we find all these explanations. It is only our bad temper that we put down to being tired or worried or hungry; we put our good temper down to ourselves. → *must thank God for that.*

These, then, are the two points I wanted to make. First, that human beings, all over the earth, have this curious idea that they ought to behave in a certain way, and cannot really get rid of it. Secondly, that they do not in fact behave in that way. They know the Law of Nature; they break it. These two facts are the foundation of all clear thinking about ourselves and the universe we live in.

* *for Christian, should I dare say all know the simple command of love god and love your neighbor, yet they Break it.*

CHAPTER 18

The Moral Argument

Paul Copan

French Catholic philosopher Jacques Maritain helped draft the United Nations Declaration of Human Rights (1948), which recognizes "the inherent dignity" and "the equal and inalienable rights of all members of the human family." Further, it affirms: "All human beings are born free and equal in dignity and rights. They are endowed with reason and conscience and should act towards one another in a spirit of brotherhood." What is missing, though, is any foundation or basis for human dignity and rights. In light of the philosophical discussion behind the drafting of the Declaration, Maritain wrote: "We agree on these rights, providing we are not asked why. With the 'why,' the dispute begins.[1]

The dispute about morality involves a host of questions about whether objective/universal moral values exist and whether humans have dignity and rights—and if so, what their source is. Are moral values emergent properties, supervening upon natural processes and social configurations, or are beliefs about moral values an adaptation hard-wired into human beings who, like other organisms, fight, reed, flee, and reproduce? Does God offer any metaphysical foundation for moral values and human dignity, or can a Platonic, Aristotelian, categorical imperative (Kantian), or Ideal Observer ethic adequately account for them?

This essay argues, *first,* that objective moral values are an inescapable, properly basic bedrock. Moral subjectivism is inadequate to account for our fundamental intuitions, including ones about evil. *Second,*

certain naturalistic moral realists commonly confuse the *order of knowing* with the *order of being.* Since all humans are God's image-bearers, it isn't surprising that they are capable of recognizing or knowing the same sorts of moral values—whether theists or not. The metaphysical question is the more fundamental: How did there come to *be* morally responsible persons in the absence of God and as products of value-less processes? I would maintain that a moral universe is far less likely—indeed extremely difficult to come by—if God does not exist. Naturalism provides a poor context for objective moral values, duties, and human dignity.

Third, in various ways, naturalism undermines objective ethics despite attempts to root it in science. *Fourth,* a naturalistic evolutionary account of morality fails to engage our deepest moral intuitions about right and wrong, and it leaves us skeptical about whether we can have confidence about fundamental epistemic and moral convictions. Any confidence would borrow metaphysical capital from a worldview like theism, as humans have been made in the image of a faithful, truthful, and rational Being. *Finally,* despite the claims of naturalistic moral realists, any appeals to Plato's Euthyphro dilemma fail to render God superfluous in accounting for the source of objective moral values.

A moral universe and human dignity are best explained in the context of a morally excellent, worship-worthy Being as their metaphysical foundation, as opposed to nontheistic alternatives,[2] and naturalism

---

1. Jacques Maritain, *Man and the State* (Chicago: University of Chicago Press, 1951), 77.

2. These nontheistic alternatives such as Jainism, Taoism, or Buddhism have difficulty grounding human rights and dignity and

objective moral values. An *impersonal* ultimate reality, it seems, cannot adequately ground *personal* virtues such as love, kindness, and compassion. Ninian Smart, scholar of Asian philosophy and religion, observes that the "concept of the importance of the historical in particular.[3] If objective moral values and human dignity and rights are a reality (and there is very good reason to think they are), then it is extremely likely that some intrinsically valuable Being and Creator exists.

The Proper Basicality of Moral Values

We are wise to assume that our senses, our powers of reasoning, and our most fundamental moral instincts are not systematically deceiving us. We should — and typically do — take for granted their adequate function. Indeed, even the most radical skeptic assumes this as he confidently draws his skeptical conclusions. He appropriates various logical laws to prove his point and, no doubt believing those claiming to have knowledge to be in error, presumes that others ought to share his inferences. Whatever epistemological blunders humans may make, they are not sufficient to justify a deep skepticism. Yes, humans may misperceive or make logical missteps. However, such mistakes hardly call into question the general reliability of our sense or reasoning powers; indeed, they presuppose it. The ability to detect error presumes an awareness of truth.

Likewise, despite flawed moral judgments, there still are certain moral truths that we can't *not* know — unless we suppress our conscience or engage in self-deception.[4] We possess an in-built "yuck factor" — basic moral intuitions about the wrongness of torturing babies for fun, of raping, murdering, or abusing children. We can also recognize the virtue of kindness or selflessness, the obligation to treat others as we would want to be treated, and the moral difference between Mother Teresa and Josef Stalin. Those not recognizing such truths as properly basic are simply wrong and morally dysfunctional. We need no social contract or established methodology to recognize the rights of all humans before the law as well as the wrongness of racism or ethnocentrism. For instance, blacks had value before any civil rights legislation in the United States or South Africa. We can agree with Nicholas Rescher, who observes that if members of a particular tribe think that sacrificing firstborn children is acceptable, "then their grasp on the conception of morality is somewhere between inadequate and nonexistent."[5]

Morality isn't a superficial feature of our world. Atheist David O. Brink asserts, "Our commitment to the *objectivity of ethics* is a deep one."[6] Kai Nielsen deems such a moral awareness to be "bedrock":

> It is more reasonable to believe such elemental things [as wife-beating and child abuse] to be evil than to believe any skeptical theory that tells us we cannot know or reasonably believe any of these things to be evil.... I firmly believe that this is bedrock and right and that anyone who does not believe it cannot have probed deeply enough into the grounds of his moral beliefs.[7]

That is, basic moral principles are *discovered,* not *invented,* and persons with a decently functioning conscience can get a lot of moral things right. As C. S. Lewis has pointed out, law codes across civilizations and throughout history (Egyptian, Babylonian, Greek, Native American, and so on) reveal a continual resurfacing of the same basic moral standards — do not murder, break promises, take another's property,

process is largely foreign to these faiths," adding that "the notion of a personal God is altogether less prominent." Ninian Smart, "Religion as a Discipline," in *Concept and Empathy,* ed. Donald Wiebe (New York: New York University Press, 1986), 161. So, though I respond to naturalism here, my argument would apply to any nonpersonal metaphysic of ultimate reality.

3. Incidentally, I respond to various Humean sorts of objections that attempt to diminish the force of objections to natural theology: see chap. 8 in Paul Copan, *Loving Wisdom: Christian Philosophy of Religion* (St. Louis: Chalice, 2007); idem, "Hume and the Moral Argument," in *In Defense of Natural Theology: A Post-Humean Assessment,* ed. James F. Sennett and Douglas Groothuis, 2005),

200 – 225; and Paul Copan and Paul K. Moser, "Introduction," in *The Rationality of Theism* (London: Routledge, 2003), 1 – 10.

4. J. Budziszewski, *What We Can't Not Know* (Dallas: Spence, 2003).

5. Nicholas Rescher, *Moral Absolutes: An Essay on the Nature and Rationale of Morality,* Studies in Moral Philosophy, vol. 2 (New York: Peter Lang, 1989), 43.

6. O. Brink, "The Autonomy of Ethics," in *The Cambridge Companion to Atheism,* ed. Michael Martin (Cambridge: Cambridge University Press, 2006), 149.

7. Kai Nielsen, *Ethics without God,* rev. ed. (Buffalo: Prometheus, 1990), 10 – 11.

or defraud.[8] Despite our faulty moral judgments, we would be wrong to abandon the quest for goodness or become moral skeptics: "we cannot always or even usually be totally mistaken about goodness," Robert Adams affirms.[9]

Such an affirmation of human dignity, rights,[10] and duties is something we would readily expect if God exists — but *not* if humans have emerged from valueless, mindless processes (more below). The Jewish-Christian Scriptures assume that humans are morally responsible agents who can generally know what is good and that we ought to do it. The prophet Amos delivers severe divine warnings to surrounding Gentile nations for their atrocities and crimes against humanity — ripping open pregnant women, breaking treaties, acting treacherously, stifling compassion. The underlying assumption is that these nations — even without God's special revelation — should have known better (Amos 1 – 2). The same perspective is expressed more explicitly by Paul, who speaks of Gentiles without the Law of Moses who still have a law — a conscience — "written in their hearts" (Rom. 2:14 – 15).

Philosopher Thomas Reid argued that basic moral principles such as, "treat another as you desire to be treated," are simply commonsensical — obvious to those who have not ignored their conscience. He claimed he did not know by what reasoning — demonstrative or probable — he could convince the epistemic or moral skeptic:

> The sceptic asks me, Why do you believe the existence of the external object which you perceive? This belief, sir, is none of my manufacture; it came from the mint of Nature; it bears her image and superscription; and, if it is not right, the fault is not mine. I ever took it upon trust, and without suspicion.[11]

According to Reid, morality begins with certain axioms or first principles, which are self-evident to the properly functioning human being. To reject God's law written on our hearts (the conscience with its fundamental inclinations) is to act unnaturally.[12] Being God's image-bearer, the atheist can recognize the same moral truths as the theist because this "faculty [is] given him by God." If God had not bestowed this faculty upon humans, none of us would be "a moral and accountable being."[13] Although basic moral principles — to be kind, selfless, and compassionate; to avoid torturing for fun, raping, or taking innocent human life — are accessible and knowable to morally sensitive human beings, some improperly functioning individuals may be self-deceived or hard-hearted sophists.

Thus, we should reasonably believe what is apparent or obvious to us unless there are overriding reasons to dismiss it (the credulity principle) a belief that applies to our *sense* perception, our *reasoning* faculty, and our *moral* intuitions/perceptions. In general, we take for granted the innocence of these capacities until they are proven guilty. We should accept their testimony *unless* we have strong reasons to doubt them. Indeed, the common argument from evil launched against belief in God still takes for granted a fundamental standard of goodness or a design-plan, which is difficult to account for if God does not exist and the material universe is the sum total of reality.

Robert Audi offers a description of how such moral intuitions function. They are (1) *noninferential or directly apprehended;* (2) *firm* (they must be believed as propositions); (3) *comprehensible* (intuitions are formed in the light of an adequate understanding of their propositional objects); and (4) *pretheoretical*

---

8. Appendix, C. S. Lewis, *The Abolition of Man* (San Francisco: HarperSanFrancisco, 2001), 83 – 101.

9. Robert M. Adams, *Finite and Infinite Goods: Framework for Ethics* (New York: Oxford University Press, 1999), 20.

10. Robert Audi notes that *dignity* is the ground of *rights*. When those rights are not observed, this violates one's dignity. "Dignity … provides a bridge between the axiological and the deontic, between value and obligation." *Moral Knowledge and Ethical Character* (New York: Oxford University Press, 1997), 263, 264.

11. In *Thomas Reid's Inquiry and Essays*, ed. Keith Lehrer

and Ronald E. Beanblossom (Indianapolis: Bobbs-Merrill, 1975), 84 – 85.

12. See Essay 3 in Thomas Reid, "Of the First Principles of Morals," in *Essays on the Active Powers of the Human Mind*, intro. B. A. Brody (Cambridge, Mass.: MIT Press, 1969), 364 – 67.

13. Thomas Reid, Essay 7 in "Whether Morality Be Demonstrable," in "Essays on the Intellectual Powers of Man," ed., D. Stewart, *The Works of Thomas Reid*, vol. 2 (New York: Bangs and Mason, 1822), 381.

(not dependent on theories nor themselves theoretical hypotheses). Such moral knowledge emerges not from reflection on abstract principles but from reflecting on particular moral cases. And however strong, these prima facie intuitions are *not* thereby indefeasible. That is, they may be adjusted or refined in light of other considerations or overriding circumstances. For instance, keeping a promise may be overridden by circumstances preventing me from keeping it, but I still have a duty to explain to my friend why I could not keep the promise.[14]

Consider Daniel Dennett's declaration that, given our evolution, ethical decision-making "holds out scant hope of our ever discovering a formula or an algorithm for doing right." Rather than despairing, he advocates using our "mind-tools" to "design and redesign ourselves" as we continually search for better solutions to the sorts of moral challenges we face.[15] This point is well taken, and the pursuit of universal moral agreement is not going to be achievable. However, the discerning moral realist will take into account circumstances, motives, and conflicting moral duties — not to mention the importance of moral dialogue and the moral lessons learned from history and moral reforms. We can reject a simplistic "algorithm" approach while acknowledging genuine moral duties and the importance of virtuous character. So we can still live wisely and morally despite moral puzzles and challenges.[16] The existence of "gray areas" doesn't mean that we cannot readily recognize basic objective moral values. We must begin with the clear and move to the unclear, not vice versa — and proceed as wisely as we can. Dr. Samuel Johnson reminds us: the fact that there is such a thing as twilight does not mean that we cannot distinguish between day and night.[17]

Knowing versus Being, Metaphysical Contexts, and Choosing the Better Alternative

Knowing versus Being

Certain atheists may question how God's nonexistence would adversely affect the goodness of compassion, mercy, justice, and other virtues. Richard Dawkins — despite his moral subjectivism — maintains that we do not need a God nor must we believe God is constantly policing us in order to be good. In fact, if belief in God would suddenly vanish from the world, people wouldn't become "callous and selfish hedonists, with no kindness, no charity, no generosity."[18]

Likewise, Daniel Dennett (a moral realist) challenges the notion that goodness is opposed to scientific materialism: "There is *no reason at all* why a disbelief in the immateriality or immortality of the soul should make a person less caring, less moral, less committed to the well-being of everybody on Earth than somebody who believes in 'the spirit.'" He adds that a "good scientific materialist" can be concerned about "whether there is plenty of justice, love, joy, beauty, political freedom, and yes, even religious freedom" as the "deeply spiritual."[19] And he quite rightly observes that those calling themselves spiritual can be "cruel, arrogant, self-centered, and utterly unconcerned about the moral problems of the world."[20]

According to naturalistic moral realists, one can *both* affirm objective moral values (for example, that kindness is a virtue) *and* deny the existence of God — with perfect consistency. David O. Brink insists that "the objectivity of ethics is not hostage to the truth of theism."[21] William Rowe, another atheist, asserts that

14. Robert Audi, *Moral Knowledge and Ethical Character*, part 3.

15. Daniel Dennett, *Darwin's Dangerous Idea* (New York: Simon and Schuster, 1995), 510.

16. For some explorations on this topic. see Gerard Casey, "Ethics and Human Nature," *American Catholic Philosophical Quarterly* 77, no. 4 (Fall 2003): 521–33. James B. Reichmann, *Evolution, Animal "Rights," and the Environment* (Washington. D.C.: Catholic University of America Press, 2000).

17. See Alvin Plantinga, *Warranted Christian Belief* (New York:

Oxford University Press, 2001), 202.

18. Richard Dawkins, *The God Delusion* (Boston: Houghton Mifflin, 2006), 226, 227.

19. Daniel C. Dennett, *Breaking the Spell: Religion as a Natural Phenomenon* (New York: Viking, 2006), 305 (his italics).

20. Ibid.

21. Brink, "The Autonomy of Ethics," 150. Brink gives a list of what he calls "commonsense morality" (cp. properly basic moral intuitions mentioned in the first section): "compliance with norms

morality (or logic or mathematics) has the same objective status for atheist and theist alike: "the claim that God is needed for morality to be objective is absurd."[22] Christians will give the same reasons as atheists about, say, the immorality of rape (for example, "rape violates the victim's rights and undermines societal cohesion"). No need to appeal to God's existence![23]

However, theists can readily admit that nonbelievers can *know* moral truths. But *knowing* (epistemology) must be distinguished from *being* (ontology), the latter being the more fundamental. *Epistemologically*, the atheist is right: because *all* humans have been made in God's image (Gen. 1:26–27, 9:3; James 3:9)[24] and are thus intrinsically valuable (endowed with dignity, conscience, rights, duties, and the basic capacity to recognize right and wrong), it is no surprise that nontheists of all stripes know the same sorts of moral truths as believers. *Ontologically*, however, a nontheistic metaphysic (that is, the *actual ground* or *basis* that makes moral knowledge possible) is inadequate: Why think impersonal/physical, valueless processes will produce valuable, rights-bearing persons?[25]

Theism has the metaphysical wherewithal to account for such values: there is an intimate connection between *(a)* a good God and Creator (the metaphysical foundation) and *(b)* human dignity/rights, and general moral obligations. God is the necessarily good Source of all finite goods.[26] So anyone can *know* that humans have rights and dignity and obligations. But, more crucially, how did they come to *be* that way

— particularly if they are the result of valueless, cause-and-effect physical processes from the big bang until now? Theism offers the requisite foundations.

The Metaphysical Context

The more plausible metaphysical context for grounding human rights and dignity is this: we have been *created* with a *moral constitution* by a supremely valuable being, and we are "hard-wired" to function properly by living moral, deeply relational lives. So if humans have intrinsic, rather than instrumental (or no) value, the deeper, more natural context offering a smoother transition is a personal, supremely valuable God as the source of goodness and creator of morally responsible agents. The naturalist's context of a series of impersonal, valueless causes and effects producing valuable beings is shocking — an utterly incongruous outcome given the context.

Various naturalist moral realists have claimed that moral properties or objective moral values somehow emerge or supervene upon a sufficiently neurologically complex organism[27] — or once certain complex social configurations arise (what Richard Boyd calls "homeostatic property clusters").[28] For instance, the racial injustice of apartheid would supervene upon certain (natural) social, legal, and economic conditions.[29]

Despite such claims, problems regarding the emergence of dignity and duties remain. If intrinsic value does not exist from the outset, its emergence from nonvaluable processes is difficult to explain. It doesn't

---

prohibiting aggression (at least, unprovoked aggression), enjoining cooperation, fidelity, and aid, and condemning individuals who free-ride on the compliance of others" (157). Cp. Audi's list of "basic duties": fidelity (promise-keeping, truth-telling), "non-injury, reparation, justice, gratitude, beneficence, and self-improvement" (*Moral Knowledge and Ethical Character*, 279).

22. William Rowe, "Reflections on the Craig-Flew Debate," in *Does God Exist? The Craig-Flew Debate*, ed. Stan W. Wallace (Burlington, Vt.: Ashgate, 2003), 66.

23. For such reasoning, see Michael Martin, *Atheism, Morality, and Meaning* (Amherst, N.Y.: Prometheus, 2002). This rape example is found in Michael Martin, "Atheism, Christian Theism, and Rape". Available at www.infidels.org/library/modern/michael_martin/rape.html, accessed 21 May 2008.

24. Even though, as this tradition argues, human sin has intro-

duced evil and corruption into the world, the goodness of human nature, though damaged and distorted by evil, still remains. On how Christian theism best helps us come to terms with evil, see Gordon Graham, *Evil and Christian Ethics* (Cambridge: Cambridge University Press, 2001).

25. See Paul Copan, "The Moral Argument," in *The Rationality of Theism*, ed. Copan and Moser, 69–74.

26. Cp. Adams, Finite and Infinite Goods.

27. David O. Brink, *Moral Realism and the Foundation of Ethics* (Cambridge: Cambridge University Press, 1989); and Martin. *Atheism, Morality, and Meaning*.

28. Richard N. Boyd, "How to Be a Moral Realist," in *Essays on Moral Realism*, ed. Geoffrey Sayre-McCord (Ithaca: Cornell University Press, 1988).

29. Brink, "The Autonomy of Ethics," 153.

matter how many nonpersonal and nonvaluable components we happen to stack up: from valuelessness, valuelessness comes.

Brink suggests a parallel to support his naturalistic moral realism — namely, the supervenience of the *mental* upon a complex *physical* brain and nervous system: "Assuming materialism is true, mental states supervene on physical states, yet few think that mental states are metaphysically queer."[30] Such optimism is exceedingly unwarranted, though, as many naturalists themselves admit. For instance, Ned Block acknowledges that we have "no conception" — "zilch" — that enables us to explain subjective experience or to *begin* to account for conscious life: "Researchers are *stumped.*[31] Jaegwon Kim wonders how "a series of physical events, little particles jostling against one another, electric current rushing to and fro" could blossom into "conscious experience": "Why should *any* experience emerge when these neurons fire?"[32] Consciousness *is* metaphysically queer given naturalism! Colin McGinn avers that the emergence of consciousness "strikes us as miraculous, eerie, even faintly comic."[33] So Brink's confidence is ill placed. By contrast, the theist has no such challenges if a supremely self-aware Being exists — from consciousness, consciousness comes.

The same applies to moral values. Instead of a supervenience model, theists can plausibly argue that a *personal* Creator, who makes human *persons* in the Creator's image, serves as the ontological basis for the existence of objective moral values, moral obligation, human dignity, and rights. Consider: (1) Without the existence of a personal God, there would be no persons at all. (Indeed, God is the sufficient reason for why anything exists at all; for if the universe came into existence a finite time ago, as physicist Paul Davies suggests, the only options appear to be that it was simply uncaused — a metaphysical impossibility — or that something outside the universe caused its existence.)[34] And (2) if no persons would exist, then no moral properties would be instantiated or realized in our world.

Without this personal God and Creator of other persons, it is extraordinarily difficult to account for the instantiation of moral properties. Moral values — the instantiation of moral properties — and personhood are intertwined: moral properties are instantiated through personhood, which is ontologically rooted in God's personhood.

Now various nontheistic moral realists — not to mention some theists[35] — maintain that statements such as "Murder is wrong" would hold true even if God does not exist. They are simply brute facts and necessary truths. In reply, we could offer the following responses:

1. *Simplicity:* If naturalistic moral realists assume (*a*) a preexistent (Platonic) moral realm of brute facts and the eventual evolution of (*b*) valuable human beings corresponding to it, we have two utterly unconnected moral realities. Theism, however, offers a ready and for simpler connection: humans have been made in the image of a good God — the source of objective moral values.

2. *Asymmetrical Necessity:* Even if "Murder is wrong" is a necessary truth, it, first, need not be analytic (compare "water is H_2O"), and, second, a necessary truth may require some kind of explanation (for example, "Water is necessarily H_2O" still

30. Brink, *Moral Realism*, 120, 156 – 67.

31. Ned Block, "Consciousness," in *A Companion to the Philosophy of Mind*, ed. Samuel Guttenplan (Oxford: Blackwell, 1994), 211 (his italics).

32. Jaegwon Kim, *Philosophy of Mind* (Boulder: Westview, 1996), 8.

33. Colin McGinn, *The Problem of Consciousness* (Oxford: Blackwell, 1990), 10 – 11.

34. Paul Davies, "The Birth of the Cosmos," in *God, Cosmos, Nature and Creativity,* ed. Jill Gready (Edinburgh: Scottish Academic Press, 1995), 8 – 9.

35. Richard Swinburne, *The Coherence of Theism* (Oxford: Oxford University Press, 1977), 204; Keith Yandell, "Theism, Atheism, and Cosmology," in *Does God Exist?* ed. Stan Wallace, 96; Louis P. Pojman, *Philosophy of Religion* (Mountain View, Calif.: Mayfield, 2001), 167; Stephen C. Layman, *The Shape of the Good: Christian Reflections and the Foundation of Ethics* (Notre Dame, Ind.: University of Notre Dame Press, 1994), 44 – 52. Layman does acknowledge, however, that human value is difficult to account for given naturalism.

requires an explanation for water's existence and structure).[36] In the case of morality, we are still left wondering how value and obligation came to be thrust upon a valueless context of unguided matter in motion to have a context for the truth of "Murder is wrong." Third, certain necessary truths are logically prior to or more metaphysically basic than others, which may derive from or be entailed by them.[37] Likewise, the necessity of moral truths does not diminish their need for grounding in the character of a personal God. God, who necessarily exists in all possible worlds, is the source of all necessary moral (and logical) truths that stand in asymmetrical relation to God's necessity. God's existence and nature are explanatorily prior to any necessary truths, whether moral or logical.[38]

3. *Cosmic Coincidence (or Arbitrariness):* If moral facts are just brute givens and necessarily true, there is left unexplained a huge cosmic coincidence between the existence of these *moral facts* and the eventual emergence of *morally responsible agents* who are obligated to them. That this moral realm appears to be *anticipating* our emergence is a staggering cosmic concurrence that begs an explanation. The naturalistic moral realist may prefer another scenario, however: she may simply argue that certain a priori truths emerge based on the make-up of naturalistically evolved human beings. Dennett appeals to the parallel of certain "a priori" and "timeless" truths about the game of chess; *once the game is devised, certain fixed truths pertain to it.*[39] In response, not only does such a perspective actually imply belief in essentialism (that humans have a fixed *nature)* — something Dennett and his ilk repudiate. But we are also left with the *arbitrariness* problem: humans could have evolved differ-

ently (see below) and thus could have developed different — even opposing — moral "truths" appropriate to them.

4. *Accounting for Human Value:* The naturalist's position still offers no good reason to think that valuable, morally responsible human beings should emerge from valueless processes. Theism offers a far more plausible context for human value.

Deciding between Naturalism and Theism

Let us try to bring a few of these strands together. In deciding which hypothesis — naturalism or theism — presents the most plausible context for objective moral values and human dignity, we should consider at least three guidelines for preferring one over the other: Which is the more natural, the more unifying, and the more basic?

1. *We should prefer the theory that affords the more natural (that is, less ad hoc) transition from the overall theory to the entity in question.* Theism offers a more suitable context for objective moral values, which flow readily from a wise, supremely valuable Being to that Being's valuable image-bearers. Naturalism affords no such smooth transition from a context of undirected valueless processes to objective moral values and human dignity.

2. *We should prefer a worldview that is a kind of grand unifying factor for a wide range of features.* Better explanations are unified and interconnected rather than fragmented and unrelated. The existence of objective moral values and human dignity are only part of the bigger picture that is better explained by God's existence.

How then do we best account for the existence of valuable, morally responsible, self-aware, reasoning,

---

36. As Saul Kripke argued, there is a *metaphysical* necessity that, in this case, is discovered a posteriori. On this and the moral argument, see C. Stephen Evans, "Moral Arguments," in *Companion to Philosophy of Religion,* ed. Philip Quinn and Charles Taliaferro (Oxford: Blackwell, 1997), 346–47.

37. "*Addition is possible* is necessarily true because *Numbers exist* is necessarily true and numbers have certain essential properties," notes William Lane Craig. He also points out that theistic thinkers like Swinburne and Yandell *also* hold the problematic belief that "God exists" is not true in every possible world. Thus, their failure

to make the intrinsic connection between God and objective moral values is not surprising. See Craig's final comments in *The Craig-Flew Debate,* ed. Stan W. Wallace (Burlington, Vt.: Ashgate, 2003), 168–73; and his "Theistic Critiques of Atheism," in *The Cambridge Companion to Atheism,* ed. Michael Martin, 83–84.

38. Ibid.

39. Dennett made this point at *The Future of Atheism* conference (the Greer-Heard Forum) in New Orleans on 24 February 2007, where he reinforced his rejection of *essentialism!*

truth-seeking, living human beings who inhabit a finely tuned, beautiful universe that came to exist a finite time ago? Is this best explained naturalistically — namely, the result of disparate valueless, mindless, lifeless physical processes in a universe that came into existence from nothing? Or is the better unifying explanation a supremely valuable, supremely aware, logical, truthful, powerful, intelligent, beautiful Being? This Being serves as a natural unifier and thus the superior explanation and grounding to the naturalistic alternative of a remarkable string of highly contingent features.[40] (As Dennett writes, "just the tiniest amount" of change in the universe's variables would mean life could not have emerged: "we almost didn't make it!")[41] As philosopher of science Del Ratzsch observes, "When a value is produced by a long, tricky, precarious process, when it is generated and preserved by some breathtaking complexity, when it is realized against all odds, then intent — even design — suddenly becomes a live and reasonable question."[42]

3. *We should prefer a hypothesis/worldview whose relevant features are deeper or more basic than those in alternative worldviews.* Any hypothesis will have an explanatory stopping point. The question is: Which hypothesis most adequately furnishes the deepest ontological foundations or more ultimate explanations for its relevant features? For example, is the "miraculous, eerie, even faintly comic"[43] phenomenon of consciousness or the staggering breadth and variety of beauty a mere surd, or is there some deeper, more

basic explanation to account for its existence? What if we can go a *step further* to account for it?

We could say the same about human dignity and rights or reason. Naturalism's metaphysic seems inadequate to offer a deep account for such features in our world.[44] A deeper, more stable explanation is available through theism, which "offers suggestions for answers to a wide range of otherwise intractable questions."[45] George Mavrodes rightly observes that moral values and obligations cannot be deep in a world of matter, energy, natural laws, and chance.[46] By contrast, a world created by God has goodness and purpose deeply embedded within it.

Theism has a distinct advantage over gradualistic naturalistic accounts of morality as Dennett, Martin, or Brink might espouse. (We should add that theism need not be viewed as inherently incompatible with an evolutionary process, which God could have initiated; as we note below, Darwin himself believed that God was responsible for getting the evolutionary ball rolling.) Theism oils the more "natural" moral context to move us seamlessly from value to value instead of naturalism's attempt move from valuelessness to value.

The Inadequacy of Various Naturalistic Moral Systems

We should mention the red herring of naturalistic philosophers, who appeal to various objectivistic ethical systems that purportedly can safely overcome

---

40. Louis P. Pojman, "A Critique of Contemporary Egalitarianism: A Christian Perspective." *Faith and Philosophy* 8 (October 1991): 501.

41. Daniel C. Dennett, "Atheism and Evolution," in *The Cambridge Companion to Atheism*, ed. Martin, 144. With remarkable confidence, Dennett latches on to an oscillating model of the universe, which means an infinite number of opportunities to produce life: "It had to happen eventually" (146, 147). Such optimism is misplaced, as it is contradicted by the physical evidence (the Hawking-Penrose Singularity Theorem in 1970 helped lead to the demise of this theory): the universe is not eternal. As Stephen Hawking reminds us: "Almost everyone now believes that the universe, and *time itself* had a beginning at the Big Bang." Stephen Hawking and Roger Penrose, *The Nature of Space and Time* (Princeton: Princeton University Press, 1996), 20. For an examination of this and other

cosmological models, see chaps. 7 and 8 in Paul Copan and William Lane Craig, *Creation Out of Nothing: A Biblical, Philosophical, and Scientific Exploration* (Grand Rapids/Leicester, UK: Baker Academic/Apollos, 2004).

42. Del Ratzsch, *Nature, Design, and Science* (Albany: State University of New York Press, 2001), 68.

43. McGinn, *The Problem of Consciousness*, 10–11.

44. See Vance G. Morgan, "The Metaphysics of Naturalism," *American Catholic Philosophical Quarterly* 75, no. 3 (Summer 2001): 409–31.

45. Alvin Plantinga, "Natural Theology," in *Companion to Metaphysics*, ed. Jaegwon Kim and Ernest Sosa (Cambridge: Blackwell, 1995), 347.

46. Mavrodes, "Religion and the Queerness of Morality," 225, 226.

any essential God-morality connection. Again, such confidence is poorly placed.

Consider Aristotle's eudaimonistic virtue ethic. Despite his rich ethical discussion and even his mention of God, critical gaps and shortcomings remain: (*a*) the questionable notion of *intellectual* activity (as opposed to loving relationships) as central to our natural human task *(ergon)* and fulfilling our goal *(telos)*; (*b*) the radical evil embedded in human nature that inclines us to self-centeredness and profound evil — what comes "naturally" may often undermine human flourishing; and (*c*) the inability to account for human value and rights. Despite Aristotle's valuable insights, his system is both incomplete and fraught with significant problems.[47]

Neither can naturalists take comfort in Kant's categorical imperative and kingdom of ends. First, the often-misunderstood Kant actually posits God, freedom, and immortality in order to make sense of morality; his is not a secular ethical system but one that requires God's existence.[48] Second, the more fundamental question for those who take a secularized Kantian position is, "Why should humans be treated as ends rather than means? Why think they should have value given their valueless origins?" Indeed, Kant's system *presupposes* and *posits* human dignity and personal responsibility; naturalism lacks the necessary metaphysical resources to account for them.

Despite the naturalistic appeal of a Rawlsian neo-contractarianism with its wide reflective equilibrium[49] or an Ideal Observer theory (a "good" is what an ideal observer would approve under ideal conditions),[50] such theories are long on epistemology but short on ontology: they specify how to *recognize* moral duties and virtues, but equally fail to provide a decent metaphysical account of human dignity and rights or make sense of moral obligation given naturalism's metaphysic. They lack ontological completeness.

Naturalistic Evolutionary Ethics

Though a moral realist, Daniel Dennett maintains that the human fixation on human rights is a misguided, though fortuitous, "rule worship" that contributes to human well-being and social cohesion. The presumption of "natural and imprescriptible rights" is nothing more than (good and useful) "nonsense upon stilts," to use Jeremy Bentham's dismissive phrase.[51]

According to Michael Ruse, a moral subjectivist, we merely *think* morality is objective, but Ruse informs us that isn't so.[52] We believe the *illusion* of moral realism and moral obligation; without this strong impulse, Ruse declares, we would disregard or disobey morality. "If you think about it, you will see that the very essence of an ethical claim, like 'Love little children,' is that, whatever its truth status may be, we think it binding upon us *because we think it has an objective status.*"[53] This is a *corporate illusion* that has been "fobbed off on us by our genes to get us to cooperate."[54]

Despite the arguments of naturalistic moral realists, their naturalistically rooted ethic presents two problems: we are faced with the apparent arbitrariness of our moral beliefs, and we appear to be justi-

47. C. Stephen Layman, *The Shape of the Good*, 138–44.

48. See John E. Hare, *The Moral Gap: Kantian Ethics, Human Limits, and God's Assistance* (Oxford: Clarendon Press, 1996); John E. Hare, *God and Morality: A Philosophical History* (Oxford: Blackwell, 2007), 122–83.

49. Martin's *Atheism, Morality, and Meaning* makes much use of this approach. For a response, see Paul Copan, "Morality and Meaning Without God: Another Failed Attempt," *Philosophia Christi* n.s. 6. no. 2 (2004): 295–304.

50. See Roderick Firth, "Ethical Absolutism and the Ideal Observer," *Philosophy and Phenomenological Research* 12 (1952): 317–45. Firth, a Quaker, considered the Ideal Observer theory to be harmonious with belief in God as the Ideal Observer: "an ideal observer will be a partial description of God, if God is conceived to

be an infallible moral judge" (333). (Firth's religious affiliation was pointed out to me by Firth's former student at Brown University, Charles Taliaferro [24 May 1999].)

51. Dennett, *Darwin's Dangerous Idea,* 507. Dennett writes: "It might seem then that 'rule worship' of a certain kind is a good thing, at least for agents designed like us. It is good not because there is a certain rule, or set of rules, which is probably the best, or which always yields the right answer, but because having rules works — somewhat — and not having rules doesn't work at all" (507).

52. Michael Ruse, "Evolutionary Ethics: A Phoenix Arisen," in *Issues in Evolutionary Ethics*, ed. Paul Thompson (Albany: State University of New York Press, 1995), 236.

53. Ibid., 235.

54. Michael Ruse and E. O. Wilson, "The Evolution of Ethics,"

fied in our skepticism or agnosticism concerning moral living. Note also that my argument would be opposed only to *naturalistic* evolution, not evolution per se. In his *Origin of Species,* Darwin himself is not writing as an intellectually fulfilled atheist![55] Besides affirming that God impressed laws upon nature and breathed life into creation, Darwin uses the word "creation" over 100 times and (in the *Origin's* inscription) approvingly cites Francis Bacon's acknowledgment of both the "book of God's word" (special revelation) and "book of God's works" (divine revelation in nature). Even if naturalists can furnish (1) a complete gradualistic biological account of evolutionary development and (2) an account of ever-increasing moral awareness in human minds, this need not conflict with God as Creator or the source of objective moral values, Daniel Dennett notwithstanding. As we have argued, value from value is more "natural" than value from valuelessness.

Arbitrary Morality?

Given naturalism, it appears that humans could have evolved differently and inherited rather contrary moral beliefs ("rules") for the "chess game" of survival. Whatever those rules, they would still direct us toward surviving and reproducing. Ruse (with E. O. Wilson) gives an example: instead of evolving from "savannah-dwelling primates," we, like termites, could have evolved needing "to dwell in darkness, eat each other's faeces, and cannibalise the dead." If the latter

were the case, we would "extol such acts as beautiful and moral" and "find it morally disgusting to live in the open air, dispose of body waste and bury the dead."[56] So our awareness of morality ("a sense of right and wrong and a feeling of obligation to be thus governed") is of "biological worth," serves as "an aid to survival," and "has no being beyond this."[57] Though rare in human societies, Eskimos permit infanticide in the face of scant resources for the sake of survival. And what of suttee (widow burning), honor killings, or female circumcision? Or should we think of Larry Arnhart's serial monogamy as "natural" — as opposed to lifelong monogamy, which frustrates natural, promiscuous desires in males?[58] Should such practices be prohibited or condemned? It is hard to see how Ruse could protest.

Take another example: *A Natural History of Rape*[59] (coauthored by a biologist and an anthropologist) maintains that rape can be explained biologically: when a male cannot find a mate, his subconscious drive to reproduce his own species pushes him to force himself upon a female. Such acts happen in the animal kingdom (for example, male mallards or scorpion flies). Now the authors do not advocate rape; in fact, they claim that rapists are not excused for their (mis)behavior. To say that rape is good because it is biologically advantageous ("natural") is to commit the naturalistic fallacy (moving from *is* to *ought*).

However, if the rape impulse happens to be embedded into human nature from antiquity and if it confers

in *Religion and the Natural Sciences,* ed. J. E. Huchingson (Orlando: Harcourt Brace, 1993), 310–11. For discussion on this, see Matthew H. Nitecki and Doris V. Nitecki, *Evolutionary Ethics* (Albany: State University of New York Press, 1993), 8.

55. In *The Origin of Species,* Darwin himself speaks of "laws impressed on matter by the Creator" and of life "having been originally breathed by the Creator into a few forms or into one." *Origin of Species* (New York: Thomas Y. Crowell, n.d. [corr. ed.]), 459, 460.

56. Ruse and Wilson, "Evolution of Ethics," 311. This example can also be found in Ruse's "Evolutionary Ethics: A Phoenix Arisen," 241–42, where he humorously refers to the termites' "rather strange foodstuffs"!

57. Michael Ruse, *The Darwinian Paradigm* (London: Routledge, 1989), 262, 268.

58. Larry Arnhart advocates some counterintuitive problems given his naturalistic view of human morality, which he takes to be

rooted entirely in our animal nature. If, as Arnhart argues, the good is desirable and the desirable is that which humans generally desire, we are left with difficult moral pills to swallow: besides this point of implicitly encouraging males to act according to their promiscuous inclinations. Amhart's moral perspective (a) denies a universal "altruistic selflessness" as normative but instead advocates a more restrictive love of one's own kinship group as an extension of self-love (which seems to encourage tribalism); and (b) he agrees with Aristotle that power, wealth, and prestige are "naturally" desired by humans (but it is a non sequitur to say these are therefore good). See Larry Arnhart, *Darwinian Natural Right: The Biological Ethics of Human Nature* (Albany: State University of New York Press, 1998). For a response to Arnhart, see Hare, *God and Morality,* 65–72.

59. Randy Thornhill and Craig T. Palmer, *A Natural History of Rape: Biological Bases of Sexual Coercion* (Cambridge, Mass.: MIT Press, 2000).

biological advantage, how can the authors suggest that this behavior *ought* to be ended? Is this not committing the naturalistic fallacy as well? Indeed, the authors' resistance to rape, despite its "naturalness," suggests objective moral values not rooted in nature.

An ethic rooted in nature appears to leave us with arbitrary morality. Theism, on the other hand, *begins* with value; so bridging the is-ought gulf is a nonissue.

Skepticism about Ethics

An ethic rooted in naturalistic evolution ends up being subjectivistic and ultimately reduces to relativism. Ethics is simply illusory, as Ruse argues (and, as Dennett notes, naturalistic evolution doesn't leave room for genuine natural rights). So Westerners may find abhorrent practices such as female circumcision or a widow's self-immolation on the funeral pyre of her husband (outlawed in India under the British Raj). But why presuppose moral duties or human dignity and rights? On what metaphysical basis should one oppose such practices? If ethical beliefs are simply hardwired into us for our fitness and survival, we have no reason to think these beliefs are *true;* they simply *are.* If, as Francis Crick argues, human identity ("you") is simply "the behavior of a vast assembly of nerve cells and their associated molecules,"[60] then such a perspective is only accidentally correct. After all, this belief itself is the result of "the behavior of a vast assembly of nerve cells and their associated molecules"!

Whether the naturalist holds a realistic or nonrealistic view of morality, one can legitimately ask: *Can we even trust our minds if we are nothing more than the products of naturalistic evolution trying to fight,* *feed, flee, and reproduce?*[61] Darwin himself was deeply troubled by this:

> With me the horrid doubt always arises whether the convictions of man's mind, which has been developed from the mind of the lower animals, are of any value or at all trustworthy. Would anyone trust in the convictions of a monkey's mind, if there are any convictions in such a mind?[62]

Regarding ethics, Darwin claimed: "Thus at last man comes to feel, through acquired and perhaps inherited habit, that it is best for him to obey his more persistent impulses."[63] The evolutionary process, however, is interested in fitness and survival, not in true belief. The problem with naturalistic evolution is that not only is *objective morality* undermined; so is *rational thought.* Our beliefs — moral or epistemic — may help us *survive,* but we can have no confidence that they are *true.*[64]

So we *may believe* that we have intrinsic value and moral duties and that our free actions make a difference, and these beliefs *could well help* us survive as a species; but they may be *completely false.* If we are blindly hard-wired by nature to accept certain beliefs because of their survival-enhancing value, then we would not have access to the *truth-status* of these beliefs. They may aid our survival, but how could we know whether they are true or false?

Along these lines, Elliott Sober rejects two chief arguments used to argue that ethics must be subjective — the naturalistic (is-ought) fallacy and the genetic fallacy ("ethical beliefs can't be true if they're the product of evolution").[65] However, all of this seems beside the

---

60. Francis Crick, *The Astonishing Hypothesis* (New York: Scribner's, 1994), 3.

61. On this problem, see Victor Reppert, *C. S. Lewis's Dangerous Idea: In Defense of the Argument from Reason* (Downers Grove, Ill.: InterVarsity, 2003).

62. Charles Darwin, "Letter to William Graham Down" (3 July 1881), in *The Life and Letters of Charles Darwin Including an Autobiographical Chapter.* vol. 1, ed. F. Darwin (London: John Murray, Abermarle Street, 1887), 1:315–16.

63. Charles Darwin, *Descent of Man,* 2d ed (London: Murray, 1874), 486. David Hume's position anticipates Darwinism: Reason is "the slave of the passions, and can never pretend to any other office

than to serve and obey them." Morality itself is "more properly felt than judg'd of." For Hume, one can never locate vice "till you turn your reflexion into your own breast, and find a sentiment of disapprobation, which arises in you, towards this action." *A. Treatise of Human Nature,* ed. L. A Selby-Bigge (Oxford: Clarendon, 1740; repr. 1888), 2.3.3;415; 3.1.2, 470, 468–69.

64. George I. Mavrodes, "Religion and the Queerness of Morality," in *Rationality, Religious Belief, and Moral Commitment,* ed. Robert Audi and William J. Wainwright (Ithaca, N.Y.: Cornell University Press, 1986), 219.

65. Elliott Sober, *Philosophy of Biology* (Boulder, Colo.: Westview, 1993), 202–08.

point if naturalism is true. We *still* can't be confident about which — if any — of our beliefs are true. If they are true, it is by accident rather than through some epistemic virtue. *And* we are still left wondering how a valueless universe should produce objective moral values and rights-bearing moral beings to appreciate them. At best, Sober's analysis leaves us agnostic as to the existence of objective moral values.

So, the fact that we do not proceed as (global) skeptics about reason or sense perception or fundamental moral beliefs suggests borrowing from a worldview like theism (in that we have been made in the image of a truthful God). And, again, if one takes the skeptical route, one still relies on the very cognitive faculties whose unreliability is the conclusion of one's skeptical argument.[66] One assumes a trustworthy reasoning process to arrive, ironically, at the conclusion that reasoning cannot be trusted.

The fact that humans can be interested in truth seeking, not merely survival, flies in the face of naturalistic Darwinism. Commenting on the notion of our "increated" orientation toward truth, Richard Rorty calls this as "un-Darwinian" as the notion of humans having "a built-in moral compass" or conscience.[67] Thus, it appears that a naturalistic evolutionary process cannot sufficiently explain — or explain away — certain bedrock moral beliefs or our quest for truth. And if we claim that such basic beliefs should be questioned in the name of our impulse to survive and reproduce, then this skeptical conclusion is itself the result of those same impulses.

Naturalism does not inspire confidence in our belief-forming mechanisms. Indeed, naturalism has the potential to undermine our conviction that rationality and objective moral values exist. If our *beliefs* — moral or epistemic — are survival-enhancing byproducts of Darwinistic evolution, why think that we actually *have* dignity, rights, and obligations — or that we are thinking rationally? A theistic worldview, on the other hand, does inspire confidence that we can *know* moral (and rational) truths — even if they do not contribute one whit to our survival.

Naturalism's Undermining of Ethics

Despite its appeal to "science," naturalism's materialist ontology not only fails to produce moral values, but positively undermines them. This becomes apparent as we examine the properties of matter, the nature of scientific description, and the notable representation of naturalists who deny objective goodness (even if they may prefer it). Further, naturalism has embedded within it a number of features that could readily undercut moral motivation.

Moral Values Defy Physical Description

Naturalists seem increasingly to take their worldview to involve a strict materialism. As Kai Nielsen puts it, "[Naturalism] is the view that anything that exists is ultimately composed of physical components."[68] However, material or physical properties such as extension, color, shape, or size are far different from moral values, which are not blue, ten centimeters long, or rough to the touch. No physics textbook will include "moral value" in its attempted description of matter. Michael Martin claims that there is "no a priori reason why objective moral values could not be constituted by matter."[69] But there is. There is a *background* or *contextual* problem for the naturalist who believes in objective moral values: How do we move from a universe that originates from no prior matter into a universe of valueless matter and energy, eventually arriving at moral values, including human rights, human dignity, and moral obligation? It is hard to see how the naturalist could bridge this chasm. Matter just does not have moral properties, let alone mental ones.

Goodness Is Scientifically Superfluous

Some naturalistic moral realists believe that recent

66. Plantinga, *Warranted Christian Belief,* 219 n.29.

67. Richard Rorty, "Untruth and Consequences," *The New Republic* (31 July 1995): 32 – 36.

68. Kai Nielsen, "Naturalistic Explanations of Theistic Belief," in *A Companion to Philosophy of Religion,* ed. Quinn and Taliaferro, 402.

69. Martin, *Atheism, Morality, and Meaning,* 45.

developments in the philosophy of science — together with "naturalistic" developments in epistemology and philosophy of language — can help in the articulation and defense of moral realism: "moral realism can be shown to be a more attractive and plausible position if recent developments in realist philosophy of science are brought to bear in its defense."[70] Other naturalists are not so sanguine about naturalism's ability to pull goodness out of the ontological hat. Thomas Nagel puts it candidly: "There is no room for agency in a world of neural impulses, chemical reactions, and bone and muscle movements." Given naturalism, it is hard not to conclude that we're "helpless" and "not responsible" for our actions.[71] Zoologist Richard Dawkins admits, "Science has no methods for deciding what is ethical."[72] Harvard's Marc Hauser, who believes that we come evolutionarily equipped with an "innate moral grammar," claims much the same thing — that science is about making *descriptions,* not moral prescriptions.[73] Though not a naturalist, Derk Pereboom nicely summarizes naturalism's perspective on moral responsibility: "our best scientific theories indeed have the consequence that we are not morally responsible for our actions .... [We are] more like machines than we ordinarily suppose."[74]

Contrary to what naturalistic moral realists claim, "scientific explanation" seems to call for rejecting the existence of objective moral values rather than bloating their ontology. A methodologically naturalistic science would require stripping off: Why insert objective moral values (*ought*) when bare scientific descriptions (*is*) seem to be all that is required? Why not use *non*moral terms and explanations of certain events

that naturalistic moral realists typically take as morally weighted? Why not eliminate objective morality in the name of simplicity?

Naturalistic moral realists claim that moral facts help explain certain actions performed by individuals — for example, "Hitler killed millions of Jews because he was morally depraved." But are such moral facts explanatorily *necessary*? Perhaps a "strictly scientific" response should simply stop with a nonmoral description: Hitler, being bitter and angry, held many false beliefs about the Jews (for example, that they were responsible for Germany's defeat in WWI). Hitler sought to destroy the Jews as a way of releasing his hostilities.[75] While moral facts may be *relevant,* they are not necessary to *explain* Hitler's behavior. Thus, in the spirit of Ockham's razor, why multiply entities or explanations unnecessarily? Why can't natural, descriptive facts do the explanatory work? The scientific account suggests that moral facts are dispensable.[76]

It is difficult to see why the naturalist must resort to moral explanations when parsimony suggests another course — the descriptive one. If we are going the route of "facts" and "science," then why get side-tracked by the prescriptive? The is-ought problem still seems difficult for the naturalist to overcome.

Naturalists Themselves Confess ...

Science's metaphysical failure to account for goodness is further reinforced by a large portion of naturalists who admit that natural processes without God cannot bring us to moral responsibility and goodness: these don't square well with naturalism. We have

70. Richard Boyd, "How To Be a Moral Realist," 106. See also Russ Shafer-Landau, *Moral Realism: A Defence* (New York: Oxford University Press, 2005).

71. Thomas Nagel, *The View from Nowhere* (New York: Oxford University Press, 1986), 111, 113.

72. Richard Dawkins, *A Devil's Chaplain* (Boston: Houghton Mifflin, 2003), 34. Ironically, Dawkins waxes quite "unscientific" in his book *The God Delusion,* in which he rails against "religious morality."

73. Marc D. Hauser, *Moral Minds* (New York: HarperCollins, 2006).

74. Derk Pereboorn, *Living without Free Will* (Cambridge: Cambridge University Press, 2001), xiii – xiv.

75. Summarized from Thomas L. Carson, *Value and the Good Life* (Notre Dame, Ind.: University of Notre Dame Press, 2000), 194.

76. Ibid., 198. Carson adds that nothing is *explained* by assuming that moral properties are constituted by natural facts: "The best explanations of human behavior available to us at the present time do not make use of claims to the effect that moral facts are constituted by natural facts ... and it is a mystery how those properties cause or explain observable phenomena" (198 – 99). Simply to *posit* that moral properties have been instantiated by nature — that they have emerged from (or "supervened upon") natural ones — is a far cry from *explaining* how this is so.

already cited Nagel, Dawkins, and Hauser. In addition, Bertrand Russell believed that "the whole subject of ethics arises from the pressure of the community on the individual."[77] E. O. Wilson locates moral feeling in "the hypothalamus and the limbic system"; it is a "device of survival in social organisms."[78] Jonathan Glover considers morality a "human creation" and calls on humans to "re-create ethics."[79]

If humans are simply more developed animals, why think there are moral duties to which they must subscribe — or that they are even morally responsible? John Searle admits that we have an intuition of freedom (that "we could have done something else"), but he rejects libertarian freedom because of his commitment to the "scientific" approach to reality. Otherwise, we would have to postulate a self that could potentially disrupt the "causal order of nature."[80]

Given such a perspective, no wonder Simon Blackburn confesses that he cannot adequately answer the relativist's challenge: "Nature has no concern for good or bad, right or wrong .... We cannot get behind ethics." Questions of moral knowledge and moral progress can only be answered "from within our own moral perspective." Blackburn prefers "dignity" to "humiliation."[81] If, however, we have been created in the image of a good, supremely valuable, and free being and have been endowed with moral value and "certain unalienable rights," then the theist is able to offer a much more plausible context for affirming human dignity, rights, and responsibility than the naturalist who wants to be a realist but doesn't quite know how. Atheist J. L. Mackie had it right when he affirmed that objective goodness, given naturalism, is "odd" and "unlikely"; if it exists, it must be rooted in "an all-powerful god."[82] He opted for the idea that human beings "invent" right and wrong.[83]

Naturalism May Undercut Moral Motivation

The popular writer Michael Shermer affirms that our remote ancestors have genetically passed on to us our sense of moral obligation within, and this is (epigenetically) reinforced by group pressure. Ultimately, to ask, "Why should we be moral?" is like asking, "Why should we be hungry or horny?"[84] C. S. Lewis noted that given such conditions, moral impulses are no more true (or false) "than a vomit or a yawn."[85] Thinking "I ought" is on the same level of "I itch." Indeed, "my impulse to serve posterity is just the same sort of thing as my fondness for cheese" or preferring mild or bitter beer.[86] Naturalism's inability to get beyond descriptions of human behavior and psychology does not inspire confidence for grounding moral obligation. At best, one should remain agnostic about it — which doesn't do much to encourage the pursuit of virtue.

Furthermore, if, as can be argued, humans could have evolved a different set of moral beliefs that might nevertheless enhance survival (for example, rape as biologically beneficial), then this, too, takes the wind out of the sails of moral motivation. If we are simply animals, why refrain from raping or practicing infanticide[87] when this is "natural" or "widespread" in nature? It seems that those who vehemently resist such practices are smuggling in metaphysical capital from

77. Bertrand Russell, *Human Society in Ethics and Politics* (London: Allen & Unwin, 1954), 124.

78. Edward O. Wilson, *Consilience* (New York: Random House, 1998), 268, 269.

79. Jonathan Glover, *Humanity: A Moral History of the Twentieth Century* (London: Jonathan Cape, 1999), 41, 42.

80. John Searle, *Minds, Brains, and Science* (Cambridge, Mass.: Harvard University Press, 1986 repr.), 87, 88, 92.

81. Simon Blackburn, *Being Good: A Short Introduction to Ethics* (New York: Oxford University Press. 2001),133, 134.

82. J. L. Mackie, *The Miracle of Theism* (Oxford: Clarendon, 1982), 115.

83. J. L. Mackie, *Ethics: Inventing Right and Wrong* (London:

Penguin, 1977). Mackie argued that even if ethics is subjective — or even false — a person could still remain firmly committed to them (16)! But surely this commitment may be irrelevant or even harmful (consider Stalin or Pol Pot, who were committed — wrongly — to their perverse moral vision).

84. Michael Shermer, *The Science of Good and Evil: Why People Cheat, Gossip, Care, Share, and Follow the Golden Rule* (New York: Henry Holt, 2004), 56–57.

85. C. S. Lewis, *Miracles* (New York: Macmillan, 1960), 37.

86. Ibid., 38, 37.

87. Elliott Sober and David Sloan Wilson, *Unto Others* (Cambridge, Mass.: Harvard University Press, 1998), 301–2.

another worldview that clearly demarcates valuable, responsible moral agents from environment-bound, instinct-guided animals.

The Euthyphro Problem

In a *Calvin and Hobbes* cartoon strip,[88] the mischievous imp Calvin is pondering the lyrics of "Santa Claus Is Coming to Town": "... He knows if you've been bad or good; so be good, for goodness's sake!" Calvin reports his musings to Hobbes, his striped sidekick and co-conspirator. "This Santa Claus stuff bothers me ... especially the judge and jury bit." Why, Calvin wonders, does Santa carry such moral authority? "Who appointed Santa? How do we know he's impartial? What criteria does he use for determining bad or good?"

Along these lines, Socrates, in Plato's *Euthyphro* dialogue (l0a), once asked: "Is what is holy holy because the gods approve it, or do they approve it because it is holy?" Various philosophers of religion have followed up on this question to show that no necessary connection exists between God and objective morality. They present the dilemma in (roughly) this way: either God's commands are *arbitrary* (something is good *because* God commands it — and God could have commanded "You *shall* murder/commit adultery") — or there must be some *autonomous moral standard* (which God consults in order to command). Robin Le Poidevin maintains that "we can, apparently, only make sense of these doctrines [that God is good and wills us to do what is good] if we think of goodness as being defined independently of God."[89] Steven Pinker, who believes that our evolutionary hard-wiring fully accounts for our moral beliefs and sense of moral obligation, claims that Plato made quick work of the idea that God is "in charge of morality" since God's dictates would be "divine whims."[90]

Such claims, though, are misguided. Why think our alternatives are reduced to these two — (a) a moral standard that exists completely independently of God (which God must apparently consult when issuing commands) or (b) divine arbitrariness or capriciousness?

Although divine commands may serve as a partial guide to living rightly (for example, God's civil laws to theocratic Israel),[91] God's good character with accompanying "divine motivations"[92] is the more ultimate and underlying reality; God's moral nature is more fundamental to God's worship-worthiness than God's commands — a point nontheistic philosophers seem to ignore.[93] Even divine command theorist Robert Adams points out, "It matters what God's attributes are.... It makes a difference if you think of commands as coming from someone who completely understands both us and our situation. It matters not only that God is loving but also that he is just."[94] Elsewhere Adams speaks of God's commands springing from a good design and purpose; such commands are conducive to human flourishing: "It matters to the plausibility of

---

88. Taken from Bill Watterson, *The Authoritative Calvin and Hobbes: A Calvin and Hobbes Treasury* (New York: Universal Press Syndicate, 1990), 105.

89. Robin Le Poidevin, *Arguing for Atheism* (London: Routledge, 1996), 86.

90. Steven Pinker, "The Moral Instinct," *New York Times* (January 13, 2008). Available at http://www. nytimes.com/2008/01/13/ magazine / I3Psychology-t. html?_r=1&oref=slogin&pagewanted= print. accessed February 1, 2008.

91. In addition to considerations of diet, clothing, ceremonial purity, and the like, we should keep in mind that Old Testament ethics (Mosaic legislation in particular) commonly assumes a departure from the divine ideals in Genesis 1 – 2 (the implications of the divine image and lifelong monogamous commitment). The Law of Moses often takes for granted human hard-heartedness (cp. Matthew 19:8) and a divine accommodation to, and the regulation or restriction of,

negative ancient Near East social structures (e.g., polygamy, slavery, patriarchalism, primogeniture, and the like) *without* approving them. That said, Mosaic legislation often presents a vast improvement over other ancient Near East cultures, including the elevated status of women and slaves, the accountability of all persons under the law (including kings and nobles), and far less severe punishments. For a detailed discussion, see Paul Copan, "Is Yahweh a Moral Monster? The New Atheists and Old Testament Ethics," *Philosophia Christi* n.s. 10, no. 1 (2008): 7 – 37.

92. See Linda Zagzebski, *Divine Motivation Theory* (Cambridge: Cambridge University Press, 2004).

93. One egregious example is David Brink's "The Autonomy of Ethics."

94. Robert M. Adams, "Divine Commands and Obligation," *Faith and Philosophy* 4 (1988): 272.

a divine command theory, for example, that we do not believe that God demands cruelty."[95]

Indeed, the ultimate resolution to this Euthyphro dilemma is that *God's good character* or *nature* sufficiently grounds objective morality. So we do not need to look elsewhere for such a standard. We have been made in the divine image; without it we would neither be moral beings (let alone exist) nor have the capacity to recognize objective moral values. The ultimate solution to the Euthyphro dilemma shifts the grounding of morality from the *commands of God* to something more basic — that is, the *nature* or *character* of God. Thus, we human beings (who have been made to resemble God in certain ways) have the capacity to recognize this, and thus God's commands — far from being arbitrary — are in accordance with that nature and also with how we have been designed. We would not *know* goodness without God's granting us a moral *constitution*. We have rights, dignity, freedom, and responsibility because God has designed us this way. And we can grant Pinker's assumption that fundamental moral convictions that prohibit torturing babies for fun or raping are hard-wired into us evolutionarily while rejecting the notion that this hard-wiring grounds human morality. Such hard-wiring is quite compatible with God's existence, but it runs into trouble if morality is strictly natural, as we noted above.

As an aside, God's designs for us are for our good and well-being, not our harm (Deut, 6:24; 10:13). Contrary to the skeptic's caricatures of God as a divine police officer or cosmic killjoy, God issues commands that are rooted in God's good nature and are in line with the maximal function and flourishing of human beings. Indeed, these commands spring from the love and self-giving nature of God, who is *pro nobis* (for us).

Furthermore, in light of (1) our ability to recognize basic moral values and ideals, as well as (2) our moral failures to live up to these ideals, this "moral gap" suggests the need for (3) divine grace to enable us to live

as we ought. So, rather than Kant's "ought implies can," we failing humans may still cast ourselves upon God's mercy and grace; that is, "ought implies can — *with* divine assistance."[96]

There are other points to ponder. What if the naturalistic (or nontheistic) moral realist pushes the Euthyphro dilemma further? What if she calls God's character itself into question? Is the very *character of God* good because it happens to be God's, or is God's character good because it conforms to some external standard of goodness? I briefly respond below.

- If the naturalistic (or nontheistic) moral realist is correct about there needing to be some moral standard external to God, then she herself cannot escape a similar dilemma, *mutatis mutandis:* Are these moral values good simply because they are good, or is there an independent standard of goodness to which *they* conform? Her argument offers her no actual advantage over theism. And if two entities are sufficient to establish a relation (here, God's good character and moral values), inserting yet a third entity — some moral standard independent of God to assess the connection between them becomes superfluous. The skeptic's demand is unwarranted.
- The naturalist's query is pointless in this regard also: we must eventually arrive at some self-sufficient and self-explanatory stopping point beyond which the discussion cannot go. Why is this "independent moral standard" any less arbitrary a stopping point than God's nature?
- God, who is essentially perfect, does not have obligations to some external moral standard; God simply acts, and it is good. God naturally does what is good. God does not fulfill moral obligations but simply expresses the goodness of the divine nature. As H. O. Mounce suggests, "God cannot hold anything good unless he *already* values it. But then his valuing cannot *depend* all on its being good."[97]
- The idea that God could be evil or command evil is utterly contrary to the very definition of God

---

95. Adams, *Infinite and Finite Goods,* 255.
96. John Hare, *The Moral Gap.*
97. H. O. Mounce, "Morality and Religion," in *Philosophy of Reli-*

gion, ed. Brian Davies (Washington, D.C.: Georgetown University Press, 1998), 278.

(who is intrinsically morally excellent, maximally great, and worthy of worship); if we are really talking about "God," then this God cannot be some evil creator of the universe.

- The acceptance of objective values assumes a kind of ultimate goal or design plan for human beings. This would make little sense given naturalism (since we are the products of mindless, unguided processes), but it makes much sense given theism, which presumes a design plan or ideal standard for human beings.

- Even if there were some moral standard independent of God, it still would fail to account for how humans, given their valueless, unguided, materialistic origins came to be morally valuable, rights-bearing, morally responsible beings. There seems to be no reason to think that the Euthyphro dilemma poses a serious threat to a theistically rooted ethic.[98]

For all their huffing and puffing, naturalistic moral realists are mistaken about the "threat" that the Euthyphro dilemma poses for God's being the ground of objective moral values.

Conclusion

Unlike the UN Universal Declaration of Human Rights, which takes human rights and moral obligations for granted, another historic document — the Declaration of Independence — presents the essential grounding for "certain unalienable" human rights and dignity. These are rooted in "our Creator," a personal Being who has uniquely made human beings. Without God, it seems exceedingly difficult to account for objective moral values, obligations, human rights, and human dignity.

John Rist has observed that there is "widely admitted to be a crisis in contemporary Western debate about ethical foundations."[99] It seems that taking seriously a personal God and Creator, who is the infinite Good and source of all finite goods — including human dignity — would go a long way in providing the needed metaphysical foundation for human rights and objective moral values. Apart from such a move, it seems that the crisis may become only more pronounced.

Maritain argued that God and objective morality cannot plausibly be separated since God, the Creator of valuable, morally responsible human beings, is the very source of value. Ethical systems — and official documents regarding human rights — that ignore this foundation will necessarily be incomplete. To close with Jacques Maritain:

> The truths which I have just recalled were not discovered and formulated by moral philosophy. They spring from a higher source. They correspond, nevertheless, to an aspiration (a trans-natural aspiration) so deeply rooted in man that many philosophers have undergone its attraction, and have tried to transpose it into purely rational terms, an attempt which, lacking the indispensable data, could only be disappointing.[100]

If objective moral values exist, we have good reason for believing in God. Of course, a successful moral argument does not reveal that the God of Abraham, Isaac, Jacob, and Jesus exists — a full-blown and robust theism. The moral argument, however, can be supplemented with other successful theistic arguments and with God's specific revelation in Jesus of Nazareth. That said, the moral argument does point us to a supreme personal moral Being who is worthy of worship, who has made us with dignity and worth, to whom we are personally accountable, and who may reasonably be called "God."

---

98. On the Euthyphro question, see William P. Alston, "Some Suggestions for Divine Command Theorists," in *Christian Theism and the Problems of Philosophy*, ed. Michael D. Beaty (Notre Dame, Ind.: University of Notre Dame Press, 1990); Thomas V. Morris, "Duty and Divine Goodness" and "The Necessity of God's Goodness," in *Anselmian Explorations* (Notre Dame, Ind.: University of Notre Dame Press, 1987); Paul Copan, "The Moral Argument," in *The Rationality of Theism*; and William J. Wainwright, *Religion and Morality* (Burlington, Vt.: Ashgate, 2005).

99. John M. Rist, *Real Ethics: Rethinking the Foundations of Morality* (Cambridge: Cambridge University Press, 2001), 1.

100. Jacques Maritain, *Moral Philosophy* (New York: Scribner's, 1964), 439.

CHAPTER 19

Experiencing God

Teresa of Avila

Chapter XXVIII

Treats of the great favours, which the Lord bestowed upon her, and of His first appearance to her. Describes the nature of an imaginary vision. Enumerates the important effects and signs which this produces when it proceeds from God. This chapter is very profitable and should be carefully noted.

Returning to our subject: I spent some days, though only a few, with that vision continually in my mind, and it did me so much good that I remained in prayer unceasingly and contrived that everything I did should be such as not to displease Him Who, as I clearly perceived, was a witness of it. And, although I was given so much advice that I sometimes became afraid, my fear was short-lived, for the Lord reassured me. One day, when I was at prayer, the Lord was pleased to reveal to me nothing but His hands, the beauty of which was so great as to be indescribable. This made me very fearful, as does every new experience that I have when the Lord is beginning to grant me some supernatural favour. A few days later I also saw that Divine face, which seemed to leave me completely absorbed. I could not understand why the Lord revealed Himself gradually like this since He was later to grant me the favour of seeing Him wholly, until at length I realized that His Majesty was leading me according to my natural weakness. May He be blessed forever, for so much glory all at once would have been more than so base and wicked a person could bear: knowing this, the compassionate Lord prepared me for it by degrees.

Your Reverence may suppose that it would have needed no great effort to behold those hands and that beauteous face. But there is such beauty about glorified bodies that the glory which illumines them throws all who look upon such supernatural loveliness into confusion. I was so much afraid, then, that I was plunged into turmoil and confusion, though later I began to feel such certainty and security that my fear was soon lost.

One year, on Saint Paul's Day, when I was at Mass, I saw a complete representation of this most sacred Humanity, just as in a picture of His resurrection body, in very great beauty and majesty; this I described in detail to Your Reverence in writing, at your very insistent request. It distressed me terribly to have to do so, for it is impossible to write such a description without a disruption of one's very being, but I did the best I could and so there is no reason for me to repeat the attempt here. I will only say that, if there were nothing else in Heaven to delight the eyes but the extreme beauty of the glorified bodies there, that alone would be the greatest bliss. A most especial bliss, then, will it be to us when we see the Humanity of Jesus Christ; for, if it is so even on earth, where His Majesty reveals Himself according to what our wretchedness can bear, what will it be where the fruition of that joy is complete? Although this vision is imaginary, I never saw it, or any other vision, with the eyes of the body, but only with the eyes of the soul.

Those who know better than I say that the type of vision already described[1] is nearer perfection than

---

1. I.e., the intellectual vision. By "this," of course, is meant the imaginary vision.

this, while this in its turn is much more so than those which are seen with the eyes of the body. The last-named type, they say, is the lowest and the most open to delusions from the devil. At that time I was not aware of this, and wished that, as this favour was being granted me, it could have been of such a kind as was visible to the eyes of the body, and then my confessor would not tell me I was imagining it. And no sooner had the vision faded — the very moment, indeed, after it had gone — than I began to think the same thing myself — that I had imagined it — and was worried at having spoken about it to my confessor and wondered if I had been deceiving him. Here was another cause for distress, so I went to him and consulted him about it. He asked me if I had told him what the vision really looked like to me or if I had meant to deceive him. I said I had told him the truth, for I felt sure I had not been lying or had had any such intention; I would not think one thing and say another for the whole world. This he well knew, and so he managed to calm me. It worried me so much to have to go to him about these things that I cannot imagine how the devil could ever have suggested to me that I must be inventing them and thus be torturing myself. But the Lord made such haste to grant me this favour and to make its reality plain that my doubt about its being fancy left me immediately and since then it has become quite clear to me how silly I was. For, if I were to spend years and years imagining how to invent anything so beautiful, I could not do it, and I do not even know how I should try, for, even in its whiteness and radiance alone, it exceeds all that we can imagine.

It is not a radiance which dazzles, but a soft whiteness and an infused radiance which, without wearying the eyes, causes them the greatest delight; nor are they wearied by the brightness which they see in seeing this Divine beauty. So different from any earthly light is the brightness and light now revealed to the eyes that, by comparison with it, the brightness of our sun seems quite dim and we should never want to open our eyes again for the purpose of seeing it. It is as if we were to look at a very clear stream, in a bed of crystal, reflecting the sun's rays, and then to see a very muddy stream, in an earthy bed and overshadowed by clouds. Not that the sun, or any other such light, enters into the vision: on the contrary, it is like a natural light and all other kinds of light seem artificial. It is a light which never gives place to night, and, being always light, is disturbed by nothing. It is of such a kind, indeed, that no one, however powerful his intellect, could, in the whole course of his life, imagine it as it is. And so quickly does God reveal it to us that, even if we needed to open our eyes in order to see it, there would not be time for us to do so. But it is all the same whether they are open or closed: if the Lord is pleased for us to see it, we shall do so even against our will. There is nothing powerful enough to divert our attention from it, and we can neither resist it nor attain to it by any diligence or care of our own. This I have conclusively proved by experience, as I shall relate.

I should like now to say something of the way in which the Lord reveals Himself through these visions. I do not mean that. I shall describe how it is that He can introduce this strong light into the inward sense and give the understanding an image so clear that it seems like reality. That is a matter for learned men to explain. The Lord has not been pleased to grant me to understand how it is; and I am so ignorant, and my understanding is so dull that, although many attempts have been made to explain it to me, I have not yet succeeded in understanding how it can happen, There is no doubt about this: I have not a keen understanding, although Your Reverence may think I have; again and again I have proved that my mind has to be spoon-fed, as they say, if it is to retain anything. Occasionally my confessor used to be astounded at the depths of my ignorance, and it never became clear to me how God did this and how it was possible that He should; nor, in fact, did I want to know, so I never asked anyone about it, though, as I have said, I have for many years been in touch with men of sound learning. What I did ask them was whether certain things were sinful or no: as for the rest, all I needed was to remember that God did everything and then I realized that I had no reason to be afraid and every reason to praise Him. Difficulties like that only arouse devotion in me, and the greater they are, the greater is the devotion.

I will describe, then, what I have discovered by experience. How the Lord effects it, Your Reverence will explain better than I and will expound everything obscure of which I do not know the explanation. At certain times it really seemed to me that it was an image I was seeing; but on many other occasions I thought it was no image, but Christ Himself, such was the brightness with which He was pleased to reveal Himself to me. Sometimes, because of its indistinctness, I would think the vision was an image, though it was like no earthly painting, however perfect, and I have seen a great many good ones. It is ridiculous to think that the one thing is any more like the other than a living person is like his portrait: however well the portrait is done, it can never look completely natural: one sees, in fact, that it is a dead thing. But let us pass over that, apposite and literally true through it is.

I am not saying this as a comparison, for comparisons are never quite satisfactory: it is the actual truth. The difference is similar to that between something living and something painted, neither more so nor less. For if what I see is an image it is a living image — not a dead man but the living Christ. And He shows me that He is both Man and God — not as He was in the sepulchre, but as He was when He left it after rising from the dead. Sometimes He comes with such majesty that no one can doubt it is the Lord Himself; this is especially so after Communion, for we know that He is there, since the Faith tells us so. He reveals Himself so completely as the Lord of that inn, the soul, that it feels as though it were wholly dissolved and consumed in Christ. O my Jesus, if one could but describe the majesty with which Thou dost reveal Thyself! How completely art Thou Lord of the whole world, and of the heavens, and of a thousand other worlds, and of countless worlds and heavens that Thou hast created! And the majesty with which Thou dost reveal Thyself shows the soul that to be Lord of this is nothing for Thee.

Here it becomes evident, my Jesus, how trifling is the power of all the devils in comparison with Thine, and how he who is pleasing to Thee can trample upon all the hosts of hell. Here we see with what reason the devils trembled when Thou didst descend into Hades: well might they have longed for a thousand deeper hells in order to flee from such great Majesty! I see that Thou art pleased to reveal to the soul the greatness of Thy Majesty, together with the power of this most sacred Humanity in union with the Divinity. Here is a clear picture of what the Day of Judgment will be, when we shall behold the Majesty of this King and see the rigour of His judgment upon the wicked. Here we find true humility, giving the soul power to behold its own wretchedness, of which it cannot be ignorant. Here is shame and genuine repentance for sin; for, though it sees God revealing His love to it, the soul can find no place to hide itself and thus is utterly confounded. I mean that, when the Lord is pleased to reveal to the soul so much of His greatness and majesty, the vision has such exceeding great power that I believe it would be impossible to endure, unless the Lord were pleased to help the soul in a most supernatural way by sending it into a rapture or an ecstasy, during the fruition of which the vision of that Divine Presence is lost. Though it is true that afterwards the vision is forgotten, the majesty and beauty of God are so deeply imprinted upon the soul that it is impossible to forget these — save when the Lord is pleased for the soul to suffer the great loneliness and aridity that I shall describe later; for then it seems even to forget God Himself. The soul is now a new creature: it is continuously absorbed in God; it seems to me that a new and living love of God is beginning to work within it to a very high degree; for, though the former type of vision which, as I said, reveals God without presenting any image of Him, is of a higher kind, yet, if the memory of it is to last, despite our weakness, and if the thoughts are to be well occupied, it is a great thing that so Divine a Presence should be presented to the imagination and should remain within it. These two kinds of vision almost invariably occur simultaneously, and, as they come in this way, the eyes of the soul see the excellence and the beauty and the glory of the most holy Humanity. And in the other way which has been described it is revealed to us how He is God, and that He is powerful, and can do all things, and commands all things, and rules all things, and fills all things with His love.

This vision is to be very highly esteemed, and, in my view, there is no peril in it, as its effects show that the devil has no power over it. Three or four times, I think, he has attempted to present the Lord Himself to me in this way, by making a false likeness of Him. He takes the form of flesh, but he cannot counterfeit the glory which the vision has when it comes from God. He makes these attempts in order to destroy the effects of the genuine vision that the soul has experienced; but the soul, of its own accord, resists them: it then becomes troubled, despondent and restless; loses the devotion and joy which it had before; and is unable to pray. At the beginning of my experiences, as I have said, this happened to me three or four times. It is so very different from a true vision that I think, even if a soul has experienced only the Prayer of Quiet, it will become aware of the difference, from the effects which have been described in the chapter on locutions. The thing is very easy to recognize; and, unless a soul wants to be deceived, I do not think the devil will deceive it if it walks in humility and simplicity. Anyone, of course, who has had a genuine vision from God will recognize the devil's work almost at once; he will begin by giving the soul consolations and favours, but it will thrust them from it. And further, I think, the devil's consolations must be different from those of God: there is no suggestion in them of pure and chaste love and it very soon becomes easy to see whence they come. So, in my view, where a soul has had experience, the devil will be unable to do it any harm.

Of all impossibilities, the most impossible is that these true visions should be the work of the imagination. There is no way in which this could be so: by the mere beauty and whiteness of a single one of the hands which we are shown the imagination is completely transcended. In any case, there is no other way in which it would be possible for us to see in a moment things of which we have no recollection, which we have never thought of, and which, even in a long period of time, we could not invent with our imagination, because, as I have already said, they far transcend what we can comprehend on earth. Whether we could possibly be in any way responsible for this will be clear from what I shall now say. If, in a vision, the representation proceeded from our own understanding, quite apart from the fact that it would not bring about the striking effects which are produced when a vision is of God, or, indeed, any effects at all, the position would be like that of a man who wants to put himself to sleep but stays awake because sleep has not come to him. He needs it — perhaps his brain is tired — and so is anxious for it; and he settles down to doze, and does all he can to go off to sleep, and sometimes thinks he is succeeding, but if is not real sleep it will not restore him or refresh his brain — indeed, the brain sometimes grows wearier. Something like that will be the case here: instead of being restored and becoming strong, the soul will grow wearier and become tired and peevish. It is impossible for human tongue to exaggerate the riches which a vision from God brings to the soul: it even bestows health and refreshment on the body.

I used to put forward this argument, together with others, when they told me, as they often did, that I was being deceived by the devil and that it was all the work of my imagination. I also drew such comparisons as I could and as the Lord revealed to my understanding. But it was all too little purpose, because there were some very holy persons in the place, by comparison with whom I was a lost creature; and, as God was not leading these persons by that way, they were afraid and thought that what I saw was the result of my sins. They repeated to one another what I said, so that before long they all got to know about it, though I had spoken of it only to my confessor and to those with whom he had commanded me to discuss it.

I once said to the people who were talking to me in this way that if they were to tell me that a person whom I knew well and had just been speaking to was not herself at all, but that I was imagining her to be so, and that they knew this was the case, I should certainly believe them rather than my own eyes. But, I added, if that person left some jewels with me, which I was actually holding in my hands as pledges of her great love, and if, never having had any before, I were thus to find myself rich instead of poor, I could not possibly believe that this was delusion, even if I wanted to. And, I said, I could show them these jewels — for all who knew me were well aware how my soul had changed: my confessor himself testified to this, for the difference was very great in every respect, and no fancy, but such as all could clearly see. As I had previously been so wicked, I concluded, I could not believe that, if the devil were doing this to delude me and drag me down to hell, he would make use of means which so completely defeated their own ends by taking away my vices and making me virtuous and strong; for it was quite clear to me that these experiences had immediately made me a different person.

CHAPTER 20

On Perceiving God

William Alston

I want to explore and defend the idea that the experience, or, as I shall say, the *perception,* of God plays an epistemic role with respect to beliefs about God importantly analogous to that played by sense perception with respect to beliefs about the physical world. The nature of that latter role is, of course, a matter of controversy, and I have no time here to go into those controversies. It is admitted, however, on (almost) all hands that sense perception provides us with knowledge (justified belief) about current states of affairs in the immediate environment of the perceiver and that knowledge of this sort is somehow required for any further knowledge of the physical world. The possibility I wish to explore is that what a person takes to be an experience of God can provide him/her with knowledge (justified beliefs) about what God is doing, or how God is "situated," vis-a-vis that subject at that moment. Thus, by experiencing the presence and activity of God, S can come to know (justifiably believe) that God is sustaining her in being, filling her with His love, strengthening her, or communicating a certain message to her. Let's call beliefs as to how God is currently related to the subject *M-beliefs* ("M" for manifestation); these are the "perceptual beliefs" of the theological sphere. I shall suppose that here too the "perceptual" knowledge one acquires from experience is crucial for whatever else we can learn about God, though I won't have time to explore and defend that part of the position; I will have my hands full defending the claim that M-beliefs are justified. I will just make two quick points about the role of M-beliefs in the larger scheme. First, just as with our knowledge of the physical world, the recognition of a crucial role for perceptual knowledge is compatible with a wide variety of views as to just how it figures in the total system and as to what else is involved. Second, an important difference between the two spheres is that in the theological sphere perceptual beliefs as to what God has "said" (communicated, revealed) to one or another person play a major role.

I have been speaking alternatively of perceptual *knowledge* and of the *justification* of perceptual beliefs. In this paper I shall concentrate on justification, leaving to one side whatever else is involved in knowledge. It will be my contention that (putative) experience of God is a source of justification for M-beliefs, somewhat in the way that sense experience is a source of justification for perceptual beliefs. Again, it is quite controversial what this latter way is. I shall be thinking of it in terms of a direct-realist construal of sense perception, according to which I can be justified in supposing that my dog is wagging his tail just because something is visually presenting itself to me as (looks like) my dog wagging his tail; that is, it looks to me in such a way that I am thereby justified in thereby supposing it to be my dog wagging his tail. Analogously I think of the "experience of God" as a matter of something's presenting itself to one's experience as God (doing so and so); so that here too the subject is justified in believing that God is present to her, or is doing so and so vis-a-vis her, just because that is the way in which the object is presented to her experience. (For the purposes of this paper let's focus on those cases in which this presentation is not via any *sensory* qualities or sensorily perceivable objects. The experience involved will be nonsensory in character.) It is because I think of the experience of God as having basically the same structure as the sense perception of physical objects that I feel entitled to speak of "perceiving God." But though I construe the matter in direct-realist terms, most of what I have to say here will be relevant to a defense of the more general claim that the experiential justification of M-beliefs is importantly parallel to the experiential justification of perceptual beliefs about the physical environment, on any halfway plausible construal of the latter, at least on any halfway plausible realist construal.

I shall develop the position by way of responding to a number of objections. This procedure reflects my conviction that the very considerable incidence of putative perceptions of God creates a certain initial presumption that these experiences are what they seem to be and that something can thereby be learned about God.

Objection I. What reason do we have for supposing that anyone ever does really perceive God? In order for S to perceive God it would have to be the case that (1) God exists, and (2) God is related to S or to his experience in such a way as to be perceivable by him. Only after we have seen reason to accept all that will we take seriously any claim to perceive God.

Answer. It all depends on what you will take as a reason. What you have in mind, presumably, are reasons drawn from some source other than perceptions of God, e.g., metaphysical arguments for the existence and nature of God. But why do you think you are justified in that restriction? We don't proceed in this way with respect to sense perception. Although in determining whether a particular alleged perception was genuine we don't make use of the results of *that* perception, we do utilize what has been observed in many other cases. And what alternative is there? The conditions of veridical sense perception have to do with states of affairs and causal interactions in the physical world, matters to which we have no cognitive access that is not based on sense perception. In like fashion, if there is a divine reality why suppose that the conditions of veridically perceiving it could be ascertained without relying on perceptions of *it*? In

requiring external validation in this case but not the other you are arbitrarily imposing a double standard.

Objection II. There are many contradictions in the body of M-beliefs. In particular, persons report communications from God that contradict other reported communications. How, then, can one claim that all M-beliefs are justified?

Answer. What is (should be) claimed is only *prima facie* justification. When a person believes that God is experientially present to him, that belief is justified *unless* the subject has sufficient reasons to suppose it to be false or to suppose that the experience is not, in these circumstances, sufficiently indicative of the truth of the belief. This is, of course, precisely the status of individual perceptual beliefs about the physical environment. When, seeming to see a lake, I believe there to be a lake in front of me, my belief is thereby justified unless I have sufficient reason to suppose it false or to suppose that, in these circumstances, the experience is not sufficiently indicative of the truth of the belief.

Objection III. It is rational to form beliefs about the physical environment on the basis of the way that environment appears to us in sense experience (call this practice of belief formation *SP)* because that is a generally reliable mode of belief formation. And it is reliable just because, in normal conditions, sense experience varies concomitantly with variations in what we take ourselves to be perceiving. But we have no reason to suppose any such regular covariation for putative perception of God. And hence we lack reason for regarding as rational the parallel practice of forming M-beliefs on the basis of what is taken to be a perception of God (call that practice *RE).*

Answer. This is another use of a double standard. How do we know that normal sense experience varies concomitantly with perceived objects? We don't know this a priori. Rather, we have strong empirical evidence for it. That is, by relying on sense perception for our data we have piled up evidence for the reliability of SP. Let's call the kind of circularity exhibited here *epistemic circularity*. It is involved whenever the premises in an argument for the reliability or rationality of a belief-forming practice have themselves been acquired by that practice.[1] If we allow epistemically circular arguments, the reliability of RE can be supported in the same way. Among the things people have claimed to learn from RE is that God will enable people to experience His presence and activity from time to time in a veridical way. By relying on what one learns from the practice of RE, one can show that RE is a reliable belief-forming practice. On the other hand, if epistemically circular arguments are not countenanced, there can be no significant basis for a reliability claim in either case.

Objection IV. A claim to perceive X, and so to form reliable perceptual beliefs about X on the basis of this, presupposes that the experience involved is best explained by the activity of X, *inter alia*. But it seems that we can give adequate explanations of putative experiences of God in purely naturalistic terms, without bringing God into the explanation at all. Whereas we can't give adequate explanations of normal sense experience without bringing the experienced external objects into the explanation. Hence RE, but not SP, is discredited by these considerations.

Answer. I do not believe that much of a case can be made for the adequacy of any naturalistic explanation of experiences of God. But for present purposes I want to concentrate on the way in which this objection once more depends on a double standard. You will have no case at all for your claim unless you, question-beggingly, restrict yourself to sources of evidence that exclude RE. For from RE and systems built up on its output we learn that God is involved in the explanation of every fact whatever. But you would not proceed in that way with SP. If it is a question of determining the best explanation of sense experience you will, of course, make use of what you think you have learned from SP. Again, you have arbitrarily applied different standards to the two practices.

Here is another point. Suppose that one could give a purely psychological or physiological explanation of the experiences in question. That is quite compatible with God's figuring among their causes and, hence, coming into an ideally complete explanation. After all, it is presumably possible to give an adequate causal explanation of sense experience in terms of what goes on within the skull, but that is quite compatible with the external perceived objects' figuring further back along the causal chain.

Objection V. You have been accusing me of *arbitrarily* employing a double standard. But I maintain that RE differs from SP in ways that make different standards appropriate. SP is a pervasive and inescapable feature of our lives. Sense experience is insistent, omnipresent, vivid, and richly detailed. We use it as a source of information during all our waking hours. RE, by contrast, is not universally shared; and even for its devotees its practice is relatively infrequent. Moreover, its deliverances are, by comparison, meager, obscure, and uncertain. Thus when an output of RE does pop up, it is naturally greeted with more skepticism, and one properly demands more for its validation than in the case of so regular and central a part of our lives as SP.

Answer. I don't want to deny either the existence or the importance of these differences. I want to deny only that they have the alleged bearing on the epistemic situation. Why should we suppose that a cognitive access enjoyed only by a part of the population is less likely to be reliable than one that is universally distributed? Why should we suppose that a source that yields less detailed and less fully understood beliefs is more suspect than a richer source? A priori it would seem just as likely that some aspects of reality are accessible only to persons that satisfy certain conditions not satisfied by all human beings as that some aspects are equally accessible to all. A priori it would seem just as likely that some aspects of reality are humanly graspable only in a fragmentary and opaque manner as that some aspects are graspable in a

1. See my "Epistemic Circularity," *Philosophy and Phenomenological Research*, XLVII, 1 (September 1986): 1 – 30.

more nearly complete and pellucid fashion. Why view the one sort of cognitive claim with more suspicion than the other? I will agree that the spotty distribution of RE calls for explanation, as does the various cognitively unsatisfactory features of its output. But, for that matter, so does the universal distribution and cognitive richness of SP. And in both cases explanations are forthcoming, though in both cases the outputs of the practices are utilized in order to achieve those explanations. As for RE, the limited distribution may be explained by the fact that many persons are not prepared to meet the moral and other "way of life" conditions that God has set for awareness of Himself. And the cognitively unsatisfactory features of the doxastic output are explained by the fact that God infinitely exceeds our cognitive powers.

Objection VI. When someone claims to see a spruce tree in a certain spot, the claim is checkable. Other people can take a look, photographs can be taken, the subject's condition can be diagnosed, and so on. But there are no comparable checks and tests available in RE. And how can we take seriously a claim to have perceived an objective state of affairs if there is, in principle, no intersubjective way of determining whether that claim is correct?

Answer. The answer to this objection is implicit in a point made earlier, viz., that putative experience of God yields only prima facie justification, justification (unqualifiedly) provided there are no sufficient overriding considerations. This notion has a significant application only where there is what we may call an *overrider system*, i.e., ways of determining whether the facts are such as to indicate a belief from the range in question to be false and ways of determining whether conditions are such that the basis of the belief is sufficiently indicative of its truth. SP does contain such a system. What about RE? Here we must confront a salient difference between the two spheres. If we consider the way in which a body of beliefs has been developed on the basis of SP we find pretty much the same system across all cultures. But our encounters with God have spawned a number of different religious communities with beliefs and practices of worship which are quite different, though with some considerable overlap. These differences carry with them differences in overrider systems. But it remains true that if we consider any particular religious community which exhibits a significant commonality in doctrine and worship it will feature a more or less definite overrider system. For concreteness let's think of what I will call the *mainline Christian community*. (From this point onward I will use the term 'RE' for the practice of forming M-beliefs as it goes on in this community.) In that community a body of doctrine has developed concerning the nature of God, His purposes, and His interactions with mankind, including His appearances to us. If an M-belief contradicts this system that is a reason for deeming it false. Moreover there is a long and varied history of experiential encounters with God, embodied in written accounts as well as oral transmission. This provides bases for regarding particular experiences as more or less likely to be veridical, given the conditions, psychological or otherwise, in which they occurred, the character of the subject, and the effects in the life of the subject. Thus a socially established religious doxastic practice like RE will contain a rich system of overriders that provides resources for checking the acceptability of any particular M-belief.

But perhaps your point is rather that there are no *external* checks on a particular report, none that do not rely on other claims of the same sort. Let's agree that this is the case. But why suppose that to be any black mark against RE? Here is the double standard again. After all, particular claims within SP cannot be checked without relying on what we have learned from SP. Suppose I claim to see a fir tree in a certain spot. To check on this one would have to rely on other persons' perceptual reports as to what is at that spot, our general empirical knowledge of the likelihood of a fir tree in that locality, and so on. Apart from what we take ourselves to have learned from SP, we would have nothing to go on. One can hardly determine whether my report was accurate by intuiting self-evident truths or by consulting divine revelation. But if SP counts as having a system of checks even though this system involves relying on some outputs of the practice in order to put others to the test, why should RE be deemed to have no such system when its procedures exhibit the same structure? Once more you are, arbitrarily, setting quite different requirements for different practices.

Perhaps your point was that RE's system of checks is unlike SP's. In particular, the following difference can be discerned. Suppose I report seeing a morel at a certain spot in the forest. Now suppose that a number of qualified observers take a good look at that spot at that time and report that no morel is to be seen. In that case my report would have been decisively disconfirmed. But nothing like that is possible in RE. We can't lay down any conditions (of a sort the satisfaction of which we can determine) under which a properly qualified person will experience the presence of God if God is "there" to be experienced. Hence a particular report cannot be decisively disconfirmed by the experience of others.

But what epistemic relevance does this difference have? Why should we suppose that RE is rendered dubious for lacking checkability of this sort? Let's consider what makes this kind of intersubjective test possible for SP. Clearly it is that we have discovered fairly firm regularities in the behavior of physical things, including human sense perception. Since there are stable regularities in the ways in which physical objects disclose themselves to our perception, we can be assured that if X exists at a certain time and place and if S satisfies appropriate conditions then S is sure to perceive X. But no such tight regularities are discoverable in God's appearances to our experience. We can say something about the way in which such matters as the distribution of attention and the moral and spiritual state of the subject are conducive to such appearances; but these most emphatically do not add up to the sort of lawlike connections we get with SP. Now what about this difference? Is it to the epistemic discredit of RE that it does not enable us to discover such regularities? Well, that all depends on what it would be reasonable to expect if RE does put us

into effective cognitive contact with God. Given what we have learned about God and our relations to Him (from Re, supplemented by whatever other sources there be), should we expect to be able to discover such realities if God really exists? Clearly not. There are several important points here, but the most important is that it is contrary to God's plans for us to give us that much control, cognitive and practical. Hence it is quite understandable, if God exists and is as RE leads us to suppose, that we should not be able to ascertain the kinds of regularities that would make possible the kinds of intersubjective tests exhibited by SP. Hence, the epistemic status of RE is in no way diminished by its lack of such tests. Once more RE is subjected to an inappropriate standard. This time, however, it is not a double standard, but rather an inappropriate single standard. RE is being graded down for lacking positive features of other practices, where these features cannot reasonably be supposed to be generally necessary conditions of epistemic excellence, even for experiential practices. Thus my critic is exhibiting what we might term *epistemic chauvinism*, judging alien forms of life according to whether they conform to the home situation, a procedure as much to be deplored in the epistemic as in the political sphere.

Objection VII. How can it be rational to take RE as a source of justification when there are incompatible rivals that can lay claim to that status on exactly the same grounds? M-beliefs of different religious communities conflict to a considerable extent, particularly those concerning alleged divine messages, and the bodies of doctrine they support conflict even more. We get incompatible accounts of God's plans for us and requirements on us, of the conditions of salvation, and so on. This being the case, how can we pick out just one of these communal practices as yielding justified belief?

Answer. I take this to be by far the most serious difficulty with my position. I have chosen to concentrate on what I take to be less serious problems, partly because their consideration brings out better the main lineaments of the position, and partly because any serious treatment of this last problem would spill beyond the confines of this paper.[2] Here I shall have to content myself with making one basic point. We are not faced with the necessity of choosing only one such practice as yielding prima facie justified M-beliefs. The fact that there are incompatibilities between systems of religious beliefs, in M-beliefs and elsewhere, shows that not all M-beliefs can be true, but not that they cannot all be prima facie justified. After all, incompatible beliefs *within* a system can all be prima facie justified; that's the point of the prima facie qualification. When we are faced with a situation like that, the hope is that the overrider system and other winnowing devices will weed out the inconsistencies. To be sure, intersystem winnowing devices are hazier and more meager than those which are available within a system; but consistency, consonance with other well-entrenched beliefs and doxastic practices, and general reasonability and plausibility give us something to go on. Moreover, it may be that some religious ways of life fulfill their own promises more fully than others. Of course, there is never any guarantee that a unique way of resolving incompatibilities will present itself, even with a system. But where there are established practices of forming beliefs on the basis of experience, I believe the rational course is to regard each such belief as thereby prima facie justified, hoping that future developments, perhaps unforeseeable at present, will resolve fundamental incompatibilities.

In conclusion I will make explicit the general epistemological orientation I have been presupposing in my defense of RE. I take our human situation to be such that we engage in a plurality of basic doxastic practices, each of which involves a distinctive sort of input to belief-forming "mechanisms," a distinctive range of belief contents (a "subject matter" and ways of conceiving it), and a set of functions that determine belief contents as a function of input features. Each practice is socially established: socially shared, inculcated, reinforced, and propagated. In addition to expe-

riential practices, with which we have been concerned in this paper, there are, e.g., inferential practices, the input of which consists of beliefs, and the practice of forming memory beliefs. A doxastic practice is not restricted to the formation of first-level beliefs; it will also typically involve criteria and procedures of criticism of the beliefs thus formed; here we will find the "overrider systems" of which we were speaking earlier. In general, we learn these practices and engage in them long before we arrive at the stage of explicitly formulating their principles and subjecting them to critical reflection. Theory is deeply rooted in practice.

Nor, having arrived at the age of reason, can we turn our back on all that and take a fresh start, in the Cartesian spirit, choosing our epistemic procedures and criteria anew, on a purely "rational" basis.

Apart from reliance on doxastic tendencies with which we find ourselves, we literally have nothing to go on. Indeed, what Descartes did, as Thomas Reid trenchantly pointed out, was arbitrarily to pick one doxastic practice he found himself engaged in — accepting propositions that seem self-evident — and set that as a judge over all the others, with what results we are all too familiar. This is not to say that we must acquiesce in our prereflective doxastic tendencies in every respect. We can tidy things up, modify our established practices so as to make each more internally consistent and more consistent with the others. But, on the whole and for the most part, we have no choice but to continue to form beliefs in accordance with these practices and to take these ways of forming beliefs as paradigmatically conferring epistemic justification. And this is the way that epistemology has in fact gone, except for some arbitrary partiality. Of course it would be satisfying to economize our basic commitments by taking one or a few of these practices as basic and using them to validate the others; but we have made little progress in this enterprise over the centuries. It is not self-evident that sense perception is reliable, nor can we establish its reliability if

---

2. For an extended treatment of this issue see my "Religious Experience and Religious Diversity," forthcoming in *Christian Scholars' Review*.

we restrict ourselves to premises drawn from introspection; we cannot show that deductive reasoning is valid without using deductive reasoning to do so; and so on. We are endowed with strong tendencies to engage in a number of distinct doxastic practices, none of which can be warranted on the basis of others. It is clearly the better part of wisdom to recognize beliefs that emerge from these practices to be rational and justified, at least once they are properly sifted and refined.

In this paper I have undertaken to extend this account to doxastic practices that are not universally practiced. Except for that matter of distribution and the other peripheral matters mentioned in Objection V and except for being faced with actually existing rivals, a religious experiential doxastic practice like RE seems to me to be on all fours with SP and other universal practices. It too involves a distinctive range of inputs, a range of belief contents, and functions that map features of the former onto contents of the latter.

It is socially established within a certain community. It involves higher level procedures of correction and modification of its first-level beliefs. Though it *may* be acquired in a deliberate and self-conscious fashion, it is more typically acquired in a practical, prereflective form. Though it is obviously evitable in a way SP, e.g., is not, for many of its practitioners it is just about as firmly entrenched.

These similarities lead me to the conclusion that if, as it seems we must concede, a belief is prima facie justified by virtue of emerging from one of the universal basic practices, we should also concede the same status to the products of RE. I have sought to show that various plausible-sounding objections to this position depend on the use of a double standard or reflect arbitrary epistemic chauvinism. They involve subjecting RE to inappropriate standards. Once we appreciate these points, we can see the strength of the case for RE as one more epistemically autonomous practice of belief formation and source of justification.

QUESTIONS AND FURTHER READINGS

Questions for Discussion

1. In the First Way argument, is Aquinas arguing that the universe could not be temporally infinite and so must have a cause? Explain.

2. Do you find any of the cosmological arguments in this section compelling? Why or why not?

3. Does the universe need a cause? If so, why does God not also need a cause?

4. Do you find any of the design arguments offered here convincing? Explain.

5. How does the theory of evolution affect the design argument?

6. Is Michael Behe's irreducible complexity argument a "God of the Gaps" fallacy?

7. Do you think Collins's version of the fine-tuning argument is successful? Why or why not?

8. Many argue that the presence of evil and chaos in the universe provides a defeater for the design argument. What is your response?

9. How would you describe the ontological argument in your own words?

10. In response to the ontological argument, it has been argued that if the concept of a perfect island does not prove that it exists, then the concept of God does not prove God exists. Do you agree or disagree, and why?

11. Explain the central argument presented by Bahnsen. Do you think this argument is successful? Why or why not?

12. What are some objections that come to mind to Pascal's Wager? Should one gamble on faith? Explain.

13. How does religious pluralism affect the plausibility of this wager?

14. If you were writing to a friend and wanted to present the moral argument, how would you explain and defend it?

15. Is it reasonable to believe that absolute morals exist and a personal God does not exist? Explain.

16. Do exceptional cases (lying to save a life) negate moral absolutes? If so, why? If not, why not?

17. In Plato's *Euthyphro*, Socrates asks, "Do the gods command the good because it is good, or is it good because it is commanded by the gods?" In theistic terms, the question would be, "Does God command the good because it is good, or is it good because it is commanded by God?" How does Copan address this issue, and what is your analysis of it?

18. Can the kind of religious experiences that Teresa of Avila had, along with countless other Christians, be used as evidence for the veracity of the Christian faith? Why or why not?

19. With respect to Alston's article, do you think that his view of the value of personal experiences of God adds to the validity of Christianity? Explain.

20. Antony Flew, one of the most renowned atheists of the twentieth century, says that he converted to theism because of the evidence (you can read his story at www.biola.edu/antonyflew/). What role do you think evidence plays in faith? Is faith contrary to evidence and reason?

Further Readings

Copan, Paul (2004). "Morality and Meaning without God: Another Failed Attempt," *Philosophia Christi* 6:295 – 304. (A review essay on the work of atheist Michael Martin.)

Craig, William Lane (2000). *The Kalam Cosmological Argument.* Eugene, OR: Wipf & Stock. (A historical overview and defense of the kalam argument.)

Craig, William Lane (2001). *The Cosmological Argument from Plato to Leibniz.* Eugene, OR: Wipf & Stock. (Analyzes the cosmological arguments of thirteen major proponents, including significant Jewish and Islamic thinkers.)

Everitt, Nicholas (2004). *The Non-Existence of God.* London: Routledge. (Critically assesses traditional and recent arguments about God's existence.)

Frame, John M. (1994). *Apologetics to the Glory of God: An Introduction.* Presbyterian & Reformed. (An introduction to apologetics from a Reformed perspective that emphasizes the transcendental argument.)

Graham, Gordon (2001). *Evil and Christian Ethics.* Cambridge: Cambridge University Press. (An insightful discussion of goodness and evil.)

Leadership University. www.leaderu.com. (A website dedicated to theology and the integration of faith and learning; contains many academic papers on arguments for the existence of God.)

Leibniz, Gottfried W. (1714; reprint, 1898/1951). "Monadology," in *The Monadology and Other Philosophical Writings.* Translated by Robert Latta. Oxford: Oxford University Press. (Contains Leibniz's "sufficient reasons" version of the cosmological argument.)

Plato ([c. 360 BC] 1988). *Laws.* Chicago: University of Chicago Press. (Contains one of the earliest versions of the cosmological argument — see specifically Stephanus pagination numbers 893 – 96.)

Rowe, William (1975). *The Cosmological Argument.* Princeton, NJ: Princeton University Press. (A critical study of versions of the cosmological argument.)

Sorley, W. R. (1921). *Moral Values and the Idea of God.* 2nd ed. New York: Macmillan. (A classic defense of the moral argument.)

Wainwright, William J. (2005). *Religion and Morality.* Burlington, VT: Ashgate. (Focuses on the Euthyphro argument and various aspects of divine command theory.)

PART 3

THE TRINITY

The doctrine of the Trinity is a fundamental teaching of Christianity. While the term *Trinity* does not appear in the pages of the Bible, Christians affirm that it is rooted in the Bible, most especially in the New Testament. The Trinity, as a doctrine, developed during the first few centuries of Christianity as the early Christians reflected on the biblical teachings and as they engaged in the practices of worshiping God the Father, Jesus, and the Holy Spirit. Due to various difficulties and disagreements that arose regarding the doctrine, church councils were formed to establish agreed-upon teachings. Ecumenical councils were established, which created creeds to reflect the orthodox understanding of the Trinity; and throughout the centuries Christians have continually discussed and debated various issues related to this orthodox understanding, including the meaning of a person, a nature, and a substance.

The first selection offered in this section is that of Origen, an early Christian theologian of the late second/early third centuries. He was a brilliant scholar and apologist and was schooled in biblical studies and Greek philosophy. In this piece, he articulates and defends many aspects of the view of God as Trinity, including the generation of the Son from the Father, the unitary substance of God, and the activity of creation by God through the Son.

Next, two historic Trinitarian creeds are given: the Athanasian and Nicene (or more accurately, Nicene-Constantinopolitan) Creeds. The Athanasian Creed is a statement of faith that focuses on the Trinity and Christology. It is the first creed in which the equality of the three persons of the Trinity is explicitly stated. While it is not widely used by Eastern Christians, it is so by Christians in the West and has been liturgically since the sixth century.

The Nicene Creed (so called because it was adopted in the city of Nicea, the location of which is in modern Turkey) was originally formulated by the first ecumenical council in AD 325. A formal statement of doctrine of the Christian faith to defend orthodoxy from Arianism, this creed is widely used in Christian liturgy and is normative for the Eastern Orthodox Church, the Roman Catholic Church, the Anglican Church, and most Protestant denominations. Interestingly, the Eastern version of the creed says that the Holy Spirit proceeds from the Father. The Western version states that the Holy Spirit proceeds not only from the Father, but from the Father and the Son (Latin, *filioque*). This disputed issue remains unresolved to this day.

Thomas Aquinas, one of the most influential theologians of the medieval church, wrote extensively about the Trinity. His general apologetic approach regarding the Trinity includes the attempt to demonstrate that, while God is one, nevertheless each of the persons of the Godhead is distinct. His selections that we have included examine the relations between the persons of the Trinity, the meaning of the terms *person* and *essence*, and whether the knowledge of the Trinity can be known by natural reason.

The next piece was written by Richard of St. Victor. While many theologians have maintained that the doctrine of the Trinity can only be accepted as a confession dependent on divine revelation, Richard offers an argument for it. His argument, in brief, is that the nature of God is perfect love, and as such it must reflect a trinity of persons — a community where perfect love can be expressed.

The final essay in this section was written by a contemporary philosopher/theologian, Thomas Morris. He first contrasts the Christian understanding of God as existing in threefold form — three persons in the unity of one divine nature — with the heresies of modalism and polytheism. He then argues for the doctrine of the Trinity, responding to *the problem of the lonely God* in his defense. He discusses both singularity theories and social theories and concludes by noting that the doctrine of the Trinity is not an opaque mystery impenetrable by human thought. He claims that we can make important headway in our attempts to understand the most distinctive Christian claims about God.

Regarding the Trinity

Origen

Chapter IV

28. It is now time, after the rapid consideration which to the best of our ability we have given to the topics discussed, to recapitulate, by way of summing up what we have said in different places, the individual points, and first of all to restate our conclusions regarding the Father, and the Son, and the Holy Spirit.

Seeing God the Father is invisible and inseparable from the Son, the Son is not generated from Him by prolation, as some suppose. For if the Son be a prolation of the Father (the term prolation being used to signify such a generation as that of animals or men usually is), then, of necessity, both He who prolated and He who *was* prolated are corporeal. For we do not say, as the heretics suppose, that some part of the substance of God was converted into the Son, or that the Son was procreated by the Father out of things non-existent, i.e., beyond His own substance, so that there once was a time when He did not exist; but, putting away all corporeal conceptions, we say that the Word and Wisdom was begotten out of the invisible and incorporeal without any corporeal feeling, as if it were an act of the will proceeding from the understanding. Nor, seeing He is called the Son of (His) love, will it appear absurd if in this way He be called the Son of (His) will. Nay, John also indicates that God is Light, and Paul also declares that the Son is the splendour of everlasting light. As light, accordingly, could never exist without splendour, so neither can the Son be understood to exist without the Father; for He is called the express image of His person, and the Word and Wisdom. How, then, can it be asserted that there once was a time when He was not the Son? For that

is nothing else than to say that there was once a time when He was not the Truth, nor the Wisdom, nor the Life, although in all these He is judged to be the perfect essence of God the Father; for these things cannot be severed from Him, or even be separated from His essence. And although these qualities are said to be many in understanding, yet in their nature and essence they are one, and in them is the fullness of divinity. Now this expression which we employ — that there never was a time when He did not exist — is to be understood with an allowance. For these very words "when" or "never" have a meaning that relates to time, whereas the statements made regarding Father, Son, and Holy Spirit are to be understood as transcending all time, all ages, and all eternity. For it is the Trinity alone which exceeds the comprehension not only of temporal but even of eternal intelligence; while other things which are not included in it are to be measured by times and ages. This Son of God, then, in respect of the Word being God, which was in the beginning with God, no one will logically suppose to be contained in any place; nor yet in respect of His being Wisdom, or Truth, or the Life, or Righteousness, or Sanctification, or Redemption: for all these properties do not require space to be able to act or to operate, but each one of them is to be understood as meaning those individuals who participate in His virtue and working.

29. Now, if any one were to say that, through those who are partakers of the Word of God, or of His Wisdom, or His Truth, or His Life, the Word and Wisdom itself appeared to be contained in a place, we should have to say to him in answer, that there is no doubt that Christ, in respect of being the Word or Wisdom, or all other things, was in Paul, and that he therefore

said, Do you seek a proof of Christ speaking in me? and again, I live, yet not I, but Christ lives in me. Seeing, then, He was in Paul, who will doubt that He was in a similar manner in Peter and in John, and in each one of the saints; and not only in those who are upon the earth, but in those also who are in heaven? For it is absurd to say that Christ was in Peter and in Paul, but not in Michael the archangel, nor in Gabriel. And from this it is distinctly shown that the divinity of the Son of God was not shut up in some place; otherwise it would have been in it only, and not in another. But since, in conformity with the majesty of its incorporeal nature, it is confined to no place; so, again, it cannot be understood to be wanting in any. But this is understood to be the sole difference, that although He is in different individuals as we have said — as Peter, or Paul, or Michael, or Gabriel — He is not in a similar way in all beings whatever. For He is more fully and clearly, and, so to speak, more openly in archangels than in other holy men. And this is evident from the statement, that when all who are saints have arrived at the summit of perfection, they are said to be made like, or equal to, the angels, agreeably to the declaration in the Gospels. Whence it is clear that Christ is in each individual in as great a degree as the amount of his deserts allows.

30. Having, then, briefly restated these points regarding the nature of the Trinity, it follows that we notice shortly this statement also, that by the Son are said to be created all things that are in heaven, and that are in earth, visible and invisible, whether they be thrones, or dominions, or principalities, or powers: all things were created by Him, and for Him; and He is before all, and all things consist by Him, who is the Head. In conformity with which John also in his Gospel says: All things were created by Him; and without Him was not anything made. And David, intimating that the mystery of the entire Trinity was (concerned) in the creation of all things, says: By the Word of the Lord were the heavens made; and all the host of them by the Spirit of His mouth.

After these points we shall appropriately remind (the reader) of the bodily advent and incarnation of the only-begotten Son of God, with respect to whom we are not to suppose that all the majesty of His divinity is confined within the limits of His slender body, so that all the word of God, and His wisdom, and essential truth, and life, was either rent asunder from the Father, or restrained and confined within the narrowness of His bodily person, and is not to be considered to have operated anywhere besides; but the cautious acknowledgment of a religious man ought to be between the two, so that it ought neither to be believed that anything of divinity was wanting in Christ, nor that any separation at all was made from the essence of the Father, which is everywhere. For some such meaning seems to be indicated by John the Baptist, when he said to the multitude in the bodily absence of Jesus, There stands one among you whom you know not: He it is who comes after me, the latchet of whose shoes I am not worthy to unloose. For it certainly could not be said of Him, who was absent, so far as His bodily presence is concerned, that He was standing in the midst of those among whom the Son of God was not bodily present.

31. Let no one, however, suppose that by this we affirm that some portion of the divinity of the Son of God was in Christ, and that the remaining portion was elsewhere or everywhere, which may be the opinion of those who are ignorant of the nature of an incorporeal and invisible essence. For it is impossible to speak of the parts of an incorporeal being, or to make any division of them; but He is in all things, and through all things, and above all things, in the manner in which we have spoken above, i.e., in the manner in which He is understood to be either wisdom, or the word, or the life, or the truth, by which method of understanding all confinement of a local kind is undoubtedly excluded. The Son of God, then, desiring for the salvation of the human race to appear unto men, and to sojourn among them, assumed not only a human body, as some suppose, but also a soul resembling our souls indeed in nature, but in will and power resembling Himself, and such as might unfailingly accomplish all the desires and arrangements of the word and wisdom. Now, that He had a soul, is most clearly

shown by the Saviour in the Gospels, when He said, No man takes my life from me, but I lay it down of myself. I have power to lay down my life, and I have power to take it again. And again, My soul is sorrowful even unto death. And again, Now is my soul troubled. For the Word of God is not to be understood to be a sorrowful and troubled soul, because with the authority of divinity He says, I have power to lay down my life. Nor yet do we assert that the Son of God was in that soul as he was in the soul of Paul or Peter and the other saints, in whom Christ is believed to speak as He does in Paul. But regarding all these we are to hold, as Scripture declares, No one is clean from filthiness, not even if his life lasted but a single day. But this soul which was in Jesus, before it knew the evil, selected the good; and because He loved righteousness, and hated iniquity, therefore God anointed Him with the oil of gladness above His fellows. He is anointed, then, with the oil of gladness when He is united to the word of God in a stainless union, and by this means alone of all souls was incapable of sin, because it was capable of (receiving) well and fully the Son of God; and therefore also it is one with Him, and is named by His titles, and is called Jesus Christ, by whom all things are said to be made. Of which soul, seeing it had received into itself the whole wisdom of God, and the truth, and the life, I think that the apostle also said this: Our life is hidden with Christ in God; but when Christ, who is our life, shall appear, then shall we also appear with him in glory. For what other Christ can be here understood, who is said to be hidden in God, and who is afterwards to appear, except Him who is related to have been anointed with the oil of gladness, i.e., to have been filled with God essentially, in whom he is now said to be hidden? For on this account is Christ proposed as an example to all believers, because as He always, even before he knew evil at all, selected the good, and loved righteousness, and hated iniquity, and therefore God anointed Him with the oil of gladness; so also ought each one, after a lapse or sin, to cleanse himself from his stains, making Him his example, and, taking Him as the guide of his journey, enter upon the steep way of virtue, that so perchance by this means,

as far as possible we may, by imitating Him, be made partakers of the divine nature, according to the words of Scripture: He that says that he believes in Christ, ought so to walk, as He also walked.

This word, then, and this wisdom, by the imitation of which we are said to be either wise or rational (beings), becomes all things to all men, that it may gain all; and because it is made weak, it is therefore said of it, Though He was crucified through weakness, yet He lives by the power of God. Finally, to the Corinthians who were weak, Paul declares that he knew nothing, save Jesus Christ, and Him crucified.

32. Some, indeed, would have the following language of the apostle applied to the soul itself, as soon as it had assumed flesh from Mary, viz., Who, being in the form of God, thought it not robbery to be equal with God, but divested Himself (of His glory) taking upon Himself the form of a servant; since He undoubtedly restored it to the form of God by means of better examples and training, and recalled it to that fullness of which He had divested Himself.

As now by participation in the Son of God one is adopted as a son, and by participating in that wisdom which is in God is rendered wise, so also by participation in the Holy Spirit is a man rendered holy and spiritual. For it is one and the same thing to have a share in the Holy Spirit, which is (the Spirit) of the Father and the Son, since the nature of the Trinity is one and incorporeal. And what we have said regarding the participation of the soul is to be understood of angels and heavenly powers in a similar way as of souls, because every rational creature needs a participation in the Trinity.

Respecting also the plan of this visible world — seeing one of the most important questions usually raised is as to the manner of its existence — we have spoken to the best of our ability in the preceding pages, for the sake of those who are accustomed to seek the grounds of their belief in our religion, and also for those who stir against us heretical questions, and who are accustomed to bandy about the word matter, which they have not yet been able to understand; of which subject I now deem it necessary briefly to remind (the reader).

33. And, in the first place, it is to be noted that we have nowhere found in the canonical Scriptures, up to the present time, the word "matter" used for that substance which is said to underlie bodies. For in the expression of Isaiah, And he shall devour ὕλη, i.e., matter, like hay, when speaking of those who were appointed to undergo their punishments, the word "matter" was used instead of sins. And if this word "matter" should happen to occur in any other passage, it will never be found, in my opinion, to have the signification of which we are now in quest, unless perhaps in the book which is called the Wisdom of Solomon, a work which is certainly not esteemed authoritative by all. In that book, however, we find written as follows: For your almighty hand, that made the world out of shapeless matter, wanted not means to send among them a multitude of bears and fierce lions. Very many, indeed, are of opinion that the matter of which things are made is itself signified in the language used by Moses in the beginning of Genesis: In the beginning God made heaven and earth; and the earth was invisible, and not arranged: for by the words invisible and not arranged Moses would seem to mean nothing else than shapeless matter. But if this be truly matter, it is clear then that the original elements of bodies are not incapable of change. For those who posited atoms — either those particles which are incapable of subdivision, or those which are subdivided into equal parts — or any one element, as the principles of bodily things, could not posit the word "matter" in the proper sense of the term among the first principles of things. For if they will have it that matter underlies every body — a substance convertible or changeable, or divisible in all its parts — they will not, as is proper, assert that it exists without qualities. And with them we agree, for we altogether deny that matter ought to be spoken of as unbegotten or uncreated, agreeably to our former statements, when we pointed out that from water, and earth, and air or heat, different kinds of fruits were produced by different kinds of trees; or when we showed that fire, and air, and water, and earth were alternately converted into each other, and that one element was resolved into another by a kind of mutual consanguinity; and also when we proved that from the food either of men or animals the substance of the flesh was derived, or that the moisture of the natural seed was converted into solid flesh and bones — all which go to prove that the substance of the body is changeable, and may pass from one quality into all others.

34. Nevertheless we must not forget that a substance never exists without a quality, and that it is by an act of the understanding alone that this (substance) which underlies bodies, and which is capable of quality, is discovered to be matter. Some indeed, in their desire to investigate these subjects more profoundly, have ventured to assert that bodily nature is nothing else than qualities. For if hardness and softness, heat and cold, moisture and aridity, be qualities; and if, when these or other (qualities) of this sort be cut away, nothing else is understood to remain, then all things will appear to be qualities. And therefore also those persons who make these assertions have endeavoured to maintain, that since all who say that matter was uncreated will admit that qualities were created by God, it may be in this way shown that even according to them matter was not uncreated; since qualities constitute everything, and these are declared by all without contradiction to have been made by God. Those, again, who would make out that qualities are superimposed from without upon a certain underlying matter, make use of illustrations of this kind: e.g., Paul undoubtedly is either silent, or speaks, or watches, or sleeps, or maintains a certain attitude of body; for he is either in a sitting, or standing, or recumbent position. For these are accidents belonging to men, without which they are almost never found. And yet our conception of man does not lay down any of these things as a definition of him; but we so understand and regard him by their means, that we do not at all take into account the reason of his (particular) condition either in watching, or in sleeping, or in speaking, or in keeping silence, or in any other action that must necessarily happen to men. If any one, then, can regard Paul as being without all these things which are capable of happening, he will in the same way also be able to understand this

underlying (substance) without qualities. When, then, our mind puts away all qualities from its conception, and gazes, so to speak, upon the underlying element alone, and keeps its attention closely upon it, without any reference to the softness or hardness, or heat or cold, or humidity or aridity of the substance, then by means of this somewhat simulated process of thought it will appear to behold matter clear from qualities of every kind.

35. But some one will perhaps inquire whether we can obtain out of Scripture any grounds for such an understanding of the subject. Now I think some such view is indicated in the Psalms, when the prophet says, My eyes have seen your imperfection; by which the mind of the prophet, examining with keener glance the first principles of things, and separating in thought and imagination only between matter and its qualities, perceived the imperfection of God, which certainly is understood to be perfected by the addition of qualities. Enoch also, in his book, speaks as follows: I have walked on even to imperfection; which expression I consider may be understood in a similar manner, viz., that the mind of the prophet proceeded in its scrutiny and investigation of all visible things, until it arrived at that first beginning in which it beheld imperfect matter (existing) without qualities. For it is written in the same book of Enoch, I beheld the whole of matter; which is so understood as if he had said: I have clearly seen all the divisions of matter which are broken up from one into each individual species either of men, or animals, or of the sky, or of the sun, or of all other things in this world. After these points, now, we proved to the best of our power in the preceding pages that all things which exist were made by God, and that there was nothing which was not made, save the nature of the Father, and the Son, and the Holy Spirit; and that God, who is by nature good, desiring to have those upon whom He might confer benefits, and who might rejoice in receiving His benefits, created creatures worthy (of this), i.e., who were capable of receiving Him in a worthy manner, who, He says, are also begotten by Him as his sons. He made all things, moreover, by number and measure. For there is nothing before God without either limit or measure. For by His power He comprehends all things, and He Himself is comprehended by the strength of no created thing, because that nature is known to itself alone. For the Father alone knows the Son, and the Son alone knows the Father, and the Holy Spirit alone searches even the deep things of God. All created things, therefore, i.e., either the number of rational beings or the measure of bodily matter, are distinguished by Him as being within a certain number or measurement; since, as it was necessary for an intellectual nature to employ bodies, and this nature is shown to be changeable and convertible by the very condition of its being created (for what did not exist, but began to exist, is said by this very circumstance to be of mutable nature), it can have neither goodness nor wickedness as an essential, but only as an accidental attribute of its being. Seeing, then, as we have said, that rational nature was mutable and changeable, so that it made use of a different bodily covering of this or that sort of quality, according to its merits, it was necessary, as God foreknew there would be diversities in souls or spiritual powers, that He should create also a bodily nature the qualities of which might be changed at the will of the Creator into all that was required. And this bodily nature must last as long as those things which require it as a covering: for there will be always rational natures which need a bodily covering; and there will therefore always be a bodily nature whose coverings must necessarily be used by rational creatures, unless some one be able to demonstrate by arguments that a rational nature can live without a body. But how difficult — nay, how almost impossible — this is for our understanding, we have shown in the preceding pages, in our discussion of the individual topics.

36. It will not, I consider, be opposed to the nature of our undertaking, if we restate with all possible brevity our opinions on the immortality of rational natures. Every one who participates in anything, is unquestionably of one essence and nature with him who is partaker of the same thing. For example, as all eyes participate in the light, so accordingly all eyes which partake of the light are of one nature; but

although every eye partakes of the light, yet, inasmuch as one sees more clearly, and another more obscurely, every eye does not equally share in the light. And again, all hearing receives voice or sound, and therefore all hearing is of one nature; but each one hears more rapidly or more slowly, according as the quality of his hearing is clear and sound. Let us pass now from these sensuous illustrations to the consideration of intellectual things. Every mind which partakes of intellectual light ought undoubtedly to be of one nature with every mind which partakes in a similar manner of intellectual light. If the heavenly virtues, then, partake of intellectual light — i.e., of divine nature, because they participate in wisdom and holiness, and if human souls, have partaken of the same light and wisdom, and thus are mutually of one nature and of one essence — then, since the heavenly virtues are incorruptible and immortal, the essence of the human soul will also be immortal and incorruptible. And not only so, but because the nature of Father, and Son, and Holy Spirit, in whose intellectual light alone all created things have a share, is incorruptible and eternal, it is altogether consistent and necessary that every substance which partakes of that eternal nature should last forever, and be incorruptible and eternal, so that the eternity of divine goodness may be understood also in this respect, that they who obtain its benefits are also eternal. But as, in the instances referred to, a diversity in the participation of the light was observed, when the glance of the beholder was described as being duller or more acute, so also a diversity is to be noted in the participation of Father, Son, and Holy Spirit, varying with the degree of zeal or capacity of mind. If such were not the case, we have to consider whether it would not seem to be an act of impiety to say that the mind which is capable of (receiving) God should admit of a destruction of its essence; as if the very fact that it is able to feel and understand God could not suffice for its perpetual existence, especially since, if even through neglect the mind fall away from a pure and complete reception of God, it nevertheless contains within it certain seeds of restoration and renewal to a better understanding,

seeing the inner, which is also called the rational man, is renewed after the image and likeness of God, who created him. And therefore the prophet says, All the ends of the earth shall remember, and turn unto the Lord; and all the kindreds of the nations shall worship before You.

37. If any one, indeed, venture to ascribe essential corruption to Him who was made after the image and likeness of God, then, in my opinion, this impious charge extends even to the Son of God Himself, for He is called in Scripture the image of God. Or he who holds this opinion would certainly impugn the authority of Scripture, which says that man was made in the image of God; and in him are manifestly to be discovered traces of the divine image, not by any appearance of the bodily frame, which is corruptible, but by mental wisdom, by justice, moderation, virtue, wisdom, discipline; in fine, by the whole band of virtues, which are innate in the essence of God, and which may enter into man by diligence and imitation of God; as the Lord also intimates in the Gospel, when He says, Be therefore merciful, as your Father also is merciful; and, Be perfect, even as your Father also is perfect. From which it is clearly shown that all these virtues are perpetually in God, and that they can never approach to or depart from Him, whereas by men they are acquired only slowly, and one by one. And hence also by these means they seem to have a kind of relationship with God; and since God knows all things, and none of things intellectual in themselves can elude His notice (for God the Father alone, and His only-begotten Son, and the Holy Spirit, not only possess a knowledge of those things which they have created, but also of themselves), a rational understanding also, advancing from small things to great, and from things visible to things invisible, may attain to a more perfect knowledge. For it is placed in the body, and advances from sensible things themselves, which are corporeal, to things that are intellectual. But lest our statement that things intellectual are not cognisable by the senses should appear unbecoming, we shall employ the instance of Solomon, who says, You will find also a divine sense; by which he shows that those things

which are intellectual are to be sought out not by means of a bodily sense, but by a certain other which he calls divine. And with this sense must we look on each of those rational beings which we have enumerated above; and with this sense are to be understood those words which we speak, and those statements to be weighed which we commit to writing. For the divine nature knows even those thoughts which we revolve within us in silence. And on those matters of which we have spoken, or on the others which follow from them, according to the rule above laid down, are our opinions to be formed.

CHAPTER 22

Trinitarian Creeds

The Athanasian Creed

1. Whosoever will be saved, before all things it is necessary that he hold the catholic faith;

2. Which faith except every one do keep whole and undefiled, without doubt he shall perish everlastingly.

3. And the catholic faith is this: That we worship one God in Trinity, and Trinity in Unity;

4. Neither confounding the persons nor dividing the substance.

5. For there is one person of the Father, another of the Son, and another of the Holy Spirit.

6. But the Godhead of the Father, of the Son, and of the Holy Spirit is all one, the glory equal, the majesty coeternal.

7. Such as the Father is, such is the Son, and such is the Holy Spirit.

8. The Father uncreated, the Son uncreated, and the Holy Spirit uncreated.

9. The Father incomprehensible, the Son incomprehensible, and the Holy Spirit incomprehensible.

10. The Father eternal, the Son eternal, and the Holy Spirit eternal.

11. And yet they are not three eternals but one eternal.

12. As also there are not three uncreated nor three incomprehensible, but one uncreated and one incomprehensible.

13. So likewise the Father is almighty, the Son almighty, and the Holy Spirit almighty.

14. And yet they are not three almighties, but one almighty.

15. So the Father is God, the Son is God, and the Holy Spirit is God;

16. And yet they are not three Gods, but one God.

17. So likewise the Father is Lord, the Son Lord, and the Holy Spirit Lord;

18. And yet they are not three Lords but one Lord.

19. For like as we are compelled by the Christian verity to acknowledge every Person by himself to be God and Lord;

20. So are we forbidden by the catholic religion to say; There are three Gods or three Lords.

21. The Father is made of none, neither created nor begotten.

22. The Son is of the Father alone; not made nor created, but begotten.

23. The Holy Spirit is of the Father and of the Son; neither made, nor created, nor begotten, but proceeding.

24. So there is one Father, not three Fathers; one Son, not three Sons; one Holy Spirit, not three Holy Spirits.

25. And in this Trinity none is afore or after another; none is greater or less than another.

26. But the whole three persons are coeternal, and coequal.

27. So that in all things, as aforesaid, the Unity in Trinity and the Trinity in Unity is to be worshipped.

28. He therefore that will be saved must thus think of the Trinity.

29. Furthermore it is necessary to everlasting salvation that he also believe rightly the incarnation of our Lord Jesus Christ.

30. For the right faith is that we believe and confess that our Lord Jesus Christ, the Son of God, is God and man.

31. God of the substance of the Father, begotten

before the worlds; and man of substance of His mother, born in the world.

32. Perfect God and perfect man, of a reasonable soul and human flesh subsisting.

33. Equal to the Father as touching His Godhead, and inferior to the Father as touching His manhood.

34. Who, although He is God and man, yet He is not two, but one Christ.

35. One, not by conversion of the Godhead into flesh, but by taking of that manhood into God.

36. One altogether, not by confusion of substance, but by unity of person.

37. For as the reasonable soul and flesh is one man, so God and man is one Christ;

38. Who suffered for our salvation, descended into hell, rose again the third day from the dead;

39. He ascended into heaven, He sits on the right hand of the Father, God, Almighty;

40. From thence He shall come to judge the quick and the dead.

41. At whose coming all men shall rise again with their bodies;

42. And shall give account of their own works.

43. And they that have done good shall go into life everlasting and they that have done evil into everlasting fire.

44. This is the catholic faith, which except a man believe faithfully he cannot be saved.

The Nicene (Nicene-Constantinopolitan) Creed

I believe in one God, the Father Almighty, Maker of heaven and earth, and of all things visible and invisible.

And in one Lord Jesus Christ, the only begotten Son of God, begotten of the Father before all worlds; God of God, Light of Light, very God of very God; begotten, not made, being of one substance with the Father, by whom all things were made.

Who, for us men for our salvation, came down from heaven, and was incarnate by the Holy Spirit of the virgin Mary, and was made man; and was crucified also for us under Pontius Pilate; He suffered and was buried; and the third day He rose again, according to the Scriptures; and ascended into heaven, and sits on the right hand of the Father; and He shall come again, with glory, to judge the quick and the dead; whose kingdom shall have no end.

And I believe in the Holy Ghost, the Lord and Giver of Life; who proceeds from the Father *and the Son*; who with the Father *and the Son* together is worshipped and glorified; who spoke by the prophets.

And I believe one holy catholic and apostolic Church. I acknowledge one baptism for the remission of sins; and I look for the resurrection of the dead, and the life of the world to come. Amen.

CHAPTER 23

Treatise on the Most Holy Trinity

Thomas Aquinas

Procession of the Divine Persons

We have previously studied about the unity of the divine essence; we now study about the trinity of persons in God. And since the divine persons are distinguished by their relations of origin, the order of our exposition is completely outlined; we shall have to consider: 1. the origin or procession; 2. the relations of origin; 3. the persons.

On the topic of procession, five questions come up: 1. Is there any procession in God? 2. Is there in God a procession that can be called begetting? 3. Besides begetting, can there be any other procession in God? 4. Can this procession be called begetting? 5. Are there only these two processions in God?

Summa of Theology I, q. 27, Prologue

Two Processions

There are two processions in God: that of the Word, and another. To show this, let us realize that in God the only procession is the action remaining in the agent himself rather than toward any external term. And in an intellectual nature, this immanent action is realized in the act of knowing and of willing. The procession of the Word belongs to the act of knowing. As to the will's action, it is within us the case of another procession: the procession of love, which makes the beloved be in the lover just as the procession of the Word makes what is said or known be within the knower. So that besides the procession of the Word there is in God another procession: This is the procession of love.

Summa of Theology I, q. 27, a. 3, c

... Although in God will is one with intellect, the procession of love keeps a distinction of order from the procession of the Word, because it is essential to love to proceed from an intellectual knowing.

Summa of Theology I, q. 27, a. 3, ad. 3

... Hence that which proceeds in God by way of love does not proceed as a begotten term, nor as a son, but rather as a "spirit": this word evokes a kind of *élan* or vital impulse, insofar as we say that love moves us and urges us to do something.

Summa of Theology I, q. 27, a. 4, c

Divine Relations

Relations really exist in God. To make this evident, let us consider that the category of relative predicates is the only one that is founded merely on reason and not on reality. This is not the case with other kinds; those like quantity and quality signify formally and properly something inhering in a subject, while relative predicates signify formally and properly only a relationship to another thing. This relationship sometimes exists in the very nature of things, namely, when realities are by nature ordered to each other and tend toward each other. Such relations are necessarily real. So a heavy body tends and is ordered to the center of the earth; consequently there is in the heavy body a relationship to the central place. It is the same in other similar cases. But sometimes also the relationship signified by the relative predicate exists only in reason's apprehension, which establishes a comparison between one thing and another. It is then only a relation of reason, as when the mind, comparing "man" to "animal," considers it the species of a genus.

But when a thing proceeds from a principle of like nature, both — that which proceeds and its principle

— belong necessarily to the same order; and therefore real relations exist between them. Since then in God the processions are realized in identity of nature … necessarily the relations considered from the fact of these processions are real relations.

Summa of Theology I, q. 28, 1

Relations Considered

To clarify this question let us first note that in each of the nine kinds of accident there are two aspects to consider. There is, first of all, the being *(esse)* appropriate to each of them as an accident; and for all, this consists in existing within the subject; indeed, accidental being is existing in another. The other aspect to be considered in each of these is the formal reason proper to each one of these kinds. But in the kinds other than relation (for example, in quantity and quality), the proper formal reason is found in the relation to the subject: So we say that the quantity is a measure of the substance, and quality of its disposition. On the contrary, the proper formal reason of relation is not found in its relationship to the subject in which it exists; it is found in its relation to something external. If then we consider relations, even in created things, as relations, under this aspect they are found *assistantes* (adjacent) and not fixed from within, i.e., that they signify a relationship closely connected in some way to the thing referred to, since through relationship it tends to the other. While if we consider the relation as accident, it is thus inherent in the subject and has in it an accidental being. Gilbert of Porré considered relation only under the first aspect.

But that which in creature possesses an accidental being, when transferred to God possesses in him substantial being; for nothing in God exists as an accident in a subject; anything existing in God is his essence. Whence if one considers relation under that aspect which in created things gives it accidental being in the subject, in this way the relation that really exists in God gets its being from the divine essence and makes only one with him. But as a relation, it does not signify a relationship to the essence, but indeed to its opposite.

Thus it is clear that real relation in God is really identical with the essence, and differs from it only by mental consideration; inasmuch as the relation evokes a relationship to its opposite, it does not evoke the term "essence." It is also apparent that in God there is no distinguishing of relative being and essential being; this is one and the same being.

Summa of Theology I, q. 28, 2, c

Relation in God

In God's case as with creatures, relation implies not only reference to another, but also something absolute, yet there is a difference. What is present in the creature over and above what is present in the meaning of relation is something other than the relation; but in God there is no distinction, but both are one and the same; and this is not perfectly clarified by the word "relation," as though understood in the usual meaning of that term. For it was previously shown (q. 13, a. 2), in discussing the divine names, that more is present in the perfection of the divine essence than can be signified by any name. Thus there consequently does not exist in God anything in reality besides relation, but only in the various names given by us.

Summa of Theology I, q. 29, 2, ad. 2

Relations Really Distinct

In God, said Boethius, "substance contains unity, relation multiplies the trinity." If then relations are not really distinguished from one another, there will be no real trinity in God; there will merely be a trinity of reason. But this is Sabellius's error.

To attribute a predicate to a subject is necessarily to attribute to it everything contained in the predicate's definition. For example, if the predicate "man" is attributed to someone, the predicate "reasonable" is also necessarily attributed. But relation, by definition, involves a relationship to another, relationship that relatively opposes the thing to that other. Whence, because there is real relation in God, there must also be real opposition. But relative opposition includes in its very definition a distinction. So there must be real distinction in God, not, certainly, from the viewpoint of the essence wherein the highest unity and simplicity are verified, but according to its relative reality.

Summa of Theology I, q. 28, a. 3, c

Opposite Relationships

According to the philosopher (*Physics* III), there are limits to this argument, and only if the identity is real and logical is it true that two things identical with the same thing are identical with each other (as, for example, a tunic and a garment); but not if they differ logically. So in the same spot he states that although action is the same as motion, and passion also; yet it does not follow that passion and action are the same; for action implies reference in the thing moved to motion *from which;* whereas passion implies that something is *from another.* So, although fatherhood, like sonship, is really the same as the divine essence, yet these two in their own proper idea and definitions imply opposite relationships. So they are distinguished from each other.

Summa of Theology I, q. 28, Require Distinction a. 4, ad. 1

Divine Relations Based on Action

… A real relation in God can be based only upon action. These relations are not based upon God's action in reference to any extrinsic procession, inasmuch as God's relations to creatures are not real in him (q. 13, a. 7). Consequently real relations in God are understood only in reference to those actions by which there are intrinsic, not extrinsic processions in God. These are only two: … one coming from the intellect's action, the procession of the Word, and the other from the will's action, the procession of love. Two opposite relations arise in reference to each of these processions: One of these is the relation of the person proceeding from the principle, the other is the relation of the principle himself. The procession of the Word is called begetting in the proper sense of the term, and thus it is applied to living things. Now, in perfect living beings, the relation of the principle of begetting is called fatherhood, and the relation of the one proceeding from the principle is called sonship. But the procession of love has not its own proper name, so neither have the relations derived from it. We

give the name "spiration" to the relation of the principle of this procession, and that of *procession* to the relation of the proceeding term, although these two names are properly those of procession or of origin, and not of relation.

Summa of Theology I, q. 28, a. 4, c

Word Really Proceeds

Wherever the knowing and the known, the willing and the willed are two, there can be a real relation of intellect to the thing known, of will to the thing willed. But in God knowing and known are absolutely one, for in knowing himself, God knows all things. It is the same with his will and the object of his will. Thus it follows that these kinds of relations are not real in God; neither is the relation of the thing to itself. Yet the relation to the Word is a real relation, inasmuch as the Word is what we understand to proceed from an intelligent action, and is not the thing known. In fact, what we call "word" when we know a stone is what the intellect conceives of the thing known.

Summa of Theology I, q. 28, a. 4, ad. 1

Procedure in Study of Persons

We have first of all set forth the notions that seemed prerequisite with regard to processions and relations; we must now begin the study of the persons. It will comprise two parts: the persons considered in themselves and the persons in relation to one another. About the first, we should primarily consider persons in general, then each person in particular. The study of persons in general comprises four questions: 1. the meaning of the term "person"; 2. the number of persons; 3. the attributes that this number implies or excludes, such as those that call for difference, solitude, etc.; 4. our knowledge of the persons.

On the topic of the meaning of the word "person" we shall see: 1. the definition of person; 2. the comparison of this term with those of essence, of subsistence, and of hypostasis; 3. whether the term "person" is appropriate for God; 4. what it signifies in him.

Summa of Theology I, q. 29, Prologue

Person and God

Essence, hypostasis, subsistence ... what these three names signify in common with the entire genus of substances, this name *person* signifies in the genus of rational substance.

ad. 1. As used by the Greeks, the strict meaning of "hypostasis" refers to any individual substance, but custom has associated with it a certain dignity, so that it refers to an individual being of rational nature.

ad. 2. Just as we refer in the plural to three "persons" and three "subsistences" in God, so the Greeks refer to three hypostases. But the word "substance" which, strictly speaking, is equivalent in meaning to "hypostasis," is equivocal in our usage, inasmuch as it refers at times to "essence" and at other times to "hypostasis"; in order to avoid misunderstanding they chose to translate "hypostasis" by "subsistence" rather than by "substance."

ad. 3. Strictly speaking, the definition expresses the essence.

A definition includes specific but not individual principles. It follows that essence in things composed of matter and form refers neither to the form alone nor to the matter alone but to what is composed of both matter and form in general, as principles of the species. But what is composed of this matter and this form is characterized as an hypostasis or a person; for whereas soul, flesh, and bones belong to the meaning of "man," *this* soul, *this* flesh, and *these* bones belong to the meaning of *this* man. So "hypostasis" and "person" add individual principles to the notion of the essence, and in things composed of matter and form these are not identical with the essence, as we noted when speaking of the divine simplicity.

ad. 4. Boethius says that genera *subsist*, since if it belongs to certain individuals to subsist, they do this as subjects of genera and species comprised in the category, substance; the genera and species do not themselves subsist except in the theory of Plato, who made the essences of things subsist apart from singulars. On the contrary, the function of *substare* belongs to the same individuals with regard to accidents, which make no part of the definition of genera and species.

The individual composed of matter and form has the function of subject for accidents properly from its matter. So Boethius says that the form cannot be a subject (*On the Trinity*, 2). It subsists by itself through its form. This is not an addition to something already subsisting, but gives actual being to matter so that the individual can subsist. This is why Boethius relates *hypostasis* to matter and act-of-being or *subsistentia* to form: This is because the matter is principle of *substare*, and the form principle of *subsistere*.

Summa of Theology I, q. 29, a. 2, and ad. 1,2,3,4

"Person" refers to that which is most perfect in the whole of nature, namely, to that which subsists in rational nature. Now, because God's nature has all perfection, and thus every kind of perfection should be attributed to him, it is fitting to use the word "person" to speak of God; yet when used of God it is not used exactly as it is of creatures, but in a higher sense, just as is the case with other words naming creatures, as was clarified when we treated of the names of God.

ad. 1. So the word "person" is not discovered in the text of the Old or New Testament as referring to God. Yet what this word means is often present in Holy Scripture, namely, that his is the peak of self-existence and most perfect in wisdom. If we were restricted to speaking of God only in the words used in Holy Scripture, it would follow that no one could speak of God in any other language than the one used in the Old and the New Testaments. Because we must dialogue with nonbelievers, it is necessary for us to discover new words about God expressing the ancient belief. Nor should we avoid such innovation as profane, i.e., as out of harmony with the scriptural meaning. What St. Paul tells us to avoid are profane verbal innovations.

ad. 2. Although we may not use "person" in its original meaning of God, we may extend this acceptably for our present purpose. Since famous men were represented in comedies and tragedies, the word' "person" (*persona:* mask) came to be used to refer to men of high rank. In the ecclesiastical world there grew up the custom of referring to personages of rank. For this reason some theologians define person as "a hypostasis distinguished by dignity." To subsist in rational nature is characterized by dignity and so, as we said, every individual with rational nature is spoken of as "person." Certainly the dignity of divine nature surpasses every nature, and thus it is entirely suitable to speak of God as "person."

Summa of Theology I, q. 29, 3, c, and ad. 1,2,3,4

"Person" as Common Noun

… This is usually understood of the divine persons: that each of them subsists distinct from the others in the divine nature. Thus the term "person" is common in our understanding of the three divine persons.

Summa of Theology I, q. 30, a.1, ad.1

Significance of "Trinity"

In its etymological meaning, the word "Trinity" evidently signifies the one essence of the three persons, in that "trinity" means triune unity. But strictly speaking, it rather signifies the number of persons in one essence; and hence we cannot say that the Father is the Trinity, as he is not three persons. Yet it does not mean the relations themselves of the persons, but rather the number of persons related to one another, so that the word is not expressive of relativity.

Summa of Theology I, q. 31, a. 1, ad. 1

Careful Use of the Word "Trinity"

Because as Jerome notes (Ep. 57), words badly used run the risk of heresy, in speaking of the Trinity we must do so carefully and modestly: "Nowhere," says St. Augustine, "is error more dangerous, the search more arduous, the finding more fruitful." But in speaking of the Trinity we should avoid two contrary errors and proceed with care between them — namely Arius' error, a making of the Trinity of persons a trinity of substances; and that of Sabellius, who made of the unity of essence a unity of person.

To avoid Arius' error we should avoid speaking of "diversity" or of "difference" in God — this would ruin the unity of essence. We can, however, appeal to the term "distinction" because of the relative opposition; it is in this sense that one should interpret the expressions "diversity" or "difference" of persons when encountered in a reliable text. Moreover, to preserve the simplicity of the divine essence, we should avoid the terms of "separation" and "division" that belong to the parts of a whole; lest equality be lost, we avoid using the word "disparity"; and to preserve likeness we should avoid the terms "alien" and "divergent." For Ambrose says (*On Faith* I), "in the Father and in the Son" there is no divergence, but one Godhead, and according to St. Hilary there is nothing separable in God.

But to avoid Sabellius's error, we should not use the word "singularity" (isolatedness), which would deny the communicability of the divine essence; according to St. Hilary, in fact, it is a sacrilege to call the Father and the Son "a singular God." We should also avoid the term "unique," which would deny the plurality of persons; St. Hilary says in the same place: "We exclude from God the idea of singularity or uniqueness." Yet we do say the "only Son," for there is no plurality of sons in God. But we do not say the "only God," for Godhead is common to several. We avoid the word "confused" to respect the order of nature among the persons. So Ambrose says: "What is one is not confused; and there is no multiplicity where there is no difference." We should also avoid the word "solitary" lest we detract from the society of the three persons; for, as Hilary says (*On the Trinity* IV), "We confess neither a solitary nor a diverse God."

But the masculine meaning of other (*alius*) denotes only a distinction of *suppositum;* and so we can properly say that the Son is other than the Father, because he is another *suppositum* of the divine nature, as he is another person and another hypostasis.

Summa of Theology I, q. 31, a. 1, ad. 1

Trinitarian God Transcends Reason

It is impossible to reach the knowledge of the Trinity by natural reason. For, as previously explained (q. 12, a: 4, a. 12), man through natural reason cannot reach any knowledge of God except from creatures. But we go from creatures to knowing God as from effects to their cause. So by natural reason we can only know of God what necessarily belongs to him as the principle of all things.... Now, the creative power of God is common to the entire Trinity; and so it belongs to the unity of the essence and not to the distinction of the persons. So by natural reason we can know what belongs to the unity of the essence but not what belongs to the distinction of persons....

Summa of Theology I, q. 32, a. 1, c

Need to Know God as Trinity

The knowledge of the divine persons was necessary for two reasons. The first was to give us the right idea of creation. To assert that God made all things through his Word is to reject the error according to which God produced things by natural need; and to place in him the procession of love is to show that if God has produced creatures, this is not because he needed them for himself nor for any other cause extrinsic to him; it is through love of his goodness [the desire to share].

Also Moses, after having written: "In the beginning God created heaven and earth," added, "God said, 'Let there be light,'" to manifest the divine Word; and then said: "God saw the light that it was good," to show the approval of the divine love. And in the same way he describes the production of the other works.

The second reason and the principal one was to give us a true notion of the salvation of the human race, salvation which is accomplished by the incarnation of the Son and by the gift of the Holy Spirit.

Summa of Theology I, q. 32, 1, ad. 3

Appropriate Terms

... Since we confess the Father, the Son, and the Holy Spirit to be one God and three persons, to those who ask: "Whereby are they one God?" and "Whereby are they three persons?" we answer that they are one in essence or Godhead; so there must be some abstract terms whereby we may answer that the persons are distinguished; and these are the properties or notions signified by the abstract terms, as fatherhood and sonship. Thus the divine essence is signified as "what"; and the person as "who"; and the property as "whereby."

Summa of Theology I, q. 32, 2, c

So-Called "Notions" in God

A notion is the proper idea whereby we know a divine person. But the divine persons are multiplied by reason of their origin, and origin includes the idea of someone *from whom another comes* and of *someone who comes from another,* and by these two ways a person can be known. So the person of the Father cannot be known by the fact that he is from another but by the fact that he is from no one; and so the notion that pertains to him is unbegottenness. As the source of another, he is knowable in two ways, for insofar as the Son is from him, the Father is known by the notion of *fatherhood*; and as the Holy Spirit is from him, he is known by the notion of *common spiration*. The Son is knowable as begotten by another, and so he is known by *sonship* and is also known through another person proceeding from him, the Holy Spirit, so that he is known in the same way the Father is known, by *common spiration:* The Holy Spirit is known from the fact that he is from another or from others; hence he is known by *procession;* but not by the fact that another is from him, as no divine person proceeds from him.

So in God there are five notions: unbegottenness, fatherhood, sonship, common spiration, and procession. Only four of these are relations, for unbegottenness is not a relation, unless by reduction, as is seen later (q. 33, a. 4, ad. 3). Only four are properties. For common spiration is no property, inasmuch as it belongs to two persons. Three are personal notions, i.e., constituting persons: *fatherhood, sonship,* and *procession.* Common spiration and unbegottenness are spoken of as notions of persons, but not personal notions, as we shall see (q. 40, a. 1, ad. 1).

ad. 2. The divine essence is signified as a reality; the persons are also signified as realities; whereas the notions indicate ideas intimating the persons. So, although God is one by unity of essence, and triune by trinity of persons, he is not fivefold by the five notions.

ad. 3. Because real plurality in God is based upon relative opposition, the several properties of one person, since they are not relatively opposed to each other, do not really differ. Nor can we predicate them of each other, since they are mentally distinct....

Summa of Theology I, q. 32, 3, c, and ad. 2, 3

Discussion
of Trinity Still Open

... Anyone may hold contrary opinions about the notions, if he does not intend to uphold anything at variance with the faith. But if anyone should hold a false opinion about the notions, knowing or believing that what is contrary to the faith would follow, he would fall into heresy.

Summa of Theology I, q. 32, a. 4, c

Person of the Father

The word *principle* signifies only that from which something proceeds: for we call anything from which anything in any way proceeds a principle, and vice versa. Since the Father is the one from which another proceeds, it follows that the Father is a principle.

ad. 1. The Greeks use indifferently the words "cause" and "principle" when referring to God; on the contrary, the Latin doctors avoid the word "cause" and use only that of "principle." This is the reason. "Principle" is more general than "cause," the latter being itself more general than element; in fact, the first term or even the first part of a thing is called the "principle" but not the "cause." But the more general a term, the more it can be used of God, for the more specialized names are, the more appropriate they are to the creature. So the word "cause" implies diversity of substance and a dependence of effect upon cause, which the name "principle" does not imply; for whatever be the kind of causality, there is always between cause and effect a kind of distance in perfection or in power. On the contrary, the word "principle" is used even when there is no such difference; it is enough that order is discernible. So we say that the point is the principle of the line, or even that the first part of a line is the principle of it.

ad. 2. It is true that the word "principle," considered etymologically, appears taken from a priority; however, it does not signify priority, but origin. Do not confuse the signification of the word with what was its origin or the occasion for its creation.

Summa of Theology I, q. 33, 1, c, and ad. 1, 3

"Unbegotten" Signifies Relation

... Since "begotten" implies relation in God, "unbegotten" belongs also to relation. Hence it does not follow that the unbegotten Father is substantially distinguished from the begotten Son, but only by relation, that is, as the relation of Son is denied of the Father.

Summa of Theology I, q. 33, a. 4, ad. 3

And Things Spoken in the Word

... For the Father, by understanding himself and the Son and the Holy Spirit and everything else comprised in this knowledge, conceives the Word; in this way, then, the whole Trinity is *spoken* in the Word; and likewise are all creatures also, just as the intellect of a man by the word he conceives in the act of understanding a stone, speaks a stone ... So only the person who utters the Word is *speaker* in God, although each person understands and is understood, and so is spoken by the Word.

Summa of Theology I, q. 33, a. l, ad. 3

"Word" Is Proper Name of Son

"Word" used of God in its proper meaning is used personally, and is the proper name of the person of the Son; for it signifies an emanation of intellect, and the person who in God proceeds through intellect's emanation is called the Son; and this procession is called begetting....

Summa of Theology I, q. 34, a. 2, c

Word Is God's Being

To be and to understand are in us not the same thing. So in us whatever has intellectual being does not belong to our nature. But in God "to be" and "to understand" are one and the same; thus the Word of God is not an accident in him or his effect but belongs to his very nature. Hence it has to be something subsistent, for anything in the nature of God subsists; and so Damascene says *(On Orthodox Faith* I, 18) that the "Word of God is substantial and has a hypostatic being; but other words (like ours) are activities of the soul."

Summa of Theology I, q. 34, a.2, ad. l

Creatures Somehow within the Word

Augustine says (*Eighty-three Questions,* 63) "the name 'Word' signifies not only relation to the Father, but also relation to those beings which are made through the Word by his operative power."

So "Word" implies relation to creatures. In knowing himself, God knows every creature. But the word conceived in thought expresses all that the subject knows in act; so in us there are as many different words as there are different things that we understand. On the contrary, God knows in one sole act himself and all things; his one Word does not only express the Father, but even all creatures. While with God the divine thought is pure knowledge, with creatures it is knowledge and cause; so the Word of God is a pure expression of the mystery of the Father, but it is expression and cause of creatures. Whence the Psalmist said (Ps. 32:9): "He spake, and they were made," because in the Word is found the operative idea of what God makes.

Summa of Theology I, q. 34, a. 3, c

Nontemporal Character of Relationship through the Word

Since relations result from actions, some names carry a relation of God to the creature following from God's transitive actions, i.e., terminating at an extrinsic effect such as to create, to govern the world; names of this kind are attributed to God in time. But others carry a relation following from an action not passing into an extrinsic effect but remaining within the agent — as to know and to will. These are not applied to God in time, and this kind of relation to creatures is implied in the name of the Word. Nor is it true that all names relative to the created are attributed to God in time, but only those that imply a relation following upon a transitive action.

Summa of Theology I, q. 34, a. 3, ad. 2

Requisites for Imaging

Likeness belongs to the notion of image. Yet not any kind of likeness is sufficient for the notion of image, but only likeness of species, or at least of some specific sign. And in corporeal things the sign characteristic of the species is chiefly the figure. For we notice that the species of various animals are of various figures; but not of various colors. So if the color of a thing is placed upon the wall, we do not call this an image unless the figure is also pictured there. Moreover, more is needed for an image than likeness of species or figure, and this is origin; for, as Augustine says (*Eighty-three Questions,* 74): "One egg is not the image of another, because it is not derived from it." To be truly an image of another, it is necessary to proceed from it so as to resemble it in species or at least in a sign of the species. But the attributes that imply procession or origin in God are personal names. Hence the name "image" is a name of a person.

Summa of Theology I, q. 35, 1, c

Whether the Name of Image Is Proper to the Son

Augustine says (*On the Trinity* VI, 2): "The Son alone is the image of the Father."

The Greek doctors usually say that the Holy Spirit is the image both of the Father and of the Son, but the Latin doctors attribute to the Son alone the name "image." For in the canonical Scripture it is only found as applied to the Son, as in the words: "Who is the image of the invisible God, the firstborn of creatures" (Col. 1:15); and also: "Who being the brightness of his glory, and the figure of his substance" (Heb. 1:3).

Summa of Theology I, q. 35, a. 2, c

A thing may be an image in two ways. In one way as of the same specific nature, as the image of the king is found in his son. In another way as when it is something of a different nature, as the king's image on the coin. In the first way the Son is the image of the Father; in the second way man is called the image of God; and to express the imperfect character of the divine image in man, man is not merely called the image, but "to the image," whereby there is expressed a certain motion of tendency to perfection. But we cannot say that the

Son of God is "to the image," because he is the perfect image of the Father.

Summa of Theology I, q., 35, a. 2, ad. 3

Holy Spirit

... To signify the divine person who proceeds by way of love, this name "Holy Spirit" is suitable to him through scriptural usage. The appropriateness of the name is seen in two ways. First, because the person called "Holy Spirit" has something in common with the other persons. For, as Augustine says (*On the Trinity* XV, 17: V, 11): "Because the Holy Spirit is common to both, he himself is called that properly which both are called in common. For the Father also is a spirit and the Son is a spirit; and the Father is holy and the Son is holy."

Second, from the proper signification of the name. For in bodily things the name "spirit" apparently signifies impulse and motion; for we give the name "spirit" to breath and wind. Now, love moves and urges the lover's will toward the beloved. Moreover, holiness is attributed to whatever is directed to God. So because the divine person proceeds by way of the love by which God is loved, that person is most properly named the "Holy Spirit."

Summa of Theology I, q., 36, 1

Suitability of the Term "Spirit"

Although this name "Holy Spirit" does not indicate a relation, yet it substitutes for a relative term one suitable to signify a person distinct from the others by relation only. Yet one can see a relation in this term by considering the Holy Spirit as being breathed (*spiratus*).

Summa of Theology I, q. 36, 1, ad. 2

Why the Holy Spirit Is Said to Be "from the Son"

It must be said that the Holy Spirit is from the Son. For if he were not, he could in no way be distinguished from the Son.... the divine persons are distinguished from one another only by the relations. Now, relations cannot distinguish the persons unless they are oppo-site relations.... Now, there cannot be in God any relations opposed to each other except relations of origin. And opposite relations of origin are to be understood as of a *principle,* and of what is *from a principle.* So we must conclude that it is necessary to say either that the Son is from the Holy Spirit, which no one says, or that the Holy Spirit is from the Son, as we confess...

Summa of Theology I, q. 36, a. 2, c

The Holy Spirit is distinguished personally from the Son insofar as the origin of one is distinguished from the origin of the other; but the difference itself of origin is found in the fact that the Son is only from the Father, but the Holy Spirit is from the Father and the Son; for otherwise the processions would not be distinguished from each other....

Summa of Theology I, q. 36, 2, ad. 7

Spirit Proceeding "through the Son" Also Valid Expression

... Because it is from what the Son receives from the Father that the Holy Spirit proceeds from him, it can be said that the Father spirates the Holy Spirit through the Son or that the Holy Spirit proceeds from the Father through the Son, which means the same thing.

Summa of Theology I, q. 36, a. 3

Augustine says (*On the Trinity* XIV) that the Father and the Son are not two principles but one principle of the Holy Spirit.

The Father and the Son are one in everything when there is no distinction between them of opposite relation. Thus since there is no relative opposition between them as the principle of the Holy Spirit, it follows that the Father and the Son are one principle of the Holy Spirit.

Summa of Theology I, q. 36, 4, c

Love as Notional Term

... Insofar as love signifies only the relation of the lover to the beloved, "love" and "to love" are said of the essence, as "understanding" and "to understand"; but insofar as these words are used to express the relation to its principle, of what proceeds by way of love, and vice versa, so that by "love" is understood the "love proceeding," and by "to love" is understood the "spiration of the love proceeding," in that sense "love" is the name of the person and "to love" is a notional term, like "to speak" or "to beget."

Summa of Theology I, q. 37, 1, c

Love, a Bond

ad. 2. Although "to know," "to will," and "to love" are used as verbs signifying actions passing to their objects [transitive verbs], they are really immanent actions, connoting within the agent itself a relation to the object. Likewise, even in us, love is something that remains within the lover, and the mental word is something remaining within the one who "speaks" it while connoting a relation to the thing expressed or loved. But in God, in whom there is nothing accidental, their condition is still better: the Word and love are there subsistent. So when we say that the Holy Spirit is the love of the Father *for* the Son or *for* anything else, we do not mean anything passing into another, but only the relation of love to the beloved, as also the Word connotes the relationship of the Word to the thing expressed in this Word.

ad. 3. We say that the Holy Spirit is the bond of the Father and the Son, inasmuch as he is love. In fact, it is by the one love (*unica dilectione)* that the Father loves both himself and the Son — and reciprocally; consequently it is as love that the Holy Spirit calls forth a reciprocal relationship between the Father and the Son, that of lover to the beloved. But from the fact that the Father and the Son love each other, their mutual love, in other words, the Holy Spirit, must proceed from both. If then we consider origin, the Holy Spirit is not in the middle but is the third person of the Trinity. But if we consider the relationship we are discussing, he is between the two other persons as the bond that unites them, while proceeding from each of them.

Summa of Theology I, q. 37, 1, ad. 2, 3

Creatures Grounded in Trinitarian Love

... Since in God "to love" is understood in two ways,

essentially and notionally, when it is understood essentially, it means that the Father and the Son love each other not by the Holy Spirit but by their essence. So Augustine says (*On the Trinity* XV, 7): "Who dares to say that the Father loves neither himself nor the Son nor the Holy Spirit except by the Holy Spirit?..."

If, on the contrary, the word "love" is understood in the notional sense, it only means "to spirate love"; just as "to speak" signifies "to produce a word," and "to flower," "to produce flowers." So then as we say that a tree flowers by its flowers, so we say, "The Father speaks by his Word or by the Son himself and the creature"; and we say, "The Father and the Son love themselves and us by the Holy Spirit or by the love that proceeds."

ad. 3. Not only does the Father love his Son by the Holy Spirit, but even himself and us; for, as we said, "to love" in the notional sense does not only connote the production of a divine person, it connotes the person produced by way of love; and love implies relationship to the thing loved. That is why, just as the Father speaks, by the Word that he begets, himself and every creature — since the Word begotten by him suffices to represent the Father and every creature, so also he loves himself and every creature by the Holy Spirit, since the Holy Spirit proceeds as love from that first goodness that is the reason for the Father loving himself as well as every creature.

So it is clear that relation to the creature is implied both in the Word and in the love that proceeds; although in a secondary way; for the divine truth and goodness are the principle of God's knowledge and love of the creature.

Summa of Theology I, q. 37, a. 2, c, and ad. 3

Personal Signification of the Term "Gift"

The term "gift" implies a personal distinction, inasmuch as "gift" implies something belonging to another through its origin. Yet the Holy Spirit gives himself insofar as he is his own and can use or rather enjoy himself, as a free man likewise belongs to himself. And as Augustine says (on Jn. 29): "What is more yours than yourself?" Or we could more appropriately say that a gift should in a way belong to the giver. But this relationship of "belonging," "to be someone's" can be verified in many ways. First, by identity, as Augustine says, and in this sense "gift" is the same as "the giver," but not the same as "the one to whom it is given." The Holy Spirit in this sense gives himself. In another sense, something is another's as a possession, or as a slave, and "gift" in that sense is essentially distinct from "the giver." Understood this way, the gift of God is a created thing. In a third sense "this is someone's" only through its origin, and in this sense the Son is the Father's, and the Holy Spirit belongs to both. So inasmuch as in this sense "gift" signifies the possession of the giver, it is personally distinguished from the giver, and is a personal name.

Summa of Theology I, q. 38, a. 1, ad. 1

Understood in its personal sense in God, Gift is the Holy Spirit's proper name. And for these reasons, according to the philosopher, there is properly a gift when there is a donation without return, i.e., when one gives without expecting any return; "gift" therefore implies a gratuitous donation. But love is the reason for a gratuitous donation: why do we give anything to anyone gratuitously? Because we wish them well. The first gift that we offer, therefore, is the love that makes us wish them well. We see then that love constitutes the first gift by virtue of which all gratuitous gifts are given. So, since the Holy Spirit proceeds as love, he proceeds as first Gift. Thus Augustine says (*On the Trinity* XV, 24): "By the gift which is the Holy Spirit, many particular gifts are distributed to the members of Christ."

Summa of Theology I, q. 38, 2, c

Relations Are Realities

… It was shown previously (q. 3, a. 3) that the divine simplicity requires in God that essence be identical with *suppositum,* which is nothing else than person in intellectual beings. What is apparently difficult here is that with several persons, the essence keeps its unity.

And as, according to Boethius (*On the Trinity* I), "relation multiplies the Trinity of persons," some considered that in God essence and person differ, since they thought of the relations as (*assistentes*) adjacent, seeing only in relation the notion of "reference to another," forgetting that relations are also realities.

But as previously shown, although in creatures relations inhere as accidents, in God they are the very divine essence. It follows that in God essence is not really distinct from person; and yet the persons are really distinguished from one another. For "person" … signifies relation as subsisting in the divine nature. But "relation," in reference to the essence, does not really differ from it, but only through our thinking about it; whereas in reference to an opposite relation, it is really distinct from it by virtue of the opposition. So there is one essence and there are three persons.

Summa of Theology I, q. 39, 1, c

Relations Denote Individuals

ad. 2. … the relations themselves are not distinguished from one another insofar as they are identified with the essence.

ad. 3. Divine realities are named by us after the manner of created ones … So because created natures are individualized by matter, which is the subject of the specific nature, it follows that individuals are called "subjects," "supposita," or "hypostases." So the divine persons are spoken of as "supposita" or "hypostases," but not because there really exists any real supposition or subjection.

Summa of Theology I, q. 39, 1, ad. 1, 3

Scriptural Source of Trinitarian Doctrine

Although in Holy Scripture we do not find the literal expression "three Persons of one essence," yet we find this meaning there with the words: "I and the Father are one" (Jn. 10: 30); and "I am in the Father, and the Father in Me"; and in many similar texts.

Summa of Theology I, q. 39, a. 2, ad. 2

CHAPTER 24

On the Trinity

Richard of St. Victor[1]

Up to now we have discussed as best we could the unity and proper attributes of the divine substance. In what follows however we propose to examine what we ought to think about the plurality of persons and their properties.

The first question it seems we should discuss is whether in that true and simple divinity there is a plurality of persons and whether they are three in number as we believe. [...]

We have learned from what was said earlier [in Book Two] that in the highest and universally perfect good there is the plenitude and perfection of all goodness. Where the fullness of goodness exists, however, true and supreme charity or love cannot be absent, for nothing is better or more perfect than charity. Now no one is said to have charity by virtue of the private love he has for himself, since to be charity, love must tend towards another; and where there are not several persons, charity simply cannot exist.

But perhaps you will say: Even if there were but a single person in that true divinity, he still could, and indeed would have charity towards creatures. But surely he could not have the supreme degree of charity for a person who was created. For if he loved supremely one unworthy of supreme love, his charity would be inordinate. But it is impossible that inordinate charity should exist in goodness that is also supremely wise. A divine person then could not have the highest charity towards a person unworthy of supreme love. For charity to be supreme and all-perfect then, it must be so great that it could not be greater and of such quality that it could not be better. But as long as one loves only himself, this private love he bears himself shows he has yet to reach the highest degree of charity. A divine person would have no one he could fittingly love as himself had he no deserving person his peer. But no person who was not God would be a worthy peer of a divine person. In order to have the plenitude of charity in that true divinity, therefore, what any divine person must have is the companionship of a person who is his peer in dignity and who is therefore divine.

See how easily then reason proves a plurality of persons must be present in true divinity. Certainly God alone is supremely good; God alone then is to be loved supremely. A divine person consequently could not display the highest love towards a person who lacked divinity. But the fullness of divinity could not be present if complete goodness was missing; and complete goodness could not be present without the fullness of charity, nor the complete charity without a plurality of divine persons. [...]

It is clear that there is a plurality of divine persons, but it is not yet evident that they constitute a trinity. For there can be plurality without a trinity. Duality itself is a plurality. Let us ask the same witnesses about trinity that attested to the presence of a plurality. And, if you will, let us see first what sovereign charity has to say on the subject.

Sovereign charity must be perfect on all counts. To be supremely perfect, however, charity must be such that it can be neither greater nor better. No degree or kind of excellence could be missing. Now to wish that

---

1. This selection by Richard of St. Victor, "On the Trinity," is reprinted with the permission of The Free Press, a Division of Simon and Schuster, Inc., from *Medieval Philosophy: From St.*

Augustine to Nicholas of Cosa, edited by John F. Wippel and Allan B. Wolter. Copyright © 1969 by The Free Press. All rights reserved.

another be loved as we are loved seems to be the sort of thing that should be present in true charity. Where love is ardent and mutual, nothing is rarer, nothing more admirable than the desire that another be loved to the same degree as you by the one whom you love supremely and by whom you are supremely loved. The proof of consummate charity then is this desire to share the love shown to oneself. Surely one who loves supremely and desires to be loved supremely would be wont to find perfect joy in the fulfillment of that desire, in obtaining the love desired. Never to have the satisfaction of sharing such perfect joy, therefore, is proof that perfect charity is not present. To be unable to enjoy this companionship of love is a sign of weakness. But if it is great to be *able* to do so, it is still greater to do so *in fact,* and greatest of all if one *must* do so. The first is a great good, the second a greater good, the third the greatest good. Such excellence we owe to the Supreme Being; to the best we owe the best.

Our earlier discussion revealed the presence of two persons united in mutual love. The perfection of each, however, if it is to be consummate, requires that each for the same reason have someone to share the love shown to himself. For if either did not want what perfect goodness requires, where would the plenitude of power be? Hence reason clearly reveals that where some defect of power or will precludes such sharing in love, such participation of perfect joy, there the supreme degree of charity and plenitude of goodness cannot exist. Each of these persons who is and should be supremely loved must needs require by common desire a third person to be loved and must needs possess such a one in perfect harmony as they desire.

See then how the consummation of charity demands a trinity of persons without which it could not subsist whole and entire! Where something universally perfect is present in its entirety, neither integral charity nor true trinity can be absent. Hence there is not only plurality but also true trinity in true unity, and true unity in true trinity....

Note indeed in these divine persons that the perfection of one demands it be joined to another and consequently the perfection of the pair requires their union with a third. For, as we said above, if each of the pair deserves the supreme love of the other, each must be supremely perfect. As the pair must be one in wisdom and power, so too in supreme generosity. But the hallmark of the highest and most perfect generosity is that it share with another the full measure of its richness. But if each of the two has the same generosity, they must share the same desire for the same reasons; both require a third partner to share their supreme joy. For where a loving pair are seized by supreme desire and each delighted by the supreme love of the other, then the supreme joy of the one comes from his intimate love of the other, and conversely, the supreme joy of the second stems from his intimate love of the first. But so long as one is loved only by the other, he seems to be the sole possessor of his Supremely sweet delight. Similarly with the other, so long as he has no partner in the love shown him, he misses sharing this supreme joy. *But* that both can share their own delight, they need another loved one. Where such colovers are so generous, then, that they Want to share whatever perfection they possess, both, by common desire and for equal reasons, need to have another who is loved even as they and, by virtue of the plenitude of their power, to possess what they desire.

CHAPTER 25

The Doctrine of the Trinity

Thomas V. Morris

We already have indicated, in the briefest way possible, what the doctrine of the Trinity is. Now is the time to lay it out a bit more carefully. The threefold Christian experience of God, as recorded in the New Testament, has led to the Christian understanding of God as existing in threefold form — three persons in the unity of one divine nature. Jesus, as we have seen, is believed to be divine, God Incarnate. But he himself often indicated that he saw himself as standing in relation to a distinct divine person. He seems often to have prayed to God and to have said of himself that he had been sent by his heavenly father. So Christians have come to recognize, at the level of deity, both God the Father and God the Son, who have also come to be known, respectively, as the First Person and the Second Person of the divine Trinity. The special Comforter, whom Jesus promised his followers after his departure and who was believed to have come upon the church at Pentecost, endowing those early Christians with supernatural gifts, drawing others to Christ and working sanctification in the lives of all true believers, is identified in Christian theology as the Third Person of the divine Trinity, God the Holy Spirit. So we have as the object of Christian faith and worship three divine persons. But Christians have insisted from the earliest days that this is in no important way like pagan polytheism; it is not the worship of three independent gods.[1]

In any attempt to understand the doctrine of the Incarnation, the challenge is to secure the unity of the person of Christ while at the same time acknowledging the real distinctness of his two natures. In understanding the doctrine of the Trinity, the challenge is to balance the distinctness of the persons with the real unity of the divine nature, a unity sufficient to justify the Christian insistence that monotheism has not been utterly abandoned, that, in the words of Deuteronomy, "The LORD our God is one God" (Deut 6:4). But how is this to be done?

Throughout the centuries, many theologians and philosophers have tried to explain both the threeness and the oneness of the Trinity, while staying within the boundaries for an acceptable account laid down by the early church. In reaction against the views of the popular theologian Arius, who had claimed that at the deepest level of his being Jesus the Christ was a created being, brought into existence by God the Father at a particular time, the Council of Nicaea (A.D. 325) declared:

> We believe in one God, the Father almighty, maker of all things, visible and invisible;
>
> And in one Lord Jesus Christ, the Son of God, only-begotten, that is, from the substance of the Father, God from God, light from light, true God from true God, begotten not made, of one substance with the Father, through whom all things came into being, things in heaven and things on earth, who because of us men and because of our salvation came down and

---

1. For a clear presentation of the development of this doctrine, as well as the doctrine of the Incarnation, see J. N. D. Kelly, *Early Christian Doctrines*, rev. ed. (New York: Harper and Row, 1978). For the rejection of polytheism, see Cornelius Plantinga, Jr., "Social Trinity and Tritheism," in *Trinity, Incarnation and Atonement*, ed. Ronald J. Feenstra and Cornelius Plantinga, Jr. (Notre Dame: University of Notre Dame Press, 1989), pp. 21–47.

became incarnate, becoming man, suffered and rose again on the third day, ascended to the heavens, and will come to judge the living and the dead;

And in the Holy Spirit.

But as for those who say, there was when He was not and, before being born He was not, and that He came into existence out of nothing, or who assert that the Son of God is from a different hypostasis or substance, or is created, or is subject to alteration or change — these the Catholic church anathematizes.[2]

The fully divine status of the Holy Spirit, who is no more than mentioned here (since the controversy addressed was over the Son), was made clear at the Council of Constantinople a few years later in 381. As the trinitarian language came to be developed in the Western church, the Son was said to have been eternally "begotten" by the Father, whereas the Spirit eternally "proceeded" from the Father and the Son. So, although the three persons were regarded as equally divine, there was believed to be a hierarchy of dependence relations within the exalted realm of divinity.

All the attempts to spell out the doctrine of the Trinity can be thought of as located along a spectrum, at one end of which is the error of *modalism*, and at the other end of which is *polytheism*. The heresy of modalism is the claim that the three "persons" are merely three appearances of God, or three roles God plays in salvation history. It is a view which holds that really there is only one divine individual, one ultimate bearer of the properties of divinity beneath these three "masks" or "modes of appearance." And, of course, polytheism is the belief in two or more distinct and independent deities. Modalism and polytheism are the Scylla and Charybdis between which all orthodox accounts of the Trinity must steer.

Within this range, we can distinguish between *singularity theories of the Trinity*, which attempt to stress the unity of the divine nature, without falling into modalism, and *social theories of the Trinity*, which

attempt to highlight the diversity or distinctness of the three persons, without falling into polytheism. A social theory represents the Trinity as a community of three distinct persons, each with a distinct center of consciousness and will, yet all existing with the others in as close a relation of harmony and love as it is possible to stand in.

In a recent essay, "Could There Be More Than One God?" Richard Swinburne develops a fascinating version of a social theory.[3] Swinburne calls our attention to the fact that one important aspect of perfect goodness is perfect love. Now love must have an object, but, even more importantly, love must be shared. For in self-love one's love has an object, but surely, in order to be a fully loving person, any individual must extend his or her love beyond the bounds of self alone. Divine love is not only complete, it is eternal and necessary. So there must exist on the part of God some sharing of love which is both eternal and necessary.... Some philosophers and theologians have argued that, because of the requirements of perfect love, God must of necessity create some contingent being or other, or some world of contingent beings, with whom to share his love. Otherwise, his love would not be complete. But this conclusion runs counter to the firmly held traditional claim that God was free not to create any contingent things at all. Let us refer to this problem as the *problem of the lonely God*.

Swinburne offers a solution to the problem of the lonely God which blocks this argument and avoids the conclusion that God needed to create something contingent like you or me. Suppose, he begins, that there is a primordial divine being with such attributes as omnipotence, omniscience, necessity and perfect goodness. Suppose this being eternally and necessarily exemplifies all the attributes constitutive of deity. He could not exemplify them all, however, without sharing love in the deepest and most complete way possible. But the deepest and most complete way of sharing love would be to share of oneself in giving

---

2. Kelly, *Early Christian Doctrines*, p. 232.

3. Richard Swinburne, "Could There Be More Than God?" *Faith and Philosophy* 5 (July 1988): 225–41.

being to another from one's own being. This divine individual thus eternally and necessarily begets, from his own being, a distinct person who, as so begotten, is a true Son of the Father, divine from divine being. We thus have a conception of a primordial divine being's giving existence, eternally and necessarily, to a second divine person with whom love can be perfectly shared. But there is another element of love, or form of love, yet to be attended to. Not only is it possible for one person to share love with a second person, it is possible for two people to join together in sharing mutual love with a third. Think of the way in which married couples naturally seek to express their love in the giving and nurturing of a distinct life. This seems to be a form of love, or a richness of love, distinct from the sharing which goes on only between one person and another. But the perfection of divine love must encompass every basic form, or level of richness, possible for love. So we must suppose that a third divine person proceeds from the Father and the Son, eternally and necessarily, as the object of the mutuality of their ultimate giving and sharing. This divine person, the Holy Spirit, both is loved by, and in turn loves, each of the other persons of the Trinity. And there is completeness in mutual love. The Father and Son love the Spirit. The Son and Spirit love the Father. The Father and Spirit love the Son. All the forms and depths of love are manifest within divinity, and there is no need of any other divine person to make possible the complete manifestation of love. On this view, there are necessarily three distinct persons within divinity, and just as necessarily, there are no others. Thus, there exists the divine Trinity worshiped by Christians.

Some philosophers have suggested that there could not possibly exist more than one omnipotent being, for if there were two or more, their wills could potentially conflict.[4] But there could not be any possible resolution of a conflict between omnipotent beings.

So, these philosophers have thought, we must conclude that there cannot be more than one omnipotent individual. What exactly follows, however, is just that if there is more than one omnipotent being, they must be necessarily harmonious in will. But from where will that harmony come? What will be the principle of division of labor, or who will set the rules, so to speak, for the patterns of co-operation among equally omnipotent beings? Swinburne suggests that among omnipotent beings, there must be a hierarchy of responsibility or authority over such matters, and that this in itself indicates that there could not be a multiplicity of divine beings unless their ontology was much like what he argues to be the case in the Trinity. For Father, Son and Holy Spirit, the coordination responsibilities, or authority, will lie with the Father, as the primordial member of the Trinity. It would be a condition of the eternal and necessary existence of the other two persons that in some metaphysically prior way, the matters of coordination and harmonious function had already been settled. So they must eternally and necessarily derive from the Father. The New Testament itself contains reflections of this, as God the Son Incarnate seems clearly to defer to the Father and to the authority of the Father.[5]

On this view of the Trinity as consisting in a society of divine persons, we must therefore understand the possible exercise of the omnipotent power of each of the persons as constrained by the opportunities provided by whatever rules of coordination the Father lays down. Since such rules are necessary and come from a perfectly good person, Swinburne argues, each of the other members of the Trinity would necessarily welcome them and abide by them. And this is no unfortunate limitation on the freedom of each of the divine persons, as it is a necessary condition of the highest form of existence, encompassing the completeness of perfect goodness and love.

---

4. For an example of this sort of argument, and other related arguments, see William J. Wainwright, "Monotheism," in *Rationality, Religious Belief, and Moral Commitment*, ed. Robert Audi and William J. Wainwright (Ithaca, N.Y.,: Cornell University Press, 1986), pp. 289–314.

5. See, for example, John 5:37, 45; 6:57; 14:10; 15:10, and many other such passages in the Gospels.

But a few final words of clarification are needed if we are to hope to attain a good grasp of this sort of social theory of the Trinity. The decree of Nicaea insisted that the Son was not made of previously existing created material, and that he was not created *ex nihilo* at some point in time, as presumably is the case with every contingent object. The *generation* of the Son and what has been called the *spiration* of the Spirit are viewed as sharings of the being or substance of God the Father, sufficient for the eternal and necessary coexistence of two divine persons distinct from the Father, himself a divine person. Each of them has all the attributes constitutive of deity. But it is obvious that our understanding of aseity, or ontological independence, must be qualified somewhat on this view. For the Son depends on the Father, and the Spirit depends on the Father and the Son. Only the Father's existence is primordial and underived. But as we have seen on this view, insofar as being perfectly good is a condition of his existence, and the existence of the Son and Spirit as objects and sharers in love is necessary for his goodness, he bears some sort of dependence relation to them. But neither the Trinity itself, nor any of the members of the Trinity, stands in any relation of ontological dependence on any source of being prior to, or independent of, either the Father or the community all three form. The divine Trinity itself is ontologically independent and thus self-sufficient.

On this view, each member of the Trinity can be viewed as a greatest possible being, such that no other being could possibly be greater. Or we could judge there to be an internal hierarchy of greatness within the Trinity, such that no being outside the Trinity can be as great as the Spirit or the Son, but God the Father is greater than all (as some readings of John 10:29 might be taken to suggest) in the interpretive context of trinitarian doctrine. But in order to avoid another heresy, that of *subordinationism*, this latter view would have to insist on the underlying divine unity, that each of the persons of the Trinity is indeed fully divine. Another distinct application of the Anselmian perspective could specify that it is the Trinity itself which is properly considered the greatest possible being. My point here is only that social trinitarians could make various moves at this point to square their theory with the perspective of perfect being theology.

To avoid polytheism of the sort rejected by the early church fathers, social trinitarians must insist on the unity of the divine essence (the persons all share the attributes of deity), the unity of the divine substance (they all share in the being of the Father), and the unity that exists on the level of divine activity: What one member of the Trinity performs, all are said to share in performing, each in his own way, so full and deep is their cooperation.

But social trinitarians are nonetheless often said to be polytheists, however strongly they protest and proclaim their monotheism. Many theologians and Christian philosophers are very uncomfortable with any social theory of the Trinity, and thus seek to develop instead some form of what I have called a singularity theory of God's tri-unity. The heresies associated with singularity theories involve holding that the threeness of God consists only in his manner of presentation of himself to us. Christian orthodoxy has insisted that the diversity of the divine be not just a matter of appearance, but a matter of eternal, ontological reality. Numerous biblical passages seem to suggest this (Jn 1:1–3; 8:58; 17:1–26), and the problem of the lonely God seems to demand it. But singularity theories have faced difficulties in attempting an account of the Trinity adequate for accommodating those New Testament passages and avoiding that problem.

Singularity theories stress the oneness of God as a single ultimate bearer of properties, a sole metaphysical individual. On this sort of view, the three persons of the Trinity are not to be conceived as any sort of society or community of severally divine individuals or entities. The threeness which we have come to talk of as "persons" is rather to be understood as some less distinct internal relatedness within the life of the one God. As the greatest of singularity theorists, Augustine (A.D. 354–430), put it, Father, Son and Holy Spirit are themselves somehow just existent relations within the Godhead. In so categorizing the members of the Trinity, Augustine was drawing upon an ancient understanding of the status, or metaphysics, of relations, which is nowadays quite difficult for us to find at all plausible or even intelligible.

But Augustine offered some analogies to help us to grasp this view of the Trinity.[6] It was his view that the nature of God is mirrored in the nature of his creation, to the extent that even the tri-unity of the divine will be found reflected in creatures. He reminds us that God is referred to in the plural in an important passage in Genesis and is represented as saying: "Let *us* make man in *our* image" (Gen 1:26). So it is primarily to the life of human beings that we should look for analogies to help us understand the Trinity. Ideally, we need to find a triad of elements, the first of which begets the second, and the third of which binds the other two together, suggests Augustine. He offers such varied examples as: (1) an external object perceived, (2) the mind's representation of it, (3) the act of concentrating or focusing the mind on it; (1) the self as lover, (2) the object loved (which can be within that same self), (3) the love that binds; (1) the mind's memory *knowledge* of itself, (2) the mind's *understanding* of itself, (3) the mind's *will*, or love, of itself; and (1) the mind as remembering God, (2) the mind as knowing God, and (3) the mind as loving God.

But the most obvious problem with all these analogies is that they involve some sort of process or internal relatedness within the life of one person, and the doctrine of the Trinity is that, in some remotely plausible sense of "person," there are three persons which exist as the one God over all. Augustine thought that this, however, was about the best we can do. The Trinity is ultimately a mystery which we cannot hope to fathom fully, at least in this life.

Are these sorts of psychological analogies the best a singularity theory of the Trinity can manage? Well, Augustine and the many medieval philosophers who endorsed some form of singularity theory were typically pressured away from any recognition of a deeper diversity within the divine by their acceptance of a doctrine of divine simplicity, according to which there is no real ontological complexity or composition within the life of God.... And it is difficult to see how anyone who endorses divine simplicity in the full-blown sense can accept even the analogies Augustine has given us as reflecting anything really to be found in the oneness of the divine. For these theorists, there can be no genuine ontological diversity, if strict simplicity really holds. Perhaps the best move for a singularity theorist who wants a plausible account of the Trinity, explicable by psychological analogies having to do with diversity within the sphere of individuality, is to jettison the constraints of the ancient doctrine of divine simplicity. When this is done, a new sort of analogy becomes available for the elaboration of a singularity theory.

Recall the two-minds view of God Incarnate developed in the previous section. Something like a multimind perspective could be used to explicate the doctrine of the Trinity as well. Suppose that there is only one ultimate divine bearer of properties, one fundamental individual who is God. If, as we argued in the previous section, it is compatible with the unity of the person of Christ that he have two minds, or two distinct spheres of mentality, then it should also be compatible with the unity of the one individual who is God that he have three divine minds, or three distinct spheres of perfect mentality, each capable of awareness and the initiation of action. And as the human mind of Christ was hierarchically answerable to the divine mind, imagine here a three-level hierarchy of answerability, with the mind designated as God the Father filling the role of overarching consciousness.

At this point the picture could be developed in different ways. Remembering that on any singularist theory, there is really only one divine individual, there is no conceptual pressure to assign each of the attributes constitutive of deity to each sphere of mentality within deity. Thus, it could be held that only the overarching consciousness of God the Father holds all the riches

---

6. For a convenient summary and references, see Kelly, *Early Christian Doctrines*, pp. 271–79.

of omniscient knowledge. On this view, Christ need not have been speaking only of the limitations of his earthly mind when he talked of the passing away of heaven and earth and said: "But of that day or hour no one knows, not even the angels in heaven, nor the Son, but the Father alone" (Mk 13:32).

Likewise, it is possible for this sort of view to be developed in such a way that omnipotence is not assigned differentially to each sphere of mentality, thereby avoiding the coordination of activity problems of three omnipotent agents. The Son and the Spirit would then be divine, not in virtue of severally exemplifying all the attributes essential to deity, but rather through being centers of mentality belonging to the one true God as spheres of his own mindedness.

But there is nothing intrinsic to the multimind version of a singularity theory that would preclude our seeing each divine mind as enjoying the riches of omniscience and omnipotence. Each would be eternal, necessary components of the divine life. And each can be thought of as internally involved in contributing to the character and activities to be found in each of the others. The attribute of aseity, or ontological independence, could be reserved for the individual who exists with this multiminded richness of interior life, or could rather be attributed in qualified form to each of the spheres of mindedness. Neither Father, nor Son, nor Spirit depends for its existence on anything extra-trinitarian, outside the life of divinity. But if there is ontologically only one ultimate divine entity, an individual God with these three spheres of mentality, it would be this single individual who most directly would answer to Anselm's concept of *the* greatest possible being and creation theology's concept of a single source of all.

Singularity theories seek to secure unambiguous monotheism, in line with the clear Judaic background of Christian theology. As such, there is much to be said for them. But it is difficult to render any confident judgment that any such theory can accommodate naturally the full data of biblical revelation and Christian experience. And it is a bit hard to see how any such theory will suffice to block what we have called the problem of the lonely God. Could I be said to experience the fullness of love just through my conscious mind's having a high regard for my unconscious mind, which in turn appreciated the conscious sphere? It is hard to see how even a richly differentiated self-love could suffice to capture all the facets that could possibly characterize the goodness of a full and perfect love. And if singularity theories are found inevitably wanting in this regard, it will be incumbent upon the Christian theist to find some form of a social theory to explicate the relation between threeness and oneness in the life of the triune God.

The main point that needs to be made here is that neither the doctrine of the Trinity nor the doctrine of the Incarnation is just an opaque mystery totally impenetrable to human thought. In each case we have seen that we can construct alternative, intelligible models or theories which offer quite interesting interpretations of initially paradoxical-looking ideas. As we have seen in the case of some of the attributes definitive of the divine, a fairly high degree of confidence concerning our conception of God at one level is compatible with having alternative explications, and thus with some degree of tentativeness, at a more fine-grained level of theological specificity. What is important to stress here, though, is that just as we can make progress in our efforts to think about the various basic attributes conceptually constitutive of our idea of deity, so, likewise, we can make important headway in our attempts to understand the most distinctive Christian claims about the greatest possible source of all.

QUESTIONS AND FURTHER READINGS

Questions for Discussion

1. How would you explain, in your own words, the doctrine of the Trinity?

2. Describe something significant you learned from the essay by Origen. Is it relevant for today? Explain.

3. What are two important points you gleaned from the Aquinas reading?

4. How are the creeds relevant to the Trinity doctrine?

5. What are several important biblical passages that support the Trinity doctrine? Would a Jehovah's Witness be satisfied with these passages? Should they be? Explain.

6. In a paragraph or so, explain Richard of St. Victor's argument for the Trinity. Do you find it persuasive? Why or why not?

7. What would you say to a Muslim who claims that the Trinity doctrine is tritheism — the belief in three gods?

8. Has Thomas Morris adequately defended the coherence of the Trinity, in your view? If so, how? If not, why not?

9. Briefly describe the difference between *singularity theories of the Trinity* and *social theories of the Trinity*. Which theory do you believe makes the most sense, and which is most biblical? Explain.

10. How would you defend the doctrine of the Trinity?

Further Readings

Augustine (1991). *The Trinity*. Translated, with an introduction and notes, by E. Hill. New York: New City Press. (Augustine's classic work on the subject.)

Brower, Jeffrey E., and Michael C. Rea (2005). "Material Constitution and the Trinity." *Faith and Philosophy* 22:57 – 76. (Argues that the divine essence is like matter that is individuated into three persons by three distinct properties.)

Brown, David (1985). *The Divine Trinity*. London: Duckworth. (A widely discussed book on the Trinity.)

Davis, Stephen T., Daniel Kendall, and Gerald O'Collins, eds. (2002). *The Trinity: An Interdisciplinary Symposium on the Trinity*. Oxford: Oxford University Press. (A seminal collection of essays on the Trinity.)

Erickson, Millard J. (2000). *Making Sense of the Trinity: Three Crucial Questions*. Grand Rapids: Baker. (Leading evangelical theologian focuses on three central and difficult questions.)

McGrath, Alister (1994). *Christian Theology: An Introduction*. Oxford: Blackwell. (Recommended for those with little or no background in theology or the history of Christian thought.)

Moltmann, Jürgen (1981). *The Trinity and the Kingdom*. Translated by M. Kohl. San Francisco: Harper & Row.

Olson, Roger E., and Christopher A. Hall (2002). *The Trinity*. Grand Rapids: Eerdmans.

Rusch, William, ed. (1980). *The Trinitarian Controversy*. Philadelphia: Fortress. (A collection of important early documents on the Trinity.)

Zizioulas, John D. (1985). *Being as Communion*. Crestwood, NY: St. Vladimir's Seminary Press. (A contemporary Eastern Orthodox statement of the Trinity.)

PART 4

THE INCARNATION

The doctrine of the incarnation is essentially that Jesus Christ is God incarnate. Jesus was more than a prophet, more than an adopted "son of God," even more than a pre-eminent creature who came into existence by the will of the Father. More than any of this, the incarnation is the view that the human being Jesus of Nazareth is God — the eternal Second Person of the Holy Trinity — incarnate. Many questions arise from this doctrine, including the following: How could the omnipotent, immutable, omnipresent God "become" a human being? And why would God do so? Does Jesus, God incarnate, have both a divine nature and a human nature? A divine mind and a human mind? If so, how can we make sense of these ideas? In answering these and a number of other related questions, many heresies arose in the early centuries of the church. The Council of Chalcedon in 451 proclaimed what became the received traditional view.

While Christian theologians and philosophers have agreed that the incarnation is in some ways a mystery beyond human comprehension, nevertheless many also maintain that much can be said in an attempt to better understand it. Christian apologists have for many centuries defended the doctrine of the incarnation, making the case that it is neither illogical nor debasing to God.

In the first selection, the early apologist Athanasius develops an elaborate apologetic for the incarnation. Since his work is often ignored in our day, we thought it beneficial to include here a significant portion of his apologetic as it was penned (or perhaps "quilled") by him so many centuries ago. These issues are, for the most part, timeless. The selections we have chosen include such issues as why Christ died the way he did, how through his death he proved to be conqueror of death, why he came in human form, and what some of his amazing works were as the Word incarnate.

One of the great defenders of the traditional understanding of the incarnation was Saint Anselm of Canterbury (1033 – 1109). In this classic work, Anselm, who continually affirmed that reason can and should be used to explain and defend the Christian faith, interacts with his interlocutor Boso as he offers an advanced apologetic for the incarnation. As with Athanasius's work, he too deals with a number of relevant issues. He also attempts to prove that the incarnation *had* to happen.

In the third and final essay in this part, Thomas Morris explains and defends the traditional doctrine of the incarnation. Morris notes that it first appears that the incarnation — the claim that Jesus was both *fully* God and *fully* man — seems metaphysically and logically impossible. However, he argues that distinguishing between individual essences and kind essences provides a needed distinction for this possibility. He outlines two main views of the incarnation: kenotic Christology and the two-minds view. In the former, Christ freely chose to empty himself of his divinity for a time. For Morris, this unsatisfactorily redefines what it means to be deity. On the two-minds view, taking on a human body and mind did not require or involve relinquishing the proper resources of divinity. Instead, the incarnation involved a duality of abstract natures, as well as a duality of consciousness.

CHAPTER 26

On the Incarnation

Athanasius of Alexandria

Chapter I

Introductory. The subject of this treatise: the humiliation and incarnation of the Word. Presupposes the doctrine of Creation, and that by the Word. The Father has saved the world by Him through Whom He first made it.

1. Whereas in what precedes we have drawn out — choosing a few points from among many — a sufficient account of the error of the heathen concerning idols, and of the worship of idols, and how they originally came to be invented; how, namely, out of wickedness men devised for themselves the worshipping of idols: and whereas we have by God's grace noted somewhat also of the divinity of the Word of the Father, and of His universal Providence and power, and that the Good Father through Him orders all things, and all things are moved by Him, and in Him are quickened: come now, Macarius,[1] (worthy of that name), and true lover of Christ, let us follow up the faith of our religion,[2] and set forth also what relates to the Word's becoming Man, and to His divine Appearing amongst us, which Jews traduce and Greeks laugh to scorn, but we worship; in order that, all the more for the seeming low estate of the Word, your piety toward Him may be increased and multiplied.

2. For the more He is mocked among the unbelieving, the more witness does He give of His own Godhead; inasmuch as He not only Himself demonstrates as possible what men mistake, thinking impossible, but what men deride as unseemly, this by His own goodness He clothes with seemliness, and what men, in their conceit of wisdom, laugh at as merely human, He by His own power demonstrates to be divine, subduing the pretensions of idols by His supposed humiliation — by the Cross — and those who mock and disbelieve invisibly winning over to recognise His divinity and power.

3. But to treat this subject it is necessary to recall what has been previously said; in order that you may neither fail to know the cause of the bodily appearing of the Word of the Father, so high and so great, nor think it a consequence of His own nature that the Saviour has worn a body; but that being incorporeal by nature, and Word from the beginning, He has yet of the loving-kindness and goodness of His own Father been manifested to us in a human body for our salvation.

4. It is, then, proper for us to begin the treatment of this subject by speaking of the creation of the universe, and of God its Artificer, that so it may be duly perceived that the renewal of creation has been the work of the self-same Word that made it at the beginning. For it will appear not inconsonant for the Father to have wrought its salvation in Him by Whose means He made it.

[…]

---

1. Archibald Robertson, ed., *St. Athanasius,* trans. Cardinal Newman, *A Select Library of Nicene and Post-Nicene Fathers of the Christian Church,* ed. Henry Wace and Philip Schaff (Oxford: Parker, 1892), 4:36–38, 48–50, 52–67.

See *Contra Gentes,* i. The word (*macaria*) may be an adjective only, but its occurrence in *both* places seems decisive. The name was very common (*Apol. c. Ar.* passim). "Macarius" was a Christian as the present passage shews: he is presumed (*c. Gent.* i. 7) to have access to Scripture.

2. *teis eusebeias.* See 1 Tim. 3:16.

Chapters IV, V

Our creation and God's Incarnation most intimately connected. As by the Word man was called from non-existence into being, and further received the grace of a divine life, so by the one fault which forfeited that life they again incurred corruption and untold sin and misery filled the world.

1. You are wondering, perhaps, for what possible reason, having proposed to speak of the Incarnation of the Word, we are at present treating of the origin of mankind. But this, too, properly belongs to the aim of our treatise.

2. For in speaking of the appearance of the Saviour amongst us, we must needs speak also of the origin of men, that you may know that the reason of His coming down was because of us, and that our transgression[3] called forth the loving-kindness of the Word, that the Lord should both make haste to help us and appear among men.

3. For of His becoming Incarnate we were the object, and for our salvation He dealt so lovingly as to appear and be born even in a human body.

[…]

Chapter XXI

Death brought to nought by the death of Christ. Why then did not Christ die privately, or in a more honourable way? He was not subject to natural death, but had to die at the hands of others. Why then did He die? Nay but for that purpose He came, and but for that, He could not have risen.

6. […] Since it was not fit, either, that the Lord should fall sick, who healed the diseases of others; nor again was it right for that body to lose its strength, in which He gives strength to the weaknesses of others also.

7. Why, then, did He not prevent death, as He did sickness? Because it was for this that He had the body, and it was unfitting to prevent it, lest the Resurrection also should be hindered, while yet it was equally unfitting for sickness to precede His death, lest it should be thought weakness on the part of Him that was in the body. Did He not then hunger? Yes; He hungered, agreeably to the properties of His body. But He did not perish of hunger, because of the Lord that wore it. Hence, even if He died to ransom all, yet He saw not corruption. For [His body] rose again in perfect soundness, since the body belonged to none other, but to the very Life.

Chapter XXII

But why did He not withdraw His body from the Jews, and so guard its immortality? (1) It became Him not to inflict death on Himself, and yet not to shun it. (2) He came to receive death as the due of others, therefore it should come to Him from without. (3) His death must be certain, to guarantee the truth of His Resurrection. Also, He could not die from infirmity, lest He should be mocked in His healing of others.

1. But it were better, one might say, to have hidden from the designs of the Jews, that He might guard His body altogether from death. Now let such an one be told that this too was unbefitting the Lord. For as it was not fitting for the Word of God, being the Life, to inflict death Himself on His own body, so neither was it suitable to fly from death offered by others, but rather to follow it up unto destruction, for which reason He naturally neither laid aside His body of His own accord, nor, again, fled from the Jews when they took counsel against Him.

2. But this did not shew weakness on the Word's part, but, on the contrary, shewed Him to be Saviour and Life; in that He both awaited death to destroy it, and hasted to accomplish the death offered Him for the salvation of all.

3. And besides, the Saviour came to accomplish not His own death, but the death of men; whence He did not lay aside His body by a death of His own — for He was Life and had none — but received that death which came from men, in order perfectly to do away with this when it met Him in His own body [John 10:17 – 18].

---

3. Cf. *Orat.* ii. 54, note 4.

4. Again, from the following also one might see the reasonableness of the Lord's body meeting this end. The Lord was especially concerned for the resurrection of the body which He was set to accomplish. For what He was to do was to manifest it as a monument of victory over death, and to assure all of His having effected the blotting out of corruption, and of the incorruption of their bodies from thenceforward; as a gage of which and a proof of the resurrection in store for all, He has preserved His own body incorrupt.

5. If, then, once more, His body had fallen sick, and the word had been sundered from it in the sight of all, it would have been unbecoming that He who healed the diseases of others should suffer His own instrument to waste in sickness. For how could His driving out the diseases of others have been believed[4] in if His own temple fell sick in Him?[5] For either He had been mocked as unable to drive away diseases, or if He could, but did not, He would be thought insensible toward others also.

[...]

Chapter XXIV

Further objections anticipated. He did not choose His manner of death; for He was to prove Conqueror of death in all or any of its forms: (simile of a good wrestler). The death chosen to disgrace Him proved the Trophy against death: moreover it preserved His body undivided.

1. But what others also might have said, we must anticipate in reply. For perhaps a man might say even as follows: If it was necessary for His death to take place before all, and with witnesses, that the story of His Resurrection also might be believed, it would have been better at any rate for Him to have devised for Himself a glorious death, if only to escape the ignominy of the Cross.

2. But had He done even this, He would give ground for suspicion against Himself, that He was not powerful against every death, but only against the

death devised for[6] Him; and so again there would have been a pretext for disbelief about the Resurrection all the same. So death came to His body, not from Himself, but from hostile counsels, in order that whatever death they offered to the Saviour, this He might utterly do away.

3. And just as a noble wrestler, great in skill and courage, does not pick out his antagonists for himself, lest he should raise a suspicion of his being afraid of some of them, but puts it in the choice of the onlookers, and especially so if they happen to be his enemies, so that against whomsoever they match him, him he may throw, and be believed superior to them all; so also the Life of all, our Lord and Saviour, even Christ, did not devise a death for His own body, so as not to appear to be fearing some other death; but He accepted on the Cross, and endured, a death inflicted by others, and above all by His enemies, which they thought dreadful and ignominious and not to be faced; so that this also being destroyed, both He Himself might be believed to be the Life, and the power of death be brought utterly to nought.

4. So something surprising and startling has happened; for the death, which they thought to inflict as a disgrace, was actually a monument of victory against death itself. Whence neither did He suffer the death of John, his head being severed, nor, as Esaias, was He sawn in sunder; in order that even in death He might still keep His body undivided and in perfect soundness, and no pretext be afforded to those that would divide the Church.

Chapter XXV

Why the Cross, of all deaths? (1) He had to bear the curse for us. (2) On it He held out His hands to unite all, Jews and Gentiles, in Himself (3) He defeated the "Prince of the powers of the air" in his own region, clearing the way to heaven and opening for us the everlasting doors.

1. And thus much in reply to those without who

---

4. Cf. Matt. 27:42.

5. *i.e.*, when sustained by its union with Him.

6. *i.e.*, suggested as *endoxon* (*supra*, 1); a reading *par eautou* has been suggested: (devised) "by Himself."

pile up arguments for themselves. But if any of our own people also inquire, not from love of debate, but from love of learning, why He suffered death in none other way save on the Cross, let him also be told that no other way than this was good for us, and that it was well that the Lord suffered this for our sakes.

2. For if He came Himself to bear the curse laid upon us, how else could He have "become a curse" [Gal. 3:13], unless He received the death set for a curse? And that is the Cross. For this is exactly what is written: "Cursed is he that hangeth on a tree" [Deut. 21:23].

3. Again, if the Lord's death is the ransom of all, and by His death "the middle wall of partition" [Eph. 2: 14] is broken down, and the calling of the nations is brought about, how would He have called us to Him, had He not been crucified? For it is only on the cross that a man dies with his hands spread out. Whence it was fitting for the Lord to bear this also and to spread out His hands, that with the one He might draw the ancient people, and with the other those from the Gentiles, and unite both in Himself.

4. For this is what He Himself has said, signifying by what manner of death He was to ransom all: "I, when I am lifted up," He saith, "shall draw all men unto Me" [John 12:32].

5. And once more, if the devil, the enemy of our race, having fallen from heaven, wanders about our lower atmosphere, and there bearing rule over his fellow-spirits, as his peers in disobedience, not only works illusions by their means in them that are deceived, but tries to hinder them that are going up (and about this[7] the Apostle says: "According to the prince of the power of the air, of the spirit that now worketh in the sons of disobedience"); while the Lord came to cast down the devil, and clear the air and prepare the way for us up into heaven, as said the Apostle: "Through the veil, that is to say, His flesh" [Heb. 10:20] — and this must needs be by death — well, by what other kind of death could this have come to pass, than by one which took place in the air, I mean the cross?

For only he that is perfected on the cross dies in the air. Whence it was quite fitting that the Lord suffered this death.

6. For thus being lifted up He cleared the air[8] of the malignity both of the devil and of demons of all kinds, as He says: "I beheld Satan as lightning fall from heaven" [Luke 10:18]; and made a new opening of the way up into heaven, as He says once more: "Lift up your gates, O ye princes, and be ye lift up, ye everlasting doors."[9] For it was not the Word Himself that needed an opening of the gates, being Lord of all; nor were any of His works closed to their Maker; but we it was that needed it, whom He carried up by His own body. For as He offered it to death on behalf of all, so by it He once more made ready the way up into the heavens.

[…]

Chapter XXX

The reality of the Resurrection proved by facts: (1) the victory over death described above: (2) the Wonders of Grace are the work of one Living, of One who is God: (3) if the gods be (as alleged) real and living, a fortiori He Who shatters their power is alive.

1. What we have so far said, then, is no small proof that death has been brought to nought, and that the Cross of the Lord is a sign of victory over him. But of the Resurrection of the body to immortality thereupon accomplished by Christ, the common Saviour and true Life of all the demonstration by facts is clearer than arguments to those whose mental vision is sound.

2. For if, as our argument shewed, death has been brought to nought, and because of Christ all tread him under foot, much more did He Himself first tread him down with His own body, and bring him to nought. But supposing death slain by Him, what could have happened save the rising again of His body, and its being displayed as a monument of victory against death? or how could death have been shewn to be brought to nought unless the Lord's body had risen? But if this demonstration of the Resurrection seem to

---

7. Eph. 2:2, and see the curious visions of Antony, *Vit. Ant.,* 65, 66.

8. Cf. Lightfoot on Coloss. 2:15, also the fragment of *Letter* 22, and *Letter* 60.7.

9. Ps. 24:7, Septuagint.

anyone insufficient, let him be assured of what is said even from what takes place before his eyes.

3. For whereas on a man's decease he can put forth no power, but his influence lasts to the grave and thenceforth ceases; and actions, and power over men, belong to the living only; let him who will, see and be judge, confessing the truth from what appears to sight.

4. For now that the Saviour works so great things among men, and day by day is invisibly persuading so great a multitude from every side, both from them that dwell in Greece and in foreign lands, to come over to His faith, and all to obey His teaching, will anyone still hold his mind in doubt whether a Resurrection has been accomplished by the Saviour, and whether Christ is alive, or rather is Himself the Life?

5. Or is it like a dead man to be pricking the consciences of men, so that they deny their hereditary laws and bow before the teaching of Christ? Or how, if he is no longer active (for this is proper to one dead), does he stay from their activity those who are active and alive, so that the adulterer no longer commits adultery, and the murderer murders no more, nor is the inflicter of wrong any longer grasping, and the profane is henceforth religious? Or how, if He be not risen but is dead, does He drive away, and pursue, and cast down those false gods said by the unbelievers to be alive, and the demons they worship?

6. For where Christ is named, and His faith, there all idolatry is deposed and all imposture of evil spirits is exposed, and any spirit is unable to endure even the name, nay even on barely hearing it flies and disappears. But this work is not that of one dead, but of one that lives-and especially of God.

7. In particular, it would be ridiculous to say that while the spirits cast out by Him and the idols brought to nought are alive, He who chases them away, and by His power prevents their even appearing, yea, and is being confessed by them all to be Son of God, is dead.

[…]

Chapter XXXII

But who is to see Him risen, so as to believe? Nay, God is ever invisible and known by His works only: and here the works cry out in proof. If you do not believe, look at those who do, and perceive the Godhead of Christ. The demons see this, though men be blind. Summary of the argument so far.

1. But if, because He is not seen, His having risen at all is disbelieved, it is high time for those who refuse belief to deny the very course of Nature. For it is God's peculiar property at once to be invisible and yet to be known from His works, as has been already stated above.

2. If, then, the works are not there, they do well to disbelieve what does not appear. But if the works cry aloud and shew it clearly, why do they choose to deny the life so manifestly due to the Resurrection? For even if they be maimed in their intelligence, yet even with the external senses men may see the unimpeachable power and Godhead of Christ.

3. For even a blind man, if he see not the sun, yet if he but take hold of the warmth the sun gives out, knows that there is a sun above the earth. Thus let our opponents also, even if they believe not as yet, being still blind to the truth, yet at least knowing His power by others who believe, not deny the Godhead of Christ and the Resurrection accomplished by Him.

4. For it is plain that if Christ be dead, He could not be expelling demons and spoiling idols; for a dead man the spirits would not have obeyed. But if they be manifestly expelled by the naming of His name, it must be evident that He is not dead; especially as spirits, seeing even what is unseen by men, could tell if Christ were dead and refuse Him any obedience at all.

5. But as it is, what irreligious men believe not, the spirits see — that He is God — and hence they fly and fall at His feet, saying just what they uttered when He was in the body: "We know Thee Who Thou art, the Holy One of God" [Luke 4:34]; and, "Ah, what have we to do with Thee, Thou Son of God? I pray Thee, torment me not" [Mark 5:7].

6. As then demons confess Him, and His works bear Him witness day by day, it must be evident, and let none brazen it out against the truth, both that the Saviour raised His own body, and that He is the true Son of God, being from Him, as from His Father, His

own Word, and Wisdom, and Power, Who in ages later took a body for the salvation of all, and taught the world concerning the Father, and brought death to nought, and bestowed incorruption upon all by the promise of the Resurrection, having raised His own body as a first-fruits of this, and having displayed it by the sign of the Cross as a monument of victory over death and its corruption.

[...]

Chapter XXXIV

Prophecies of His passion and death in all its circumstances.

1. Nor is even His death passed over in silence: on the contrary, it is referred to in the divine Scriptures, even exceeding clearly. For to the end that none should err for want of instruction in the actual events, they feared not to mention even the cause of His death — that He suffers it not for His own sake, but for the immortality and salvation of all, and the counsels of the Jews against Him and the indignities offered Him at their hands.

2. They say then: "A man in stripes, and knowing how to bear weakness, for his face is turned away: he was dishonoured and held in no account. He beareth our sins, and is in pain on our account; and we reckoned him to be in labour, and in stripes, and in ill-usage; but he was wounded for our sins, and made weak for our wickedness. The chastisement of our peace was upon him, and by his stripes we were healed" [Isa. 53:3 – 5]. O marvel at the loving-kindness of the Word, that for our sakes He is dishonoured, that we may be brought to honour. "For all we," it says, "like sheep were gone astray; man had erred in his way; and the Lord delivered him for our sins; and he openeth

not his mouth, because he hath been evilly intreated. As a sheep was he brought to the slaughter, and as a lamb dumb before his shearer, so openeth he not his mouth: in his abasement his judgment was taken away"[10] [Isa. 53:6 – 8].

3. Then lest any should from His suffering conceive Him to be a common man, Holy Writ anticipates the surmises of man, and declares the power (which worked) for Him,[11] and the difference of His nature compared with ourselves saying: "But who shall declare his generation? For his life is taken away from the earth. From the wickedness of the people was he brought to death. And I will give the wicked instead of his burial, and the rich instead of his death; for he did no wickedness, neither was guile found in his mouth. And the Lord will cleanse him from his stripes."

Chapter XXXV

Prophecies of the Cross. How these prophecies are satisfied in Christ alone.

1. But, perhaps, having heard the prophecy of His death, you ask to learn also what is set forth concerning the Cross. For not even this is passed over: it is displayed by the holy men with great plainness.

2. For first Moses predicts it, and that with a loud voice, when he says: "Ye shall see[12] your Life hanging before your eyes, and shall not believe."

3. And next, the prophets after him witness of this, saying: "But I as an innocent lamb brought to be slain" [Jer. 11: 9], "knew it not; they counselled an evil counsel against me, saying, Hither and let us cast a tree upon his[13] bread, and efface him from the land of the living."

4. And again: "They pierced my hands and my feet, they numbered all my bones ... they parted my gar-

---

10. Or, "exalted."

11. *Tein hyper autou dynamin.* The Ben. version simplifies this difficult expression by ignoring the hyper. Mr. E. N. Bennett has suggested to me that the true reading may be *hyperaulon* for *hyper autou* (*hyperaulos* in Philo). I would add the suggestion that *autou* stood after *hyperaulon*, and that the similarity of the five letters in MS. caused the second word to be dropped out. "*His* exceeding immaterial power" would be the resulting sense. (See *Class. Review*, 1890, No. iv. P. 182).

12. Deut. 28:66, see *Orat.* ii. 16, note 1.

13. Properly "let us destroy the tree with its bread" (*i.e.*, fruit). The Septuagint translates *belahmo* "*upon* his bread," which is possible in itself; but they either mistook the verb, or followed some wrong reading. Their rendering is followed by all the Latin versions. For a comment on the latter see Tertull. *Adv. Marc.* iii. 19, iv. 40.

ments among them, and for my vesture they cast lots" [Ps. 22:16 – 18].

5. Now a death raised aloft, and that takes place on a tree, could be none other than the Cross: and again, in no other death are the hands and feet pierced, save on the Cross only.

6. But since by the sojourn of the Saviour among men all nations also on every side began to know God; they did not leave this point, either, without a reference: but mention is made of this matter as well in the Holy Scriptures. For "there shall be," he saith "the root of Jesse, and he that riseth to rule the nations, on him shall the nations hope" [Isa. 11:10]. This then is a little in proof of what has happened.

7. But all Scripture teems with refutations of the disbelief of the Jews. For which of the righteous men and holy prophets, and patriarchs, recorded in the divine Scriptures, ever had his corporal birth of a virgin only? Or what woman has sufficed without man for the conception of human kind? Was not Abel born of Adam, Enoch of Jared, Noe of Lamech, and Abraham of Tharra, Isaac of Abraham, Jacob of Isaac? Was not Judas born of Jacob, and Moses and Aaron of Ameram? Was not Samuel born of Elkana, was not David of Jesse, was not Solomon of David, was not Ezechias of Achaz, was not Josias of Amos, was not Esaias of Amos, was not Jeremy of Chelchias, was not Ezechiel of Buzi? Had not each a father as author of his existence? Who then is he that is born of a virgin only? For the prophet made exceeding much of this sign.

8. Or whose birth did a star in the skies forerun, to announce to the world him that was born? For when Moses was born, he was hid by his parents: David was not heard of, even by those of his neighbourhood, inasmuch as even the great Samuel knew him not, but asked, had Jesse yet another son? Abraham again became known to his neighbours as[14] a great man only subsequently to his birth. But of Christ's birth the witness was not man, but a star in that heaven whence He was descending.

[...]

Chapter XLII

His union with the body is based upon His relation to Creation as a whole. He used a human body, since to man it was that He wished to reveal Himself.

1. For just as, while the whole body is quickened and illumined by man, supposing one said it were absurd that man's power should also be in the toe, he would be thought foolish; because, while granting that he pervades and works in the whole, he demurs to his being in the part also; thus he who grants and believes that the Word of God is in the whole Universe, and that the whole is illumined and moved by Him, should not think it absurd that a single human body also should receive movement and light from Him.

2. But if it is because the human race is a thing created and has been made out of nothing, that they regard that manifestation of the Saviour in man, which we speak of, as not seemly, it is high time for them to eject Him from creation also; for it too has been brought into existence by the Word out of nothing.

3. But if, even though creation be a thing made, it is not absurd that the Word should be in it, then neither is it absurd that He should be in man. For whatever idea they form of the whole, they must necessarily apply the like idea to the part. For man also, as I said before, is a part of the whole.

4. Thus it is not at all unseemly that the Word should be in man, while all things are deriving from Him their light and movement and light, as also their authors say, "In him we live and move and have our being" [Acts 17:28].

5. So, then, what is there to scoff at in what we say, if the Word has used that, wherein He is, as an instrument to manifest Himself? For were He not in it, neither could He have used it; but if we have previously allowed that He is in the whole and in its parts, what is there incredible in His manifesting Himself in that wherein He is?

6. For by His own power He is united[15] wholly with each and all, and orders all things without stint, so that no one could have called it out of place for Him to

---

14. Or "only after he had grown great," i.e., to man's estate.

15. *epibainon*, see supra, note 24.

speak, and make known Himself and His Father, by means of sun, if He so willed, or moon, or heaven, or earth, or waters, or fire;[16] inasmuch as He holds in one all things at once, and is in fact not only in all, but also in the part in question, and there invisibly manifests Himself. In like manner, it cannot be absurd if, ordering as He does the whole, and giving life to all things, and having willed to make Himself known through men, He has used as His instrument a human body to manifest the truth and knowledge of the Father. For humanity, too, is an actual part of the whole.

7. And as Mind, pervading man all through, is interpreted by a part of the body, I mean the tongue, without anyone saying, I suppose, that the essence of the mind is on that account lowered, so if the Word, pervading all things, has used a human instrument, this cannot appear unseemly. For, as I have said previously, if it be unseemly to have used a body as an instrument, it is unseemly also for Him to be in the Whole.

Chapter XLIII

He came in human rather than in any nobler form, because (1) He came to save, not to impress; (2) Man alone of creatures had sinned. As men would not recognise His works in the Universe, He came and worked among them as a Man; in the sphere to which they had limited themselves.

1. Now, if they ask, Why then did He not appear by means of other and nobler parts of creation, and use some nobler instrument, as the sun, or moon, or stars, or fire, or air, instead of man merely? let them know that the Lord came not to make a display, but to heal and teach those who were suffering.

2. For the way for one aiming at display would be, just to appear, and to dazzle the beholders; but for one seeking to heal and teach the way is, not simply to sojourn here, but to give himself to the aid of those in want, and to appear as they who need him can bear it; that he may not, by exceeding the requirements of the sufferers, trouble the very persons that need him, rendering God's appearance useless to them.

3. Now, nothing in creation had gone astray with regard to their notions of God, save man only. Why, neither sun, nor moon, nor heaven, nor the stars, nor water, nor air had swerved from their order; but knowing their Artificer and Sovereign, the Word, they remain as they were made.[17] But men alone, having rejected what was good, then devised things of nought instead of the truth, and have ascribed the honour due to God, and their knowledge of Him, to demons and men in the shape of stones.

4. With reason, then, since it were unworthy of the Divine Goodness to overlook so grave a matter, while yet men were not able to recognise Him as ordering and guiding the whole, He takes to Himself as an instrument a part of the whole, His human body, and unites[18] Himself with that, in order that since men could not recognise Him in the whole, they should not fail to know Him in the part; and since they could not look up to His invisible power, might be able, at any rate, from what resembled themselves to reason to Him and to contemplate Him.

5. For, men as they are, they will be able to know His Father more quickly and directly by a body of like nature and by the divine works wrought through it, judging by comparison that they are not human, but the works of God, which are done by Him.

6. And if it were absurd, as they say, for the Word to be known through the works of the body, it would likewise be absurd for Him to be known through the works of the universe. For just as He is in creation, and yet does not partake of its nature in the least degree, but rather all things partake[19] of His power; so while He used the body as His instrument He partook of

---

16. The superfluous *pepoiekenai* is ignored, being untranslatable as the text stands. For a less simple conjecture, see the Bened. Note.

17. This thought is beautifully expressed by Keble:

"All true, all faultless, all in tune, Creation's wondrous choir
Opened in mystic unison, to last till time expire.
And still it lasts: by day and night with one consenting voice

All hymn Thy glory, Lord, aright, all worship and rejoice:
Man only mars the sweet accord …"

('Christian Year,' Fourth Sunday after Trinity.)

18. Cf. 41.5, note 27.

19. Cf. Orig. *c. Cels.* Vi.64, where there is the same contrast between *metekein* and *metekesthai*.

no corporeal property, but, on the contrary, Himself sanctified even the body.

7. For if even Plato, who is in such repute among the Greeks, says[20] that its author, beholding the universe tempest-tossed, and in peril of going down to the place of chaos, takes his seat at the helm of the soul and comes to the rescue and corrects all its calamities; what is there incredible in what we say, that mankind being in error, the Word lighted down[21] upon it and appeared as man, that He might save it in its tempest by His guidance and goodness?

[…]

Chapter XLVIII

Further facts. Christian continence of virgins and ascetics. Martyrs. The power of the Cross against demons and magic. Christ by His Power shews Himself more than a man, more than a magician, more than a spirit. For all these are totally subject to Him. Therefore He is the Word of God.

1. Now these arguments of ours do not amount merely to words, but have in actual experience a witness to their truth.

2. For let him that will, go up and behold the proof of virtue in the virgins of Christ and in the young men that practise holy chastity,[22] and the assurance of immortality in so great a band of His martyrs.

3. And let him come who would test by experience what we have now said, and in the very presence of the deceit of demons and the imposture of oracles and the marvels of magic, let him use the Sign of that Cross which is laughed at among them, and he shall see how by its means demons fly, oracles cease, all magic and witchcraft is brought to nought.

4. Who, then, and how great is this Christ, Who by His own Name and Presence casts into the shade and brings to nought all things on every side, and is alone strong against all, and has filled the whole world with His teaching? Let the Greeks tell us, who are pleased to laugh, and blush not.

5. For if He is a man, how then has one man exceeded the power of all whom even themselves hold to be gods, and convicted them by His own power of being nothing? But if they call Him a magician, how can it be that by a magician all magic is destroyed, instead of being confirmed? For if He conquered particular magicians, or prevailed over one only, it would be proper for them to hold that He excelled the rest by superior skill;

6. but if His Cross has won the victory over absolutely all magic, and over the very name of it, it must be plain that the Saviour is not a magician, seeing that even those demons who are invoked by the other magicians fly from Him as their Master.

7. Who He is, then, let the Greeks tell us, whose only serious pursuit is jesting. Perhaps they might say that He, too, was a demon, and hence His strength. But say this as they will, they will have the laugh against them, for they can once more be put to shame by our former proofs. For how is it possible that He should be a demon who drives the demons out?

8. For if He simply drove out particular demons, it might properly be held that by the chief of demons He prevailed against the lesser, just as the Jews said to Him when they wished to insult Him. But if, by His Name being named, all madness of the demons is uprooted and chased away, it must be evident that here, too, they are wrong, and that our Lord and Saviour Christ is not, as they think, some demoniacal power.

9. Then, if the Saviour is neither a man simply, nor a magician, nor some demon, but has by His own Godhead brought to nought and cast into the shade both the doctrine found in the poets and the delusion of the demons and the wisdom of the Gentiles, it must be plain and will be owned by all, that this is the true Son of God, even the Word and Wisdom and Power of the Father from the beginning. For this is why His works also are no works of man, but are recognised to be above man, and truly God's works, both from the facts in themselves, and from comparison with [the rest of] mankind.

---

20. Ath. paraphrases loosely Plat. *Politic*. 273 D. See Jowett's Plato (ed. 2), vol. iv, pp. 515, 553.

21. Lit. "sat down," as three lines above.
22. Cf. *Hist. Arian*. 25, *Apol. Const*. 33.

[...]

Chapter LIII

The whole fabric of Gentilism levelled at a blow by Christ secretly addressing the conscience of man.

1. And to mention one proof of the divinity of the Saviour, which is indeed utterly surprising — what mere man or magician or tyrant or king was ever able by himself to engage with so many, and to fight the battle against all idolatry and the whole dernoniacal host and all magic, and all the wisdom of the Greeks, while they were so strong and still flourishing and imposing upon all, and at one onset to check them all, as was our Lord, the true Word of God, Who, invisibly exposing each man's error, is by Himself bearing off all men from them all, so that while they who were worshipping idols now trample upon them, those in repute for magic burn their books, and the wise prefer to all studies the interpretation of the Gospels?

2. For whom they used to worship, them they are deserting, and Whom they used to mock as one crucified, Him they worship as Christ, confessing Him to be God. And they that are called gods among them are routed by the Sign of the Cross, while the Crucified Saviour is proclaimed in all the world as God and the Son of God. And the gods worshipped among the Greeks are falling into ill repute at their hands, as scandalous beings; while those who receive the teaching of Christ live a chaster life than they.

3. If, then, these and the like are human works, let him who will point out similar works on the part of men of former time, and so convince us. But if they prove to be, and are, not men's works, but God's, why are the unbelievers so irreligious as not to recognise the Master that wrought them?

4. For their case is as though a man, from the works of creation, failed to know God their Artificer. For if they knew His Godhead from His power over the universe, they would have known that the bodily works of Christ also are not human, but are the works of the Saviour of all, the Word of God. And did they thus know, "they would not," as Paul said, "have crucified the Lord of glory" [1 Cor. 2:8].

Chapter LIV

The Word Incarnate, as is the case with the Invisible God, is known to us by His works. By them we recognise His deifying mission. Let us be content to enumerate a few of them, leaving their dazzling plentitude to him who will behold.

1. As, then, if a man should wish to see God, Who is invisible by nature and not seen at all, he may know and apprehend Him from His works: so let him who fails to see Christ with his understanding, at least apprehend Him by the works of His body, and test whether they be human works or God's works.

2. And if they be human, let him scoff; but if they are not human, but of God, let him recognise it, and not laugh at what is no matter for scoffing; but rather let him marvel that by so ordinary a means things divine had been manifested to us, and that by death immortality has reached to all, and that by the Word becoming man, the universal Providence has been known, and its Giver and Artificer the very Word of God.

3. For He was made man that we might be made God;[23] and He manifested Himself by a body that we might receive the idea of the unseen Father; and He endured the insolence of men that we might inherit immortality. For while He Himself was in no way injured, being impassible and incorruptible and very Word and God, men who were suffering, and for

---

23. *theopoiethomen.* See *Orat.* ii.70, note 1, and many other passages in those Discourses, as well as *Letters* 60.4, 61.2 (Eucharistic reference), de *Synodis* 51, note 7. (Compare also Iren. IV. xxxviii. 4, "non ab initio dii facti sum us, sed primo quidem homines. tunc demum dii." d. *ib.* praef. 4 *fin.* also V. ix.2, "sublevat in vitam Dei." Origen *eels.* iii.28 *fin.* touches the same thought, but Ath. is here in closer affinity to the idea of Irenaeus than to that of Origen.) The New Test. reference is 2 Pet. 1:4, rather than Heb. 2:9 sqq.; the Old Test., Ps. 82:6, which seems to underlie *Orat.* iii.25 (note 5). In spite of the last mentioned passage, "God" is far preferable as a rendering, in most places, to "gods," which has heathenish associations. To us (1 Cor. 8:6) there are no such things as "gods." (The best summary of patristic teaching on this subject is given by Harnack, *Dg.* ii. p. 46 note.)

whose sakes He endured all this, He maintained and preserved in His own impassibility.

4. And, in a word, the achievements of the Saviour, resulting from His becoming man, are of such kind and number, that if one should wish to enumerate them, he may be compared to men who gaze at the expanse of the sea and wish to count its waves. For as one cannot take in the whole of the waves with his eyes, for those which are coming on baffle the sense of him that attempts it; so for him that would take in all the achievements of Christ in the body, it is impossible to take in the whole, even by reckoning them up, as those which go beyond his thought are more than those he thinks he has taken in.

5. Better is it, then, not to aim at speaking of the whole, where one cannot do justice even to a part, but, after mentioning one more, to leave the whole for you to marvel at. For all alike are marvellous, and wherever a man turns his glance, he may behold on that side the divinity of the Word, and be struck with exceeding great awe.

Chapter LV

Summary of foregoing. Cessation of pagan oracles, etc.: propagation of the faith. The true King has come forth and silenced all usurpers.

1. This, then, after what we have so far said, it is right for you to realize, and to take as the sum of what we have already stated, and to marvel at exceedingly; namely, that since the Saviour has come among us, idolatry not only has no longer increased, but what there was is diminishing and gradually coming to an end: and not only does the wisdom of the Greeks no longer advance, but what there is is now fading away: and demons, so far from cheating any more by illusions and prophecies and magic arts, if they so much as dare to make the attempt, are put to shame by the sign of the Cross.

2. And to sum the matter up: behold how the Saviour's doctrine is everywhere increasing, while all idolatry and everything opposed to the faith of Christ is daily dwindling, and losing power, and falling. And thus beholding, worship the Saviour, "Who is above

all" and mighty, even God the Word; and condemn those who are being worsted and done away by Him.

3. For as, when the sun is come, darkness no longer prevails, but if any be still left anywhere it is driven away; so, now that the divine Appearing of the Word of God is come, the darkness of the idols prevails no more, and all parts of the world in every direction are illumined by His teaching.

4. And as, when a king is reigning in some country without appearing but keeps at home in his own house, often some disorderly persons, abusing his retirement, proclaim themselves; and each of them, by assuming the character, imposes on the simple as king, and so men are led astray by the name, hearing that there is a king, but not seeing him, if for no other reason, because they cannot enter the house; but when the real king comes forth and appears, then the disorderly impostors are exposed by his presence, while men, seeing the real king, desert those who previously led them astray:

5. In like manner, the evil spirits formerly used to deceive men, investing themselves with God's honour; but when the Word of God appeared in a body, and made known to us His own Father, then at length the deceit of the evil spirits is done away and stopped, while men, turning their eyes to the true God, Word of the Father, are deserting the idols, and now coming to know the true God.

6. Now this is a proof that Christ is God the Word, and the Power of God. For whereas human things cease, and the Word of Christ abides, it is clear to all eyes that what ceases is temporary, but that He Who abides is God, and the true Son of God, His only-begotten Word.

Chapter LVI

Search then, the Scriptures, if you can, and so fill up this sketch. Learn to look for the Second Advent and Judgment.

1. Let this, then, Christ-loving man, be our offering to you, just for a rudimentary sketch and outline, in a short compass, of the faith of Christ and of His Divine appearing to usward. But you, taking occasion

by this, if you light upon the text of the Scriptures, by genuinely applying your mind to them, will learn from them more completely and clearly the exact detail of what we have said.

2. For they were spoken and written by God, through men who spoke of God. But we impart of what we have learned from inspired teachers who have been conversant with them, who have also become martyrs for the deity of Christ, to your zeal for learning, in turn.

3. And you will also learn about His second glorious and truly divine appearing to us, when no longer in lowliness, but in His own glory — no longer in humble guise, but in His own magnificence — He is to come, no more to suffer, but thenceforth to render to all the fruit of His own Cross, that is, the resurrection and incorruption; and no longer to be judged, but to judge all, by what each has done in the body, whether good or evil; where there is laid up for the good the kingdom of heaven, but for them that have done evil everlasting fire and outer darkness.

4. For thus the Lord Himself also says: "Henceforth ye shall see the Son of Man sitting at the right hand of power, and coming on the clouds of heaven in the glory of the Father" [Matt. 26:64].

5. And for this very reason there is also a word of the Saviour to prepare us for that day, in these words: "Be ye ready and watch, for He cometh at an hour ye know not" [Matt. 24:42].[24] For, according to the blessed Paul: "We must all stand before the judgment-seat of Christ, that each one may receive according as he hath done in the body, whether it be good or bad" [2 Cor. 5:10].[25]

Chapter LVII

Above all, so *live that you may have the right to eat of* *this tree* of *knowledge and life, and* so *come to eternal joys. Doxology.*

1. But for the searching of the Scriptures and true knowledge of them, an honourable life is needed, and a pure soul, and that virtue which is according to Christ; so that the intellect guiding its path by it, may be able to attain what it desires, and to comprehend it, in so far as it is accessible to human nature to learn concerning the Word of God.

2. For without a pure mind and a modelling of the life after the saints, a man could not possibly comprehend the words of the saints.

3. For just as, if a man wished to see the light of the sun, he would at any rate wipe and brighten his eye, purifying himself in some sort like what he desires, so that the eye, thus becoming light, may see the light of the sun; or as, if a man would see a city or country, he at any rate comes to the place to see it; thus he that would comprehend the mind of those who speak of God must needs begin by washing and cleansing his soul, by his manner of living, and approach the saints themselves by imitating their works; so that, associated with them in the conduct of a common life, he may understand also what has been revealed to them by God, and thenceforth, as closely knit to them, may escape the peril of the sinners and their fire at the day of judgment, and receive what is laid up for the saints in the kingdom of heaven, which "Eye hath not seen, nor ear heard, neither have entered into the heart of man" [1 Cor. 2:9], whatsoever things are prepared for them that live a virtuous life, and love the God and Father, in Christ Jesus our Lord: through Whom and with Whom be to the Father Himself, with the Son Himself, in the Holy Spirit, honour and might and glory for ever and ever. Amen.

---

24. Cf. Mark 13:35.

25. Cf. Rom. 14:10.

CHAPTER 27

On the Incarnation

Anselm of Canterbury

Chapter I

The question on which the whole work rests.

I have been often and most earnestly requested by many, both personally and by letter, that I would hand down in writing the proofs of a certain doctrine of our faith, which I am accustomed to give to inquirers; for they say that these proofs gratify them, and are considered sufficient. This they ask, not for the sake of attaining to faith by means of reason, but that they may be gladdened by understanding and meditating on those things which they believe; and that, as far as possible, they may be always ready to convince anyone who demands of them a reason of that hope which is in us. And this question, both infidels are accustomed to bring up against us, ridiculing Christian simplicity as absurd; and many believers ponder it in their hearts; for what cause or necessity, in sooth, God became man, and by his own death, as we believe and affirm, restored life to the world; when he might have done this, by means of some other being, angelic or human, or merely by his will. Not only the learned, but also many unlearned persons interest themselves in this inquiry and seek for its solution. Therefore, since many desire to consider this subject, and, though it seem very difficult in the investigation, it is yet plain to all in the solution, and attractive for the value and beauty of the reasoning; although what ought to be sufficient has been said by the holy fathers and their successors, yet I will take pains to disclose to inquirers what God has seen fit to lay open to me. And since investigations, which are carried on by question and answer, are thus made more plain to many, and especially to less quick minds, and on that account are more gratifying, I will take to argue with me one of those persons who agitate this subject; one, who among the rest impels me more earnestly to it, so that in this way Boso may question and Anselm reply.

Chapter V

How the redemption of man could not be effected by any other being but God.

Boso: If this deliverance were said to be effected somehow by any other being than God (whether it were an angelic or a human being), the mind of man would receive it far more patiently. For God could have made some man without sin, not of a sinful substance, and not a descendant of any man, but just as he made Adam, and by this man it should seem that the work we speak of could have been done.

Anselm: Do you not perceive that, if any other being should rescue man from eternal death, man would rightly be adjudged as the servant of that being? Now if this be so, he would in no wise be restored to that dignity which would have been his had he never sinned. For he, who was to be through eternity only the servant of God and an equal with the holy angels, would now be the servant of a being who was not God, and whom the angels did not serve.

Chapter XI

What it is to sin, and to make satisfaction for sin.

Anselm: We must needs inquire, therefore, in what manner God puts away men's sins; and, in order to do this more plainly, let us first consider what it is to sin, and what it is to make satisfaction for sin.

Boso: It is yours to explain and mine to listen.

Anselm: If man or angel always rendered to God his due, he would never sin.

Boso: I cannot deny that.

Anselm: Therefore to sin is nothing else than not to render to God his due.

Boso: What is the debt which we owe to God?

Anselm: Every wish of a rational creature should be subject to the will of God.

Boso: Nothing is more true.

Anselm: This is the debt which man and angel owe to God, and no one who pays this debt commits sin; but everyone who does not pay it sins. This is justice, or uprightness of will, which makes a being just or upright in heart, that is, in will; and this is the sole and complete debt of honor which we owe to God, and which God requires of us. For it is such a will only, when it can be exercised, that does works pleasing to God and when this will cannot be exercised, it is pleasing of itself alone, since without it no work is acceptable. He who does not render this honor which is due to God, robs God of his own and dishonors him; and this is sin. Moreover, so long as he does not restore what he has taken away, he remains in fault; and it will not suffice merely to restore what has been taken away, but, considering the contempt offered, he ought to restore more than he took away. For as one who imperils another's safety does not enough by merely restoring his safety, without making some compensation for the anguish incurred; so he who violates another's honor does not enough by merely rendering honor again, but must, according to the extent of the injury done, make restoration in some way satisfactory to the person whom he has dishonored. We must also observe that when any one pays what he has unjustly taken away, he ought to give something which could not have been demanded of him, had he not stolen what belonged to another. So then, everyone who sins ought to pay back the honor of which he has robbed God; and this is the satisfaction which every sinner owes to God.

Boso: Since we have determined to follow reason in all these things, I am unable to bring any objection against them, although you somewhat startle me.

Chapter XII

Whether it were proper for God to put away sins by compassion alone, without any payment of debt.

Anselm: Let us return and consider whether it were proper for God to put away sins by compassion alone, without any payment of the honor taken from him.

Boso: I do not see why it is not proper.

Anselm: To remit sin in this manner is nothing else than not to punish; and since it is not right to cancel sin without compensation or punishment; if it be not punished, then is it passed by undischarged.

Boso: What you say is reasonable.

Anselm: It is not fitting for God to pass over anything in his kingdom undischarged.

Boso: If I wish to oppose this, I fear to sin.

Anselm: It is, therefore, not proper for God thus to pass over sin unpunished.

Boso: Thus it follows.

Anselm: There is also another thing which follows if sin be passed by unpunished, viz., that with God there will be no difference between the guilty and the not guilty; and this is unbecoming to God.

Boso: I cannot deny it.

Anselm: Observe this also. Everyone knows that justice to man is regulated by law, so that, according to the requirements of law, the measure of award is bestowed by God.

Boso: This is our belief.

Anselm: But if sin is neither paid for nor punished, it is subject to no law.

Boso: I cannot conceive it to be otherwise.

Anselm: Injustice, therefore, if it is cancelled by compassion alone, is more free than justice, which seems very inconsistent. And to these is also added a further incongruity, viz. , that it makes injustice like God. For as God is subject to no law, so neither is injustice.

Boso: I cannot withstand your reasoning. But when

God commands us in every case to forgive those who trespass against us, it seems inconsistent to enjoin a thing upon us which it is not proper for him to do himself.

Anselm: There is no inconsistency in God's commanding us not to take upon ourselves what belongs to Him alone. For to execute vengeance belongs to none but Him who is Lord of all; for when the powers of the world rightly accomplish this end, God himself does it who appointed them for the purpose.

Boso: You have obviated the difficulty which I thought to exist; but there is another to which I would like to have your answer. For since God is so free as to be subject to no law, and to the judgment of no one, and is so merciful as that nothing more merciful can be conceived; and nothing is right or fit save as he wills; it seems a strange thing for us to say that he is wholly unwilling or unable to put away an injury done to himself, when we are wont to apply to him for indulgence with regard to those offences which we commit against others.

Anselm: What you say of God's liberty and choice and compassion is true; but we ought so to interpret these things as that they may not seem to interfere with His dignity. For there is no liberty except as regards what is best or fitting; nor should that be called mercy which does anything improper for the Divine character. Moreover, when it is said that what God wishes is just, and that what He does not wish is unjust, we must not understand that if God wished anything improper it would be just, simply because he wished it. For if God wishes to lie, we must not conclude that it is right to lie, but rather that he is not God. For no will can ever wish to lie, unless truth in it is impaired, nay, unless the will itself be impaired by forsaking truth. When, then, it is said: "If God wishes to lie," the meaning is simply this: "If the nature of God is such as that he wishes to lie;" and, therefore, it does not follow that falsehood is right, except it be understood in the same manner as when we speak of two impossible things: "If this be true, then that follows; because neither this nor that is true;" as if a man should say: "Supposing water to be dry, and fire to be moist; " for neither is the case. Therefore, with regard to these things, to speak the whole truth: If God desires a thing, it is right that he should desire that which involves no unfitness. For if God chooses that it should rain, it is right that it should rain; and if he desires that any man should die, then is it right that he should die. Wherefore, if it be not fitting for God to do anything unjustly, or out of course, it does not belong to his liberty or compassion or will to let the sinner go unpunished, who makes no return to God of what the sinner has defrauded him.

Boso: You remove from me every possible objection which I had thought of bringing against you.

Anselm: Yet observe why it is not fitting for God to do this.

Boso: I listen readily to whatever you say.

Chapter XV

Whether God suffers his honor to be violated even in the least degree.

Boso: What you say satisfies me. But there is still another point which I should like to have you answer. For if, as you make out, God ought to sustain his own honor, why does he allow it to be violated even in the least degree? For what is in any way made liable to injury is not entirely and perfectly preserved.

Anselm: Nothing can be added to or taken from the honor of God. For this honor which belongs to him is in no way subject to injury or change. But as the individual creature preserves, naturally or by reason, the condition belonging, and, as it were, allotted to him, he is said to obey and honor God; and to this, rational nature, which possesses intelligence, is especially bound. And when the being chooses what he ought, he honors God; not by bestowing anything upon him, but because he brings himself freely under God's will and disposal, and maintains his own condition in the universe, and the beauty of the universe itself, as far as in him lies. But when he does not choose what he ought, he dishonors God, as far as the being himself is concerned, because he does not submit himself freely to God's disposal. And he disturbs the order and beauty of the universe, as relates to himself, although he cannot injure nor tarnish the power and majesty of God. For if those things which are held together in the circuit of the heavens desire to be elsewhere than under the heavens, or to be further removed from the heavens, there is no place where they can be but under the heavens, nor can they fly from the heavens without also approaching them. For both whence and whither and in what way they go, they are still under the heavens; and if they are at a greater distance from one part of them, they are only so much nearer to the opposite part. And so, though man or evil angel refuse to submit to the Divine will and appointment, yet he cannot escape it; for if he wishes to fly from a will that commands, he falls into the power of a will that punishes. And if you ask whither he goes, it is only under the permission of that will; and even this wayward choice or action of his becomes subservient, under infinite wisdom, to the order and beauty of the universe before spoken of. For when it is understood that God brings good out of many forms of evil, then the satisfaction for sin freely given, or if this be not given, the exaction of punishment, hold their own place and orderly beauty in the same universe. For if Divine wisdom were not to insist upon these things, when wickedness tries to disturb the right appointment, there would be, in the very universe which God ought to control, an unseemliness springing from the violation of the beauty of arrangement, and God would appear to be deficient in his management. And these two things are not only unfitting, but consequently impossible; so that satisfaction or punishment must needs follow every sin.

Boso: You have relieved my objection.

Anselm: It is then plain that no one can honor or dishonor God, as he is in himself; but the creature, as

far as he is concerned, appears to do this when he submits or opposes his will to the will of God.

Boso: I know of nothing which can be said against this.

Anselm: Let me add something to it.

Boso: Go on, until I am weary of listening.

Chapter XIX

How man cannot be saved without satisfaction for sin.

Anselm: It was fitting for God to fill the places of the fallen angels from among men.

Boso: That is certain.

Anselm: Therefore there ought to be in the heavenly empire as many men taken as substitutes for the angels as would correspond with the number whose place they shall take, that is, as many as there are good angels now; otherwise they who fell will not be restored, and it will follow that God either could not accomplish the good which he begun, or he will repent of having undertaken it; either of which is absurd.

Boso: Truly it is fitting that men should be equal with good angels.

Anselm: Have good angels ever sinned?

Boso: No.

Anselm: Can you think that man, who has sinned, and never made satisfaction to God for his sin, but only been suffered to go unpunished, may become the equal of an angel who has never sinned?

Boso: These words I can both think of and utter, but can no more perceive their meaning than I can make truth out of falsehood.

Anselm: Therefore it is not fitting that God should take sinful man without an atonement, in substitution for lost angels; for truth will not suffer man thus to be raised to an equality with holy beings.

Boso: Reason shows this.

Anselm: Consider, also, leaving out the question of equality with the angels, whether God ought, under such circumstances, to raise man to the same or a similar kind of happiness as that which he had before he sinned.

Boso: Tell your opinion, and I will attend to it as well as I can.

Anselm: Suppose a rich man possessed a choice pearl which had never been defiled, and which could not be taken from his hands without his permission; and that he determined to commit it to the treasury of his dearest and most valuable possessions.

Boso: I accept your supposition.

Anselm: What if he should allow it to be struck from his hand and cast in the mire, though he might have prevented it; and afterwards taking it all soiled by the mire and unwashed, should commit it again to his beautiful and loved casket; will you consider him a wise man?

Boso: How can I? For would it not be far better to keep and preserve his pearl pure, than to have it polluted?

Anselm: Would not God be acting like this, who held man in paradise, as it were in his own hand, without sin, and destined to the society of angels, and allowed the devil, inflamed with envy, to cast him into the mire of sin, though truly with man's consent? For, had God chosen to restrain the devil, the devil could not have tempted man. Now I say, would not God be acting like this, should he restore man, stained with the defilement of sin, unwashed, that is, without any satisfaction, and always to remain so; should He restore him at once to paradise, from which he had been thrust out?

Boso: I dare not deny the aptness of your comparison, were God to do this, and therefore do not admit that he can do this. For it should seem either that he could not accomplish what he designed, or else that he repented of his good intent, neither of which things is possible with God.

Anselm: Therefore, consider it settled that, without satisfaction, that is, without voluntary payment of the debt, God can neither pass by the sin unpunished, nor can the sinner attain that happiness, or happiness like that, which he had before he sinned; for man cannot in this way be restored, or become such as he was before he sinned.

Boso: I am wholly unable to refute your reasoning.

But what say you to this : that we pray God, "put away our sins from us," and every nation prays the God of its faith to put away its sins. For, if we pay our debt, why do we pray God to put it away? Is not God unjust to demand what has already been paid? But if we do not make payment, why do we supplicate in vain that he will do what he cannot do, because it is unbecoming?

Anselm: He who does not pay says in vain: "Pardon" but he who pays makes supplication, because prayer is properly connected with the payment; for God owes no man anything, but every creature owes God; and, therefore, it does not become man to treat with God as with an equal. But of this it is not now needful for me to answer you. For when you think why Christ died, I think you will see yourself the answer to your question.

Boso: Your reply with regard to this matter suffices me for the present. And, moreover, you have so clearly shown that no man can attain happiness in sin, or be freed from sin without satisfaction for the trespass, that, even were I so disposed, I could not doubt it.

Chapter XX

That satisfaction ought to be proportionate to guilt; and that man is of himself unable to accomplish this.

Anselm: Neither, I think, will you doubt this, that satisfaction should be proportionate to guilt.

Boso: Otherwise sin would remain in a manner exempt from control (Inordinatum), which cannot be, for God leaves nothing uncontrolled in his kingdom. But this is determined, that even the smallest unfitness is impossible with God.

Anselm: Tell me, then, what payment you make God for your sin?

Boso: Repentance, a broken and contrite heart, Self-denial, various bodily sufferings, pity in giving and forgiving, and obedience.

Anselm: What do you give to God in all these?

Boso: Do I not honor God, when, for his love and fear, in heartfelt contrition I give up worldly joy, and despise, amid abstinence and toils, the delights and ease of this life, and submit obediently to him, freely bestowing my possessions in giving to and releasing others?

Anselm: When you render anything to God which you owe him, irrespective of your past sin, you should not reckon this as the debt which you owe for sin. But you owe God every one of those things which you have mentioned. For, in this mortal state there should be such love and such desire of attaining the true end of your being, which is the meaning of prayer, and such grief that you have not yet reached this object, and such fear lest you fail of it, that you should find joy in nothing which does not help you or give encouragement of your success. For you do not deserve to have a thing which you do not love and desire for its own sake, and the want of which at present, together with the great danger of never getting it, causes you no grief. This also requires one to avoid ease and worldly pleasures such as seduce the mind from real rest and pleasure, except so far as you think suffices for the accomplishment of that object. But you ought to view the gifts which you bestow as a part of your debt, since you know that what you give comes not from yourself, but from him whose servant both you are and he also to whom you give. And nature herself teaches you to do to your fellow servant, man to man, as you would be done by; and that he who will not bestow what he has ought not to receive what he has not. Of forgiveness, indeed, I speak briefly, for, as we said above, vengeance in no sense belongs to you, since you are not your own, nor is he who injures you yours or his, but you are both the servants of one Lord, made by him out of nothing. And if you avenge yourself upon your fellow servant, you proudly assume judgment over him when it is the peculiar right of God, the judge of all. But what do you give to God by your obedience, which is not owed him already, since he demands from you all that you are and have and can become?

Boso: Truly I dare not say that in all these things I pay any portion of my debt to God.

Anselm: How then do you pay God for your transgression?

Boso: If in justice I owe God myself and all my powers, even when I do not sin, I have nothing left to render to him for my sin.

Anselm: What will become of you then? How will you be saved?

Boso: Merely looking at your arguments, I see no way of escape. But, turning to my belief, I hope through Christian faith, "which works by love," that I may be saved, and the more, since we read that if the sinner turns from his iniquity and does what is right, all his transgressions shall be forgotten.

Anselm: This is only said of those who either looked for Christ before his coming, or who believe in him since he has appeared. But we set aside Christ and his religion as if they did not exist, when we proposed to inquire whether his coming were necessary to man's salvation.

Boso: We did so.

Anselm: Let us then proceed by reason simply.

Boso: Though you bring me into straits, yet I very much wish you to proceed as you have begun.

Chapter XXII

What contempt man brought upon God, when he allowed himself to be conquered by the devil; for which he can make no satisfaction.

Anselm: Man being made holy was placed in paradise, as it were in the place of God, between God and the devil, to conquer the devil by not yielding to his temptation, and so to vindicate the honor of God and put the devil to shame, because that man, though weaker and dwelling upon earth, should not sin though tempted by the devil, while the devil, though stronger and in heaven, sinned without any to tempt him. And when man could have easily effected this, he, without compulsion and of his own accord, allowed himself to be brought over to the will of the devil, contrary to the will and honor of God.

Boso: To what would you bring me?

Anselm: Decide for yourself if it be not contrary to the honor of God for man to be reconciled to Him, with this calumnious reproach still heaped upon God; unless man first shall have honored God by overcoming the devil, as he dishonored him in yielding to the devil. Now the victory ought to be of this kind, that, as in strength and immortal vigor, he freely yielded to the devil to sin, and on this account justly incurred the penalty of death; so, in his weakness and mortality, which he had brought upon himself, he should conquer the devil by the pain of death, while wholly avoiding sin. But this cannot be done, so long as from the deadly effect of the first transgression, man is conceived and born in sin.

Boso: Again I say that the thing is impossible, and reason approves what you say.

Anselm: Let me mention one thing more, without which man's reconciliation cannot be justly reflected, and the impossibility is the same.

Boso: You have already presented so many obligations which we ought to fulfill, that nothing which you can add will alarm me more.

Anselm: Yet listen.

Boso: I will.

Chapter XXIII

What man took from God by his sin, which be has no power to repay.

Anselm: What did man take from God, when he allowed himself to be overcome by the devil?

Boso: Go on to mention, as you have begun, the evil things which can be added to those already shown for I am ignorant of them.

Anselm: Did not man take from God whatever He had purposed to do for human nature?

Boso: There is no denying that.

Anselm: Listen to the voice of strict justice; and judge according to that whether man makes to God a real satisfaction for his sin, unless, by overcoming the devil, man restore to God what he took from God in allowing himself to be conquered by the devil; so that, as by this conquest over man the devil took

what belonged to God, and God was the loser, so in man's victory the devil may be despoiled, and God recover his right.

Boso: Surely nothing can be more exactly or justly conceived.

Anselm: Think you that supreme justice can violate this justice?

Boso: I dare not think it.

Anselm: Therefore man cannot and ought not by any means to receive from God what God designed to give him, unless he return to God everything which he took from him; so that, as by man God suffered loss, by man also. He might recover His loss. But this cannot be effected except in this way: that, as in the fall of man all human nature was corrupted, and, as it were, tainted with sin, and God will not choose one of such a race to fill up the number in his heavenly kingdom; so, by man's victory, as many men may be justified from sin as are needed to complete the number which man was made to fill. But a sinful man can by no means do this, for a sinner cannot justify a sinner.

Boso: There is nothing more just or necessary; but, from all these things, the compassion of God and the hope of man seems to fail, as far as regards that happiness for which man was made.

Anselm: Yet wait a little.

Boso: Have you anything further?

BOOK SECOND

Chapter VI

How no being, except the God-man, can make the atonement by which man is saved.

Anselm: But this cannot be effected, except the price paid to God for the sin of man be something greater than all the universe besides God.

Boso: So it appears.

Anselm: Moreover, it is necessary that he who can give God anything of his own which is more valuable than all things in the possession of God, must be greater than all else but God himself.

Boso: I cannot deny it.

Anselm: Therefore none but God can make this satisfaction.

Boso: So it appears.

Anselm: But none but a man ought to do this, otherwise man does not make the satisfaction.

Boso: Nothing seems more just.

Anselm: If it be necessary, therefore, as it appears, that the heavenly kingdom be made up of men, and this cannot be effected unless the aforesaid satisfaction be made, which none but God can make and none but man ought to make, it is necessary for the God man to make it.

Boso: Now blessed be God! We have made a great discovery with regard to our question. Go on, therefore, as you have begun. For I hope that God will assist you.

Anselm: Now must we inquire how God can become man.

Chapter VII

How necessary it is for the same being to be perfect God and perfect man.

Anselm: The Divine and human natures cannot alternate, so that the Divine should become human or the human Divine; nor can they be so commingled as that a third should be produced from the two which is neither wholly Divine nor wholly human. For, granting that it were possible for either to be changed into the other, it would in that case be only God and not man, or man only and not God. Or, if they were so commingled that a third nature sprung from the combination of the two (as from two animals, a male and a female of different species, a third is produced, which does not preserve entire the species of either parent, but has a mixed nature derived from both), it would neither be God nor man. Therefore the God-man, whom we require to be of a nature both human and Divine, cannot be produced by a change from one into the other, nor by an imperfect commingling of both in a third; since these things cannot be, or, if they could be, would avail nothing to our purpose.

Moreover, if these two complete natures are said to be joined somehow, in such a way that one may be Divine while the other is human, and yet that which is God not be the same with that which is man, it is impossible for both to do the work necessary to be accomplished. For God will not do it, because he has no debt to pay; and man will not do it, because he cannot. Therefore, in order that the God-man may perform this, it is necessary that the same being should be perfect God and perfect man, in order to make this atonement. For he cannot and ought not to do it, unless he be very God and very man. Since, then, it is necessary that the God-man preserve the completeness of each nature, it is no less necessary that two natures be united entire in one person, just as a body and a reasonable soul exist together in every human being; for otherwise it is impossible that the same being should be very God and very man.

Boso: All that you say is satisfactory to me.

Chapter XIV

How his death outweighs the number and greatness of our sins.

Boso: Now I ask you to tell me how his death can outweigh the number and magnitude of our sins, when the least sin we can think of you have shown to be so monstrous that, were there an infinite number of worlds as full of created existence as this, they could not stand, but would fall back into nothing, sooner than one look should be made contrary to the just will of God.

Anselm: Were that man here before you, and you knew who he was, and it were told you that, if you did not kill him, the whole universe, except God, would perish, would you do it to preserve the rest of creation?

Boso: No! Not even were an infinite number of worlds displayed before me.

Anselm: But suppose you were told: "If you do not kill him, all the sins of the world will be heaped upon you."

Boso: I should answer, that I would far rather bear all other sins, not only those of this world, past and future, but also all others that can be conceived of, than this alone. And I think I ought to say this, not only with regard to killing him, but even as to the slightest injury which could be inflicted on him.

Anselm: You judge correctly; but tell me why it is that your heart recoils from one injury inflicted upon him as more heinous than all other sins that can be thought of, inasmuch as all sins whatsoever are committed against him?

Boso: A sin committed upon his person exceeds beyond comparison all the sins which can be thought of, that do not affect his person.

Anselm: What say you to this, that one often suffers freely certain evils in his person, in order not to suffer greater ones in his property?

Boso: God has no need of such patience, for all things lie in subjection to his power, as you answered a certain question of mine above.

Anselm: You say well; and hence we see that no enormity or multitude of sins, apart from the Divine person, can for a moment be compared with a bodily injury inflicted upon that man.

Boso: This is most plain.

Anselm: How great does this good seem to you, if the destruction of it is such an evil?

Boso: If its existence is as great a good as its destruction is an evil, then is it far more a good than those sins are evils which its destruction so far surpasses.

Anselm: Very true. Consider, also, that sins are as hateful as they are evil, and that life is only ami-able in proportion as it is good. And, therefore, it follows that that life is more lovely than sins are odious.

Boso: I cannot help seeing this.

Anselm: And do you not think that so great a good in itself so lovely, can avail to pay what is due for the sins of the whole world?

Boso: Yes! It has even infinite value.

Anselm: Do you see, then, how this life conquers all sins, if it be given for them?

Boso: Plainly.

Anselm: If, then, to lay down life is the same as to suffer death, as the gift of his life surpasses all the sins of men, so will also the suffering of death.

Chapter XX

How great and how just is God's compassion.

Now we have found the compassion of God which appeared lost to you when we were considering God's holiness and man's sin; we have found it, I say, so great and so consistent with his holiness, as to be incomparably above anything that can be conceived. For what compassion can excel these words of the Father, addressed to the sinner doomed to eternal torments and having no way of escape: "Take my only begotten Son and make him an offering for yourself"; or these words of the Son: "Take me, and ransom your souls." For these are the voices they utter, when inviting and leading us to faith in the Gospel. Or can anything be more just than for him to remit all debt since he has earned a reward greater than all debt, if given with the love which he deserves.

CHAPTER 28

The Coherence of the Incarnation

Thomas V. Morris

In this chapter we shall turn our attention to some claims about God made by Christians alone. In particular, we shall focus in on two theological doctrines that together define what is distinctive about the Christian idea of God: the doctrine of the Incarnation and the doctrine of the Trinity.

The Doctrine of the Incarnation

By any reasonable account, the short life and ministry of Jesus of Nazareth had an extremely powerful impact on the people around him. Because of their experience of his life and teaching, and especially of the extraordinary events surrounding the end of his earthly career, his followers came to believe that creaturely categories were inadequate for conceptualizing who he is. Thus was born the distinctively Christian conviction that Jesus was, and is, both divine and human, God and man. The doctrine of the Incarnation is just the claim that in the case of Jesus the Christ, we are confronted by one person with two natures, human nature and the divine nature.

So the uniquely Christian proclamation was that Jesus is God Incarnate. Yet, he himself prayed to God and told his followers that when he left the earthly stage another comforter would come. This led to a threefold experience of divinity on the part of Christians, and a firm conviction that there is multiplicity within the unity of deity. It was this conviction that gave rise to the theologically precise doctrine of the Trinity, the belief that within the unity of the divine nature, God exists as three persons: God the Father, God the Son and God the Holy Spirit. With this devel-

opment in the distinctively Christian view of deity, it was then possible to state the doctrine of the Incarnation with more precision. The claim is specifically that a properly divine person, God the Son, the second person of the divine Trinity, has taken on a human nature for us and our salvation. Before the time of the Incarnation, this person existed from all eternity as fully divine. Then, in the days of Herod the king, he took upon himself a fully human form of existence, yet never therein ceasing to be that which he eternally was. The early Christian experience of Christ thus finally led the Council of Chalcedon to decree in the year 451 that:

> Following therefore the holy Fathers, we confess one and the same our Lord Jesus Christ, and we all teach harmoniously [that he is] the same perfect in Godhead, the same perfect in manhood, truly God and truly man, the same of a reasonable soul and body; consubstantial with the Father in Godhead, and the same consubstantial with us in manhood, like us in all things except sin ... one and the same Christ, Son, Lord, unique; acknowledged in two natures without confusion, without change, without division, without separation — the difference of the natures being by no means taken away because of the union, but rather the distinctive character of each nature being preserved, and (each) combining in one person ... not divided or separated into two persons, but one and the same Son and only-begotten God, Word, Lord Jesus Christ; as the prophets of old and the Lord Jesus Christ himself taught us about him, and the symbol of the Fathers has handed down to us.[1]

---

1. Edward R. Hardy, ed., *Christology of the Later Fathers*, Library of Christian Classics (Philadelphia: Westminster Press, 1954), p. 373.

By so speaking, the Council presented the Christian church with the definition of orthodoxy on the ontology of Christ.

But, of course, the central philosophical problem which quickly arises here is not difficult to discern. In the Judeo-Christian vision of reality, no beings could be more different from each other than God, the creator of all, and any kind of creature. And even granting the doctrine that human beings are created in the image of God, humanity and divinity can certainly seem to be so different as to render it metaphysically and even logically impossible for any single individual to be both human and divine, *truly* God and *truly* man.... God is omnipotent, omniscient, omnipresent, eternal, ontologically independent, and absolutely perfect. We human beings, of course, have none of these properties. And this surely seems to be no accident. Could I possibly have been a greatest possible being? Could you have been uncreated, eternally existent, and omnipresent in all of creation? Surely the logical complements, or opposites, of these divine properties are essential to you and to me. We could not exist without certain sorts of metaphysical limitations and dependencies — limitations and dependencies which are necessarily alien to the divine form of existence as it is conceived in Jewish and Christian theology. From this, critics of Chalcedon have concluded that there are properties necessary for being divine that no human being could possibly have, and properties essential for being human that no divine being could possibly have. The dramatic story told by Chalcedon is then viewed as a metaphysical impossibility.

The tension inherent in the two-natures doctrine of Christ was felt from the very earliest days of reflective Christian theology, and led to the existence of many conflicting opinions about Christ. The philanthropists denied that Jesus was truly divine. The docetists concluded that he was not really human. The Arians denied that he was literally either. Apollinarians tried to whittle down the humanity to make room for the divinity. And Nestorians speculated on a composite Christ, one individual human person and one individual divine person, distinct from one another but acting in the closest possible relation of moral harmony. The church at large rejected all these strategies of partial or complete capitulation and insisted again and again on the Chalcedonian formula: one person, two natures — truly God and truly man.[2]

The philosophical question here is whether orthodoxy embraces a possibility. Can the doctrine even possibly be true? In recent years many critics of the doctrine have claimed that it is clearly incoherent. But I believe that a strategy of defense is available which, surprisingly, is fairly simple.[3] The initial operative assumption is that, in trying to understand the doctrine, we should indeed begin with the most exalted conception of divinity, a down-to-earth conception of humanity, and the metaphysical constraints passed on to us by the early ecumenical councils of the church. Given these starting points, the procedure is then to turn back the philosophical arguments against the Incarnation's possibility by the use of conceptual distinctions and metaphysical postulations that flout no strong, reflectively held intuitions, and that together succeed in providing a picture of the metaphysics of God Incarnate that will accord with the portrayal of Christ in the documents of the New Testament.

In our attempt to understand and defend the doctrine of the Incarnation, we shall continue to use the most exalted conception of deity possible, that conception captured by perfect being theology. That is to say, we shall begin by thinking of any divine being as a greatest possible, or maximally perfect being. Divinity, or deity, we shall continue to construe as analogous to a

---

2. More on the ancient Christian heresies can be found in such standard texts as Charles Gore, *The Incarnation of the Son of God* (London: John Murray, 1891); H. M. Relton, *A Study in Christology* (London: SPCK, 1917); E. G. Jay, *Son of Man, Son of God* (Montreal: McGill University Press, 1965); and J. N. D. Kelly, *Early Christian Doctrines*, rev. ed. (New York: Harper and Row, 1978). The heresy of psilanthropism is pronounced "sill-AN-throw-pism" and comes from two Greek words meaning "mere man." Docetism is pronounced "DOE-seh-tizm."

3. See Thomas V. Morris, *The Logic of God Incarnate* (Ithaca, N.Y.: Cornell University Press, 1986), for a full deployment of this strategy.

natural kind, and thus as comprising a kind-essence, a cluster of properties individually necessary and jointly sufficient for belonging to the kind, or in this case, for being divine. We shall thus continue to think of omnipotence and omniscience, for example, as properties essential to deity. And, following the standard Anselmian intuitions ..., we shall take the strongly modalized properties of *necessary* omnipotence (omnipotence in all possible worlds, and at all times in any such worlds) and *necessary* omniscience to be ingredient in deity as well. Thus, on this picture, ... no individual could possibly be God without being omnipotent. And no being could count as literally divine without having that attribute necessarily. The picture of God we are assuming thus holds that such properties as omnipotence, omniscience, omnipresence, eternality, moral perfection and ontological independence must belong to any individual who is divine, and must be had with the strongest possible modal status. If such an exalted conception of divinity can be squared with the doctrine of the Incarnation, then presumably more modest conceptions could be as well.

All other things being equal, it would seem that the more extreme a conception we have of deity, the more trouble we are going to have mapping out a coherent account of a divine Incarnation. But I do not think critics of the Incarnation usually go wrong by having too exalted a conception of divinity. Rather, I think they most commonly come to judge the Incarnation an impossibility mainly on account of an incorrect, metaphysically flawed conception of humanity. Only if we assume that it is necessary for being human, or for having a human nature, that an individual lack *any* of those properties ingredient in deity, do we have an obvious logical and metaphysical obstacle to the orthodox two-natures view of Christ. And I believe that the critics of the doctrine have come to hold such a conception of human nature only by missing some fairly simple distinctions and by ignoring some intriguing metaphysical possibilities.

First, there is the fairly well-known distinction between an *individual-essence* and a *kind-essence*. An *individual-essence* is a cluster of properties essential for an individual's being the particular entity it is, properties without which it would not exist. A *kind-essence* is that cluster of properties without which ... an individual would not belong to the particular natural kind it distinctively exemplifies. Of necessity, an individual can have no more than one individual-essence, or individual nature, but it does not follow from this, and is not, so far as I can tell, demonstrable from any other quarter, that an individual can have no more than one kind-essence. And this is surely a good thing, for if such an argument could be made out, it would block from the start the doctrine of the Incarnation, at least the orthodox two-natures view, without the need of turning to consider the specifics of divinity and humanity.

Once we have recognized a distinction like that between individual-essences and kind-essences, we can see that necessities intuitively thought to characterize individual human beings cannot automatically be deemed to be such in virtue of those beings' common human nature, as part of the kind-essence of humanity. You and I, and any of our neighbors, may be such that we necessarily are noneternal, created beings, and we may share that modal characterization with all of the human beings living on the surface of the earth today without its at all following that this necessity constitutes part of what it is to have a human nature. It may be the case that all of our individual essences incorporate these modal properties of limited metaphysical status without its being the case that these properties are metaphysical prerequisites for exemplifying the natural kind of being human. Of course, critics of the Incarnation have discerned such necessities while thinking about human beings, have identified them simply as ingredients in human nature, and, pointing out that quite contrary necessities form the divine nature, have gone on to conclude that it is impossible for a properly divine being to take on human nature.[4] But more caution is needed here

4. For an example, see A. D. Smith, "God' Death," *Theology* 80 (July 1979): 262–68.

than is customarily exercised. In drawing their conclusions about what is essential for being human, critics of the Incarnation have, I think, made some errors which can be highlighted and then avoided by the use of two more straightforward distinctions.

In trying to enumerate the properties essential for being human, some theologians have included the property of being sinful, but this is a property the decree of Chalcedon explicitly denies of Christ. Why would anyone ever think it is part of the kind-essence of humanity? Probably because they have employed a very simple and very inadequate method for determining the elements of human nature, a method that we can call the *look-around-town approach*: Look around town, and what do you see? Every human being you come across shares numerous properties with every other human in town, including, most likely, the property of being sinful. To conclude that being sinful is thus a part of human nature is, however, to miss a simple distinction. There are properties which happen to be *common* to members of a natural kind, and which may even be *universal* to all members of that kind, without being *essential* to membership in the kind. Mere observation alone can suffice to establish commonality. Thought experiments and modal intuitions must be drawn upon to determine necessity, or kind-essentiality. Once these distinctions are properly drawn, we can acknowledge the commonality of sinfulness among human beings while at the same time following Chalcedon in denying both its strict universality and its presence in the kind-essence which we call human nature.

Such properties as those of being contingent, created, noneternal, nonomnipotent, nonomniscient and nonomnipresent are certainly common to human beings. Apart from the case of Christ, they are even, presumably, universal human properties. But I submit that they are not kind-essential human properties. It is not true that an individual must be a contingent being, noneternal and nonomnipotent in order to exemplify human nature. It is possible for an individual to be human without being characterized by any of these limitation properties. And so it is possible for an individual who essentially lacks such properties, an individual who is properly divine, to take up at the same time a human nature.

The many properties of metaphysical limitation and dependence that characterize you and me do so, then, not because they are essential elements in our common human nature. They may characterize you and me necessarily. Presumably, they do. But it is not in virtue of our being human; rather, it is in virtue of our being the humans we are. Such properties may partially comprise our respective individual essences, or, more likely, may characterize us in virtue of the fact that we created human beings are *merely human* — we are no more than human. Humanity crowns our ontological status as the greatest foothold we have in the grand scheme of things. We are *fully human*: we have all the properties constituting the kind-essence of humanity. But we are merely human as well: we have certain limitation properties in virtue of being God's creatures. Those limitations need not be ingredient in our humanness, only in our creatureliness. Thus, God the Son, through whom all things are created, need not have taken on any of those limitation properties distinctive of our creatureliness in order to take on a human nature. He could have become fully human without being merely human.

Now, all these distinctions and defensive moves may be fine, each taken in itself, one by one. But the net result of applying them to a full defense of the Incarnation can appear problematic in the extreme. When we consult the pages of the New Testament, we see in the portrait of Jesus the workings of a mind which, extraordinarily wise and discerning as it may be, seems less than omniscient, and which appears, for all its strength, to lack the power of omnipotence in itself, having to turn heavenward for resources just as we do. We see a mind apparently conditioned by the first-century Palestinian worldview. We see a man who shared the anguish and joys of the human condition. Our metaphysical distinctions cannot be allowed to blind us to this. And it would be both foolish and heterodox to minimize it. We need a picture of the Incarnation that will account for all of these appearances.

Two Pictures of God Incarnate

We are completely clear on what it means to begin with an exalted conception of divinity. It may not be clear at all what I meant when I added above that we should also start with a down-to-earth conception of humanity. Now is the time to make it clear. Taking on a human nature involves taking on a human body and a human mind, no more and no less. What essentially constitutes a human body and a human mind we wait upon a perfected science, or a more complete revelation, to say. We have neither a very full-blown nor a very fine-grained understanding of either at this point. But we do know well enough what a human body is, and what a human mind is, for it to be informative to be told that taking on such a body and mind is taking on a human nature. It is both necessary and sufficient for being human. This is almost embarrassingly simple as metaphysics goes. No modal razzle-dazzle, no ontological arcana: If you have a human body and mind, you have a human nature — you exemplify the kind-essence of humanity. This is surely a down-to-earth conception of humanity if anything is.

For God the Son to become human, he thus had to take on a human body and a human mind, with all that entails. He did not have to become a created, contingent being. He just had to take on a created, contingent body and mind of the right sort. And so he was born of Mary the virgin and lived a human life.

But how did he manage this? Isn't it clear that taking on a human body and mind in order to live a human life involves taking on limitations of knowledge, power and presence? And aren't such limitations incompatible with divinity? As we have noted, the New Testament pictures an extraordinary individual living out a life among his fellows from limited human resources. How is this to be reconciled with his being divine? Some philosophers and theologians have believed that Jesus' limits force us to tone down a bit our conception of what deity consists in. They have come to think that facing up to what the New Testament shows us concerning Jesus' real limits requires us to conclude that in becoming incarnate he — that is, God the Son

— gave up temporarily some of his unrestricted divine attributes, for example, his omniscience, his omnipotence and his omnipresence. This, they think, was required in order for him to take on the limitations involved in living a genuinely human life and sharing fully in our common human condition. This is the story told by *kenotic Christology* (from the Greek word *kenosis*, or "emptying"). If kenotic Christology is true, if God the Son temporarily empties himself, giving up his properly divine power, relinquishing his complete knowledge, and restricting his presence to the confines of his mortal shell while nonetheless remaining divine, it cannot be that divinity necessarily comprises or requires omnipotence, omniscience and omnipresence. For if during the early sojourn, the Second Person of the Trinity was divine but was without these exalted properties, they cannot be among those things required for true deity. As kenotic Christology is incompatible with seeing divinity as, at least in part, constituted by necessary omnipotence, necessary omniscience and necessary omnipresence, so it is also incompatible with holding all the simple, nonmodalized properties of omnipotence, omniscience and omnipresence to be requisites of divinity.

Well, then, on the kenotic view, what *are* the necessary truths about divinity? What is it to be God? The kenotic suggestion, perhaps, is something like this: In order to be literally divine, it is necessary for an individual to have in all possible worlds the property of *being omnipotent unless freely and temporarily choosing to be otherwise*, the property of *being omniscient unless freely and temporarily choosing to be otherwise*, and likewise for omnipresence. On this modally less extreme view of divinity, a divine being is not necessarily invulnerable to ignorance and weakness. He can render himself vulnerable to these deficiencies, he can take them on, while yet remaining truly divine.

Kenotic Christology began to be developed during the nineteenth century and continues to be refined today despite numerous critics — many of whom have just failed to grasp the subtlety with which the position can be deployed. And it must be said in behalf of the kenotic strategy that (1) what it seeks to accommodate in the biblical portrayal of Christ is indeed crucial to preserve, and (2) it is altogether legitimate and proper for a Christian to apply his convictions arising out of divine revelation and the events of salvation history to his philosophical theology, and in particular to his philosophical conception of God. There must be a dynamic interaction between what *a priori*, intuitive, or purely philosophical constraints there are on philosophical theology and the agreed data of revelation. The kenotic maneuver presents us with an intriguing possibility, yet I must admit that I have a hard time finding it satisfactory. It presents us with a far less exalted and less theoretically satisfying conception of Christ's deity. Its way of redefining the basic divine attributes seems extremely *ad hoc*, an exercise in metaphysical gerrymandering reflective of no more general philosophical distinctions. And my misgivings about such an account of Christ's deity are not without parallel in the weightiest theological treatises.

During the early years of the fifth century, Pope Leo wrote an essay on the Incarnation which the Council of Chalcedon embraced as properly capturing the two-natures view of Christ. Known as *The Tome of Leo*, it says of Christ that, among other things:

> He took on him "the form of a servant" without the defilement of sins, augmenting what was human, not diminishing what was divine; because that "emptying of himself," whereby the Invisible made himself visible, and the Creator and Lord of all things willed to be one among mortals, was a stooping down of compassion, not a failure of power. Accordingly, the same who, remaining in the form of God, made man, was made Man in the form of a servant, so the form of a servant does not impair the form of God.[5]

A sophisticated kenotic Christology can be argued to preserve the letter of Leo's claims, but I have difficulty seeing how it can be thought to be true to the spirit of those claims. But in case this is unclear, consider the great theologian Athanasius (c. A.D. 293 – 373), who wrote earlier concerning the incarnate Christ:

> He was not, as might be imagined, circumscribed in the body, nor, while present in the body, was he absent elsewhere; nor, while he moved the body, was the universe left void of his working and providence; but, thing most marvelous, Word as he was, so far from being contained by anything, he rather contained all things himself; and just as while present in the whole of creation, he is at once distinct in being from the universe, and present in all things by his own power, … thus, even while present in a human body and himself quickening it, he was, without inconsistency, quickening the universe as well.[6]

So, for Athanasius, it seems that Christ was not limited in power, knowledge and effect to the workings of his human mind and body during the time of the Incarnation. There is no restricting of his being to the confines of the human alone. This is surely no kenotic, metaphysical emptying or relinquishing of the properly divine status or functioning. While having a human body and mind and living out a human life on this terrestrial globe, Christ nonetheless retained all of the resources and prerogatives of divinity in the most robust sense.

But can we make sense of such a view? Can we indeed have it all, the fullness of humanity and the fullness of divinity? I think so, for there is an alternative to the kenotic picture of Christ, an alternative which has been called the *two-minds view*.[7] On this account of the Incarnation, taking on a human body and mind did not require or involve relinquishing the proper resources of divinity. Just as we saw that God the Son's taking on of a created, contingent body and mind does not entail that he himself was a created, contingent being, so, on the two-minds view, his taking on of a body and mind limited in knowledge, power and presence does not entail that he himself, in his deepest continuing mode of existence, was limited in knowledge, power or presence. Rather, in the

---

5. Hardy, *Christology of the Later Fathers*, pp. 363 – 364.
6. Ibid., pp. 70 – 71.

7. See *The Logic of God Incarnate*, pp. 102 – 7 and 149 – 62.

case of God Incarnate we must recognize something like two distinct minds or systems of mentality. There is first what we can call the eternal mind of God the Son, with its distinctively divine consciousness, whatever that might be like, encompassing the full scope of omniscience, empowered by the resources of omnipotence, and present in power and knowledge throughout the entirety of creation. And in addition to this divine mind, there is the distinctly earthly mind with its consciousness that came into existence and developed with the conception, human birth and growth of Christ's earthly form of existence. The human mind drew its visual imagery from what the eyes of Jesus saw, and its concepts from the languages he learned. This earthly mind, with its range of consciousness and self-consciousness, was thoroughly human, Jewish and first-century Palestinian in nature. By living out his earthly life from only the resources of his human body and mind, he took on the form of our existence and shared in the plight of our condition.

So, on the two-minds view, the Incarnation involved not just a duality of abstract natures, but a duality of consciousness or mentality, which was introduced into the divine life of God the Son. The two minds of Christ should be thought of as standing in something like an asymmetric accessing relation: The human mind was contained by, but did not itself contain, the divine mind; or, to portray it from the other side, the divine mind contained, but was not contained by, the human mind. Everything present to the human mind of Christ was thereby present to the divine mind as well, but not vice versa. There was immediate, direct access from the human mind to the divine mind, but no such converse immediacy of access. Insofar as Christ normally chose to live his earthly life out of his human resources alone, the words he spoke and the actions he performed by means of the body were words and actions arising out of his human mind. He had all the mental, intellectual, emotional and volitional resources we all have, lacking none. And it was these, not his divine resources, that he typically drew on for the personal history he enacted on this earth. But this living of a human life

through human resources was, on the two-minds view, going on at the same time that he, in his properly divine form of existence, was continuing to exercise his omnipotence, with the wisdom of his omniscience, in his omnipresent activities throughout creation.

Can we, however, really hope to understand the two-minds view? Can we attain any firm grasp of what it might have been like for God Incarnate to have at one and the same time a limited human consciousness and an overarching divine mind? To some extent, I think we can. There are numerous earthly phenomena with which we are familiar that can be taken to provide very helpful, partial analogies to the two-minds view of Christ. There seem to exist, for example, cases of dreams in which the dreamer both plays a role within the environs of the dream story, operating with a consciousness formed from within the dream, and yet at the same time, *as* dreamer, retains an overarching consciousness that the drama of the dream is just that — only a dream. Another sort of analogy can be provided by thought experiments dealing with artificial intelligence, in which two physical systems are each such as to be credited with mentality, and yet stand in such an asymmetric accessing relation that one can be considered a subsystem of the other, with its own distinctive origin and functions, but at the same time belonging to the unity of a larger system of mentality. And then there are numerous, powerful, partial analogies available in the literature dealing with human cases of multiple personality. In many such cases, there seem to be different centers or spheres of consciousness standing in an asymmetric accessing relation to an overarching or executive self, and ultimately belonging to one person. Of course, human cases of multiple personality involve severe dysfunction and undesirable traits starkly disanalogous to anything we want to acknowledge in the Incarnation. But this just helps us to see where the specific limits of this sort of analogy lie.

There are also certain phenomena having to do with hypnosis, brain commissurotomy, self-deception and *akrasia,* or weakness of will, in which there seem to be operative different levels or spheres of awareness, information retention and processing, or, in general, mentality which are, in important metaphysical ways, analogous to what the two-minds view recognizes in the case of the Incarnation. Again, it must be stressed that the negative aspects of these extraordinary, worldly cases of multiple mentality are not meant at all to characterize the Incarnation, and in fact can be argued decisively not to cloud Christ's case in the least. These are only partial analogies, which provide us with some imaginative grip on the two-minds picture.

One of the best analogies may be provided by the claim of twentieth-century psychologists that every normal human being partakes of a variety of levels of mentality. Consider for example the very simple distinction of the conscious human mind, the seat of occurrent awareness, from the unconscious mind. In most standard accounts of such a distinction, the unconscious mind stands to the conscious mind in much the same relation that the two-minds view sees between the divine and human minds in the case of Christ. God the Son, on this picture, took on every normal level or sphere of human mentality, but enjoyed the extra depth as well of his properly divine mindedness.

One interesting feature of all these analogies which have to do with human psychological phenomena is that they point toward what some theorists are calling a "multimind" view of persons in general.[8] On this sort of a view, a person is, or at least it is inevitable that a person potentially has, *a system of systems of mentality*, to use the broadest possible terminology. This systems view of the person is in close accord with the more generalized view of all of life as involving hierarchically stratified systems of organization and control, but is arrived at with evidence of its own, not as just the application of the more general view to the case of persons.

We can develop a systems view here in such a way that all finite mental systems are metaphysically open-ended for hierarchical subsumption by deeper, or higher, systems — use whichever vertical metaphor you prefer. Epistemologically, we typically come to recognize the existence of a multiplicity of mental systems in the case of a human being only when things go awry, as in multiple personality, commissurotomy, or what is called self-deception. But the systems view is that what we thus come to recognize, the multiplicity of systems of mentality, is always there in some form in normal cases as well, although functioning very differently, and thus being manifested very differently, if at all, to normal observation.

It is, of course, not my claim that a systems view of mentality proves the two-minds view of Christ, that it serves as any evidence for the truth of this theological view, or even that it establishes the possibility of this picture of the Incarnation. It only provides us with a general account of mentality that is thoroughly consonant with the main features of the metaphysical postulations distinctive of the two-minds view, and thus gives us a vantage point from which to come to better understand the view. It also helps to answer some questions that can otherwise seem to yield troubling problems for the view.

Did Christ have erroneous beliefs, such as would have been acquired through the natural functioning of his human mind in the social and intellectual environment in which he lived? Did he have a geocentric picture of the cosmos? Did he really not know who touched the hem of his garment? He had a limited human mind and a divine mind, so what is the answer, yes or no? Our ordinary practices and locutions for belief ascription can lead to puzzling questions concerning God Incarnate. But I think the two-minds view, rather than creating such puzzlement, actually helps us to see through it. First of all, we must be cautious about assuming that our ordinary linguistic practices are completely in order here, in such a way that they can act as altogether reliable touchstones of truth. If it is asked exactly what Christ believed, the two-minds view will direct us to ask what information was contained in his earthly mind, and

---

8. For a popular presentation of this sort of view, see Robert Ornstein, *Multimind* (Boston: Houghton Mifflin, 1986).

then what information was contained in his divine mind. And this sort of response is to be expected on any multimind view of the person, or on any multisystems approach to mentality. Our ordinary, simple ways of posing and answering such questions in mundane contexts may provide less than absolutely reliable guidance where such metaphysical precision is required, as in the doctrine of the Incarnation.

But if the question is pressed concerning what the person God the Son himself believed on this or that issue, evading the question by appealing to the duality of minds can appear to threaten the unity of the person, and thus the coherence of the whole picture. The response of dividing the question does remind us of something important. God the Son Incarnate had two minds and chose to live out the life of the body on this earth normally through the resources of the human mind alone. That was the primary font of most of his earthly behavior and speech. Nevertheless, if the question is really pressed, if it is insisted that we be prepared, in principle, to say what he, the individual person, believed about this or that, we must appeal to the feature of hierarchical organization endemic to a systems view of mentality and, recognizing the priority of the divine, represent God the Son's ultimate belief state as captured in his divine omniscience. This feature of hierarchical organization thus does not leave us in puzzlement concerning the final story about the person.

This move seems to indicate a compatibility between metaphysical double-mindedness and personal unity. But what exactly does the personal unity of Christ consist in on the two-minds view? What makes the human mind of Jesus a mind of God the Son? A critic of this account of the Incarnation could point out, for example, that on the standard view of God as utterly omniscient, any divine person stands in a direct, immediate and complete asymmetric accessing relation to the mind of every human being. If standing in this relation is what makes Jesus' earthly mind a mind of God, all our minds are minds of God, and thus we are all divine incarnations. If this were a safe inference from the two-minds view, I think it is

safe to say it would serve as an effective refutation of the view, demonstrating its unacceptability.

The accessing relation alone, however, is not intended by the two-minds view to count as a sufficient condition of Incarnation. Information flow by itself does not constitute mental, metaphysical ownership. So, what does? I must admit that I am no more sure about how to spell out what constitutes metaphysical ownership in the case of the Incarnation than I am about how to spell out exactly what it is for a range of mentality to be a part of my own mind, or to belong to me. There are mysteries here in any case, not just in the case of what the two-minds view claims about the Incarnation. But, fortunately, this is not all there is to be said.

What we can refer to as my human mental system was intended by God to define a person. If my human mental system is subsumed or overridden by any other causal system, my personal freedom is abrogated. The complete human mental system of Jesus was not intended alone to define a person. It was created to belong to a person with a divine mind as well as the ultimate, hierarchically maximal mental system. At any point during the metaphysical event of the Incarnation, it is thus possible that the human capacities of Christ, or the entirety of what we are calling his human mental system, be subsumed and overridden by the divine mind, without its being the case that any person's freedom is thereby abrogated. And this is a crucial difference between Jesus and any other human being, indeed, between Jesus and any free-willed *creature* of God. When our attention has been directed to this, it has been directed to the distinctiveness of the metaphysics of God Incarnate.

We are always in danger of misunderstanding the doctrine of the Incarnation, and the two-minds view of Christ in particular, if we forget that here, as in other properly metaphysical contexts, 'person' is an ultimate, ontological status term, not a composition term. The entirety of the human mental system of God the Son did not serve to compose a human person distinct from the person who was and is properly divine, because having the status of exemplifying a human body-mind composite was not the deepest truth about the ontological status of that individual. The personhood of Jesus was a matter of his ultimate ontological status and nothing less. This is the claim of the Christian tradition.

The two-minds view of Christ is extraordinarily interesting, philosophically and theologically, and, at least *prima facie*, it seems to me strongly preferable to the alternative of kenotic Christology. Something like one or the other of these pictures of the Incarnation is necessary, I think, if we are to make full sense of the manifest earthly career of Jesus from the perspective of a commitment to his divinity; or, to put it the other way around, if we are to make full sense of a belief in his divinity from the perspective of the manifest, earthly career of Jesus. From either point of view, we need some such account of the metaphysics of God Incarnate.

QUESTIONS AND FURTHER READINGS

Questions for Discussion

1. What is the doctrine of the Incarnation?

2. How would you defend the doctrine on biblical grounds?

3. Describe several of the points made by Athanasius. Are they relevant today? Explain.

4. Why did the Incarnation have to happen, as argued by Anselm? Do you agree? Why or why not?

5. On the traditional view of the Incarnation, is Jesus more than one person? And how many natures does he have?

6. Did God change at the Incarnation? Explain.

7. Was the Incarnation necessary for salvation to be possible? Why or why not?

8. Which of the two views — kenotic Christology or the two-minds view — do you find most reasonable? Why?

9. For the two-minds view, what makes Jesus one person rather than two persons? Is it a logical contradiction to believe that Jesus had an omniscient mind and a non-omniscient mind? Why or why not?

10. How does the doctrine of the Incarnation affect Christian worship? How does it affect your own Christian experience?

Further Readings

Anselm of Canterbury (d. 1109; reprint, 1998). *Why God Became Man*. In *Anselm of Canterbury: The Major Works*, ed. Brian Davies and G. R. Evans. Oxford: Oxford University Press. (Anselm's classic work on this issue.)

Boethius (d. 525; reprint, 1973). *A Treatise against Eutyches and Nestorius*. Translated by H. F. Stewart, E. K. Rand, and S. J. Tester. In *Boethius*. Cambridge: Harvard University Press.

Brown, David (2004). "Anselm on Atonement." Pages 279 – 302 in *The Cambridge Companion to Anselm*, ed. Brian Davies and Brian Leftow. Cambridge: Cambridge University Press.

Hebblethwaite, Brian (1987). *The Incarnation: Collected Essays in Christology*. Cambridge: Cambridge University Press. (A philosophical defense of the orthodox doctrine.)

Hick, John (2006). *The Metaphor of God Incarnate: Christology in a Pluralistic Age*. Louisville, KY: Westminster John Knox. (A critical look at the traditional doctrine of the incarnation.)

Morris, Thomas (1986). *The Logic of God Incarnate*. Ithaca, NY: Cornell University Press. (An accessible and articulate defense of the incarnation.)

Norris, Richard (1980). *The Christological Controversy*. Minneapolis: Augsburg Fortress. (Classical readings in early development of the doctrine of the incarnation.)

Rogers, Katherin (2000). *Perfect Being Theology*. Edinburgh: Edinburgh University Press. (Argues for the God of classical theism.)

Weinandy, Thomas (1985). *Does God Change? Studies in Historical Theology*. Vol. 4. Still River, MA: St. Bede's.

PART 5

THE BIBLE

The Bible is the foundational set of "books" of the Christian tradition — the established canon of faith and practice. The whole of it was officially adopted as the authoritative canon in the mid-fourth century and was understood by the church to be divinely inspired in authorship and content. The Bible has been understood historically by the Christian church to be the written words of God, crafted by prophets and apostles under the inspiration of the Holy Spirit of God. It is the fundamental guide to spiritual discernment and has final authority for Christians.

Throughout the centuries, the Bible has been challenged on many fronts, both within and without the church. How were the books of the Bible selected for inclusion in the canon? What criteria were used, and how can we be sure these are the books that were inspired by God? Is there external evidence that what the Bible says is, in fact, reliable and true? These and many other questions have been raised about the Bible. One of the tasks of the Christian apologist, both in the past and today, is to defend the reliability and authority of the Bible. In the selections in this section we get a glimpse of how this has been and continues to be done.

In the essay by Augustine, he describes a standard for affirming the canonical books: that they are received by all the catholic (i.e., orthodox) churches. If they are not received by all, the ones that are received by the greater number have more weight than those received by fewer. He also discusses the importance of studying the Bible, various ways of interpretation, and the need to know biblical languages.

In the next selection, John Calvin makes a case for the credibility of the Bible. He argues that the Bible has its authority from God and that the witness of the Holy Spirit is stronger than any proof that the Scriptures are from God. Scripture, he claims, is self-authenticating. He also argues that the church itself is grounded on the Bible, not the other way around. He then provides further reasons for affirming the credibility of the Bible, including miracles and prophecy.

Contemporary biblical scholar R. T. France offers a defense of the reliability of the Gospels as support for the historical reality of Jesus of Nazareth. He argues that while there are very few early references to Jesus outside the Gospels, nevertheless given their literary genre, the nature of tradition utilized, and a theistic worldview, we have good reason to take the Gospels seriously as a source of information concerning the life and teaching of Jesus and the historical origins of Christianity.

Next, Old Testament scholar Eugene Carpenter provides cutting-edge research on biblical archaeology at the end of the twentieth century and the beginning of the twenty-first century and its effects on Old Testament scholarship. He notes that the methods, perspectives, and approaches utilized in archaeological work have made significant progress over the past couple of centuries and are enjoying, but are also frustrated by, an information explosion of both artifacts and texts. The cache of ancient Near Eastern material has helped scholars better understand the backdrop of worldviews present during Old Testament times, and this aids in situating the Old Testament in a context for better understanding its history and theology. From all this, we can arguably conclude that the Old Testament is reliable and trustworthy, especially when considering the literary and historiographical perspectives of its narratives.

CHAPTER 29

On the Canon

Augustine

CHAPTER 8
The Canonical Books

12. But let us now go back to consider the third step here mentioned, for it is about it that I have set myself to speak and reason as the Lord shall grant me wisdom. The most skillful interpreter of the sacred writings, then, will be he who in the first place has read them all and retained them in his knowledge, if not yet with full understanding, still with such knowledge as reading gives — those of them, at least, that are called canonical. For he will read the others with greater safety when built up in the belief of the truth, so that they will not take first possession of a weak mind, nor, cheating it with dangerous falsehoods and delusions, fill it with prejudices adverse to a sound understanding. Now, in regard to the canonical Scriptures, he must follow the judgment of the greater number of Catholic churches; and among these, of course, a high place must be given to such as have been thought worthy to be the seat of an apostle and to receive epistles. Accordingly, among the canonical Scriptures he will judge according to the following standard: to prefer those that are received by all the Catholic churches to those which some do not receive. Among those, again, which are not received by all, he will prefer such as have the sanction of the greater number and those of greater authority, to such as are held by the smaller number and those of less authority. If, however, he shall find that some books are held by the greater number of churches, and others by the churches of greater authority (though this is not a very likely thing to happen), I think that in such a case the authority on the two sides is to be looked upon as equal.

13. Now the whole canon of Scripture on which we say this judgment is to be exercised, is contained in the following books — five books of Moses, that is, Genesis, Exodus, Leviticus, Numbers, Deuteronomy; one book of Joshua the son of Nun; one of Judges; one short book called Ruth, which seems rather to belong to the beginning of Kings; next, four books of Kings, and two of Chronicles — these last not following one another, but running parallel, so to speak, and going over the same ground. The books now mentioned are history, which contains a connected narrative of the times, and follows the order of the events. There are other books which seem to follow no regular order, and are connected neither with the order of the preceding books nor with one another, such as Job, and Tobias, and Esther, and Judith, and the two books of Maccabees, and the two of Ezra, which last look more like a sequel to the continuous regular history which terminates with the books of Kings and Chronicles. Next are the Prophets, in which there is one book of the Psalms of David; and three books of Solomon, viz., Proverbs, Song of Songs, and Ecclesiastes. For two books, one called Wisdom and the other Ecclesiasticus, are ascribed to Solomon from a certain resemblance of style, but the most likely opinion is that they were written by Jesus the son of Sirach. Still they are to be reckoned among the prophetical books, since they have attained recognition as being authoritative. The remainder are the books which are strictly called the Prophets: twelve separate books of the prophets which are connected with one another, and having never been disjoined, are reckoned as one book; the names of these prophets are as follows: Hosea, Joel, Amos,

273

Obadiah, Jonah, Micah, Nahum, Habakkuk, Zephaniah, Haggai, Zechariah, Malachi; then there are the four greater prophets, Isaiah, Jeremiah, Daniel, Ezekiel. The authority of the Old Testament is contained within the limits of these forty-four books. That of the New Testament, again, is contained within the following: four books of the Gospel, according to Matthew, according to Mark, according to Luke, according to John; fourteen epistles of the Apostle Paul—one to the Romans, two to the Corinthians, one to the Galatians, to the Ephesians, to the Philippians, two to the Thessalonians, one to the Colossians, two to Timothy, one to Titus, to Philemon, to the Hebrews; two of Peter; three of John; one of Jude; and one of James; one book of the Acts of the Apostles; and one of the Revelation of John.

CHAPTER 9
How We Should Proceed in Studying Scripture

14. In all these books those who fear God and are of a meek and pious disposition seek the will of God. And in pursuing this search the first rule to be observed is, as I said, to know these books, if not yet with the understanding, still to read them so as to commit them to memory, or at least so as not to remain wholly ignorant of them. Next, those matters that are plainly laid down in them, whether rules of life or rules of faith, are to be searched into more carefully and more diligently; and the more of these a man discovers, the more capacious does his understanding become. For among the things that are plainly laid down in Scripture are to be found all matters that concern faith and the manner of life—to wit, hope and love, of which I have spoken in the previous book. After this, when we have made ourselves to a certain extent familiar with the language of Scripture, we may proceed to open up and investigate the obscure passages, and in doing so draw examples from the plainer expressions to throw light upon the more obscure, and use the evidence of passages about which there is no doubt to remove all hesitation in regard to the doubtful passages. And in

this matter memory counts for a great deal; but if the memory be defective, no rules can supply the want.

CHAPTER 10
Unknown or Ambiguous Signs Prevent Scripture from Being Understood

15. Now there are two causes which prevent what is written from being understood: its being veiled either under unknown, or under ambiguous signs. Signs are either proper or figurative. They are called proper when they are used to point out the objects they were designed to point out, as we say bos when we mean an ox, because all men who with us use the Latin tongue call it by this name. Signs are figurative when the things themselves which we indicate by the proper names are used to signify something else, as we say bos, and understand by that syllable the ox, which is ordinarily called by that name; but then further by that ox understand a preacher of the gospel, as Scripture signifies, according to the apostle's explanation, when it says: "You shall not muzzle the ox that treads out the grain."

CHAPTER 11
Knowledge of Languages, Especially of Greek and Hebrew, Necessary to Remove Ignorance of Signs

16. The great remedy for ignorance of proper signs is knowledge of languages. And men who speak the Latin tongue, of whom are those I have undertaken to instruct, need two other languages for the knowledge of Scripture, Hebrew and Greek, that they may have recourse to the original texts if the endless diversity of the Latin translators throw them into doubt. Although, indeed, we often find Hebrew words untranslated in the books as for example, Amen, Halleluia, Racha, Hosanna, and others of the same kind. Some of these, although they could have been translated, have been preserved in their original form on account of the more sacred authority that attaches to it, as for example, Amen and Halleluia. Some of them, again, are said

to be untranslatable into another tongue, of which the other two I have mentioned are examples. For in some languages there are words that cannot be translated into the idiom of another language. And this happens chiefly in the case of interjections, which are words that express rather an emotion of the mind than any part of a thought we have in our mind. And the two given above are said to be of this kind, Racha expressing the cry of an angry man, Hosanna that of a joyful man. But the knowledge of these languages is necessary, not for the sake of a few words like these which it is very easy to mark and to ask about, but, as has been said, on account of the diversities among translators. For the translations of the Scriptures from Hebrew into Greek can be counted, but the Latin translators are out of all number. For in the early days of the faith every man who happened to get his hands upon a Greek manuscript, and who thought he had any knowledge, were it ever so little, of the two languages, ventured upon the work of translation.

CHAPTER 12
A Diversity of Interpretations Is Useful: Errors Arising from Ambiguous Words

17. And this circumstance would assist rather than hinder the understanding of Scripture, if only readers were not careless. For the examination of a number of texts has often thrown light upon some of the more obscure passages; for example, in that passage of the prophet Isaiah, one translator reads: "And do not despise the domestics of your seed;" another reads: "And do not despise your own flesh." Each of these in turn confirms the other. For the one is explained by the other; because "flesh" may be taken in its literal sense, so that a man may understand that he is admonished not to despise his own body; and "the domestics of your seed" may be understood figuratively of Christians, because they are spiritually born of the same seed as ourselves, namely, the Word. When now the meaning of the two translators is compared, a more likely sense of the words suggests itself, viz., that the command is not to despise our kinsmen, because when one brings the expression "domestics of your seed"

into relation with "flesh," kinsmen most naturally occur to one's mind. Whence, I think, that expression of the apostle, when he says, "If by any means I may provoke to emulation them which are my flesh, and might save some of them;" Romans 11:14 that is, that through emulation of those who had believed, some of them might believe too. And he calls the Jews his "flesh," on account of the relationship of blood. Again, that passage from the same prophet Isaiah: "If you will not believe, you shall not understand," another has translated: "If you will not believe, you shall not abide." Now which of these is the literal translation cannot be ascertained without reference to the text in the original tongue. And yet to those who read with knowledge, a great truth is to be found in each. For it is difficult for interpreters to differ so widely as not to touch at some point. Accordingly here, as understanding consists in sight, and is abiding, but faith feeds us as babes, upon milk, in the cradles of temporal things (for now we walk by faith, not by sight); 2 Corinthians 5:7 as, moreover, unless we walk by faith, we shall not attain to sight, which does not pass away, but abides, our understanding being purified by holding to the truth — for these reasons one says, "If you will not believe, you shall not understand;" but the other, "If you will not believe, you shall not abide."

18. And very often a translator, to whom the meaning is not well known, is deceived by an ambiguity in the original language, and puts upon the passage a construction that is wholly alien to the sense of the writer. As for example, some texts read: "Their feet are sharp to shed blood" (Romans 3:15), for the word ὀξύς among the Greeks means both sharp and swift. And so he saw the true meaning who translated: "Their feet are swift to shed blood." The other, taking the wrong sense of an ambiguous word, fell into error. Now translations such as this are not obscure, but false; and there is a wide difference between the two things. For we must learn not to interpret, but to correct texts of this sort. For the same reason it is, that because the Greek word μόσχος means a calf, some have not understood that μοσχεύματα are shoots of trees, and have translated the word "calves;" and this error has crept into so

many texts, that you can hardly find it written in any other way. And yet the meaning is very clear; for it is made evident by the words that follow. For "the plantings of an adulterer will not take deep root," is a more suitable form of expression than the "calves;" because these walk upon the ground with their feet, and are not fixed in the earth by roots. In this passage, indeed, the rest of the context also justifies this translation.

CHAPTER 30

The Authority and Credibility of Scripture

John Calvin

Chapter VII

The Testimony of the Spirit Necessary to Confirm the Scripture, in Order to the Complete Establishment of its Authority. The Suspension of its Authority on the Judgment of the Church, an Impious Function

I. The authority of Scripture comes from God, not the Church[1]

Before I proceed any further, it is proper to introduce some remarks on the authority of the Scripture, not only to prepare the mind to regard it with due reverence, but also to remove every doubt. For, when it is admitted to be a declaration of the word of God, no man can be so deplorably presumptuous, unless he be also destitute of common sense and of the common feelings of men, as to dare to derogate from the credit due to the speaker. But since we are not favoured with daily oracles from heaven, and since it is only in the Scriptures that the Lord hath been pleased to preserve his truth in perpetual remembrance, it obtains the same complete credit and authority with believers, when they are satisfied of its divine origin, as if they heard the very words pronounced by God himself. The subject, indeed, merits a diffuse discussion, and a most accurate examination. But the reader will pardon me if I attend rather to what the design of this work admits, than to what the extensive nature of the present subject requires. But there has very generally prevailed a most pernicious error, that the Scriptures have only so much weight as is conceded to them by the suffrages of the Church; as though the eternal and inviolable truth of God depended on the arbitrary will of men. For thus, with great contempt of the Holy Spirit, they inquire, Who can assure us that God is the author of them? Who can with certainty affirm that they have been preserved safe and uncorrupted to the present age? Who can persuade us that this book ought to be received with reverence, and that expunged from the sacred number, unless all these things were regulated by the decisions of the Church? It depends, therefore, (say they) on the determination of the Church to decide both what reverence is due to the Scripture, and what books are to be comprised in its canon. Thus sacrilegious men, while they wish to introduce an unlimited tyranny under the name of the Church, are totally unconcerned with what absurdities they embarrass themselves and others, provided they can extort from the ignorant this one admission, that the Church can do everything. But, if this be true, what will be the condition of those wretched consciences, which are seeking a solid assurance of eternal life, if all the promises extant concerning it rest only on the judgment of men? Will the reception of such an answer cause their fluctuations to subside, and their terrors to vanish? Again, how will the impious ridicule our faith, and all men call it in question, if it be understood to possess only a precarious authority depending on the favour of men!

II. The Church is grounded on Scripture

But such cavillers are completely refuted even by one word of the Apostle. He testifies that the Church

---

1. Heading titles have been added throughout this document for clarity.

is "built upon the foundation of the apostles and prophets." If the doctrine of the prophets and apostles be the foundation of the Church, it must have been certain, antecedently to the existence of the Church. Nor is there any foundation for this cavil, that though the Church derive its origin from the Scriptures, yet it remains doubtful what writings are to be ascribed to the prophets and apostles, unless it be determined by the Church. For if the Christian Church has been from the beginning founded on the writings of the prophets and the preaching of the apostles, wherever that doctrine is found, the approbation of it has certainly preceded the formation of the Church; since without it the Church itself had never existed. It is a very false notion, therefore, that the power of judging of the Scripture belongs to the Church, so as to make the certainty of it dependent on the Church's will. Wherefore, when the Church receives it, and seals it with her suffrage, she does not authenticate a thing otherwise dubious or controvertible; but, knowing it to be the truth of her God, performs a duty of piety by treating it with immediate veneration. But with regard to the question, How shall we be persuaded of its divine original, unless we have recourse to the decree of the Church? This is just as if anyone should inquire, How shall we learn to distinguish light from darkness, white from black, sweet from bitter? For the Scripture exhibits as clear evidence of its truth, as white and black things do of their colour, or sweet and fitter things of their taste.

III. The authority of Augustine cannot be used as evidence against this view

I know, indeed, that they commonly cite the opinion of Augustine, where he says, "that he would not believe the Gospel unless he were influenced by the authority of the Church." But how falsely and unfairly this is cited in support of such a notion, it is easy to discover from the context. He was in that contending with the Manichees, who wished to be credited, without any controversy, when they affirmed the truth to be on their side, but never proved it. Now, as they made the authority of the Gospel a pretext in

order to establish the credit of their Manichasus, he inquires what they would do if they met with a man who did not believe the Gospel; with what kind of persuasion they would convert him to their opinion. He afterwards adds, "Indeed, I would not give credit to the Gospel," intending that he himself, when an alien from the faith, could not be prevailed on to embrace the Gospel as the certain truth of God, till he was convinced by the authority of the Church. And is it surprising that any one, yet destitute of the knowledge of Christ, should pay a respect to men? Augustine, therefore, does not there maintain that the faith of the pious is founded on the authority of the Church, nor does he mean that the certainty of the Gospel depends on it; but simply, that unbelievers would have no assurance of the truth of the Gospel that would win them to Christ, unless they were influenced by the consent of the Church. And a little before, he clearly confirms it in these words: "When I shall have commended my own creed, and derided yours, what judgment, think you, ought we to form, what conduct ought we to pursue, but to forsake those who invite us to acknowledge things that are certain, and afterwards command us to believe things that are uncertain; and to follow those who invite us first to believe what we cannot yet clearly see, that, being strengthened by faith, we may acquire an understanding of what we believe: our mind being now internally strengthened and illuminated, not by men, but by God himself?" These are the express words of Augustine; whence the inference is obvious to everyone, that this holy man did not design to suspend our faith in the Scriptures on the arbitrary decision of the Church, but only to show (what we all confess to be true) that they who are yet unilluminated by the Spirit of God are, by a reverence for the Church, brought to such a docility as to submit to learn the faith of Christ from the Gospel; and that thus the authority of the Church is an introduction to prepare us for the faith of the Gospel. For we see that he will have the certainty of the pious to rest on a very different foundation. Otherwise I do not deny his frequently urging on the Manichees the universal consent of the Church, with a view to prove the truth of the Scripture, which they rejected. Whence his rebuke of Faustus, "for not submitting to the truth of the Gospel, so founded, so established, so gloriously celebrated, and delivered through certain successions from the apostolic age." But he nowhere insinuates that the authority which we attribute to the Scripture depends on the definitions or decrees of men: he only produces the universal judgment of the Church, which was very useful to his argument, and gave him an advantage over his adversaries. If any one desire a fuller proof of this, let him read his treatise "Of the Advantage of Believing," where he will find that he recommends no other facility of believing, than such as may afford us an introduction, and be a proper beginning of inquiry, as he expresses himself; yet that we should not be satisfied with mere opinion, but rest upon certain and solid truth.

IV. The witness of the Holy Spirit supersedes evidence

It must be maintained, as I have before asserted, that we are not established in the belief of the doctrine till we are indubitably persuaded that God is its Author. The principal proof, therefore, of the Scriptures is everywhere derived from the character of the Divine Speaker. The prophets and apostles boast not of their own genius, or any of those talents which conciliate the faith of the hearers; nor do they insist on arguments from reason, but bring forward the sacred name of God, to compel the submission of the whole world. We must now see how it appears, not from probable supposition, but from clear demonstration, that this use of the divine name is neither rash nor fallacious. Now, if we wish to consult the true interest of our consciences, that they may not be unstable and wavering, the subjects of perpetual doubt; that they may not hesitate at the smallest scruples — this persuasion must be sought from a higher source than human reasons, or judgments, or conjectures, even from the secret testimony of the Spirit. It is true that, if we were inclined to argue the point, many things might be adduced which certainly evince, if there be any God in heaven, that he is the Author of the Law, and the Prophecies, and the Gospel. Even though men

of learning and deep judgment rise up in opposition, and exert and display all the powers of their minds in this dispute, yet, unless they are wholly lost to all sense of shame, this confession will be extorted from them, that the Scripture exhibits the plainest evidences that it is God who speaks in it, which manifests its doctrine to be divine. And we shall soon see that all the books of the sacred Scripture very far excel all other writings. If we read it with pure eyes and sound minds, we shall immediately perceive the majesty of God, which will subdue our audacious contradictions and compel us to obey him. Yet it is acting a preposterous part to endeavour to produce sound faith in the Scripture by disputations. Though, indeed, I am far from excelling in peculiar dexterity or eloquence; yet, if I were to contend with the most subtle despisers of God, who are ambitious to display their wit and their skill in weakening the authority of Scripture, I trust I should be able, without difficulty, to silence their obstreperous clamour. And, if it were of any use to attempt a refutation of their cavils, I would easily demolish the boasts which they mutter in secret corners. But though any one vindicates the sacred word of God from the aspersions of men, yet this will not fix in their hearts that assurance which is essential to true piety. Religion appearing, to profane men, to consist wholly in opinion, in order that they may not believe anything on foolish or slight grounds, they wish and expect it to be proved by rational arguments that Moses and the prophets spake by divine inspiration. But I reply that the testimony of the Spirit is superior to all reason. For, as God alone is a sufficient witness of himself in his own word, so also the word will never gain credit in the hearts of men, till it be confirmed by the internal testimony of the Spirit. It is necessary, therefore, that the same Spirit who spake by the mouths of the prophets should penetrate into our hearts, to convince us that they faithfully delivered the oracles which were divinely entrusted to them. And this connection is very suitably expressed in these words: "My Spirit that is upon thee, and my word which I have put in thy mouth, shall not depart out of thy mouth, nor out of the mouth of thy seed, nor out of the mouth of thy seed's seed, forever." Some good men are troubled that they are not always prepared with clear proof to oppose the impious, when they murmur with impunity against the divine word; as though the Spirit were not therefore denominated a "seal," and "an earnest," for the confirmation of the faith of the pious; because, till he illuminate their minds, they are perpetually fluctuating amidst a multitude of doubts.

V. Scripture offers an authentication of its own

Let it be considered, then, as an undeniable truth, that they who have been inwardly taught by the Spirit feel an entire acquiescence in the Scripture, and that it is self-authenticated, carrying with it its own evidence, and ought not to be made the subject of demonstration and arguments from reason; but it obtains the credit which it deserves with us by the testimony of the Spirit. For though it conciliate our reverence by its internal majesty, it never seriously affects us till it is confirmed by the Spirit in our hearts. Therefore, being illuminated by him, we now believe the divine original of the Scripture, not from our own judgment or that of others; but we esteem the certainty, that we have received it from God's own mouth by the ministry of men, to be superior to that of any human judgment, and equal to that of an intuitive perception of God himself in it. We seek not arguments or probabilities to support our judgment, but submit our judgments and understandings as to a thing concerning which it is impossible for us to judge; and that not like some persons, who are in the habit of hastily embracing what they do not understand, which displeases them as soon as they examine it, but because we feel the firmest conviction that we hold an invincible truth; nor like those unhappy men who surrender their minds captives to superstitions, but because we perceive in it the undoubted energies of the Divine power, by which we are attracted and inflamed to an understanding and voluntary obedience, but with a vigour and efficacy superior to the power of any human will or knowledge. With the greatest justice, therefore, God

exclaims by Isaiah, that the prophets and all the people were his witnesses; because, being taught by prophecies, they were certain that God had spoken without the least fallacy or ambiguity. It is such a persuasion, therefore, as requires no reasons; such a knowledge as is supported by the highest reason, in which, indeed, the mind rests with greater security and constancy than in any reasons; it is, finally, such a sentiment as cannot be produced but by a revelation from heaven. I speak of nothing but what every believer experiences in his heart, except that my language falls far short of a just explication of the subject. I pass over many things at present, because this subject will present itself for discussion again in another place. Only let it be known here, that that alone is true faith which the Spirit of God seals in our hearts. And with this one reason every reader of modesty and docility will be satisfied: Isaiah predicts that "all the children" of the renovated Church "shall be taught of God." Herein God deigns to confer a singular privilege on his elect, whom he distinguishes from the rest of mankind. For what is the beginning of true learning but a prompt alacrity to hear the voice of God? By the mouth of Moses he demands our attention in these terms: "Say not in thine heart, Who shall ascend into heaven? or, Who shall descend into the deep? The word is even in thy mouth." If God hath determined that this treasury of wisdom shall be reserved for his children, it is neither surprising nor absurd that we see so much ignorance and stupidity among the vulgar herd of mankind. By this appellation I designate even those of the greatest talents and highest rank, till they are incorporated into the Church. Moreover, Isaiah, observing that the prophetical doctrine would be incredible, not only to aliens, but also to the Jews, who wished to be esteemed members of the family, adds, at the same time, the reason — because the arm of the Lord will not be revealed to all. Whenever, therefore, we are disturbed at the paucity of believers, let us, on the other hand, remember that none, but those to whom it was given, have any apprehension of the mysteries of God.

Chapter VIII

Rational Proofs to Establish the Belief of the Scripture

I. Scripture is superior to the wisdom of human beings

Without this certainty, better and stronger than any human judgment, in vain will the authority of the Scripture be either defended by arguments, or established by the consent of the Church, or confirmed by any other supports; since, unless the foundation be laid, it remains in perpetual suspense. Whilst, on the contrary, when, regarding it in a different point of view from common things, we have once religiously received it in a manner worthy of its excellence, we shall then derive great assistance from things which before were not sufficient to establish the certainty of it in our minds. For it is admirable to observe how much it conduces to our confirmation, attentively to study the order and disposition of the Divine Wisdom dispensed in it, the heavenly nature of its doctrine, which never savours of anything terrestrial, the beautiful agreement of all the parts with each other, and other similar characters adapted to conciliate respect to any writings. But our hearts are more strongly confirmed, when we reflect that we are constrained to admire it more by the dignity of the subjects than by the beauties of the language. For even this did not happen without the particular providence of God, that the sublime mysteries of the kingdom of heaven should be communicated, for the most part, in a humble and contemptible style; lest, if they had been illustrated with more of the splendour of eloquence, the impious might cavil that their triumph is only the triumph of eloquence. Now, since that uncultivated and almost rude simplicity procures itself more reverence than all the graces of rhetoric, what opinion can we form, but that the force of truth in the sacred Scripture is too powerful to need the assistance of verbal art? Justly, therefore, does the apostle argue that the faith of the Corinthians was founded, "not in the wisdom of men, but in the power of God," because his preaching among them was "not with enticing words of man's wisdom, but in demonstration of the Spirit and of power." For the truth is vindicated from every doubt, when, unassisted by foreign aid, it is sufficient for its own support. But that this is the peculiar property of the Scripture appears from the insufficiency of any human compositions, however artificially polished, to make an equal impression on our minds. Read Demosthenes or Cicero; read Plato, Aristotle, or any others of that class; I grant that you will be attracted, delighted, moved, and enraptured by them in a surprising manner; but if, after reading them, you turn to the perusal of the sacred volume, whether you are willing or unwilling, it will affect you so powerfully, it will so penetrate your heart, and impress itself so strongly on your mind, that, compared with its energetic influence, the beauties of rhetoricians and philosophers will almost entirely disappear; so that it is easy to perceive something divine in the sacred Scriptures, which far surpasses the highest attainments and ornaments of human industry.

II. Content is fundamental

I grant, indeed, that the diction of some of the prophets is neat and elegant, and even splendid; so that they are not inferior in eloquence to the heathen writers. And by such examples the Holy Spirit hath been pleased to show that he was not deficient in eloquence, though elsewhere he hath used a rude and homely style. But whether we read David, Isaiah, and others that resemble them, who have a sweet and pleasant flow of words, or Amos the herdsman, Jeremiah, and Zechariah, whose rougher language savours of rusticity — that majesty of the Spirit, which I have mentioned, is everywhere conspicuous. I am not ignorant that Satan in many things imitates God, in order that, by the fallacious resemblance, he may more easily insinuate himself into the minds of the simple; and has therefore craftily disseminated, in unpolished and even barbarous language, the most impious errors, by which multitudes have been miserably deceived, and has often used obsolete forms of speech as a mask to conceal his impostures. But the vanity and fraud of such affectation are visible to all men of moderate understanding. With respect to the sacred Scripture, though presumptuous men try to cavil at various passages, yet it is evidently replete with sentences which are beyond the powers of human conception. Let all the prophets be examined; not one will be found who has not far surpassed the ability of men; so that those to whom their doctrine is insipid must be accounted utterly destitute of all true taste.

III. The antiquity of Scripture is significant

This argument has been copiously treated by other writers; wherefore it may suffice at present merely to hint at a few things which chiefly relate to the subject in a general view. Beside what I have already treated on, the antiquity of the Scripture is of no small weight. For, notwithstanding the fabulous accounts of the Greek writers concerning the Egyptian theology, yet there remains no monument of any religion, but what is much lower than the age of Moses. Nor does Moses invent a new deity; he only makes a declaration of what the Israelites had, through a long series of years, received by tradition from their forefathers concerning the eternal God. For what does he aim at, but to recall them to the covenant made with Abraham? If he had advanced a thing till then unheard of, it would not have been received; but their liberation from the servitude in which they were detained must have been a thing well known to them all; so that the mention of it immediately excited universal attention. It is probable also that they had been informed of the number of four hundred years. Now, we must consider, if Moses (who himself preceded all other writers by such a long distance of time) derives the tradition of his doctrine from so remote a beginning, how much the sacred Scripture exceeds in antiquity all other books.

IV. The role of Moses's example

Unless any would choose to credit the Egyptians, who extend their antiquity to six thousand years

before the creation of the world. But since their garrulity has been ridiculed even by all the profane writers, I need not trouble myself with refuting it. Josephus, in his book against Appion, cites from the most ancient writers testimonies worthy of being remembered; whence we may gather that the doctrine contained in the law has, according to the consent of all nations, been renowned from the remotest ages, although it was neither read nor truly understood. Now, that the malicious might have no room for suspicion, nor even the wicked any pretence for cavilling, God hath provided the most excellent remedies for both these dangers. When Moses relates what Jacob had, almost three hundred years before, by the spirit of inspiration pronounced concerning his posterity, how does he disgrace his own tribe! He even brands it, in the person of Levi, with perpetual infamy. "Simeon," says he, "and Levi instruments of cruelty are in their habitations. O my soul, come not thou into their secret: unto their assembly, mine honour, be not thou united." He certainly might have been silent on that disgraceful circumstance, not only to spare his father, but also to avoid aspersing himself, as well as all his family, with part of the same ignominy. How can any suspicion be entertained of him, who, voluntarily publishing, from the inspiration of the Holy Spirit, that the first of the family from which he was descended was guilty of detestable conduct, neither consults his own personal honours, nor refuses to incur the resentment of his relations, to whom this must undoubtedly have given offence? When he mentions also the impious murmurings of Aaron, his brother, and Miriam, his sister, shall we say that he spake according to the dictates of the flesh, or obeyed the command of the Holy Spirit? Besides, as he enjoyed the supreme authority, why did he not leave to his own sons, at least, the office of the high-priesthood, but place them in the lowest station? I only hint at a *few* things out of many. But in the law itself many arguments will everywhere occur, which challenge a full belief that, without controversy, the legation of Moses was truly divine.

V. Miracles and authority

Moreover, the miracles which he relates, and which are so numerous and remarkable, are so many confirmations of the law which he delivered, and of the doctrine which he published. For that he was carried up into the mountain in *a* cloud; that he continued there forty days, deprived of all human intercourse; that, in the act of proclaiming the law, his face shone as with the rays of the sun; that lightnings flashed all around; that thunders and various noises were heard through the whole atmosphere; that a trumpet sounded, but a trumpet not blown by human breath; that the entrance of the tabernacle was concealed from the view of the people by an intervening cloud; that his authority was so miraculously vindicated by the horrible destruction of Korah, Dathan, and Abiram, and all their impious faction; that a rock smitten with a rod immediately emitted a river; that manna rained from heaven at his request — are not all these so many testimonies from heaven of his being a true prophet? If any one object that I assume, as granted, things which are the subjects of controversy, this cavil is easily answered. For, as Moses published all these things in an assembly of the people, what room was there for fiction among those who had been witnesses of the events? Is it probable that he would make his appearance in public, and, accusing the people of infidelity, contumacy, ingratitude, and other crimes, boast that his doctrine had been confirmed in their sight by miracles which they had never seen?

VI. The miracles of Moses are indisputable

For this also is worthy of being remarked, that all his accounts of miracles are connected with such unpleasant circumstances, as were calculated to stimulate all the people, if there had been but the smallest occasion, to a public and positive contradiction; whence it appears, that they were induced to coincide with him only by the ample conviction of their own experience. But since the matter was too evident for profane writers to take the liberty of denying the performance of miracles by Moses, the father of lies has suggested the calumny of ascribing them to magical arts. But by what kind of conjecture can they pretend to charge him with having been a magician, who had so great an abhorrence of that superstition, as to command, that he who merely consulted magicians and soothsayers should be stoned? Certainly no impostor practises such juggling tricks who does not make it his study, for the sake of acquiring fame, to astonish the minds of the vulgar. But what is the practice of Moses? Openly avowing that himself and his brother Aaron are nothing, but that they only execute the commands of God, he sufficiently clears his character from every unfavourable aspersion. Now, if the events themselves be considered, what incantation could cause manna to rain daily from heaven sufficient to support the people, and, if any one laid up more than proper quantity, cause it to putrefy, as a punishment from God for his unbelief? Add also the many serious examinations which God permitted his servant to undergo, so that the clamour of the wicked can now be of no avail. For as often as this holy servant of God was in danger of being destroyed, at one time by proud and petulant insurrections of all the people, at another by the secret conspiracies of a few — how was it possible for him to elude their inveterate rage by any arts of deception? And the event evidently proves, that by these circumstances his doctrine was confirmed to all succeeding ages.

VII. Fulfilled prophecies

Moreover, who can deny that his assigning, in the person of the patriarch Jacob, the supreme power to the tribe of Judah, proceeded from a spirit of prophecy, especially if we consider the eventual accomplishment of this prediction? Suppose Moses to have been the first author of it; yet after he committed it to writing, there elapsed four hunched years in which we have no mention of the sceptre in the tribe of Judah. After the inauguration of Saul, the regal power seemed to be fixed in the tribe of Benjamin. When Samuel anointed

David, what reason appeared for transferring it? Who would have expected a king to arise out of the plebeian family of a herdsman? And of seven brothers, who would have conjectured that such an honour was destined for the youngest? And by what means did he attain any hope of the kingdom? Who can assert that this unction was directed by human art, or industry, or prudence, and was not rather a completion of the prediction of heaven? And in like manner do not his predictions, although obscure, concerning the admission of the Gentiles into the covenant of God, which were accomplished almost two thousand years after, clearly prove him to have spoken under a divine inspiration? I omit other predictions, which so strongly savour of a divine inspiration, that all who have the use of their reason must perceive that it is God who speaks. In short, one song of his is a clear mirror in which God evidently appears.

VIII. The confirmation of God

But in the other prophets this is yet far more conspicuous. I shall only select a few examples, for to collect all would be too laborious. When, in the time of Isaiah, the kingdom of Judah was in peace, and even when they thought themselves safe in the alliance of the Chaldeans, Isaiah publicly spake of the destruction of the city and the banishment of the people. Now, even if to predict long before things which then seemed false, but have since appeared to be true, were not a sufficiently clear proof of a divine inspiration, to whom but God shall we ascribe the prophecies which he uttered concerning their deliverance? He mentions the name of Cyrus, by whom the Chaldeans were to be subdued, and the people restored to liberty. More than a century elapsed after this prophecy before the birth of Cyrus; for he was not born till about the hundredth year after the prophet's death. No man could then divine, that there would be one Cyrus, who would engage in a war with the Babylonians, who would subjugate such a powerful monarchy, and release the people of Israel from exile. Does not this bare narration, without any ornaments of diction, plainly demonstrate that Isaiah delivered the undoubted oracles

of God, and not the conjectures of men? Again, when Jeremiah, just before the people were carried away, limited the duration of their captivity to seventy years, and predicted their liberation and return, must not his tongue have been under the direction of the Spirit of God? What impudence must it be to deny that the authority of the prophets has been confirmed by such proofs, or that what they themselves assert, in order to vindicate the credit due to their declarations, has been actually fulfilled! "Behold, the former things are come to pass, and new things do I declare: before they spring forth, I tell you of them." I shall not speak of Jeremiah and Ezekiel, who, living in distant countries, but prophesying at the same time, so exactly accord in their declarations, as though they had mutually dictated the words to each other. What shall we say of Daniel? Has not he prophesied of the events of nearly six hundred years in such a connected series, as if he were composing a history of transactions already past and universally known? If pious men properly consider these things, they will be sufficiently prepared to curb the petulance of the wicked; for the demonstration is too clear to be liable to any cavils.

IX. The preservation and transmission of the law of Moses

I know what is objected by some clamorous men, who would ostentatiously display the force of their understanding in opposing divine truth. For they inquire, Who has assured us that Moses and the prophets actually wrote those books which bear their names? They even dare to question whether such a man as Moses ever existed. But if any man should call in question the existence of Plato, or Aristotle, or Cicero, who would deny that such madness ought to receive corporal punishment? The law of Moses has been wonderfully preserved, rather by the providence of heaven than by the endeavours of men. And though, through the negligence of the priests, it lay for a short time concealed, since it was found by the pious king Josiah, it has continued in the hands of men through every succeeding age. Nor, indeed, did Josiah produce it as a thing unknown or new, but as what had always been public, and the memory of which was then famous. The photograph had been appointed to be kept in the temple, and a transcript of it to be deposited in the royal archives; only the priests had discontinued their ancient custom of publishing the law, and the people themselves had neglected their wonted reading of it yet there scarcely passed an age in which its sanction was not confirmed and renewed. Were they, who had the writings of David, ignorant of Moses? But, to speak of all at once, it is certain that their writings descended to posterity only from hand to hand, so to speak, through a long series of years transmitted from the fathers, who partly had heard them speak, and partly learned from others who heard them, while it was fresh in their memory, that they had thus spoken.

X. The Law and the Prophets preserved

With regard to what they object from the history of the Maccabees, to diminish the credit of the Scripture, nothing could be conceived more adapted to establish it. But first let us divest it of their artificial colouring, and then retort upon them the weapon which they direct against us. When Antiochus, say they, commanded all the books to be burned, whence proceeded the copies which we now have? I, on the contrary, inquire where they could so speedily be fabricated. For it is evident that, as soon as the persecution subsided, they immediately appeared and were, without controversy, acknowledged as the same by all pious men; who, having been educated in their doctrine, had been familiarly acquainted with them. Nay, even when all the impious, as if by a general conspiracy, so wantonly insulted the Jews, no man ever dared to charge them with forging their books. For, whatever be their opinion of the Jewish religion, yet they confess that Moses was the author of it. What, then, do these clamorous objectors, but betray their own consummate impudence, when they slander, as supposititious, books whose sacred antiquity is confirmed by the consent of all histories? But, to waste no more useless labour in refuting such stale calumnies, let us rather consider how carefully the Lord preserved

his own word, when, beyond all hope, he rescued it from the fury of the most cruel of tyrants, as from a devouring fire — that he endued the pious priests and others with so much constancy, that they hesitated not to redeem this treasure, if necessary, with their lives to transmit it to posterity; and that he frustrated the most diligent inquisition of so many governors and soldiers. Who is there but must acknowledge it to have been an eminent and wonderful work of God, that those sacked monuments, which the impious had flattered themselves were utterly destroyed, were soon public again, as it were, fully restored to mankind, and, indeed, with far greater honour? For soon after followed the Greek Translation, which published them throughout the world. Nor was God's preserving the tables of his covenant from the sanguinary edicts of Antiochus, the only instance of his wonderful operation, but that, amidst such various miseries, with which the Jewish nation was diminished and laid waste, and at last nearly exterminated, these records still remained entire. The Hebrew language lay not only despised, but almost unknown; and surely, had not God consulted the interest of religion, it had been totally lost. For how much the Jews, after their return from captivity, departed from the genuine use of their native language, appears from the prophets of that age; which it is therefore useful to observe, because this comparison more clearly evinces the antiquity of the law and the prophets. And by whom hath God preserved to us the doctrine of salvation contained in the law and the prophets, that Christ might be manifested in due time? By his most inveterate enemies, the Jews; whom Augustine therefore v justly denominates the librarians of the Christian Church, because they have furnished us with a book of which themselves make no use.

XI. The solid foundations of the New Testament

If we proceed to the New Testament, by what solid foundations is its truth supported? Three Evangelists recite their history in a low and mean style. Many proud men are disgusted with that simplicity, because they attend not to the principal points of doctrine; whence it were easy to infer, that they treat of heavenly mysteries which are above human capacity. They who have a spark of ingenuous modesty will certainly be ashamed, if they peruse the first chapter of Luke. Now, the discourses of Christ, a concise summary of which is comprised in these three Evangelists, easily exempt their writings from contempt. But John, thundering from his sublimity, more powerfully than any thunderbolt, levels to the dust the obstinacy of those whom he does not compel to the obedience of faith. Let all those censorious critics whose supreme pleasure consists in banishing all reverence for the Scripture out of their own hearts and the hearts of others, come forth to public view. Let them read the Gospel of John: whether they wish it or not, they will there find numerous passages, which, not least, arouse their indolence; and which will even imprint a horrible brand on their consciences to restrain their ridicule. Similar is the method of Paul and of Peter, in whose writings, though the greater part be blind, yet their heavenly majesty attracts universal attention. But this one circumstance raises their doctrine sufficiently above the world, that Matthew, who had before been confined to the profit of his table, and Peter and John, who had been employed in fishing-boats — all plain, unlettered men — had learned nothing in any human school which they could communicate to others. And Paul, from not only a professed, but a cruel and sanguinary enemy, being converted to a new man, proves, by his sudden and unhoped for change, that he was constrained by a command from heaven to vindicate that doctrine which he had before opposed. Let these men deny that the Holy Spirit descended on the Apostles; or, at least, let them dispute the credibility of the history; yet the fact itself loudly proclaims that they were taught by the Spirit, who, though before despised as some of the meanest of the people, suddenly began to discourse in such a magnificent manner on the mysteries of heaven.

XII. The testimony of the Church

Besides, there are also other very substantial reasons why the consent of the Church should have its weight. For it is not an unimportant consideration that, since the publication of the Scripture, so many generations of men should have agreed in voluntarily obeying it; and that however Satan together with the whole world, has endeavoured by strange methods to suppress or destroy it, or utterly to erase and obliterate it from the memory of man, yet it has always, like a palm tree, risen superior to all opposition, and remained invincible. Indeed, there has scarcely ever been a sophist or orator of more than common abilities, who has not tried his strength in opposing it; yet they have all availed nothing. All the powers of the earth have armed themselves for its destruction; but their attempts have all evaporated into smoke. How could it have so firmly resisted attacks on every quarter, if it had been supported only by human power? Indeed, an additional proof of its Divine origin arises from this very circumstance, that, notwithstanding all the strenuous resistance of men, it has, by its own power, risen superior to every danger. Moreover, not one city, or one nation, only, has conspired to receive and embrace it; but, as far as the world extends, it has obtained its authority by the holy consent of various nations, who agreed in nothing besides. And as such an agreement of minds, so widely distant in place, and so completely dissimilar in manners and opinions, ought to have great influence with us, since it is plain that it was effected only by the power of heaven, so it acquires no small weight from a consideration of the piety of those who unite in this agreement; not indeed of all, but of those who, it hath pleased the Lord, should shine as luminaries in his Church.

XIII. Martyrs died for Scripture

Now, with what unlimited confidence should we submit to that doctrine, which we see confirmed and witnessed by the blood of so many saints! Having once received it, they hesitated not, with intrepid boldness, and even with great alacrity, to die in its defence: transmitted to us with such a pledge, how should we not receive it with a firm and unshaken conviction? Is it therefore no small confirmation of the Scripture, that it has been sealed with the blood of so many martyrs? Especially when we consider that they died to bear testimony to their faith, not through intemperate fanaticism, as is sometimes the case with men of erroneous minds, but through a firm and constant, yet sober zeal for God. There are other reasons, and those neither few nor weak, by which the native dignity and authority of the Scripture are not only maintained in the minds of the pious, but also completely vindicated against the subtleties of calumniators; but such as alone are not sufficient to produce firm faith in it, till the heavenly Father, discovering his own power therein, places its authority beyond all controversy.

Wherefore the Scripture will then only be effectual to produce the saving knowledge of God, when the certainty of it shall be founded on the internal persuasion of the Holy Spirit. Thus those human testimonies, which contribute to its confirmation, will not be useless, if they follow that first and principal proof, as secondary aids to our imbecility. But those persons betray great folly, who wish it to be demonstrated to infidels that the Scripture is the word of God, which cannot be known without faith. Augustine therefore justly observes, that piety and peace of mind ought to precede, in order that a man may understand somewhat of such great subjects.

CHAPTER 31

The Gospels as Historical Sources for Jesus

R. T. France[1]

1. The Four Canonical Gospels Are Indispensable

1.1 The *lack of relevant evidence outside the gospels* makes them the necessary starting-point of any investigation of the historical Jesus.

1.1.1 In the first century or so after the death of Jesus there are very few *references to Jesus in non-Christian literature.*

(a) The brief notice in Tacitus *Annals* xv.44 mentions only his title, *Christus,* and his execution in Judea by order of Pontius Pilatus. Nor is there any reason to believe that Tacitus bases this on independent information — it is what Christians would be saying in Rome in the early second century. Suetonius and Pliny, together with Tacitus, testify to the significant presence of Christians in Rome and other parts of the empire from the mid-sixties onwards, but add nothing to our knowledge of their founder. No other clear pagan references to Jesus can be dated before AD 150,[2] by which time the source of any information is more likely to be Christian propaganda than an independent record.

(b) The only clear non-Christian Jewish reference in this period is that of Josephus *Antiquities* XVIII.63 – 64, the so-called *Testimonium Flavianum.* Virtually all scholars are agreed that the received text is a Christian rewriting, but most are prepared to accept that in the original text a brief account of Jesus, perhaps in a less complimentary vein, stood at this point.[3] Josephus' passing mention of "Jesus, the so-called Messiah" in *Antiquities* XX.200 is hard to explain without some previous notice of this Jesus, especially since Josephus elsewhere makes no reference to Christianity, nor even uses the term *Christos* of any other figure. The different and less "committed" version of the *Testimonium* preserved in a tenth-century Arabic quotation from Josephus,[4] while it is unlikely to represent the original text, does testify to the existence of an account of Jesus in Josephus' work underlying the Christianized text. But reconstruction of what Josephus wrote is necessarily speculative.

(c) Rabbinic traditions about Jesus[5] recall him as a sorcerer who gained a following and "led Israel astray," and so "was hanged on the eve of the Passover." Some of the relevant passages may date from the second century AD, but they are very obscure, and bear little relation to the Jesus his own followers remembered. Their polemical nature and their lack of interest in factual data does not create confidence in their potential as historical evidence for Jesus.

1.1.2 *Early Christian references to Jesus outside the canonical gospels* fall into two categories.

---

1. For further development of the ideas and material presented in this article, see R.T. France, *The Evidence for Jesus,* co-published by Hodder & Stoughton and InterVarsity Press, 1986, reprinted by Regent Publishing, Vancouver, 2006.

2. For other suggested references in the history of Thallus and in a letter by an otherwise unknown Mara bar Serapion see F.F. Bruce, *Jesus and Christian Origins outside the New Testament* (London: Hodder, 1984) 29 – 31; neither is certainly a reference to Jesus or Christianity.

3. For a survey of scholarly views up to 1969 see P. Winter's excursus in E. Schürer, *The History of the Jewish People in the Age of Jesus Christ,* vol. 1 (new edition by G. Vermes, F. Millar, and M. Black. Edinburgh: T&T Clark, 1973) 428 – 441.

4. S. Pines, *An Arabic Version of the Testimonium Flavianum and its Implications* (Jerusalem: Israel Academy of Sciences and Humanities, 1971).

5. The main passages are Babylonian Talmud, *Sanhedrin* 43a, 107b, and the uncensored text of *Sanhedrin* 67a. Also Tosefta, *Hullin* 2:22 – 24.

(a) Practically all surviving Christian writings of the *first century* are found in the New Testament. In the letters of Paul, in the early preaching as Luke reports it in the Acts of the Apostles, and in various references in the other New Testament books, we gain a basic perspective on Jesus as the Jewish Messiah, crucified and raised from death, on whom the early Christians based their hope of salvation. These references to Jesus are made in a context of faith, to which biographical interest takes second place. They do in fact add up to a fairly consistent, if minimal, portrait of Jesus as a remembered figure of history, and their factual content is not negligible.[6] But a historian who had only this material to work on could hope for only the most meager record of Jesus' life and teaching.

(b) From the *second century* and later come a large number of Christian writings, many of which purport to give an account of what Jesus said and did. These "apocryphal gospels" vary from novelistic accounts of improbable marvels surrounding Jesus' birth and childhood (especially the *Protevangelium of James* and the *Infancy Gospel of Thomas*) to elaborate discourses on Gnostic cosmology presented as the post-resurrection teaching of Jesus to his disciples (several such were found at Nag Hammadi, notably the *Sophia of Jesus Christ*). A high percentage of these works are clearly written within the framework of a Gnosticized Christianity (indeed some are Christian adaptations of pagan Gnostic writings),[7] and their portrait of Jesus is tailored accordingly. The difference in tone from first-century Christian writings is thus remarkable and leaves the historian with a fundamental choice: either she accepts the earlier accounts and so dismisses the "Gnostic" Jesus as a later perversion, or she alleges a large-scale cover-up by "orthodox" Christianity which successfully suppressed earlier evidence of a Jesus whose magical propensities and esoteric teaching formed the historical basis of the "Gnostic" version of Christianity — a more authentic version which is now labelled "heretical" only because it had the misfortune to be the eventual loser in the battle with "orthodoxy."[8] This paper proceeds on the assumption that the earlier evidence is to be preferred. This is not to deny, however, that some authentic tradition about Jesus may have been preserved outside the New Testament. This is in fact inherently likely, and scholars have argued that some stories, such as that of the encounter of Jesus in the temple with Levi the Pharisee,[9] or sayings such as the frequently quoted "Be approved money-changers,"[10] are likely to have a basis in fact. Such isolated fragments, however, are not a significant contribution to our knowledge of Jesus.

1.1.3 *Archeological evidence* for Jesus is in the nature of the case only background evidence. It may tell us much about the world he lived in; it may illuminate the background to certain stories in the gospels;[11] it may help us in deciding between suggested locations of places mentioned in the gospels.[12] But it cannot be expected to offer us direct evidence of a figure whose position in society was not such as to make him the subject of inscriptions.

1.2 The *explanation for this lack of evidence* is to be found in the nature and scale of the early Christian movement.

1.2.1 From the point of view of Roman history of the first century, Jesus was a nobody. A man of

---

6. This aspect of the New Testament is explored by G.N. Stanton, *Jesus of Nazareth in New Testament Preaching* (SNTS Monograph 27; Cambridge University Press, 1974).

7. E.g. the *Sophia of Jesus Christ* is apparently a Christianized version of the *Letter of Eugnostos the Blessed*, a non-Christian Gnostic work found in the same collection of Gnostic writings at Nag Hammadi.

8. This is the approach especially of Morton Smith, *Jesus the Magician* (London: Gollancz, 1978). At a more popular level it is used in I. Wilson, *Jesus: the Evidence* (London: Weidenfeld & Nicolson, 1984).

9. The story, contained in Oxyrhynchus Papyrus 840, may be found, with discussion, in J. Finegan, *Hidden Records of the Life of Jesus* (Philadelphia: Pilgrim Press, 1969) 226 – 230.

10. The saying occurs as a quotation some fifteen times in patristic literature between the second and fifth century. For references see G.W.H. Lampe, *A Patristic Greek Lexicon* (Oxford University Press, 1961) 1400. For discussion see J. Jeremias, *Unknown Sayings of Jesus* (London: SPCK, 1957) 89 – 93.

11. E.g. the pool of Bethesda, described in John 5:2f. See J. Wilkinson, *Jerusalem as Jesus Knew It* (London: Thames & Hudson, 1978) 95 – 104.

12. E.g. the rival locations for Jesus' crucifixion and burial; see J. Wilkinson, ibid. 144 – 150.

no social standing, who achieved brief local notice in a remote and little-loved province as a preacher and miracle-worker, and who was duly executed by order of a minor provincial governor, could hardly be expected to achieve mention in the Roman head-lines. Even his fellow-countrymen who did not respond to his mission would not be likely to think much of him once his execution had put paid to his claims.

1.2.2 If Jesus was to be noticed it would more likely be through the success of the movement which he founded. As we noted above, it is Christianity rather than Jesus which first makes an appearance in Roman records. In the light of the political prominence which Christianity achieved in the fourth century, it is natural for us to envisage it as an imposing movement from the beginning. But sociological studies indicate first-century Christianity as a predominantly lower-class movement, with only a very limited appeal to the influential classes. And the careful reader of Paul's letters and of the Acts of the Apostles does not gain the impression of a mass movement, but rather of small, rather isolated groups of Christians banding together for mutual support in a hostile environment. Such groups are not the stuff of which news stories are made.

1.2.3 Christianity was a religious movement which did not in its early years have political ambitions. We are surrounded by such movements today. For all our awareness of their presence, it is seldom that we feel it necessary to mention them in ordinary speech and writing. They may be quite large, and for their adherents they may be the focus of all that is important; some of them may, for all we know, be destined to become world-changing forces. But for those of us who are outside them they are, for the time being, barely worthy of notice.

1.3 Seen in this light, the scanty nature of early non-Christian evidence for Christianity, and for Jesus in particular, is hardly surprising. It rings true

to the historical reality of the situation. And if that is the case, it is inevitable that our knowledge of the beginnings of Christianity will be dependent almost entirely on Christian records. We are fortunate that quite full early Christian records have in fact survived, in the form of the four first-century gospels. Indeed the availability of four separate records by different authors of the same person in ancient history is a rare, if not a unique, phenomenon.

2. The Acceptability of the Gospels As Historical Sources

2.1 The literary genre of the gospels.

2.1.1 It has long been an accepted dictum of New Testament scholars that the gospels are not *biographies*. In the sense that they do not set about their task in the way a modern biographer does this is undoubtedly true. Their records are highly selective, have only a loose chronological framework, focus one-sidedly on matters of theological significance, and tell us little or nothing about their subject's psychology or personal development. In these ways, however, they are much closer to the type of "biography" which was fashionable in the ancient world.[13] To commend the teaching and example of a great man by means of a selective and "moralizing" anthology of his sayings and deeds was an accepted approach. Many such "biographies" were of heroes long ago, and are largely mythical and valueless as historical sources; but in the case of a more recent figure there is no reason *a priori* why authentic historical reminiscences should not form the basis for such a "life."

2.1.2 The primary cultural milieu for the gospels is Jewish, and prominent among Jewish literary techniques of the early Christian period is *midrash*.[14] This category has been applied to the gospels, with the suggestion that the source of much that they attribute to Jesus is a scripturally-inspired imagination rather than historical tradition. It must be insisted, however, (a)

---

13. C.H. Talbert, *What is a Gospel?* (Philadelphia: Fortress, 1977) has argued for a close literary relationship between the gospels and Greco-Roman biographies. Despite important criticisms of Talbert's total thesis by D.E. Aune in R.T. France & D. Wenham (ed.), *Gospel Perspectives II* (Sheffield: JSOT Press, 1981) 9 – 60,

much of his comparative material is relevant to a literary categorization of the gospels.

14. See especially M.D. Goulder, *Midrash and Lection in Matthew* (London: SPCK, 1974); J. Drury, *Tradition and Design in Luke's Gospel* (London: Darton Longman & Todd, 1976).

that "midrash" (however that slippery word is defined) was far from being the dominant factor in Jewish writing about recent history, however strongly it may have influenced their retelling of ancient, sacred stories, and (b) that while the framework around which midrash was composed was a pre-existing sacred text, the framework of the gospels is a narrative about Jesus, into which scriptural elements may be introduced as the narrative suggests them, rather than vice versa. There may be much to be learned by comparing the gospel writers' methods with those of midrashists, but there is no meaningful sense in which the gospels in themselves can be described in literary terms as midrash.[15]

2.1.3 It is in fact widely agreed that there is no pre-existing literary category into which the gospels will fit. While they may use elements of existing techniques, and may in various respects resemble other genres, in themselves they are *sui generis,* a specifically Christian literary development. This means that their aims and methods are to be assessed not by extrapolation from those of other literature, but by studying them in their own terms.

2.2 The *nature of the tradition* incorporated in the gospels.

2.2.1 The *length of time* between the events and their recording in the gospels is not much more than two generations, even on the latest dating now proposed. The majority of New Testament scholars still date Mark's gospel shortly before or shortly after AD 70, Matthew and Luke roughly 80 – 90, and John close to the end of the first century. No part of this scheme, however, is uncontested, both the relative dating of the gospels[16] and the overall period of their composition being increasingly debated. While J.A.T. Robin-

son's view that all the gospels were completed before AD 70 has few adherents in its entirety, many are now prepared to argue that both Matthew and Luke could have been written in the sixties (and therefore, for most scholars, Mark would be still earlier).[17] This would give barely more than one generation between the events and the final Synoptic record of them.

2.2.2 The view of the nature of the tradition during this period which has been dominant in twentieth-century scholarship has been that associated with *the form-critical school* of Rudolf Bultmann. According to this view most of the stories and sayings of Jesus were remembered as independent oral "pericopes," which were preserved or altered as the needs of the various churches required, with little concern for the historical basis of the material. During this oral period much was lost, much was changed, and much may have been added to the tradition which had no origin in the historical ministry of Jesus. When the material came to be written down and organized into a continous "narrative," the shape of this narrative was contributed by the writer's literary skill rather than by historical reminiscence. Thus what we may expect to find in the gospels is primarily the beliefs of the second- and third- generation churches, rather than the history of Jesus. Such historical material as may be preserved in the gospels must be specifically detected by the application of agreed "criteria of authenticity,"[18] on the assumption that what does not pass such a test may not be claimed as historical evidence for Jesus.

2.2.3 At the opposite extreme is what has come to be known as *the Scandinavian approach.*[19] This view is based on the observation that oral tradition as it was practised in rabbinic circles was by no means as fluid

---

15. *Gospel Perspectives III* (ed. France & Wenham; Sheffield: JSOT Press, 1983) is devoted to a critique of the approach to the gospels as "midrash".

16. In particular the recent revival of the Griesbach Hypothesis, which puts Matthew first and Mark last among the Synoptic Gospels. See especially W.R. Farmer, *The Synoptic Problem* (Dillsboro: Western North Carolina Press, 1976), and many subsequent studies.

17. For a recent and persuasive argument for a date in the early sixties for both Matthew and Luke see R.H. Gundry, *Matthew: A Commentary on His Literary and Theological Art* (Grand Rapids: Eerdmans, 1982) 559 – 609.

18. The standard approach, based on that of Bultmann, is set out in N. Perrin, *Rediscovering the Teaching of Jesus* (London: SCM, 1967) 38 – 47. For a full survey and criticism see R.H. Stein in France & Wenham (ed.), *Gospel Perspectives 1* (Sheffield: JSOT Press, 1980) 225 – 263.

19. This approach is associated particularly with the work of H. Riesenfeld and B. Gerhardsson. The most substantial work is B. Gerhardsson, *Memory and Manuscript* (Acta Seminarii Neotestamentici Upsaliensis 22; Uppsala, 1961), while the results of this study for the gospels are popularly presented in idem, *The Origins of the Gospel Traditions* (Philadelphia: Fortress, 1979).

as the form-critical approach suggests. Large tracts of legal and other teaching material were memorized verbatim, and transmitted unaltered from generation to generation by men specially trained for the purpose. It is suggested that Jesus selected and trained his apostles as guardians of a tradition which was designed for easy memorization, a tradition which included not only his teaching but also key incidents of his ministry. On this view we have in the gospels not the result of a haphazard process, but the tradition as Jesus intended it to be remembered. This view has rightly been criticized on the grounds that Jesus and his disciples were not apparently a rabbinic school dealing in legal formulae, that much of what we have in the gospels is more in the nature of anecdote than of formal tradition, and that in any case a verbatim transmission is ruled out by the considerable variations between accounts of the same incident or teaching in the different gospels. It is, however, questionable whether the original proponents of this approach ever intended such an exact analogy between the gospels and the products of rabbinic schools. But they have done us the service of reminding us that in the Jewish world oral tradition is not synonymous with unreliability. Their study has recently been extended to the area of Jewish primary education, where the same emphasis on accurate memorization has been observed.[20] In such a milieu we might expect a much closer relationship between the gospel records and the historical ministry of Jesus than form-criticism has typically envisaged.

2.2.4 A recent modification of this approach has been to compare the gospel traditions with the phenomena of *informal tradition in a Middle Eastern peasant culture*.[21] Here, while the formal controls of rabbinic tradition are lacking, and in some types of oral material a considerable degree of latitude may be allowed in the telling of a story, the main structure and key phrases, sayings, etc. are fixed by community memory to the extent that however often a story may be told in different circles with varying detail or coloring, it will still remain in all essentials the same story, with the same punch line etc., as when it started. Other material in such a culture will have a more unvarying form, where the exact words matter, as in proverbs or poems. This mixture, it is suggested, is closer to the phenomena of the gospels than either of the previously considered approaches, and encourages a strong confidence in the essential reliability of the gospels while allowing for a considerable variation in detail which gives full play to the individual personality and views of each gospel writer.

2.2.5 It should be noted that all these models assume an essentially or even entirely *oral* tradition for most of the period before the writing of the gospels. This is an assumption which should at least be questioned. There is no *a priori* reason why written records of Jesus' teaching and actions may not have been preserved from shortly after the events themselves. Most scholars in fact speak of a written source or sources (in addition to Mark) used by Matthew and Luke. It is not clear why this lost "document" (known for convenience as "Q") should be the only or the earliest such record. May we not give more weight to Luke's statement (Luke 1:1) that "many" had already attempted to compile accounts of Jesus' ministry?

2.3 The *roots of skepticism* as to the historical value of the gospels.

2.3.1 *Problems in harmonizing with external data.* A notorious case is Luke's reference to a Roman census under the governorship of Quirinius at the time of Jesus' birth. The historical problems are well known, and the case against Luke's accuracy here is a strong one.[22] But such problems are few, because in the nature of the case the vast majority of the content of the gospels simply does not overlap with secular history. It should be pointed out, moreover, that the same Luke whose

---

20. R. Riesner, *Jesus als Lehrer* (WUNT 7; Tubingen: J.C.B. Mohr, 1981).

21. In a significant paper by K.E. Bailey entitled "Informal, Controlled Oral Tradition and the Synoptic Gospels", *Themelios* 20/2 (Jan 1995), 4–11.

22. The case against Luke is forcefully put in the classic excursus in E. Schurer, *op. cit.,* vol. I pp. 339–427. For an assessment more favourable to Luke see I.H. Marshall, *The Gospel of Luke* (New International Greek Testament Commentary; Grand Rapids: Eerdmans, 1978) 99–104.

work is criticized on account of the census problem also wrote the Acts of the Apostles, where the overlap with recorded history is far greater, and in this area Luke's accuracy in referring to the details of political institutions and appointments in Asia Minor and Greece was sufficient to cause the archeologist Sir William Ramsay to change from an inherited skepticism to a warm regard for Luke as a careful and responsible historian.[23] The bearing of external data on the historical reliability of the gospel writers is not all in one direction.

2.3.2 *Problems in harmonization between the gospels.* Perhaps the most notorious example here is that of the four gospels' accounts of the finding of the empty tomb, and of Jesus' subsequent appearances to selected disciples. It is well known that the details of these stories vary so widely that most scholars have declared any complete harmonization impossible. Be that as it may, it should not be allowed to obscure the fact that the essential story, the finding of an empty tomb early on the first day of the week by women who had reason to expect to find the body of Jesus there, is common to all the accounts. The same is true in general of discrepancies between the gospels: they concern details rather than the essential content (and in most cases the discrepancy in detail is far less than in the case of the resurrection stories). Often the discrepancy is over the apparent chronological order of the events — but it is questionable how far a chronological order is always what the writers intended in the first place. Generally the narrative discrepancies are of the type mentioned above in Middle Eastern story-telling, which leave the essential storyline unaffected. Problems of harmonization are the regular experience of any ancient historian who is fortunate enough to have two sources to compare, and do not in themselves lead him to question the integrity of his sources. Interpreters of the gospels will differ over the weight they assign to such discrepancies, but it would be hard to justify the view that they are sufficient to cast doubt on the essential portrait of Jesus which the gospels share.

2.3.3 *Theology and history.* Modern study of the gospels has rightly emphasized the role of the gospel writers as theologians. They are not dispassionate compilers of traditions, but write with a message to convey. Their theological interpretation of Jesus and his teaching can be discerned in the distinctive way each has "angled" his account, both in order to draw out aspects of Jesus which are important to the author himself, and also in order to make the record relevant to the needs and interests of the church for which he is writing. From this observation it has seemed a natural step to some to assume that their theological motivation has taken precedence over, or even eliminated, their historical interest. The simplistic equation, "If a theologian then not a historian," while seldom explicit, seems to have been at the root of much recent writing on the gospels. It need only be stated to be seen to be absurd. There is no logical incompatibility between having an axe to grind (whether theological or other) and writing careful and accurate history. Indeed it may be questioned how many of the world's great historians have been dispassionate chroniclers, with no message to convey to their readers other than the bare facts.

2.3.4 *The perspective of early Christianity.* The belief that the gospel materials would have been significantly modified and expanded during the period between Jesus' life and the writing of the gospels presupposes that primitive Christianity was unconcerned with the historicity of its traditions. It supposes that when a story or saying was presented in a significantly altered form, this would either not have been noticed, or would have been accepted and approved, and no one would have objected, "But it wasn't like that." Such a view fits well with a modern existentialist philosophy for which faith must be independent of history, and truth consists more in the effect on the hearer than in correspondence with the way things happened. But it is questionable how far such a view fits the concerns of early Christianity, as we can reconstruct them from the New Testament itself.[24] It may be suggested that

---

23. See W.W. Gasque, *Sir William M. Ramsay: Archeologist and New Testament Scholar* (Grand Rapids: Baker, 1966).

24. For interest in the "biography" of Jesus in the first century church see G.N. Stanton, *op. cit.*; also C.F.D. Moule, *The Phenomenon of the New Testament* (London: SCM, 1967) 100–114.

the more immediately applicable models are those proposed above of the Jewish world of Jesus' day and of the continuing values of Middle Eastern peasant culture. Here "getting the facts right" is an essential part of good teaching and story-telling, and it must be proved rather than assumed that this was not also the case in the early Christian church.

2.3.5 *The supernatural dimension.* Undoubtedly the most powerful motive for questioning the historical reliability of the gospels has been the fact that they record ideas and events which are foreign to most modern Western scholars' conception of what may be accepted as "historical." At the narrative level we find angels, miracles, the raising of the dead, a visionary experience of Jesus speaking with men who died centuries earlier, and Jesus' own bodily resurrection. At the level of thought, the gospels envisage a God who controls events, to whom man is accountable, with a future prospect of heaven or hell, and Jesus as the one who determines a man's destiny. Here is a total world-view with which modern secular culture cannot be comfortable, and which in the view of many scholars has forfeited any claim to be regarded as "historical." Even if the men of those days believed in such a world, modern science would seem to rule out such happenings, and those who wrote as if such things really happened are *ipso facto* discredited as purveyors of history. But it is a matter of fact that there are many in the world today, yes even in the scholarly world, for whom such a world-view is not excluded. They may have doubts about this or that specific incident or saying, but they would regard the *a priori* exclusion of the "supernatural" dimension as a dogmatic prejudice. The issue thus boils down ultimately to a difference of views not only over literary conventions or tradition technique but more fundamentally over the view of reality which the gospels presuppose.

2.4 On such grounds as we have noted, it may be argued that at the level of their literary and historical character we have good reason to treat the gospels seriously as a source of information on the life and teaching of Jesus, and thus on the historical origins of Christianity. Ancient historians have sometimes commented that the degree of skepticism with which New Testament scholars approach their sources is far greater than would be thought justified in any other branch of ancient history.[25] Indeed many ancient historians would count themselves fortunate to have four such responsible accounts, written within a generation or two of the events, and preserved in such a wealth of early manuscript evidence as to be, from the point of view of textual criticism, virtually uncontested in all but detail.[26] Beyond that point, the decision as to how far a scholar is willing to accept the record they offer is likely to be influenced more by his or her openness to a "supernaturalist" world-view than by strictly historical considerations.

3. Conclusion

If the argument sketched out above is valid, any responsible reconstruction of Christian origins must find its starting-point in the first-century gospel records, not in the hints of an alternative view of Jesus contained in second-century literature from the Gnostic wing of Christianity, nor in the attempt to assimilate Jesus to non-Christian parallels in the history of religions. The four canonical gospels will not answer all the questions we would like to ask about the founder of Christianity; but, sensitively interpreted, they do give us a rounded portrait of a Jesus who is sufficiently integrated into what we know of first-century Jewish culture to carry historical conviction, but at the same time sufficiently remarkable and distinctive to account for the growth of a new and potentially world-wide religious movement out of his life and teaching.

25. A.N. Sherwin-White, *Roman Society and Roman Law in the New Testament* (Oxford University Press, 1963) 186 – 192. Cf. the remarks of the Hanson brothers in A.T. Hanson (ed.), *Vindications* (London: SCM, 1966) 41f, 94f.

26. Two significant passages in the traditional text of the gospels are textually doubtful, viz. Mark 16:9 – 20 and John 7:53 – 8:11. What is significant is that it is precisely as exceptions that these two stand out. No other passage of more than a verse or two is seriously contested as part of the original text.

CHAPTER 32

Archaeology and the Old Testament

Eugene Carpenter

Archaeological endeavors in the Middle East go as far back as Napoleon's ventures into Egypt (1798), where he took with him a team of specialists to record its ancient wonders and marvels. The Rosetta Stone (1799) was discovered; the study of its three languages provided an unexpected key to the decipherment of Egyptian hieroglyphics by Thomas Young (1819) and Jean-Francois Champollion (1822). When this success was reported, it stirred new interest in the ancient world. In fact, it opened a veritable floodgate of interest into the wonders of the Ancient Near East (ANE) and, especially, into the light those wonders might shed upon the best known and greatest religious, literary, and historical production of the ANE — the Bible. The ancient Akkadian Semitic language was soon deciphered (Rawlinson, 1845) using the Behistun Inscription (518 B.C.) that was, interestingly, also inscribed in three languages. Other ancient languages were also soon deciphered.

After that, "biblical archaeology," a subset of Syria-Palestinian archaeology, soon prospered and drew worldwide attention. Archaeologists, scholars, and treasure hunters were amazed at the discovery of creation stories, flood stories, legal documents, law codes, ancient civilizations (e.g., Hittites) and additional languages, religious and theological epics and rituals, sacrificial rituals, plans for tabernacles, plans for temples, palaces, wisdom literature, covenants and covenantal forms, war stories and manuals of religions, birth stories of famous kings, king lists, pagan prophetic activity, annalistic literature, omen literature, and much more. These massive and revealing discoveries have over the decades pulled back the curtain of antiquity and revealed the ANE world of the Old Testament.

These texts and artifacts have helped shape and set the agenda for the study and understanding of the Old Testament.

Since the Old Testament is an ANE monumental document itself — an ANE book and artifact — this is not really surprising. The growth of archaeological methodology has been slow, and the placing of the ANE discoveries into distinct archaeological eras has been laborious. The results have influenced biblical studies and have led to a better understanding of the biblical texts and their world. Although these divisions are constantly under further refinement, some key eras have been labeled: the *Bronze Age* (Early Bronze, 3200 – 2200 B.C.; Middle Bronze, 2200 – 1550 B.C.; Late Bronze, 1550 – 1200 B.C.), *Iron Age* (roughly 1200 – 586 B.C.), *Persian Age* (538 – 332 B.C.), *Greek (Hellenistic) Age* (332 – 68 B.C.), and *Roman Era* (68 B.C.). Many of the major texts and artifacts that have been discovered and that touch upon the Old Testament in some significant way are listed in the chart below. Most of these items are texts, but even texts must be interpreted, to say nothing of the challenge of interpreting a mute artifact. In the list below, canonical compositions, monumental inscriptions, and archival documents are included.

The methods, perspectives, and approaches employed to do archaeology have made significant progress over the past two centuries. The scientific study of ancient "tells" (mounds of dirt and cultural debris compacted together to form strata over the centuries and millennia that witness to the various times when these tells were occupied by humans) began with W. F. Flinders Petrie (1890) in Palestine when he adopted and used methods H. Schliemann had used at ancient Troy in modern day Turkey. According to this approach, the various strata or layers of occupation of a tell are unearthed, analyzed, placed in a broad context and interpreted.

From Petrie's day to about 1950 archaeology in Palestine flourished. "Treasure hunting" was now over and appropriate goals, concerns and scientific techniques, tools, purposes, skilled experts, and improved record keeping developed. From 1950 until today an architectural approach and method pioneered by Wheeler-Kenyon (the extensive use of case balks) continued to evolve. Today a combination of these methods is usually employed. But, more than ever, multicultural and interdisciplinary activities are plugged into these basic methodologies. Scholars from many disciplines now take part in an archaeological expedition (paleographers, linguists, osteologists, geologists, zoologists, pottery experts, surveyors, satellite technology, technical dating devices, etc.), and archaeological teams are often international in flavor. More recently "surface surveying" examines whole regions; these surface surveys have proven quite productive, and large areas of Syria-Palestine have been covered with good results that help indicate where more detailed excavations would be most fruitful.

Archaeology at the end of the twentieth century and the beginning of the twenty-first century is enjoying, but is also frustrated by, a huge information explosion of both artifacts and texts. These artifacts and texts must be deciphered and interpreted by persons living in our era and competent to exercise judgment in doing so. Every item must be placed into its larger Syria-Palestinian context and, for biblical studies, must be cautiously placed in a proper relationship to relevant biblical materials. Properly identified and interpreted archaeological materials may *illustrate, illuminate, demonstrate, and (sometimes at some level) confirm or challenge* certain aspects of a biblical text and its worldview. And it remains humbling to realize that the context of a given text or artifact may never be totally available to us. Moreover, usually these same texts or artifacts cannot be used at a theological level to "prove" the specific religious/theological claims

of a biblical text, but may surround a particular text with a supportive world that illuminates and suggests strongly the veracity, historically and theologically, of the text in question. These materials can make plausible and confirm certain historical perspectives and claims of biblical texts.

The following list is not complete, and there is no other way to experience these texts except to read them. All the texts listed below are available in English translation and reading them begins to open up a window of perception that illuminates and illustrates many of the texts of the Old Testament. On the literary level alone, these texts illustrate the multiplicity of literary genres through which the Old Testament world is richly and effusively presented. On the other hand, an encounter with these texts also, just as helpfully, reveals the contrasts that the documents of the Old Testament exhibit when set against their ANE counterparts, both in thought and in form and style.

This list of key ANE texts and artifacts has helped scholars paint, with a broad brush at least (and in some cases with some detail), a broad backdrop of worldviews that were present during the time of the Old Testament across the centuries and millennia — worldviews that help place the Old Testament into a context that enables us to better understand its history, its literary qualities, and even its theological claims and perspectives. From this impressive accumulation of ANE data, some scholars have attempted to present at least preliminary contours of the world of the Old Testament. This is buttressed firmly by the facts from this huge cache of ANE materials that make the reliability of the Old Testament arguably firm and trustworthy, especially so given the literary and historiographical perspectives of its narratives. Certain of these materials show Israel as a fellow participant in the ANE of her day, yet also distinct from that world at crucial points where they intersect. She shared in the worldviews of those cultures and eras. But just as firmly certain materials, texts and artifacts show striking contrasts between Israel and the world in which she lived — a world in which she believed that her God, Yahweh, guided her and (continued, p. 307)

Key Ancient Archaeological Texts and Artifacts Relating to the Old Testament

Title/Topic	Date Found/ Published	Date of Artifact	Provenance	Description	Ancient Sources (English Translation)	OT References
Enuma Elish	1848–76	Ca. 1000 B.C.	Nineveh, Ashur, Kish	**Akkadian:** Hymn: cosmology, Marduk, creation, ordering of creation, humans created.	COS 1.111 / ANET, 60–72, 501–3 / RANE #6	Gen. 1–2
Gilgamish Epic	1872; 1930, 1933	1900 B.C.	Sumer, Babylon	**Sumerian; Akkadian:** flood, death, divine/human, Utnapishtim, search for life, Babylonian Noah.	COS 1.132 / DBA ANET, 72–98 / OTP, **11–20** / RANE 66–70	Gen. 3, 6–9. Noah, Ark
Sumerian King Lists	1923	Ca. 18th Cent. B.C.	Sumer	**Sumerian:** Kingship from the gods; Kings before flood, long life spans; illustrates literary structure of O.T.	ANET, 265–66 / RANE, #45 / ROT, 423, 441–47 / OTP, 21–32	Gen. 5; Gen. 1–11; cf. kingship in Deut., 1 Sam. 8, 12
Hymn to Enlil	1959	2000–1595 B.C.	Nippur	**Sumerian:** A powerful hymn to the god over the gods, Enlil, in Nippur, in the temple Ekur. He is praised as the shepherd and keeper of all mankind, all things. The gods cannot look upon him.	ANET, 573–76 / Cf. RANE, #74	Illustrates the praise given to gods; cf. various Pss in OT
Hymn to Shamash	1889, 1901	Late 2d Millennium B.C.	Babylon	**Akkadian:** Hymns that praise the sun god, Shamash, who is the keeper of justice, including just weights and measures.	COS 1.117 / RANE, #75 / ANET, 387–89	OT concern for justice, just business dealings; Lev. 19:15; Deut. 25–13–16
Memphite Creation	Ca. 1830	2700 B.C.	Memphis, Egypt	**Egyptian:** Creation by heart/tongue, creation spoken into creation through senses; god Ptah.	COS 1.15 / RANE 62–65 / ANET, 4–6 / OTP, **3–6**	Gen. 1–2
Ra and The Serpent	1936	2400 B.C.	Thebes, Egypt	**Egyptian:** Pictures the Sun and a Serpent in opposition to each other; Ra creates in communion with his heart and humans come from his tears; serpent goes on its belly.	OTP, 28–31 / ANET, 6–7 / COS 1.9; 1.21	Gen. 1:1–2:4a / Gen. 3
Seven Year Famines (Famine Stele)		2700 B.C. (text: Ptolemaic Era)	Sehel Island	**Egyptian:** 7 years of famine motif; theological issues between Pharaoh/god involved; tradition is found elsewhere as well.	ANET, 31–2 / COS 1.53	Gen. 12:41
Beni Hassan	1902–1904	2000 B.C	Beni Hassan, Egypt	**Picture:** Presents a group of 37 people coming to Egypt from Palestine to sell eye paint. Helps recreate, illustrate, and illuminate the world of patriarchs. Some suggest patriarchal culture and dress is well illustrated here.	AOT, 94	Possible culture, lives, appearance of patriarchs / Gen. 12–50

Title/Topic	Date Found/ Published	Date of Artifact	Provenance	Description	Ancient Sources (English Translation)	OT References
Tale of Two Brothers	1855	1225 B.C.	Egypt	**Egyptian:** Brother rejects advances of sister-in-law.	ANET, 23 – 25 COS 1.40	Gen. 39; Joseph
Dream Interpretation	1935	1300 B.C. (or much earlier, 2000 B.C.)	Thebes	**Egyptian:** A short list of how to interpret a dream that concerns oneself in a dream.	ANET, 495 COS 1.33	Gen. 40 – 41 and Joseph's dream interpretations
Dream Omens/Oracles	1954 1850 1871	Ca. 1350 B.C. Ca. 1050 B.C. 648 B.C.	Ugarit Cairo Ashur	**Ugaritic:** Seems to attempt to conceive the world in terms of dreams. **Egyptian:** A dream sent from a god reveals to Thutmose IV that he will be king if he removes sand from Sphinx. **Akkadian:** A seer's dream/vision reveals to Ashurbanipal that as king Ishtar would favor him and give him success in war and politics.	COS 1.93 ANET, 449 ANET, 451	Shows the importance of dreams in the ANE and in the OT: prophets, revelation
Gudea Temple Instructions	1877, 1900	Late 3d Millennium B.C.	Sumer	**Sumerian:** Two cylinders give the dream conditions under which Gudea received a command and instructions to build a temple for his god Ningirsu of Lagash. It is an extensive temple building document.	COS 2.155 ANET, 268 – 9 ANETOT, 63	Cf. 2 Sam. 7 – 8; 1 Kgs. 6 and also the instructions for the Tabernacle in Exod. 25 – 31, 35 – 40
Sargon Legend		3d Millennium B.C.	Sumer	**Akkadian:** Sargon I, rescued from river in a reed basket; certain other comparisons and contrasts to Moses' birth and rescue.	COS 1.133 RANE 75 – 6 OTP, 55 – 8 ANET, 119	Exod. 2
Construction of New Temple	1906	13th Century B.C.	Hattusus	**Hittite:** A record describing the construction of a new temple setting for a goddess.	COS 1.70	Cf. construction of Tabernacle and Temple in OT (Exod., 1 Kgs., Ezra)
Rituals Against Reptiles	1929 – 37	1350 B.C.	Ugarit	**Ugaritic:** Records requests to 12 gods to render serpent's venom powerless, but only the final 12th ritual is effective.	COS 1.94	Various refs. to serpents in OT, but note Num. 21:4 – 9; Deut. 32:33
Hittite Treaties	1903 – 10	1400 – 1200 B.C.	Anatolia; Hattusus (Turkey)	**Hittite:** Illustrates covenantal forms evidenced in covenants of ANE and OT. Rameses II & Hattusilus III's covenant is a good example out of many (30+).	ANET, 199 – 206, 529 – 41; 659 – 61 COS 2.17 – 8; 2.82; 2.127 – 9; RANE 97 – 100 OTP, 49 – 54	Deut., Josh. 24; Exod. 19 – 24
Laws of Hammurabi	1901	1750 B.C. (and earlier)	Susa	**Akkadian:** ANE laws that parallel (contrast & compare) Mosaic Laws; includes prologue and epilogue.	ANET, 163 – 79 OTP, 62 – 7; RANE 111 – 14 COS 2.131	Deut. 12 – 26 Exod. 20 – 24 Lev. 16 – 26, etc.

Title/Topic	Date Found/Published	Date of Artifact	Provenance	Description	Ancient Sources (English Translation)	OT References
Merneptah Stele	1896	1209 B.C.	Thebes, Egypt	**Egyptian:** 1st mention of Israel outside of OT. Pharaoh Merneptah; huge monument recording massive campaigns of this Pharaoh.	ANET, 376–78; OTP, 81–4; COS 2.6; RANE #50	Joshua; entrance into Canaan (ca. 1400/1200 B.C.)
Herem: A Thing Devoted	1906	13th Century B.C.	Hattusus	**Hittite:** Records installation of Storm god and things and persons "devoted" to him for destruction/use. Mesha Inscription describes Mesha's devotion of Nebo to his god Chemosh for destruction.	COS 1.72; Cf. Stele of Mesha, Moabite Stone below and entries there; also found at Mari	Similar to the "herem" or ban in Joshua of the cities/peoples "devoted to the Lord"
Hittite Laws	Ca. 1893	1650–1200 B.C.	Hattusus	**Hittite:** Laws that compare/contrast to OT laws; contain casuistic laws arranged by topics; scapegoat laws and levirate laws present.	OTP, 70–2; ANET, 188–196; COS 2.19; RANE 115–16	Exod. 19–24; Deut. 12–26; Lev. 17–26, etc.
Urim and Thummin	1906	1250–1200 B.C.	Hattusus	**Hittite:** Omen text relating the use of extipicy/bird omens to discover the god's will using a "favorable/unfavorable" options scheme.	COS 1.78	Use of Urim and Thummin, Exod. 28:30; Lev. 8:8; Deut. 33:8; Ezra 2.63; Neh. 7:65
Urim and Thummin	1992	650 B.C. 833, 823 B.C.	Assur, Assyria	**Akkadian:** First text describes a divination process using two stones, one white, one black. Second text describes use of lots to choose a limmu leader in Assyria.	COS 1.127; COS 2.1130	Use of Urim and Thummin, Exod. 28:30; Lev. 8:8; Deut. 33:8; Ezra 2.63; Neh. 7:65; Esth. 3:7
Urim and Thummin		Ca. 1287	Egypt	**Egyptian:** During the time of Rameses II, this text describes how a god could indicate his desire by a visible sign, yes/no.	ANET, 448	Use of Urim and Thummin, Exod. 28:30; Lev. 8:8; Deut. 33:8; Ezra 2.63; Neh. 7:65
Story of Aqhat	1929–37	1350 B.C.	Ugarit	**Ugaritic:** Illustrates Canaanite literature, poetry, gods, religion, importance of royal heir; mentions Noah, Job, Danel.	OTP, 85–94; ANET, 149–55; COS 1.103; RANE #19	Judg.; pre-Israel cultural and religious aspects of Canaan; patriarchal need for heirs; Daniel in Ezek. 4; 14; 28; Dan. 1–12
Gezer Alphabet/Calendar	1908	900 B.C.	Gezer	**Canaanite (old Hebrew):** Oldest example and illustrates writing, letters of that era; agricultural cycles.	OTP, 104–8; ANET, 320; COS 2.85; RANE 171	Agricultural picture of OT is helpful; linguistic data helpful
Travels of Sinuhe	1916	1800–1000 B.C.	Egypt	**Egyptian:** This narrative includes descriptions of Canaan and Syria and the people; it is considered a novella by many; promotes Egyptian life; shows an Egyptian "in exile" in Canaan.	ANET, 18–22; COS 1.38; OTP, 129–33; RANE 76–82	Gen. 12–50; Joseph esp. Literary, cultural insights

Title/Topic	Date Found/Published	Date of Artifact	Provenance	Description	Ancient Sources (English Translation)	OT References
Travels of Wenamun	1899	1090 B.C.	Egypt	**Egyptian:** Travels of Wenamun includes descriptions of Canaan and insights into culture, religion, prophets; some burial customs; caution is needed since it is semi-fictional.	ANET, 25–9 COS 1.41 OTP, 323–30 RANE #83	Gen. 34; general cultural milieu in certain sections of patriarchal narratives
Shoshenk I, Inscription	1825	920 B.C.	Egypt, Karnak Temple	**Egyptian:** Shoshenk (Shishak) raids/invades/quells Palestine, removes wealth from Jerusalem; provides lists of cities in this area, including Israelite cities.	ANET, 242–43, ROT, 63–4 AOT, 300–2 ATSHB, 390	1 Kgs. 11:40; 14:25–28
Stele of Mesha, King of Moab Moabite Stone	1868	850 B.C.	Dibon, Moab	**Moabite:** Omri, Ahab, and King Mesha listed, house of David (possible); national theology of Moab toward their god Chemosh is set forth to compare/contrast to Israel's; use of "devoted to destruction" (cherem) is present.	ANET, 320–1 COS 2.23 OTP, 157–9 RANE #51; ROT, 92–3	Deut. 7:26; Josh. "cherem" 6:17, 40; 1 Kgs. 11:44 (16:21–28)–2 Kgs. (3:4) 25:30
Black Obelisk	1846	827 B.C.	Calah, Assyria	**Akkadian:** Describes success0r of Shalmaneser III; Jehu, Ahab involved; Jehu (or envoy) pays tribute to Shalmaneser.	OTP, 122–24 COS 2.113f ANET, 281 RANE #4	1 Kgs. 19:16; 2 Kgs. 8:7–15; 9:1–13; 10:31–36
Annals of Sargon II	1843–54	Ca. 722 B.C.	Khorsabad, Assyria	**Akkadian:** Sargon II conquers Samaria; takes 27,290 prisoners and many chariots; deported Israelites.	OTP, 127–29 RANE #42 ANET, 284–87 COS 2.118	2 Kgs. 17:3–6; 18:11
Siloam Inscription	1880	701 B.C.	Jerusalem	**Hebrew:** Describes completion of Hezekiah's tunnel; incidentally records the earliest use of matres lectionis in Hebrew.	OTP, 130–1 RANE, 171–2 ANET, 321 COS 2.28	2 Kgs. 20:20 2 Chr. 32:30
Sennacherib Prism	1830	701 B.C.	Nineveh	**Akkadian:** Describes Sennacherib's siege of Jerusalem and raiding of 46 other cities.	ANET, 287–88 COS 2.119b OTP, 139–40 RANE, #43	2 Kgs. 18–20 Isa. 36:1–39:8
Lachish Ostraca	1935 1938	589–586 B.C.	Tell ed Duwer/ Lachish	**Hebrew:** Over 19 letters describe the plight of those under siege by Assyrians and also give glimpses of royal military administration and personal issues; reading is evidenced as a skill and a portion of a prophet's name may refer to Jeremiah.	ANET, 321–22 COS 3.42 a-f OTP, 134–36 RANE #56 ATSHB, 460	1 Kgs. 17:19; 19:7 Jer. 26:20–22; 34:6–7 Language and literary issues are gleaned from these meager documents

Title/Topic	Date Found/Published	Date of Artifact	Provenance	Description	Ancient Sources (English Translation)	OT References
Kuntillet Ajrud Texts (Graffiti)	1975–76	9th–8th Century B.C.	Northwest Sinai	**Hebrew, Phoenician:** Texts illustrate well the syncretism and trafficking against; prophets of Israel railed against; graffiti-like figures of the Egyptian God Bes on jars; Yahweh name with "his" consort mentioned.	ROT, 413–15, 588–89; IR, 283–89	Illuminates the mixed nature of the religion of certain Israelites' beliefs in the OT; Yahweh/Baal identity seems likely; influence of Asherah in OT illuminated
Baruch's Seal	1975	Ca. 600 B.C.	Jerusalem	A clay seal found with Baruch's name; other seals (bulla) bear names found in Jeremiah.	AOT, 364	Jer. 36, 40
Babylonian Chronicles	1887	745 to late Seleucid era B.C.	Babylon	**Akkadian:** Yearly records covering reign of Nabopolassar and first 13 years of Nebuchadnezzar's reign: deportation of Jehoiachin in 597 B.C. Certain years of the chronicle are especially helpful: 727, 722, 681, 605, 598/97, and 539. Cyrus' conquest of Babylon is recorded.	ANET, 301–7; 563–4; COS 1.137; OTP, 182–4; RANE #49	1 Kgs. 2:10; 11:43; 2 Kgs. 17:3–6; 18:8–12; 19:37; 20:12; 24:1–7, 10–17; Jer. 37:1; Dan. 5:30; 6:28
Nabonidas and His God	1956	556–539 B.C.	Harran	**Akkadian:** Depicts the last Babylonian king in his "apostasy" worshipping the moon god Sin.	ANET, 312–14; 562–3; COS 1.89	General background of Babylonian period: Daniel's exile, 4; Dan. 5, Belshazzar
Babylonian Administrative Document	1938	595–568 B.C.	Babylon	**Akkadian (cf. Chronicles above):** Certain documents describe the good fortune of Jehoiachin, exiled king of Judah, and his recognition at the court of Evil-Merodach, Babylonian king in 561 B.C. along with several other persons.	ANET, 308; ATSHB, 378–9	2 Kgs. 25:27–30
Nabonidus' Recognition of Sin as Supreme God	1976	6th Century B.C.	Ur, Ziggurat of Ur	**Akkadian:** Records Nabonidus' rebuilding of Zizzurat of Ur and his recognition of Sin ("gods") as god of gods, which demotes Marduk. Belshazzar, his son, is mentioned.	COS 2.123B	Background of pre-exilic period in Babylon; Dan. 5
Nabonidus Chronicle	1882	556–539 B.C.	Babylon	**Akkadian:** Relates the stay of Nabonidus, last king of Babylon, in Tema and his final return to Babylon; fall of Babylon; fate of Nabonidus.	ANET, 305–7; COS 1.89 (cf.)	Dan. 5 Belshazzar; background for Daniel and Babylonian era
Cyrus Cylinder	1879	518 B.C.	Babylon	**Akkadian:** Records conquest of city of Babylon 586/7 B.C. and gives his theological explanation of the events. His policies allowed Jews and all other conquered peoples to return to their homelands and rebuild temples and worship.	ANET, 315–16; COS 2.124; OTP, 193–95; RANE #44	Dan. 5:30; 6:28; II Chron. 36:22–23; Ezra 1:1–4; 6:1–15; Isa. 44:26–8
Elephantine Papyri	1907	5th Century B.C.	Elephantine, Egypt	**Aramaic:** Describes religious, everyday, and political life among Jews who fled to Egypt after fall of Jerusalem. Communication with Jews in Samaria and Judah. Temple in Egypt built/demolished. Dream report is recorded on an ostracon.	ANET, 222, 491, 548–9; COS 3.51; 3.52; 3.53; 3.68, 3.88	cf. Ezra, Neh., Hag.; cf. Daniel 2; 4; 7:28; 10; Jer. 42–44

Title/Topic	Date Found/Published	Date of Artifact	Provenance	Description	Ancient Sources (English Translation)	OT References
Dead Sea Scrolls	1947	3d Century B.C. – 1st Century A.D.	Northwest corner of Dead Sea	**Aramaic, Hebrew, Greek:** Some of oldest copies of OT mss and many extra-canonical documents; documents help us understand the state of OT mss in this era and the social-religious structures of this era.	*Dead Sea Scroll Bible*; The Dead Sea Scrolls in translation, Vermes, etc.	Insights into various ways this group interpreted the biblical texts for their era; linguistic insights
The Shipwrecked Sailor	1927	2040 – 1640 B.C.	Egypt (original provenance unknown)	**Middle Egyptian:** Narrates a story of a sailor's misfortune but eventual recovery and deliverance; fictional elements illustrate a moral to follow.	COS 1.39 AEL, 1:211 – 14 ATSHB, 257 – 8	Narrative style and beauty; literary devices, features of OT world
Balaam Inscription	1967	700 B.C.	Deir 'Alla, Jordan	**Dialect of Aramaic:** The name Balaam, a "good prophet" in this text, recalls the Balaam of the OT. He also dies as a result of his actions as does Balaam in OT. Theological issues in general are raised.	COS 2.27 OTP, 124 – 6 RANE, #91	Lamentations Num. 22 – 24; 26; Gen. 6 – 8
Annals and Stele of Thutmose III	1940	1468 B.C.	Egypt	**Egyptian:** Describes his siege of Megiddo and other battles in Palestine using an Egyptian daybook scribal tradition. Divine intervention by god Ashur using a "star" or "light" is recorded.	ANET, 234 – 41 COS 2.2A, 2.2B OTP, 142 – 45 ROT, 175, 541 – 42	OT battle reports: Sam – Kgs; Josh. 1 – 6, 7 – 11; esp. 10:28 – 42; 11:10 – 14
Battle of Qadesh; Annals of Rameses II	1928, 1935	1275 B.C.	Egypt: On major temples in Egypt and Nubia	**Egyptian:** Description of the Battle of Qadesh in Syria; some find early "deuteronomistic" type theology in Rameses's attitude and actions toward his god, Amun. Use of numbers: millions, hundreds of thousands, etc. and idioms like a "locust-swarm" in number are informative.	COS 2.5 ROT, 255 – 56 ANET, 255	General background of divine intervention in war; deuteronomistic theology; hyperbolic use of numbers
Annals of Rameses III	Ca. 1800	Ca. 1200 B.C.	Egypt	**Egyptian:** Describes battle(s) of Rameses III with the Sea Peoples including the future Philistines.	ANET, 262 – 3 OTP, 151 – 54 ROT, 140 – 43; 535 – 6	Judg. 13:1 – 16:31; 1 – 2 Sam, Samuel/David stories
Weidner Chronicle	1926	Late 2d Millennium	Ashur and Sippar	**Akkadian:** A "theology of history" is embedded in these texts from Mesopotamia. The Marduk Temple and Babylon and their treatment is the key to historical success. Many see its historiography similar to the books of Josh.– 2 Kgs.	COS 1.138 RANE #47	Evaluation of kings in OT historiography of Israel and ANE: Kings, Chronicles
Limmu (Official) List Assyrian Eponym Canon	1941	910 – 612 B.C.	Assyria	**Akkadian:** A list across 300 years that records a selected official for each year. Both relative and absolute chronology (763 B.C. eclipse) are made possible with this list.	ANET, 274 COS 2.1131	OT dating by correlation: kings, events, etc.
Annals of Shalmaneser III	1846, 1861	Ca. 850 – 824 B.C.	Ashur	**Akkadian:** Describes the incursions of Shalmaneser III into Syria-Palestine. Ahab of Israel and Hadadezer of Syria are mentioned.	ANET, 276 – 81 COS 2.113A-H OTP, 176 – 81	1 Kgs. 16:29 – 22 2 Kgs. 9:1 – 10:33

Title/Topic	Date Found/Published	Date of Artifact	Provenance	Description	Ancient Sources (English Translation)	OT References
Annals of Sargon II	1843, 1852–4	721–706 B.C.	Khorsabad	**Akkadian:** These are illustrative of annalistic records kept by the Assyrian kings; the mention of broken treaties, idols and their indwelling gods, eunuchs, and tribute picture the political/religious inner-workings of the historical/religious thinking of those eras.	COS 2.118A ANET, 284–87 OTP 127–9 RANE #42	General historiography; 2 Kgs. 17:1–24; 18:1–2; Isa. 10:27–32; 14:4b–21; 20:1
Annals of Tiglath-Pileser IV (Pul)	1906–7	744–727 B.C.	Calah (Nimrud), Assyria	**Akkadian:** Records 17 years of this king's reign who founded the Neo-Assyrian Empire. His encounters with Israel are significant.	COS 2.117 ANET, 282–4 OTP, 125–6 RANE #41	Kings: Menahem, Pekah, Hoshea, 2 Kgs. 15–16; Isa. 7: 8:1–10; 2 Chr. 28:16–21; etc.
Mari	1933	18th Century B.C.	Mari (Tell Hariri) on Middle Euphrates River	**Akkadian:** Correspondence between famous kings: Zimri-Lim and Babylon; Habiru noted; conditions during patriarchal eras probably reflected. Prophetic texts and activity. Religious perspectives revealed. Includes female prophetesses. Contain various genres of archival materials; concept of herem is mentioned.	OTP, 318–22 ANETOT, 78 RANE #79 ANET, 482–3, 623–26	Sets forth a context for Israels' prophets for contrast, comparison overall. Terms for prophets are helpful; several other general concepts, such as herem
Emar	1972–76, 78	1550–1200 B.C	Emar on Euphrates River	**Akkadian:** Especially important for its ritual and religious texts. Legal texts are present. The *Zukru Festival* marking new beginnings for the year is especially important for a Syrian perspective on such a festival. Also *kissu* festivals are recorded for recognition of god(s).	COS 1.123; 1.126; 2.137 IR, 114–123	Especially: Lev. 8:30; 23; Num. 28–29; Deut. 16; 31; 32 Nabu, = OT term for prophet; cf. Passover, Unleavened Bread
Nuzi Tablets	1925–31	15th Century B.C.	Nuzi	**Hurrian (dialect of Akkadian):** Texts describe various social, religious, legal customs on familial and political levels. Often private documents. Private family pictures of Hurrians in Mitanni. Reflects practices from before *and* after the 15th century.	ANET, 219–20 COS 3.121 AOT, 102–3 RANE #14.	Provides a large backdrop for OT. Baal references and cult. Also Elijah, Elisha cycles.
Ugarit (Ras Shamra)	1929–37	15th Century B.C.	Ugarit	**Ugaritic:** Hundreds of tablets that help understand the religious milieu there and perhaps in Canaan. The Baal Cycle, Tale of Aqhat, Tale of Kirtu, are key religious texts, but many other texts are relevant: sacrifice, cult, ritual, mythology, pantheons, royal roles, tabernacle, culture – all these and more are included.	COS 1.88; 1.104 IR, 95–6; 97, 98–109, 204–5, 164–5, 156–7, 228, 328–9 OTP, 263–74	Provides a broad window for OT pagan religious practices: Baal refs. and cult; Elijah and Elisha cycles; literary significance; Baal/Yahweh contrasts and comparisons are helpful
Amarna Letters and Tell El-Amarna Tablets	1887	1550–1150 B.C.	Tell-el-Amarna	**Akkadian:** Letters (540) from kings in Palestine seeking help from Pharaoh Akhenaton against enemies & from Amenophis III. Habiru appear. Includes Canaanite words and phrases. "God of my father" mentioned in one text.	OTP, 77–80 IR, 94–5 TSB, Excursus 7.1 RANE 166–68	Reflect conditions in Canaan before or during Israel's arrival in Joshua and Judges. "God of my father" text

Title/Topic	Date Found/ Published	Date of Artifact	Provenance	Description	Ancient Sources (English Translation)	OT References
Ebla Archives	1968, 1974–76	Ca. 2500 B.C.	Ebla, Syria	**Sumerian, Eblaite:** A huge cache of texts that picture an important part of the pre-patriarchal biblical world in many areas of culture and history. "God of fathers" noted, various gods, some family deities.	OTP, 240–3; IR, 82–3, 148	Reflects larger world of Middle East in pre-patriarchal eras Gods of OT tied to Ebla gods is possible. Designation Nabi'utum, "prophet" attested.
Instructions of Ptah Hotep	1900	Ca. 2500 B.C.	Egypt	**Egyptian:** Gives the wisdom of one of Egypt's greatest wise men, who teaches his son using metaphor/analogy on how to succeed in life and vocation.	OTP, 283–88; ANET, 412–14; ATSHB, 67; RANE 182–4	Parallels in Proverbs, Ecclesiastes; esp. Prov. 2, 6, 23, 25, 26
Atrahasis Epic	1880	18th Cent. B.C.	Assyria	**(Sumerian: original) Akkadian:** Creation in place, multiplication of life, flood. Humans created to serve in hard labor for gods. God sends flood to wipe out a noisome humanity. A king builds a boat and rescues himself and humanity; a new era or beginning is recorded. (Also, the Eridu Genesis inscription).	COS 1.130; OTP, 31–40; RANE #5; ANET, 104–5, 512–14; ATSOT, 313	GEN. 1–11, esp. Ex. 2
Instructions for Amenemope	1926	7th–6th Century B.C.	Thebes, Egypt	**Egyptian:** This wisdom didactic literature encourages self-control, kindness, altruism, lack of covetousness. Its 30 chapters also stress the ideal man. Its composition was in the Ramesside era.	OTP, 274–82; COS 1.47; RANE #69; ANET, 421–25	Esp. Prov. 22–23; 24
Ludlul Bel Nemeqi	1929, 1960	2d Millennium B.C.	Babylon	**Akkadian:** The sufferings of a noble Babylonian are somewhat reminiscent of the biblical Job. He, like Job, is restored.	COS 1.153; ANET, 434, 596–600; RANE #64	Job; Wisdom; Pss.
Lament over City of Ur	1888	Ca. 2000 B.C.	Nippur	**Sumerian:** A person that laments the fall of the city of Ur, capital of Ur III empire, making it an early "genre" like Lamentations. A sense of abandonment by the gods is strong. Gives insights into Sumer.	COS 1.166; ANET, 455–63; 611–19; OTP, 247–55; RANE 222–25	Jer., Ezek., Lamentations (over) Jerusalem; Babylon; Ur from which Abraham came
Hymn to Aten (Son Disk)	1891; 1911–14	14th Century B.C.	Amarna, Egypt	**Egyptian:** A poem that praises the sun with terminology that recalls Psalm 104.	COS 1.28; ANET, 369–71; OTP, 257–61; RANE, #73	Psalm 104
Negative Confessions of Innocence	1937	500 B.C. and back to 2500 B.C.	Egypt	**Egyptian:** Shows a deceased person asserting their innocence by giving an exhaustive list of what they have not done.	ANET, 34–6; COS 2.12; OTP, 219–22	Background for the OT's assertion that after death, each person will be judged

Title/Topic	Date Found/Published	Date of Artifact	Provenance	Description	Ancient Sources (English Translation)	OT References
Mortuary Texts (Pyramid Texts, Coffin Texts, Book of the Dead, Tomb and Grave Inscriptions)	Various	2550 B.C. and after	Egypt	**Egyptian:** Various texts reveal what the ancient Egyptians thought about the final state of the deceased.	COS 2.8 – 14	Contrast and Comparison with the OT concept of Sheol, etc. and the final state of the deceased
Inanna's Descent to the Netherworld	1937, 1942	1st half of 2d Millennium B.C.	Nippur	**Sumerian:** The goddess descends into the netherworld and its character and contents are encountered along the way.	ANET, 52 – 57 COS 1:108	Cf. OT description of Sheol
Ishtar's Descent to Netherworld	1949, 1917	1st Millennium B.C.	Ashur, Nineveh	**Akkadian:** Borrows and transforms to some extent the Inanna classic text.	COS 1.108 ANET, 106 – 8 ANETOT, 45	Cf. OT description of Sheol
Middle Assyrian Laws	1903	12th Century B.C.	Assyria	**Akkadian:** Laws of the Middle-Assyrian Empire ca. 12th Century B.C.	COS 2.132 ANET, 180 – 8 OTP, 114 – 23 RANE, #31	Various laws in OT: Exod. 19 – 24; Deut. 12 – 26; Lev. 17 – 26
Lipit-Ishtar Laws	1948	19th Century B.C.	Babylonia	**Sumerian:** A collection of laws to compare/contrast to biblical laws; they also contain a prologue and epilogue.	COS 2.154 ANET, 159 – 60 RANE #106 – 109	Various laws in OT: Exod. 19 – 24; Deut. 12 – 26, etc.
Murashu Tablets	1898, 1904	5th Century B.C.	Nippur	**Akkadian:** Describes economic transactions between Murashu and Sons (Babylonian company) with Jews who remained in exile and other persons. Illustrates post exilic issues.	GS, 209 ATSHB, 41 ABD, 4:927 – 8	Insights in exile period, 538 – 404 B.C. Ezra-Neh.
Babylonian Theodicy	1960	Early 1st Millennium B.C.	Babylon	**Akkadian:** A sufferer and a companion engage each other in dialogue about life; classic issues of universal wisdom literature.	COS 1.154 ANET, 601 – 4 OTP, 223 – 28 RANE #65	Job, Eccl.
Dialogue of Pessimism	1960	Early 1st Millennium B.C.	Babylon	**Akkadian:** A slave and his master discuss the lack of real value in anything. Death is as good an option as any and is inevitable.	COS 1.155 ANET, 600 – 1	Job
Egyptian Love Poetry	1932, 1945	11th – 14th Century B.C.	Egypt	**Egyptian:** Fifty items in monologue form report in sensual exotic language.	ANET, 467 – 69; RANE 192 – 3 OTP, 297 – 301	Song of Songs (Solomon)
Specific Love Songs	1985	11th – 14th Century B.C.	Egypt	**Egyptian:** May be entertainment songs; boy, girl verbal exchanges featured and some monologue.	COS 1.49, 50, 51, 52	Song of Songs (Solomon)
Love Song to King	1947	2000 – 1500 B.C.	Nippur	**Sumerian:** A long song composed by a priestess in honor of the king, Shu Sin.	ANET, 496	Song of Songs and Love hymns in general in OT

Title/Topic	Date Found/Published	Date of Artifact	Provenance	Description	Ancient Sources (English Translation)	OT References
Ritual of Opening/ Washing of the Mouth	1960; 2001	1st Millennium B.C.; Old Kingdom	Babylon; Egypt	**Akkadian; Egyptian:** These are the classic texts describing the production of an image (idol) in Babylon and earlier (1600 B.C.) in Ur III to the beginning of its oracular life and the opening of the idol's mouth in Egypt.	ANETOT, 58. ATSHB, 147 – 49	Isa. 6; Isa. 40 – 55; idolatry in general in prophets; purification of prophets lips
Tell Dan Inscription	1993 – 4	Ca. 850 B.C.	Dan	**Aramaic:** This inscription contains the first reference to David outside the OT. The phrase is "house of David."	COS 2.39 OTP, 160 – 61 RANE #54 ROT, 17, 92 IR, 62, 199	Historical reign of David: 1 – 2 Sam., 1 Kgs., etc.; 1 Kgs. 19:16 – 17; 2 Kgs. 9 – 10; Hos. 1:4
Yavneh Yam (workman's plea)	1960	Late 7th Century	Mesad Hashavyahu	**Hebrew:** This short letter on an ostracon contains the request for a fieldworker to have his cloak returned to him which his supervisor had confiscated unjustly.	COS 3.41 RANE #58 OTP, 331 – 32	Ex. 22:25 – 5; Deut. 24:12 – 17; Prov. 14:9; 25:20
Sumerian Proverbs	1980, 1997	2600 – 2000 B.C.	Sumer/Assyria/ Babylon	**Sumerian:** Illustrates the ancient nature and subject matter of proverbs in the Ancient NE across cultures.	COS 1.174; 1.175	Proverbs; Ecclesiastes (Proverbs)
Hittite Proverbs	1960 1984 1986 1992	13th Century (?)	Hattusas	**Hittite:** Various proverbs scattered throughout Hittite literature and a bilingual wisdom text.	COS 1.81, 82	OT proverbs in general, Proverbs, Jer. 31:29; Ezek. 18:2
Wisdom of Ahiqar	1906	700 – 650 B.C.	Assyrian Court	**Aramaic:** In addition to an intriguing Assyrian court tale, the words of this wise court official give proverbial instructions for training children, piety, humility, and maintaining controlled speech.	ANET, 427 – 30 OTP, 283 – 88 RANE #70	Court story and historical narrative; proverbs and wisdom literature; cf. also Judg. 9:8 – 15; 2 Kgs. 14:9; Prov., Job, Eccl., and Joseph, Daniel, Mordecai
Neo-Assyrian Prophecy	1912 1916	8th – 7th Century	Assyria	**Akkadian:** Texts record how prophets/prophetesses functioned under Esarhaddon/Asshurbanipal. Ishtar intercedes for her favored king and also does battle for him.	RANE #80 ANET, 449 – 51; 605 – 6 ATSHB, 227 – 29	Illustrates functions of prophecy, prophets outside Israel
Prophecies of Neferti	1900	Ca. 1990 B.C.	Egypt	**Egyptian:** Neferti relates the downfall of the king to Pharaoh Snefru (2680 – 2564 B.C.) and predicts the rise of the great Pharaoh Amenemhet I (1991 – 1960 B.C.).	OTP, 235 – 40 ANET, 444 – 46 COS 1.45 RANE 210 – 12 ATSHB, 245	Cf. Dan. 2 – 6; 1 Kgs. 13
Zakkur Inscription	1907 – 8	800 B.C.	North Syria	**Aramaic:** Zakkur, king of Hamath, gives due recognition to his god, Baal-Shamayin. Shows devotion to a god by a faithful king. Mentions Ben-Hadad, son of Hazael, historical figure from the OT.	ANET, 655 – 56 COS 2.35; RANE 163 – 5	Kgs. 15; 19; 20; 2 Kings: 6; 8; 13

desired for her, through her placement in that culture, to point the surrounding nations to the LORD, the God of creation, history, culture, politics, economics, sociology, psychology, nature; that is, to the God of gods.

The column labeled "Ancient Sources" provides readers with ample materials that will enable them to read the primary materials in English translation. The primary and secondary list of resources below includes further discussions of these materials and their significance for the study of the OT. In addition, taken as a whole, the secondary resources direct readers to exhaustive listings of many more ancient texts/artifacts for the study of the OT and its conceptual world.

Primary Texts Relating to the Old Testament (in English Translation)

Bill T. Arnold & Bryan E. Beyer, *Readings from the Ancient Near East: Primary Sources for OT Study* (Grand Rapids: Baker Academic, 2002). (RANE)

William W. Hallo, ed., K. L. Younger, Jr., assoc. ed., *The Context of Scripture*, 3 vols. (Boston: 2003). (COS)

Miriam Lichtheim, *Ancient Egyptian Literature*, 3 vols. (Berkley: University of California Press, 1971–80). (AEL)

James B. Pritchard, ed., *Ancient Near Eastern Texts Relating to the Old Testament*, 3d ed. (Princeton, NJ: Princeton University Press, 1969). (ANET)

Secondary Sources That Discuss and Provide Additional Readings of Primary Materials and Old Testament

David W. Baker & Bill T. Arnold, eds., *The Face of Old Testament Studies* (Grand Rapids: Baker Books, 1999). (FOTS)

John D. Currid, *Doing Archaeology in the Land of the Bible: A Basic Guide* (Grand Rapids: Baker Books, 1999).

David N. Freedman, ed., *The Anchor Bible Dictionary*, 6 vols. (New York: Doubleday, 1992). (ABD)

Rachel S. Hallote, *Death, Burial, and Afterlife in the Biblical World* (Chicago: Ivan R. Dee, 2001). (DBA)

Richard S. Hess, *Israelite Religions: An Archaeological and Biblical Survey* (Grand Rapids: Baker Academic, 2007). (IR)

Alfred J. Hoerth, *Archaeology and the Old Testament* (Grand Rapids: Baker Academic, 1998). (AOT)

David M. Howard, Jr., & Michael A. Grisanti, eds., *Giving the Sense: Understanding and Using Old Testament Historical Texts* (Grand Rapids: Kregel, 2003) (GS)

K. A. Kitchen, *On the Reliability of the Old Testament* (Grand Rapids: William B. Eerdmans, 2003). (ROT)

Victor H. Matthews & Don C. Benjamin, eds, *Old Testament Parallels: Laws and Stories from the Ancient Near East* (New York: Paulist Press, 1991, *1997* [cited in italic pagination], **2006** [cited in bold pagination]). (OTP)

Anson R. Rainey and R. S. Notley, *The Sacred Bridge* (Carta, Jerusalem: Carta, 2006). (SB)

Suzanne Richard, *Near Eastern Archaeology: A Reader* (Winona Lake, IN: Eisenbrauns, 2003). (NEA)

Kenton L. Sparks, *Ancient Texts for the Study of the Hebrew Bible* (Peabody, MA: Hendrickson Pub., 2005). (ATSHB)

John H. Walton, *Ancient Israelite Literature in Its Cultural Context* (Grand Rapids: Zondervan, 1989). (AILCC)

John H. Walton, *Ancient Near Eastern Thought and the Old Testament: Introducing the Conceptual World of the Hebrew Bible* (Grand Rapids: Baker Academic, 2006). (ANETOT)

QUESTIONS AND FURTHER READINGS

Questions for Discussion

1. What is the Bible? How would you describe it to someone in an apologetics context (choose the context: atheism, agnosticism, Islam, Buddhism, etc.)?

2. In an apologetics engagement, do you think it is best as a general rule to present evidence for a theistic worldview before tackling the subject of the Bible? Why or why not?

3. What is a central standard, according to Augustine, for affirming the canonical books? Do some research on other criteria utilized in the development of the canon. How is this point relevant to an apologetic discussion on the formation of the canon?

4. John Calvin argues that the witness of the Holy Spirit is stronger than any proof that the Scriptures are from God. If you adopt this approach, how would you reply to someone from another faith who says that God (or Brahman or Allah) reveals to them in their spirit that their Scriptures are the true ones? Explain Calvin's approach and why you think it should or should not be adopted.

5. How is the material presented by Eugene Carpenter beneficial as an apologetic for the reliability of the Old Testament? Of the Bible in general?

6. How is the material presented by R. T. France evidence for the life and teachings of Jesus? What are some reasons for believing that we have actual history here rather than mere bias or myth?

7. How is the material presented by R. T. France beneficial as an apologetic for the reliability of the New Testament? Of the Bible in general?

8. Does the oral history utilized in ancient culture mean that major fabrications of key Christian teachings took place? Explain.

9. How would you explain and defend the *reliability* of the Bible? Provide an outline for your approach and explain why you prefer this approach.

10. How would you explain and defend the *authority* of the Bible? Provide an outline for your approach and explain why you prefer this approach.

Further Readings

Bruce, F. F. (1988). *The Canon of Scripture*. Downers Grove, IL: InterVarsity Press. (The classical evangelical work on how the books of the Bible came to be recognized as holy Scripture.)

Dever, William (2003). *Who Were the Early Israelites and Where Did They Come From?* Grand Rapids: Eerdmans. (Dever holds to a "middle-of-the-road" position between minimalists and conservatives.)

Finkelstein, Israel, and Neil Asher Silberman (2002). *The Bible Unearthed*. New York: Touchstone. (A defense of the "minimalist" camp; probably the leading accessible work against the reliability of the Old Testament.)

Friedman, Richard E. (1997). *Who Wrote the Bible?* Reprint edition. New York: HarperSanFrancisco. (A fairly recent defense of the Documentary Hypothesis.)

Geisler, Norman, and William E. Nix (1986). *A General Introduction to the Bible*. Revised edition. Chicago: Moody Press. (A helpful book detailing the development of the Bible; also provides a defense of its authenticity and reliability.)

Hoffmeier, James K. (1996). *Israel in Egypt: The Evidence for the Authenticity of the Exodus Tradition*. New York: Oxford University Press. (One of the leading biblical archaeologists of our time critiques the minimalist position and defends the historicity of such biblical patriarchs as Joseph and Moses as well as the exodus itself.)

Kitchen, K. A. (2003). *On the Reliability of the Old Testament*. Grand Rapids: Eerdmans. (This tome is *the* major contemporary work defending the reliability of the Old Testament against the minimalist camp; detailed and fairly technical.)

Lightfoot, Neil R. (2003). *How We Got the Bible*. 3rd ed. Grand Rapids: Baker. (An up-to-date and concise exposition of the development of the Bible.)

Metzger, Bruce, and Bart D. Ehrman (2005). *The Text of the New Testament: Its Transmission, Corruption, and Restoration*. 4th ed. New York: Oxford University Press. (A well-researched and scholarly work on the subject; fairly technical, but well worth a careful read.)

Swinburne, Richard (2007). *Revelation: From Metaphor to Analogy*. 2nd ed. Oxford: Oxford University Press. (Examines major issues involved in establishing the credibility of central Christian claims about divine revelation.)

Wolterstorff, Nicholas (1995). *Divine Discourse: Philosophical Reflections on the Claim That God Speaks*. Cambridge: Cambridge University Press, 1995. (An extensive and penetrating philosophical discussion of the idea of divine revelation.)

PART 6

MIRACLES

A miracle (from the Latin *mirari*, "to wonder") is, loosely defined, an event that cannot be explained by natural causes alone. A person may claim, for example, to have been "miraculously" healed by God of some disease or ailment. On a grander scale, an appeal to miracles may be utilized in support of the truth of a particular religion. Christianity, for example, has historically been grounded on belief in the miracle of the resurrection of Jesus of Nazareth. A nonbeliever may claim that the suggestion of a miracle, whether small or large, is based on unwarranted bias, and that a naturalistic (i.e., scientific) explanation — even if that explanation is not yet known — is always a more reasonable choice in our scientific age and should be sought accordingly.

In the first essay, John Locke begins by famously defining a miracle as a "sensible operation, which, being above the comprehension of the spectator, and in his opinion contrary to the established course of nature, is taken by him to be divine." The ancient Greek and Roman religions, with their many gods, did not seem to be concerned with how their religion was established, or by what authority. While they contained "miraculous" elements, they were fanciful tales, not events meant to be rooted in actual history. The monotheistic religions (Judaism, Christianity, and Islam) declare that there is only one true God who has provided us with one true message via divine revelation. According to Locke, we can acquire knowledge of the existence of God by examining the evidence available to us, most significantly the evidence from miracles. Even further, the miracles in support of Christianity are strong, he says: "So likewise the number, variety and greatness of the miracles, wrought for the confirmation of the doctrine delivered by Jesus Christ, carry with them such strong marks of an extraordinary divine power, that the truth of his mission will stand firm and unquestionable." Miracles are crucial for faith, Locke says. They are "that foundation on which the believers of any divine revelation must ultimately bottom their faith."

In the next selection, Norman Geisler argues that, while for the last several centuries many people have affirmed that the belief in miracles and a commitment to modern science are incompatible, this need not be the case. In examining the arguments of anti-supernaturalists from the Enlightenment to today, he argues that there is in fact a way to affirm the integrity of science while also affirming the reality of the supernatural.

In the third essay, Richard Swinburne argues that if there are good reasons to believe that God exists (and he thinks there are and argues so in a number of books and articles), and if God is perfectly good and loving (which he believes God to be), then we should expect miracles. We should expect, he argues, that God will interact with us on a personal level in answering prayers and meeting our needs. God will intervene in the natural order of things, although not very often as this would make it impossible to predict the consequences of our actions. Natural laws are important, but just as loving parents sometimes rightly break their own rules for special reasons, so too we can expect God to break his rules as he intervenes in history.

CHAPTER 33

A Discourse on Miracles

John Locke

To discourse of miracles without defining what one means by the word miracle, is to make a shew, but in effect to talk of nothing. A miracle then I take to be a sensible operation, which, being above the comprehension of the spectator, and in his opinion contrary to the established course of nature, is taken by him to be divine.

He that is present at the fact, is a spectator. He that believes the history of the facts, puts himself in the place of a spectator.

This definition, 'tis probable, will not escape these two exceptions.

1. That hereby what is a miracle is made very uncertain; for it depending on the opinion of the spectator, that will be a miracle to one which will not be so to another.

In answer to which, it is enough to say, that this objection is of no force, but in the mouth of one who can produce a definition of a miracle not liable to the same exception, which I think not easy to do; for it being agreed, that a miracle must be that which surpasses the force of nature in the established, steady laws of causes and effects, nothing can be taken to be a miracle but what is judged to exceed those laws. Now everyone being able to judge of those laws only by his own acquaintance with Nature; and notions of its force (which are different in different men) it is unavoidable that that should be a miracle to one, which is not so to another.

2. Another objection to this definition, will be, that the notion of a miracle thus enlarged, may come sometimes to take in operations that have nothing extraordinary or supernatural in them, and thereby invalidate the use of miracles for the attesting of divine revelation.

To which I answer, not at all, if the testimony which divine revelation receives from miracles be rightly considered.

To know that any revelation is from God, it is necessary to know that the messenger that delivers it is sent from God, and that cannot be known but by some credential given him by God himself. Let us see then whether miracles, in my sense, be not such credentials, and will not infallibly direct us right in the search of divine revelation.

It is to be considered, that divine revelation receives testimony from no other miracles, but such as are wrought to witness his mission from God who delivers the revelation. All other miracles that are done in the world, how many or great soever, revelation is not concerned in. Cases wherein there has been, or can be need of miracles for the confirmation of revelation, are fewer than perhaps is imagined. The heathen world, amidst an infinite and uncertain jumble of deities, fables and worships, had no room for a divine attestation of anyone against the rest. Those owners of many gods were at liberty in their worship; and no one of their divinities pretending to be the one only true God, no one of them could be supposed in the pagan scheme to make use of miracles to establish his worship alone, or to abolish that of the other; much less was there any use of miracles to confirm any articles of faith, since no one of them had any such to propose as necessary to be believed by their votaries. And therefore I do not remember any miracles recorded in the Greek or Roman writers, as done to confirm anyone's mission or doctrine. Conformable hereunto we find St. Paul, I Cor. 1:22, takes notice that the Jews ('tis true) required miracles, but as for the Greeks they looked after something else; they knew no need or use there was of miracles to recommend any religion to them. And indeed it is an astonishing mark how far the God of this world had blinded men's minds, if we consider that the Gentile world received and stuck to a religion, which, not being derived from reason, had no sure foundation in revelation. They knew not its original, nor the authors of it, nor seemed concerned to know from whence it came, or by whose authority delivered; and so had no mention or use of miracles for its confirmation. For though there were here and there some pretences to revelation, yet there were not so much as pretences to miracles that attested it.

If we will direct our thoughts by what has been, we must conclude that miracles, as the credentials of a messenger delivering a divine religion, have no place but upon a supposition of one only true God; and that it is so in the nature of the thing, and cannot be otherwise, I think will be made to appear in the sequel of this discourse. Of such who have come in the name of the one only true God, professing to bring a law from him, we have in history a clear account but of three, viz. Moses, Jesus and Mahomet. For what the Persees say of their Zoroaster, or the Indians of their Brama (not to mention all the wild stories of the religions farther east) is so obscure, or so manifestly fabulous, that no account can be made of it. Now of the three before-mentioned, Mahomet having none to produce, pretends to no miracles for the vouching of his mission; so that the only revelations that come attested by miracles, being only those of Moses and Christ, and they confirming each other, the business of miracles, as it stands really in matter of fact, has no manner of difficulty in it; and I think the most scrupulous or sceptical cannot from miracles raise the least doubt against the divine revelation of the gospel.

But since the speculative and learned will be putting of cases which never were, and it may be presumed never will be; since scholars and disputants will be raising of questions where there are none, and enter upon debates whereof there is no need; I crave leave to say, that he who comes with a message from God to be delivered to the world, cannot be refused belief if he vouches his mission by a miracle, because his credentials have a right to it. For every rational thinking man must conclude as Nicodemus did, "We know that thou art a teacher come from God, for no man can do these signs which thou doest, except God be with him."

For example, Jesus of Nazareth professes himself sent from God: He with a word calms a tempest at sea. This one looks on as a miracle, and consequently cannot but receive his doctrine. Another thinks this might be the effect of chance, or skill in the weather and no miracle, and so stands out; but afterwards seeing him walk on the sea, owns that for a miracle and believes; which yet upon another has not that force, who suspects it may possibly be done by the assistance of a spirit. But yet the same person, seeing afterwards Our Saviour cure an inveterate palsy by a word, admits that for a miracle, and becomes a convert. Another overlooking it in this instance, afterwards finds a miracle in his giving sight to one born blind, or in raising the dead, or his raising himself from the dead, and so receives his doctrine as a revelation coming from God. By all which it is plain, that where the miracle is admitted, the doctrine cannot be rejected; it comes with the assurance of a divine attestation to him that allows the miracle, and he cannot question its truth.

The next thing then is, what shall be a sufficient inducement to take any extraordinary operation to be a miracle, i.e., wrought by God himself for the attestation of a revelation from him?

And to this I answer, the carrying with it the marks of a greater power than appears in opposition to it. For:

First, this removes the main difficulty where it presses hardest, and clears the matter from doubt, when extraordinary and supernatural operations are brought to support opposite missions, about which me thinks more dust has been raised by men of leisure than so plain a matter needed. For since God's power is paramount to all, and no opposition can be made against him with an equal force to his; and since his honour and goodness can never be supposed to suffer his messenger and his truth to be born down by the appearance of a greater power on the side of an impostor, and in favour of a lie; wherever there is an opposition, and two pretending to be sent from heaven clash, the signs, which carry with them the evident marks of a greater power, will always be a certain and unquestionable evidence, that the truth and divine mission are on that side on which they appear. For though the discovery, how the lying wonders are or can be produced, be beyond the capacity of the ignorant, and often beyond the conception of the most knowing spectator, who is therefore forced to allow them in his apprehension to be above the force of natural causes and effects; yet he cannot but know they are not seals set by God to his truth for the attesting of it, since they are opposed by miracles that carry the evident marks of a greater and superior power, and therefore they cannot at all shake the authority of one so supported. God can never be thought to suffer that a lie, set up in opposition to a truth coming from him, should be backed with a greater power than he will shew for the confirmation and propagation of a doctrine which he has revealed, to the end it might be believed. The producing of serpents, blood and frogs, by the Egyptian sorcerers and by Moses, could not to the spectators but appear equally miraculous, which of the pretenders then had their mission from God: and the truth on their side could not have been determined if the matter had rested there. But when Moses's serpent ate up theirs, when he produced lice which they could not, the decision was easy. 'Twas plain Jannes and Jambres acted by an inferior power, and their operations, how marvellous and extraordinary soever, could not in the least bring in question Moses's mission; that stood the firmer for this opposition, and remained the more unquestionable after this, than if no such signs had been brought against it.

So likewise the number, variety and greatness of the miracles, wrought for the confirmation of the doctrine delivered by Jesus Christ, carry with them such strong marks of an extraordinary divine power, that the truth of his mission will stand firm and unquestionable, till anyone rising up in opposition to him shall do greater miracles than he and his apostles did. For anything less will not be of weight to turn the scales in the opinion of anyone, whether of an inferior or more exalted understanding. This is one of those palpable truths and trials, of which all mankind are judges; and there needs no assistance of learning, no deep thought to come to a certainty in it. Such care has God taken that no pretended revelation should stand in competition with what is truly divine, that we need but open our eyes to see and be sure which came from him. The marks of his over-ruling power accompany it; and therefore to this day we find, that wherever the gospel comes, it prevails to the beating down the strongholds of Satan, and the dislodging the Prince of the Power of Darkness, driving him away with all his living wonders; which is a standing miracle, carrying with it the testimony of superiority.

What is the uttermost power of natural agents or created beings, men of the greatest reach cannot discover; but that it is not equal to God's omnipotency is obvious to everyone's understanding; so that the superior power is an easy, as well as sure guide to divine revelation, attested by miracles where they are brought as credentials to an embassy from God.

And thus upon the same grounds of superiority of power, uncontested revelation will stand too.

For the explaining of which, it may be necessary to premise:

1. That no mission can be looked on to be divine, that delivers anything derogating from the honour of the one, only, true, invisible God, or inconsistent with natural religion and the rules of morality: because God having discovered to men the unity and majesty of his eternal Godhead, and the truths of natural religion and morality by the light of reason, he cannot be supposed to back the contrary by revelation; for that would be to destroy the evidence and the use of reason, without which men cannot be able to distinguish divine revelation from diabolical imposture.

2. That it cannot be expected that God should send anyone into the world on purpose to inform men of things indifferent, and of small moment, or that are knowable by the use of their natural faculties. This

would be to lessen the dignity of his majesty in favour of our sloth, and in prejudice to our reason.

3. The only case then wherein a mission of any-one from heaven can be reconciled to the high and awful thoughts men ought to have of the deity, must be the revelation of some supernatural truths relating to the glory of God, and some great concern of men. Supernatural operations attesting such a revelation may, with reason, be taken to be miracles, as carrying the marks of a superior and over-ruling power, as long as no revelation accompanied with marks of a greater power appears against it. Such supernatural signs may justly stand good, and be received for divine, i.e., wrought by a power superior to all, 'till a mission attested by operations of a greater force shall disprove them: because it cannot be supposed, God should suffer his prerogative to be so far usurped by any inferior being, as to permit any creature, depending on him, to set his seals, the marks of his divine authority, to a mission coming from him. For these supernatural signs being the only means God is conceived to have to satisfy men as rational creatures of the certainty of anything he would reveal, as coming from himself, can never consent that it should be wrested out of his hands, to serve the ends and establish the authority of an inferior agent that rivals him. His power being known to have no equal, always will, and always may be safely depended on, to shew its superiority in vindicating his authority, and maintaining every truth that he hath revealed. So that the marks of a superior power accompanying it, always have been, and always will be a visible and sure guide to divine revelation; by which men may conduct themselves in their examining of revealed religions, and be satisfied which they ought to receive as coming from God; though they have by no means ability precisely to determine what it is, or is not above the force of any created being; or what operations can be performed by none but a divine power, and require the immediate hand of the Almighty. And therefore we see 'tis by that Our Saviour measures the great unbelief of the Jews, John 15:24, saying, "If I had not done among them the works which no other man did, they had not had sin,

but now have they both seen and hated both me and my Father"; declaring, that they could not but see the power and presence of God in those many miracles he did, which were greater than ever any other man had done. When God sent Moses to the children of Israel with a message, that now according to his promise he would redeem them by his hand out of Egypt, and furnished him with signs and credentials of his mission; it is very remarkable what God himself says of those signs, Exod. 4:8, "And it shall come to pass, if they will not believe thee, nor hearken to the voice of the first sign" (which was turning his rod into a serpent) "that they will believe, and the voice of the latter sign" (which was the making his hand leprous by putting it in his bosom); God further adds, ver. 9, "And it shall come to pass, if they will not believe also these two signs, neither hearken unto thy voice, that thou shalt take of the water of the river and pour upon the dry land: And the water which thou takest out of the river shall become blood upon the dry land." Which of those operations was or was not above the force of all created beings, will, I suppose, be hard for any man, too hard for a poor brick-maker to determine; and therefore the credit and certain reception of the mission, was annexed to neither of them, but the prevailing of their attestation was heightened by the increase of their number; two supernatural operations shewing more power than one, and three more than two. God allowed that it was natural, that the marks of greater power should have a greater impression on the minds and belief of the spectators. Accordingly the Jews, by this estimate judged of the miracles of Our Saviour, John 7:31, where we have this account, "and many of the people believed on him, and said when Christ cometh will he do more miracles than these which this man hath done?" This perhaps, as it is the plainest, so it is also the surest way to preserve the testimony of miracles in its due force to all sorts and degrees of people. For miracles being the basis on which divine mission is always established, and consequently that foundation on which the believers of any divine revelation must ultimately bottom their faith, this use of them would be lost, if not to all mankind, yet at least to the simple and illiterate (which is the far greatest part) if miracles be defined to be none but such divine operations as are in themselves beyond the power of all created beings, or at least operations contrary to the fixed and established laws of Nature. For as to the latter of those, what are the fixed and established laws of Nature, philosophers alone, if at least they can pretend to determine. And if they are to be operations performable only by divine power, I doubt whether any man learned or unlearned, can in most cases be able to say of any particular operation, that can fall under his senses, that it is certainly a miracle. Before he can come to that certainty, he must know that no created being has a power to perform it. We know good and bad angels have abilities and excellencies exceedingly beyond all our poor performances or narrow comprehensions. But to define what is the utmost extent of power that any of them has, is a bold undertaking of a man in the dark, that pronounces without seeing, and sets bounds to his narrow cell to things at an infinite distance from his model and comprehension.

Such definitions therefore of miracles, however specious in discourse and theory, fail us when we come to use, and an application of them in particular cases.

These thoughts concerning miracles, were occasioned by my reading Mr. Fleetwood's *Essay on Miracles*, and the letter writ to him on that subject. The one of them defining a miracle to be an extraordinary operation performable by God alone: and the other writing of miracles without any definition of a miracle at all.

CHAPTER 34

Miracles and Modern Scientific Thought

Norman Geisler

Since the "Enlightenment" it is widely accepted that the belief in miracles and a commitment to modern scientific methodology are incompatible. This study will examine the arguments of important anti-supernatural thinkers from Spinoza to the present with a view to finding any common threads. Next, we will analyze the nature of miracles in the light of scientific methodology to see if they are irresolvably incompatible. Finally, we will see if a way can be found to retain the integrity of science without denying the credibility of the supernatural.

I. The Arguments against Miracles

A. Benedict Spinoza (1632–1677)

We will begin our study with the Jewish philosopher, Benedict Spinoza. Arguing from a Newtonian concept of nature, Spinoza insisted that "nothing then, comes to pass in nature in contravention to her universal laws, nay, nothing does not agree with them and follow from them, for ... she keeps a fixed and immutable order." In fact "a miracle, whether in contravention to, or beyond, nature, is a mere absurdity." Spinoza was dogmatic about the impossibility of miracles when he proclaimed, "We may, then, be absolutely certain that every event which is truly described in Scripture necessarily happened, like everything else, according to natural laws."[1]

In support of his crucial premise Spinoza insisted that Nature "keeps a fixed and *immutable* Order." That is to say, everything "*necessarily* happened ... according to natural laws." And "nothing comes to pass in nature in contravention to her *universal* laws ..."[2]

Spinoza's argument can be summarized as follows:

1. Miracles are violations of natural laws.
2. Natural laws are immutable.
3. It is impossible for immutable laws to be violated.
4. Therefore, miracles are impossible.

Put in this form it is clear that the second premise is crucial: natural laws are universal or immutable. Just how does one know this? Laying aside for the moment Spinoza's deductive rationalism, from a strictly empirical point of view Spinoza's answer is: we know this by *universal observation*. That is, we *always* observe physical objects fall in accordance with Newton's law of gravitation. There are *no known exceptions*. But a miracle would be an exception. Hence, miracles are contrary to universal scientific observation.

B. David Hume (1711–1776)

Next, let us consider briefly Hume's argument against miracles. David Hume said of his argument: "I flatter myself that I have discovered an argument ... which, if just, will, with the wise and learned, be an everlasting check to all kinds of superstitious delusion, and consequently will be useful as long as the world endures."[3]

Just what is this "final" argument against the miraculous? In Hume's own words:

1. "A miracle is a violation of the laws of nature."

1. Benedict de Spinoza, *Tractatus Theologica-Pliticus*, in *The Chief Works of Benedict de Spinoza*, trans. R. H. M. Elwes (London: George Bell and Sons, 1883), 1:83, 87, 92.

2. Ibid., p. 83.
3. David Hume, *An Inquiry Concerning Human Understanding*, ed. C. W. Hendel (New York: Bobbs-Merrill, 1955), 10.1.118.

2. "Firm and unalterable experience has established these laws."

3. "A wise man proportions his belief to the evidence."

4. Therefore, "the proof against miracles ... is as entire as any argument from experience can possibly be imagined."[4]

In this form the crucial premise is the second one which Hume explains as follows: "There must, therefore, be a uniform experience against every miraculous event. Otherwise the event would not merit that appellation." So "nothing is esteemed a miracle if it ever happened in the common course of nature."[5]

Here again the essence of the argument depends on man's repeated observation. For the common course of nature provides us with uniform experience of natural regularities. However, there is a difference between Hume and Spinoza. For Spinoza a scientific law was *universal* and immutable; hence, miracles were absolutely *impossible*. For Hume human experience is *uniform* and, thus, miracles may be possible but they are *incredible*. So between Spinoza and Hume there was a softening of the basis for naturalism which corresponds to the later softening of the understanding of a scientific law. A scientific law is not necessarily universal (with no *possible* exception); it is simply *uniform* (with no credible exception). But even in this weaker form, Hume's argument rests upon the *regularity* of nature as opposed to the claim for highly irregular events (such as miracles).

C. Immanuel Kant (1724 – 1804)

There is a widely neglected argument against miracles tucked away in Kant's famous book, *Religion Within the Limits of Reason Alone*. In his own words, Kant reasons this way:

Those whose judgment in these matters is so inclined that they suppose themselves to be helpless without miracles, believe that they soften the blow which reason suffers from them by holding that they happen but *seldom*. [but we can ask] *How seldom?* Once in a hundred years? ... Here we can determine nothing on the basis of knowledge of the object ... but only on the basis of the maxims which are necessary to the use of our reason. Thus, miracles must be admitted as [occurring] *daily* (though indeed hidden under the guise of natural events) or else *never* ... Since the former alternative [that they occur daily] is not at all compatible with reason, nothing remains but to adopt the later maxim — for this principle remains ever a mere maxim for making judgments, not a theoretical assertion. [For example, with regard to the] admirable conservation of the species in the plant and animal kingdoms, ... no one, indeed, can claim to comprehend whether or not the direct influence of the Creator is required on each occasion. [Kant insists] they are *for us*, ... nothing but natural effects and *ought* never to be adjudged otherwise ... To venture beyond these limits is rashness and immodesty....[6]

The heart of Kant's argument can be summarized as follows:

1. Everything in our experience (the world *to us*) is determined by practical reason.

2. Practical reason operates according to universal laws.

3. Miracles occur either (1) daily, (2) seldom, or (3) never.

4. But what occurs daily is not a miracle since it occurs regularly according to natural laws.

5. And what occurs seldom is not determined by any law.

6. But all scientific knowledge must be determined by practical reason which operates on universal laws.

7. Therefore, it is rationally necessary for us to conclude that miracles *never* occur.

8. Stated this way the critical premise is the second one which claims that practical reason operates according to universal laws. In support of this premise Kant wrote, "In the affairs of life, therefore, it is impossible for us to count on miracles or

---

4. Ibid., pp. 118 – 123.
5. Ibid., pp. 10.1.122 – 123.

6. Immanuel Kant, *Religion Within the Limits of Reason Alone*, 2nd ed., trans. T. M. Green and H. H. Hudon (New York: Harper Torchbook, 1960), pp. 83 – 84.

to take them into consideration at all in our use of reason (and reason must be used in every incident of life).”[7]

In brief, miracles are theoretically possible but they are *practically* impossible. We must live *as if* they never occur. If we lived any other way it would overthrow the dictates of practical reason and erode the basis for both science and morality. For both science and morality are based on universal principles. Once more we can see that the key element in the anti-supernatural argument is the regularity of the operational laws of the universe. Kant believed these regular events to be universal. To deny them by admitting miracles, Kant thought, would be to deny the very basis of a rational and moral life.

D. Antony Flew (1923 –)

In his article on “Miracles” in *The Encyclopedia of Philosophy*, Flew notes that “Hume was primarily concerned, not with the question of fact, but with that of evidence. The problem was how the occurrence of a miracle could be proved, rather than whether any such events had ever occurred.” However, adds Flew, “our sole ground for characterizing the reported occurrence as miraculous is at the same time a sufficient reason for calling it physically impossible.” Why is this so? Because “the critical historian, confronted with some story of a miracle, will usually dismiss it out of hand . . . .” On what grounds? Flew answers, “To justify his procedure he will have to appeal to precisely the principle which Hume advanced: the ‘absolute impossibility or miraculous nature’ of the events attested must, ‘in the eyes of all reasonable people . . . alone be regarded as a sufficient refutation.’ ” In short, even though miracles are not *logically* impossible, they are *scientifically* impossible. “For it is only and precisely by presuming that the laws that hold today held in the past . . . that we can rationally interpret the *detritus*

[fragments] of the past as evidence and from it construct our account of what actually happened.”[8]

Flew’s argument against miracles can be summarized this way:

1. Miracles are by nature particular and unrepeatable.
2. Natural events are by nature general and repeatable.
3. Now, in practice, the evidence for the general and repeatable is always greater than that for the particular and unrepeatable.
4. Therefore, in practice, the evidence will always be greater against miracles than for them.

Like the arguments of Spinoza, Hume, and Kant, the key to Flew’s argument is premise number 3 which counts as greater evidence events which are regular or repeatable. For science by its very nature is not based on the exceptional or the odd but on the normal and the usual.

E. Alastair McKinnon

Other contemporary philosophers have offered arguments with similar premises against supernatural acts. Alastair McKinnon’s argument is an example. It can be summarized as follows:[9]

1. A scientific law is a generalization based on observation.
2. Any exception to a scientific law invalidates that law as such and calls for a revision of it.
3. A miracle is an exception to a scientific law.
4. Therefore, a “miracle” would call for a revision of a law and the recognition of a broader law (which thereby explains the “miracle” as a natural event).

Here the critical premise is the second one. It is admitted by all that a scientific law is a generalization based on observation. But not all would insist that a single exception would invalidate a law. Even some anti-supernaturalists admit that “This a priori argument can be refuted by noting that a supernaturally caused exception to a scientific law would *not* invali-

---

7. Ibid., p. 82.
8. Anthony Flew, “Miracles” in *The Encyclopedia of Philosophy*, ed. Paul Edwards (New York: The Macmillan Company and The Free Press, 1967), 5.346 – 353.

9. Alastair McKinnon, “‘Miracle’ and ‘Paradox’” in *American Philosophical Quarterly* 4 (Oct. 1967), 308 – 14.

date it, because scientific laws are designed to express *natural* regularities."[10] But in the case of a miracle we have "a special and non-repeatable" exception.

From a strictly scientific perspective a non-repeatable exception is an anomaly. And scientists do not overthrow established laws on the basis of singular, unrepeated anomalies. In fact, they are more likely to attribute the anomaly to faulty observation. At any rate, scientists do not revise laws based on unrepeated exceptions, since scientifically the irregular never outweighs the regular.

F. The Common Thread

Even in this admittedly unsuccessful anti-supernatural argument is hidden the premise of an apparently successful one, namely the evidence for the regular and repeatable is always greater than that for the irregular and singular. Science is based on uniform experience, not anomalies. Regularity is the basis of a scientific understanding. Therefore, science as such can never accept the miraculous. Thus the principle of regularity seems to be the common thread of the anti- supernatural arguments.

II. The Nature of Science

A. Two Fundamental Principles of Science

It seems beyond question that science involves at least two things: *observation* and *repetition*. No scientific law emerges unless there has been some observation of natural phenomena. This observation need not be strictly empirical. Microscopes and telescopes are legitimate extensions of man's empirical senses. Nor need one observe the actual event directly, as long as there are observed phenomena associated with the event. But there must be observation of some recurring pattern or else there is no scientific basis for drawing conclusions.

The events of the past, such as are indicated by the rock and fossil record, are not an exception to the need for observation. There were no human scientific observers of the origin of the universe or the origin of living things. However, our scientific understanding of these events is dependent, nonetheless, on observations. It is not dependent on past observation of these events but on present observation of similar events. That is, all understanding of the past is based on the principle of uniformity, to wit, "the present is the key to the past."[11] This principle of uniformity means that processes observed in the present are the basis for a scientific approach to unobserved processes in the past. So even in the case of unavailable past events science is based on observation of similar events which repeatedly happen in the present.

B. Repetition and the Odd

Science is so firmly based in regular repeatable events in the present that even when an odd event occurs scientists do not consider it part of a scientific explanation. Thus experiments that cannot be repeated are given little or no validity. At least unrepeatable events are never made the basis for an operational law of science.

In a thought provoking article on miracles one contemporary philosopher argued that:[12]

1. No event can be attributed to a rational agent unless its occurrence is regular and repeatable.
2. Miracles are by nature not regular or repeatable.
3. Therefore, no miracle can be attributed to any rational agent (e.g., to God).

The crux of the argument is what he called the "repeatability requirement."[13] Unless an event can be repeated over and over again we have no right to claim we know who (or what) caused it. For example, one

---

10. Malcolm L. Diamond, "Miracles," *Religious Studies* 9 (Sept., 1973), 316 – 317.

11. Charles Lyell (1797 – 1876), the father of modern uniformitarianism, wrote: "It may be necessary in the present state of science to supply some part of the assumed course of nature hypothetically; but if so, this must be done without any violation of probability, and always consistently with the analogy of what is known both of the past and present economy of our system." See his *Principles of Geology* (New York: D. Appleton and Company, 1887), p. 229.

12. George D. Chryssides, "Miracles and Agents," *Religious Studies* 11 (Sept., 1975), 319 – 27.

13. Ibid., p. 322.

should not make a causal connection between the golfer's type of swing and a once-in-a-lifetime-hole-in-one he shot. Rather than drawing a direct causal connection between them, we would consider it a lucky shot. And scientific analysis is not based on fluke relations but on repeated relations. This is why scientists use the principle of concomitant variation. For unless there is a direct correlation between the presence and absence of the cause and the presence and absence of the effect, then there is here no scientific basis for believing it is the cause.

This same point applies whether the cause is a natural force or an intelligent being. With regard to an intelligent cause, certainly no one would believe that there is a scientifically established causal connection between one's intellectual ability to pick a winning horse and a one-time win at the racetrack. For unless the intelligent being can do it over and over we would believe the result was a matter of luck, not a matter of scientific intelligence. Likewise, with regard to non-intelligent causes, there is no scientific basis for belief in a causal connection between spilt letters of alphabet cereal and a fan which blew them into the word "careful." Unless the fan does this repeatedly with randomly dropped letters we would consider this one-time event an anomaly. In such a case no scientific causal connection will be drawn between the apparent message and the fan.

So whether we are dealing with non-intelligent or intelligent causes, there must be a relationship repeatedly observed before one can consider the connection scientifically based. But this repeated relation is precisely what we do not — indeed, cannot — have with miracles because they are *one-time* events. Hence, by nature, singularities such as miracles would seem to be ruled out of the realm of science.

III. Science and the Supernatural

If all scientific understanding of the universe is based on observed repetitions and if miracles are by nature singularities, then are not miracles automatically ruled out on scientific grounds? For miracles are by nature singular (unusual) events which are caused by an intelligent being (namely, God) beyond the realm of natural law.

A. Are Miracles a Matter of Faith?

For the supernaturalist there seem to be two basic avenues of escape from this argument. First, he could simply admit there is no scientific basis for belief in miracles. Simply because miracles are not subject to repetition does not mean they do not occur. After all, a hole-in-one has happened; desperation shots have gone through the hoop, and some have won at the lottery on the first ticket. So all the theist needs to admit is that singular events (such as miracles) are not subject to scientific analysis. That is, there may be no way to have a scientific understanding of them; they might be understood only by "faith." In this sense, what the non-supernaturalist would call a "fluke" the supernaturalist may choose (by faith) to see as the "hand of God." Thus the theist could admit that there is no *scientific way* to differentiate between a natural statistical improbability and a miracle. Both would have the same empirical data associated with them and neither would be based in the scientific principle of repeatability.

Of course, if the theist admits this then the naturalist has won a major victory. For the theist has admitted that there is no *scientific* basis for a belief in either the creation of the universe or of life, to say nothing of the resurrection of Christ. Further, the anti-supernaturalist could press his argument that there is no *rational* or *evidential* grounds for belief in miracles either. For all rational connections seem to be based on previously observed causal connections. And all empirical evidence is likewise dependent on empirical observations of regular events. In brief, if the supernaturalist admits there is no regularly observed phenomena as a basis for miracles, then he has given up any basis for *knowing* they have happened. It has become simply a matter of unjustifiable *faith* in believing they have happened. If this is so then his faith is empirically unfalsifiable. This would not differ in principle from someone who claims his watch works because a little invisible green gremlin changes the time each second.

B. A Scientific Basis for the Miraculous

However, before all is given up to fideism let us suggest another possibility which offers a *scientific* basis for belief in miracles. This approach is grounded on the most fundamental principle of science-the very principle of regularity used to argue against miracles. In order to understand this approach let us first try to pinpoint the basic problem in the arguments against miracles. The essence of the argument goes like this:

1. Only what is observed to occur over and over again can be the basis for a scientific understanding of what caused the event.[14]
2. Singular events like miracles are not repeated over and over again.
3. Therefore, there is no scientific basis for an understanding of what caused a singularity such as a miracle.

1. Antisupernaturalism Proves Too Much

The first and most obvious problem with this argument is that it seems to prove too much. For if the argument is valid, then it would prove that there is no scientific basis for some events considered to be scientific by non-supernaturalistic scientists. For example, the Big Bang theory is considered by most astronomers to be a viable scientific explanation of the origin of the universe,[15] but so far as the scientific evidence goes the Big Bang occurred only once. It has not been repeated. It is a singularity. Hence, if the repeatability requirement is pressed it would eliminate one of the most widely held scientific views on the origin of the universe.

Further, most non-supernaturalist scientists believe in the spontaneous generation of first life on earth.[16] And even naturalists who believe life began in outer space, must acknowledge that it began by spontaneous generation somewhere out there. But to bring the problem back down to earth, most scientists believe that life began here only once. At the very least the spontaneous generation of life has not happened over and over again. What is more, we do not observe it happening spontaneously over and over again in the present. But if repeatability in the present is essential to a scientific understanding of an event, then the belief in spontaneous generation is not scientific either.[17]

The same logic applies to the naturalistic theory of macro-evolution. According to this belief, the evolutionary development of life occurred only once. Each new forward development occurred only once. For example fish evolved into reptiles only once, and reptiles evolved into birds only once, and so on. These events have never happened again. Yet naturalistic scientists believe it is scientific to speak of macro-evolution. Some even call evolution a "fact," not merely a theory.[18] But if it is unscientific to believe in singularities, then it would also be unscientific to

---

14. This point was made by Paley in his famous watchmaker argument, but it seems to have been largely lost in the subsequent arguments against God. For example, Paley used phrases like "we observe," "our observer," "each observation," "our observation" over and over again. He even used the phrase "uniform experience" as the basis for his belief in an intelligent Designer of nature. (See William Paley, *A View of the Evidences of Christianity* (Cambridge: J. Hall & Sons, 1875), 6th ed., pp. 10, 11, 20, 29, and especially 37–38.

15. See Robert Jastrow, *God and the Astronomers* (New York: W. W. Norton & Company, Inc., 1978), especially pp. 14, 111, 116 and 120f.

16. George Wald wrote, "We tell this story [about Pasteur's experiments] to beginning students of biology as though it represents a triumph of reason over mysticism. In fact it is very nearly the opposite. The reasonable view was to believe in spontaneous generation; the only alternative, to believe in a single, primary act of supernatural creation. There is no third position." See "The Origin of Life" in *Scientific American* (Aug., 1954), p. 48; reprinted in *Life:* *Origin and Evolution*, ed. C. E. Folsome (San Francisco: W. H. Freeman and Company, 1979).

17. Many scientists recognize this point. J. W. N. Sullivan wrote: "So far as actual evidence goes, this is still the only possible conclusion. But since it is a conclusion that seems to lead back to some supernatural creative act, it is a conclusion that scientific men find very difficult of acceptance" (*The Limitations of Science*, New York: Mentor Book, 1963, p . 94). Speaking of spontaneous generation, Robert Jastrow said, the "theory is also an act of faith. The act of faith consists in assuming that the scientific view of the origin of life is correct, without having concrete evidence to support that belief" (*Until the Sun Dies*, New York: W. W. Norton and Company, 1977, p. 63).

18. Isaac Asimov said, "Scientists who deal with evolution as their field of specialization may argue over the mechanism behind evolutionary development, but none questions the fact of evolution itself" (*Science Digest*, October, 1981, p. 86).

believe in macro-evolution. In short, the naturalist's argument against singularities proves too much; it proves that even some of his naturalistic explanations are not science either.

2. Naturalism Neglects Uniformity

In one of the strangest ironies in the history of thought, naturalism has destroyed its own argument by its own basic premise. For we have seen that from Spinoza to the present the repeatability or regularity requirement has been part of the anti-supernaturalists' argument against miracles. Scientific laws are based on repetition of events. Miracles are not repeated over and over. Therefore, miracles are not scientific.

Not only do naturalists hold to the need for regularities but they also believe there are scientific explanations for singular events (such as the origin of life). But how do they know this? The answer seems to be the principle of uniformity. That is, they insist that we can understand past *singularities* in terms of present *regularities*. For we observe over and over in the present that when certain chemicals (gases) are put together under certain circumstances that amino acids, which are the basic elements of life, are the result. Hence, we can assume that the same thing would occur under similar circumstances in the past.

The same is true of macro-evolution. Scientists have observed over and over in the present that small changes occur in animals. Hence, they assume that given long periods of time in the past these small changes could add up to the large changes needed to explain a common ancestry of all life. So here too the principle of uniformity is the key. That is, even though the past event is a *singularity* which the naturalist did not observe, nevertheless, there are present *regularities* (which are observed to occur over and over again) which are used as the scientific basis for understanding these past singularities. In this way what is repeated in the present is the key to understanding what hap-

pened only once in the past. Thus, the naturalist can avoid the charge that his view about past singularities is unscientific. It is scientific, they can insist, because their understanding of a singular event is based on similar regular events which happen all the time.

What is true of past singularities is also true of present ones. For example, one need only see one Mount Rushmore to know that some intelligence carved these faces on the mountain. For *repeated* experiences of similar situations are a sufficient basis for knowing that what caused this *singular* event must have been intelligent. There is an analogous situation here to the astronomical search for extra-terrestrial intelligence. Carl Sagan believes that even a *single* message from outer space would prove the existence of highly intelligent beings there.[19] How does he know this? Because he has *repeated* experiences of similar messages caused by intelligent beings. So the general principle can be stated as follows: *all singularities must be understood in terms of similar regularities.*

This being the case, the objection of the supernaturalist about their belief in singularities without a scientific basis in repetition seems to have collapsed. For if one can know there is an intelligent cause of a single message (or event), based on repeated experience of similar situations, then why cannot one know there was an intelligent cause for the origin of life? In short, the answer of the naturalist opens the door wide for a scientific explanation for a supernatural origin of life. For if repetition is the key to understanding singularities, then a supernaturalist can argue that there was a supernatural cause for the origin of first life. For this reasoning is also based on repeated observation. The argument has two sides, both of which are based in repeated observation.

First, all observational evidence indicates that the non-living never produces the living. Pasteur's experiments disproved spontaneous generation long ago. There is a *uniform* and universally available experi-

---

19. Sagan wrote: "There are others who believe that our problems are soluble, that humanity is still in its childhood, that one day soon we will grow up. The receipt of a *single message* from space would show that it is possible to live through such technological adolescence: the transmitting civilization, after all, has survived. Such knowledge, it seems to me, might be worth a great price" (*Broca's Brain*, New York: Random House, 1979, p. 275, emphasis added).

ence as a basis for this conclusion, and there are no verified exceptions. Hence, the argument against spontaneous generation is as firmly scientific as any such argument can be.

There appears to be one exception to this principle that life only produces life. Are not scientists able to produce life? That is, cannot life be created by intelligent beings? In response to this two things should be noted. First of all, scientists have not yet created life from non-living chemicals. They have only succeeded in producing some biologically interesting chemicals, such as amino acids. Furthermore, even in these experiments the role of the experimenters plays a crucial role in the success of the experiment.[20] Thus intelligent intervention is necessary in the production of these results. Hence, even if scientists could produce life, it would show that it took an intelligent form of life to produce a less than intelligent form of life. And the production of an intelligent robot would also show that only intelligence produces intelligence. So in any event, the creation of life (whether non-intelligent or intelligent life) always takes an intelligent source of life to accomplish it. But if this is so, then here again scientific observation would lead us to believe that the first living thing must have had an intelligent cause.

Second, this leads us to the other side of this scientific argument for an intelligent origin of life.

1. The only cause repeatedly observed to be adequate to produce information is intelligence.
2. Now the information in the first single cell which emerged on earth would fill a whole volume of an encyclopedia.[21]
3. But observation of regularities are the scientific basis for understanding singularities.
4. Hence, there is a scientific basis (in repeated observation) for believing that first life was caused by some intelligence beyond the natural world.
5. But since this kind of singularity produced by a

supernatural intelligent being would be a miracle by definition, then we have a firm scientific basis for believing in miracles.

In short, repetition in the present does give us a firm scientific basis for believing in an intelligent intervention into the natural world. To borrow Hume's term, we have "uniform experience" on which to base our belief in the miraculous origin of life. For we never observe an encyclopedia resulting from an explosion in a printing shop. We never observe a fan blowing on alphabet cereal produce a scientific research paper. No one would conclude Mount Rushmore resulted from wind or rain erosion. Why? Our uniform experience teaches us that the kind of information conveyed on Mount Rushmore never results from natural laws but only from intelligent intervention.

IV. Summary and Conclusion

Since the rise of modern science anti-supernatural arguments have stressed the principle of uniformity. They have argued that:

1. Scientific understanding is always based on constant repetition of events.
2. Miracles are not constantly repeated.
3. Therefore, there is no scientific way to understand miracles.

Two things should be noted about this argument. First, this form of the argument does not deny that unusual events like miracles may occur, any more than it denies a hole-in-one may occur. It simply says that scientific law is based on regularities. And until one can establish a constant conjunction between antecedent and consequent factors there is no scientific basis for assuming a causal connection between them.

Second, neither does this argument deny that there is any scientific way to analyze singularities, such as the origin of the universe, or the origin of life, or

20. See the excellent new book by some creative scientists on this point: Charles Thaxton, Walter Bradley, and Roger Olsen, *The Mystery of Life's Origin: Reassessing Current Theories* (New York: Philosophical Library, 1984).

21. The information in a complex form of life is much greater. Carl Sagan pointed out that "If written out in English, say, that information [in the human brain] would fill some twenty million volumes, as many as in the world's largest libraries" (*Cosmos*, New York: Random House, 1980, p. 278).

receiving one message from outer space. It simply says that *observed regularities* must be the basis for analyzing *singularities*. For example, if we observe over and over again that a certain kind of effect regularly results from a certain kind of cause then when we discover even a *singular* case of this kind of effect (whether from the past or present), we have a scientific basis for assuming it had the same kind of cause too. This same assumption is behind the naturalists' search for a chemical basis for the origins of life and an evolutionary basis for the origin of species. In both cases repeatable observations in the present are used as a basis for understanding the singularity of origin in the past. Without this principle of uniformity there would be no way of getting at singularities in either the past or the present.

Certainly we must grant that this is a legitimate procedure to base all scientific understanding in the principle of regularity. However, the question is this: Does such a procedure eliminate a scientific understanding of miracles? In order to better understand our answer to this question let us reformulate the naturalist argument in the light of the two qualifications noted above.

1) Scientific understanding is always based on constant repetition of events.

1a) This repetition need not be a repetition of the event we are analyzing but only of other similar events.

2) Miracles are not constantly repeated events.

3b) Therefore, miracles need not be eliminated from the realm of scientific understanding.

Once the argument is put in this form we can see that all one needs to do to establish a basis for singularities such as miracles is to find some constantly repeated process as a basis for understanding them. This we believe can be done by adding these premises:

4) Constant repetition informs us that wherever complex information is conveyed there was an intelligent cause.

5) There are some scientific singularities (such as the origin of first life) where complex information is conveyed.

6) Therefore, there is a scientific basis for positing an intelligent non-natural cause for the origin of first life.

Certainly no one can reasonably deny the information comes from an informer. This is a uniform experience. The only apparent exceptions are flukes which cannot be repeated constantly. So firmly established is our uniform experience that only intelligence causes information that we would consider it highly unscientific for a geology teacher to insist that his students continue to study the faces on Mount Rushmore until they can find some natural law of erosion which can explain them. Furthermore, one does not have to see more than one Mount Rushmore to know that it was formed by intelligence, not by natural processes of erosion. For uniform experience of similar situations indicates that these kinds of forms on rocks always result from intelligent intervention. Likewise, if a single sentence or paragraph is repeatedly observed to result from intelligence, then the encyclopedia full of information contained in the first simple form of life surely must have had an intelligent cause too.

Should someone protest that there is still a chance — remote as it may be — that life arose naturally, we need only remind them that science is not based on flukes or anomalies. It is based on regularities and repetition. And we have no observed regularly repeated conjunctions that would provide a scientific basis for us to believe in such an unrepeated singularity. In brief, the principle of repeatability which naturalists use to attack miracles actually boomerangs to support the miraculous. Naturalism is defeated at its own game of science on its own principles.

CHAPTER 35

A Case for Miracles

Richard Swinburne

I have argued so far that the claim that God created and sustains our universe is the hypothesis that best accounts for its general structure — its very existence, its conformity to natural laws, its being fine-tuned to evolve animals and humans, and these latter being conscious beings with sensations, thoughts, beliefs, desires, and purposes who can make great differences to themselves and the world in deeply significant ways. I have argued too that the existence of evil of the kind we find on earth does not count against that claim. The evidence considered so far, therefore, gives a significant degree of probability to that claim — that there is a God. However, if there is a God, who, being perfectly good, will love his creatures, one would expect him to interact with us occasionally more directly on a personal basis, rather than merely through the natural order of the world which he constantly sustains — to answer our prayers and to meet our needs. He will not, however, intervene in the natural order at all often, for, if he did, we would not be able to predict the consequences of our actions and so we would lose control over the world and ourselves. If God answered most prayers for a relative to recover from cancer, then cancer would no longer be a problem for humans to solve. Humans would no longer see cancer as a problem to be solved by scientific research — prayer would be the obvious method of curing cancer. God would then have deprived us of the serious choice of whether to put money and energy into finding a cure for cancer or not to bother; and of whether to take trouble to avoid cancer (e.g. by not smoking) or not to bother. Natural laws determining that certain events will cause good effects and other ones cause bad effects enable us to discover which produce which

and to use them for ourselves. Natural laws are like rules, instituted by parents, schools, or governments, stating that these actions will be punished and those ones rewarded. Once we discover the rules, we acquire control over the consequences of our actions — we can then choose whether to be rewarded or to risk being punished. But loving parents will rightly occasionally break their own rules in answer to special pleading — it means that they are persons in interaction, not just systems of rules. And for a similar reason one might expect God occasionally to break his own rules, and intervene in history.

Miracles and Natural Laws

One might expect God occasionally to answer prayer when it is for a good cause — such as the relief of suffering and restoration to health of mind or body, and for awareness of himself and of important spiritual truths. And one might also expect him to intervene occasionally without waiting for our prayer — to help us to make the world better in various ways when we have misused our freedom. A divine intervention will consist either in God acting in areas where natural laws do not determine what happens (perhaps our mental life is not fully determined by natural laws), or in God temporarily suspending natural laws. Let us call interventions of the latter kind miracles and interventions of the former kind non-miraculous interventions. A miracle is a violation or suspension of natural laws, brought about by God. Does human history contain events of a kind which God, if he exists, would be expected to bring about and yet which do not occur as a result of the operation of natural laws? It certainly contains large numbers of events of the kind which

God would be expected to bring about, but about which we have no idea whether they occurred as a result of the operation of natural laws or not. I pray for my friend to get better from cancer and he does. Since we do not normally know in any detail the exact state of his body when he had cancer, nor do we know in any detail the natural laws which govern the development of cancer, we cannot say whether the recovery occurs as a result of natural laws or not. The pious believer believes that God intervened, and the hard-headed atheist believes that only natural laws were at work. Human history also contains *reports* of many events which, *if* they occurred as reported, clearly would not have occurred as a result of natural laws, and which are also events of a kind that God might be expected to bring about. The Second Book of Kings records that a sick and doubting King Hezekiah sought a sign of encouragement from God that he, Hezekiah, would recover and that God would save Jerusalem from the Assyrians. In response to the prayer of the prophet Isaiah that God would give Hezekiah a sign, the shadow cast by the sun reportedly went 'backwards ten steps' (2 Kgs. 20:11). The latter can only have happened if the laws of mechanics (governing the rotation of the earth on its axis, and so the direction of the sun from Jerusalem), or the laws of light (governing how light from the sun forms shadows in the region of Hezekiah's palace), had been suspended.

I suggest that, in so far as we have other reason to believe that there is a God, we have reason to believe that God intervenes in history in some such cases (we may not know which) and so that some of the events happened as described, although not necessitated to do so by natural laws. It would be odd to suppose that God, concerned for our total well-being, confined his interventions to those areas (if any) where natural laws leave it undetermined what will happen — for example, confined his interventions to influencing the mental lives of human beings. If he has reason to interact with us, he has reason very occasionally to intervene to suspend those natural laws by which our life is controlled; and in particular, since the bodily processes which determine our health are fairly evi-

dently subject to largely deterministic natural laws, he has reason very occasionally to intervene in those. Conversely, in so far as we have other reason to believe that there is no God, we have reason to believe that natural processes are the highest-level determinants of what happens and so that no events happen contrary to laws of nature. In other words, background knowledge (our other reasons for general belief about how the world works — e.g., reasons for believing that there is a God, or that there is no God) is rightly a very important factor in assessing what happened on particular occasions (more so here than in assessing the worth of large scientific or religious theories ...).

Background Knowledge and Historical Evidence

But, while background knowledge must be a powerful factor in determining what is reasonable to believe about what happened on particular occasions, it is not, of course, the only factor. We have the detailed historical evidence of what observers seem to recall having happened, what witnesses claim to have observed, and any physical traces of past events (documents, archaeological remains, and so on).

That background knowledge must weigh heavily in comparison with the detailed historical evidence in assessing particular claims about the past can be seen from innumerable non-religious examples. If a well-established scientific theory leads you to expect that stars will sometimes explode, then some debris in the sky of a kind which could have been caused by an exploding star but which (though improbably) just might have some other cause may be reasonably interpreted as debris left by an exploding star. But, if a well-established theory says that stars cannot explode, you will need very strong evidence that the debris could not have had another cause before interpreting it as debris of an exploding star. However, in the case of purported miraculous interventions, the background knowledge will be of two kinds. It will include the scientific knowledge of what are the relevant laws of nature — for example, the laws of light and the laws governing the rotation of the earth, which (since laws of nature operate almost all the time) lead us to expect that on that particular occasion Hezekiah's shadow did not move backwards. But it will also include the other evidence that there is a God able and having reason sometimes (but not necessarily on any one particular occasion) to intervene to suspend the operation of natural laws. In view of these conflicting bodies of background knowledge, we would need quite a bit of particular historical evidence to show that, on any particular occasion, God intervened in a miraculous way. The historical evidence could be backed up by argument that that particular purported miracle was one which God had strong reason for bringing about.

To balance detailed historical evidence against background evidence of both kinds to establish what happened on any particular occasion is a difficult matter on which we are seldom going to be able to reach a clear verdict. But detailed historical evidence about what happened could in principle be substantial. To take a simple, imaginary, and not especially religiously significant example, we ourselves might have apparently seen someone levitate (that is, rise in the air, not as a result of strings or magnets or any other known force for which we have checked). Many witnesses, proved totally trustworthy on other occasions where they would have had no reason to lie, might report having observed such a thing. There might even be traces in the form of physical effects which such an event would have caused — for example, marks on the ceiling which would have been caused by a levitating body hitting it. But against all this there will still be the background knowledge of what are the laws of nature, in this case the laws of gravity; and all the evidence in favour of these being the laws of nature will be evidence that they operated at the time in question, and so that no levitation occurred.

Note that any detailed historical evidence that the levitation occurred will, as such, be evidence against the laws of gravity being the laws of nature — just as evidence that some piece of metal did not expand when heated would be evidence that it is not a law of nature that all metals expand when heated. But if, much though we may try, we fail to find further

exceptions to our purported law — if, for example, we cannot produce another levitation by recreating the circumstances in which the former one purportedly occurred — that will be grounds for believing that, if the former occurred, it was not an event in accord with some hitherto undiscovered law of nature, but rather a violation or suspension of a law.

In such cases, we would, I think, be most unlikely to have enough detailed historical evidence that the event occurred to outweigh the scientific background knowledge that such events cannot occur, unless we also had substantial religious background knowledge showing not merely that there is a God but that he had very good reason on this particular occasion to work this particular miracle. In the case of a purported levitation, I doubt that we would ever have such evidence. That is not, of course, to say that levitations do not occur, only that we are most unlikely to have enough reason to believe that one did occur on any particular occasion. Note that in all such cases what we are doing is to seek the simplest theory of what happened in the past which leads us to account for the data (what I have here called the detailed historical evidence), and which fits in best with our background knowledge . . . .

I am, however, inclined to think that we do have enough historical evidence of events occurring contrary to natural laws of a kind which God would have reason to bring out to show that probably some of them (we do not know which) are genuine miracles. There are many reports of purported miracles, ancient and modern, some of them quite well documented. (See for example, the cure of the Glasgow man from cancer described in D. Hickey and G. Smith, *Miracle* [1978], or some of the cases discussed in Rex Gardiner, *Healing Miracles* [1986]. For a more sceptical account of some purported Lourdes miracles, see, for contrast, D. J. West, *Eleven Lourdes Miracles* [1957].) Or, rather, we have enough detailed historical evidence in some such cases given that we have a certain amount of background evidence to support the claim that there is a God, able and willing to intervene in history. But, of course, the reader must consider the evidence in such cases for himself or herself. The occurrence of such detailed historical evidence is itself further evidence of the existence of God ... because one would expect to have it if there is a God but not otherwise — for if natural laws are the highest-level determinants of what happens, there is every reason to expect that they will not be suspended.

Evidence and the Existence of God

It is so often said in such cases that we 'may be mistaken'. New scientific evidence may show that the event as reported was not contrary to natural laws — we simply misunderstood what were the natural laws. Maybe we have just misunderstood how cancer develops; a patient sometimes 'spontaneously' recovers by purely natural processes. Or, if many people claim to have observed someone levitate, maybe they have all been subject to hallucination. Maybe. But the rational enquirer in these matters, as in all matters, must go on the evidence available. If that evidence shows that the laws of nature are such and such, that if the event happened as described it was contrary to them, that the new evidence had no tendency to show that the supposed laws are not the true laws (because in all other similar cases they are followed), that there is very strong historical evidence (witnesses, and so on) that the event occurred, then it is rational to believe that a miracle occurred. We are rational to believe, while allowing the possibility that evidence might turn up later to show that we are mistaken. 'We may be mistaken' is a knife which cuts both ways — we may be mistaken in believing that an event is not a divine intervention when really it is, as well as the other way round.

Historians often affirm that, when they are investigating particular claims about past events important to religious traditions — for example, about what Jesus did and what happened to him — they do so without making any religious or anti-religious assumptions. In practice most of them do not live up to such affirmations. Either they heavily discount such biblical claims as that Jesus cured the blind on the grounds that such

things do not happen; or (more commonly in past centuries) they automatically accept the testimony of witnesses to what Jesus did, on the grounds that biblical witnesses are especially reliable. But what needs to be appreciated is that background evidence ought to influence the investigator — as it does in all other areas of enquiry. Not to allow it to do so is irrational.

The existence of detailed historical evidence for the occurrence of violations of natural laws of a kind which God, if there is a God, would have had reason to bring about is itself evidence for the existence of God. Though not nearly enough on its own, it makes its contribution; and with other evidence [...] it could be enough to establish the existence of God, if the other evidence is not enough on its own. Consider, by analogy, a detective investigating a crime and considering the hypothesis that Jones committed the crime. Some of his clues will be evidence for the occurrence of some event, an event which, if it occurred, would provide evidence in its turn for the hypothesis that Jones committed the crime. The former might, for example, be the evidence of witnesses who claim to have seen Jones near the scene of the crime. Even if Jones was near the scene of the crime, that is in its turn on its own fairly weak evidence that he committed the crime. Much more evidence is needed. But because the testimony of witnesses is evidence for Jones having been near the scene of the crime, and Jones having been near the scene is some evidence that he committed it, the testimony of the witnesses is nevertheless some (indirect) evidence for his having committed the crime. Likewise, evidence of witnesses who claim to observe a violation of natural laws is indirect evidence for the existence of God, because the occurrence of such violations would be itself more direct evidence for the existence of God. If the total evidence becomes strong enough, then it will justify asserting that God exists, and hence that the event in question was not merely a violation, but brought about by God and thus a miracle.

QUESTIONS AND FURTHER READINGS

Questions for Discussion

1. Describe the difference between a miracle and a non-miraculous intervention. Might there be reason to believe in one and not the other? Why or why not?

2. What are some relevant factors to consider in determining what is reasonable to believe about a particular alleged miracle?

3. If a natural explanation is available for an event, can it still be considered a miracle?

4. Suppose that some event occurred that, at first blush, you and a number of others took to be a miracle. How can you be justified in believing that it was a miracle as opposed to, say, an event that occurred based on a natural law of which we are currently unaware (or based on a misunderstanding of current natural laws)? How should the rational inquirer approach such matters?

5. What reason could God possibly have for violating the laws of nature, especially given that he is an all-good and all-powerful God and therefore would have arranged for things to happen in a good way?

6. Evaluate John Locke's central argument. Do you find it persuasive? Why or why not?

7. Is prophecy a miracle (e.g., God revealing the future to the prophets)? Explain.

8. Richard Swinburne gives some principles we can use to evaluate the claims of the miraculous. Do you agree with them? Explain your answer.

9. How does one's worldview affect belief in miracles? How should it affect such belief?

10. There are many claims made about miracles, even today. Are you ever skeptical of them? Why? What are some legitimate reasons for being skeptical of miraculous claims?

Further Readings

Basinger, David, and Randall Basinger (1986). *Philosophy and Miracle: The Contemporary Debate.* Lewiston, NY: Edwin Mellen. (An overview and assessment of various issues on the topic.)

Geivett, R. Douglas, and Gary Habermas (1997). *In Defense of Miracles: A Comprehensive Case for God's Action in History.* Downers Grove, IL: InterVarsity Press. (An excellent collection of articles by leading scholars.)

Greenleaf, Simon (1847). *An Examination of the Testimony of the Four Evangelists, by the Rules of Evidence Administered in Courts of Justice.* 2nd ed. London: A. Maxwell & Son. (A classic work on evidence and miracle.)

Hume, David (1777; reprint, 1977). "On Miracles." In *An Enquiry Concerning Human Understanding,* ed. Eric Steinberg. Indianapolis: Hackett. (The classic critique of miracles.)

Lewis, C. S. (1960; reprint, 2001). *Miracles.* New York: HarperCollins. (A defense of belief in miracles; responds to Hume's arguments.)

Montgomery, John Warwick (1978). "Science, Theology, and the Miraculous." *Journal of the American Scientific Association* 30:145–53. (A short, insightful piece on the subject.)

Swinburne, Richard (1996). *Is There a God?* Oxford: Oxford University Press. (An accessible defense of theism; the selection above was taken from this book.)

Swinburne, Richard, ed. (1989). *Miracles.* New York: Macmillan. (A helpful collection of essays on miracles.)

PART 7

THE RESURRECTION OF JESUS

Throughout Christian history it has been widely affirmed that Jesus' resurrection is the epicenter of Christianity and fundamental to Christian theology and practice. In the New Testament, the resurrection was a central teaching, as is reflected in 1 Corinthians 15, where Paul claims that if Jesus was not raised from the dead, then Christian faith is useless. So unlike many other religions, the heart of Christianity is rooted in historical events. If those events are false (and this one in particular), Christianity is false. Given the central role of this historical event, it is not surprising that many of those who deny the truth of Christianity attempt to disprove the resurrection. On the other hand, if there is solid evidence for the resurrection, as many Christians have claimed, then this provides evidence for believers' life after death. Indeed, some have even argued that it provides evidence for the existence of God.

In the first selection in this section, Thomas Aquinas — the "Angelic Doctor," as he is often referred to — methodically works through several major issues (major issues for his time and place) related to the resurrection of Jesus. In his characteristic logical fashion, he argues that it was necessary for Jesus to rise from the dead, that it was fitting that he should rise on the third day, and that he was the first person to rise from the dead.

Next, J. W. Montgomery uses legal reasoning and the law of evidence to argue for Christian faith. The advantage of this jurisprudential approach, he argues, is that it is difficult to ignore or jettison the legal standards of proof by a preponderance of evidence and proof beyond reasonable doubt. He argues that Jesus' resurrection can be established on legal grounds, even outside a theistic structure.

In the next selection, Gary Habermas notes that for a number of reasons, most contemporary scholars (both believers and critics) maintain that, after Jesus' death, his disciples believed they had seen appearances of the risen Jesus. But do the beliefs of the disciples offer any clues about what, in fact, really happened? He notes three chief options to account for the appearances, and he argues that Jesus' disciples were convinced that they had seen the risen Jesus and that a number of solid reasons support the historicity of these beliefs.

In the final essay, William Lane Craig contests the claim that from Paul's testimony about Jesus' resurrection body, we can conclude that it was an unextended, immaterial, and intangible spiritual body. Craig argues that, to the contrary, the information that Paul provides confirms the Gospels' narratives of Jesus' bodily resurrection.

CHAPTER 36

The Resurrection of Jesus

Thomas Aquinas

Third Part; Question 53

Article 1. *Whether it was necessary for Christ to rise again?*

Objection 1. It would seem that it was not necessary for Christ to rise again. For Damascene says (De Fide Orth. iv): "Resurrection is the rising again of an animate being, which was disintegrated and fallen." But Christ did not fall by sinning, nor was His body dissolved, as is manifest from what was stated above (Question 51, Article 3). Therefore, it does not properly belong to Him to rise again.

Objection 2. Further, whoever rises again is promoted to a higher state, since to rise is to be uplifted. But after death Christ's body continued to be united with the Godhead, hence it could not be uplifted to any higher condition. Therefore, it was not due to it to rise again.

Objection 3. Further, all that befell Christ's humanity was ordained for our salvation. But Christ's Passion sufficed for our salvation, since by it we were loosed from guilt and punishment, as is clear from what was said above (49, 1, 3). Consequently, it was not necessary for Christ to rise again from the dead.

On the contrary, it is written (Luke 24:46): "It behooved Christ to suffer and to rise again from the dead."

I answer that, it behooved Christ to rise again, for five reasons.

First of all; for the commendation of Divine Justice, to which it belongs to exalt them who humble themselves for God's sake, according to Luke 1:52: "He hath put down the mighty from their seat, and hath exalted the humble." Consequently, because Christ humbled Himself even to the death of the Cross, from love and obedience to God, it behooved Him to be uplifted by God to a glorious resurrection; hence it is said in His Person (Psalm 138:2): "Thou hast known," i.e., approved, "my sitting down," i.e., My humiliation and Passion, "and my rising up," i.e., My glorification in the resurrection; as the gloss expounds.

Secondly, for our instruction in the faith, since our belief in Christ's Godhead is confirmed by His rising again, because, according to 2 Corinthians 13:4, "although He was crucified through weakness, yet He liveth by the power of God." And therefore it is written (1 Corinthians 15:14): "If Christ be not risen again, then is our preaching vain, and our [Vulgate: 'your'] faith is also vain": and (Psalm 29:10): "What profit is there in my blood?" that is, in the shedding of My blood, "while I go down," as by various degrees of evils, "into corruption?" As though He were to answer: "None. 'For if I do not at once rise again but My body be corrupted, I shall preach to no one, I shall gain no one,'" as the gloss expounds.

Thirdly, for the raising of our hope, since through seeing Christ, who is our head, rise again, we hope that we likewise shall rise again. Hence it is written (1 Corinthians 15:12): "Now if Christ be preached that He rose from the dead, how do some among you say, that there is no resurrection of the dead?" And (Job 19:25–27): "I know," that is with certainty of faith, "that my Redeemer," i.e., Christ, "liveth," having risen from the dead; "and" therefore "in the last day I shall rise out of the earth … this my hope is laid up in my bosom."

Fourthly, to set in order the lives of the faithful: according to Romans 6:4: "As Christ is risen from the dead by the glory of the Father, so we also may walk in newness of life": and further on; "Christ rising from the dead dieth now no more; so do you also reckon that you are dead to sin, but alive to God."

Fifthly, in order to complete the work of our salvation: because, just as for this reason did He endure evil things in dying that He might deliver us from evil, so was He glorified in rising again in order to advance us towards good things; according to Romans 4:25: "He was delivered up for our sins, and rose again for our justification."

Reply to Objection 1. Although Christ did not fall by sin, yet He fell by death, because as sin is a fall from righteousness, so death is a fall from life: hence the words of Micah 7:8 can be taken as though spoken by Christ: "Rejoice not thou, my enemy, over me, because I am fallen: I shall rise again." Likewise, although Christ's body was not disintegrated by returning to dust, yet the separation of His soul and body was a kind of disintegration.

Reply to Objection 2. The Godhead was united with Christ's flesh after death by personal union, but not by natural union; thus the soul is united with the body as its form, so as to constitute human nature. Consequently, by the union of the body and soul, the body was uplifted to a higher condition of nature, but not to a higher personal state.

Reply to Objection 3. Christ's Passion wrought our salvation, properly speaking, by removing evils; but the Resurrection did so as the beginning and exemplar of all good things.

Article 2. *Whether it was fitting for Christ to rise again on the third day?*

Objection 1. It would seem unfitting that Christ should have risen again on the third day. For the members ought to be in conformity with their head. But we who are His members do not rise from death on the third day, since our rising is put off until the end of the world. Therefore, it seems that Christ, who is our head, should not have risen on the third day, but that His Resurrection ought to have been deferred until the end of the world.

Objection 2. Further, Peter said (Acts 2:24) that "it was impossible for Christ to be held fast by hell" and death. Therefore it seems that Christ's rising ought not to have been deferred until the third day, but that He ought to have risen at once on the same day; especially since the gloss quoted above (Article 1) says that "there is no profit in the shedding of Christ's blood, if He did not rise at once."

Objection 3. The day seems to start with the rising of the sun, the presence of which causes the day. But Christ rose before sunrise: for it is related (John 20:1) that "Mary Magdalen cometh early, when it was yet dark, unto the sepulchre": but Christ was already risen, for it goes on to say: "And she saw the stone taken away from the sepulchre." Therefore Christ did not rise on the third day.

On the contrary, it is written (Matthew 20:19): "They shall deliver Him to the Gentiles to be mocked, and scourged, and crucified, and the third day He shall rise again."

I answer that, as stated above (Article 1) Christ's Resurrection was necessary for the instruction of our faith. But our faith regards Christ's Godhead and humanity, for it is not enough to believe the one without the other, as is evident from what has been said (36, 4; cf. II-II, 2, 7,8). Consequently, in order that our faith in the truth of His Godhead might be confirmed it was necessary that He should rise speedily, and that His Resurrection should not be deferred until the end of the world. But to confirm our faith regarding the truth of His humanity and death, it was needful that there should be some interval between His death and rising. For if He had risen directly after death, it might seem that His death was not genuine and consequently neither would His Resurrection be true. But to establish the truth of Christ's death, it was enough for His rising to be deferred until the third day, for within that time some signs of life always appear in one who appears to be dead whereas he is alive.

Furthermore, by His rising on the third day, the perfection of the number "three" is commended, which is "the number of everything," as having "beginning, middle, and end," as is said in De Coelo i. Again in the mystical sense we are taught that Christ by "His one death" (i.e., of the body) which was light, by reason of His righteousness, "destroyed our two deaths" (i.e., of soul and body), which are as darkness on account of sin; consequently, He remained in death for one day and two nights, as Augustine observes (De Trin. iv).

And thereby is also signified that a third epoch began with the Resurrection: for the first was before the Law; the second under the Law; and the third under grace. Moreover the third state of the saints began with the Resurrection of Christ: for, the first was under figures of the Law; the second under the truth of faith; while the third will be in the eternity of glory, which Christ inaugurated by rising again.

Reply to Objection 1. The head and members are likened in nature, but not in power; because the power of the head is more excellent than that of the members. Accordingly, to show forth the excellence of Christ's power, it was fitting that He should rise on the third day, while the resurrection of the rest is put off until the end of the world.

Reply to Objection 2. Detention implies a certain compulsion. But Christ was not held fast by any necessity of death, but was "free among the dead": and therefore He abode a while in death, not as one held fast, but of His own will, just so long as He deemed necessary for the instruction of our faith. And a task is said to be done "at once" which is performed within a short space of time.

Reply to Objection 3. As stated above (51, 4, ad 1,2), Christ rose early when the day was beginning to dawn, to denote that by His Resurrection He brought us to the light of glory; just as He died when the day was drawing to its close, and nearing to darkness, in order to signify that by His death He would destroy the darkness of sin and its punishment. Nevertheless He is said to have risen on the third day, taking day as a natural day which contains twenty-four hours. And as Augustine says (De Trin. iv): "The night until the dawn, when the Lord's Resurrection was proclaimed, belongs to the third day. Because God, who made the light to shine forth from darkness, in order that by the grace of the New Testament and partaking of Christ's rising we might hear this — 'once ye were darkness,

but now light in the Lord' — insinuates in a measure to us that day draws its origin from night: for, as the first days are computed from light to darkness on account of man's coming fall, so these days are reckoned from darkness to light owing to man's restoration." And so it is evident that even if He had risen at midnight, He could be said to have risen on the third day, taking it as a natural day. But now that He rose early, it can be affirmed that He rose on the third day, even taking the artificial day which is caused by the sun's presence, because the sun had already begun to brighten the sky. Hence it is written (Mark 16:2) that "the women come to the sepulchre, the sun being now risen"; which is not contrary to John's statement "when it was yet dark," as Augustine says (De Cons. Evang. iii), "because, as the day advances the more the light rises, the more are the remaining shadows dispelled." But when Mark says "'the sun being now risen,' it is not to be taken as if the sun were already apparent over the horizon, but as coming presently into those parts."

Article 3. *Whether Christ was the first to rise from the dead?*

Objection 1. It would seem that Christ was not the first to rise from the dead, because we read in the Old Testament of some persons raised to life by Elias and Eliseus, according to Hebrews 11:35: "Women received their dead raised to life again": also Christ before His Passion raised three dead persons to life. Therefore Christ was not the first to rise from the dead.

Objection 2. Further, among the other miracles which happened during the Passion, it is narrated (Matthew 27:52) that "the monuments were opened, and many bodies of the saints who had slept rose again." Therefore Christ was not the first to rise from the dead.

Objection 3. Further, as Christ by His own rising is the cause of our resurrection, so by His grace He is the cause of our grace, according to John 1:16: "Of His fullness we all have received." But in point of time some others had grace previous to Christ — for instance all the fathers of the Old Testament. Therefore some others came to the resurrection of the body before Christ.

On the contrary, It is written (1 Corinthians 15:20): "Christ is risen from the dead, the first fruits of them that sleep — because," says the gloss, "He rose first in point of time and dignity."

I answer that, Resurrection is a restoring from death to life. Now a man is snatched from death in two ways: first of all, from actual death, so that he begins in any way to live anew after being actually dead: in another way, so that he is not only rescued from death, but from the necessity, nay more, from the possibility of dying again. Such is a true and perfect resurrection, because so long as a man lives, subject to the necessity of dying, death has dominion over him in a measure, according to Romans 8:10: "The body indeed is dead because of sin." Furthermore, what has the possibility of existence, is said to exist in some respect, that is, in potentiality. Thus it is evident that the resurrection, whereby one is rescued from actual death only, is but an imperfect one.

Consequently, speaking of perfect resurrection, Christ is the first of them who rise, because by rising He was the first to attain life utterly immortal, according to Romans 6:9: "Christ rising from the dead dieth now no more." But by an imperfect resurrection, some others have risen before Christ, so as to be a kind of figure of His Resurrection.

And thus the answer to the first objection is clear: because both those raised from the dead in the old Testament, and those raised by Christ, so returned to life that they had to die again.

Reply to Objection 2. There are two opinions regarding them who rose with Christ. Some hold that they rose to life so as to die no more, because it would be a greater torment for them to die a second time than not to rise at all. According to this view, as Jerome observes on Matthew 27:52 – 53, we must understand that "they had not risen before our Lord rose." Hence the Evangelist says that "coming out of the tombs after His Resurrection, they came into the holy city, and appeared to many." But Augustine (Ep. ad Evod. clxiv) while giving this opinion, says: "I know that it appears some, that by the death of Christ the Lord the same resurrection was bestowed upon the righteous as is promised to us in the end; and if they slept not again by laying aside their bodies, it remains to be seen how Christ can be understood to be 'the first-born of the dead,' if so many preceded Him unto that resurrection. Now if reply be made that this is said by anticipation, so that the monuments be understood to have been opened by the earthquake while Christ was still hanging on the cross, but that the bodies of the just did not rise then but after He had risen, the difficulty still arises — how is it that Peter asserts that it was predicted not of David but of Christ, that His body would not see corruption, since David's tomb was in their midst; and thus he did not convince them, if David's body was no longer there; for even if he had risen soon after his death, and his flesh had not seen corruption, his tomb might nevertheless remain. Now it seems hard that David from whose seed Christ is descended, was not in that rising of the just, if an eternal rising was conferred upon them. Also that saying in the Epistle to the Hebrews (11:40) regarding the ancient just would be hard to explain, 'that they should not be perfected without us,' if they were already established in that incorruption of the resurrection which is promised at the end when we shall be made perfect": so that Augustine would seem to think that they rose to die again. In this sense Jerome also in commenting on Matthew (27:52, 53) says: "As Lazarus rose, so also many of the bodies of the saints rose, that they might bear witness to the risen Christ." Nevertheless in a sermon for the Assumption [Ep. ix ad Paul. et Eustoch.; among the supposititious works ascribed to St. Jerome] he seems to leave the matter doubtful. But Augustine's reasons seem to be much more cogent.

Reply to Objection 3. As everything preceding Christ's coming was preparatory for Christ, so is grace a disposition for glory. Consequently, it behooved all things appertaining to glory, whether they regard the soul, as the perfect fruition of God, or whether they regard the body, as the glorious resurrection, to be first in Christ as the author of glory: but that grace should be first in those that were ordained unto Christ.

CHAPTER 37

A Juridical Defense of Jesus' Resurrection

John Warwick Montgomery

Existential, blind "leaps of faith" can be and often are suicide jumps, with no criteria of truth available before the leap is made. But suppose the truth of a religious claim did not depend upon an unverifiable, subjectivistic leap of faith? What if a revelational truth-claim did not turn on questions of theology and religious philosophy — on any kind of esoteric, fideistic method available only to those who are already "true believers" — but on the very reasoning employed in the law to determine questions of fact?

The historic Christian claim differs qualitatively from the claims of all other world religions at the epistemological point: on the issue of testability. Eastern faiths and Islam, to take familiar examples, ask the uncommitted seeker to discover their truth experientially: the faith-experience will be self-validating. Unhappily, as analytical philosopher Kai Nielsen and others have rigorously shown, a subjective faith-experience is logically incapable of "validating God-talk" — including the alleged absolutes about which the god in question does the talking.[1] Christianity, on the other hand, declares that the truth of its absolute claims rests squarely on certain historical facts, open to ordinary investigation. These facts relate essentially to the man Jesus, His presentation of Himself as God in human flesh, and His resurrection from the dead as proof of His deity.

Thus the rabbinic lawyer, Christian convert, and apostle — Paul of Tarsus — offered this gospel to Stoic philosophers at Athens as the historically verifiable fulfillment of natural religion and the natural law tradition, with their vague and insufficiently defined content.

Certain Epicurean and Stoic philosophers encountered [Paul at Athens]. And some said, What will this babbler say? Others said, He seems to be setting forth strange gods — for he had been preaching Jesus and the resurrection to them. And they took him to the Areopagus, saying, May we know what this new doctrine is of which you are speaking?...

Then Paul stood at the center of the Areopagus and said, You men of Athens. I note that in all things you are too superstitious. For as I passed by and beheld your devotions, I found an altar with this inscription: TO THE UNKNOWN GOD. Whom therefore you ignorantly worship I declare to you.... The times of this ignorance God winked at, but now commands all men everywhere to repent, for he has appointed a day when he will judge the world in righteousness by the Man whom he has ordained, and he has given assurance of it to all in that he has raised him from the dead.[2]

At one point in his speech, Paul asserted that

---

1. Kai Nielsen, "Can Faith Validate God-Talk?" in *New Theology No. 1*, ed. Martin E. Marty and Dean G. Peerman (New York: Macmillan, 1964), esp. 147; C. B. Martin, "A Religious Way of Knowing," in *New Essays in Philosophical Theology*, ed. Antony Flew and Alasdair MacIntyre (London: SCM Press, 1955), 76 – 95; Frederick Ferre, *Language, Logic and God* (New York: Harper, 1961), 94 – 104. But see also in part 5 of the present volume philosopher John Hare's endeavor to rehabilitate Christian truth: "The Argument from Experience."

2. Acts 17:18 – 19, 22 – 23, 30 – 31. This and all subsequent quotations from Scripture in this chapter are from the King James Version of the Bible. Some passages may be paraphrased. The late classical scholar E. M. Blaiklock of the University of Auckland, New Zealand, in delivering the Annual Wheaton College Graduate School Lectures, 21 – 22 October 1964, on the subject of Paul's Areopagus address, noted that Paul ignored the Epicureans ("the Sadducees of the Greeks"), doubtless because of the intellectual dishonesty into which their movement had fallen, and concentrated on the Stoics, who continued to hold a high view of natural law.

human life is the product of divine creation, "as certain also of your own [Stoic] poets have said," thereby making clear that classical natural law thinking was correct as far as it went, though it did not by any means go far enough.[3] Its completion could be found in Jesus, the Man whom God ordained, and His divine character was verifiable through His resurrection from the dead.

Elsewhere I have argued this case by employing standard, accepted techniques of historical analysis.[4] Here we shall use legal reasoning and the law of evidence. The advantage of a jurisprudential approach lies in the difficulty of jettisoning it: legal standards of evidence develop as essential means of resolving the most intractable disputes in society (dispute settlement by self-help — the only alternative to adjudication — will tear any society apart.) Thus one cannot very well throw out legal reasoning merely because its application to Christianity results in a verdict for the Christian faith.[5]

Significantly, both in philosophy and in theology, there are moves to introduce juridical styles of reasoning. Stephen Toulmin, professor of philosophy at Leeds and one of the foremost analytical philosophers of our time, presents a veritable call to arms:

> To break the power of old models and analogies, we can provide ourselves with a new one. Logic is concerned with the soundness of the claims we make — with the solidity of the grounds we produce to support them, the firmness of the backing we provide for them — or, to change the metaphor, with the sort of *case* we present in defence of our claims. The legal analogy implied in this last way of putting the point can for once be a real help. So let us forget about psychology, sociology, technology and mathematics, ignore the echoes of structural engineering and *collage* in the words 'grounds' and 'backing', and take as our model the discipline of jurisprudence. Logic (we may say) is generalized jurisprudence. Arguments can be compared with law-suits, and the claims we make and argue for in extra-legal contexts with claims made in the courts, while the cases we present in making good each kind of claim can be compared with each other.[6]

Mortimer Adler, at the end of his careful discussion of the question of God's existence, employs not the traditional philosophical ideal of Cartesian absolute certainty, but the legal standards of proof by preponderance of evidence and proof beyond reasonable doubt:

> If I am able to say no more than that a preponderance of reasons favor believing that God exists, I can still say I have advanced reasonable grounds for that belief....
>
> I am persuaded that God exists, either beyond a reasonable doubt or by a preponderance of reasons in favor of that conclusion over reasons against it. I am, therefore, willing to terminate this inquiry with the statement that I have reasonable grounds for affirming God's existence.[7]

And from the jurisprudential side, Jerome Hall recognizes the potential for arbitrating central issues of religion and ethics by the sophisticated instrument of legal reasoning.

> Legal rules of evidence are reflections of "natural reason," and they could enter into dialogues in several ways, for example, to test the validity of theological arguments for the existence of God and to distinguish secular beliefs, even those held without any reasonable doubt, from faith that is so firm (Job's) that it

3. In Acts 17:28 Paul quoted Cleanthes (300 B.C.), *Hymn to Zeus 5,* and/or Aratus (270 B.C.), *Phoenom 5.* Cf. J. B. Lightfoot's essay, "St. Paul and Seneca," in his *St. Paul's Epistle to the Philippians* (Grand Rapids, Mich.: Zondervan, 1953); F. W. Farrar, *Seekers After God* (London: Macmillan, 1906); N. B. Stonehouse, *Paul Before Areopagus, and Other New Testament Studies* (Grand Rapids, Mich.: Eerdmans, 1957); B. Gartner, *The Areopagus Speech and Natural Revelation* (Lund, 1955); and J. Sevenster, *Paul and Seneca* (Leiden: Brill, 1961).

4. John Warwick Montgomery, "Jesus Christ and History," in his *Where Is History Going?* (Minneapolis, Minn.: Bethany, 1972), 37–74.

5. Cf. John Warwick Montgomery, "Legal Reasoning and Christian Apologetics," in his *The Law Above the Law* (Minneapolis, Minn.: Bethany, 1975), 84–90; and idem, *Law and Gospel: A Study in Jurisprudence* (Oak Park, Ill.: Christian Legal Society, 1978), 34–37.

6. Stephen E. Toulmin, *The Uses of Argument* (Cambridge: Cambridge University Press, 1958), 7.

7. Mortimer J. Adler, *How to Think about God* (New York: Macmillan, 1980), 150.

excludes the slightest shadow of doubt and persists even in the face of evidence that on rational grounds is plainly contradictory. In these and other ways the rationality of the law of evidence in the trial of an issue of fact joins philosophical rationalism in raising pertinent questions about faith.[8]

In terms of our discussion, what are the "pertinent questions about faith"? Four overarching questions need to be answered: (1) Are the historical records of Jesus solid enough to rely upon? (2) Is the testimony in these records concerning His life and ministry sufficiently reliable to know what He claimed about Himself? (3) Do the accounts of His resurrection from the dead, offered as proof of His divine claims, in fact establish those claims? (4) If Jesus' deity is established in the foregoing manner, does He place a divine stamp of approval on the Bible so as to render its pronouncements apodictically certain? Let us see how legal reasoning helps to answer each of these key questions.

Basic to any determination of the soundness of Christian claims is the question of the reliability of the pertinent historical documents. The documents at issue are not (*pace* the man on the Clapham omnibus) Josephus, Tacitus, Pliny the Younger, or other pagan references to Jesus, though these do of course exist. Such references are secondary at best, since none of these writers had firsthand contact with Jesus or with His disciples. The documents on which the case for Christianity depends are the New Testament writings, for they claim to have been written by eyewitnesses or by close associates of eyewitnesses (indeed, their origin in apostolic circles was the essential criterion for including them in the New Testament).

How good are these New Testament records? They handsomely fulfill the historian's requirements of *transmissional reliability* (their texts have been transmitted accurately from the time of writing to our own day), *internal reliability* (they claim to be primary-source documents and ring true as such), and *external reliability* (their authorships and dates are backed up by such solid extrinsic testimony as that of the early second-century writer Papias, a student of John the Evangelist, who was told by him that the first three Gospels were indeed written by their traditional authors).[9] Harvard's Simon Greenleaf, the greatest nineteenth-century authority on the law of evidence in the common-law world, applied to these records the "ancient documents" rule: ancient documents will be received as competent evidence if they are "fair on their face" (i.e., offer no internal evidence of tampering) and have been maintained in "reasonable custody" (i.e., their preservation has been consistent with their content). He concluded that the competence of the New Testament documents would be established in any court of law.[10]

The speculation that the Gospel records were "faked" some three hundred years after the events described in them (a viewpoint gratuitously proffered by Professor Trevor-Roper) is dismissed by Lord Chancellor Hailsham, England's highest ranking legal luminary, with an apt lawyer's illustration.

> [What] renders the argument invalid is a fact about fakes of all kinds which I learned myself in the course of a case I did in which there was in question the authenticity of a painting purporting to be by, and to be signed by. Modigliani. This painting, as the result of my Advice on Evidence, was shown to be a fake by X-ray evidence. But in the course of my researches I was supplied by my instructing solicitor with a considerable bibliography concerning the

---

8. Jerome Hall, "Religion, Law and Ethics — A Call for Dialogue," *Hastings Law Journal* 29 (July 1978): 1273. We are not persuaded that Job's faith was quite as firm — or as irrational — as Hall suggests, but the reference to Job is in any case an *obiter dictum*!

9. Montgomery, "Jesus Christ and History"; F. F. Bruce, *The New Testament Documents: Are They Reliable?* 5th ed. (London: Inter-Varsity, 1960); John Warwick Montgomery, "The Fourth Gospel Yesterday and Today," in his *The Suicide of Christian Theology* (Minneapolis, Minn.: Bethany, 1971), 428–65. On the extra-biblical

evidence, see C. R. Haines, *Heathen Contact with Christianity During Its First Century and a Half: Being All References to Christianity Recorded in Pagan Writings During That Period* (Cambridge, England: Deighton, Bell, 1923); and Gary R. Habermas, *Ancient Evidence for the Life of Jesus* (Nashville, Tenn.; Thomas Nelson, 1984).

10. Simon Greenleaf, *The Testimony of the Evangelists, Examined by the Rules of Evidence Administered in Courts of Justice,* reprinted in Montgomery, *The Law Above the Law,* 91ff.

nature of fakes of all kinds and how to detect them. There was one point made by the author of one of these books which is of direct relevance to the point I am discussing. Although fakes can often be made which confuse or actually deceive contemporaries of the faker, the experts, or even the not so expert, of a later age can invariably detect them, whether fraudulent or not because the faker cannot fail to include stylistic or other material not obvious to contemporaries because they are contemporaries, but which stand out a mile to later observers because they reflect the standards, or the materials, or the styles of a succeeding age to that of the author whose work is being faked.[11]

As for the skepticism of the so-called higher critics (or redaction critics) in the liberal theological tradition, it stems from an outmoded methodology (almost universally discarded today by classical and literary scholars and by specialists in comparative Near Eastern studies), and from unjustified philosophical presuppositions (such as anti-supernaturalistic bias and bias in favor of religious evolution).[12] A. N. Sherwin-White, a specialist in Roman law, countered such critics in his 1960–61 Sarum Lectures at the University of London.

It is astonishing that while Graeco-Roman historians have been growing in confidence, the twentieth-century study of the Gospel narratives, starting from the no less promising material, has taken so gloomy a turn in the development of form-criticism that the more advanced exponents of it apparently maintain — so far as an amateur can understand the matter — that the historical Christ is unknowable and the history of His mission cannot be written. This seems very curious when one compares the case for the best-known contemporary of Christ, who like Christ is a

well-documented figure — Tiberius Caesar. The story of his reign is known from four sources, the *Annals* of Tacitus and the biography of Suetonius, written some eighty or ninety years later, the brief contemporary record of Velleius Paterculus, and the third century history of Cassius Dio. These disagree amongst themselves in the wildest possible fashion, both in major matters of political action or motive and in specific details of minor events. Everyone would admit that Tacitus is the best of all the sources, and yet no serious modern historian would accept at face value the majority of the statements of Tacitus about the motives of Tiberius. But this does not prevent the belief that the material of Tacitus can be used to write a history of Tiberius.[13]

The conclusion is inescapable: if one compares the New Testament documents with universally accepted secular writings of antiquity, the New Testament is more than vindicated. Some years ago, when I debated philosophy professor Avrum Stroll of the University of British Columbia on this point,[14] he responded: "All right. I'll throw out my knowledge of the classical world." At which the chairman of the classics department cried: "Good Lord, Avrum, not *that!*"

If, as we have seen, the New Testament records are sound historical documents, how good is their testimony of Jesus? This is a question of great importance, since the accounts tell us plainly that Jesus claimed to be nothing less than God-in-the-flesh, come to earth to reveal God's will for the human race and to save human beings from the penalty of their sins. Moreover, the same testimony meticulously records Jesus' post-resurrection appearances, so a decision as to its reliability will also bear directly on our third major question, the historicity of the resurrection.

11. Lord Hailsham (Quintin Hogg), *The Door Wherein I Went* (London: Collins. 1975), 32–33; the theological and apologetic portion of Lord Hailsham's autobiography has been photolithographically reproduced in *The Simon Greenleaf Law Review* 4 (1984–85): 1–67, with editorial introduction by John Warwick Montgomery.

12. C. S. Lewis, "Modern Theology and Biblical Criticism," in *Christian Reflections,* ed. Walter Hooper (Grand Rapids, Mich.: Eerdmans, 1967), 152–66; Gerhard Maier, *The End of the Historical-Critical Method,* trans. E. W. Leverenz and R. F. Norden

(St. Louis, Mo.: Concordia, 1977); and cf. John Warwick Montgomery, "Why Has God Incarnate Suddenly Become Mythical?" in *Perspectives on Evangelical Theology,* ed. Kenneth S. Kantzer and Stanley N. Gundry (Grand Rapids, Mich.: Baker Book House, 1979), 57–65.

13. A. N. Sherwin-White, *Roman Society and Roman Law in the New Testament* (Oxford: Clarendon Press, 1963), 187.

14. My lectures and Professor Stroll's are published in Montgomery, *Where Is History Going?* 37–74 and 207–21.

In a court of law, admissible testimony is considered truthful unless impeached or otherwise rendered doubtful. This is in accord with ordinary life, where only the paranoiac goes about with the bias that everyone is lying. (Think of Cousin Elmo, convinced that he is followed by Albanians.) The burden, then, is on those who would show that the New Testament testimony to Jesus is not worthy of belief. Let us place the Gospel testimony to Jesus under the legal microscope to see if its reliability can be impeached.

Here we employ a construct for attacking perjury that has been labeled "the finest work on that subject."[15] McCloskey and Schoenberg offer a fourfold test for exposing perjury, involving a determination of *internal* and *external* defects in the *witness himself* on the one hand and in the *testimony itself* on the other.[16] We can translate their schema into diagrammatic form thusly:

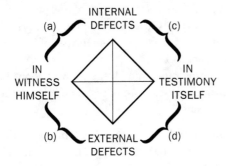

Figure 6.2a. A Construct for Exposing Perjury

(a) Internal defects in the witness himself refer to any personal characteristics or past history tending to show that the "witness is inherently untrustworthy, unreliable, or undependable." Were the apostolic witnesses to Jesus persons who may be disbelieved because they were "not the type of persons who can be trusted"? Did they have criminal records or is there reason to think they were pathological liars? If anything, their simple literalness and directness is almost painful. They seem singularly poor candidates for a James Bond thriller or for being cast in the role of "Spy and Counterspy." But perhaps they were mythomanes — people incapable of distinguishing fact from fantasy? They themselves declare precisely the contrary: "We have not followed cunningly devised fables [Gk. *mythoi*, 'myths']," they write, "when we made known unto you the power and coming of our Lord Jesus Christ, but were eyewitnesses of his majesty."[17]

(b) But perhaps the apostolic witnesses suffered from external defects, that is, "motives to falsify"?

Not all perjurers have committed prior immoral acts or prior crimes. Frequently, law abiding citizens whose pasts are without blemish will commit perjury, not because they are inherently unworthy, but because some specific present reason compels them to do so in the case at bar. Motive, then, becomes the common denominator. There is a motive for every act of perjury. The second major way in which the cross-examiner can seek to expose perjury, therefore, is to isolate the specific motive which causes the witness to commit perjury.[18]

Surely no sensible person would argue that the apostolic witnesses would have lied about Jesus for monetary gain or as a result of societal pressure. To the contrary: they lost the possibility both of worldly wealth and of social acceptability among their Jewish peers because of their commitment to Jesus.[19] Might that very affection for and attachment to Jesus serve

---

15. Alan Saltzman, "Criminal Law: How to Expose Perjury Through Cross-Examination," *Los Angeles Daily Journal*, 4 November 1982.

16. Patrick L. McCloskey and Ronald L. Schoenberg, *Criminal Law Advocacy* (New York: Matthew Bender, 1984), vol. 5, para. 12.01 [b].

17. 2 Pet. 1:16. In vv. 17–18, Peter states expressly that he was with Jesus when He was transfigured (Matt. 17:2; Mark 9:2; Luke 9:29).

18. McCloskey and Schoenberg, *Criminal Law Advocacy*, vol. 5, para. 12.03.

19. A point made as early as the fourth century by the historian Eusebius of Caesarea, and reiterated by such classical apologists as Hugo Grotius ("the father of international law"), in "The Resurrection of Christ proved from credible testimony," in his *The Truth of the Christian Religion*, trans. John Clarke (new ed.; London: William Baynes, 1825), bk. 2. sec. 6, 85–88; this section of Grotius's work is photolithographically reproduced in John Warwick Montgomery, ed., *Jurisprudence: A Book of Readings* (Orange, Calif.: Simon Greenleaf School of Law, 1980), 327–30.

as a motive to falsify? Not when we remember that their Master expressly taught them that lying was of the devil.[20]

(c) Turning now to the testimony itself, we must ask if the New Testament writings are internally inconsistent or self-contradictory. Certainly, the Four Gospels do not give identical, verbatim accounts of the words or acts of Jesus. But if they did, that fact alone would make them highly-suspect, for it would point to collusion.[21] The Gospel records view the life and ministry of Jesus from four different perspectives — just as veridical witnesses to the same accident will present different but complementary accounts of the same event. If the objection is raised that the same occurrence or pericope is sometimes found at different times or places in Jesus' ministry, depending upon which Gospel one consults, the simple answer is that no one Gospel contains or was ever intended to contain the complete account of Jesus' three-year ministry.[22] Furthermore, Jesus (like any preacher) certainly spoke the same messages to different groups at different times. And suppose He did throw the moneychangers out of the Temple twice: is it not strange, in light of their activity and His principles, that He *only* threw them out twice? (We would have expected it every Saturday — Sabbath — night.) Observe also how honestly and in what an unflattering manner the apostolic company picture themselves in these records. Mark, Peter's companion, describes him as having a consistent case of foot-in-the-mouth disease; and the Apostles in general are presented (in Jesus' own words) as "slow of heart to believe all that the prophets have spoken."[23] To use New Testament translator J. B. Phillips's expression, the internal content of the New Testament records has "the ring of truth."[24]

(d) Finally, what about external defects in the testimony itself, i.e., inconsistencies between the New Testament accounts and what we know to be the case from archaeology or extra-biblical historical records? Far from avoiding contact with secular history, the New Testament is replete with explicit references to secular personages, places, and events. Unlike typical sacred literature, myth, and fairytale ("Once upon a time ..."), the Gospel story begins with "There went out a decree from Caesar Augustus that all the world should be taxed."[25] Typical of the New Testament accounts are passages such as the following:

> Now in the fifteenth year of the reign of Tiberius Caesar, Pontius Pilate being governor of Judea, and Herod being tetrarch of Galilee, and his brother Philip, tetrarch of Itoraea and of the region of Trachonitis, and Lysanias the tetrarch of Abilene.
>
> Annas and Caiaphas being the high priests, the word of God came unto John the son of Zacharias in the wilderness.
>
> And he came into all the country about Jordan preaching the baptism of repentance for the remission of sins.[26]

Modern archaeological research has confirmed again and again the reliability of New Testament geography, chronology, and general history.[27] To take but a single, striking example: After the rise of liberal biblical criticism, doubt was expressed as to the historicity of Pontius Pilate, since he is mentioned even by pagan historians only in connection with Jesus' death. Then, in 1961, came the discovery at Caesarea of the now

20. John 8:44, etc.

21. "People just do not see things in an identical way when their positions and chances for observation vary. [If so,] the case is a frame up." F. Lee Bailey and Henry B. Rothblatt, *Fundamentals of Criminal Advocacy* (San Francisco: Bancroft-Whitney, 1974), para. 500, p. 240.

22. John 20:30–31; 21:25. See Edmund H. Bennett. *The Four Gospels from a Lawyer's Standpoint* (Boston: Houghton, Mifflin, 1899); photolithographically reproduced with editorial introduction by John Warwick Montgomery in *The Simon Greenleaf Law Review* 1 (1981–82).

23. Luke 24:25.

24. J. B. Phillips, *Ring of Truth: A Translator's Testimony* (New York: Macmillan, 1967).

25. Luke 2:1. See John Warwick Montgomery, *Myth, Allegory and Gospel* (Minneapolis, Minn.: Bethany, 1974), 11–31, 116–18.

26. Luke 3:1–3.

27. See, for example, E. M. Blaiklock, *The Archaeology of the New Testament* (Grand Rapids, Mich.: Zondervan, 1970); and Edwin M. Yamauchi, *The Stones and the Scriptures* (Grand Rapids, Mich.: Baker Book House, 1981).

famous "Pilate inscription," definitely showing that, as usual, the, New Testament writers were engaged in accurate historiography.

Thus on no one of the four elements of the McCloskey-Schoenberg construct for attacking perjury can the New Testament witnesses to Jesus be impugned.

Furthermore, one should realize (and non-law-yers seldom do realize) how difficult it is to succeed in effective lying or misrepresentation when a cross-examiner is at work. Richard A. Givens, in his standard work, *Advocacy,* in the McGraw-Hill Trial Practice Series, diagrams ordinary truthful communication and then contrasts it with the tremendous complexities of deceitful communication (figures 6.2b and 6.2c).[28]

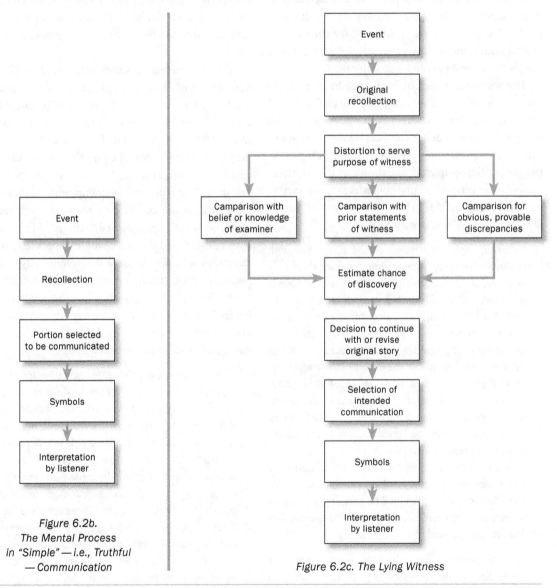

Figure 6.2b.
The Mental Process
in "Simple" — i.e., Truthful
— Communication

Figure 6.2c. The Lying Witness

28. Richard A. Givens, *Advocacy* (New York: McGraw-Hill, 1980), 13 – 14.

Observe that the witness engaged in deception must, as it were, juggle at least three balls simultaneously, while continually estimating his chances of discovery: he must be sure he doesn't say anything that contradicts what his examiner knows (or what he thinks his examiner knows); he must tell a consistent lie ("liars must have good memories"); and he must take care that nothing he says can be checked against contradictory external data. Givens's point is that successful deception is terribly difficult, for the psychological strain and energy expended in attempting it makes the deceiver exceedingly vulnerable.

The wider the angles of divergence between these various images, the more confusing the problem, and the more "higher mathematics" must be done in order to attempt to avoid direct conflicts between these elements. The greater the angle of deception employed, the greater the complexity and the lower the effectiveness of these internal mental operations. If this is conscious, we attribute this to lying. If it is unconscious we lay it to the "bias" of the witness.

> If one is lying or strongly biased, it is not enough to simply dredge up whatever mental trace there may be of the event and attempt to articulate it in answer to a question. Instead, all of the various elements mentioned must be weighed, a decision made as to the best approach, a reply contrived that is expected to be most convincing, and then an effort made to launch this communication into the minds of the audience.
>
> The person with a wide angle of divergence between what is recalled and the impression sought to be given is thus at an almost helpless disadvantage, especially if confronting a cross-examiner who understands the predicament.
>
> If the audience includes both a cross-examiner and a tribunal, the number of elements to be considered becomes even greater. The mental gymnastics required rise in geometric proportion to the number of elements involved.[29]

Now, wholly apart from the question as to whether the New Testament witnesses to Jesus were the kind of people to engage in such deception (and we have already seen in examining them for possible internal and external defects, that they were not): *had* they attempted such a massive deception, *could they have gotten away with it?* Admittedly, they were never put on a literal witness stand, but they concentrated their preaching on synagogue audiences. This put their testimony at the mercy of the hostile Jewish religious leadership who had had intimate contact with Jesus' ministry and had been chiefly instrumental in ending it.

Such an audience eminently satisfies Givens's description of "both a cross-examiner and a tribunal": they had the *means*, *motive*, and *opportunity* to expose the apostolic witness as inaccurate and deceptive if it had been such. The fact that they did not can only be effectively explained on the ground that they *could not*. It would seem, for example, inconceivable that the Jewish religious leadership, with their intimate knowledge of the Old Testament, would have sat idly by as the Apostles proclaimed that Jesus' life and ministry had fulfilled dozens of highly specific Old Testament prophecies (birth at Bethlehem, virgin birth, flight to Egypt, triumphal entry, sold by a friend for thirty pieces of silver, etc., etc.), had that not been true. Professor F. F. Bruce of the University of Manchester underscores this fundamental point as to the evidential significance of the hostile witnesses:

> It was not only friendly eyewitnesses that the early preachers had to reckon with; there were others less well disposed who were also conversant with the main facts of the ministry and death of Jesus. The disciples could not afford to risk inaccuracies (not to speak of willful manipulation of the facts), which would at once be exposed by those who would be only too glad to do so. On the contrary, one of the strong points in the original apostolic preaching is the confident appeal to the knowledge of the hearers; they not only said, "We are witnesses of these things," but also, "As you yourselves also know" (Acts 2:22). Had there been any tendency to depart from the facts in

---

29. Ibid., 12.

any material respect, the possible presence of hostile witnesses in the audience would have served as a further corrective.[30]

We do not waste time on the possibility that the disciples were suffering from insane delusions. First, because the law presumes a man sane, and there is no suggestion in the accounts the Apostles were otherwise. Second, because the point Professor Bruce has just stressed concerning the hostile witnesses applies with equal force to the insanity suggestion: had the disciples distorted Jesus' biography for *any* reason, including a deluded state of mind, the hostile witnesses would surely have used this against them.

The functional equivalence of hostile witnesses with formal cross-examination goes far to answer the occasionally voiced objection that the apostolic testimony to Jesus would be rejected by a modern court as "hearsay:" i.e., out-of-court statements tendered to prove the truth of their contents. Let us note at the outset the most severe problem with hearsay testimony: the originator of it is not in court and so cannot be subjected to searching cross-examination. Thus even when New Testament testimony to Jesus would technically fall under the axe of the hearsay rule, the hostile witnesses as functional cross-examiners reduce the problem to the vanishing point .

In the second place, the hearsay rule exists in Anglo-American common law (no such rule is a part of the Continental civil law tradition), especially as a technical device to protect juries from secondhand evidence. Following the virtual abolition of the civil jury in England, the Civil Evidence Act of 1968 in effect eliminated the hearsay rule by statute from civil trials — on the ground that judges can presumably sift even secondhand testimony for its truth-value.[31] In the United States, and in English criminal trials, the exceptions to the hearsay rule have almost swallowed up the rule, and one of these exceptions is the "ancient documents" rule (to which we referred earlier), by which the New Testament documents would indeed be received as competent evidence.

To be sure, the underlying principle of the hearsay rule remains vital: that a witness ought to testify "of his own knowledge or observation," not on the basis of what has come to him indirectly from others. And the New Testament writers continually tell us that they are setting forth that "which we have heard, which we have seen with our eyes, which we have looked upon, and our hands have handled ... the Word of life."[32]

Simon Greenleaf's summation of the testimonial case for Jesus' life, ministry, and claims about Himself offers a perennial challenge to the earnest seeker for truth.

> All that Christianity asks of men on this subject, is, that they would be consistent with themselves; that they would treat its evidences as they treat the evidence of other things; and that they would try and judge its actors and witnesses, as they deal with their fellow men, when testifying to human affairs and actions, in human tribunals. Let the witnesses be compared with themselves, with each other, and with surrounding facts and circumstances; and let their testimony be sifted, as if it were given in a court of justice, on the side of the adverse party, the witness being subjected to a rigorous cross-examination. The result, it is confidently believed, will be an undoubting conviction of their integrity, ability, and truth. In the course of such an examination, the undesigned coincidences will multiply upon us at every step in our progress; the probability of the veracity of the witnesses and of the reality of the occurrences which they relate will increase, until it acquires, for all practical purposes, the value and force of demonstration.[33]

At the heart of the apostolic testimony and proclamation is the alleged resurrection of Jesus Christ from the dead. During His ministry, Jesus offered His

30. Bruce, *New Testament Documents,* 45 – 46.

31. Peter Murphy, *A Practical Approach to Evidence* (London: Financial Training, 1982), 23 – 24; cf. George B. Johnston, "The Development of Civil Trial by Jury in England and the United States," *Simon Greenleaf Law Review* 4 (1984 – 85): 69 – 92.

32. 1 John 1:1.

33. Greenleaf, *Testimony of the Evangelists,* 132 – 22.

forthcoming resurrection as the decisive proof of His claim to deity.[34] Did the Resurrection in fact occur?[35]

First, consider the written records of the Resurrection and of detailed post-resurrection appearances which occurred over a forty-day period.[36] What is important here is that these accounts are all contained in the very New Testament documents whose historical reliability we have already confirmed and are testified to by the same apostolic witnesses whose veracity we have just established. To do an abrupt *volte-face* and now declare those documents and witnesses to be untrustworthy because they assert that Jesus rose from the dead would be to substitute a dubious metaphysic ("resurrections from the dead are cosmically impossible" — and how does one establish *that* in a relativistic, Einsteinian universe?) for careful historical investigation. We must not make the mistake of eighteenth-century philosopher David Hume, who thought he could avoid evidential drudgery by deductively reasoning from the gratuitous premise that "a firm and unalterable experience has established the laws of nature" to the (entirely circular) conclusions: "There must be a uniform experience against every miraculous event" and "That a dead man should come to life has never been observed in any age or country."[37]

Second, we should reflect upon the force of the "missing body" argument of Frank Morison,[38] who was converted to Christianity through his investigation of the evidence for the Resurrection. His argument proceeds as follows: (1) If Jesus didn't rise, someone must have stolen the body; (2) the only people involved were the Roman authorities, the Jewish religious leaders, and Jesus' disciples; (3) the Romans and the Jewish religious leaders would certainly not have taken the body, since to do so would have been against their own interests (the Romans wanted to keep Palestine quiet, and the Jews wanted to preserve their religious influence);[39] and (4) the disciples would hardly have stolen the body and then died for what they knew to be untrue; (5) *Ergo* — by process of elimination — Jesus rose from the dead just as the firsthand accounts declare.

I have shown elsewhere that Antony Flew's attempt to avoid the impact of this argument is unsuccessful.[40] When Flew says that Christians simply prefer a biological miracle (the Resurrection) to a psychological miracle (the disciples dying for what they knew to be false), he completely misses the point. The issue is not metaphysical preference; it is testimonial evidence. No such evidence exists to support a picture of psychologically aberrant disciples, while tremendously powerful testimonial evidence exists to the effect that Jesus physically rose from the dead.

During the last few years, more inventive attempts to explain away the Resurrection have appeared. Schonfield's *Passover Plot* argues that Jesus induced His own crucifixion, drugging Himself so as to survive just long enough in the tomb to convince the fuddled disciples that He had risen.[41] (*Quaere:* How does this square with Jesus' own moral teachings? And does

---

34. Matt. 12:38–40; 16:4; Luke 11:29; John 2:18–22.

35. I.e., did the resurrection occur in *ordinary* history? We do not deal here with the unverifiable vagaries of "hyper-history" or "supra-history" (as in the thought of Karl Barth and certain of his neoorthodox followers), or with "existential" resurrections (Rudolf Bultmann and the post-Bultmannians). I have discussed elsewhere these modern theological attempts to have one's cake and eat it too: John Warwick Montgomery, "Karl Barth and Contemporary Theology of History," in his *Where Is History Going?* 100–117; cf. idem, "Faith, History and the Resurrection," in ibid., 225–39; idem, "Luther's Hermeneutic vs. the New Hermeneutic," in his *In Defense of Martin Luther* (Milwaukee, Wis.: Northwestern Publishing House, 1970), 40–85.

36. Concerning the historical and evidential value of these appearances, see Merrill C. Tenney, *The Reality of the Resurrection* (New York: Harper, 1963); Josh McDowell, *The Resurrection Fac-*

tor (San Bernardino, Calif.: Here's Life Publishers, 1981); Richard Riss, *The Evidence for the Resurrection of Jesus Christ* (Minneapolis, Minn.: Bethany, 1977); and Sir Norman Anderson, *The Evidence for the Resurrection* (London: Inter-Varsity, 1966).

37. David Hume, "Of Miracles," in his *An Enquiry Concerning Human Understanding* (1748); for critique, see C. S. Lewis, *Miracles* (New York: Macmillan, 1947), esp. chaps. 8 and 13; and John Warwick Montgomery, *The Shape of the Past*, revised ed. (Minneapolis, Minn.: Bethany, 1975), 289–93.

38. Frank Morison, *Who Moved the Stone?* (London: Faber & Faber, 1944).

39. Cf. Matt. 27:62–66.

40. John Warwick Montgomery, "Science, Theology, and the Miraculous," in his *Faith Founded on Fact* (Nashville, Tenn.: Thomas Nelson, 1978), 43–73, esp. 54.

41. See Edwin M. Yamauchi, "Passover Plot or Easter Triumph?

it not leave us with precisely the same problem as to what finally happened to the body?) Von Daniken — who turned to pseudo-scientific writing while serving a prison sentence in Switzerland for embezzlement, fraud, and forgery[42] — "explains" the Resurrection by suggesting that it was the product of a close encounter of the third kind: Jesus was a kind of Martian cleverly dressed in a Jesus suit who knew a few tricks such as how to appear to rise from the dead.

Aren't such hypotheses *possible?* Doubtless, in our contingent universe, anything is possible (as one philosopher said) except squeezing toothpaste back into the tube. But legal reasoning operates on *probabilities,* not possibilities: preponderance of evidence in most civil actions; evidence beyond reasonable (not beyond *all*) doubt in criminal matters.[43] The *Federal Rules of Evidence* defines relevant evidence as "evidence having any tendency to make the existence of any fact that is of consequence to the determination of the action more probable or less probable than it would be without the evidence."[44] Suppose a jury brought in a verdict of "innocent" because it is always *possible* that invisible Martians, not the accused, were responsible for the crime! Judges in the United States carefully instruct juries to pay attention *only* to the evidence in the case, and to render verdicts in accord with it. A guilty verdict in a criminal matter should be rendered only if the jury cannot find any reasonable explanation of the crime (i.e., any explanation *in accord with the evidence)* other than that the accused did it. May we suggest that the tone and value of discussions about Jesus' resurrection would be considerably elevated if equally rigorous thinking were applied thereto?

Can we base ultimates (Jesus' deity, our commitment to Him for time and eternity) on mere probabilities? The analytical philosophers have shown that we have no other choice: only formal ("analytic") truths (e.g., the propositions of deductive logic and of pure mathematics) can be demonstrated absolutely — and the absoluteness here is due to the definitional nature of their axiomatic foundations, as with Euclid's geometry. All matters of fact ("synthetic" assertions) are limited to probabilistic confirmation, but this does not immobilize us in daily life. We still put our very lives in jeopardy every day on the basis of probability judgments (crossing the street, consuming packaged foods and drugs, flying in airplanes, etc.). And the law in every land redistributes property and takes away liberty (if not life) by verdicts and judgments rooted in the examination of evidence and probabilistic standards of proof.

But the issue here is a *miracle:* a resurrection. How much evidence ought a reasonable man to require in order to establish such a fact? Could evidence ever justify accepting it? Thomas Sherlock, Master of the Temple Church (owned by two of the four guilds of English barristers, the Honourable Societies of the Inner and Middle Temple) and Bishop of London, well answered these questions in the eighteenth century:

Suppose you saw a Man publickly executed, his Body afterwards wounded by the Executioner, and carry'd and laid in the Grave; that after this you shou'd be told, that the Man was come to Life again: What wou'd you suspect in this Case? Not that the Man had never been dead; for that you saw your self: But you wou'd suspect whether he was now alive. But wou'd you say, this Case excluded all human Testimony; and that Men could not possibly discern, whether one with whom they convers'd familiarly, was alive or no? Upon what Ground cou'd you say this? A Man rising from the Grave is an Object of Sense, and can give the same

A Critical Review of H. Schonfield's Recent Theory," in *Christianity for the Tough-Minded,* ed. John Warwick Montgomery (Minneapolis, Minn.; Bethany, 1973), 261–71.

42. Von Daniken had "obtained the money [over $130,000 in debts] by misrepresentation of his financial situation, falsifying the hotel's books to make it appear solvent. A court psychiatrist examined von Daniken and found him a prestige-seeker, a liar and an unstable and criminal psychopath with a hysterical character, yet fully accountable for his acts" (Richard R. Lingeman, "Erich von Daniken's Genesis," *New York Times Book Review,* 31 March 1974, 6.

43. Probability reasoning is virtually universal in the law: it operates both in common law and in non-common law systems of jurisprudence, and in "civilized" and "primitive" legal systems indiscriminately. See Montgomery, *Law and Gospel,* 35–36.

44. *Federal Rules of Evidence* 401. This definition was derived from Professor James Bradley Thayer's classic *Preliminary Treatise on Evidence* (1898).

Evidence of his being alive, as any other Man in the World can give. So that a Resurrection consider'd only as a Fact to be proved by Evidence, is a plain Case; it requires no greater Ability in the Witnesses, than that they be able to distinguish between a Man dead, and a Man alive: A Point, in which I believe every Man living thinks himself a Judge.[45]

Bishop Sherlock is certainly correct that a resurrection does not in principle create any insuperable evidential difficulty. Phenomenally (and this is all we need worry about for evidential purposes) a resurrection can be regarded as *death followed by life.*

D, then L.

Normally, the sequence is reversed, thus:

L, then D.

We are well acquainted with the phenomenal meaning of the constituent factors (though we do not understand the "secret" of life or why death must occur). Furthermore, we have no difficulty in establishing evidential criteria to place a person in one category rather than in the other. Thus the eating of fish[46] is sufficient to classify the eater among the living, and a crucifixion is enough to place the crucified among the dead. In Jesus' case, the sequential order is reversed, but that has no epistemological bearing on the weight of evidence required to establish death or life. And if Jesus was dead at point A, and alive again at point B, then resurrection has occurred: *res ipsa loquitur.*[47]

However, does not the unreliability of eyewitness testimony cast doubt on an event as extraordinary as the Resurrection? Psychologists such as Loftus have pointed up genuine dangers in eyewitness testimony.[48] Nonetheless, as we have already seen, it remains the cornerstone of legal evidence. As for the reliability of identifying acquaintances (the precise issue in the disciples' post-resurrection identifications of Jesus), specialists on the subject agree that "the better acquainted a witness is with a subject, the more likely it is that the witness' identification will be accurate." These same authorities add that "in an eyewitness context, the greatest challenge to the advocate's power of persuasion is presented by the attempt to argue, without support from expert testimony, the unreliability of an unimpeached eyewitness's identification of a prior acquaintance."[49] And this is precisely what we have in the case under consideration: disciples like Thomas provide "unimpeached eyewitness identification" of the resurrected Jesus with whom they had had the most intimate acquaintance for the immediately preceding three-year period.[50] No advocate's "power of persuasion" is going to make a difference to that kind of identification evidence.

Finally, the objection may be offered: even granting Jesus' resurrection, is that fact alone enough to establish His deity and the truth of His claims? Theological presuppositionalists Carl F. H. Henry and Ronald H. Nash tell us that there are no self-interpreting facts,[51] and Calvinists R. C. Sproul and John Gerstner, as well as evangelical neo-Thomist Norman L. Geisler, insist that an independent theistic structure must be established to make any theological sense out of Jesus' resur-

45. Thomas Sherlock, *The Tryal of the Witnesses of the Resurrection of Jesus* (London: J. Roberts, 1729), 62; Sherlock's book is photolithographically reproduced in Montgomery, *Jurisprudence.*

46. See Luke 24:36 – 43.

47. I have applied proof by *res ipsa loquitur* to the resurrection in my *Law and Gospel,* 35.

48. Elizabeth F. Loftus, *Eyewitness Testimony* (Cambridge, Mass.: Harvard University Press, 1979); cf. her popular article on this subject in *Psychology Today* 18, no. 2 (February 1984): 22 – 26.

49. Edward B. Arnolds, et al., *Eyewitness Testimony: Strategies and Tactics* (New York: McGraw-Hill, 1984), 400 – 401.

50. John 20:19 – 28.

51. Carl F. H. Henry, *God: Revelation and Authority* (Waco, Tex; Word Books, 1976), 1:220 – 23, 230 – 38, 256 – 63; 2:313 – 34; Ronald

H. Nash, "The Use and Abuse of History in Christian Apologetics," *Christian Scholar's Review* 1, no. 3 (Spring 1971): 217 – 26; Ronald H. Nash, *Christian Faith and Historical Understanding,* 2d ed. (Dallas, Tex.: Probe Books, 1989). I have responded to Carl Henry in Montgomery, *Faith Founded on Fact,* xvii – xxv. Paul D. Feinberg wrote a devastating critique of Nash's "Use and Abuse of History" in "History: Public or Private? A Defense of John Warwick Montgomery's Philosophy of History," *Christian Scholar's Review* 1, no. 4 (Summer 1971): 325 – 31; it is reprinted in Montgomery, *Shape of the Past,* 375 – 82. Nash's book, *Christian Faith and Historical Understanding* (which, sadly, does not seem to have benefitted in any way from Feinberg's insights), has been critically reviewed by Francis I. Beckwith: "Does Evidence Matter?" *Simon Greenleaf Law Review* 4 (1984 – 85): 231 – 35.

rection.[52] We profoundly disagree. Even Rat — famous for his leading role in Kenneth Grahame's *The Wind in the Willows,* but hardly an accomplished epistemologist — becomes exasperated with his companion for not recognizing that facts can be self-interpreting:

"Do-you-mean-to-say," cried the excited Rat, "that this doormat doesn't *tell* you anything?"

"Really, Rat," said the Mole quite pettishly, "I think we've had enough of this folly. Who ever heard of a doormat *telling* anyone anything? They simply don't do it. They are not that sort at all. Doormats know their place."

"Now look here, you — you thick-headed beast," replied the Rat, really angry, "this must stop. Not another word, but scrape — scrape and scratch and dig and hunt round, especially on the sides of the hummocks, if you want to sleep dry and warm tonight, for it's our last chance!"

Elsewhere we have argued in detail that facts — historical and otherwise — "in themselves provide adequate criteria for choosing among variant interpretations of them."[53] Philosopher Paul D. Feinberg has defended that case with inexorable logic:

Let us consider an example from recent history. It can be substantiated that some 6 million Jews died under German rule in the second World War. Let me suggest two mutually exclusive interpretations. First, these events may be interpreted as the actions of a mad man who was insanely anti-Semitic. The deaths were murders, atrocities. Second, it might be asserted that Hitler really loved the Jews. He had a deep and abiding belief in heaven and life after death. After reviewing Jewish history, Hitler decided that the Jews had been persecuted enough, and because of his love for them he was seeking to help them enter eternal blessedness. If no necessity exists between events and

interpretation, then there is no way of determining which meaning is correct. We would never be justified in claiming that one holding the latter view is wrong. This is both repugnant and absurd. There must be an empirical necessity that unites an event or fact with its correct interpretation.[54]

Beyond this, we merely remind the reader that the very nature of legal argument (judgments rendered on the basis of factual verdicts) rests on the ability of facts to speak for themselves. As a single illustration, taking the leading U.S. Supreme Court case of *Williams v. North Carolina* (the "second Williams case"), which stands for the proposition that a divorce on substituted or constructive service in one state need only be given full faith and credit by another state when the parties have acquired a bona fide domicile in the divorcing state. In the course of its opinion, the Court declared:

Petitioners, long time residents of North Carolina, came to Nevada, where they stayed in an auto-court for transients, filed suits for divorce as soon as the Nevada law permitted, married one another as soon as the divorces were obtained, and promptly returned to North Carolina to live. *It cannot reasonably be claimed that one set of inferences rather than another regarding the acquisition by petitioners of new domicils [sic] in Nevada could be drawn from the circumstances attending their Nevada divorces.*[55]

Geisler misrepresents us when he says that we hold that "the resurrection is so bizarre, so odd, that only a supernatural explanation will adequately account for it."[56] In our view there are two compelling reasons to accept Jesus' resurrection as implicating His deity. First, "this miracle deals effectively with the most fundamental area of man's universal need, the conquest of death"[57] — truth recognized in law by the "dying declaration" exception to the hearsay rule (even the

52. R. C. Sproul, John Gerstner, and Arthur Lindsley, *Classical Apologetics* (Grand Rapids, Mich.: Zondervan, 1984); Norman L. Geisler, *Miracles and Modern Thought,* with a response by R. C. Sproul (Dallas, Tex.: Probe Books, 1982).

53. John Warwick Montgomery, "Gordon Clark's Historical Philosophy," in Montgomery, *Where Is History Going?* esp. 164.

54. Feinberg, "History: Public or Private?" 379.

55. *Williams v. North Carolina,* 325 U.S. 226, 65 Sup. Ct. 1092, 157 A.L.P. 1366 (italics added).

56. Geisler, *Miracles and Modern Thought,* 66. Remarkably, Geisler seems entirely unacquainted with my detailed treatment of this issue in my book *Faith Founded on Fact,* 43–73, even though my book was published four years before his.

57. Ibid., 61.

declaration of the homicide victim without religious faith is admissible in evidence, on the ground that one is particularly likely to tell the truth when conscious of the immanence of that most terrible of existential events).[58] If death is indeed that significant, then "not to worship One who gives you the gift of eternal life is hopelessly to misread what the gift tells you about the Giver."[59]

In the second place, there are logically only two possible kinds of explanation or interpretation of the fact of the Resurrection: that given by the person raised, and that given by someone else. Surely, if only Jesus was raised, He is in a far better position (indeed, in the *only* position!) to interpret or explain it. Until Von Daniken, for example, rises from the dead, we will prefer Jesus' account of what happened. And Jesus tells us that His miraculous ministry is explicable because He is no less than God in human form: "I and *my* Father are one"; "He who has seen me has seen the Father."[60] Theism then becomes the proper inference from Jesus' resurrection as He Himself explained it — not a prior metaphysical hurdle to jump in order to arrive at the proper historical and evidential interpretation of that event.

Jesus' deity in itself establishes the truth of the Christian message, over against competing religions and secular world-views. And Jesus' teachings per se, being God's teachings, represent an infallible guide to human life and conduct. But Jesus does more even than this. By His direct statements concerning the Old Testament as divine revelation[61] and by His consistent quoting of it as trustworthy and divinely authorita-tive in all respects,[62] Jesus put upon it His (i.e., God's) *imprimatur*. By giving His Apostles a special gift of the Holy Spirit to recall infallibly what He had taught them,[63] and, by implication, to recognize apostolic-ity in others, He proleptically stamped with approval as divine revelation the future writings of Apostles (the original twelve, minus Judas Iscariot, plus Paul — grafted in as Apostle to the Gentiles)[64] and writings by their associates (Mark, Luke, etc.) whose accuracy the Apostles were in a position to verify. As a result, the entire Bible — Old Testament and New — becomes an unerring source of absolute principles.[65]

Two objections may be raised to the argument we have just presented. First, why should the mere fact that God says something guarantee its truth? Second, what if the incarnate Christ was so limited to the human ideas of His time that His stamp of approval on the Bible represents no guarantee of its absolute accuracy?

The first of these arguments is reflected in Descartes's discussion of God as a possible "Evil Genius" — a cosmic liar. But if He were, He would be a divine and, therefore, consummate liar, so you would be incapable of catching Him at it. In short, He would be a better liar than you are a detective. So the very idea of God-as-liar is meaningless — an analytically unverifiable notion in principle. Once you have met God incarnate, you have no choice but to trust Him: as to the way of salvation and as to the reliability of the entire Bible.

The suggestion that Jesus was limited to human and fallible ideas (the so-called Kenotic theory[66] of liberal theology) also collapses under its own weight.

---

58. See, for example, *State v. Elliott*, 45 Iowa 486.

59. Montgomery, *Faith Founded on Fact*, 61.

60. John 10:30; 14:8 – 9, slightly paraphrased; cf. Mark 2:5 – 7; 14:61 – 64.

61. E.g., Matt. 4:4; 5:17 – 19; John 5:39; 10:35.

62. For example, Matt. 12:38 – 42; 19:3 – 6; 24:37 – 39; Luke 24:25 – 27.

63. John 14:26; 16:12 – 15. Swiss theologian Oscar Cullmann has made much of the apostolic memory as the inspired link between Jesus' ministry and the New Testament scriptures.

64. Acts 1:21 – 26; 9:26 – 27; Gal. 2:11 – 13; 2 Peter 3:15 – 16.

65. See John Warwick Montgomery, ed., *God's Inerrant Word: An International Symposium on the Trustworthiness of Scripture*

(Minneapolis, Minn.: Bethany, 1974); idem, *Crisis in Lutheran Theology*, 2d ed., 2 vols. (Minneapolis. Minn.: Bethany, 1973); idem, *Shape of the Past*, 138 – 45.

66. From the Greek noun *kenosis*, whose verb form ("empty oneself/divest oneself of privileges") is applied to Christ in Philippians 2:6 – 8. However, biblical teaching on incarnation has no resemblance to the liberal theological theory of Jesus' fallibility. Theological liberals — typically — developed the theory to have their cake (a divine Jesus) and eat it too (simultaneous rejection of Jesus' conservative view of scriptural authority). Cf. Montgomery, *Crisis in Lutheran Theology*, 1:91 – 93. It is perhaps worth noting that the well-known passage in the Gospels in which Jesus states that He does not know the hour of His Second Coming (Mark 13:32)

On Kenotic reasoning, either Jesus chose to conform His statements to the fallible ideas of His time (in which case He was an opportunist who, in the spirit of Lenin, committed one of the most basic of all moral errors, that of allowing the end to justify the means);[67] or He couldn't avoid self-limitation in the very process of Incarnation (in which case Incarnation is of little or no value to us, since there is then no guarantee that it reveals anything conclusive). And note that if such a dubious Incarnation mixed absolute wheat with cul-turally relative chaff, we would have no sufficient criterion for separating them anyway, so the "absolute" portion would do us no good!

To meet man's desperate need for apodictic principles of human conduct, an incarnate God must not speak with a forked tongue. And, as we have seen, no divine stuttering has occurred. To the contrary: His message can be relied upon as evidentially established, a sure light shining in a dark world, illuminating the path to eternity.[68]

---

is no confirmation of Kenotic theory, for (1) only a single, eschatological item of knowledge is involved, and (2) Jesus' disclaimer of knowledge on this point shows that in His incarnate state He was nonetheless fully aware of the boundaries of His knowledge, and being in control of His knowledge He would not have advertently or inadvertently given false or misleading information when He did make positive assertions (e.g., on the reliability of the Bible).

67. John Warwick Montgomery. "The Marxist Approach to Human Rights: Analysis and Critique," *Simon Greenleaf Law Review* 3 (1983–84): 51–53, 138–41.

68. This chapter is reprinted, with slight changes, from chapter 6 of the author's *Human Rights and Human Dignity* (Dallas, Tex.: Probe Books, 1986).

CHAPTER 38

Experiences of the Risen Jesus

Gary R. Habermas

Introduction

Having specialized for several decades in critical studies of the resurrection of Jesus, I recently decided to update my Bibliography. What began rather modestly evolved into a five year study of well over 2000 sources on this topic, published from 1975 to the present in German, French, and English. I was most interested in scholarly trends, resulting in a survey of well over 100 sub-issues.

One area of concentration was the common historical content recognized by virtually all researchers. For a variety of reasons, contemporary scholars widely conclude that after his death, Jesus' followers at least *thought* that they had seen appearances of the risen Jesus. Do the disciples' *beliefs* that they had witnessed resurrection appearances provide any clues as to what may really have occurred? The answer depends on how one accounts for these experiences. Here, where scholarship differs widely, three chief options prevail. In spite of these differences, it is my contention that this is the single most crucial aspect of the historical question.

During the examination of this subject, I will attempt to clarify some of the relevant issues in order to narrow the major options. While I will not choose between these answers regarding the underlying cause, my chief task is to tighten the focus of the discussion. In the process, I will use chiefly those data to which the vast majority of recent researchers agree, at least in principle, regardless of their theological positions. Due to the volume of relevant material, I will often resort to summarized conclusions of recent scholarly trends. The endnotes provide additional background information, perspectives, argumentation, and other details.

The Disciples' Experiences of the Risen Jesus

The substantially unanimous verdict of contemporary critical scholars is that Jesus' disciples at least believed that Jesus was alive, resurrected from the dead. Reginald Fuller refers to the disciples' belief in Jesus' resurrection as "one of the indisputable facts of history." Upon what was their claim based? Fuller continues that it is clear that the disciples had real experiences, characterized as appearances or visions of the risen Jesus. Whether these are explained naturally or supernaturally, this experience "is a fact upon which both believer and unbeliever may agree."[1]

In recent studies of the historical Jesus, this aspect has enjoyed the support of a broad scholarly consensus. E.P. Sanders declares that the "equally secure facts" indicate that Jesus' disciples "saw him (in what sense is not certain) after his death…. Thereafter his followers saw him."[2]

That the vast majority of scholars, in spite of extensive disagreements in other areas, recognizes that the disciples had some sort of experience is a significant starting point. How these experiences are explained is another matter. But there are some rather impressive reasons that explain such a widespread, initial conclusion. We will begin by listing eight pointers, four from Paul and four more from various other sources.

---

1. Fuller, *The Foundations of New Testament Christology* (New York: Scribner's, 1965), 142.

2. E.P. Sanders, *The Historical Figure of Jesus* (London: Penguin, 1993), 11, 13.

(1) Contemporary critical scholars agree that the apostle Paul is the primary witness to the early resurrection experiences. A former opponent (1 Cor. 15:9; Gal. 1:13 – 14; Phil. 3:4 – 7), Paul states that the risen Jesus appeared personally to him (1 Cor. 9:1; 15:8; Gal. 1:16). The scholarly consensus here is attested by atheist Michael Martin, who avers: "However, we have only one contemporary eyewitness account of a postresurrection appearance of Jesus, namely Paul's."[3]

(2) In addition to Paul's own experience, few conclusions are more widely recognized than that, in 1 Corinthians 15:3ff., Paul records an ancient oral tradition(s). This pre-Pauline report summarizes the early Gospel content, that Christ died for human sin, was buried, rose from the dead, and then appeared to many witnesses, both individuals and groups.

Paul is clear that this material was not his own but that he had passed on to others what he had received earlier, as the center of his message (15:3). There are many textual indications that the material pre-dates Paul. Most directly, the apostle employs *paredoka* and *parelabon*, the equivalent Greek terms for delivering and receiving rabbinic tradition (cf. 1 Cor. 11:23). Indirect indications of a traditional text(s) include the sentence structure and verbal parallelism, diction, and the triple sequence of *kai hoti*. Further, several non-Pauline words, the proper names of Cephas (cf. Lk. 24:34) and James, and the possibility of an Aramaic

original are all significant. Fuller attests to the unanimity of scholarship here: "It is almost universally agreed today that Paul is here citing tradition."[4] Critical scholars agree that Paul received the material well before this book was written.[5]

The most popular view is that Paul received this material during his trip to Jerusalem just three years after his conversion, to visit Peter and James, the brother of Jesus (Gal. 1:18 – 19), both of whose names appear in the appearance list (1 Cor. 15:5; 7). An important hint here is Paul's use of the verb *historesai* (1:18), a term that indicates the investigation of a topic.[6] The immediate context both before and after reveals this subject matter: Paul was inquiring concerning the nature of the Gospel proclamation (Gal. 1:11 – 2:10), of which Jesus' resurrection was the center (1 Cor. 15:3 – 4, 14, 17; Gal. 1:11, 16).

Critical scholars generally agree that this pre-Pauline creed(s) may be the earliest in the New Testament. Ulrich Wilckens asserts that it "indubitably goes back to the oldest phase of all in the history of primitive Christianity."[7] Joachim Jeremias agrees that it is, "the earliest tradition of all."[8] Perhaps a bit too optimistically, Walter Kasper even thinks that it was possibly even "in use by the end of 30 AD...."[9]

Indicating the wide approval on this subject, even more skeptical scholars frequently agree. Gerd Ludemann maintains that "the elements in the tradition are

3. Michael Martin, *The Case Against Christianity* (Philadelphia: Temple University, 1991), 81.

4. Reginald Fuller, *The Formation of the Resurrection Narratives* (New York: Macmillan, 1980), 10.

5. Of the vast number of scholars who agree, some examples include John Kloppenborg, "An Analysis of the Pre-Pauline Formula in 1 Cor 15:3b – 5 in Light of Some Recent Literature," *Catholic Biblical Quarterly*, Vol. 40 (1978), especially 351, 360; Jerome Murphy-O'Connor, "Tradition and Redaction in 1 Cor 15:3 – 7," *Catholic Biblical Quarterly*, Vol. 43 (1981), 582 – 589; John Meier, *A Marginal Jew: Rethinking the Historical Jesus* (New York: Doubleday, 2001), Vol. 2:139; Sanders, *The Historical Figure of Jesus*, 277; Pinchas Lapide, *The Resurrection of Jesus: A Jewish Perspective* (Minneapolis: Augsberg, 1983), 97 – 99.

6. Several studies on the meaning of *historesai* in Gal. 1:18 have reached similar conclusions. See William Farmer, "Peter and Paul, and the Tradition Concerning 'The Lord's Supper' in I Cor. 11:23 – 25," *Criswell Theological Review*, Vol. 2 (1987), 122 – 130,

in particular, and 135 – 138 for an apostolic, Petrine source for the pre-Pauline tradition. Also helpful is an older but still authoritative study by G.D. Kilpatrick, "Galatians 1:18 historesai Kephan" in *New Testament Essays: Studies in Memory of Thomas Walter Manson*, A.J.B. Higgins, editor (Manchester: Manchester University, 1959), 144 – 149. Paul Barnett reports that this same term appears in Herodotus, Polybius, and Plutarch, for whom it meant to inquire (41). Similar ideas are contained in J. Dore, "La Resurrection de Jesus: A L'Epreuve du Discours Theologique," *Recherches de Science Religieuse*, Vol. 65 (1977), 291, endnote 11.

7. Ulrich Wilckens, *Resurrection: Biblical Testimony to the Resurrection: An Historical Examination and Explanation* (Edinburgh: St. Andrew, 1977), 2.

8. Joachim Jeremias, "Easter: The Earliest Tradition and the Earliest Interpretation," *New Testament Theology*, trans. John Bowden (New York: Scribner's, 1971), 306.

9. Walter Kaspar, *Jesus the Christ*, new ed., trans. V. Green (Mahweh: Paulist, 1976), 125.

to be dated to the first two years after the crucifixion of Jesus ... not later than three years ... *the formation of the appearance traditions mentioned in I Cor.15.3 – 8 falls into the time between 30 and 33 CE....*"[10] Similarly, Michael Goulder thinks that it "goes back at least to what Paul was taught when he was converted, a couple of years after the crucifixion."[11] Thomas Sheehan agrees that this tradition "probably goes back to at least 32 – 34 C.E., that is, to within two to four years of the crucifixion."[12] Others clearly consent.[13]

Overall, my recent overview of critical sources mentioned above indicates that those who provide a date generally opt for Paul's reception of this report relatively soon after Jesus' death, by the early to mid-30s A.D.[14] This provides an additional source that appears just a half step removed from eyewitness testimony.

(3) Paul was so careful to assure the content of his Gospel message, that he made a second trip to Jerusalem (Gal. 2:1 – 10) specifically to be absolutely sure that he had not been mistaken (2:2). The first time he met with Peter and James (Gal. 1:18 – 20). On this occasion, the same two men were there, plus the apostle John (2:9). Paul was clearly doing his research by seeking out the chief apostles. As Martin Hengel notes, "Evidently the tradition of I Cor. 15.3 had been subjected to many tests" by Paul.[15]

These four apostles were the chief authorities in the early church, and each is represented in the list of those who had seen the resurrected Jesus (1 Cor. 15:5 – 7).

So their confirmation of Paul's Gospel preaching (Gal. 2:9), especially given the apostolic concern to insure doctrinal truth in the early church, is certainly significant. On Paul's word, we are again just a short distance from a firsthand report.

(4) Not only do we have Paul's account that the other major apostles confirmed his Gospel message, but he provides the reverse testimony, too. After listing Jesus' resurrection appearances, Paul tells us he also knew what the other apostles were preaching regarding Jesus' appearances, and it was the same as his own teaching on this subject (1 Cor. 15:11). As one, they proclaimed that Jesus was raised from the dead (15:12, 15). So Paul narrates both the more indirect confirmation of his Gospel message by the apostolic leaders, plus his firsthand, direct approval of their resurrection message.

(5) Critical scholars usually recognize that James, the brother of Jesus, was a rather skeptical unbeliever prior to Jesus' crucifixion (Mk. 3:21 – 35; Jn. 7:5). Not long afterwards, James is a leader of the Jerusalem church, where Paul finds him during his two visits (Gal. 1:18 – 19; 2:1 – 10; cf. Acts 15:13 – 21). In between, the pre-Pauline statement in 1 Corinthians 15:7 states that the risen Jesus appeared to James.

Scholars find several reasons for believing that James was an unbeliever before this event. John Meier points out that James' unbelief is multiply attested. Further, the criterion of embarrassment is probably the strongest consideration, since it would be highly

10. Gerd Ludemann, *The Resurrection of Jesus*, trans. John Bowden (Minneapolis: Fortress, 1994), 38 (Ludemann's emphasis).

11. Michael Goulder, "The Baseless Fabric of a Vision," in Gavin D'Costa, editor, *Resurrection Reconsidered* (Oxford: Oneworld, 1996), 48.

12. Thomas Sheehan, *The First Coming: How the Kingdom of God Became Christianity* (New York: Random House, 1986), 118; cf. 110 – 111.

13. For instances, see A.J.M. Wedderburn, *Beyond Resurrection* (Peabody: Hendrickson, 1999), 274, note 265; Robert Funk, Roy W. Hoover, and the Jesus Seminar, *The Five Gospels* (New York: Macmillan, 1993), 24; Jack Kent, *The Psychological Origins of the Resurrection Myth* (London: Open Gate, 1999), 16 – 17; G.A. Wells, *Did Jesus Exist?* (London: Pemberton, 1986), 30.

14. Besides those listed above, a few of the many others include: Meier, *A Marginal Jew*, 2:139; Fuller, *The Formation of the Resurrection Narratives*, 10, 14, 48; Raymond Brown, *The Virginal Conception and Bodily Resurrection of Jesus* (New York: Paulist, 1973), 81; Francis X. Durrwell, *La Resurrection de Jesus: Mystere de Salut* (Paris: Les edtions du Cerf, 1976), 22; Peter Stuhlmacher, *Jesus of Nazareth — Christ of Faith*, trans. Siegfried S. Schatzmann (Peabody: Hendrickson, 1993), 8; C.E.B. Cranfield, "The Resurrection of Jesus Christ," *Expository Times*, Vol. 101 (1990), 169; James D.G. Dunn, *The Evidence for Jesus* (Louisville: Westminster, 1985), 70; Leander E. Keck, *Who is Jesus? History in Perfect Tense* (Columbia: University of South Carolina, 2000), 139; Helmut Merklein, "Die Auferweckung Jesu und die Anfange der Christologie (Messias bzw. Sohn Gottes und Menschensohn)," *Zeitschrift fur die Neutestamentliche Wissenschaft und die Kunde der alteren Kirche*, Vol. 72 (1981), reprint, 2.

15. Martin Hengel, *The Atonement: The Origins of the Doctrine in the New Testament*, trans. John Bowden (Philadelphia: Fortress, 1981), 38.

unlikely that the early church would otherwise sponsor what would potentially be some "deeply offensive" statements regarding Jesus' brother, as well as a major leader. To a lesser extent, the criterion of coherence indicates a similarity between Jesus' frequent call to place God before one's family, and Jesus' own example, in that he did the same although some of his own family members were unbelievers.[16]

Surprisingly, Fuller concludes that even if the New Testament had not referenced the resurrection appearance to James, "we should have to invent" one in order to account for his conversion and his promotion to his lofty position in the Jerusalem church![17] The majority of recent scholars, including many rather skeptical ones, agree that James was converted from unbelief by Jesus' personal appearance.[18]

(6) Many other early creedal texts are found throughout the New Testament. Many scholars think that the Book of Acts incorporates some of these early traditions, located in the sermons contained there.[19] They are generally identified by factors such as their compactness, theological simplicity, and because the structure, style, and/or diction reflect word patterns other than the author's. Not as widely accepted as the pre-Pauline tradition(s) in 1 Corinthians 15:3ff., it still appears that a majority of critical scholars conclude that some of these snippets reflect the early preaching of the Gospel message.[20] The risen Jesus is the center of each tradition, and Jesus' appearances are mentioned frequently.[21]

These Acts traditions are often dated very early. Gerald O'Collins thinks that this book "incorporates resurrection formulae which stem from the thirties."[22] John Drane concludes that this material "almost certainly goes back to the time immediately after the resurrection event is alleged to have taken place."[23]

(7) Virtually no critical scholar questions that the disciples' convictions regarding the risen Jesus caused their radical transformation, even being willing to die for their beliefs. Their change does not evidence the resurrection appearances per se, but it is a clear indication that the disciples at least *thought* that they had experienced the risen Jesus.[24] Alternatives must account for this belief.

16. Meier, *A Marginal Jew*, 2:68 – 71.

17. Fuller, *The Formation of the Resurrection Narratives*, 37.

18. Of the many examples, see Ludemann, *The Resurrection of Jesus*, 109; Helmut Koester, *Introduction to the New Testament* (Philadelphia: Fortress, 1982), Vol. 2:84; Robert Funk, *Honest to Jesus* (San Francisco: Harper Collins, 1996), 33; Wedderburn, 116; John Shelby Spong, *The Easter Moment* (San Francisco: Harper and Row, 1987), 68; Peter Stuhlmacher, "The Resurrection of Jesus and the Resurrection of the Dead," trans. Jonathan M. Whitlock, *Ex Auditu*, Vol. 9 (1993), 49; E.P. Sanders, "But Did it Happen?" *The Spectator*, Vol. 276 (1996), 17.

19. The most popular candidates for these condensed confessional segments are located within the sermon material in Acts 1:21 – 22; 2:22 – 36; 3:13 – 16; 4:8 – 10; 5:29 – 32; 10:39 – 43; 13:28 – 31; 17:1 – 3; 17:30 – 31.

20. For some examples, see Gerd Ludemann, *Early Christianity According to the Traditions in Acts: A Commentary*, trans. John Bowden (Minneapolis: Fortress, 1989), especially 47 – 49, 112 – 115; Hengel, 34; Kloppenborg, 361; John Alsup, *The Post-Resurrection Appearance Stories of the Gospel Tradition: A History-of-Traditions Analysis with Text-Synopsis*, Calwer Theologische Monographien 5 (Stuttgart: Calwer Verlag, 1975), 64 – 65, 81 – 85; Merklein, 2; Raymond E. Brown, *An Introduction to New Testament Christology* (Mahweh: Paulist, 1994), 112 – 113, 164; Durrwell, 22; Ben F. Meyer, *The Aims of Jesus* (London: SCM, 1979), 61, 64, 66; Fuller, *The Formation of the Resurrection Narratives*, 44 – 45; Pheme Perkins,

Resurrection: New Testament Witness and Contemporary Reflection (Garden City: Doubleday, 1984), 90, 228 – 231; Max Wilcox, *The Semitisms of Acts* (Oxford: Clarendon, 1965), esp. 79 – 80, 164 – 165; Luke Timothy Johnson, *Living Jesus: Learning the Heart of the Gospel* (San Francisco: Harper Collins, 1999), 34; C.H. Dodd, *The Apostolic Preaching and its Developments* (Grand Rapids: Baker, reprint, 1980), 17 – 31.

21. For examples, mentions of Jesus' appearances are found in Acts 2:31 – 32; 3:15; 10:39 – 41; 13:29 – 37.

22. Gerald O'Collins, *Interpreting Jesus* (London: Geoffrey Chapman, 1983), 109 – 110.

23. John Drane, *Introducing the New Testament* (San Francisco: Harper and Row, 1986), 99.

24. For critical agreement in various elements here, see Willi Marxsen, *Jesus and Easter* (Nashville: Abingdon, 1990), 66; J. Dore, "Croire en la Resurrection de Jesus-Christ," *Etudes*, Vol. 356 (1982), 536 – 537; Funk, *Honest to Jesus*, especially 270; Wedderburn, 46 – 47; Hengel, 65; J.K. Elliott, "The First Easter," *History Today*, Vol. 29 (1979), 210, 215, 218; Wolfhart Pannenberg, *Jesus — God and Man*, second ed., trans. Lewis L. Wilkins and Duane A. Priebe (Philadelphia: Westminster, 1977), 96; Michael Grant, *Saint Peter: A Biography* (New York: Scribner, 1994), pp. 89, 96; Sanders, 11, 276 – 280; Hugh Jackson, "The Resurrection Belief of the Earliest Church: A Response to the Failure of Prophecy," *The Journal of Religion*, Vol. 55 (1975), 419 – 422; Elaine Pagels, *The Gnostic Gospels* (New York: Random House, 1979), 8.

(8) In the study mentioned at the outset of this essay, I found that approximately 75% of the surveyed scholars accept one or more arguments for the historicity of the empty tomb. The remaining 25% accept one or more arguments against the early church's knowledge of an empty tomb. If the majority is correct that Jesus' burial tomb was later found empty, this perhaps adds some credibility to the disciples' claim that they saw the risen Jesus. If the minority view is correct, this reason would of course not support Jesus' appearances.[25]

The survey revealed almost two dozen reasons supporting Jesus' empty tomb. These include the potentially embarrassing but unanimous agreement in all four Gospels that women were the earliest witnesses, Jerusalem being the least-likely place for a resurrection proclamation, the attestation by multiple sources, the early pre-Pauline creed (1 Cor. 15:3 – 4) implying an empty tomb (cf. the possible early tradition in Acts 13:29 – 31, 36 – 37), along with the later report that the Jewish leaders conceded it (Matt. 28:11 – 15).[26]

The minority position that accepted one or more reasons against the empty tomb cited a total of about a dozen opposing considerations. These tend to center on the lateness of the Gospel reports, Paul's lack of discussion (and perhaps knowledge) of the empty tomb, and that the report served apologetic purposes in Christian preaching.

The empty tomb is not as widely held as are the other historical reasons for the disciples' experiences, which are seldom disputed. Still, most critical scholars agree that Jesus' tomb was found empty. James D.G. Dunn concludes: "I have to say quite forcefully: the probability is that the tomb was empty. As a matter of historical reconstruction, the weight of evidence points firmly to the conclusion...." Potential alternative explanations are not feasible.[27] Historian Michael

Grant surprisingly states that "the historian ... cannot justifiably deny the empty tomb" because normally applied historical criteria indicate that "the evidence is firm and plausible enough to necessitate the conclusion that the tomb was indeed found empty."[28]

These eight reasons indicate why virtually all recent scholars conclude that the disciples thought that they had seen the risen Jesus. Paul's eyewitness testimony, the early date of the pre-Pauline creed(s) in 1 Corinthians 15:3ff., scrutinizing his Gospel message at least twice before the chief apostles who were also witnesses, and Paul's knowledge of their eyewitness teaching on the resurrection appearances produces a simply astounding, interconnected line of evidence nearly unheard of in ancient documents. Howard Clark Kee surprisingly remarks that Paul's research "can be critically examined and compared with other testimony from eyewitnesses of Jesus, just as one would evaluate evidence in a modern court or academic setting."[29]

Further, four additional reasons include the conversion of James from unbelief after witnessing an appearance from his brother Jesus, other early creedal texts in Acts and elsewhere, the disciples' transformation, and the possibility of the empty tomb. It is clear that the disciples were thoroughly convinced that Jesus was raised from the dead and that they had seen him. Still other factors could be mentioned, but these are sufficient for our purposes.[30]

No other thesis viably opposes the conclusion that the disciples at least *thought* that Jesus was raised from the dead. This was what Fuller termed "one of the indisputable facts of history." The disciples thought that they had witnessed Jesus' appearances, which, however they are explained, "is a fact upon which both believer and unbeliever may agree."[31] Fuller adds that "[e]ven the most skeptical historian" must do one more thing: "postulate some other event" that is

25. This data is summarized in my forthcoming article, "The Empty Tomb of Jesus: Recent Critical Arguments."

26. Similar reports are also found in Justin Martyr, *Dialogue with Trypho* 108 and Tertullian, *On Spectacles* 30.

27. Dunn, 68.

28. Michael Grant, *Jesus: An Historian's Review of the Gospels* (New York: Collier, 1992), 176.

29. Howard Clark Kee, *What Can We Know about Jesus?* (Cambridge: Cambridge University, 1990), 1 – 2.

30. For details on all of these reasons, as well as other pertinent information, see Gary R. Habermas, *The Risen Jesus and Future Hope* (Lanham: Rowman and Littlefield, 2003), Chapter 1.

31. Fuller, *The Foundations of New Testament Christology*, 142.

not the disciples' faith, but the reason for their faith, in order to account for their experiences. Of course, both natural and supernatural options have been proposed.[32]

For the remainder of this article, we will survey the major categorical options that propose explanations to account for the disciples' *belief* that they had actually seen the risen Jesus. Although we will not decide here on a specific cause, it is my contention that even narrowing the options can be of great assistance in addressing the single most crucial aspect of these historical issues.

Accounting for the Disciples' Experiences

Each of the eight reasons above argues clearly for the belief that Jesus was *seen* alive after his crucifixion. The widespread view of contemporary scholars is that a *visual claim* was being made, either as a perceived revelation or as some type of presence. The disciples proclaimed that they had seen appearances of Jesus. This is what Paul clearly attested. The pre-Pauline creed lists Peter, James, and the other apostles as recipients. Peter, James, and John were all present when Paul's Gospel was affirmed. Paul knew of their preaching on Jesus' appearances. Most scholars agree that Jesus' tomb was empty. As a result, these disciples were transformed.

Recent scholars agree. Helmut Koester points out that, "We are on much firmer ground with respect to the appearances of the risen Jesus and their effect." Jesus' appearances "cannot very well be questioned."[33] Bart Ehrman declares: "we can say with complete certainty that some of his disciples at some later time insisted that ... he soon appeared to them, convincing them that he had been raised from the dead."[34] Ehrman adds: "Historians, of course, have no difficulty whatsoever speaking about the belief in Jesus' resurrection, since this is a matter of public record."[35] Holtz thinks that the disciples' "experience of resurrection ... is in fact an undeniable historical event."[36] Ludemann reminds us that the appearance language employed by Paul is that of sight: "active sensual perception.... Paul is claiming a visual side to the appearance...."[37] More specifically, Paul thinks that Jesus appeared in his "transformed spiritual resurrection corporeality."[38]

It seems clear that the disciples were utterly persuaded that the risen Jesus had appeared to them. The data are strong enough that this is granted by virtually all critical scholars. Can we get any closer to the nature of the experience that convinced the disciples? We will mention three avenues, each of which presents its own problems.

Those who deny (or question) whether the disciples actually saw Jesus in some sense would seemingly sever the connection between what the disciples thought, and what really happened. They generally move in either of two directions, by directly or indirectly positing their solution.

(1) The more popular of the two skeptical approaches, reaching its heyday in nineteenth century thought, posed a naturalistic theory to account for the data. Such a move basically accepted the strongest historical facts, while veering off in a natural direction instead of affirming the resurrection.[39]

However, in spite of a minority resurgence at present,[40] this approach has proven to be the most difficult. In fact, the vast majority of critical scholars reject this

---

32. Fuller, *The Formation of the Resurrection Narratives*, 2, 169, respectively; cf. 181.

33. Koester, 2:84.

34. Bart Ehrman, *Jesus: Apocalyptic Prophet of the New Millennium* (New York: Oxford University, 1999), 230.

35. Ehrman, 231.

36. My translation of the German text in Traugott Holtz, "Kenntnis von Jesus und Kenntnis Jesu: Eine Skizze zum Verhältnis zwischen historisch-philologischer Erkenntnis und historisch-theologischem Verständnis," *Theologische Literaturzeitung*, Vol. 104 (1979), 10.

37. Ludemann, *The Resurrection of Jesus*, 50; cf. 37.

38. Gerd Ludemann, *What Really Happened to Jesus: A Historical Approach to the Resurrection*, with Alf Özen, trans. John Bowden (Louisville: Westminster John Knox, 1995), 103.

39. For details, see Gary R. Habermas, "The Late Twentieth-Century Resurgence of Naturalistic Responses to Jesus' Resurrection," *Trinity Journal*, new series, Vol. 22 (2001), 179–196.

40. Represented by the works of Ludemann, Goulder, and Kent above.

option. They are often well aware that the weight of the known historical facts opposes each of the proposals, and comparatively few attempt it. Scholars generally concede that there are multiple historical problems with each of the options.

For instance, Raymond Brown refers to these theses as "gratuitous charges."[41] James D.G. Dunn charges that these "alternative interpretations of the data fail to provide a more satisfactory explanation."[42] Stephen Davis agrees: "All of the alternative hypotheses with which I am familiar are historically weak; some are so weak that they collapse of their own weight once spelled out.... the alternative theories that have been proposed are not only weaker but far weaker at explaining the available historical evidence...."[43] John A.T. Robinson admits that, "It is indeed very difficult to dismiss [Jesus' appearances] and still find a credible explanation."[44]

(2) Another option is the agnostic plea that we do not (or cannot) really know what happened.[45] The disciples indeed were sincere in their belief that they saw Jesus, but we cannot determine the cause.

This position sometimes seems to reject even the possibility of actual appearances, rather than following the data to its conclusion. The approach is difficult to maintain, since its question mark could be answered by the many factual considerations. Perhaps we have plenty of evidence already to decide the case, especially since we used only those minimal data that virtually all critical scholars accept, including agnostics. So critics must not reject, or pull up short of, the results that are indicated by their own research, which may clearly indicate that more than an undefined "something" occurred to Jesus' disciples.

Recognized historical particulars must be accounted for in a viable manner. For example, perhaps the eight areas mentioned above could settle the matter of the *cause* of the disciples' experiences. But simply to label these data as insufficient does not explain them — they may be precisely what is capable of solving the historical issue. With Fuller, many scholars counter that we are capable of positing a cause for the disciples' faith beyond the faith itself.[46]

(3) In my study mentioned at the outset of this essay, by far the most popular option at present is that Jesus was actually raised in some form, either as an objective vision or in a transformed body.[47] The former view was more popular a few decades ago, while the latter appears clearly to be the majority view at present. Reasons such as those listed here are most frequently mentioned for establishing this position, each of which points to a visual event that changed the disciples' lives, completely convincing them that they had seen the risen Jesus.

Besides the rejoinders posed by the naturalistic hypotheses, various a priori objections have been proposed. While seldom addressed specifically to the resurrection, these philosophical misgivings are aimed at miracles in general. For example, naturalists or more deistic thinkers object that miraculous events do not occur. Or, these reservations might concern background information (as with Bayes Theorem), or issues regarding the nature of the evidence. While favored by some philosophers, these responses are also opposed by many.[48]

---

41. Brown, *An Introduction to New Testament Christology*, 163; cf. 163 – 167.

42. Dunn, 76. Cf. N.T. Wright, "Christian Origins and the Resurrection of Jesus: The Resurrection of Jesus as a Historical Problem," *Sewanee Theological Review*, Vol. 41 (1998), 118 – 122.

43. Stephen T. Davis, "Is Belief in the Resurrection Rational?" *Philo*, Vol. 2 (1999), 57 – 58.

44. John A.T. Robinson, *Can We Trust the New Testament?* (Grand Rapids: Eerdmans, 1977), 124.

45. Represented by the works of Marxsen and Wedderburn above.

46. Fuller, *The Formation of the Resurrection Narratives*, 2, 169, 181.

47. The first is favored by Jeremias and the second by Wright above.

48. For examples of each, see Rodney D. Holder, "Hume on Miracles: Bayesian Interpretation, Multiple Testimony, and the Existence of God," *British Journal for the Philosophy of Science*, Volume 49 (1998), especially 60 – 62; George N. Schlesinger, "Miracles and Probabilities," *Nous*, Volume 21 (1987), especially 219, 230 – 232; John Earman, "Bayes, Hume, and Miracles," *Faith and Philosophy*, Volume 10 (1993), especially 293, 305 – 306; Richard Otte, "Schlesinger and Miracles," *Faith and Philosophy*, Volume 10 (1993), especially 93, 97; David Owen, "Hume Versus Price on Miracles and Prior Probabilities," *Philosophical Quarterly*, Vol. 37 (1987), 187 – 202.

Conclusion

I have argued that at the center of the historical issue regarding the resurrection appearances is that Jesus' disciples were totally convinced that they had seen the risen Jesus. Many strong reasons support the historicity of these beliefs. Virtually all critical scholars agree that the disciples' *convictions* are thoroughly historical.

Do the disciples' beliefs that they had experienced resurrection appearances provide any clues as to what caused these convictions? We have outlined three chief options. It is not our purpose here to choose between these general paths that purport to account for the cause of the disciples' experiences.

One option might potentially show itself to be superior. For example, since many researchers accept the maxim that a viable natural hypothesis is to be accepted before a supernatural one, postulating and checking alternative scenarios by the known data will probably continue. This process makes sense. On the other hand, if alternative theses continually fail amid dissatisfaction with agnostic reluctance, the reasons favoring the disciples' experiences might indicate that the most likely scenario is that the disciples actually did see the risen Jesus.

In general, the more thoroughly one option fails, the more likely the others become. And the more strongly an option is established, the more the others diminish. Even without a final solution here, however, there is still value in honing our instruments and narrowing our options.

CHAPTER 39

The Bodily Resurrection of Jesus

William Lane Craig

It has been argued on the basis of Paul's testimony that Jesus's resurrection body was spiritual in the sense of being unextended, immaterial, intangible, and so forth. But neither the argument appealing to the nature of Paul's Damascus Road experience nor the argument from Paul's doctrine of the resurrection body supports such a conclusion. On the contrary, Paul's information serves to confirm the gospels' narratives of Jesus's bodily resurrection. Not only is the gospels' physicalism well-founded, but it is also, like Paul's doctrine, a nuanced physicalism.[1]

There are probably few events in the gospels for which the historical evidence is more compelling than for the resurrection of Jesus. Historical-critical studies during the second half of this century, increasingly freed from the lingering Deistical presuppositions that largely determined in advance the results of resurrection research during the previous 150 years, have reversed the current of scepticism concerning the historical resurrection, such that the trend among scholars in recent years has been acceptance of the historical credibility of Jesus's resurrection.

Nevertheless, there is still one aspect of the resurrection that a great number of scholars simply cannot bring themselves to embrace: that Jesus was raised from the dead *physically*. The physicalism of the gospels' portrayal of Jesus's resurrection body accounts, I think, more than any other single factor

for critical skepticism concerning the historicity of the gospel narratives of the bodily resurrection of Jesus. Undoubtedly the prime example of this is Hans Grass's classic *Ostergeschehen und Osterberichte*.[2] Inveighing against the *'massiven Realismus'* of the gospel narratives, Grass brushes aside the appearance stories as thoroughly legendary and brings every critical argument he can summon against the empty tomb. Not that Grass would construe the resurrection, at least overtly, merely in terms of the survival of Jesus's soul; he affirms a bodily resurrection, but the body is 'spiritual' in nature, as by the apostle Paul, not physical. Because the relation between the old, physical body and the new, spiritual body is *totaliter-aliter*, the resurrection entails, not an emptying of the tomb, but the creation of a new body. Because the body is spiritual, the appearances of Christ were in the form of heavenly visions caused by God in the minds of those chosen to receive them.

It is difficult to exaggerate the extent of Grass's influence. Though few have been willing to join him in denying the empty tomb, since the evidence inclines in the opposite direction, one not infrequently finds statements that because the resurrection body does not depend upon the old body, we are not compelled to believe in the empty tomb. And it is everywhere asserted, even by those who staunchly defend the empty tomb, that the spiritual nature of the resurrec-

1. This article was originally published as "The Bodily Resurrection of Jesus," in *Gospel Perspectives I*, pp. 47–74. Edited by R.T. France and D. Wenham. Sheffield, England: JSOT Press, 1980. This research was made possible through a generous grant from the Alexander von Humboldt Foundation and was conducted at the Universität München and Cambridge University. The full results of

this research will appear in two forthcoming volumes, *The Historical Argument for the Resurrection of Jesus: Its Rise, Decline, and Contribution* and *The Historicity of the Resurrection of Jesus*.

2. Hans Grass, *Ostergeschehen und Osterberichte* (4th ed.; Göttingen: Vandenhoeck & Ruprecht, 1970).

tion body precludes physical appearances such as are narrated in the gospels. John Alsup remarks that '… no other work has been so widely used or of such singular importance for the interpretation of the gospel accounts … as Grass' ….[3] But, Alsup protests, Grass's insistence that the heavenly vision type of appearance underlies the physical appearances of the gospels 'is predicated upon the impossibility of the material realism of that latter form as an acceptable answer to the "what happened" question.… Grass superimposes this criterion over the gospel appearance accounts and judges them by their conformity or divergence from it.'[4] As a result, '… the contemporary spectrum of research on the gospel resurrection appearances displays a proclivity to the last century (and Celsus of the second century) in large measure under the influence of Grass' approach. In a sense the gospel stories appear to be something of an embarrassment: their "realism" is offensive.'[5]

What legitimate basis can be given to such a viewpoint? Those who deny the physical resurrection body of Jesus have developed a line of reasoning that has become pretty much stock-in-trade:

> The New Testament church does not *agree* about the nature of Christ's resurrected body. Material in Luke and John perhaps suggest this body to be corporeal in nature [Luke 24.39–43; John 20.26–38]. Paul, on the other band, clearly argues that the body is a spiritual body. If any historical memory resides in the accounts of Paul's conversion in Acts, he must not have understood the appearance of Christ to have been a corporeal appearance. Most critics identify this conversion with the event referred to in I Cor. 15:8: 'Last of all, as to one untimely born, he appeared also to me. The arguments in verses 47–50 of this chapter for the identity between Christ's body and the spiritual body of the resurrection indicate that for the Apostle his Lord rose from the dead in a spiritual body. Most importantly, Paul has equated the appearance of Christ to him with the appearances to

the other apostles. The resurrected Christ, as he was manifested to the church is thus a spiritual body.[6]

We can formulate this reasoning as follows:

1. Paul's information is at least *prima facie* more reliable than the gospels, for he stands in closer temporal and personal proximity to the original events.

2. Paul's information, in contrast to the gospels, indicates Jesus possessed a purely spiritual resurrection body.

a. First Argument:

(1) Paul equated the appearance of Jesus to him with the appearances of Jesus to the disciples.

(2) The appearance of Jesus to Paul was a non-physical appearance.

(3) Therefore, the appearances of Jesus to the disciples were non-physical appearances.

b. Second Argument:

(1) Paul equated Jesus's resurrection body with our future resurrection bodies.

(2) Our future resurrection bodies will be spiritual bodies.

(3) Therefore, Jesus's resurrection body was a spiritual body.

3. Therefore, Jesus possessed a purely spiritual resurrection body.

In this way the gospel accounts of the physical resurrection may be dismissed as legendary.

Now it is my conviction that this reasoning cannot bear the weight placed upon it by those who would reject the physical resurrection. I shall not in this essay contest the first premise. But I wish to take sharp issue with the second. Neither of the two supporting arguments, it seems to me, is sound; on the contrary, they embody serious misconceptions.

With regard to the first supporting argument, concerning the appearance of Jesus to Paul, it seems to me that both premises (1) and (2) are highly questionable.

3. John E. Alsup, *The Post-Resurrection Appearance Stories of the Gospel-Tradition* (Stuttgart: Calwer Verlag, 1975), 32.
4. Ibid., 34.

5. Ibid., 54.
6. Robin Scroggs, *The Last Adam* (Oxford: Basil Blackwell, 1966), 92–3.

Taking the premises in reverse order, what is the evidence for (2) *The appearance of Jesus to Paul was a non-physical appearance?* Usually appeal is made to the accounts of this incident in Acts, where, it is said, the appearance is to be understood as a visionary experience (Acts 9.1 – 19; 22.3 – 16; 26.9 – 23). As a matter of fact, however, the appearance in Acts, while involving visionary elements, cannot without further ado be characterized as purely visionary, since in all three accounts it is accompanied by extra-mental phenomena, namely, the light and the voice, which were experienced by Paul's companions. Grass dismisses these as due to Luke's objectifying tendencies.[7] This is, however, very doubtful, since Luke does not want to objectify the *post*-ascension visions of Jesus; it is the *pre*-ascension appearances whose extra-mental reality Luke emphasizes. Had Luke had no tradition that included Paul's companions, then we should have another vision like Stephen's, lacking extra-mental phenomena. And secondly, if Luke had invented the extra-mental aspects of the appearance to Paul, we should have expected him to be more consistent and not to construct such discrepancies as that Paul's companions heard and did not hear the voice. These inconsistencies suggest that the extra-mental phenomena were part of Luke's various traditions.

Grass further maintains that Luke had before him a tradition of Paul's experience that could not be assimilated to the more physical appearances of Christ to the disciples and that therefore the tradition is reliable; the extra-mental aspects are the result of mythical or legendary influences.[8] But one could argue that precisely the opposite is true: that because the appearance to Paul is a post-ascension experience Luke is forced to construe it as a heavenly vision, since Jesus has physically ascended. Grass's anthropomorphic parallels from Greek mythology (Homer *Illiad* a 158; idem *Odyssey* p. v. 161; Apollonius *Argonauts* 4. 852) bear little resemblance to Paul's experience; a genealogical tie between them is most unlikely. Thus, no appeal to the Acts accounts of the appearance to Paul can legitimately be made as proof that that appearance was purely visionary in nature.

Paul himself gives us no firm clue as to the nature of Christ's appearance to him. But it is interesting to note that when Paul speaks of his 'visions and revelations of the Lord' (II Cor 12.1 – 7) he does *not* include Jesus's appearance to him. Paul and the early Christian community as a whole were familiar with religious visions and sharply differentiated between these and an appearance of the risen Lord.[9] But what was the difference? Grass asserts that the only difference was in *content*: in an appearance the exalted Christ is seen.[10] But surely there must have been religious visions of the exalted Christ, too. Both Stephen's vision and the book of Revelation show that claims to visions of the exalted Christ which were not resurrection appearances were made in the church. Nor can it be said that the distinctive element in an appearance was the commissioning, for appearances were known which lacked this element (the Emmaus disciples, the 500 brethren). It seems to me that the most natural answer is that an appearance involved extra-mental phenomena, something's actually appearing, whereas a vision, even if caused by God, was purely in the mind. If this is correct, then Paul, in claiming for himself an appearance of Christ as opposed to a vision of Christ, is asserting to have seen something, not merely in the mind, but actually 'out there' in the real world. For all we know from Paul, this appearance could conceivably have been as physical as those portrayed in the gospels; and it is not impossible that Luke then 'spiritualized' the appearance out of the necessity of his pre- and post-ascension scheme! At any rate, it would be futile to attempt to prove that either Acts or Paul supports a purely visionary appearance to the apostle on the Damascus road.

But suppose this is altogether wrong. Suppose the appearance to Paul was purely visionary. What grounds are there for believing premise (1), *Paul*

---

7. Grass, *Ostergeschehen*, 222.
8. Ibid., 219 – 20.

9. See ibid., 189 – 207.
10. Ibid., 229 – 32.

equated the appearance of Jesus to him with the appearances of Jesus to the disciples? Usually appeal is made to the fact that Paul places himself in the list of witnesses of the appearances; hence, the other appearances must have also been visionary appearances like his own. This, however, does not seem to follow. First, in placing himself in the list of witnesses, Paul does not imply that the foregoing appearances were the same sort of appearance as the one to him. He is not concerned here with the how of the appearances, but with who appeared. He wants to list witnesses of the risen Christ, and the mode of the appearance is entirely incidental. But second, in placing himself in the list, Paul is not trying to put the appearances to the others on a plane with his own; rather he is trying to level up his own experience to the objectivity and reality of the others. Paul's detractors doubted or denied his apostleship (I Cor 9.1 – 2; II Cor 11.5; 12.11) and his having seen Christ would be an important argument in his favor (Gal 1.1, 11 – 12, 15 – 16; I Cor 9.1 – 2; 15.8 – 9). His opponents might tend to dismiss Paul's experience as a mere subjective vision, not a real appearance, and so Paul is anxious to include himself with the other apostles as a recipient of a genuine, objective appearance of the risen Lord. By putting himself in the list, Paul is saying that what *he* saw was every bit as much a real appearance of Jesus as what *they* saw. In fact, one could argue that Paul's adding himself to the list is actually a case of special pleading! At any rate, it is a *non sequitur* to infer that because Paul includes himself in the list of witnesses, all the other appearances must be of the same mode as the appearance to Paul.

Hence, the first argument against Jesus's physical resurrection seems doubly unsound. Not only does the evidence run against a purely visionary appearance to Paul, but there is no indication that Paul equated the mode of the appearance of Jesus to himself with the mode of the appearances to the other disciples.

Let us turn then to the second supporting argument for a purely spiritual resurrection body of Jesus: the argument from Paul's term σωμα πνευματικον. Premise (1), *Paul equated Jesus's resurrection body with our future resurrection bodies,* is surely correct (Phil 3.21; I Cor 15.20; Col 1.18). But the truth of premise (2), *our future resurrection bodies will be spiritual bodies,* depends upon how one defines its terms. Therefore, before we look more closely at Paul's discussion of the resurrection body in I Cor 15.35 – 57, a word ought to be said about Paul's anthropological terms σωμα, σαρξ and ψυχη.

The most important term in the second half of I Cor 15 is σωμα.[11] During the nineteenth century under the influence of idealism, theologians interpreted the σωμα as the form of a thing and the σαρξ as its substance.[12] In this way they could avoid the objectionable notion of a physical resurrection, for it was the form that was raised from the dead endowed with a new spiritual substance. Hence, in the old commentaries one finds that the σωμα πνευματικον was conceived to be a body made out of *himmlischer Lichtsubstanz.* This understanding has now been all but abandoned.[13] The view of σωμα as merely form and σαρξ as its substance cannot be exegetically sustained; σωμα is the body, form and substance. This does not mean, however, that twentieth-century theologians take σωμα to mean the physical body. Rather under the influence of existentialism, particularly as adopted by Bultmann, they take σωμα when used theologically, as the whole person conceived abstractly in existentialist categories of self-understanding. Thus, σωμα does not equal the physical body, but the person, and hence, a bodily resurrection means not a resurrection of the physical body, but of the person. In this way the doctrine of physical resurrection is avoided as adroitly as it was in the days of philosophical idealism. It is the burden of Gundry's study to show that this understanding is

---

11. The outstanding work on this concept, which I follow here, is Robert H. Gundry, *Soma in Biblical Theology* (Cambridge: Cambridge University Press, 1976).

12. C. Rolsten, *Zum Evangelium des Paulus und des Petrus* (Rostock: Stiller, 1868); Hermann Lüdemann, *Die Anthropologie des*

Apostels Paulus und ihre Stellung innerhalb seiner Heilslehre (Kiel: Universitätsverlag, 1872); remarkably so also Hans Conzelmann, *Der erste Brief en die Korinther* (KEKNT 5; Göttingen: Vandenhoeck & Ruprecht, 1969), 335.

13. See the six point refutation in Gundry, *Soma*, 161 – 2.

drastically wrong. Even if his exegesis suffers at times from over-kill,[14] Gundry succeeds admirably in carrying his main point: that σωμα is never used in the New Testament to denote the whole person in isolation from his physical body, but is much more used to denote the physical body itself or the man with special emphasis on the physical body. Gundry's conclusion is worth quoting:

> The soma denotes the physical body, roughly synonymous with 'flesh' in the neutral sense. It forms that part of man in and through which he lives and acts in the world. It becomes the base of operations for sin in the unbeliever, for the Holy Spirit in the believer. Barring prior occurrence of the Parousia, the soma will die. That is the lingering effect of sin even in the believer. But it will also be resurrected. That is its ultimate end, a major proof of its worth and necessity to wholeness of human being, and the reason for its sanctification now.[15]

The importance of this conclusion cannot be overemphasized. Too long we have been told that for Paul σωμα is the ego, the 'I' of a man. Like a dash of cold water, Gundry's study brings us back to the genuine anthropological consciousness of first-century man. The notion of body as the 'I' is a perversion of the biblical meaning of σωμα: Robert Jewett asserts, 'Bultmann has turned σωμα into its virtual opposite: a symbol for that structure of individual existence which is essentially non-physical.'[16] Hence, existentialist treatments of σωμα, as much as idealist treatments, have been a positive impediment to accurate historical-critical exegesis of I Cor 15 and have sacrificed theology to a philosophical fashion that is already passé.[17] To say that σωμα refers primarily to the physical body is not to say that the word cannot be used as synecdoche to refer to the whole man by reference to a part. 'The soma may represent the whole person simply because the soma lives in union with the soul/spirit.

But soma does not mean "whole person," because its use is designed to call attention to the physical object which is the body of the person rather than the whole personality.'[18] Nor does this preclude metaphorical use of the word, as in the 'body of Christ' for the church; for it is a physical metaphor: the church is not the 'I' of Christ. When we turn to I Cor 15 and inquire about the nature of the resurrection body, therefore, we shall be inquiring about a body, not about an ego, an 'I,' or a 'person' abstractly conceived apart from the body.

I have already alluded to Paul's use of σαρξ, and it will not be necessary to say much here. Theologians are familiar with σαρξ as the evil proclivity within man. This touches sensitive nerves in German theology because the Creed in German states that I believe in the resurrection of the Fleisch, not of the body as in the English translation. Hence, many theologians are rightly anxious to disassociate themselves from any doctrine that the flesh as a morally evil principle will be resurrected. But they seem prone to overlook the fact that Paul often uses σαρξ in a non-moral sense simply to mean the physical flesh or body. In this morally neutral sense the resurrection of the flesh = resurrection of the body. Now in I Cor 15 Paul is clearly speaking of σαρξ in a physical, morally neutral sense, for he speaks of the flesh of birds, animals, and fish, which would be absurd in any moral sense. Hence, understood in a physical sense, the doctrine of the resurrection of the flesh is morally unobjectionable.

Finally a brief word on the third term, ψυχη: Paul does not teach a consistent dualism of σωμα-ψυχη, but often uses πνευμα and other terms to designate the immaterial element of man. In fact in the adjectival form, ψυχικος has a meaning that does not connote immateriality at all, but rather the natural character of a thing in contradistinction to the supernatural character of God's Spirit. Thus in I Cor 2.14 – 3.3, Paul differentiates three types of men: the ανθρωπος ψυχικος

---

14. See ibid., 122, 141. Most of Gundry's texts do not support dualism, but merely aspectivalism; but when he adduces texts that clearly contemplate the separation of soul or spirit and body at death, then his argument for dualism is strong and persuasive.

15. Gundry, Soma, 50.

16. Robert Jewett, Paul's Anthropological Terms (AGAJY 10; Leiden: E.J. Brill, 1971), 211.

17. Gundry, Soma, 167.

18. Ibid., 80.

or natural man apart from God's Spirit; the ανθρωπος πνευματικος or spiritual man who is led and empowered by God's Spirit; and the ανθρωπος σαρκινος or carnal man who, though possessing the Spirit of God (I Cor 12.13), is nevertheless still under the sway of the σαρξ or evil principle in human nature. This makes it evident that for Paul ψυχικος did not have the connotations which we today associate with 'soul.'

With these terms in mind we now turn to Paul's discussion in I Cor 15.35–37. He begins by asking two polemical questions: How are the dead raised? With what kind of body do they come? (v 35; cf. II Bar 49.2–3). Paul's opponents seemed to have been unable to accept the resurrection because the resurrection of a material body was either inconceivable or offensive to their Greek minds (cf. Bultmann's 'resuscitation of a corpse'). Paul's answer steers a careful course between the crasser forms of the Pharisaic doctrine of resurrection, in which the raised will, for example, each beget a thousand children and eat the flesh of Leviathan, and the Platonistic doctrine of the immortality of the soul apart from the body. Paul will contend that the resurrection body will be radically different from this natural body, but that it will nevertheless be a *body* — Paul contemplates no release of the soul from the prison house of the body. Paul's answer is that the resurrection body will be a marvellous transformation of our present body, making it suitable for existence in the age to come — a doctrine not unusual in the Judaism of Paul's day and remarkably similar to that of the contemporary II Bar 50–51, which should be read in conjunction with Paul's argument.[19] It is highly instructive, particularly if we accept that the author of Luke-Acts was an associate of Paul, that Luke specifically identifies Paul's doctrine of the resurrection with that of the Pharisees (Acts 23.6; cf. 24.14; 16.6, 21–23).

In the first paragraph, vv 36–41, Paul searches for analogies to the resurrection of the dead (v 42). The first analogy is the analogy of the seed. The point of the analogy is simply to draw attention to how different the plant is from the seed that is buried in the ground (cf. Matt 13.31–32 for Jesus's use of a similar analogy in another context). It is a good analogy for Paul's purposes, for the sowing of the seed and its death are reminiscent of the burial of the dead man (vv 42–44). To criticize Paul's analogy from the standpoint of modern botany — saying, for example, that a seed does not really die — presses the analogy too far. Similarly some commentators criticize Paul's analogy because he lacked the modern botanical notion that a particular type of seed yields a particular type of plant; Paul thought God alone determined what plant should spring up from any seed that was sown (v 38). But this is quite unreasonable, as though Paul could think that a date-palm would conceivably spring from a grain of corn! He specifically says that God gives 'each kind of seed its own body' (v 38), which harks back to the Genesis account of creation according to kinds (Gen 1.11). At any rate this loses the whole point of the analogy: that from the mere seed God produces a wonderfully different plant.

Paul then appeals to the analogy of different sorts of flesh again in order to prove that if we recognize differences even in the physical world then the resurrection body could also be different from our present body. Paul's analogy may have in mind the creation account, but I think the Jewish distinction between clean and unclean food is closer (cf. Lev 11; animals: vv 1–8; fish: vv 9–12; birds: vv 13–19; insects: vv 20–23; swarming things: vv 29–30).[20] So I do not think σαρξ here is precisely identical with σωμα. Not only would that reduce Paul's argument to the rather banal assertion that men have different bodies from

---

19. Paul's teaching is essentially the Jewish doctrine of glorified bodies, according to Johannes Weiss, *Der erste Korintherbrief* (9th ed.; KEKNT 5; Göttingen: Vandenhoeck & Ruprecht, 1910), 345; W. D. Davies, *Paul and Rabbinic Judaism* (2d ed; London: SPCK, 1965), 305–8; Ulrich Wilckens, *Auferstehung* (Stuttgart and Berlin: Kreuz Verlag, 1970), 128–31; Joseph L. Smith, 'Resurrection

Faith Today,' *TS* 30 (1969): 406.

20. On the different types of flesh, see Tractate Chullin 8. 1, where the author explains that one cannot cook flesh in milk, unless it is the flesh of fish or of grasshoppers; fowl may be set on the table with cheese, but not eaten with it. See also Davies, *Paul*, 306.

fish, but it would also entail the false statement that all animals have the same kind of body. Rather in the present connection, σαρξ means essentially 'meat' or 'organic matter.' The old commentaries were therefore wrong in defining σαρξ *tout simple* as 'substance,' for inorganic matter would not be σαρξ; Paul would never speak of the flesh of a stone. To say that the resurrection body has therefore a different kind of flesh than the present body probably presses the analogy too far; all Paul wants to show is that as there are differences among mundane things, analogously the supernatural resurrection body could also differ from the present body.

The third analogy is that of terrestrial and celestial bodies (vv 40 – 41). There can be no doubt from v 41 that Paul means astronomical bodies, not angels. Again the point of the analogy is the same: there are radical differences among bodies in the physical world, so why should not the body in the world to come differ from the present body? Paul's analogy is particularly apt in this case because as the heavenly bodies exceed terrestrial bodies in glory, so does the resurrection body the natural body (v 43; cf. Phil 3.21).[21] The δοξα of the heavenly bodies is their brightness, which varies; there is no trace here of *Lichtsubstanz*. When applied to the resurrection body, however, δοξα seems to be honor (v 43). Paul has thus prepared the way for his doctrine of the world to come by three analogies from the present world. All of them show how things can be radically different from other things of the same kind; similarly a σωμα πνευματικον will be seen to be radically different from a σωμα ψυχικον. Moreover, Paul's analogies form an ascending scale from plant to animal to terrestrial bodies to celestial bodies; the next type of body to be mentioned will be the most wonderful and exalted of all.

From vv 42 – 50 Paul spells out his doctrine of the σωμα πνευματικον. The body that is to be differs from the present body in that it will be imperishable, glorious, powerful, and spiritual; whereas the present body is perishable, dishonourable, weak, and physical (vv 42 – 44). These are the four essential differences between the present body and the resurrection body. What do they tell us about the nature of the resurrection body?

First, it is sown εν φθορα, but it is raised εν αφθαρσια. These terms tell us clearly that Paul is not talking about egos, or 'I's,' but about bodies, for (1) the σπειρεται-εγειρεται has primary reference to the burial and raising up of a dead man's body, not the 'person' in abstraction from the body; and (2) only the body can be described as perishable (II Cor 4.16), for man's spirit survives death (II Cor 5.1 – 5; cf. Rom 8.10; Phil 1.23), Rather the disjunction under discussion concerns the radical change that will take place in our *bodies*: Paul teaches personal bodily immortality, not immortality of the soul alone (cf. vv 53 – 54). Strange as this may seem, the Christian teaching (or at least Paul's) is not that our souls will live forever, but that we will have bodies in the after-life.

Second, it is sown εν ατιμια, but it is raised εν δοξη. Our present bodies are wracked by sin, are bodies of death, groaning with the whole creation to be set free from sin and decay; we long, says Paul, for the redemption of our bodies (II Cor 5.4; Rom 8.19 – 24). This body, dishonored through sin and death, will be transformed by Christ to be like his glorious body (Phil 3.21). In a spiritual sense we already have an anticipation of this glory insofar as we are conformed inwardly to the image of Christ and are sanctified by his Spirit (II Cor 3.18), but Paul teaches that the body will not simply fall away like a useless husk, but will be transformed to partake of this glory also.

Third, it is sown εν ασθενια, but it will be raised εν δυναμει. How well Paul knew of weakness! Afflicted with a bodily malediction which was offensive to others and a burden to those around him, Paul found in his weakness the power of Christ (Gal 4.13 – 14; II

21. Cf. II Bar 51.1 – 10, where the glory of the righteous seems to be a literal brightness like the stars. For Paul the glory of the righteous seems to mean majesty, honor, exaltation, etc., not so much physical radiance, which is a mere analog. See Joseph Coppens, 'La glorification céleste du Christ dans la théologie neotestamentaire et l'attente de Jésus,' in *Resurrexit* (ed. Édouard Dhanis; Rome: Editrice Libreria Vaticana, 1974), 37 – 40.

Cor 12.7 – 10). And on his poor body which had been stoned, beaten, and scourged for the sake of the gospel, Paul bore the marks of Christ, so much so that be dared to write '... in my flesh I complete what is lacking in Christ's afflictions ...' (Col 1.24). Just as Christ 'was crucified in weakness, but lives by the power of God' (II Cor 13.4) so Paul longed to know the power of the resurrection and looked forward to the day when he, too, would receive the resurrection body (II Cor 5.1 – 4; Phil 3.10 – 11).

Fourth, it is sown a σωμα ψυχικον, but it is raised a σωμα πνευματικον. By a σωμα ψυχικον Paul clearly does not mean a body made out of ψυχη. Rather just as Paul frequently uses σαρκικος to indicate, not the physical composition of a thing, but its orientation, its dominating principle, so ψυχικος also indicates, not a composition, but an orientation. In the New Testament ψυχικος always has a negative connotation (I Cor 2.14; Jas 3.15; Jude 19); that which is ψυχικος partakes of the character and direction of natural human nature. Hence, the emphasis in σωμα ψυχικον is not that the body is *physical*, but that it is *natural*. Accordingly, σωμα ψυχικον ought rightly to be translated 'natural body;' it means our present human body. This is the body that will be sown. But it is raised a σωμα πνευματικον. And just as σωμα ψυχικον does not mean a body made out of ψυχη, neither does σωμα πνευματικον mean a body made out of πνευμα. If σωμα πνευματικον indicated a body made out of spirit, then its opposite would not be a σωμα ψυχικον, but a σωμα σαρκινον. For Paul, ψυχη and πνευμα are not substances out of which bodies are made, but dominating principles by which bodies are directed. Virtually

every modern commentator agrees on this point: Paul is not talking about a rarefied body made out of spirit or ether; he means a body under the lordship and direction of God's Spirit. The present body is ψυχικον insofar as the ψυχη is its dominating principle (cf. ανθρωπος ψυχικος, I Cor 2.14). The body which is to be will be πνευματικον, not in the sense of a spiritual substance, but insofar as the πνευμα will be its dominating principle (cf. ανθρωπος πνευματικος — I Cor 2.15). They do not differ *qua* σωμα; rather they differ *qua* orientation. Thus, philological analysis leads, in Clavier's words, to the conclusion that 'the "pneumatic body" is, in substance, the same body, this body of flesh, but controlled by the Spriit, as was the body of Jesus Christ.'[22] The contrast is not between physical body / non-physical body, but between naturally oriented body / spiritually oriented body. Hence, I think it very unfortunate that the term σωμα πνευματικον has been usually translated 'spiritual body,' for this tends to be very misleading, as Héring explains:

In French, at least, the literal translation *spiritual body* runs the risk of creating worse misunderstandings. For the majority of readers of the French language, being more or less consciously Cartesians, yield to the tendency of identifying the spiritual with the unextended and naturally also with the immaterial, which goes contrary to pauline ideas and creates in addition a *contradictio in adjecto*; for what would a body with neither extension nor matter be?[23]

Héring therefore suggests that it is better to translate σωμα πνευματικον as the opposite of natural body (σωμα ψυχικον), as *supernatural* body. Although this

---

22. R. Clavier, 'Breves remarques sur la notion de σωμα πνευματικον,' in *The Background of the New Testament and Its Eschatology* (ed. W. D. Davies and D. Daube; Cambridge: Cambridge University Press, 1956), 361. The French original is: 'le "corps pneumatique" est, en substance, le même corps, ce corps de chair, mais controlé par l'esprit, comme le fut le corps de Jésus-Christ.' Despite the philological evidence, Clavier goes for a substantial understanding of spiritual body on two grounds: (1) in the seed/plant analogy, the plant is not numerically identical with the seed, and (2) I Cor 15.50. The first reason is astounding, for the plant certainly is numerically identical with the seed! Pressing the analogy this far supports the continuity of the resurrection body with the earthly

body. Clavier sadly misunderstands v 50, as evident from his remark that Paul should have mentioned bones along with flesh and blood.

23. Jean Héring, *La première épître de saint Paul aux Corinthiens* (2d ed., CNT 7; Neuchatel, Switzerland: Delachaux et Niestlé, 1959), 147. The French original reads: En français toutefois la traduction littérale *corps spirituel* risque de créer les pires malentendus. Car la plupart des lecteurs de langue française, étant plus ou moins consciemment cartésiens, céderont à la tendence d'identifier le spirituel avec l'inétendu et naturellement aussi avec l'im-matériel, ce qui va à l'encontre des idées pauliniennes et crée de plus une *contradictio in adjecto*; car que serait un corps sans étendue ni matière?

has the disadvantage of ignoring the connotation of πνευματικος as 'Spirit-dominated,' it avoids the inevitable misunderstandings engendered by 'spiritual body.' As Héring rightly comments, this latter term, understood substantively, is practically a self-contradiction. By the same token, 'physical body' is really a tautology. Thus, natural body/supernatural body is a better rendering of Paul's meaning here.

Having described the four differences between the present body and the resurrection body, Paul elaborates the doctrine of the two Adams. His statement that the first Adam was εις ψυχην ζωσαν and the second εις πνευμα ζωοποιουν (v 45) must be understood in light of the foregoing discussion. Just as Paul does not mean Adam was a disembodied soul, neither does he mean Christ turned into a disembodied spirit. That would contradict the doctrine of the resurrection of the σωμα. Rather these terms refer once again to the natural body made at creation and the supernatural body produced by the resurrection (cf. v 43b). First we have our natural bodies here on earth as possessed by Adam, then we shall have our supernatural bodies in the age to come as possessed by Jesus (vv 46, 49; cf. vv 20–23). The fact that materiality is not the issue here is made clear in v 47: ο πρωτος ανθρωπος εκ γης χοικος, ο δευτερος ανθρωπος εξ ουρανου.

There is something conspicuously missing in this parallel between το ψυχικον and το πνευματικον (v 46): the first Adam is *from* the earth, *made* of dust; the second Adam is *from* heaven, but *made of*— ?[24] Clearly Paul recoils from saying the second Adam is made of heavenly substance. The contrast between the two Adams is their origin, not their substance. Thus, the doctrine of the two Adams confirms the philological analysis. Then comes a phrase that has caused great difficulties to many: 'I tell you this, brethren, flesh and blood cannot inherit the kingdom of God, nor does the perishable inherit the imperishable' (v 50.) Does not this clearly indicate that the resurrection body will be immaterial? Jeremias has tried to escape this conclusion by arguing that 'flesh and blood' refers to those alive at the Parousia, while the 'perishable' refers to the dead in Christ: Paul means that neither living nor dead as they are can inherit God's kingdom, but must be transformed (v 51).[25] This, however, is unlikely, for it requires that v 50 go with v 51. But not only does v 50 appear to be a summary statement of the foregoing paragraph, but v 51 introduces a new paragraph and a new thought, as is indicated by the introductory words, 'Lo! I tell you a mystery!' and by the fact that something new and previously unknown is about to be communicated. Neither need one adopt the expedient of Bornhäuser that Paul means flesh and blood will decay in the grave, but the bones will be raised.[26] This falsely assumes Paul is here speaking of anatomy. Rather commentators are agreed that 'flesh and blood' is a typical Semitic expression denoting the frail human nature.[27] It emphasizes our feeble mortality over against God; hence, the second half of v 50 is Paul's elaboration in other words of exactly the same thought. The fact that the verb is in the singular may also suggest that Paul is not talking of physical aspects of the body, but about a conceptual unity: 'flesh and blood is not able to inherit ….' Elsewhere Paul also employs the expression 'flesh and blood' to mean simply 'people' or 'mortal creatures' (Gal 1.16; Eph 6.12). Therefore, Paul is not talking about anatomy here; rather he means that mortal human beings cannot enter into God's eternal kingdom: therefore, they must become imperishable (cf. v 53). This imperishability does not connote immateriality or unextendedness; on the contrary Paul's doctrine of the world

---

24. Or alternatively, the first Adam is made of the dust of the earth; the second Adam is from heaven. The first speaks of constitution, the second of origin. See also *TWNT*, , s. v. πνευμα,' by Kleinknecht, *et. al.*

25. Joachim Jeremias, '"Flesh and Blood Cannot Inherit the Kingdom of God" (I Cor. XV. 50),' *NTS* 2 (1955–6): 151–9.

26. Karl Bornhäuser, *Die Gebeine der Toten* (BFCT 26; Gütersloh: C. Bertelsmann, 1921), 37.

27. It is found in Matt 16.17; Gal 1.16; Eph 6.12; Heb 2.14; see also Sir 14.18 and the references in Hermann L. Strack and Paul Billerbeck, eds., *Kommentar zum Neuen Testament aus Talmud und Midrasch* (5th ed., 6 vols.; München: C. H. Beck, 1969), 1: 730–1, 753. The Semitic word pair σαρξ και αιμα is first attested in Ecclesiasticus 14.18; 17.31 and occurs frequently in Rabbinic texts, especially Rabbinic parables.

to come is that our resurrection bodies will be part of, so to speak, a resurrected creation (Rom 8.18 – 23). The universe will be delivered from sin and decay, not materiality, and our bodies will be part of that universe.

In the following paragraph, Paul tells how this will be done. When he says, 'We shall not all sleep, but we shall all be changed' (v 51), it is not clear whether he means by 'all' either Christians in general or Christians alive at his time (cf. I Thess 4.15, 17). But in either case, two things are clear: (1) Paul held that the transformation would take place instantaneously at the moment of the resurrection *(v. 52)*. In this he differs sharply from II Bar 50 – 51 which holds that the resurrection yields the old bodies again which are transformed only after the judgement.[28] Paul's doctrine is that we are raised imperishable and glorified. (2) For Paul the resurrection is a *transformation*, not an *exchange*. Klappert draws the distinctions nicely:

The resurrection according Paul concerns neither (1) a revivification, that is, a new creation *out of* the old, nor (2) a creation out of nothing, that is, a new creation *in the place of* the old, but rather (3) a radical transformation of the mortal body, that is, a new creation *of* the old.[29]

In the resurrection the 'ego' of a man does not trade bodies. Rather the natural body is miraculously transformed into a supernatural body. The metaphor of the sowing and raising of the body points to this. In fact, the very concept of resurrection implies this, for in an exchange of bodies there would be nothing that would be raised. When Paul says, 'We shall all be changed,' he means the bodies of both the *dead* and the *living* alike. Paul's doctrine is that at the Parousia, the dead will rise

from their graves transformed and that those who are still alive will also be transformed (vv 51 – 52; I Thess 4.16 – 17). The concept of an exchange of bodies is a peculiarly modern notion. For the Jews the resurrection of the dead concerned the remains in the grave, which they conceived to be the bones.[30] According to their understanding while the flesh decayed, the bones endured. It was the bones, therefore, that were the primary subject of the resurrection. In this hope, the Jews carefully collected the bones of the dead into ossuaries after the flesh had decomposed. Only in a case in which the bones were destroyed, as with the Jewish martyrs, did God's creating a resurrection body *ex nihilo* come into question. It is instructive that on the question of the resurrection, Jesus sided with the Pharisees. He held that the tomb is the place where the bones repose and that the dead in the tombs would be raised (Matt 23.27; John 5.28). It is important to remember, too, that Paul was a Pharisee and that Luke identifies his doctrine of the resurrection with that of the Pharisees. Paul's language is thoroughly Pharisaic, and it is unlikely that he should employ the same terminology with an entirely different meaning. This means that when Paul says the dead will be raised imperishable, he means the dead *in the graves*. As a first-century Jew and Pharisee he could have understood the expression in no other way.

Thus, Grass is simply wrong when he characterizes the resurrection as an exchange, a re-creation, and not a transformation.[31] He mistakenly appeals to v 50; his statement that Paul has no interest in the emptying of the graves ignores the clear statements of I Thess 4.16 (which in light of v 14, which probably refers, according to the current Jewish idea, to the souls of the departed, can only have reference to the bodies in the

---

28. According to Baruch the old bodies are raised for the purpose of recognition, that the living may know that the dead have been raised. But for Paul, believers, like Christ, emerge glorified from the grave.

29. Berthold Klappert, 'Einleitung,' in *Diskussion um Kreus und Auferstehung* (ed. idea; Wuppertal: Aussaat Verlag, 1971), 15. The German original reads: Es geht also in der Auferstehung nach Paulus weder 1. um eine Wiederbelebung, d. h. um eine Neuschöpfung *aus* dem Alten, noch 2. um eine Shöpfung aus dem Nichts, d. h. um

eine Neuschöpfung *anstelle* des Alten, Sondern 3. um eine radikale Verwandlung des sterblichen leibes, d. h. um eine Neuschopfung *an* dem alten.

30. See Bornhäuser, *Gebeine*; C. F. Evans, *Resurrection in the New Testament* (SBT 2/12; London: SCM, 1970), 108; Walther Grundmann, *Das Evangelium nach Lukas* (8th ed., THKNT 3; Berlin: Evangelische Verlagsanstalt, 1978), 451.

31. Grass, *Ostergeschehen*, 154.

graves) I Cor 15.42–44, 52. He attempts to strengthen his case by arguing that the relation of the old world to the new is one of annihilation to re-creation and this is analogous to the relation of the old body to the new. But Grass's texts are chiefly non-Pauline (Heb 1.10–12; Lk 13.31; Rev 6.14; 20.11; 21.1; II Pet 3.10). As we have seen, Paul's view is a transformation of creation (Rom 8.18–23; cf. I Cor 7.31). According to Paul it is *this* creation and *this* body which will be delivered from bondage to sin and decay. Paul, therefore, believed that the bodies of those alive at the Parousia would be changed, not discarded or annihilated, and that the remains (the bones?) of the dead bodies would likewise be transformed.

But this at once raises the puzzling question: what happens to those Christians who die before the Parousia? Are they simply extinguished until the day of resurrection? The clue to Paul's answer may be found in II Cor 5.1–10. Here the earthly tent = σωμα ψυχικον, and the building from God = σωμα πνευματικον. When do we receive the heavenly dwelling? The language of v 4 is irresistibly reminiscent of I Cor 15.53–54, which we saw referred to the Parousia. This makes it evident that the heavenly dwelling is not received immediately upon death, but at the Parousia. It is unbelievable that had Paul changed his mind on the dead's receiving their resurrection bodies at the Parousia, he would not have told the Corinthians, but continued to use precisely the same language. If the body were received immediately upon death, there would be no reason for the fear of nakedness, and v 8 would become unintelligible. In short this would mean that Paul abandoned the doctrine of the resurrection of the dead: but his later letters show he continued to hold to it.

In I Cor 15 Paul did not speak of a state of nakedness; the mortal simply 'put on' (ενδυσασθαι) the immortal. But in II Cor 5 he speaks of the fear of being unclothed and the preference to be further clothed (επενδυσασθαι), as by top-clothing. It is evident that Paul is here describing losing the earthly body as being stripped and hence naked. He would rather not quit the body, but simply be transformed at the Parousia without experiencing the nakedness of death. In this

sense, putting on the new body is like putting on top-clothing; namely, one need not undress first. Taken in isolation, this might be thought to imply that the resurrection is an exchange of bodies, not a transformation; but this presses the metaphor too hard. Paul is not trying to be technical, as is evident from his use of the ordinary ενδυσαμενοι in v 3; and the notion of 'putting on' is not inconsistent with the concept of transformation, as I Cor 15.53–54 makes clear. Indeed, the 'putting on' consists precisely in being transformed. Neither the εχομεν nor the αινωιον of v 1 indicates that the new body already exists; rather they express the certitude of future possession and the subsequent eternal duration of the new body. The idea that the new body exists already in heaven is an impossible notion, for the idea of an unanimated σωμα πνευματικον, stored up in heaven until the Parousia, is a contradiction in terms, since πνευμα is the essence and source of life itself. Rather from I Cor 15 we understand that the heavenly dwelling is created at the Parousia through a transformation of the earthly tent, a point concealed by Paul's intentional contrast between the two in v 1, but hinted at in v 4 (cf. also Rom 8.10–11, 18–23). What Paul wants to express by the metaphor is that he would rather live to the Parousia and be changed than die and be naked prior to being raised.

The nakedness is thus the nakedness of an individual's soul or spirit apart from the body, a common description in Hellenistic literature. This is confirmed in vv 6–9, where Paul contrasts being at home in the body and being at home with the Lord as mutually exclusive conditions. Paul is saying that while we are in this natural body we sigh, not because we want to leave the body through death and exist as a disembodied soul, but because we want to be transformed into a supernatural body without the necessity of passing through the intermediate state. But despite the unsettling prospect of such an intermediate state, Paul still thinks it better to be away from the body and with the Lord (v 8). Christ makes all the difference; for Paul the souls of the departed are not shut up in caves or caskets until the end time as in Jewish apocalyptic, nor do they 'sleep': rather they go to be with Jesus and experience a conscious, blissful communion with him (cf. Phil 1.21, 23) until he returns to earth (I Thess 4.14). This overrides the dread of nakedness.

Paul's doctrine of the nature of the resurrection body now becomes clear. When a Christian dies, his conscious spirit or soul goes to be with Christ until the Parousia, while his body lies in the grave. When Christ returns, in a single instant the remains of the natural body are transformed into a powerful, glorious, and imperishable supernatural body under the complete lordship and direction of the Spirit, and the soul of the departed is simultaneously reunited with the body, and the man is raised to everlasting life. Then those who are alive will be similarly transformed, the old body miraculously changed intro the new without excess, and all believers will go to be with the Lord.

This doctrine teaches us much about Paul's conception of the resurrection body of Christ. In no sense did Paul conceive Christ's resurrection body to be immaterial or unextended. The notion of an immaterial, unextended body seems to be a self-contradiction; the nearest thing to it would be a shade in Sheol, and this was certainly not Paul's conception of Christ's glorious resurrection body! The only phrases in Paul's discussion that could lend themselves to a 'dematerializing' of Christ's body are 'σωμα πνευματικον' and 'flesh and blood cannot inherit the kingdom of God.' But virtually all modern commentators agree that these expressions have nothing to do with substantiality or anatomy, as we have seen. Rather the first speaks of the orientation of the resurrection body, while the second refers to the mortality and feebleness of the natural body in contrast to God.

So it is very difficult to understand how theologians can persist in describing Christ's resurrection body in terms of an invisible, intangible spirit; there seems to be a great lacuna here between exegesis and theology. I can only agree with O'Collins when he asserts in this context, 'Platonism may be hardier than we suspect.'[32] With all the best will in the world, it is extremely dif-

ficult to see what is the difference between an immaterial, unextended, spiritual 'body' and the immortality of the soul. And this again is certainly not Paul's doctrine! Therefore, the second supporting argument for Jesus's having a purely spiritual resurrection body also fails.

We have seen, therefore, that the traditions of the appearance of Jesus to Paul do not describe that event as a purely visionary experience; on the contrary, extra-mental accompaniments were involved. Paul gives no firm clue as to the nature of that appearance; from his doctrine of the nature of the resurrection body, it could theoretically have been as physical as any gospel appearance. And Paul does insist that it was an *appearance,* not a vision. Luke regarded the mode of Jesus's appearance to Paul as unique because it was a post-ascension encounter. Paul himself gives no hint that he considered the appearance to him to be in any way normative for the other appearances or determinative for a doctrine of the resurrection body. On the contrary, Paul also recognized that the appearance to him was an anomaly and was exercised to bring it up to the level of objectivity and reality of the other appearances. Furthermore, Paul conceived of the resurrection body as a powerful, glorious, imperishable, Spirit-directed *body,* created through a transformation of the earthly body or the remains thereof, and made to inhabit the new universe in the eschaton. The upshot of all this is the startling conclusion that *Paul's doctrine of the resurrection body is potentially more physical than that of the gospels, and if Christ's resurrection body is to be conceived in any less than a physical way, that qualification must come from the side of the gospels, not of Paul.*

So although many theologians try to play off the 'massiven Realismus' of the gospels against a Pauline doctrine of a spiritual resurrection body, such reasoning rests on a fundamental and drastic misunderstanding of Paul's doctrine. One cannot but suspect that the real reason for scholarly scepticism concerning the

---

32. Gerald O'Collins, *The Easter Jesus* (London: Darton, Longman & Todd, 1973), 94.

historicity of the gospel appearances is that, as Bultmann openly stated, this is offensive to 'modern man,' and that Paul has been made an unwilling accomplice in critics' attempts to find reasons to support a conclusion already dictated by *a priori* philosophical assumptions. But Paul will not allow himself to be put to this use; a careful exegesis of Pauline doctrine fully supports a physical resurrection body. And, it must be said, this was how first-century Christians apparently understood him, for the letters of Clement and Ignatius prove early wide acceptance of the doctrine of physical resurrection in first-century churches, including the very churches where Paul himself had taught. The ground is thus cut from beneath those scholars who object to the historicity of the gospel resurrection narratives because of their physicalism.

But more than that: given the temporal and personal proximity of Paul to the original witnesses of the resurrection appearances, the historicity of the bodily resurrection of Jesus can scarcely be denied. For the physicalism of the gospels cannot now be explained away as a late legendary or theological development; on the contrary, what we see from Paul is that it was there from the beginning. And if it was there from the beginning, then it must have been historically well-founded — otherwise, one is at a loss how to explain that the earliest witnesses should believe in it. Though it is constantly repeated that the physicalism of the gospels is an anti-docetic apologetic, scarcely a single piece of evidence is ever produced in favor of this assertion — and mere assertion is not proof. We have seen that both Paul's personal contact and temporal proximity with the original disciples precludes a late development of the notion of physical resurrection, which is implied by the anti-docetic hypothesis. And Paul's doctrine can hardly be explained away as an anti-docetic apologetic, for it was the crass materialism of the Jewish doctrine of resurrection that Paul's Corinthian opponents probably gagged at (I Cor 15.35), so that Paul found it necessary to emphasize the transformation of the earthly body into a supernatural body. An anti-docetic apologetic would have been counter-productive. Hence, the evidence of Paul precludes that the physical resurrection was an apologetic development of the gospels aimed at Docetism.

But this consideration aside, there are other reasons to think that in the gospel narratives Docetism is not in view: (1) For a Jew the very term 'resurrection' entailed a physical resurrection of the dead man in the tomb. The notion of a 'spiritual resurrection' was not merely unknown; it was a contradiction in terms. Therefore, in saying that Jesus was raised and appeared, the early believers must have understood this in physical terms. It was Docetism which was the response to this physicalism, not the other way around. The physical resurrection is thus primitive and prior, Docetism being the later reaction of theological and philosophical reflection. (2) Moreover, had purely 'spiritual appearances' been original, then it is difficult to see how physical appearances could have developed. For (a) the offense of Docetism would then be removed, since the Christians, too, believed in purely spiritual appearances, and (b) the doctrine of physical appearances would have been counter-productive as an apologetic, both to Jews and pagans; to Jews because they did not accept an individual resurrection within history, and to pagans because their belief in the immortality of the soul could not accommodate the crudity of physical resurrection. The church would therefore have retained its purely spiritual appearances. (3) Besides, Docetism was mainly aimed at denying the reality of the incarnation of Christ (I John 4.2 – 3; III John 7), not the physical resurrection. Docetists were not so interested in denying the physical resurrection as in denying that the divine Son perished on the cross; hence, some held the Spirit deserted the human Jesus at the crucifixion, leaving the human Jesus to die and be physically raised (Irenaeus *Against Heresies* 1.26. 1). An anti-docetic apologetic aimed at proving a physical resurrection therefore misses the point entirely. (4) The demonstrations of corporeality and continuity in the gospels, as well as the other physical appearances, were not redactional additions of Luke or John, as is evident from a comparison of Luke 24.36 – 43 with John 20.19 – 23 (it is thus incorrect to speak, for example, of 'Luke's apologetic against Gnosticism'), but were part of the traditions received by the evangelists. Docetism, however, was a later theological development, attested in John's letters. Therefore, the gospel accounts of the physical resurrection tend to ante-date the rise and threat of Docetism. In fact, not even all later Gnostics denied the physical resurrection (cf. Gospel of Philip, Letter of James, and Epistle of Rheginus). It is interesting that in the ending added to Mark there is actually a switch from material proofs of the resurrection to verbal rebuke by Jesus for the disciples' unbelief. (5) The demonstrations themselves do not evince the rigorousness of an apologetic against Docetism. In both Luke and John it is not said that either the disciples or Thomas actually accepted Jesus's invitation to touch him and prove that he was not a spirit. Contrast the statements of Ignatius that the disciples did physically touch Jesus (Ignatius *Ad Smyrnaeans* 3.2; cf. *Epistula Apostolorum* 11 – 12). As Schnackenburg has said, if an anti-docetic apology were involved in the gospel accounts, more would have to have been done than Jesus's merely *showing* the wounds.[33] (6) The incidental, off-hand character of the physical resurrection in most of the accounts shows that the physicalism was a natural assumption or presupposition of the accounts, not an apologetic point consciously being made. For example, the women's grasping Jesus's feet is not a polemical point, but just their response of worship. Similarly, Jesus says, 'Do not hold me,' though Mary is not explicitly said to have done so; this is no conscious effort to prove a physical resurrection. The appearances on the mountain and by the Sea of Tiberias just naturally presuppose a physical Jesus; no points are trying to be scored against Docetism. Together these considerations strongly suggest that the physical appearances were not an apologetic to Docetism, but always part of the church's tradition; there is no

good reason to doubt that Jesus did, in fact, show his disciples that he had been physically raised.

And it must be said that despite the disdain of some theologians for the gospels' conception of the nature of the resurrection body, it is nonetheless true that like Paul the evangelists steer a careful course between gross materialism and the immortality of the soul. On the one hand, every gospel appearance of Jesus that is narrated is a physical appearance.[34] The gospels' unanimity on this score is very impressive, especially in view of the fact that the appearance stories represent largely independent traditions; they confirm Paul's doctrine that it is the earthly body that is resurrected. On the other hand, the gospels insist that Jesus's resurrection was not simply the resuscitation of a corpse. Lazarus would die again some day, but Jesus rose to everlasting life (Matt 28.18 – 20; Luke 24.26; John 20.17). And his resurrection body was possessed of powers that no normal human body possesses. Thus, in Matthew when the angel opens the tomb, Jesus does not come forth; rather he is already gone. Similarly, in Luke when the Emmaus disciples recognize him at bread-breaking he disappears. The same afternoon Jesus appears to Peter, miles away in Jerusalem. When the Emmaus disciples finally join the disciples in Jerusalem that evening, Jesus suddenly appears in their midst. John says the doors were shut, but Jesus stood among them. A week later Jesus did the same thing. Very often commentators make the error of stating that Jesus came through the closed doors, but neither John nor Luke says this. Rather Jesus simply appeared in the room; contrast the pagan myths of gods entering rooms like fog through the keyhole (Homer *Odyssey* 6. 19 – 20; *Homeric Hymns* 3. 145)! According to the gospels, Jesus in his resurrection body had the ability to appear and vanish at will, without regard to spatial limitations.

---

33. Rudolf Schnackenburg, *Das Johannesevangelium* (3 vols., 2d ed., HTKNT 4; Freiburg: Herder, 1976), 3: 383. This goes for both the appearance to the Twelve and to Thomas, he argues.

34. Although some critics have wanted to construe Matthew's mountaintop appearance as a heavenly vision similar to Paul's, this attempt seems futile. Matthew clearly considered Jesus's appearance to be physical, as is evident from his appearance to the women (Matt 28.9, 10) and his commissioning of the disciples. Even in the appearance itself, there are signs of physicality: the disciples' worshipping Jesus recalls the act of the women in v 9 and does not suit well a heavenly appearance; and Jesus's coming toward the disciples (προσελθων) seems to indicate decisively a physical appearance.

Many scholars have stumbled at Luke's 'a spirit has not flesh and bones as you see that I have,' claiming this is a direct contradiction to Paul. In fact, Paul speaks of 'flesh and blood', not 'flesh and bones.' Is the difference significant? It certainly is! 'Flesh and blood,' as we have seen, is a Semitic expression for mortal human nature and has nothing to do with anatomy. Paul agrees with Luke on the physicality of the resurrection body. But furthermore, neither is 'flesh and bones' meant to be an anatomical description. Rather, proceeding from the Jewish idea that it is the bones that are preserved and raised (Gen R 28.3; Lev R 18.1; Eccl R 12.5), the expression connotes the physical reality of Jesus's resurrection. Michaelis writes,

> If, according the Luke, a spirit has neither flesh nor bones but the Resurrected One is no spirit, that is not to say that the Resurrected One, to use pauline terminology, has no 'spiritual (glorified, heavenly) body' but a 'psychical (natural, earthly) body.' By *flesh and bones* in the Lukan statement is rather expressed (in, it must be conceded, a powerful expression, but not one that Paul would necessarily have found 'blasphemous') what Paul expresses with the notion 'soma' (body, corporeality). Through the reference to flesh and bones the spiritual character of this body is not disputed; rather the reality of the bodily is attested. Luke also presupposes, as seen in the totality of the indications he gives (cf. 24:13ff; Acts 1:3), that in the appearances it can only have to do with encounters with the Resurrected One in his glorified corporeality.[35]

The point of Jesus's utterance is to assure the disciples that this is a real resurrection, in the proper, Jewish sense of that word, not an appearance of a bodiless pneuma. Though it stresses corporeality, its primary emphasis is not on the constituents of the body. Thus, neither Paul nor Luke are talking about anatomy, and both agree on the physicality *and* the supernaturalness of Jesus's resurrection body.

In conclusion, we have seen that the critical argument designed to drive a wedge between Paul and the gospels is fallacious. Neither the argument from the appearance to Paul nor the argument from Paul's doctrine of the resurrection body serves to set Paul against the gospels. Quite the opposite, we have seen that Paul's evidence serves to confirm the gospels' narratives of Jesus's bodily resurrection and that their physicalism is probably historically well-founded, that is to say, Jesus did rise bodily from the dead and appear physically to the disciples. And finally we have seen that the gospels present, like Paul, a balanced view of the nature of Jesus's resurrection body. On the one hand, Jesus has a body — he is not a disembodied soul. For the gospels and Paul alike the incarnation is an enduring state, not limited to the 30 some years of Jesus's earthly life. On the other hand, Jesus's body is a supernatural body. We must keep firmly in mind that for the gospels as well as Paul, Jesus rises glorified from the grave. The gospels and Paul agree that the appearances of Jesus ceased and that physically he has left this universe for an indeterminate time. During his physical absence he is present through the Holy Spirit who functions in his stead. But someday he will personally return to judge mankind and to establish his reign over all creation.

---

35. Wilhelm Michaelis, *Die Erscheinungen der Auferstandenen* (Basel: Heinrich Majer, 1944), 96. The German original reads: 'Wenn nach Lukas ein Geist weder Fleisch noch Knochen hat, der Auferstandene aber kein Geist ist, so besagt das nicht, dass der Auferstandene, mit der paulinischen Terminologie zu reden, kein "pneumatisches (verklärtes, himmlisches) Soma," sondern ein "psychisches (natürliches, irdisches) Soma" habe. Mit Fleisch und Knochen in der lukanischen Aussage ist vielmehr (wie zugeben werden muss, in einem kräftigen Ausdruck, den Paulus aber nicht unbedingt als "lästerlich" empfunden haben müsste) das ausgedrückt, was Paulus mit dem Begriff "Soma" (Leib, Leiblichkeit) ausdrückt. Durch den Hinweis auf Fleisch und Knochen soll nicht der pneumatische Charakter dieses Soma bestritten, sondern die Realität des Somatischen bezeugt werden. Auch Lukas steht, wie sich zudem aus der Gesamtheit der bei ihm sich findenen Hinweise ergibt (vgl. 24.13ff; Apg. 1.3), unter den Voraussetzung, dass es sich bei den Erscheinungen nur um Begegnungen mit dem Auferstandenen in seiner verklärten Leiblichkeit handeln kann.'

QUESTIONS AND FURTHER READINGS

Questions for Discussion

1. The apostle Paul said, "And if Christ has not been raised, our preaching is useless and so is your faith. More than that, we are then found to be false witnesses about God, for we have testified about God that he raised Christ from the dead. But he did not raise him if in fact the dead are not raised. For if the dead are not raised, then Christ has not been raised either. And if Christ has not been raised, your faith is futile; you are still in your sins. Then those also who have fallen asleep in Christ are lost. If only for this life we have hope in Christ, we are of all people most to be pitied" (1 Cor. 15:14–19). Why is the resurrection so important?

2. Thomas Aquinas provides five reasons why it was important for Jesus to rise again. Describe two or three of these reasons, and explain why you agree or disagree with them.

3. Describe the approach that John Warwick Montgomery takes in arguing for the resurrection of Jesus. Do you find it persuasive? Why or why not?

4. Does the evidence for the resurrection of Jesus provide a good apologetic for the existence of God? Explain your view on this matter.

5. Gary Habermas notes that those who deny or question that the disciples actually saw Jesus in some sense would generally move in one of two directions. What are they, and how would you respond to them?

6. Describe several of the eight reasons provided by Gary Habermas for the belief that Jesus was *seen* alive after his crucifixion. Which of them do you find most persuasive? Does this provide good evidence that Jesus actually did rise from the dead? Explain.

7. William Lane Craig argues that Jesus' resurrection was bodily and not merely spiritual. What is the crux of his argument?

8. In what way is Jesus still present to us, according to William Lane Craig? Do you agree that this is the biblical view of Jesus' presence in our lives? Explain.

9. How would you defend the resurrection of Jesus to a Muslim?

10. How would you defend the resurrection of Jesus to an agnostic or atheist?

Further Readings

Borg, Marcus, and N. T. Wright (1999). *The Meaning of Jesus: Two Visions*. New York: HarperSanFrancisco. (A brilliant dialogue between two leading scholars from radically differing perspectives on the meaning of Jesus and his resurrection. Parts 3 and 4 focus specifically on Jesus' death and resurrection.)

Craig, William Lane (1981). *The Son Rises: The Historical Evidence for the Resurrection of Jesus*. Eugene, OR: Wipf & Stock. (A well-researched and highly readable work by a leading defender of the bodily resurrection of Jesus.)

Crossan, John Dominic (1993). *The Historical Jesus: The Life of a Mediterranean Jewish Peasant*. New York: HarperSanFrancisco. (A scholarly but readable work by a leading liberal biblical scholar on Jesus' life and ministry as well as his death and cultural and religious influence.)

Davis, Stephen T. (1993). *Risen Indeed: Making Sense of the Resurrection*. Grand Rapids: Eerdmans. (Provides a defense of the Christian view of the resurrection, utilizing arguments and evidences from history, philosophy, and theology.)

Habermas, Gary R., and Michael R. Licona (2004). *The Case for the Resurrection of Jesus*. Grand Rapids: Kregel. (A user-friendly text on the resurrection evidence.)

Pannenberg, Wolfhart (1977). *Jesus — God and Man.* 2nd ed. Translated by Lewis L. Wilkins and Duane A. Priebe. Philadelphia: Westminster. (A scholarly and profound work on the resurrection.)

Spong, John Shelby (1994). *Resurrection: Myth or Reality?* New York: HarperSanFrancisco. (Bishop Spong was the Episcopal Bishop of Newark, New Jersey, for many years and has written widely on Jesus and the Bible; here he questions the literal narrative concerning the resurrection of Jesus and presents a nonliteral understanding of it.)

Strobel, Lee (1998). *The Case for Christ.* Grand Rapids: Zondervan. (Like Socrates of old, Strobel is "keen, like a Spartan hound, at chasing and running down arguments" [Plato] as he interviews leading scholars on a variety of evidences for Jesus' life, death, and resurrection.)

Swinburne, Richard (2003). *The Resurrection of God Incarnate.* New York: Oxford University Press. (A philosophical work on the resurrection.)

Wilkins, Michael J., and J. P. Moreland (1995). *Jesus under Fire: Modern Scholarship Reinvents the Historical Jesus.* Grand Rapids: Zondervan. (A critique of and response to the work of the Jesus Seminar — a liberal group of scholars who deny the literal resurrection of Jesus — by a number of evangelical scholars.)

Wright, N. T. (2003). *The Resurrection of the Son of God.* Minneapolis: Fortress. (A tome on the resurrection by one of the leading New Testament scholars; he first surveys ancient conceptions of the afterlife in contrast to Jewish concepts of resurrection before investigating the New Testament claims of Jesus' resurrection and its significance.)

PART 8

BODY, SOUL, AND THE ARGUMENT FROM MIND

Throughout Christian history most theologians have affirmed a dualistic view of the human self in which human persons are (material) body and (immaterial) soul. There is strong biblical support for such a view, even though in recent times some biblical scholars, theologians, and philosophers have argued for Christian materialism (the view that human persons are material only). In affirming dualism, Christian thinkers have not only utilized the Bible in support of their position, but have used philosophical and theological arguments as well. There are different forms of dualism, primarily the Thomistic and Cartesian versions. Both forms are represented in this section.

Another apologetic issue related to the soul, or mind (sometimes these terms are used synonymously to refer to the immaterial aspect of the self), has to do with certain conclusions that follow from the existence of a rational soul. Questions arise such as, Why should we trust our mental processes if they are simply physical activities in the brain? For if that's what mental processes are, then determinism follows. And if our thoughts are determined, then we cannot truly evaluate arguments and evidences and make inferences and come to rational conclusions. In fact, determinism seems to be self-refuting. Issues such as this are included in a family of arguments, sometimes called the argument from mind, and they point to the conclusion that the rationality of human persons implies that God must be the ground of this rationality.

In the first selection, Thomas Aquinas argues for the soul as the "form" of the body. This view is more akin to Aristotle's position than to Plato's. For Aquinas (and for Aristotle), a person is a psychological unity consisting of a body whose animating form is the soul. This is substantially different from Plato's (or at least one interpretation of Plato's) in which the soul and the body are individual, separate substances. Aquinas also argues that the human soul does not perish when the body does.

The next piece is René Descartes's second Meditation, where he offers his famous *cogito ergo sum* ("I think, therefore I am") argument. In this "meditation," Descartes expects readers to meditate with him. In doing so, he thinks readers will see the truth of the argument. In the first Meditation he argues that beliefs based on sensory experience are doubtful, including the belief that I (first-person perspective) have, or am, a physical body. So does it follow that I do not exist? No, for even if such beliefs are false, there exists an "I" that believes this! Even if I am being deceived by an evil demon, there is an I that is being deceived. What follows? "I am, I exist" is necessarily true. I can be certain that I exist as a thinking thing.

In the final selection, J. P. Moreland argues that the existence of rational minds in human beings provides evidence for God's existence. He first explains and then defends mind/body dualism, providing general arguments for dualism and honing in on an argument that attempts to demonstrate that physicalism (the view that reality in general, and humans in particular, are made up of matter only) is a self-refuting position. He next argues that the view that rational minds evolved from matter is implausible. Finally, he uses the previous material to argue that rational minds come from another rational Mind: God.

CHAPTER 40

On the Soul and Body

Thomas Aquinas

SUMMA CONTRA GENTILES

BOOK TWO: Creation

CHAPTER 68: How an Intellectual Substance Can Be the Form of the Body

[1] From the preceding arguments, then, we can conclude that an intellectual substance can be united to the body as its form.

[2] For, if an intellectual substance is not united to the body merely as its mover, as Plato held that it is, nor is in contact with it merely by phantasms, as Averroes said, but as its form; and if the intellect whereby man understands is not a preparedness in human nature, as Alexander supposed it to be, nor the temperament, according to Galen, nor a harmony, as Empedocles imagined, nor a body, nor the senses or the imagination, as the early philosophers maintained, then it remains that the human soul is an intellectual substance united to the body as its form. This conclusion can be made evident as follows.

[3] For one thing to be another's substantial form, two requirements must be met. First, the form must be the principle of the substantial being of the thing whose form it is; I speak not of the productive but of the formal principle whereby a thing exists and is called a being. The second requirement then follows from this, namely, that the form and the matter be joined together in the unity of one act of being; which is not true of the union of the efficient cause with that to which it gives being. And this single act of being is that in which the composite substance subsists: a thing one in being and made up of matter and form. Now, as we have shown, the fact that an intellectual substance is subsistent does not stand in the way of its

being the formal principle of the being of the matter, as communicating its own being to the matter. For it is not unfitting that the composite and its form should subsist in the same act of being, since the composite exists only by the form, and neither of them subsists apart from the other.

[4] Nevertheless, it may be objected that an intellectual substance cannot communicate its being to corporeal matter in such fashion that the two will be united in the same act of being, because diverse genera have diverse modes of being, and to the nobler substance belongs a loftier being.

[5] Now, this argument would be relevant if that single act of being belonged in the same way to the matter as to the intellectual substance. But it does not. For that act of being appertains to the corporeal matter as its recipient and its subject, raised to a higher level; it belongs to the intellectual substance as its principle, and in keeping with its very own nature. Nothing, therefore, prevents an intellectual substance from being the human body's form, which is the human soul.

[6] Thus are we able to contemplate the marvelous connection of things. For it is always found that the lowest in the higher genus touches the highest of the lower species. Some of the lowest members of the animal kingdom, for instance, enjoy a form of life scarcely superior to that of plants; oysters, which are motionless, have only the sense of touch and are fixed to the earth like plants. That is why Blessed Dionysius says in his work *On the Divine Names* that "divine wisdom has united the ends of higher things with the beginnings of the lower." We have, therefore, to consider the existence of something supreme in the genus of

bodies, namely, the human body harmoniously tempered, which is in contact with the lowest of the higher genus, namely, the human soul, which holds the lowest rank in the genus of intellectual substances, as can be seen from its mode of understanding; so that the intellectual soul is said to be on the horizon and confines of things corporeal and incorporeal, in that it is an incorporeal substance and yet the form of a body. Nor is a thing composed of an intellectual substance and corporeal matter less one than a thing made up of the form of fire and its matter, but perhaps it is more one; because the greater the mastery of form over matter, the greater is the unity of that which is made from it and matter.

[7] But, though the form and the matter are united in the one act of being, the matter need not always be commensurate with the form. Indeed, the higher the form, the more it surpasses matter in its being. This fact is clearly apparent to one who observes the operations of forms, from the study of which we know their natures; for, as a thing is, so does it act. That is why a form whose operation transcends the condition of matter, itself also surpasses matter in the rank of its being.

[8] For we find certain lowest-grade forms whose operations are limited to the class of those proper to the qualities which are dispositions of matter; qualities such as heat, cold, moisture and dryness, rarity and density, gravity and levity, etc. And those forms are the forms of the elements: forms which therefore are altogether material and wholly embedded in matter.

[9] Above these are found the forms of mixed bodies. Although their operations are no greater in scope than those which can be effected through qualities of the aforesaid variety, nevertheless they sometimes produce those same effects by a higher power which they receive from the heavenly bodies, and which is consequent upon the latter's species. A case in point is that of the lodestone attracting iron.

[10] One rung higher on the ladder of forms, we encounter those whose operations include some which exceed the power of the previously mentioned material qualities, although the latter assist organically in the operations of those forms. Such forms are the souls of plants, which likewise resemble not only the powers of the heavenly bodies, in surpassing the active and passive qualities, but also the movers of those bodies, the souls of plants being principles of movement in living things, which move themselves.

[11] A step above, we find other forms resembling the higher substances, not only in moving, but even, somehow, in knowing, so that they are capable of operations to which the aforesaid qualities are of no assistance, even organically, although these operations are performed only by means of a bodily organ. Such forms are the souls of brute animals. For sensation and imagination are not brought about by heating and cooling, although these are necessary for the due disposition of the organ involved.

[12] Above all these forms, however, is a form like to the higher substances even in respect of the kind of knowledge proper to it, namely, understanding. This form, then, is capable of an operation which is accomplished without any bodily organ at all. And this form is the intellective soul; for understanding is not effected through any bodily organ. That is why this principle, the intellective soul by which man understands and which transcends the condition of corporeal matter, must not be wholly encompassed by or imbedded in matter, as material forms are. This is proved by its intellectual operation, wherein corporeal matter has no part. But since the human soul's act of understanding needs powers — namely, imagination and sense — which function through bodily organs, this itself shows that the soul is naturally united to the body in order to complete the human species.

CHAPTER 69: *Solution of the Arguments Advanced above in Order to Show That an Intellectual Substance Cannot Be United to the Body As Its Form*

[1] With the preceding points in mind, it is not difficult to solve the arguments previously proposed against the union in question.

[2] In the first argument a false supposition is made, because body and soul are not two actually existing

substances; rather, the two of them together constitute one actually existing substance. For man's body is not actually the same while the soul is present and when it is absent; but the soul makes it to be actually.

CHAPTER 79: *That the Human Soul Does Not Perish When the Body Is Corrupted*

[1] From what has been said, therefore, it can be clearly shown that the human soul is not corrupted when the body is corrupted.

[2] For it was proved above that every intellectual substance is incorruptible. But man's soul is an intellectual substance, as was shown. It therefore follows that the human soul is incorruptible.

[3] Again, no thing is corrupted with respect to that wherein its perfection consists, for mutations in regard to perfection and corruption are contrary to one another. The perfection of the human soul, however, consists in a certain abstraction from the body. For the soul is perfected by knowledge and virtue, and it is perfected in knowledge the more it considers immaterial things, the perfection of virtue consisting in man's not submitting to the passions of the body, but moderating and controlling them in accordance with reason. Consequently, the soul is not corrupted by being separated from the body.

[4] Now, it may be said that the soul's perfection lies in its operational separation from the body, and its corruption in its existential separation there from. Such an argument misses the mark, for a thing's operation manifests its substance and its being, since a thing operates according as it is a being, and its proper operation follows upon its proper nature. The operation of a thing, therefore, can be perfected only so far as its substance is perfected. Thus, if the soul, in leaving the body, is perfected operationally, its incorporeal substance will not fail in its being through separation from the body.

[5] Likewise, that which properly perfects the soul of man is something incorruptible; for the proper operation of man, as man, is understanding, since it is in this that he differs from brutes, plants, and inanimate things. Now, it properly pertains to this act to apprehend objects universal and incorruptible as such. But perfections must be proportionate to things perfectible. Therefore, the human soul is incorruptible.

[6] Moreover, it is impossible that natural appetite should be in vain. But man naturally desires to exist forever. This is evidenced by the fact that being is that which all desire; and man by his intellect apprehends being not merely in the present, as brute animals do, but unqualifiedly. Therefore, man attains perpetual existence as regards his soul, whereby he apprehends being unqualifiedly and in respect of every time.

[7] Also, the reception of one thing in another accords with the recipient's manner of being. But the forms of things are received in the possible intellect according as they are actually intelligible; and they are actually intelligible according as they are immaterial, universal, and consequently incorruptible. Therefore, the possible intellect is incorruptible. The possible intellect, however, is part of the human soul, as we proved above. Hence, the human soul is incorruptible.

[8] Then, too, intelligible being is more permanent than sensible being. But in sensible things that which has the role of first recipient, namely, prime matter, is incorruptible in its substance; much more so, therefore, is the possible intellect, which is receptive of intelligible forms. Therefore, the human soul, of which the possible intellect is a part, is also incorruptible.

[9] Moreover, the maker is superior to the thing made, as Aristotle says. But the agent intellect actualizes intelligibles, as was shown above. Therefore, since intelligibles in act, as such, are incorruptible, much more will the agent intellect be incorruptible. So, too, then, is the human soul, whose light is the agent intellect, as we have previously made clear.

[10] Again, a form is corrupted by three things only: the action of its contrary, the corruption of its subject, the failure of its cause; by the action of a contrary, as when beat is destroyed by the action of cold; by the corruption of its subject, as when the power of sight is destroyed through the destruction of the eye; by the failure of its cause, as when the air's illumination fails through the failure of its cause, the sun, to be present. But the human soul cannot be corrupted by

the action of a contrary, for nothing is contrary to it; since, through the possible intellect, it is cognizant and receptive of all contraries. Nor can the human soul be destroyed through the corruption of its subject, for we have already shown that it is a form independent of the body in its being. Nor, again, can the soul be destroyed through the failure of its cause, since it can have no cause except an eternal one, as we shall prove later on. Therefore, in no way can the human soul be corrupted.

[11] Furthermore, if the soul perishes as the result of the body's corruption, then its being must be weakened through the debility of the body. But if a power of the soul is weakened for that reason, this occurs only by accident, namely, in so far as that power has need of a bodily organ. Thus, the power of sot is debilitated through the weakening of its organ-accidentally, however. The following considerations will make this point clear. If some weakness were attached to the power through itself, it would never be restored as the result of the organ's being restored; yet it is a fact of observation that, however much the power of sight may seem to be weakened, if the organ is restored, then the power is restored. That is why Aristotle says, in De anima I [4], "that if an old man were to recover the eye of a youth, he would see just as well as the youth does." Since, then, the intellect is a power of the soul that needs no organ — as we proved above — it is not weakened, either through itself or accidentally, by old age or any other bodily weakness. Now, if in the operation of the intellect fatigue occurs, or some impediment because of a bodily infirmity, this is due not to any weakness on the part of the intellect itself, but to the weakness of the powers which the intellect needs, namely, of the imagination, the memory, and the cogitative power. Clearly, therefore, the intellect is incorruptible. And since it is an intellective substance, the human soul likewise is incorruptible.

[12] This conclusion also comes to light through the authority of Aristotle. For he says in De anima I [4] that the intellect is evidently a substance and is incapable of being destroyed. And it can be inferred from what has been said already that the remark of Aristotle's cannot apply to a separate substance that is either the possible or the agent intellect.

[13] The same conclusion also follows from what Aristotle says in Metaphysics XI [3], speaking against Plato, namely, "that moving causes exist prior to their effects, whereas formal causes are simultaneous with their effects; thus when a man is healed, then health exists," and not before — Plato's position, that the forms of things exist prior to the things themselves, to the contrary notwithstanding. Having said this, Aristotle adds: But we must examine whether anything also survives afterwards. "For in some cases there is nothing to prevent this — the soul, for example, may be of this sort, not every soul, but the intellect." Since Aristotle is speaking of forms, he clearly means that the intellect, which is the form of man, remains after the matter, which is the body.

[14] It is also clear from these texts of Aristotle that, while he maintains that the soul is a form, he does not say it is non-subsistent and therefore corruptible — an interpretation which Gregory of Nyssa attributes to him. For Aristotle excludes the intellective soul from the generality of other forms, in saying that it remains after the body, and is a certain substance.

[15] The doctrine of the Catholic faith is in agreement on these matters. For in the work On the Teachings of the Church there is this statement: "We believe that man alone is possessed of a subsistent soul, which continues to live even after divesting itself of the body, and is the animating principle of the senses and powers; nor does the soul die with the body, as the Arabian asserts, nor after a short period of time, as Zeno would have it, because it is a living substance."

[16] This eliminates the error of the ungodly, in whose person Solomon says: "We are born of nothing, and after this we shall be as if we had not been" (Wis. 2:2); and in whose person again Solomon says: "The death of man and of beasts is one, and the condition of them both is equal: as man dies, so they also die: all things breathe alike, and man has nothing more than beast" (Eccl. 3:19). For Solomon clearly is not speaking in his own person but in that of the godless, since at the end of the book he adds in a decisive manner:

"Before the dusts return into its earth, from whence it was, and the spirit returns to Him Who gave it" (Eccl. 12:6–7).

[17] Furthermore, there are myriad passages of sacred Scripture which proclaim the immortality of the soul.

CHAPTER 82: That the Souls of Brute Animals Are Not Immortal

[1] This truth can be clearly inferred from what has been already said.

[2] For we demonstrated above that no operation of the sensitive part of the soul can be performed without the body. In the souls of brute animals, however, there is no operation superior to those of the sensitive part, since they neither understand nor reason. This is evident from the fact that all animals of the same species operate in the same way, as though moved by nature and not as operating by art; every swallow builds its nest and every spider spins its web, in the same manner. The souls of brutes, then, are incapable of any operation that does not involve the body. Now, since every substance is possessed of some operation, the soul of a brute animal will be unable to exist apart from its body, so that it perishes along with the body.

[3] Likewise, every form separate from matter is understood in act for the agent intellect renders species intelligible in act by way of abstraction, as we see from what was said above. But if the soul of the brute animal continues to exist after its body has passed away, then that soul will be a form separate from matter, and therefore a form understood in act. And yet, as Aristotle says in De anima III [4], with things separate from matter, that which understands is identical with that which is understood. It follows that the soul of a brute animal, if it survives the body, will be intellectual; and this is impossible.

[4] Then, too, in everything capable of attaining a certain perfection, we find a natural desire for that perfection, since good is what all things desire, yet in such fashion that each thing desires the good proper to itself. In brutes, however, we find no desire for perpetual existence, but only a desire for the perpetua-tion of their several species, since we do observe in them the desire to reproduce and thereby perpetuate the species — a desire common also to plants and to inanimate things, though not as regards desire proper to an animal as such, because animal appetite is consequent upon apprehension. For, since the apprehending power of the sensitive soul is limited to the here and now, that soul cannot possibly be cognizant of perpetual existence. Nor, then, does it desire such existence with animal appetite. Therefore, the soul of a brute animal is incapable of perpetual existence.

[5] Moreover, as Aristotle remarks in Ethics X [4], pleasures perfect operations. Hence, a thing's activity is directed to that object wherein it takes pleasure, as to its end. But all the pleasures of brute animals have reference to the preservation of their body; thus, they delight in sounds, odors, and sights only to the extent that they signify for them food or sex, the sole objects of all their pleasures. All the activities of such animals, then, have but a single end: the preservation of their bodily existence. Thus, there is in them no being whatever which is independent of the body.

[6] The teaching of the Catholic faith is in harmony with this doctrine. For in the Old Testament we read, concerning the soul of the brute animal, that "the life of all flesh is in the blood" (Lev. 17:14; cf. Gen. 9:4–5), which seemingly means that the existence of such souls depends on the permanence of the blood. And it is said in the work On the Teachings of the Church: "We declare that man alone has a subsistent soul," that is, a soul having life of itself; and that "the souls of brute animals perish along with their bodies."

[7] Aristotle likewise states, in De anima II [2], that "the intellective part of the soul differs from the other parts as the incorruptible from the corruptible."

[8] This eliminates Plato's theory that the souls even of brute animals are immortal.

[9] Nevertheless, it would seem possible to show that the souls of such animals are immortal. For, if a thing possesses an operation through itself, distinctly its own, then it is subsisting through itself. But the sensitive soul in brutes enjoys an operation through itself, wherein the body has no part, namely, motion;

for a mover is compounded of two parts, the one being mover and the other moved. Since the body is a thing moved, it remains that the soul is exclusively a mover, and, consequently, is subsisting through itself. Hence, the soul cannot be corrupted by accident, when the body is corrupted, for only those things are corrupted by accident which do not have being through themselves. Nor can the soul be corrupted through itself, since it neither has a contrary nor is composed of contraries. The result of the argument, therefore, is that the soul is altogether incorruptible.

… [20] It is, then, clearly impossible for any operation of the brute animal's soul to be independent of its body. And from this it can be inferred with necessity that the soul of the brute perishes with the body.

SUMMA THEOLOGICA 1: Q. 75

ARTICLE 2: Whether the Human Soul Is Something Subsistent?

Objection 1. It would seem that the human soul is not something subsistent. For that which subsists is said to be "this particular thing." Now "this particular thing" is said not of the soul, but of that which is composed of soul and body. Therefore the soul is not something subsistent.

Objection 2. Further, everything subsistent operates. But the soul does not operate; for, as the Philosopher says (De Anima i, 4), "to say that the soul feels or understands is like saying that the soul weaves or builds." Therefore the soul is not subsistent.

Objection 3. Further, if the soul were subsistent, it would have some operation apart from the body. But it has no operation apart from the body, not even that of understanding: for the act of understanding does not take place without a phantasm, which cannot exist apart from the body. Therefore the human soul is not something subsistent.

On the contrary, Augustine says (De Trin. x, 7): "Who understands that the nature of the soul is that of a substance and not that of a body, will see that those who maintain the corporeal nature of the soul, are led astray through associating with the soul those things without which they are unable to think of any nature — i.e., imaginary pictures of corporeal things." Therefore the nature of the human intellect is not only incorporeal, but it is also a substance, that is, something subsistent.

I answer that, it must necessarily be allowed that the principle of intellectual operation which we call the soul, is a principle both incorporeal and subsistent. For it is clear that by means of the intellect man can have knowledge of all corporeal things. Now whatever knows certain things cannot have any of them in its own nature; because that which is in it naturally would impede the knowledge of anything else. Thus we observe that a sick man's tongue being vitiated by a feverish and bitter humor, is insensible to anything sweet, and everything seems bitter to it. Therefore, if the intellectual principle contained the nature of a body it would be unable to know all bodies. Now every body has its own determinate nature. Therefore it is impossible for the intellectual principle to be a body. It is likewise impossible for it to understand by means of a bodily organ; since the determinate nature of that organ would impede knowledge of all bodies; as when a certain determinate color is not only in the pupil of the eye, but also in a glass vase, the liquid in the vase seems to be of that same color.

Therefore the intellectual principle which we call the mind or the intellect has an operation "per se" apart from the body. Now only that which subsists can have an operation "per se." For nothing can operate but what is actual: for which reason we do not say that heat imparts heat, but that what is hot gives heat. We must conclude, therefore, that the human soul, which is called the intellect or the mind, is something incorporeal and subsistent.

Reply to Objection 1. "This particular thing" can be taken in two senses. Firstly, for anything subsistent; secondly, for that which subsists, and is complete in a specific nature. The former sense excludes the inherence of an accident or of a material form; the latter excludes also the imperfection of the part, so that a hand can be called "this particular thing" in the first sense, but not in the second. Therefore, as the human soul is a part of human nature, it can indeed be called "this particular thing," in the first sense, as being something subsistent; but not in the second, for in this sense, what is composed of body and soul is said to be "this particular thing."

Reply to Objection 2. Aristotle wrote those words as expressing not his own opinion, but the opinion of those who said that to understand is to be moved, as is clear from the context. Or we may reply that to operate "per se" belongs to what exists "per se." But for a thing to exist "per se," it suffices sometimes that it be not inherent, as an accident or a material form; even though it be part of something. Nevertheless, that is rightly said to subsist "per se," which is neither inherent in the above sense, nor part of anything else. In this sense, the eye or the hand cannot be said to subsist "per se"; nor can it for that reason be said to operate "per se." Hence the operation of the parts is through each part attributed to the whole. For we say that man sees with the eye, and feels with the hand, and not in the same sense as when we say that what is hot gives heat by its heat; for heat, strictly speaking, does not give heat. We may therefore say that the soul understands, as the eye sees; but it is more correct to say that man understands through the soul.

Reply to Objection 3. The body is necessary for the action of the intellect, not as its origin of action, but on the part of the object; for the phantasm is to the intellect what color is to the sight. Neither does such a dependence on the body prove the intellect to be non-subsistent; otherwise it would follow that an animal is non-subsistent, since it requires external objects of the senses in order to perform its act of perception.

ARTICLE 4: Whether the Soul Is Composed of Matter and Form?

Objection 1: It would seem that the soul is composed of matter and form. For potentiality is opposed to actuality. Now, whatsoever things are in actuality participate of the First Act, which is God; by participation of Whom, all things are good, are beings, and are living things, as is clear from the teaching of Dionysius (Div. Nom. v). Therefore whatsoever things are in potentiality participate of the first potentiality. But the first potentiality is primary matter. Therefore, since the human soul is, after a manner, in potentiality; which appears from the fact that sometimes a man is potentially understanding; it seems that the human soul must participate of primary matter, as part of itself.

Objection 2. Further, wherever the properties of matter are found, there matter is. But the properties of matter are found in the soul — namely, to be a subject, and to be changed, for it is a subject to science, and virtue; and it changes from ignorance to knowledge and from vice to virtue. Therefore matter is in the soul.

Objection 3. Further, things which have no matter, have no cause of their existence, as the Philosopher says in Metaph. viii (Did. vii, 6). But the soul has a cause of its existence, since it is created by God. Therefore the soul has matter.

Objection 4. Further, what has no matter, and is a form only, is a pure act, and is infinite. But this belongs to God alone. Therefore the soul has matter.

On the contrary, Augustine (Gen. ad lit. vii, 7,8,9) proves that the soul was made neither of corporeal matter, nor of spiritual matter.

I answer that, the soul has no matter. We may consider this question in two ways. First, from the notion of a soul in general; for it belongs to the notion of a soul to be the form of a body. Now, either it is a form by virtue of itself, in its entirety, or by virtue of some part of itself. If by virtue of itself in its entirety, then it is impossible that any part of it should be matter, if by matter we understand something purely potential: for a form, as such, is an act; and that which is purely potentiality cannot be part of an act, since potentiality is repugnant to actuality as being opposite thereto. If, however, it be a form by virtue of a part of itself, then we call that part the soul: and that matter, which it actualizes first, we call the "primary animate."

Secondly, we may proceed from the specific notion of the human soul inasmuch as it is intellectual. For it is clear that whatever is received into something is received according to the condition of the recipient. Now a thing is known in as far as its form is in the knower. But the intellectual soul knows a thing in its nature absolutely: for instance, it knows a stone absolutely as a stone; and therefore the form of a stone absolutely, as to its proper formal idea, is in the intellectual soul. Therefore the intellectual soul itself is an absolute form, and not something composed of matter and form. For if the intellectual soul were composed of matter and form, the forms of things would be received into it as individuals, and so it would only know the individual: just as it happens with the sensitive powers which receive forms in a corporeal organ; since matter is the principle by which forms are individualized. It follows, therefore, that the intellectual soul, and every intellectual substance which has knowledge of forms absolutely, is exempt from composition of matter and form.

Reply to Objection 1. The First Act is the universal principle of all acts; because it is infinite, virtually "pre-containing all things," as Dionysius says (Div. Nom. v). Wherefore things participate of it not as a part of themselves, but by diffusion of its processions. Now as potentiality is receptive of act, it must be proportionate to act. But the acts received which proceed from the First Infinite Act, and are participations thereof, are diverse, so that there cannot be one potentiality which receives all acts, as there is one act, from which all participated acts are derived; for then the receptive potentiality would equal the active potentiality of the First Act. Now the receptive potentiality in the intellectual soul is other than the receptive potentiality of first matter, as appears from the diversity of the things received by each. For primary matter receives individual forms; whereas the intelligence receives absolute forms. Hence the existence of such a potentiality in the intellectual soul does not prove that the soul is composed of matter and form.

Reply to Objection 2. To be a subject and to be changed belong to matter by reason of its being in potentiality. As, therefore, the potentiality of the intelligence is one thing and the potentiality of primary matter another, so in each is there a different reason of subjection and change. For the intelligence is subject to knowledge, and is changed from ignorance to knowledge, by reason of its being in potentiality with regard to the intelligible species.

Reply to Objection 3. The form causes matter to be, and so does the agent; wherefore the agent causes matter to be, so far as it actualizes it by transmuting it to the act of a form. A subsistent form, however, does not owe its existence to some formal principle, nor has it a cause transmuting it from potentiality to act. So after the words quoted above, the Philosopher concludes, that in things composed of matter and form, "there is no other cause but that which moves from potentiality to act; while whatsoever things have no matter are simply beings at once."

Reply to Objection 4. Everything participated is compared to the participator as its act. But whatever created form be supposed to subsist "per se," must have existence by participation; for "even life," or anything of that sort, "is a participator of existence," as Dionysius says (Div. Nom. v). Now participated existence is limited by the capacity of the participator; so that God alone, Who is His own existence, is pure act and infinite. But in intellectual substances there is composition of actuality and potentiality, not, indeed, of matter and form, but of form and participated existence. Wherefore some say that they are composed of that "whereby they are" and that "which they are"; for existence itself is that by which a thing is.

CHAPTER 41

The Cogito

René Descartes

MEDITATION II

Of the Nature of the Human Mind; and That It Is More Easily Known Than the Body

1. The Meditation of yesterday has filled my mind with so many doubts, that it is no longer in my power to forget them. Nor do I see, meanwhile, any principle on which they can be resolved; and, just as if I had fallen all of a sudden into very deep water, I am so greatly disconcerted as to be unable either to plant my feet firmly on the bottom or sustain myself by swimming on the surface. I will, nevertheless, make an effort, and try anew the same path on which I had entered yesterday, that is, proceed by casting aside all that admits of the slightest doubt, not less than if I had discovered it to be absolutely false; and I will continue always in this track until I shall find something that is certain, or at least, if I can do nothing more, until I shall know with certainty that there is nothing certain. Archimedes, that he might transport the entire globe from the place it occupied to another, demanded only a point that was firm and immovable; so, also, I shall be entitled to entertain the highest expectations, if I am fortunate enough to discover only one thing that is certain and indubitable.

2. I suppose, accordingly, that all the things which I see are false (fictitious); I believe that none of those objects which my fallacious memory represents ever existed; I suppose that I possess no senses; I believe that body, figure, extension, motion, and place are merely fictions of my mind. What is there, then, that can be esteemed true? Perhaps this only, that there is absolutely nothing certain.

3. But how do I know that there is not something different altogether from the objects I have now enumerated, of which it is impossible to entertain the slightest doubt? Is there not a God, or some being, by whatever name I may designate him, who causes these thoughts to arise in my mind? But why suppose such a being, for it may be I myself am capable of producing them? Am I, then, at least not something? But I before denied that I possessed senses or a body; I hesitate, however, for what follows from that? Am I so dependent on the body and the senses that without these I cannot exist? But I had the persuasion that there was absolutely nothing in the world, that there was no sky and no earth, neither minds nor bodies; was I not, therefore, at the same time, persuaded that I did not exist? Far from it; I assuredly existed, since I was persuaded. But there is I know not what being, who is possessed at once of the highest power and the deepest cunning, who is constantly employing all his ingenuity in deceiving me. Doubtless, then, I exist, since I am deceived; and, let him deceive me as he may, he can never bring it about that I am nothing, so long as I shall be conscious that I am something. So that it must, in fine, be maintained, all things being maturely and carefully considered, that this proposition (pronunciatum) I am, I exist, is necessarily true each time it is expressed by me, or conceived in my mind.

4. But I do not yet know with sufficient clearness what I am, though assured that I am; and hence, in the next place, I must take care, lest perchance I inconsiderately substitute some other object in room of what is properly myself, and thus wander from truth, even in that knowledge (cognition) which I hold to be of all others the most certain and evident. For this reason,

I will now consider anew what I formerly believed myself to be, before I entered on the present train of thought; and of my previous opinion I will retrench all that can in the least be invalidated by the grounds of doubt I have adduced, in order that there may at length remain nothing but what is certain and indubitable.

5. What then did I formerly think I was? Undoubtedly I judged that I was a man. But what is a man? Shall I say a rational animal? Assuredly not; for it would be necessary forthwith to inquire into what is meant by animal, and what by rational, and thus, from a single question, I should insensibly glide into others, and these more difficult than the first; nor do I now possess enough of leisure to warrant me in wasting my time amid subtleties of this sort. I prefer here to attend to the thoughts that sprung up of themselves in my mind, and were inspired by my own nature alone, when I applied myself to the consideration of what I was. In the first place, then, I thought that I possessed a countenance, hands, arms, and all the fabric of members that appears in a corpse, and which I called by the name of body. It further occurred to me that I was nourished, that I walked, perceived, and thought, and all those actions I referred to the soul; but what the soul itself was I either did not stay to consider, or, if I did, I imagined that it was something extremely rare and subtle, like wind, or flame, or ether, spread through my grosser parts. As regarded the body, I did not even doubt of its nature, but thought I distinctly knew it, and if I had wished to describe it according to the notions I then entertained, I should have explained myself in this manner: By body I understand all that can be terminated by a certain figure; that can be comprised in a certain place, and so fill a certain space as there from to exclude every other body; that can be perceived either by touch, sight, hearing, taste, or smell; that can be moved in different ways, not indeed of itself, but by something foreign to it by which it is touched and from which it receives the impression; for the power of self-motion, as likewise that of perceiving and thinking, I held as by no means pertaining to the nature of body; on the contrary, I was somewhat astonished to find such faculties existing in some bodies.

6. But as to myself, what can I now say that I am, since I suppose there exists an extremely powerful, and, if I may so speak, malignant being, whose whole endeavors are directed toward deceiving me ? Can I affirm that I possess any one of all those attributes of which I have lately spoken as belonging to the nature of body? After attentively considering them in my own mind, I find none of them that can properly be said to belong to myself. To recount them were idle and tedious. Let us pass, then, to the attributes of the soul. The first mentioned were the powers of nutrition and walking; but, if it be true that I have no body, it is true likewise that I am capable neither of walking nor of being nourished. Perception is another attribute of the soul; but perception too is impossible without the body; besides, I have frequently, during sleep, believed that I perceived objects which I afterward observed I did not in reality perceive. Thinking is another attribute of the soul; and here I discover what properly belongs to myself. This alone is inseparable from me. I am — I exist: this is certain; but how often? As often as I think; for perhaps it would even happen, if I should wholly cease to think, that I should at the same time altogether cease to be. I now admit nothing that is not necessarily true. I am therefore, precisely speaking, only a thinking thing, that is, a mind (mens sive animus), understanding, or reason, terms whose signification was before unknown to me. I am, however, a real thing, and really existent; but what thing? The answer was a thinking thing.

7. The question now arises, am I aught besides? I will stimulate my imagination with a view to discover whether I am not still something more than a thinking being. Now it is plain I am not the assemblage of members called the human body; I am not a thin and penetrating air diffused through all these members, or wind, or flame, or vapor, or breath, or any of all the things I can imagine; for I supposed that all these were not, and, without changing the supposition, I find that I still feel assured of my existence. But it is true, perhaps, that those very things which I suppose

to be non-existent, because they are unknown to me, are not in truth different from myself whom I know. This is a point I cannot determine, and do not now enter into any dispute regarding it. I can only judge of things that are known to me: I am conscious that I exist, and I who know that I exist inquire into what I am. It is, however, perfectly certain that the knowledge of my existence, thus precisely taken, is not dependent on things, the existence of which is as yet unknown to me: and consequently it is not dependent on any of the things I can feign in imagination. Moreover, the phrase itself, I frame an image (efffingo), reminds me of my error; for I should in truth frame one if I were to imagine myself to be anything, since to imagine is nothing more than to contemplate the figure or image of a corporeal thing; but I already know that I exist, and that it is possible at the same time that all those images, and in general all that relates to the nature of body, are merely dreams or chimeras. From this I discover that it is not more reasonable to say, I will excite my imagination that I may know more distinctly what I am, than to express myself as follows: I am now awake, and perceive something real; but because my perception is not sufficiently clear, I will of express purpose go to sleep that my dreams may represent to me the object of my perception with more truth and clearness. And, therefore, I know that nothing of all that I can embrace in imagination belongs to the knowledge which I have of myself, and that there is need to recall with the utmost care the mind from this mode of thinking, that it may be able to know its own nature with perfect distinctness.

8. But what, then, am I? A thinking thing, it has been said. But what is a thinking thing? It is a thing that doubts, understands, conceives, affirms, denies, wills, refuses; that imagines also, and perceives.

9. Assuredly it is not little, if all these properties belong to my nature. But why should they not belong to it? Am I not that very being who now doubts of almost everything; who, for all that, understands and conceives certain things; who affirms one alone as true, and denies the others; who desires to know more of them, and does not wish to be deceived; who

imagines many things, sometimes even despite his will; and is likewise percipient of many, as if through the medium of the senses. Is there nothing of all this as true as that I am, even although I should be always dreaming, and although he who gave me being employed all his ingenuity to deceive me? Is there also any one of these attributes that can be properly distinguished from my thought, or that can be said to be separate from myself? For it is of itself so evident that it is I who doubt, I who understand, and I who desire, that it is here unnecessary to add anything by way of rendering it more clear. And I am as certainly the same being who imagines; for although it may be (as I before supposed) that nothing I imagine is true, still the power of imagination does not cease really to exist in me and to form part of my thought. In fine, I am the same being who perceives, that is, who apprehends certain objects as by the organs of sense, since, in truth, I see light, hear a noise, and feel heat. But it will be said that these presentations are false, and that I am dreaming. Let it be so. At all events it is certain that I seem to see light, hear a noise, and feel heat; this cannot be false, and this is what in me is properly called perceiving (sentire), which is nothing else than thinking.

10. From this I begin to know what I am with somewhat greater clearness and distinctness than heretofore. But, nevertheless, it still seems to me, and I cannot help believing, that corporeal things, whose images are formed by thought which fall under the senses-, and are examined by the same, are known with much greater distinctness than that I know not what part of myself which is not imaginable; although, in truth, it may seem strange to say that I know and comprehend with greater distinctness things whose existence appears to me doubtful, that are unknown, and do not belong to me, than others of whose reality I am persuaded, that are known to me, and appertain to my proper nature; in a word, than myself. But I see clearly what is the state of the case. My mind is apt to wander, and will not yet submit to be restrained within the limits of truth. Let us therefore leave the mind to itself once more, and, according to it every

kind of liberty permit it to consider the objects that appear to it from without], in order that, having afterward withdrawn it from these gently and opportunely and fixed it on the consideration of its being and the properties it finds in itself, it may then be the more easily controlled.

11. Let us now accordingly consider the objects that are commonly thought to be the most easily, and likewise the most distinctly known, viz, the bodies we touch and see; not, indeed, bodies in general, for these general notions are usually somewhat more confused, but one body in particular. Take, for example, this piece of wax; it is quite fresh, having been but recently taken from the beehive; it has not yet lost the sweetness of the honey it contained; it still retains somewhat of the odor of the flowers from which it was gathered; its color, figure, size, are apparent to the sight; it is hard, cold, easily handled; and sounds when struck upon with the finger. In fine, all that contributes to make a body as distinctly known as possible, is found in the one before us. But, while I am speaking, let it be placed near the fire — what remained of the taste exhales, the smell evaporates, the color changes, its figure is destroyed, its size increases, it becomes liquid, it grows hot, it can hardly be handled, and, although struck upon, it emits no sound. Does the same wax still remain after this change? It must be admitted that it does remain; no one doubts it, or judges otherwise. What, then, was it I knew with so much distinctness in the piece of wax? Assuredly, it could be nothing of all that I observed by means of the senses, since all the things that fell under taste, smell, sight, touch, and hearing are changed, and yet the same wax remains.

12. It was perhaps what I now think, viz, that this wax was neither the sweetness of honey, the pleasant odor of flowers, the whiteness, the figure, nor the sound, but only a body that a little before appeared to me conspicuous under these forms, and which is now perceived under others. But, to speak precisely, what is it that I imagine when I think of it in this way? Let it be attentively considered, and, retrenching all that does not belong to the wax, let us see what remains. There certainly remains nothing, except something

extended, flexible, and movable. But what is meant by flexible and movable? Is it not that I imagine that the piece of wax, being round, is capable of becoming square, or of passing from a square into a triangular figure? Assuredly such is not the case, because I conceive that it admits of an infinity of similar changes; and I am, moreover, unable to compass this infinity by imagination, and consequently this conception which I have of the wax is not the product of the faculty of imagination. But what now is this extension? Is it not also unknown? For it becomes greater when the wax is melted, greater when it is boiled, and greater still when the heat increases; and I should not conceive clearly and according to truth, the wax as it is, if I did not suppose that the piece we are considering admitted even of a wider variety of extension than I ever imagined. I must, therefore, admit that I cannot even comprehend by imagination what the piece of wax is, and that it is the mind alone (mens, Lat., entendement, F.) which perceives it. I speak of one piece in particular; for as to wax in general, this is still more evident. But what is the piece of wax that can be perceived only by the understanding or mind? It is certainly the same which I see, touch, imagine; and, in fine, it is the same which, from the beginning, I believed it to be. But (and this it is of moment to observe) the perception of it is neither an act of sight, of touch, nor of imagination, and never was either of these, though it might formerly seem so, but is simply an intuition (inspectio) of the mind, which may be imperfect and confused, as it formerly was, or very clear and distinct, as it is at present, according as the attention is more or less directed to the elements which it contains, and of which it is composed.

13. But, meanwhile, I feel greatly astonished when I observe the weakness of my mind, and its proneness to error. For although, without at all giving expression to what I think, I consider all this in my own mind, words yet occasionally impede my progress, and I am almost led into error by the terms of ordinary language. We say, for example, that we see the same wax when it is before us, and not that we judge it to be the same from its retaining the same color and figure:

whence I should forthwith be disposed to conclude that the wax is known by the act of sight, and not by the intuition of the mind alone, were it not for the analogous instance of human beings passing on in the street below, as observed from a window. In this case I do not fail to say that I see the men themselves, just as I say that I see the wax; and yet what do I see from the window beyond hats and cloaks that might cover artificial machines, whose motions might be determined by springs? But I judge that there are human beings from these appearances, and thus I comprehend, by the faculty of judgment alone which is in the mind, what I believed I saw with my eyes.

14. The man who makes it his aim to rise to knowledge superior to the common, ought to be ashamed to seek occasions of doubting from the vulgar forms of speech: instead, therefore, of doing this, I shall proceed with the matter in hand, and inquire whether I had a clearer and more perfect perception of the piece of wax when I first saw it, and when I thought I knew it by means of the external sense itself, or, at all events, by the common sense (sensus communis), as it is called, that is, by the imaginative faculty; or whether I rather apprehend it more clearly at present, after having examined with greater care, both what it is, and in what way it can be known. It would certainly be ridiculous to entertain any doubt on this point. For what, in that first perception, was there distinct? What did I perceive which any animal might not have perceived? But when I distinguish the wax from its exterior forms, and when, as if I had stripped it of its vestments, I consider it quite naked, it is certain, although some error may still be found in my judgment, that I cannot, nevertheless, thus apprehend it without possessing a human mind.

15. But finally, what shall I say of the mind itself, that is, of myself? For as yet I do not admit that I am anything but mind. What, then! I who seem to possess so distinct an apprehension of the piece of wax, do I not know myself, both with greater truth and certitude, and also much more distinctly and clearly? For if I judge that the wax exists because I see it, it assuredly follows, much more evidently, that I myself am or exist, for the same reason: for it is possible that what I see may not in truth be wax, and that I do not even possess eyes with which to see anything; but it cannot be that when I see, or, which comes to the same thing, when I think I see, I myself who think am nothing. So likewise, if I judge that the wax exists because I touch it, it will still also follow that I am; and if I determine that my imagination, or any other cause, whatever it be, persuades me of the existence of the wax, I will still draw the same conclusion. And what is here remarked of the piece of wax, is applicable to all the other things that are external to me. And further, if the notion or perception of wax appeared to me more precise and distinct, after that not only sight and touch, but many other causes besides, rendered it manifest to my apprehension, with how much greater distinctness must I now know myself, since all the reasons that contribute to the knowledge of the nature of wax, or of anybody whatever, manifest still better the nature of my mind? And there are besides so many other things in the mind itself that contribute to the illustration of its nature, that those dependent on the body, to which I have here referred, scarcely merit to be taken into account.

16. But, in conclusion, I find I have insensibly reverted to the point I desired; for, since it is now manifest to me that bodies themselves are not properly perceived by the senses nor by the faculty of imagination, but by the intellect alone; and since they are not perceived because they are seen and touched, but only because they are understood or rightly comprehended by thought, I readily discover that there is nothing more easily or clearly apprehended than my own mind. But because it is difficult to rid one's self so promptly of an opinion to which one has been long accustomed, it will be desirable to tarry for some time at this stage, that, by long continued meditation, I may more deeply impress upon my memory this new knowledge.

CHAPTER 42

God and the Argument from Mind

J. P. Moreland

At the beginning of his *Institutes* of *the Christian Religion,* John Calvin observes: "No man can survey himself without forthwith turning his thoughts towards the God in whom he lives and moves; because it is perfectly obvious, that the endowments which we possess cannot possibly be from ourselves."[1] A number of thinkers have made similar observations. How could consciousness have evolved from matter? Can matter think? If we are simply material beings, then determinism is true for all human processes. But if we are determined, why should we trust our own thought processes? These questions are associated with a family of arguments which have gone by different names — the anthropological argument, the argument from mind or consciousness, or the argument from rationality. In one way or another, these arguments point out that man as a rational agent implies God as the Ground or Cause of his rationality.[2]

The purpose of this chapter is to clarify and defend a case for God's existence from the existence of rational minds in human beings. First, mind/body dualism will be explained and defended by offering general arguments for dualism and by centering in on an argument which tries to show that physicalism — the

view that reality in general, and humans in particular, are made up entirely of matter — is self-refuting. Second, we will explore the possibility that rational minds evolved from matter and try to show why this is not plausible. This will lend support to the view that our rational minds come from another rational Mind — God.

Arguments for Dualism

Dualism Defined

The mind/body problem focuses on two main issues. First, is a human being composed of just one ultimate component or two? Second, if the answer is two how do these two relate to one another? Physicalism is one solution to the problem. As a general worldview, physicalism holds that the only thing which exists is matter (where matter is defined by an ideal, completed form of physics). Applied to the mind/body problem, physicalism asserts that a human being is just a physical system. There is no mind or soul, just a brain and central nervous system.[3] Dualism is the opponent of physicalism and it asserts that in addition to the body, a human being also has a nonphysical

1. John Calvin, *Institutes of the Christian Religion* (1536; Grand Rapids: Associated Publishers and Authors, n.d.), 1.1.1.

2. See J. R. Lucas, *The Freedom of the* Will (Oxford: Clarendon Press, 1970), pp. 114–23; A. C. Ewing, *Value and Reality* (London: George Allen and Unwin, 1973), pp. 76–77, 176–78; Richard Purtill, *Reason to Believe* (Grand Rapids: Eerdmans, 1974), pp. 38–49; Stephen Clark, *From Athens* to *Jerusalem* (Oxford: Clarendon Press, 1984), pp. 96–157; C. S. Lewis, *Miracles: A Preliminary Study* (New York: Macmillan, 1947), pp. 2–39.

3. Helpful introductory works on the mind/body problem are Jerome A. Shaffer, *Philosophy of Mind,* Foundations of Philosophy series (Englewood Cliffs, N.J.: Prentice-Hall, 1968); Paul M.

Churchland, *Matter and Consciousness: A Contemporary Introduction to the Philosophy of Mind* (Cambridge, Mass.: MIT Press, 1984); Keith Campbell, *Body and Mind,* Problems in Philosophy series (Garden City, N.Y.: Doubleday, Anchor Books, 1970). Shaffer's work is a bit dated and Churchland's is heavily biased toward physicalism, but both are still helpful. Campbell's book is fairly balanced. The three main varieties of modern physicalism are the identity thesis, functionalism, and eliminative materialism. These three are discussed in David Rosenthal, ed., *Materialism and the Mind-Body Problem,* Central Issues in Philosophy series (Englewood Cliffs, N.J.: Prentice-Hall, 1971).

component called a soul, mind, or self (words which will be used interchangeably for our purposes).

There are two main varieties of dualism — property dualism and substance dualism. In order to understand the difference, we must first spell out the distinction between a property and a substance. A property is an entity: redness, hardness, wisdom, triangularity, or painfulness. A property has at least four characteristics which distinguish it from a substance.

First, a property is a universal, not a particular. It can be in more than one thing or at more than one place at the same time. Redness can be in my coat and your flag at the same time. Second, a property is immutable and does not contain opposites (hot and cold, red and green) within it. When a leaf goes from green to red, the *leaf* changes. Greenness does not become redness. Greenness leaves the leaf and redness replaces it. Greenness and redness remain the same. Third, properties can be had by something else. They can be in another thing which has them. Redness is in the apple. The apple *has* the redness. Fourth, properties do not have causal powers. They do not act as efficient causes. Properties are not agents which act on other agents in the world.

A substance is an entity like an apple, my dog Fido, a carbon atom, a leaf, or an angel. Substances contrast with properties in the four characteristics listed. First, substances are particulars. For example, my dog Fido cannot be in more than one place at the same time. Second, a substance can change and have opposites. A leaf can go from green to red or hot to cold by gaining or losing properties. During the process of change, the substance gains and loses properties, but it is still the same substance. The same leaf which was green

is now red. Third, substances are basic, fundamental existents. They are not *in* other things or *had by* other things. Fido is not a property of some more basic entity. Rather, Fido *has* properties. Fido is a unity of properties (dogness, brownness, shape), parts (paws, teeth, ears), and dispositions or capacities (law-like tendencies to realize certain properties in the process of growth if certain conditions obtain; for instance, the capacity to grow teeth if the fetus is nourished). They are all united into the substance Fido and possessed by him. Finally, a substance has causal powers. It can act as a causal agent in the world. A carbon atom can act on another atom. A dog can bark or pick up a bone. A leaf can hit the ground.

Property dualists hold that the mind is a property of the body. As Richard Taylor puts it, "A person is a living physical body having mind, the mind consisting, however, of nothing but a more or less continuous series of conscious or unconscious states and events … which are the effects but never the causes of bodily activity."[4] This view is called *epiphenomenalism*. The mind is to the body as smoke is to fire. Smoke is different from fire, but smoke does not cause anything. Smoke is a byproduct of fire. Similarly, mind is a byproduct of the body which does not cause anything. It just "rides" on top of the events in the body. Body events cause mind as a byproduct. The mind is a property of the body which ceases to exist when the body ceases to function.

Though some theists have denied it recently, the historic Christian view has been substance dualism. The mind, distinct from the body, is a real substance which can cause things to happen by acting and which can exist when the body ceases to function.[5]

---

4. Richard Taylor, *Metaphysics* (Englewood Cliffs, N.J.: Prentice-Hall, 1963), p. 28.

5. Examples of Christian writers who have denied substance dualism are Richard Bube, *The Human Quest* (Waco: Word, 1971), pp. 29–37, 134–59; Donald MacKay, *Human Science and Human Dignity* (Downers Grove: InterVarsity, 1979); David Myers, *The Human Puzzle: Psychological Research and Christian Belief* (San Francisco: Harper and Row, 1978). My own view is that substance dualism is the biblical view, but this does not mean Descartes's ver-

sion of dualism. More in line with the biblical data is the dualism of Aristotle or Aquinas. For a good treatment of the relationship between substance, soul, and mind in both Aristotle and Aquinas, see Thomas Ragusa, *The Substance Theory of Mind and Contemporary Functionalism* (Washington, D.C.: Catholic University of America, 1937). A good treatment of biblical anthropology is Robert Gundry, *Soma in Biblical Theology* (Cambridge: Cambridge University Press, 1976).

Dualism Defended

Problems with Physicalism as a General Worldview

Physicalism as a worldview holds that everything that exists is nothing but a single spatio-temporal system which can be completely described in terms of some ideal form of physics.[6] Matter/energy is all that exists. God, souls, and nonphysical abstract entities do not exist. If physicalism is true at the worldview level, then obviously, mind/body physicalism would follow. But is physicalism adequate as a worldview? Several factors indicate that it is not.

First, if theism is true, then physicalism as a worldview is false. God is not a physical being. Second, a number of people have argued that numbers exist and that they are abstract, nonphysical entities (e.g., sets, substances, or properties).[7] Several arguments can be offered for the existence of numbers, but two appear frequently. For one thing, mathematics claims to give us knowledge. But if this is so, there must be something that mathematics is about. Just as the biologist *discovers* biological truths about biological objects (organisms), so the mathematician often *discovers* mathematical truths (he does not invent them all the time) and these truths are about mathematical objects. If one denies the existence of numbers, then it is hard to rescue mathematics as a field which conveys knowledge about something. Without numbers, mathematics becomes merely an internally consistent game which is invented.

A second argument is often given for holding to the existence of numbers. Scientific laws and theories seem to assert their existence. For example, a calcium ion has a positive charge of two which is expressed in the formula $Ca+^2$. The number two here seems to be more than a mere formula for calculating relative amounts of compounds in laboratory reactions. Two expresses a property of the calcium ion itself. The property of twoness is just as much a real property of the charge of the calcium as the property of positiveness. If one denies that numbers exist, it is hard to continue to maintain that science gives us a real description of the world rather than a set of operations that work in the laboratory. In sum, without numbers, mathematical and scientific knowledge is hard to maintain. But if numbers exit, physicalism as a worldview is false because numbers are not physical entities.

Some have argued that values, in addition to God and numbers, exist and are not physical.[8] Certain objects (persons, animals) and certain events (helping a stranger, for example) have a nonphysical property of worth or goodness. Furthermore, moral laws are often held to be absolute objective realities (e.g., one should not torture babies). But if certain objects possess goodness, and if certain moral laws are objective realities, then physicalism must be false, because the property of goodness and the nature of moral laws are not physical. For example, it makes no sense to ask how much goodness weighs, or to ask where a moral law exists. Such realities are not physical.

Fourth, if physicalism is true, it is hard to see what one should make of the existence and nature of theories, meanings, concepts, propositions, the laws of logic, and truth itself. It would seem that theories themselves exist and can be discovered. The laws of logic seem to be real laws that govern the relationships between propositions. Propositions seem to exist and be the content of thoughts which become associated with the physical scratchings of a given language called sentences. Sentences may be made of black ink, be on a page, and be four inches long. But it is hard to see how the *content* of the sentence (i.e., the proposition or thought expressed by the sentence) could be on the page. Such entities seem to be nonphysical entities which can be in the mind.[9] Truth appears to be a

---

6. See D. M. Armstrong, *Nominalism and Scientific Realism*, 2 vols. (Cambridge: Cambridge University Press, 1978), 1:126–32.

7. A brief discussion of the issues involved in the existence of numbers and modern set theory can be found in Keith Campbell, *Metaphysics: An Introduction* (Encino, Calif.: Dickenson, 1976), pp. 200–205.

8. For a good treatment of how different ethical systems view the ontological status of value, see C. D. Broad, *Five Types of Ethical Theory* (London: Routledge and Kegan Paul, 1930).

9. Physicalists attempt to do away with semantic notions like "truth," "denotation," and "proposition" by reducing them to sentences (strings of physical markings) and the like. For two examples

relation of correspondence between a thought and the world. If a thought really describes the world accurately, it is true. It stands to the world in a relation of correspondence. But whatever else one wants to say about the relation of correspondence, it does not seem to be a physical relation like cause and effect.

Finally, universals seem to exist and they are not material.[10] A universal is an entity that can be in more than one place at the same time. Some universals are properties (redness, hardness, triangularity); others are relations (larger than, to the left of). Whatever else one may use to characterize the nature of matter, it is clear that a clump of matter is a particular. A piece of matter cannot be in more than one place at the same time. Physicalists deny the existence of universals at the level of general worldview, because universals are not physical entities.

The entities listed have caused a lot of difficulty for physicalists. They have spent a good deal of time trying to do away with numbers, values, propositions, laws of logic, and universals by reducing them to notions compatible with physicalism. But these reductionist attempts have failed and physicalism as a worldview cannot adequately handle the existence of these entities. Theism can embrace them, however, by holding that God created these nonphysical entities and sustains them in existence. The falsity of physicalism as a worldview does not refute mind/body physicalism.

One could hold to the existence of numbers and values but deny the existence of the soul. But much of the motivation for mind/body physicalism has been the desire to argue for physicalism at the worldview level. If physicalism at that level is false, then part of the reason for holding to mind/body physicalism is removed. For example, just because one cannot see the soul, weigh it, or say where it is, it does not follow that the soul does not exist. One cannot see, weigh, or locate numbers or values, but they still exist.[11]

Problems with Mind/Body Physicalism

In order to facilitate an understanding of some of the arguments against mind/body physicalism, we must first examine the nature of identity. Suppose you know that someone named J. P. Moreland exists and that the author of this book exists. Assume further that you do not know that J. P. Moreland wrote this book. If someone asked you whether J. P. Moreland is identical to the author of this book, how would you decide? How would you determine that the "two" individuals are identical instead of being two different people? If you could find something true of J. P. Moreland which is not true of the author of this book or vice versa, then they would be different people. They could not be identical. For example, if J. P. Moreland is married to Hope Moreland but the author of this book is not, they would be different people. On the other hand,

of this strategy, see Hartry Field, "Tarski's Theory of Truth," *The Journal of Philosophy* 69 (July 1972): 347 – 75; W. V. O. Quine, *Philosophy of Logic* (Englewood Cliffs, N.J.: Prentice-Hall, 1970), pp. 1 – 14. For a critique of such physicalist strategies, see Dallas Willard, *Logic and the Objectivity of Knowledge: Studies in Husserl's Early Philosophy* (Athens, Ohio: Ohio University Press, 1984), pp. 205 – 18. Three good defenses of the existence of propositions are Alonzo Church, "The Need for Abstract Entities in Semantic Analysis," in *Contemporary Readings in Logical Theory,* ed. Irving M. Copi and James A. Gould (New York: Macmillan, 1967), pp. 194 – 203; George Bealer, *Quality and Concept* (Oxford: Clarendon Press, 1982); Dallas Willard, "The Paradox of Logical Psychologism: Husserl's Way Out," *American Philosophical Quarterly* 9 (January 1972): 94 – 100. The question arises as to what the basic entities are which are involved in the laws of logic. For a survey of different attempts to answer that question, see Dallas Willard, "Husserl's Critique of Extensionalist Logic: 'A Logic That Does Not Understand Itself,'" *Idealistic Studies* 9 (May 1979): 143 – 64. Alvin Plantinga used the existence of prop-

ositions and truth to argue for God's existence in his presidential address ("How to Be an Anti-Realist") to the American Philosophical Association on April 29, 1982.

10. See J. P. Moreland, *Universals, Qualities, and Quality-Instances: A Defense of Realism* (Lanham, Md.: University Press of America, 1985). See also Howard Robinson, *Matter and Sense* (Cambridge: Cambridge University Press, 1982), pp. 46 – 50.

11. Matter is a difficult notion to understand, since the concept of matter has played such different roles in the history of philosophy. For different understandings of what matter is, see Ernan McMullin, ed., *The Concept of Matter in Greek and Medieval Philosophy* (Notre Dame: University of Notre Dame Press, 1963); *The Concept of Matter in Modern Philosophy* (Notre Dame: University of Notre Dame Press, 1963); M. P. Crosland, ed., *The Science of Matter* (Middlesex, England: Penguin, 1971); John Yolton, *Thinking Matter: Materialism in Eighteenth-Century Britain* (Minneapolis: University of Minnesota Press, 1984). For a criticism of several notions of matter, see Robinson, *Matter and Sense,* pp. 108 – 23.

if everything true of one is true of the other, "they" would be one person.

In general, if "two" things are identical, then whatever is true of the one is true of the other, since in reality only one thing is being discussed. However, if something is true of the one which is not true of the other, then they are two things and not one. This is sometimes called the indiscernibility of identicals and is expressed as follows:

$$(x)\ (y)\ [(x=y) \rightarrow (P)\ (Px \leftrightarrow Py)]$$

For any entities x and y, if x and y are really the same thing, then for any property P, P is true of x if and only if P is true of y. If x is the mind and y is a part or state of the body (e.g., the brain), then if physicalism is true, x must be identical to y.[12] On the other hand, if something is true of the mind which is not true of some part or state of the body, then the mind is not identical to the body and physicalism is false. This would be true even if the mind and body are inseparable. The roundness of an apple cannot be separated from its redness. One does not find redness sitting on a table by itself and roundness sitting next to it. But the redness of an apple is not identical to the roundness of the apple. One is a color and one is a shape.

Every time something happens in the mind (someone has a thought of an ice cream cone), some event may be going on in the brain which could be described by a neurophysiologist. In general, brain events may always have mental events that correlate with them and vice versa. They may be inseparable in that one does not occur without the other in an embodied person. But this does not mean that the mental thought is identical to the brain event. The redness and roundness of an apple, though inseparable, are not identical. The property of having three sides (trilaterality) and the property of having three angles (triangularity) always go together. They are inseparable. But they

are not identical. Physicalists must not only show that mental and brain phenomena are inseparable to make their case. They must also show that they are identical. With this in mind let us turn to some arguments for dualism.

The Distinctiveness of Mental and Physical Properties. Mental events include thoughts, feelings of pain, the experience of being a person, or a sense image or picture of a ball in my mind. Physical events are events in the brain or central nervous system which can be described exhaustively using terms of chemistry, physics, and (for now) biology. The difficulty for physicalism is that mental events do not seem to have properties that hold for physical events. My thought of Kansas City is not ten centimeters long, it does not weigh anything, it is not located anywhere (it is not two inches from my left ear). Nor is it identical to any behavior or tendency to behave in a certain way (shouting "Kansas City" when I hear the name George Brett). But the brain event associated with this thought may be located inside my head, it may have a certain chemical composition and electrical current, and so forth. My afterimage of a ball (the impression of the ball present to my consciousness when I close my eyes after seeing the ball) may be pink, but nothing in my brain is pink. Mental events and properties have different attributes and therefore they are not identical.

Private Access and Incorrigibility. I seem to be in a position to know my own thoughts and mental processes in a way not available to anyone else. I am in a privileged position with regard to my own mental life. I have private access to my own thoughts in a way not open to anyone else. Furthermore, my mental states seem to be incorrigible, at least some of the time. That is, I cannot be mistaken about them.[13] Suppose I am experiencing what I take to be a green rug. It is possible that the rug is not there or that the light is poor

---

12. Functionalism is somewhat illusive on this point, since it identifies a mental state with a functional state which receives certain input, gives certain output, and advances to another internal state. Thus mental states are likened to the software and not the hardware of simple computation machines (e.g., Turing machines). Nevertheless, functionalists who are materialists want to say that these states are ultimately physical in nature or are the behaviors of physical states. For an analysis and critique of various forms of functionalism, see Robinson, *Matter and Sense.*

13. See Roderick Chisholm, *The First Person: An Essay on Reference and Intentionality* (Minneapolis: University of Minnesota Press, 1981), pp. 75–91.

and the rug is really gray. I could be mistaken about the rug itself. But it does not seem to be possible for me to be mistaken that I am experiencing what I take to be a green rug right now. That is, my mental state is directly present to me and I know my own mental states immediately.

It would be possible for a brain surgeon to know more about my brain than I do. He may be looking into my brain, seeing it better than I, and knowing its operations better than I. But he does not — indeed, he cannot — know my mental life as well as I. I have private, privileged access to that. Further, it seems that one could always be wrong about his knowledge of some physical state of affairs in the world: The brain surgeon could be wrong about what is happening in my brain. But I cannot be wrong about what is currently happening in my mind. It would seem then that I have privileged private access to my mental states which is sometimes incorrigible. But neither I nor anyone else has private access to my brain states, and whatever access someone has is irreducibly third-person access (described from a standpoint outside of me) and is not incorrigible.[14]

The Experience of First-Person Subjectivity. The subjective character of experience is hard to capture in physicalist terms.[15] The simple fact of consciousness is a serious difficulty for physicalism. To see this consider the following. Suppose a deaf scientist became the world's leading expert on the neurology of hearing. It would be possible for him to know and describe everything there is to the physical processes involved in hearing. However, something would still be left out of such a description — the experience of what it is like to be a human who hears. As Howard Robinson puts it:

> The notion of *having something as an object of experience* is not *prima facie,* a physical notion: it does not figure in any physical science. *Having something as an object of experience* is the same as the subjective feel or the *what it* is *like* of experience.[16]

Subjective states of experiences exist. My experience of what it is like to be me, to hear a bird or see a tree, exists, and I have a first-person subjectivity to it. Such first-person experiences of my own self, or "I," which has experiences cannot be reduced to a third-person "he" or "it," because the latter do not describe the experience itself or its first-person standpoint. A physicalist, scientific description of the world leaves out this character of subjective awareness. Such a description characterizes the world in impersonal, third-person terms (e.g., "there exists an object with such and such properties and states") and leaves out the first-person, subjective experience itself (e.g., "I feel sad and food tastes sour to me").

Speaking of the character of subjective awareness, Thomas Nagel has this to say:

> If physicalism is to be defended, the phenomenological

---

14. See H. D. Lewis, *The Elusive Self* (Philadelphia: Westminster, 1982), pp. 20–32. On pp. 31–33 of *Matter and Consciousness,* Churchland criticizes the argument I am advancing as an example of the intensional fallacy in logic. In normal, truth-functional logic the connectives ("if, then," "if and only if," "or," "and," "not") are extensional. Equals can be substituted for equals and truth is preserved. Thus, if $P=Q$, then it is correct to say that if one has Q or S, -S, therefore Q, one can also have P or S, -S, therefore P. But in intensional contexts where one has words like "know," "believe," or "recognize," equals cannot be substituted for equals and preserve truth. I may know that Muhammad Ali was the world champion, but I may *not* know that Cassius Clay was the world champion (if I fail to know that *Clay* is identical to Ali). It is the intensional fallacy to assume that such substitutions can be made in intensional contexts. Similarly, I may know my mental states and not know my brain states, but the two may still be identical, says Churchland, if I fail to appreciate that such an identity holds. Two responses can be given to Churchland. First, my argument from private access does not turn on a supposed ignorance of an identity between mental and brain states, but on a difference in the relations I sustain with them. My mental states are directly present to me and my brain states are not, and this difference in relation is what makes the former have incorrigibility. If two entities stand in different relations with other things, they cannot be identical. Second, the very existence of irreducibly intensional contexts that defy extensional treatment is evidence for dualism. See George Bealer, "The Logical Status of Mind," in *Studies in the Philosophy of Mind,* ed. Peter A. French, Theodore Uehling, and Howard Wettstein, Midwest Studies in Philosophy, vol. 10 (Minneapolis: University of Minnesota Press, 1986), pp. 231–74.

15. Thomas Nagel, "What Is It Like to Be a Bat?" in his *Mortal Questions* (Cambridge: Cambridge University Press, 1979), pp. 165–80.

16. Robinson, *Matter and Sense,* p. 7.

features [the sounds, colors, smells, tastes of experience that make the experience what it is] must themselves be given a physical account. But when we examine their subjective character it seems that such a result is impossible. The reason is that every subjective phenomenon is essentially connected with a single point of view, and it seems inevitable that an objective, physical theory will abandon that point of view.[17]

Secondary Qualities. Secondary qualities are qualities such as colors, tastes, sounds, smells, and textures. Physicalism seems to imply that such qualities do not exist in the external world. But we do sense such qualities, so where are they, if they are not in the external world? They must exist as sense data (mental objects or images) in the mind. Frank Jackson has put the point this way:

It is a commonplace that there is an apparent clash between the picture Science gives of the world around us and the picture our senses give us. We *sense* the world as made up of coloured, materially continuous, macroscopic, stable objects; Science and, in particular, Physics, tells us that the material world is constituted of clouds of minute, colourless, highly-mobile particles.... Science forces us to acknowledge that physical or material things are not coloured.... This will enable us to conclude that sense-data are all mental, for they are coloured.[18]

In other words, science does away with secondary qualities, but since we know they do exist — we see them — they must exist in our minds as sense data. This shows that there must be minds, and sense data must be little images or pictures which exist as mental objects in minds.

I do not accept this understanding of secondary qualities, because it implies that I do not see the world when I use my senses. Rather, it implies that I see my sense images of the world.[19] But if this view is correct, then it would seem that some form of dualism is correct. If, on the other hand, one holds (as I do) that secondary qualities are real properties of objects in the world, physicalism as a worldview may still be in trouble. If macroscopic objects (regular-sized tables, apples, dogs) do have properties of color, odor, stability, continuous surfaces, and the like, then there must be more to them than what physics tells us. Physics tends to reduce objects to mere heaps of colorless, odorless, rapid-moving packets of matter/energy. But if objects have macroproperties which escape description in these terms, then these properties, call them metaphysical properties, are not physical. That does not mean that they are mental. But it does show that a full treatment of objects must appeal to metaphysical properties which deal with the objects as wholes. If physicalism reduces objects to the mere heaps of microphysics, then physicalism is incomplete as a worldview. On the other hand, if secondary qualities are in fact mental sense data, then physicalism is inadequate as a mind/body theory. Either way, physicalism as a general theory is in trouble.

Intentionality. Some have argued that the mark of the mental is intentionality. Intentionality is the mind's aboutness or ofness. Mental states point beyond themselves to other objects even if those objects do not exist. I have a thought *about* my wife, I hope *for* a new car, I dream *of* a unicorn. The mind has the ability to transcend itself and be of or about something else. This aboutness is not a property of anything physical.[20] Some physicalists have tried to reduce intention-

---

17. Nagel, p. 167. See also Geoffrey Maddell, *The Identity of the Self* (Edinburgh: The University Press, 1981). The fact that first-person subjectivity cannot be reduced to a third-person point of view without making essential reference to a mental state can be seen by noting that philosophers who reduce an A-Series view of time to a B-Series still have to refer to conscious mental states in order to account for our , experience of temporal becoming. For more on this, see Richard M. Gale, ed., *The Philosophy of Time* (New York: Humanities Press, 1968), pp. 65 – 85. Note especially pp. 73 – 74.

18. Frank Jackson, *Perception* (Cambridge: Cambridge University Press, 1977), p. 121. See also Colin McGinn, *The Subjective View* (Oxford: Clarendon Press, 1983).

19. For a critique of this view of perception, see Dallas Willard, "A Crucial Error in Epistemology," *Mind* 76 (October 1967): 513 – 23.

20. John Searle tries to argue that intentionality is just a property of a physical system. But his view leads to a denial of real intentionality and leads Searle to adopt physical determinism, a position

ality to the mere ability to receive input, give output, and advance to some other internal state. A computer receives input from a keyboard, gives output on a printer, and advances to a new internal state where it is ready to receive new input. But the computer still has no awareness of or about anything.[21] It seems, then, that physical states do not have intentionality and thus the fact of intentionality is evidence that the self is not physical but mental.

Personal Identity. Imagine a wooden table which had all its parts removed one by one and replaced by metal parts. When the top and all the legs were replaced would it still be the same table? The answer would seem to be no. In fact, it would be possible to take all the original wooden parts and rearrange them into the original table. Even when the table had just one leg replaced, it would not literally be the same table. It would be a table similar to the original

Losing old parts and gaining new ones changes the identity of the object in question. But now a question arises regarding persons. Am I literally the same self that I was a moment ago? Are my baby pictures really pictures of *me* or are they pictures of an ancestor of me who resembles me? I am constantly losing physical parts. I lose hair and fingernails; atoms are constantly being replaced, and every seven years my cells are almost entirely replaced. Do I maintain literal, absolute identity through change or not?

Substance dualists argue that persons do maintain absolute identity through change, because they have, in addition to their bodies, a soul that remains constant through change, and personal identity is constituted by sameness of soul, not sameness of body.[22]

Physicalists have no alternative but to hold that personal identity is not absolute. Usually they argue that persons are really ancestral chains of successive "selves" which are connected with one another in some way. At each moment a new self exists (since the self or physical organism is constantly in flux, losing and gaining parts) and this self resembles the self prior to and after it. The relation of resemblance between selves plus the fact that later selves have the same memories as earlier selves and the body of each self traces a continuous path through space when the whole chain of selves is put together, constitute a relative sense of personal identity.

So substance dualists hold to a literal, absolute sense of personal identity and physicalists hold to a loose, relative sense of personal identity which amounts to a stream of successive selves held together into "one" person by resemblance between each self (also called a person stage), similarity of memory, and spatial continuity. For the physicalist, a person becomes a space-time worm (i.e., a path traced through space and time). The person is the entire path marked off at the time and place of his birth and death. At any given moment and location where "I" happen to be, "I" am not a person, just a person stage. The person is the whole path. So there is no literal sameness through change.

But now certain problems arise for physicalism.[23] First, why should "I" ever fear the future? When it gets here, "I" will not be present; rather, another self who looks like me will be there but "I" will have ceased to exist. Second, why should anyone be punished? The self who did the crime in the past is not literally the

with which he is somewhat uncomfortable. See his *Minds, Brains, and Science* (Cambridge: Harvard University Press, 1985). In the same vein, Peter Smith and O. R. Jones argue that mental states can be treated as functional states which are mere physical happenings. But like Searle, they are forced to deny real human freedom and they settle for a reduced form of freedom compatible with determinism. See Peter Smith and O. R. Jones, *The Philosophy of Mind* (Cambridge: Cambridge University Press, 1986), pp. 252–68.

21. See Hilary Putnam, *Reason, Truth, and History* (Cambridge: Cambridge University Press, 1981), pp. 8–12. Putnam asks us to imagine a case where two computers are connected in such a way

that the input of one feeds into the output of the other and vice versa. In such a case, the two computers could "talk" to each other forever and "refer" to things in the world, even if the world disappeared! This example illustrates that intentionality cannot be identified with a functionalist analysis in terms of artificial intelligence.

22. This does not mean that the soul is inert and static. See David Wiggins, *Sameness and Substance* (Cambridge: Harvard University Press, 1980).

23. See Maddell, *Identity of the Self,* pp. 15–16; H. D. Lewis, *The Self and Immortality,* ed. John H. Hick, Philosophy of Religion series (New York: Seabury, Crossroad Books, 1973), pp. 29–46.

same self who is present at the time of punishment. Physicalism seems to require a radical readjustment of our common-sense notions of future expectations and past actions because both presuppose a literal identity of the same self present in past, present, and future.

Third, physicalists not only have difficulty handling the unity of the self through time, but also cannot explain the unity of the self at a given time. As Harvard philosopher W. V. O. Quine puts it, according to physicalism the self becomes a sum or heap of scattered physical parts. The unity of the self is like the unity of an assembly of building blocks. If I have a pain in my foot while I am thinking about baseball, each is a distinct experience involving different physical parts. There is no self which *has* each experience. The self is merely a bundle or heap of parts and experiences. It has no real unity. The dualist says that the soul is diffused throughout the body and it is present before each experience. The soul has each experience. The unity of consciousness is due to the fact that the same soul is the possessor of each and every experience of consciousness. But the physicalist must say that each experience is possessed by different parts of the body and there is no real unity. However, my own experience of the unity of my consciousness shows this unity to be genuine and not arbitrary. I have my experiences. They are all *mine*. Physicalism does not adequately explain this fact.

Morality, Responsibility, and Punishment. As will be shown shortly, physicalism seems to imply determinism. If I am just matter, then my actions are not the result of free choice. They are determined by the laws of chemistry and physics plus boundary conditions. For example, the position of a bullet can be calculated given Newton's laws plus the initial position and velocity of the bullet. But then it is hard to make sense of

moral obligation and responsibility. If I "ought" to do something, it seems to be necessary to suppose that I *can* do it. No one would say that I ought to jump to the top of a fifty-floor building to save a baby, since it is not possible for me to do that. But if physicalism is true, I do not have any genuine ability to choose my actions. It is safe to say that physicalism requires a radical revision of our common-sense notions of freedom, moral obligation, responsibility, and punishment.[24] If these common-sense notions are true, then physicalism is false.

This completes our survey of some of the major arguments for dualism. More could be said about each point, but perhaps enough has been offered to indicate the kinds of arguments relevant to a defense of dualism. There is, however, a major argument for dualism which may be the most important one. To this argument we now turn.

Mind/Body Physicalism Refuted

A number of philosophers have argued that physicalism must be false because it implies determinism and determinism is self-refuting.[25] Speaking of the determinist, J. R. Lucas says,

> If what he says is true, he says it merely as the result of his heredity and environment, and of nothing else. He does not hold his determinist views because they are true, but because he has such-and-such stimuli; that is, not because the *structure* of the universe is such-and-such but only because the configuration of only part of the universe, together with the structure of the determinist's brain, is such as to produce that result.... Determinism, therefore, cannot be true, because if it was, we should not take the determinists' arguments as being really arguments, but as being only conditioned reflexes. Their statements should

24. See Bruce R. Reichenbach, *Is Man the Phoenix?* (Grand Rapids: Eerdmans, 1978), pp. 105–11.

25. I am not advancing a design argument to the effect that, if our minds were not designed, we would have no reason to trust their operations and deliverances. This sort of argument was advanced in chapter 2. Evolutionists point out, in response to this form of argument that the mind's rational abilities aided the possessors of those abilities in the struggle for survival. But this is far from obvious.

Some evolutionists point out that such rational activities require an increased information-processing capacity in the nervous system which is actually a reproductive liability prenatally (such a system requires a longer and more vulnerable gestation period) and postnatally (it takes longer to raise and teach the young). See John Barrow and Frank Tipler, *The Anthropic Cosmological Principle* (Oxford: Clarendon Press, 1986), pp. 129–33.

not be regarded as really claiming to be true, but only as seeking to cause us to respond in some way desired by them.[26]

H. P. Owen states that

determinism is self-stultifying. If my mental processes are totally determined, I am totally determined either to accept or to reject determinism. But if the sole reason for my believing or not believing X is that I am causally determined to believe it I have no ground for holding that my judgment is true or false.[27]

Others have pointed out that property dualism (epiphenomenalism) suffers at the hands of this argument no less than does strict physicalism. A. C. Ewing holds that

if epiphenomenalism is true, it follows that nobody can be justified in believing it. On the epiphenomenalist view what causes a belief is always a change in the brain and never the apprehension of any reason for holding it. So if epiphenomenalism is true, neither it nor anything else can ever be believed, for any good reason whatever.[28]

Hans Jonas echoes this sentiment by saying that the epiphenomenalist

passes judgment on himself by what his thesis says about the possible validity of any thesis whatsoever and, therefore, about the validity claim of his own.

Every theory, even the most mistaken, is a tribute to the power of thought, to which in the very meaning of the theorizing act it is allowed that it can rise above the power of extramental determinations, that it can judge freely on what is given in the field of representations, that it is; first of all; capable of the *resolve* for truth, i.e., the resolve to follow the guidance of insight and not the drift of fancies. But epiphenomenalism contends the impotence of thinking and therewith its *own* inability to be independent theory. Indeed, even the extreme materialist must exempt himself *qua* thinker, so that extreme materialism as a doctrine be possible.[29]

In order to understand these statements, let us first examine the nature of self-refutation and then see why physicalism (and epiphenomenalism) is self-refuting.

What Is Self-Refutation?

A statement is about its subject matter. The statement "dogs are mammals" is about dogs. Some statements refer to themselves; that is, they are included in their own field of reference. The statement "all sentences of English are short" makes a statement about all English sentences, including itself. When a statement fails to satisfy itself (i.e., to conform to its own criteria of validity or acceptability), it is self-refuting.[30] Such statements are necessarily false. The facts which falsify them are unavoidably given with the statement when it is uttered.

26. Lucas, *Freedom of the Will*, pp. 114–15.

27. H. P. Owen, *Christian Theism* (Edinburgh: T. and T. Clark, 1984), p. 118.

28. Ewing, *Value and Reality*, p. 77.

29. Hans Jonas, *On Faith, Reason, and Responsibility* (Claremont, Calif.: The Institute for Antiquity and Christianity, 1981), p. 43. For an application of this point to evolution, see Stanley L. Jaki, *Angels, Apes, and Men* (La Salle, Ill.: Sugden, 1982), pp. 51–60. C. S. Lewis used an argument of this sort to argue for God's existence in his book on miracles. G. E. M. Anscombe subsequently critiqued Lewis's argument, which led him to revise his view. For a favorable treatment of Lewis on this point, see Richard Purtill, *C. S. Lewis's Case for the Christian Faith* (San Francisco: Harper and Row, 1981), pp. 22–27. For a critique of Lewis, see John Beversluis, *C. S. Lewis and the Search for Rational Religion* (Grand Rapids: Eerdmans, 1985), pp. 58–83. Beversluis's critique is too detailed to examine here, but it should be pointed out that he grants that Lewis refutes a rather strict form of reductionist physicalism. However,

Beversluis thinks that epiphenomenalism (he specifies his own view in terms of complementarity, not unlike Donald M. MacKay) is not refuted. But epiphenomenalism is refuted by Lewis's argument, for it is a compatiblist view of freedom which has no real agent theory of the self.

30. The following are good treatments of the nature of self-refutation: Michael Stack, "Self-Refuting Arguments," *Metaphilosophy* 14 (July/October 1983): 327–35; George Mavrodes, "Self-Referential Incoherence," *American Philosophical Quarterly* 22 (January 1985): 65–72; Carl Kordig, "Self-Reference and Philosophy," *American Philosophical Quarterly* 20 (April 1983): 207–16; Joseph Boyle, "Self-Referential Inconsistence, Inevitable Falsity, and Metaphysic Argumentation," *Metaphilosophy* 3 (January 1972): 25–42. In what follows I will not make a distinction among sentences, propositions, and statements. Such a distinction is important but too detailed for the level of discussion I am advancing. See the article by Boyle for more on this subject.

Consider some examples. "I cannot say a word of English" is self-refuting when uttered in English. "I do not exist" is self-refuting, for one must exist to utter it. The claim "there are no truths" is self-refuting. If it is false, then it is false. But if it is true, then it is false as well, for in that case there would be no truths, including the statement itself.

On the other hand, the claim "there are no moral truths" is not self-refuting, for it is not necessarily a *moral* statement. The claim becomes self-refuting if it is combined with the claim that one *ought* (morally) to be a relativist. This second claim has a morally absolute sense of "ought" which the first claim rules out. The statement "there is no knowledge" is not self-refuting, since the one uttering the claim could merely believe the statement to be true without claiming to know it to be true. But if he claims to know this statement, then his claim is self-refuting, for he now claims to know there is no knowledge. In sum, if a statement is self-refuting, it refers to itself, it fails to satisfy its own criteria of acceptability, and it cannot be true.

Why Is Physicalism Self-Refuting?

Physicalism is self-refuting in much the same way that the example about knowledge is self-refuting. Assuming that theism is false and that a coherent notion of truth can be spelled out on physicalist assumptions (I have already argued against this latter assumption), physicalism could be true and the claim that it is true is not self-refuting. The world could have had nothing but matter in it. But if one claims to know that physicalism is true, or to embrace it for good reasons, if one claims that it is a rational position which should be chosen on the basis of evidence, then this claim is self-refuting. This is so because physicalism seems to deny the possibility of rationality. To see this, let us examine the necessary preconditions which must hold if there is to be such a thing as rationality and show how physicalism denies these preconditions.

At least five factors must obtain if there are to be genuine rational agents who can accurately reflect on the world. First, minds must have intentionality; they must be capable of having thoughts *about* or *of* the world. Acts of inference are "insights into" or "knowings of" something other than themselves.

Second, reasons, propositions, thoughts, laws of logic and evidence, and truth must exist and be capable of being instanced in people's minds and influencing their thought processes. This fact is hard to reconcile with physicalism. To see this, consider the field of ethics. Morality prescribes what we ought to do; it does not merely describe what is in fact done. Objective morality makes sense if real moral laws or oughts exist and if normative, moral properties like rightness, goodness, worth, and dignity exist in acts (the act of honoring one's parents) and things (persons and animals *have* worth). If physicalism is true as a worldview, there are no moral properties or full-blooded oughts. Physical states just are, and one physical state causes or fails to cause another physical state. A physical state does not morally prescribe that another physical state ought to be. If physicalism is true, oughts are not real moral obligations telling us what one should do to be in conformity with the moral universe. Rather, "ought" serves as a mere guide for reaching a socially accepted or psychologically desired goal (e.g., "If one wants to have pleasure and avoid pain, then one 'ought' to tell the truth"). Moral imperatives become grounded in subjective preferences on the same level as a preference for Burger King over McDonald's.

In the area of rationality, there are rational oughts. Given certain forms of evidence, one ought to believe some things. Reasons and evidence imply or support certain conclusions, and if one is to be objectively rational, one "ought" to accept these conclusions. For example, if one accepts the propositions "all men are mortals" and "Socrates is a man," then one ought to believe "Socrates is a mortal." Failure to do so makes one irrational. But if physicalism is true, it is hard to see how one mental state (the state of believing the first two propositions) could stand to another mental state (the state of believing the last proposition) in an inferential relation which prescribes that one ought to have the last mental state. For these are now mere physical states in the brain. And one physical state does not logically imply another or prescribe that the other "ought" to occur logically. It either causes or fails to cause that second state. Physical states simply are; they are not things that "ought" to be. The connection between premises and conclusion is not a physical relation of cause and effect. It is a logical relation of inference.

Stephen Oark puts it this way:

Any merely materialistic or naturalistic metaphysician must have considerable difficulty in accommodating any rules of evidence. If what I think is the echo or epiphenomenon merely of material processes, so that my thought is what it is because my neural chemistry is what it is, it seems very difficult to see how that thought can be one that I ought to have or ought not to have. It might of course be better (because more accurate?) if I did, or if I did not, but I can be under no obligation to have it, whether because it is true or because it "follows" from other thoughts of mine, any more than I have an obligation to cause my heart to beat. My thoughts "follow" from other thoughts only in the sense that the causal processes which accompany them, or which (on the strictest materialist interpretation) we misdescribe as "thoughts," take place in ways that can be duplicated in test-tubes, and partially understood. True and consistent materialists ought not to claim that their arguments are ones which anyone ought to accept, or which anyone has any reason to think are true-in-fact. Materialism generates pragmatic relativism, and this in turn renders the materialist hypothesis a mere fable.[31]

Third, it is not enough for there to be propositions or reasons which stand in logical and evidential relations with one another. One must be able to "see" or have rational insight into the flow of the argument and be influenced by this act of perception in forming one's beliefs. William Hasker puts it this way:

It is clear, when we consider the matter, that rational thinking must be *guided by rational insight* in the light of principles of sound reasoning. That is to say, one must "see," rationally, that the conclusion is justified by the evidence—and one is helped to see this by principles of reasoning, such as the laws of inductive and deductive logic and the like.[32]

If physicalism is true, it is hard to make sense of this form of seeing. What sort of property of matter could one hold to which would enable matter to see in the sense of rational insight? Whatever property the physicalist comes up with, one suspects it would be an old-fashioned mental property by another name. Further, if propositions and the laws of logic do not exist, then there is nothing there to see. Most dualists hold to the existence of the laws of logic and thoughts (propositions, concepts) which can be instanced in minds and, therefore, seen with rational insight which is a capacity of a mind.

Fourth, in order for one to rationally think through a chain of reasoning such that one sees the inferential connections in the chain, one would have to be the same self present at the beginning of the thought process as the one present at the end. As Immanuel Kant argued long ago, the process of thought requires a genuine enduring "I." In the syllogism about Socrates, if there is one self who reflects on premise 1, a second self who reflects on premise 2, and a third self who reflects on the conclusion, there is literally no enduring self who thinks *through* the argument and *draws* the conclusion. Physicalism has difficulty maintaining the existence of an enduring "I" and thus it has difficulty accounting for the need for such an "I" in the process of rational reflection. Thinking is a rational experience, and as H. D. Lewis has noted, "one thing seems certain, namely that there must be someone or something at the centre of such experience to hold the terms and relations of it together in one stream of consciousness."[33]

Finally, the activity of rational thought seems to require an agent view of the self which, in turn, involves four theses:

---

31. Clark, *From Athens to Jerusalem*, pp. 96–97.
32. William Hasker, *Metaphysics: Constructing a World View* (Downers Grove: InterVarsity, 1983), p. 47.

33. Lewis, *The Self and Immortality*, p. 34.

1. I must be able to deliberate, to reflect about what I am going to do. I deliberate about my behavior and not that of others, future events, and not past ones, courses of action which I have not already settled. These facts of deliberation make sense only if I assume that my actions are "up to me" to perform or not perform.

2. I must have free will; that is, given choices *a* and *b,* I can genuinely do both. If I do *a,* I could have done otherwise. I could have chosen *b.* The past and present do not physically determine only one future. The future is open and depends, to some extent, on my free choices.

3. I am an agent. My acts are often self-caused. I am the absolute origin of my acts. My prior mental or physical states are not sufficient to determine what I will do. I must act as an agent.

4. Free will is incompatible with physical determinism. They cannot both be true at the same time.

If one is to be rational, one must be free to choose his beliefs based on reasons. One cannot be determined to react to stimuli by nonrational physical factors. If a belief is caused by entirely nonrational factors, it is not a belief that is embraced *because* it is reasonable. For a belief to be a rational one, I must be able to deliberate about whether or not I accept it, I must be free to choose it, and I must enter into the process as a genuine agent.[34]

Physical determinism is the view that, given a physical description of the world at a given time, it would be possible in principle to predict later states of the world, for they are causally settled by the laws of chemistry and physics coupled with the boundary conditions of earlier states.[35] Determinism is the thesis that, given the past and the laws of nature, there is only one possible future. There is no room for nonphysical factors like agents, evidence, reasons, or rational insight to affect the course of the world. Only causal, physical relations act. A person's output is *wholly* caused by physical factors.

In sum, it is self-refuting to *argue* that one *ought* to *choose* physicalism *because* he should *see* that the *evidence* is *good* for physicalism. Physicalism cannot be offered as a rational theory because physicalism does away with the necessary preconditions for there to be such a thing as rationality. Physicalism usually denies intentionality by reducing it to a physical relation of input/output, thereby denying that the mind is genuinely capable of having thoughts *about* the world. Physicalism denies the existence of propositions and nonphysical laws of logic and evidence which can be in minds and influence thinking. Physicalism denies the existence of a faculty capable of rational insight into these nonphysical laws and propositions, and it denies the existence of an enduring "I" which is present through the process of reflection. Finally, it denies the existence of a genuine agent who deliberates and chooses positions because they are rational, an act possible only if physical factors are not sufficient for determining future behavior.

A case has been presented for dualism, the belief that in addition to a body, a person has a soul or mind. Several general arguments have been offered in support of dualism and a case has been presented which seeks to show that physicalism is self-refuting. Some of the arguments presented can be used to establish either property dualism (epiphenomenalism) or substance dualism. However, some of them — in particular, the arguments which show that rationality requires a free agent — rule out epiphenomenalism and establish substance dualism.

The question now arises: From whence comes mind or soul? Could it evolve from matter or did it need to be created by God? To these issues we now turn.

---

34. It is interesting to read discussions of ethics with an agent theory of the self in mind. See Thomas Mappes and Jane Zembaty, *Biomedical Ethics,* 2d ed. (New York: McGraw-Hill, 1980), pp. 26 – 29.

35. See Lucas, *Freedom of the Will,* pp. 65 – 95; Peter van Inwagen, *An Essay on Free Will* (Oxford: Clarendon Press, 1983), pp. 58 – 65. The indeterminacy of quantum mechanics is not relevant here. First, it can be taken epistemologically, not ontologically. Second, if it is to be taken ontologically, then determinism still holds at the level of macro-objects. Thirds, indeterminacy of the self is not what is needed for rationality. Self-determination is what is required.

The Origin of Mind

We have seen that there are good reasons for holding that strict physicalism is false. But most physicalists are recalcitrant. If they embrace dualism at all, they embrace epiphenomenalism because, as I will show later, it is more compatible with physicalism than is substance dualism. Mind is not matter, but it comes from matter through evolution when matter reaches a suitable structural arrangement for mind to emerge.

If mind emerged from matter without the direction of a superior Intelligence, two problems arise immediately. First, why should we trust the deliverances of the mind as being rational or true, especially in the mind's more theoretical activities? No one would trust the printout of a computer if he knew that it was programmed by random forces or by nonrational laws without a mind being behind it. Theoretical activity does not seem to contribute to survival value. And less theoretical activities (e.g., sensing the world) would not need to give true information about the world to aid an organism; such activities would need only to help the organism interact with the world consistently. An amoeba which consistently sensed a large object as small and vice versa would learn which ones to avoid without having true insights into the way the world is. Further, according to epiphenomenalism, mental activities do not cause anything anyway. So even if mind emerged, it is hard to see how it could come about by aiding an organism in its evolutionary struggle for survival.[36] And even if it did, it would not need to give true information to do so. So it is hard to see why the mind should be trusted, given that it is an epiphenomenon which emerged in the process of evolution.

Second, if thinking involves having abstract entities (propositions, laws of logic, and the like) instanced in one's mind, then it seems to be incredibly unlikely that a property which emerged from matter in a struggle for survival would be the sort of thing that could *have* thoughts in it in the first place. Why this emergent property would be such that it could contain abstract entities would be a mystery. But let us set these two arguments aside. They are forms of the design argument considered in chapter 2. There are still serious difficulties with epiphenomenalism. To see these we must first clarify what epiphenomenalism involves. The view is also called holism, and when mind is seen to emerge through the coming together of matter in a certain way (for instance, through the evolution of the central nervous system and brain) the position is called the emergent property view (EPV). Here are four main features of the EPV.

The Emergent Property View

Wholes and Parts

In nature, wholes are often greater than the sum of their parts. Nature exhibits a hierarchy of systems — subatomic particles, atoms, molecules, cells, organs, whole organisms. Each level has properties of the wholes at that level which are not properties of their constituent parts. For example, water has the property of being wet, but this property is not true of either hydrogen or oxygen. Similarly, the mind is a property of the brain.[37]

Levels of Explanation and Complementarity

Each level in a hierarchy can be explained by using concepts appropriate at that level. Further, all the levels are complementary. For example, an explanation of a person's behavior could be given at a psychological level which used the concepts *beliefs, desires,* or *fears.* The same behavior could be given an explanation at the neurophysiological level using the concepts *neurons, synapses,* and so forth. These two levels of explanation are not in competition; they complement one another by offering descriptions of the same behavior at different levels.

---

36. See n. 25 regarding the survival value of rationality.

37. See MacKay, *Human Science and Human Dignity,* pp. 26–34; David Hull, *Philosophy of Biological Science* (Englewood Cliffs, N.J.: Prentice-Hall, 1974), pp. 125–41; Terence Horgan, "Supervenience and Microphysics," *Pacific Philosophical Quarterly* 63 (1982): 39.

Causation between Levels

Lower levels in the hierarchy cause things to happen at higher levels but not vice versa. When it comes to persons, events at the physical level can be characterized in terms of physical laws which make no reference to the causal efficaciousness of future events (e.g., the purposes of the agent) or higher levels of organization. The events at the physical level obey deterministic physical laws and mental events are mere byproducts.[38]

Resultant View of the Self

The self is not some mental substance added to the brain from the "outside" when the brain reaches a certain level of complexity. It is an emergent property which supervenes upon the brain.[39] The self becomes a discontinuous series of mental events when mental properties are instanced in different brain events. The self is a series of events which "ride" on top of the brain. Consider the following diagram:

$$M_1 \rightarrow M_2 \rightarrow M_3 \rightarrow M_4$$

$$B_{1\rightarrow} \rightarrow B_{2\rightarrow} \rightarrow B_{3\rightarrow} \rightarrow B_4$$

Suppose M_1 is the mental state of seeing an apple from a distance of five feet. It is a *mental* state since it involves the conscious awareness of seeing the apple, and conscious awareness is something true of minds and not matter. Now suppose M_2 is the mental state of seeing the apple from one foot, M_3 the state of feeling a pain on the toe, and M_4 the state of hearing a plane fly overhead. B_1 through B_4 are brain states which are associated with each mental state.

Three things stand out immediately. First, B_1 through B_4 stand in rigid physical, causal relations with one another. B_1 causes B_2 and so on. There is no room for a rational agent to intervene in this causal sequence. Mental agents do not act here. The physical level determines all the action. Mental states are mere byproducts of their physical states as smoke is a byproduct of fire.

Second, there is no unified, enduring self at the mental level. According to substance dualism, the self is not identical to its states; it *has* its states. The mind *has* its thoughts and experiences and the same mind can have two experiences at the same time (hearing a plane and seeing an apple) or it can have one experience followed by another. The *self* is present at both experiences and underlies the change of experiences.

When a leaf goes from green to red, green does not become red. Rather, green leaves, and is replaced by red *in* the leaf. The leaf is the same substance present at both ends of the process. When a substance gains or loses properties, it remains the same while the properties come and go. They are replaced. Red replaces green. The EPV says that M_1 through M_4 are properties of the body. There is no enduring mental substance which has them. There is just one mental property at one time which leaves and is replaced by another mental property at another time. The "self" is a series of mental events where mental properties are had by physical states.

Third, it is hard to see what sense can be given to intentionality. How is it that M_1 is of or about an apple? M_1 is just a dummy, a free rider on B_1. At best, B_1 would just be a state caused by light waves from the apple but it is hard to see how this would cause M_1 to be really a state *about* that apple. Even if it were, what difference would it make? Any further body states (the act of touching the apple or eating it) would be caused totally by brain states and make no reference to mental states at all.[40]

It should now be clear why epiphenomenalism was ruled out as an inadequate account of the necessary features of rationality. It cannot account for the existence of intentionality, it leaves no room for genuine rational agency to freely choose mental beliefs, and

---

38. See Searle, *Minds, Brains, and Science*, p. 93.

39. Emergence is roughly synonymous with supervenience, except the former is used diachronically and the latter synchronically.

40. I have said nothing about the relations which obtain among M_1 through M_4. Insofar as these mental states contain propositions and concepts, they must bear logical or epistemic relations with one another which the agent himself brings together and recognizes. It is hard to see where there is room for such relations at this level or to see where there is room for an agent to intervene at the lower level.

there is no enduring "I" to be present through the process of thought.[41]

The Origin of Mind as an Emergent Property

But let us waive these problems for the moment. Where would the mind as an emergent property come from? How can mind, the capacity to know truth, and so forth, emerge from mindless, nonrational matter?[42] Remember, mind here is not identical to the brain's structure. If it were, then the view would be some form of crude materialism or, perhaps, some unclear intermediate view between dualism and physicalism. But in either case, the position would be worse than epiphenomenalism, for it would suffer from the same deficiencies as the latter, as well as those raised earlier against physicalism in its pure form.

The EPV holds that mind is a genuine mental property (or series of properties) which supervenes on top of matter. Consider water again. Wetness emerges when hydrogen and oxygen come together into a structure known as H_2O. Wetness is not identical to that structure. Wetness is a simple quality; the structure is a set of relationships which can be quantified (spatial relations, relations of force, which can be given numerical values). So the structure is not the same thing as the wetness. Similarly, the mind is not the same thing as the brain's structure; it supervenes over that structure in the EPV view. So it is a genuinely new entity which must come into being somehow or other.

It does not seem that it could come into being from nothing. For one thing, that would violate a generally accepted principle that something does not come from nothing. Some have disputed this principle, but it still seems reasonable, especially at the macroscopic level and not the level of the microparticles of physics (though I believe it to hold at that level as well). And it is the macroscopic level that is involved when mind emerges, since it emerges over an object the size of a structured brain.

One could respond that the mind is not itself a macroscopic entity perhaps by saying that the macro/micro distinction does not hold for minds. But if the EPV view means that mind emerges over a structured brain out of nothing and that this fact is not anchored to the nature of that brain, then it is hard to see why mind emerges time and again over just this type of structured matter and not over a nickel or a bowling pin. The defender of the EPV cannot appeal to the causal efficacy of the mind itself and argue that the mind of a child comes from the mind of its parents, for this allows minds to cause something, and this is not allowed according to the EPV.

At the level of normal-sized macroscopic objects (objects visible to normal sight) things just do not pop in and out of existence. Even if mind is not such an object, its emergence seems to be tied to the brain. And the brain is such an object. So it is not very promising to account for the emergence of mind by saying it comes from nothing.

There is, however, a more promising view. Aristotle taught us long ago that when something new emerges, it does not come from nothing but from potentiality. When a leaf turns from green to red, the red does not simply come into existence; it was already in the leaf potentially. When an appleseed produces apples, the apples were in the seed potentially. In general, when a property emerges in a substance, it comes to actuality from potentiality, not from pure nonbeing. The

---

41. This has led several philosophers to radically revise our common-sense intuitions about the self in order to preserve physicalism. But in this case, as Robinson points out, the proper order between philosophy and science has been reversed. Philosophy is conceptually prior to science in a number of ways. See *Matter and Sense,* p. 109. Along these same lines, Bealer has argued that the distinction between mind and matter is logical and knowable a priori. Thus, it is a mistake to look to empirical means in the natural sciences to solve the mind/body problem. See "The Logical Status of Mind," pp. 231–74. For a brief, general treatment on the conceptual priority of philosophy over science, see John Kekes, *The Nature of Philosophy* (Totowa, N.J.: Rowman and Littlefield, 1980), pp. 147–63.

42. These are the problems that Max Delbruck proposes to answer in *Mind from Matter: An Essay on Revolutionary Epistemology,* ed. Gunther Stent and David Presti (Palo Alto, Calif.: Blackwell Scientific Publications, 1985), p. 22. After 280 pages of discussing the problem, he says: "To the question of how the mental capacity for such transcendence can have arisen in the course of biological evolution I have no satisfactory answer."

property was in the substance potentially and when it emerges, it becomes actual.

Mind must somehow be in matter potentially such that when matter reaches a certain stage of development, mind becomes actual. This is a more plausible version of the EPV, but it still has serious difficulties.

First, it is hard to see how this is compatible with the doctrines and motives of physicalism. Physicalism is embraced in part out of a desire to promote science as the ultimate, perhaps only, kind of knowledge. So physicalists often assert that the world is a network of physical causes wherein only physical causality does anything. Further, the world for a physicalist is in principle describable in strictly physical laws. But if mind is potential in matter, then physicalism seems to become some form of panpsychism, the view that mind is ultimate. Matter no longer is describable in terms of familiar physical properties and laws alone. Now it contains elusive mental potentialities.

After wrestling with this problem, Nobel Prize-winning scientist Max Delbruck argued that "our ideas about the objective character of the physical world, and hence of the nature of truth have been revised. In other words, mind looks less psychic and matter looks less materialistic."[43] So if one admits that mind is potential in matter, then one can no longer hold that reality is exhausted by the spatio-temporal physical universe.

Second, one could no longer hold that physical laws could exhaustively describe the causal processes of the universe. Richard Swinburne discusses this problem in some detail and argues that science will never be able to explain where mental properties come from or why they emerge when they do. He says,

What of mental properties? Take the simplest such property — sensations. There can be a physico-chemical explanation of how an animal's genes cause his nervous system to have a certain structure, and how a mutation in a gene can cause the nervous system of his

offspring to have a different structure. It can explain how an animal comes to have organs differentially sensitive to light of this and that range of wavelengths, sensitive to temperature or bodily damage; sensitive to these things in the sense that it responds differently to light of this wavelength from the way it responds to light of that wavelength and so on. But what physics and chemistry could not possibly explain is why the brain-events to which the impinging light gives rise, in turn give rise to sensations of blueness (as opposed to redness), a high noise rather than a low noise, this sort of smell rather than that sort of smell — why sodium chloride tastes salty, and roses look pink. And the reason why physics and chemistry could not explain these things is that pink looks, high noises, and salty tastes are not the sort of thing physics and chemistry deal in. These sciences deal in the physical (i.e., public) properties of small physical objects, and of the large physical objects which they come to form — in mass and charge, volume and spin. Yet mental properties are different from physical properties....[44]

Third, this emergent property view could not rule out the future existence of God. If mind can emerge from matter when a high-level system reaches a certain point of complexity, why is it not possible for a large-scale Mind to emerge at a later period in evolutionary development? In other words, the EPV cannot rule out Hegelianism, the view that mind emerges from matter all the way up to the emergence of God himself. This may sound far-fetched. But the point is that the EPV cannot rule it out, for the emergence of mind over brains is a startling fact which could hardly have been predicted from the properties of matter alone. So why should one think the process of emergence should stop with finite, human minds? Why could not some form of deity emerge, since mind is in some sense a basic constituent of the universe? Christian philosopher Richard Purtill has called this the God-not-yet view. And it should come as no comfort to an atheist, who is trying to

---

43. Ibid., p. 279.

44. Richard Swinburne, *The Evolution of the Soul* (Oxford: Clarendon Press, 1986), p. 186.

save some form of minimal physicalism, to be told that his view seems to imply some form of emergent theism. At the very least, emergent theism cannot be ruled out.

Finally, Clark points out that it is hard to specify just what these potential mental properties are.[45] Are these potential properties conscious? If so, then why do we have no memory from them when they emerge to form our own minds? Does it really make sense to say that my mind is composed of several particles of mind dust (i.e., little selves which came together to form my own mental life)? If these potential properties are not conscious, how are they still mental? These questions may have an answer, but they are certainly puzzling and the EPV seems to commit one to the existence of rather odd potential mental properties, odd at least from the standpoint of one who wants to maintain some form of respectable physicalism.[46]

The simple fact is that the existence of mind has always been a problem for the physicalist. As physicalist Paul M. Churchland argues,

> The important point about the standard evolutionary story is that the human species and all of its features are the wholly physical outcome of a purely physical process.... If this is the correct account of our origins, then there seems neither need, nor room, to fit any nonphysical substances or properties into our theoretical account of ourselves. We are creatures of matter.[47]

Physicalist D. M. Armstrong agrees:

> It is not a particularly difficult notion that, when the nervous system reaches a certain level of complexity, it should develop new properties. Nor would there be anything particularly difficult in the notion that when the nervous system reaches a certain level of complexity it should affect something that was already in existence in a new way. But it is a quite different matter to hold that the nervous system should have the power to create something else, of a quite different nature from itself, and create it out of no materials.[48]

Physicalism is false because it fails to adequately handle several general arguments raised against it. And it is self-refuting, for it undercuts the very prerequisites of rational thought itself. Once one grants the existence of mind, then the question arises as to where it came from. The emergent property view is one answer to this question. But it fails as an adequate theory of mind itself, and it postulates either the origin of mind from nothing or its emergence from potentiality in matter. Both options are problematic. Mind appears to be a basic feature of the cosmos and its origin at a finite level of persons is best explained by postulating a fundamental Mind who gave finite minds being and design. As Calvin put it, the endowments which we possess cannot possibly be from ourselves. They point to the ultimate Mind and ground of rationality himself.

45. Clark, *From Athens to Jerusalem*, pp. 143–46.

46. For a novel attempt to integrate emergentism with a scientific worldview without embracing substance dualism, see Roger Sperry, "Changed Concepts of Brain and Consciousness: Some Value Implications," *Zygon* 20 (March 1985): 41–57.

47. Churchland, *Matter and Consciousness*, p. 21.

48. D. M. Armstrong, *A Materialist Theory of the Mind* (London: Routledge and Kegan Paul, 1968), p. 30.

QUESTIONS AND FURTHER READINGS

Questions for Discussion

1. What is dualism on the Thomistic account (that is, on the account of Thomas Aquinas)?

2. What is Aquinas's reason for affirming that the human soul does not perish when the body does?

3. One of the difficulties with believing that we are material only and that our current bodies can be resurrected is the troubling problem of cannibals eating a person, and thus taking another person's atoms into their bodies. One materialist solution is that while *we* might not be in a position to locate and reconstitute the relevant atoms of someone's body, since God is omnipotent, *he* will be able to do so. Is this answer simply an appeal to mystery? Does the dualist have a better way of accounting for the resurrection of the person in such cases? Explain.

4. Explain Descartes' cogito argument. What is its conclusion? Is the argument successful?

5. Is Aquinas's view consistent with Descartes's? How are they similar? How are they different? Which one do you think is more consistent with the relevant biblical passages?

6. What is the difference between a substance and a property, as described by Professor Moreland? How does this distinction relate to a human person?

7. Describe in detail one of the arguments for dualism as defended by J. P. Moreland. Is it a good argument? Why or why not?

8. How is physicalism self-refuting, according to Moreland? Do you agree that it is? Explain.

9. What do you think the Bible teaches about the soul? Defend your position biblically, theologically, and philosophically.

10. Do you think the issue of whether we are body and soul or body only is an important one for the Christian? Why or why not?

Further Readings

Cooper, John W. (1989). *Body, Soul, and Life Everlasting: Biblical Anthropology and the Monism-Dualism Debate*. Grand Rapids: Eerdmans. (A study of biblical anthropology that includes theological, philosophical, and scientific discussions on the nature and destiny of human persons.)

Corcoran, Kevin, ed. (2001). *Soul, Body and Survival*. Ithaca, NY: Cornell University Press. (Includes constructive contributions on the possibility of an afterlife.)

Davis, Stephen T. (1993). *Risen Indeed: Making Sense of the Resurrection*. Grand Rapids: Eerdmans. (Provides a defense of the Christian view of the resurrection utilizing arguments and evidences from history, philosophy, and theology.)

Descartes, René (1641; reprint, 1972). *Meditations on First Philosophy*. In *The Philosophical Works of Descartes*, vol. 1. Ed. E. S. Haldane and G. R. T. Ross. Cambridge: Cambridge University Press. (Descartes offers his argument for substance dualism; note especially meditations 2 and 6.)

Edwards, Paul, ed. (1992). *Immortality*. New York: Macmillan. (A helpful collection of excerpts on immortality from different thinkers from Plato to today.)

Hasker, W. (1999). *The Emergent Self*. Ithaca, NY: Cornell University Press. (Contains a rigorous defense of property and substance dualism.)

Moreland, J. P. (2008). *Consciousness and the Existence of God: A Theistic Argument*. London: Routledge. (An advanced defense of the argument from mind.)

Moreland, J. P., and Scott B. Rae (2000). *Body and Soul: Human Nature and the Crisis in Ethics.* Downers Grove, IL: InterVarsity Press. (A defense of the Thomistic view of the soul, along with a discussion of relevant ethical issues.)

Perry, John (1978). *A Dialogue on Personal Identity and Immortality.* Indianapolis: Hackett. (A fun-to-read conversation/dialogue that fairly presents different sides of the immortality debate.)

Swinburne, Richard (1997). *The Evolution of the Soul.* Oxford: Clarendon. (A contemporary philosopher from Oxford University defends a dualist position.)

Taliaferro, Charles (1994; reprint, 2005). *Consciousness and the Mind of God.* Cambridge: Cambridge University Press. (Develops a concept of persons that allows for an afterlife.)

PART 9

THE PROBLEM OF EVIL

Perhaps the most significant challenge to Christian faith — indeed, to theism in general — is the problem of evil. God, as generally understood by theists, possesses the qualities of omniscience, omnipotence, and omnibenevolence. But the coexistence of such a God and evil raises some glaring difficulties. One type of problem is the *logical* problem of evil in which it is argued that the following two propositions are logically contradictory:

(1) God — an omnipotent, omniscient, and omnibenevolent being — exists.

and

(2) Evil — in its many manifestations — exists.

One way of spelling out the logical inconsistency is as follows:

1. If God exists, God is omnipotent (all-powerful), omniscient (all-knowing), and omnibenevolent (wholly good).
2. An omnibenevolent being would have the desire to eliminate evil.
3. An omnipotent being would have the power to eliminate evil.
4. An omniscient being would have the knowledge to eliminate evil.
5. If an omnibenevolent, omnipotent, and omniscient God exists, then evil would not exist.
6. Evil does exist.
7. Therefore, God does not exist.

A second type of problem is an *evidential* one. According to this problem, the kind and amount of evil in the world provide reasonable evidence for the belief that God, an omniscient, omnipotent, and omnibenevolent being, probably does not exist.

Two general strategies for dealing with the problem of evil are as follows. First is a *defense*, which is an attempt to demonstrate that it is not unreasonable, or illogical, to believe in the coexistence of God and evil. A second strategy for dealing with evil is called a *theodicy*, which is an attempt to justify God given the evil in the world. Unlike a defense, a theodicy is an attempt to explain the actual reasons why God created a world that includes evil.

Philosophers often make a distinction between *natural* evil and *moral* evil. Natural evils are events that occur in nature, including tornadoes, earthquakes, disease, and so forth, which cause harm or suffering to people or other sentient creatures. Natural evils are caused by impersonal forces. Moral evils are events brought about by human agents intentionally acting for the purpose of causing harm or suffering to people or other sentient creatures. Examples of moral evils include raping, torturing, and murdering innocent persons.

The first essay in this section is one of the earliest theodicies ever penned in the Christian West. It was written by Augustine (354–430) and includes his discussion with a friend named Evodius. He explains the importance of free will; how while free will is good, it nevertheless allows for the possibility of evil; how God is not responsible for evil; and what is the cause of the will.

In the next essay, Alvin Plantinga provides a response to the logical problem of evil. His defense is similar to Augustine's theodicy, most notably its inclusion of the free will of human beings. Plantinga is not attempting to justify God-given evil, however; he is not offering a theodicy. Rather, he is rebutting the atheologian's (the one who argues against belief in God) claims that there is a contradiction between the two propositions that God exists and evil exists. Plantinga also utilizes the notion of *transworld depravity* — that in every possible world, human beings freely choose to do evil. Given these two possibilities (free will and transworld depravity), he argues that it is logically possible that God could not create a world with free creatures without that world having evil in it. So there is no contradiction between the existence of God and the existence of evil. This argument is now widely taken by theists and atheists to be a solid rebuttal to the logical problem of evil.

In the third essay, John Hick spells out his soul-making theodicy. He first contrasts two different kinds of theodicies: Augustinian and Irenaean. According to the former, human beings were created by God as sinless beings in a perfect paradise. Through their free will, however, they chose to sin and so brought about the evil in the world. But God is merciful and sent his Son into the world to redeem the elect. They will spend eternity in heaven with God and no longer experience pain and suffering. The wicked, on the other hand, will experience eternal punishment separated from God.

The Irenaean theodicy, or what John Hick also calls the "soul-making" theodicy, is quite different from the Augustinian theodicy. Here, Adam (representing the first human beings) is not understood to have been created morally perfect and then to have fallen into sin. Rather, Adam is seen as an infant developing into a mature and virtuous human being over time. Developed from ideas of Irenaeus, a Greek bishop in the ancient Christian church, human history involves the unfolding story of *homo sapiens* being perfected in soul as they makes choices in the challenging environments in which they are placed. Hick argues that God is working through the evolution of humanity to create perfected souls in the eschaton. Unlike the Augustinian theodicy, which focuses primarily on moral evil, this soul-making theodicy offers a way of accounting for both moral and natural evil.

In the next selection, Peter Kreeft argues that the solution to evil and suffering is best explained in the Christian tradition: through Calvary God defeated evil. In the incarnation God entered the world of pain and experienced deep suffering, but the darkness could not overcome him. He came for love; he was victorious in love. Suffering, while still present in our lives, becomes an invitation to follow Christ.

In the final essay in this section, Marilyn Adams argues that theists need a response to the existence of evils of a particular sort: *horrendous* evils, which are so terrible that when a person experiences them she doubts that her life overall can be taken as a great good. Like Kreeft, Adams also argues that Christianity provides the resources requisite for dealing with the worst sorts of evil.

CHAPTER 43

Evil and Free Will

Augustine

BOOK II

I. 1. *Evodius* — Now explain to me, if it can be done, why God has given man free choice in willing, for if he had not received that freedom he would not have been able to sin. [...]

3. *Augustine* — [...] If man is good, and if he would not be able to act rightly except by willing to do so, he ought to have free will because without it he would not be able to act rightly. Because he also sins through having free will, we are not to believe that God gave it to him for that purpose. It is, therefore, a sufficient reason why he ought to have been given it, that without it man could not live aright. That it was given for this purpose can be understood from this fact. If anyone uses his free will in order to sin, God punishes him. That would be unjust unless the will was free not only to live aright but also to sin. How could he be justly punished who uses his will for the purpose for which it was given? Now when God punishes a sinner what else do you suppose he will say to him than "Why did you not use your free will for the purpose for which I gave it to you, that is, in order to do right?" Justice is praised as a good thing because it condemns sins and honours righteous actions. How could that be done if man had not free will? An action would be neither sinful nor righteous unless it were done voluntarily. For the same reason both punishment and reward would be unjust, if man did not have free will. But in punishing and in rewarding there must have been justice since justice is one of the good things which come from God. God, therefore, must have given and ought to have given man free will.

4. *Evodius* — I admit now that God has given us free will. But don't you think, pray, that, if it was given for the purpose of well-doing, it ought not to have been possible to convert it to sinful uses? Justice itself was given to man so that he might live rightly, and it is not possible for anyone to live an evil life by means of justice. So no one ought to be able to sin voluntarily if free will was given that we might live aright.

Augustine — God will, I hope, give me ability to answer you, or rather will give you the ability to answer your own question. Truth, which is the best master of all, will inwardly teach us both alike. But I wish you would tell me this: I asked you whether you know with perfect certainty that God has given us free will and you replied that you did. Now if we allow that God gave it, ought we to say that he ought not to have given it? If it is uncertain whether he gave it, we rightly ask whether it was good that it was given. If then we find that it was good, we find also that it was given by him who bestows all good things on men. If, however, we find that it was not a good thing we know that it was not given by him whom it is impious to accuse. If it is certain that he has given it, we ought to confess that, however it was given, it was rightly given. We may not say that it ought not to have been given or that it ought to have been given in some other way. If he has given it his action cannot in any way be rightly blamed.

5. *Evodius* — I believe all that unshakably. Nevertheless, because I do not know it, let us inquire as if it were all uncertain. I see that because it is uncertain whether free will was given that men might do right since by it we can also sin, another uncertainty arises, namely whether free will ought to have been given to us. If it is uncertain that it was given that we should act righteously, it is also uncertain that it ought to have been given at all. […]

BOOK III

45. *Augustine* — God owes nothing to any man, for he gives everything gratuitously. If anyone says God owes him something for his merits, God did not even owe him existence. Nothing could be owing to one who did not yet exist. And what merit is there in turning to him from whom you derive existence, that you may be made better by him from whom you derive existence? Why do you ask him for anything as if you were demanding repayment of a debt? If you were unwilling to turn to him, the loss would not be his but yours. For without him you would be nothing, and from him you derive such existence as you have; but on condition that, unless you turn to him, you must pay him back the existence you have from him, and become, not indeed nothing, but miserable. All things owe him, first, their existence so far as they are natural things, and secondly, that they can become better if they wish, receiving additional gifts if they wish them and being what they ought to be. No man is guilty because he has not received this or that power. But because he does not do as he ought he is justly held guilty. Obligation arises if he has received free will and sufficient power.

46. No blame attaches to the Creator if any of his creatures does not do what he ought. Indeed, that the wrong-doer suffers as he ought redounds to the praise of the Creator. In the very act of blaming anyone for not doing as he ought, he is praised to whom the debt is owed. If you are praised for seeing what you ought to do, and you only see it in him who is unchangeable truth, how much more is he to be praised who has taught you what you ought to wish, has given you the power to do it, and has not allowed you to refuse to do it with impunity? If "oughtness" depends upon what has been given, and man has been so made that he sins by necessity, then he ought to sin. So when he

sins he does what he ought. But it is wicked to speak like that. No man's nature compels him to sin, nor does any other nature. No man sins when he suffers what he does not wish. If he has to suffer justly he does not sin in suffering unwillingly. He sinned in that he did something voluntarily which involved him in suffering justly what he did not wish. If he suffers unjustly, where is the sin? There is no sin in suffering something unjustly but in doing something unjustly. So, if no one is compelled to sin either by his own nature or by another, it remains that he sins by his own will. If you want to attribute his sin to the Creator you will make the sinner guiltless because he has simply obeyed the laws of the Creator. If the sinner can be rightly defended he is not a sinner, and there is no sin to attribute to the Creator. Let us then praise the Creator whether or not the sinner can be defended. If he is justly defended he is no sinner and we can therefore praise the Creator. If he cannot be defended, he is a sinner so far as he turns away from the Creator. Therefore praise the Creator. I find, therefore, no way at all, and I assert that there is none to be found, by which our sins can be ascribed to the Creator, our God. I find that he is to be praised even for sins, not only because he punishes them, but also because sin arises only when a man departs from his truth.

Evodius — I most gladly approve all you have said, and assent with all my heart to the truth that there is no way at all of rightly ascribing our sins to our Creator.

47. But I should like to know, if possible, why those beings do not sin whom God knew beforehand would not sin, and why those others do sin whom he foresaw would sin. I do not now think that God's foreknowledge compels the one to sin and the other not to sin. But if there were no cause rational creatures would not be divided into classes as they are: those who never sin, those who continually sin, and the intermediary class of those who sometimes sin and sometimes are turned towards well-doing. What is the reason for this division? I do not want you to reply that it is the will that does it. What I want to know is what cause lies behind willing. There must be some reason why one class never wills to sin, another never lacks the will to sin, and another sometimes wills to sin and at other times does not so will. For they are all alike in nature. I seem to see that there must be some cause for this threefold classification of rational beings according to their wills, but what it is I do not know.

48. *Augustine* — Since will is the cause of sin, you now ask what is the cause of will. If I could find one, are you not going to ask for the cause of the cause I have found? What limit will there be to your quest, what end to inquiry and explanation? You ought not to push your inquiry deeper, for you must beware of imagining that anything can be more truly said than that which is written: "Avarice is the root of all evils" (I Tim. 6:10), that is, wanting more than is sufficient. That is sufficient which is demanded by the need of preserving any particular creature. Avarice, in Greek *philarguria*, derives its name from *argentum* [silver], because among the ancients coins were made of silver or more frequently with an admixture of silver. But avarice must be understood as connected not only with silver and money but with everything which is immoderately desired, in every case where a man wants more than is sufficient. Such avarice is cupidity, and cupidity is an evil will. An evil will therefore, is the cause of all evils. If it were according to nature it would preserve nature and not be hostile to it, and so it would not be evil. The inference is that the root of all evils is not according to nature. That is sufficient answer to all who want to accuse nature. But you ask what is the cause of this root. How then will it be the root of all evils? If it has a cause, that cause will be the root of evil. And if you find a cause, as I said, you will ask for a cause of that cause, and there will be no limit to your inquiry.

49. But what cause of willing can there be which is prior to willing? Either it is a will, in which case we have not got beyond the root of evil will. Or it is not a will, and in that case there is no sin in it. Either, then, will is itself the first cause of sin, or the first cause is without sin. Now sin is rightly imputed only to that which sins, nor is it rightly imputed unless it sins voluntarily. I do not know why you should want to inquire further, but here is a further point. If there is a cause of willing it is either just or unjust. If it is just, he who obeys it will not sin, if unjust he who does not obey it will not sin either.

CHAPTER 44

A Free Will Defense

Alvin Plantinga

The Free Will Defense

In what follows I shall focus attention upon the Free Will Defense. I shall examine it more closely, state it more exactly, and consider objections to it; and I shall argue that in the end it is successful. Earlier [in *God, Freedom, and Evil*] we saw that among good states of affairs there are some that not even God can bring about without bringing about evil: those goods, namely, that *entail* or *include* evil states of affairs. The Free Will Defense can be looked upon as an effort to show that there may be a very different kind of good that God can't bring about without permitting evil. These are good states of affairs that don't include evil; they do not entail the existence of any evil whatever; nonetheless God Himself can't bring them about without permitting evil.

So how does the Free Will Defense work? And what does the Free Will Defender mean when he says that people are or may be free? What is relevant to the Free Will Defense is the idea of *being free with respect to an action*. If a person is free with respect to a given action, then he is free to perform that action and free to refrain from performing it; no antecedent conditions and/or causal laws determine that he will perform the action, or that he won't. It is within his power, at the time in question, to take or perform the action and within his power to refrain from it. Freedom so conceived is not to be confused with unpredictability. You might be able to predict what you will do in a given situation even if you are free, in that situation, to do something else. If I know you well, I may be

able to predict what action you will take in response to a certain set of conditions; it does not follow that you are not free with respect to that action. Secondly, I shall say that an action is *morally significant*, for a given person, if it would be wrong for him to perform the action but right to refrain or *vice versa*. Keeping a promise, for example, would ordinarily be morally significant for a person, as would refusing induction into the army. On the other hand, having Cheerios for breakfast (instead of Wheaties) would not normally be morally significant. Further, suppose we say that a person is *significantly free*, on a given occasion, if he is then free with respect to a morally significant action. And finally we must distinguish between *moral evil* and *natural evil*. The former is evil that results from free human activity; natural evil is any other kind of evil.[1]

Given these definitions and distinctions, we can make a preliminary statement of the Free Will Defense as follows. A world containing creatures who are significantly free (and freely perform more good than evil actions) is more valuable, all else being equal, than a world containing no free creatures at all. Now God can create free creatures, but He can't *cause* or *determine* them to do only what is right. For if He does so, then they aren't significantly free after all; they do not do what is right *freely*. To create creatures capable of *moral good*, therefore, He must create creatures capable of moral evil; and He can't give these creatures the freedom to perform evil and at the same time prevent them from doing so. As it turned out,

---

1. This distinction is not very precise (how, exactly, are we to construe "results from"?), but perhaps it will serve our present purposes.

sadly enough, some of the free creatures God created went wrong in the exercise of their freedom; this is the source of moral evil. The fact that free creatures sometimes go wrong, however, counts neither against God's omnipotence nor against His goodness; for He could have forestalled the occurrence of moral evil only by removing the possibility of moral good.

I said earlier [in *God, Freedom, and Evil*] that the Free Will Defender tries to find a proposition that is consistent with

(1) God is omniscient, omnipotent, and wholly good

and together with (1) entails that there is evil. According to the Free Will Defense, we must find this proposition somewhere in the above story. The heart of the Free Will Defense is the claim that it is *possible* that God could not have created a universe containing moral good (or as much moral good as this world contains) without creating one that also contained moral evil. And if so, then it is possible that God has a good reason for creating a world containing evil.

Now this defense has met with several kinds of objections. For example, some philosophers say that *causal determinism* and *freedom*, contrary to what we might have thought, are not really incompatible.[2] But if so, then God could have created free creatures who were free, and free to do what is wrong, but nevertheless were causally determined to do only what is right. Thus He could have created creatures who were free to do what was wrong, while nevertheless preventing them from ever performing any wrong actions — simply by seeing to it that they were causally determined to do only what is right. Of course this contradicts the Free Will Defense, according to which there is inconsistency in supposing that God determines free creatures to do only what is right. But is it really possible that all of a person's actions are causally determined while some of them are free? How could that be so? According to one version of

the doctrine in question, to say that George acts freely on a given occasion is to say only this: *if George had chosen to do otherwise, he would have done otherwise.* Now George's action A is causally determined if some event E — some event beyond his control — has already occurred, where the state of affairs consisting in E's occurrence conjoined with George's *refraining* from performing A, is a causally impossible state of affairs. Then one can consistently hold both that all of a man's actions are causally determined and that some of them are free in the above sense. For suppose that all of a man's actions are causally determined and that he *couldn't*, on any occasion, have made any choice or performed any action different from the ones he did make and perform. It could still be true that if he *had* chosen to do otherwise, he would have done otherwise. Granted, he couldn't have chosen to do otherwise; but this is consistent with saying that *if* he had, things would have gone differently.

This objection to the Free Will Defense seems utterly implausible. One might as well claim that being in jail doesn't really limit one's freedom on the grounds that if one were *not* in jail, he'd be free to come and go as he pleased. So I shall say no more about this objection here.[3]

A second objection is more formidable. In essence it goes like this. Surely it is possible to do only what is right, even if one is free to do wrong. It is *possible*, in that broadly logical sense, that there be a world containing free creatures who always do what is right. There is certainly no *contradiction* or *inconsistency* in this idea. But God is omnipotent; his power has no nonlogical limitations. So if it's possible that there be a world containing creatures who are free to do what is wrong but never in fact do so, then it follows that an omnipotent God could create such a world. If so, however, the Free Will Defense must be mistaken in its insistence upon the possibility that God is omnipotent but unable to create a world containing moral good

2. See, for example, A. Flew, "Divine Omnipotence and Human Freedom," in *New Essays in Philosophical Theology*, ed. A. Flew and A. MacIntyre (London: SCM, 1955), pp. 150–153.

3. For further discussion of it see Plantinga, *God and Other Minds*, pp. 132–135.

without permitting moral evil. J. L. Mackie ... states this objection:

> If God has made men such that in their free choices they sometimes prefer what is good and sometimes what is evil, why could he not have made men such that they always freely choose the good? If there is no logical impossibility in a man's freely choosing the good on one, or on several occasions, there cannot be a logical impossibility in his freely choosing the good on every occasion. God was not, then, faced with a choice between making innocent automata and making beings who, in acting freely, would sometimes go wrong; there was open to him the obviously better possibility of making beings who would act freely but always go right. Clearly, his failure to avail himself of this possibility is inconsistent with his being both omnipotent and wholly good.[4]

Now what, exactly, is Mackie's point here? This. According to the Free Will Defense, it is possible both that God is omnipotent and that He was unable to create a world containing moral good without creating one containing moral evil. But, replies Mackie, this limitation on His power to create is inconsistent with God's omnipotence. For surely it's *possible* that there be a world containing perfectly virtuous persons — persons who are significantly free but always do what is right. Surely there are *possible worlds* that contain moral good but no moral evil. But God, if He is omnipotent, can create any possible world He chooses. So it is *not* possible, contrary to the Free Will Defense, both that God is omnipotent and that He could create a world containing moral good only by creating one containing moral evil. If He is omnipotent, the only limitations of His power are *logical* limitations; in which case there are no possible worlds He could not have created.

This is a subtle and important point. According to the great German philosopher G.W. Leibniz, *this* world, the actual world, must be the best of all possible worlds. His reasoning goes as follows. Before God created anything at all, He was confronted with an enormous range of choices; He could create or bring into actuality any of the myriads of different possible worlds. Being perfectly good, He must have chosen to create the best world He could; being omnipotent, He was able to create any possible world He pleased. He must, therefore, have chosen the best of all possible worlds; and hence *this* world, the one He did create, must be the best possible. Now Mackie, of course, agrees with Leibniz that God, if omnipotent, could have created any world He pleased and would have created the best world he could. But while Leibniz draws the conclusion that this world, despite appearances, must be the best possible, Mackie concludes instead that there is no omnipotent, wholly good God. For, he says, it is obvious enough that this present world is not the best of all possible worlds.

The Free Will Defender disagrees with both Leibniz and Mackie. In the first place, he might say, what is the reason for supposing that *there is* such a thing as the best of all possible worlds? No matter how marvelous a world is — containing no matter how many persons enjoying unalloyed bliss — isn't it possible that there be an even better world containing even more persons enjoying even more unalloyed bliss? But what is really characteristic and central to the Free Will Defense is the claim that God, though omnipotent, could not have actualized just any possible world He pleased.

Was It within God's Power to Create Any Possible World He Pleased?

This is indeed the crucial question for the Free Will Defense. If we wish to discuss it with insight and authority, we shall have to look into the idea of *possible worlds*. And a sensible first question is this: what sort of thing is a possible world? The basic idea is that a possible world is a *way things could have been*; it is a *state of affairs* of some kind. Earlier we spoke of states of affairs, in particular of good and evil states of affairs. Suppose we look at this idea in more detail.

---

4. Mackie, in *The Philosophy of Religion*, pp. 100 – 101.

What sort of thing is a state of affairs? The following would be examples:

> Nixon's having won the 1972 election
>
> 7 + 5's being equal to 12
>
> All men's being mortal

and

> Gary, Indiana's, having a really nasty pollution problem.

These are *actual* states of affairs: states of affairs that do in fact *obtain*. And corresponding to each such actual state of affairs there is a true proposition — in the above cases, the corresponding propositions would be *Nixon won the 1972 presidential election, 7 + 5 is equal to 12, all men are mortal,* and *Gary, Indiana, has a really nasty pollution problem.* A proposition *p corresponds* to a state of affairs *s,* in this sense, if it is impossible that *p* be true and *s* fail to obtain and impossible that *s* obtain and *p* fail to be true.

But just as there are false propositions, so there are states of affairs that do *not* obtain or are *not* actual. *Kissinger's having swum the Atlantic* and *Hubert Horatio Humphrey's having run a mile in four minutes* would be examples. Some states of affairs that do not obtain are *impossible*: e.g., *Hubert's having drawn a square circle, 7 + 5's being equal to 75,* and *Agnew's having a brother who was an only child.* The propositions corresponding to these states of affairs, of course, are necessarily false. So there are states of affairs that *obtain* or *are actual* and also states of affairs that don't obtain. Among the latter some are *impossible* and others are possible. And a possible world is a possible state of affairs. Of course not every possible state of affairs is a possible world; *Hubert's having run a mile in four minutes* is a possible state of affairs but not a possible world. No doubt it is an *element* of many possible worlds, but it isn't itself inclusive enough to be one. To be a possible world, a state of affairs must be very large — so large as to be *complete* or *maximal.*

To get at this idea of completeness we need a couple of definitions.... [A] state of affairs A *includes* a state of affairs B if it is not possible that A obtain and B

not obtain or if the conjunctive state of affairs A *but not B* — the state of affairs that obtains if and only if A obtains and B does not — is not possible. For example, *Jim Whittaker's being the first American to climb Mt. Everest* includes *Jim Whittaker's being an American.* It also includes *Mt. Everest's being climbed, something's being climbed, no American's having climbed Everest before Whittaker did,* and the like. *Inclusion* among states of affairs is like *entailment* among propositions; and where a state of affairs A includes a state of affairs B, the proposition corresponding to A entails the one corresponding to B. Accordingly, *Jim Whittaker is the first American to climb Everest* entails *Mt. Everest has been climbed, something has been climbed,* and *no American climbed Everest before Whittaker did.* Now suppose we say further that a state of affairs A *precludes* a state of affairs B if it is not possible that *both* obtain, or if the conjunctive state of affairs A *and B* is impossible. Thus *Whittaker's being the first American to climb Mt. Everest* precludes *Luther Jerstad's being the first American to climb Everest,* as well as *Whittaker's never having climbed any mountains.* If A precludes B, then A's corresponding proposition entails the denial of the one corresponding to B. Still further, let's say that the *complement* of a state of affairs is the state of affairs that obtains just in case A does not obtain. [Or we might say that the complement (call it A*) of A is the state of affairs corresponding to the *denial* or *negation* of the proposition corresponding to A.] Given these definitions, we can say what it is for a state of affairs to be *complete*: A is a complete state of affairs if and only if for every state of affairs B, either A *includes* B or A *precludes* B. (We could express the same thing by saying that if A is a complete state of affairs, then for every state of affairs B, either A includes B or A includes B*, the complement of B.) And now we are able to say what a possible world is: a possible world is any possible state of affairs that is complete. If A is a possible world, then it says something about everything; every state of affairs S is either included in or precluded by it.

Corresponding to each possible world W, furthermore, there is a set of propositions that I'll call *the book on W*. A proposition is in the book on *W* just in case the state of affairs to which it corresponds is included in *W*. Or we might express it like this. Suppose we say that a proposition *P* is *true in a world W* if and only if *P would have been true if W had been actual* — if and only if, that is, it is not possible that *W* be actual and *P* be false. Then the book on *W* is the set of propositions true in *W*. Like possible worlds, books are *complete*; if *B* is a book, then for any proposition *P*, either *P* or the denial of *P* will be a member of *B*. A book is a *maximal consistent set* of propositions; it is so large that the addition of another proposition to it always yields an explicitly inconsistent set.

Of course, for each possible world there is exactly one book corresponding to it (that is, for a given world *W* there is just one book *B* such that each member of *B* is true in *W*); and for each book there is just one world to which it corresponds. So every world has its book.

It should be obvious that exactly one possible world is actual. At *least* one must be, since the set of true propositions is a maximal consistent set and hence a book. But then it corresponds to a possible world, and the possible world corresponding to this set of propositions (since it's the set of *true* propositions) will be actual. On the other hand there is at *most* one actual world. For suppose there were two: *W* and *W′*. These worlds cannot include all the very same states of affairs; if they did, they would be the very same world. So there must be at least one state of affairs *S* such that *W* includes *S* and *W′* does not. But a possible world is maximal; *W′*, therefore, includes the complement *S̄* of *S*. So if both *W* and *W′* were actual, as we have supposed, then both *S* and *S** would be actual — which is impossible. So there can't be more than one possible world that is actual.

Leibniz pointed out that a proposition *p* is necessary if it is true in every possible world. We may add that *p* is possible if it is true in one world and impossible if true in none. Furthermore, *p entails q* if there is no possible world in which *p* is true and *q* is false; and *p is consistent with q* if there is at least one world in which both *p* and *q* are true.

A further feature of possible worlds is that people (and other things) *exist* in them. Each of us exists in the actual world, obviously; but a person also exists in many worlds distinct from the actual world. It would be a mistake, of course, to think of all of these worlds as somehow "going on" at the same time, with the same person reduplicated through these worlds and actually existing in a lot of different ways. This is not what is meant by saying that the same person exists in different possible worlds. What is meant, instead, is this: a person Paul exists in each of those possible worlds *W* which is such that, if *W had been actual*, Paul would have existed — actually existed. Suppose Paul had been an inch taller than he is, or a better tennis player. Then the world that does in fact obtain would not have been actual; some other world — *W′*, let's say — would have obtained instead. If *W′* had been actual, Paul would have existed; so Paul exists in *W′*. (Of course there are still other possible worlds in which Paul does not exist — worlds, for example, in which there are no people at all.) Accordingly, when we say that Paul exists in a world *W*, what we mean is that Paul *would have* existed had *W* been actual. Or we could put it like this: Paul exists in each world *W* that includes the state of affairs consisting in Paul's existence. We can put this still more simply by saying that Paul exists in those worlds whose books contain the proposition *Paul exists*.

But isn't there a problem here? *Many* people are named "Paul": Paul the apostle, Paul J. Zwier, John Paul Jones, and many other famous Pauls. So who *goes* with "Paul exists"? Which Paul? The answer has to do with the fact that books contain *propositions* — not sentences. They contain the sort of thing sentences are used to express and assert. And the same sentence — "Aristotle is wise," for example — can be used to express many different propositions. When Plato used it, he asserted a proposition predicating wisdom of his famous pupil; when Jackie Onassis uses it, she asserts a proposition predicating wisdom of her wealthy husband. These are distinct propositions (we might even think they differ in truth value); but they are expressed by the same sentence. Normally (but not always) we don't have much trouble determining which of the several propositions expressed by a given sentence is relevant in the context at hand. So in this case a given person, Paul, exists in a world W if and only if W's book contains the proposition that says that *he* — that particular person — exists. The fact that the sentence we use to express this proposition can also be used to express *other* propositions is not relevant.

After this excursion into the nature of books and worlds we can return to our question. Could God have created just any world He chose? Before addressing the question, however, we must note that God does not, strictly speaking, *create* any possible worlds or states of affairs at all. What He creates are the heavens and the earth and all that they contain. But He has not created states of affairs. There are, for example, the state of affairs consisting in God's existence and the state of affairs consisting in His nonexistence. That is, there is such a thing as the state of affairs consisting in the existence of God, and there is also such a thing as the state of affairs consisting in the nonexistence of God, just as there are the two propositions *God exists* and *God does not exist*. The theist believes that the first state of affairs is actual and the first proposition true; the atheist believes that the second state of affairs is actual and the second proposition true. But, of course, both propositions *exist*, even though just one is true. Similarly, there are two states of affairs here, just one of which is actual. So both states of affairs *exist*, but only one *obtains*. And God has not created either one of them since there never was a time at which either did not exist. Nor has He created the state of affairs consisting in the earth's existence; there was a time when *the earth* did not exist, but none when the state of affairs consisting in the earth's existence didn't exist. Indeed, God did not bring into existence any states of affairs at all. What He did was to perform actions of a certain sort — creating the heavens and the earth, for example — which resulted in the *actuality* of certain states of affairs. God *actualizes* states of affairs.

He actualizes the possible world that does in fact obtain; He does not create it. And while He has created Socrates, He did not create the state of affairs consisting in Socrates' existence.[5]

Bearing this in mind, let's finally return to our question. Is the atheologian right in holding that if God is omnipotent, then he could have actualized or created any possible world He pleased? Not obviously. First, we must ask ourselves whether God is a *necessary* or a *contingent* being. A *necessary* being is one that exists in every possible world — one that would have existed no matter which possible world had been actual; a contingent being exists only in some possible worlds. Now if God is not a necessary being (and many, perhaps most, theists think that He is not), then clearly enough there will be many possible worlds He could not have actualized — all those, for example, in which He does not exist. Clearly, God could not have created a world in which He doesn't even exist.

So, if God is a contingent being then there are many possible worlds beyond His power to create. But this is really irrelevant to our present concerns. For perhaps the atheologian can maintain his case if he revises his claim to avoid this difficulty; perhaps he will say something like this: if God is omnipotent, then He could have actualized any of those possible worlds *in which He exists*. So if He exists and is omnipotent, He could have actualized (contrary to the Free Will Defense) any of those possible worlds in which He exists and in which there exist free creatures who do no wrong. He could have actualized worlds containing moral good but no moral evil. Is this correct?

Let's begin with a trivial example. You and Paul have just returned from an Australian hunting expedition: your quarry was the elusive double-wattled cassowary. Paul captured an aardvark, mistaking it for a cassowary. The creature's disarming ways have won it a place in Paul's heart; he is deeply attached to it. Upon your return to the States you offer Paul $500 for his aardvark, only to be rudely turned down. Later you

<hr>

5. Strict accuracy demands, therefore, that we speak of God as *actualizing* rather than creating possible worlds. I shall continue to use both locutions, thus sacrificing accuracy to familiarity. For more

about possible worlds see my book *The Nature of Necessity* (Oxford: The Clarendon Press, 1974), chaps. 4 – 8.

ask yourself, "What would he have done if I'd offered him $700?" Now what is it, exactly, that you are asking? What you're really asking in a way is whether, under a *specific set of conditions*, Paul would have sold it. These conditions include your having offered him $700 rather than $500 for the aardvark, everything else being as much as possible like the conditions that did in fact obtain. Let S' be this set of conditions or state of affairs. S' includes the state of affairs consisting in your offering Paul $700 (instead of the $500 you did offer him); of course it does not include his *accepting* your offer, and it does not include his *rejecting* it; for the rest, the conditions it includes are just like the ones that did obtain in the actual world. So, for example, S' includes Paul's being free to accept the offer and free to refrain; and if in fact the going rate for an aardvark was $650, then S' includes the state of affairs consisting in the going rate's being $650. So we might put your question by asking which of the following conditionals is true:

(23) If the state of affairs S' had obtained, Paul would have accepted the offer

(24) If the state of affairs S' had obtained, Paul would not have accepted the offer.

It seems clear that at least one of these conditionals is true, but naturally they can't both be; so exactly one is.

Now since S' includes neither Paul's accepting the offer nor his rejecting it, the antecedent of (23) and (24) does not entail the consequent of either. That is,

(25) S' obtains

does not entail either

(26) Paul accepts the offer

or

(27) Paul does not accept the offer.

So there are possible worlds in which both (25) and (26) are true, and other possible worlds in which both (25) and (27) are true.

We are now in a position to grasp an important fact. Either (23) or (24) is in fact true; and either way there are possible worlds God could not have actualized. Suppose, first of all, that (23) is true. Then it was beyond the power of God to create a world in which (1) Paul is free to sell his aardvark and free to refrain, and in which the other states of affairs included in S' obtain, and (2) Paul does not sell. That is, it was beyond His power to create a world in which (25) and (27) are both true. There is at least one possible world like this, but God, despite His omnipotence, could not have brought about its actuality. For let W be such a world. To actualize W, God must bring it about that Paul is free with respect to this action, and that the other states of affairs included in S' obtain. But (23), as we are supposing, is true; so if God had actualized S' and left Paul *free* with respect to this action, he would have sold: in which case W would not have been actual. If, on the other hand, God had *brought it about* that Paul didn't sell or had *caused him* to refrain from selling, then Paul would not have been free with respect to this action; then S' would not have been actual (since S' includes Paul's being free with respect to it), and W would not have been actual since W includes S'.

Of course if it is (24) rather than (23) that is true, then another class of worlds was beyond God's power to actualize — those, namely, in which S' obtains and Paul *sells* his aardvark. These are the worlds in which both (25) and (26) are true. But either (23) or (24) is true. Therefore, there are possible worlds God could not have actualized. If we consider whether or not God could have created a world in which, let's say, both (25) and (26) are true, we see that the answer depends upon a peculiar kind of fact; it depends upon what Paul would have freely chosen to do in a certain situation. So there are any number of possible worlds such that it is partly up to Paul whether God can create them.[6]

That was a past tense example. Perhaps it would be useful to consider a future tense case, since this might

---

6. For a fuller statement of this argument see Plantinga, *The Nature of Necessity*, chap. 9, secs. 4–6.

seem to correspond more closely to God's situation in choosing a possible world to actualize. At some time t in the near future Maurice will be free with respect to some insignificant action — having freeze-dried oatmeal for breakfast, let's say. That is, at time t Maurice will be free to have oatmeal but also free to take something else — shredded wheat, perhaps. Next, suppose we consider S', a state of affairs that is included in the actual world and includes Maurice's being free with respect to taking oatmeal at time t. That is, S' includes Maurice's being free at time t to take oatmeal and free to reject it. S' does not include Maurice's taking oatmeal, however; nor does it include his rejecting it. For the rest S' is as much as possible like the actual world. In particular there are many conditions that do in fact hold at time t and are *relevant* to his choice — such conditions, for example, as the fact that he hasn't had oatmeal lately, that his wife will be annoyed if he rejects it, and the like; and S' includes each of these conditions. Now God no doubt knows what Maurice will do at time t, if S obtains; He knows which action Maurice would freely perform if S were to be actual. That is, God knows that one of the following conditionals is true:

(28) If S' were to obtain, Maurice will freely take the oatmeal

or

(29) If S' were to obtain, Maurice will freely reject it.

We may not know which of these is true, and Maurice himself may not know; but presumably God does.

So either God knows that (28) is true, or else He knows that (29) is. Let's suppose it is (28). Then there is a possible world that God, though omnipotent, cannot create. For consider a possible world W' that shares S' with the actual world (which for ease of reference I'll name "Kronos") and in which Maurice does *not* take oatmeal. (We know there *is* such a world, since S' does not include Maurice's taking the oatmeal.) S' obtains in W' just as it does in Kronos. Indeed, everything in

W' is just as it is in Kronos up to time t. But whereas in Kronos Maurice takes oatmeal at time t, in W' he does not. Now W' is a perfectly possible world; but it is not within God's power to create it or bring about its actuality. For to do so He must actualize S'. But (28) is in fact true. So if God actualizes S' (as He must to create W') and leaves Maurice free with respect to the action in question, then he will take the oatmeal; and then, of course, W' will not be actual. If, on the other hand, God causes Maurice to *refrain* from taking the oatmeal, then he is not *free* to take it. That means, once again, that W' is not actual; for in W' Maurice is free to take the oatmeal (even if he doesn't do so). So if (28) is true, then this world W' is one that God can't actualize; it is not within His power to actualize it even though He is omnipotent and it is a possible world.

Of course, if it is (29) that is true, we get a similar result; then too there are possible worlds that God can't actualize. These would be worlds which share S' with Kronos and in which Maurice *does* take oatmeal. But either (28) or (29) *is* true; so either way there is a possible world that God can't create. If we consider a world in which S' obtains and in which Maurice freely chooses oatmeal at time t, we see that whether or not it is within God's power to actualize it depends upon what Maurice would do if he were free in a certain situation. Accordingly, there are any number of possible worlds such that it is partly up to Maurice whether or not God can actualize them. It is, of course, up to God whether or not to create Maurice and also up to God whether or not to make him free with respect to the action of taking oatmeal at time t. (God could, if He chose, cause him to succumb to the dreaded *equine obsession*, a condition shared by some people and most horses, whose victims find it *psychologically impossible* to refuse oats or oat products.) But if He creates Maurice and creates him free with respect to this action, then whether or not he actually performs the action is up to Maurice — not God.[7]

Now we can return to the Free Will Defense and

7. For a more complete and more exact statement of this argument see Plantinga, *The Nature of Necessity*, chap. 9, secs. 4–6.

the problem of evil. The Free Will Defender, you recall, insists on the possibility that it is not within God's power to create a world containing moral good without creating one containing moral evil. His atheological opponent — Mackie, for example — agrees with Leibniz in insisting that *if* (as the theist holds) God is omnipotent, then it *follows* that He could have created any possible world He pleased. We now see that this contention — call it "Leibniz' Lapse" — is a mistake. The atheologian is right in holding that there are many possible worlds containing moral good but no moral evil; his mistake lies in endorsing Leibniz' Lapse. So one of his premises — that God, if omnipotent, could have actualized just any world He pleased — is false.

Could God Have Created a World Containing Moral Good but No Moral Evil?

Now suppose we recapitulate the logic of the situation. The Free Will Defender claims that the following is possible:

(30) God is omnipotent, and it was not within His power to create a world containing moral good but no moral evil.

By way of retort the atheologian insists that there are possible worlds containing moral good but no moral evil. He adds that an omnipotent being could have actualized any possible world he chose. So if God is omnipotent, it follows that He could have actualized a world containing moral good but no moral evil; hence (30), contrary to the Free Will Defender's claim, is not possible. What we have seen so far is that his second premiss — Leibniz' Lapse — is false.

Of course, this does not settle the issue in the Free Will Defender's favor. Leibniz' Lapse (appropriately enough for a lapse) is false; but this doesn't show that (30) is possible. To show this latter we must demonstrate the possibility that among the worlds God could not have actualized are all the worlds containing moral good but no moral evil. How can we approach this question?

Instead of choosing oatmeal for breakfast or selling an aardvark, suppose we think about a morally significant action such as taking a bribe. Curley Smith, the mayor of Boston, is opposed to the proposed freeway route; it would require destruction of the Old North Church along with some other antiquated and structurally unsound buildings. L. B. Smedes, the director of highways, asks him whether he'd drop his opposition for $1 million. "Of course," he replies. "Would you do it for $2?" asks Smedes. "What do you take me for?" comes the indignant reply. "That's already established," smirks Smedes; "all that remains is to nail down your price." Smedes then offers him a bribe of $35,000; unwilling to break with the fine old traditions of Bay State politics, Curley accepts. Smedes then spends a sleepless night wondering whether he could have bought Curley for $20,000.

Now suppose we assume that Curley was free with respect to the action of taking the bribe — free to take it and free to refuse. And suppose, furthermore, that he would have taken it. That is, let us suppose that

(31) If Smedes had offered Curley a bribe of $20,000, he would have accepted it.

If (31) is true, then there is a state of affairs S' that (1) includes Curley's being offered a bribe of $20,000; (2) does not include either his accepting the bribe or his rejecting it; and (3) is otherwise as much as possible like the actual world. Just to make sure S' includes every relevant circumstance, let us suppose that it is a *maximal world segment*. That is, add to S' any state of affairs compatible with but not included in it, and the result will be an entire possible world. We could think of it roughly like this: S' is included in at least one world W in which Curley takes the bribe and in at least one world W' in which he rejects it. If S' is a maximal world segment, then S' is what remains of W when *Curley's taking the bribe* is deleted; it is also what remains of W' when *Curley's rejecting the bribe* is deleted. More exactly, if S' is a maximal world segment, then every possible state of affairs that includes S', but isn't included by S', is a possible world. So if (31) is true, then there is a maximal world segment S' that (1) includes Curley's being offered a bribe of $20,000; (2) does not include either his accepting the bribe or his rejecting it; (3) is otherwise as much as possible like the actual world — in particular, it includes Curley's being free with respect to the bribe; and (4) is such that if it were actual then Curley would have taken the bribe. That is,

(32) If S′ were actual, Curley would have accepted the bribe

is true.

Now, of course, there is at least one possible world W′ in which S′ is actual and Curley does not take the bribe. But God could not have created W′; to do so, He would have been obliged to actualize S′, leaving Curley free with respect to the action of taking the bribe. But under these conditions Curley, as (32) assures us, would have accepted the bribe, so that the world thus created would not have been S′.

Curley, as we see, is not above a bit of Watergating. But there may be worse to come. Of course, there are possible worlds in which he is significantly free (i.e., free with respect to a morally significant action) and never does what is wrong. But the sad truth about Curley may be this. Consider W′, any of these worlds: in W′ Curley is significantly free, so in W′ there are some actions that are morally significant for him and with respect to which he is free. But at least one of these actions — call it A — has the following peculiar property. There is a maximal world segment S′ that obtains in W′ and is such that (1) S′ includes Curley's being free re A but neither his performing A nor his refraining from A; (2) S′ is otherwise as much as possible like W′; and (3) if S′ had been actual, Curley would have gone wrong with respect to A.[8] (Notice that this third condition holds in fact, in the actual world; it does not hold in that world W′.)

This means, of course, that God could not have actualized W′. For to do so He'd have been obliged to bring it about that S′ is actual; but then Curley would go wrong with respect to A. Since in W′ he always does what is right, the world thus actualized would not be W′. On the other hand, if God *causes* Curley to go right with respect to A or *brings it about that* he

does so, then Curley isn't free with respect to A; and so once more it isn't W′ that is actual. Accordingly God cannot create W′. But W′ was just any of the worlds in which Curley is significantly free but always does only what is right. It therefore follows that it was not within God's power to create a world in which Curley produces moral good but no moral evil. Every world God can actualize is such that if Curley is significantly free in it, he takes at least one wrong action.

Obviously Curley is in serious trouble. I shall call the malady from which he suffers *transworld depravity*. (I leave as homework the problem of comparing transworld depravity with what Calvinists call "total depravity.") By way of explicit definition:

(33) A person P suffers from transworld depravity if and only if the following holds: for every world W such that P is significantly free in W and P does only what is right in W, there is an action A and a maximal world segment S′ such that

(1) S′ includes A's being morally significant for P

(2) S′ includes P's being free with respect to A

(3) S′ is included in W and includes neither P's performing A nor P's refraining from performing A and

(4) If S′ were actual, P would go wrong with respect to A.

(In thinking about this definition, remember that (4) is to be true in fact, in the actual world — not in that world W.)

What is important about the idea of transworld depravity is that if a person suffers from it, then it wasn't within God's power to actualize any world in which that person is significantly free but does no wrong — that is, a world in which he produces moral good but no moral evil.

We have been considering a crucial contention of the Free Will Defender: the contention, namely, that

(30) God is omnipotent, and it was not within His power to create a world containing moral good but no moral evil.

---

8. A person goes wrong with respect to an action if he either wrongfully performs it or wrongfully fails to perform it.

How is transworld depravity relevant to this? As follows. Obviously it is possible that there be persons who suffer from transworld depravity. More generally, it is possible that *everybody* suffers from it. And if this possibility were actual, then God, though omnipotent, could not have created any of the possible worlds containing just the persons who do in fact exist, and containing moral good but no moral evil. For to do so He'd have to create persons who were significantly free (otherwise there would be no moral good) but suffered from transworld depravity. Such persons go wrong with respect to at least one action in any world God could have actualized and in which they are free with respect to morally significant actions; so the price for creating a world in which they produce moral good is creating one in which they also produce moral evil.

CHAPTER 45

A Soul Making Theodicy

John Hick

Can a world in which sadistic cruelty often has its way, in which selfish lovelessness is so rife, in which there are debilitating diseases, crippling accidents, bodily and mental decay, insanity, and all manner of natural disasters be regarded as the expression of infinite creative goodness? Certainly all this could never by itself lead anyone to believe in the existence of a limitlessly powerful God. And yet even in such a world, innumerable men and women have believed and do believe in the reality of an infinite creative goodness, which they call God. The theodicy project starts at this point — with an already operating belief in God, embodied in human living — and attempts to show that this belief is not rendered irrational by the fact of evil. It attempts to explain how the universe, assumed to be created and ultimately ruled by a limitlessly good and limitlessly powerful Being, is as it is, including all the pain, suffering, wickedness, and folly that we find around us and within us. The theodicy project is thus an exercise in metaphysical thinking, in the sense that it consists in the formation and criticism of large-scale hypotheses concerning the nature and process of the universe.

Since a theodicy both starts from and tests belief in the reality of God, it naturally takes different forms in relation to different concepts of God. In this paper I shall be discussing the project of a specifically Christian theodicy; I shall not be attempting the further and even more difficult work of comparative theodicy, leading in turn to the question of a global theodicy.

The two main demands upon a theodicy hypothesis are that it be (1) internally coherent, and (2) consistent with the data both of the religious tradition on which it is based, and of the world, in respect both of

the latter's general character as revealed by scientific enquiry and of the specific facts of moral and natural evil. These two criteria demand, respectively, possibility and plausibility.

Traditionally, Christian theology has centered upon the concept of God as both limitlessly powerful and limitlessly good and loving; this concept of deity gives rise to the problem of evil as a threat to theistic faith. The threat was definitively expressed in Stendhal's bombshell, "The only excuse for God is that he does not exist!" The theodicy project is the attempt to offer a different view of the universe that is both possible and plausible and which does not ignite Stendhal's bombshell.

Christian thought has always included a certain range of variety, and in the area of theodicy it offers two broad types of approach. The Augustinian approach, representing until fairly recently the majority report of the Christian mind, hinges upon the idea of the fall as the origin of moral evil, which has in turn brought about the almost universal carnage of nature. The Irenaean approach, representing in the past a minority report, hinges upon the creation of humankind through the evolutionary process as an immature creature living in a challenging and therefore person-making world. I shall indicate very briefly why I do not find the first type of theodicy satisfactory, and then spend the remainder of this paper exploring the second type.

In recent years the free-will defense has dominated the philosophical discussion of the problem of evil. Alvin Plantinga and a number of other Christian philosophers have made a major effort to show that it is logically *possible* that a limitlessly powerful and limitlessly good God is responsible for the existence of this world and that all evil may ultimately result from misuses of creaturely freedom. But, they add, it may nevertheless be better for God to have created free than unfree beings; and it is logically possible that any and all free beings whom God might create would, as a matter of contingent fact, misuse their freedom by falling into sin. In that case it would be logically *impossible* for God to have created a world containing free beings and yet not containing sin and the suffering that sin brings with it. Thus it is logically possible, despite the fact of evil, that the existing universe is the work of a limitlessly good creator.

These writers are in effect arguing that the traditional Augustinian type of theodicy, based upon the fall from grace of free finite creatures — first angels and then human beings — and a consequent going wrong of the physical world, is not logically impossible. I am in fact doubtful whether their argument is sound, and I will return to the question later. But even if the Augustinian approach is sound, I suggest that their argument wins only a Pyrrhic victory, since the logical possibility that it would establish is one that, for very many people today, is fatally lacking in plausibility. Most educated inhabitants of the modern world regard the biblical story of Adam and Eve, and their temptation by the devil, as myth rather than as history; they believe further that far from having been created finitely perfect and then falling, humanity evolved out of lower forms of life, emerging in a morally, spiritually, and culturally primitive state. Further, they reject as incredible the idea that earthquake and flood, disease, decay, and death are consequences either of the human fall or of a prior fall of angelic beings who are now exerting an evil influence upon the earth. They see all this as part of a prescientific worldview, along with such stories as the world having been created in six days and of the sun standing still for twenty-four hours at Joshua's command. One cannot, strictly speaking, disprove any of these ancient biblical myths and sagas, or refute their elaboration in the medieval Christian picture of the universe. But people for whom the resulting theodicy, even if logically possible, is rad-

ically implausible, must look elsewhere for light on the problem of evil.

I believe that we find the light that we need in the main alternative strand of Christian thinking, which goes back to important constructive suggestions by the early Hellenistic Fathers of the church, particularly St. Irenaeus (120 – 202 A.D.). Irenaeus himself did not develop a theodicy, but he did together with other Greek-speaking Christian writers of that period, such as Clement of Alexandria, build a framework of thought within which a theodicy becomes possible that does not depend upon the idea of the fall, and which is consonant with modern knowledge concerning the origins of the human race. This theodicy cannot, as such, be attributed to Irenaeus. We should rather speak of a type of theodicy, presented in varying ways by different subsequent thinkers (the greatest of whom has been Friedrich Schleiermacher), of which Irenaeus can properly be regarded as the patron saint.

The central theme out of which this Irenaean type of theodicy has arisen is the two-stage conception of the creation of humankind, first in the "image" and then in the "likeness" of God. Re-expressing this concept in modern terms, the first stage was the gradual production of *homo sapiens,* through the long evolutionary process, as intelligent ethical and religious animals. The human being is one of the varied forms of earthly life and continuous as such with the whole realm of animal existence. But a human is uniquely intelligent, having evolved a large and immensely complex brain. Further, humans are ethical; that is, gregarious as well as intelligent animals, able to realize and respond to the complex demands of social life. They are also religious animals, with an innate tendency to experience the world in terms of the presence and activity of supernatural beings and powers. This portrayal, then, is early *homo sapiens,* the intelligent social animal capable of awareness of the divine. But early *homo sapiens* does not include the Adam and Eve of Augustinian theology, living in perfect harmony with self, with nature, and with God. On the contrary, the life of early *homo sapiens* must have been a constant struggle against a hostile environment, necessitating the capacity for savage violence against their fellow human beings, particularly outside their own immediate group. This being's concepts of the divine were primitive and often bloodthirsty. Existence "in the image of God" was thus a *potentiality* for knowledge of and relationship with one's Maker, rather than such knowledge and relationship as a fully realized state. In other words, people were created as spiritually and morally immature creatures, at the beginning of a long process of further growth and development, which constitutes the second stage of God's creative work.

In this second stage, of which we are a part, intelligent, ethical, and religious animals are being brought through their own free responses into what Irenaeus called the divine "likeness." Irenaeus's own terminology *(eikon, homoiosis; imago, similitude)* has no particular merit, based as it is on a misunderstanding of the Hebrew parallelism in Genesis 1:26, but his conception of a two-stage creation of humanity, with perfection lying in the future rather than in the past, is of fundamental importance.

The notion of the Fall was not basic to this picture, although it later became basic to the great drama of salvation depicted by St. Augustine and accepted within Western Christendom, including the churches stemming from the Reformation, until well into the nineteenth century. Irenaeus himself could not, however, in the historical knowledge of his time, question the fact of the Fall, though he treated it as a relatively minor lapse — a youthful error — rather than as the infinite crime and cosmic disaster that has ruined the whole creation. But today we can acknowledge that no evidence at all exists of a period in the distant past when humankind was in the ideal state of a fully realized "child of God." We can accept that, so far as actual events in time are concerned, a fall from an original righteousness and grace never occurred. If we want to continue to use the term "fall," because of its hallowed place in the Christian tradition, we must use it to refer to the immense gap between what we actually are and what in the divine intention we are eventually to become. But we must not blur our awareness that

the ideal state is not something already enjoyed and lost, but is a future and as-yet-unrealized goal. The reality is not a perfect creation that has gone tragically wrong, but a still continuing creative process whose completion lies in the eschaton.

Let us now try to formulate a contemporary version of the Irenaean type of theodicy, based on this suggestion of the initial creation of humankind, not as finitely perfect, but as an immature creature at the beginning of a long process of further growth and development. We may begin by asking why humanity should have been created as an imperfect and developing creature rather than as the perfect being whom God is intending to create. The answer, I think, consists in two considerations that converge in their practical implications, one concerned with our relationship to God and the other with our relationship to other human beings. As to the first, we could have the picture of God creating finite beings, whether angels or humans, directly in the divine presence, so that in being conscious of that which is other than oneself the creature is automatically conscious of God, the limitless reality and power, goodness and love, knowledge and wisdom, towering above oneself. In such a situation the disproportion between Creator and creatures would be so great that the latter would have no freedom in relation to God; they would indeed not exist as independent autonomous persons. For what freedom could finite beings have in an immediate consciousness of the presence of the one who has created them, who knows them through and through, who is limitlessly powerful as well as limitlessly loving and good, and who claims their total obedience? In order to be a person, exercising some measure of genuine freedom, the creature must be brought into existence, not in the immediate divine presence, but at a "distance" from God. This "distance" cannot of course be spatial, for God is omnipresent. The distance must be epistemic, a distance in the cognitive dimension. And the Irenaean hypothesis is that this "distance" consists, in the case of humans, in their existence within and as part of a world that functions as an autonomous system and from within which God is not overwhelmingly evident. The world exists, in Bonhoeffer's phrase, *etsi deus non daretur,* as if there were no God. Or rather, the world is religiously ambiguous, capable of being seen either as a purely natural phenomenon or as God's creation and experienced as mediating his presence. In such a world one can exist as a person over against the Creator. One has space to exist as a finite being, a space created by this epistemic distance from God and protected by one's basic cognitive freedom, one's freedom to open or close oneself to the dawning awareness of God that is experienced naturally by a religious animal. This Irenaean picture corresponds, I suggest, to our actual human situation. Emerging within the evolutionary process as part of the continuum of animal life, in a universe that functions in accordance with its own laws and whose workings can be investigated and described without reference to a creator, the human being has a genuine, even awesome, freedom in relation to one's Maker. We are free to acknowledge and worship God, and free — particularly since the emergence of individuality and the beginnings of critical consciousness during the first millennium B.C. — to doubt the reality of God.

Within such a situation the possibility enters of human beings coming freely to know and love their Maker. Indeed, if the end-state that God is seeking to bring about is one in which finite persons have come in their own freedom to know and love him, this condition requires their initial creation in a state which is not that of already knowing and loving him (or her). To create beings already in a state of having come into that state by their own free choices is logically impossible. The other consideration, which converges with this in pointing to something like the human situation as we experience it, concerns our human moral nature. We can approach it by asking why humans should not have been created at this epistemic distance from God, and yet at the same time as morally perfect beings. That persons could have been created morally perfect and yet free, so that they would always in fact choose rightly, has been argued by such critics of the free-will defense as Antony Flew and J. L. Mackie, and argued against by Alvin Plantinga and other upholders

of that theodicy. On the specific issue defined in the debate between them, it appears to me that the criticism of the free-will defense stands, that a perfectly good being, although formally free to sin, would in fact never do so. If we imagine such beings in a morally frictionless environment, involving no stresses or temptation, then we must assume that they would exemplify the ethical equivalent of Newton's first law of motion, which states that a moving body will continue in uniform motion until interfered with by some outside force. By analogy, perfectly good beings would continue in the same moral course forever, with nothing in the environment to throw them off it. And even if we suppose morally perfect beings to exist in an imperfect world, in which they are subject to temptations, it still follows that, in virtue of their moral perfection, they will always overcome those temptations — as in the case, according to orthodox Christian belief, of Jesus Christ. It is, to be sure, logically possible, as Plantinga and others argue, that a free being, simply as such, may at any time contingently decide to sin. However, a responsible free being does not act randomly, but on the basis of a moral nature, and a free being whose nature is wholly and unqualifiedly good will accordingly never in fact sin.

But if God could, without logical contradiction, have created humans as wholly good, free beings, why did God not do so? Why was humanity not initially created in possession of all the virtues, instead of having to acquire them through the long, hard struggle of life as we know it? The answer, I suggest, appeals to the principle that virtues that have been formed within the agent as a hard-won deposit of right decisions in situations of challenge and temptation are intrinsically more valuable than ready-made virtues created within her without any effort on her own part. This principle expresses a basic value judgment that cannot be established by argument but which one can only present, in the hope that it will be as morally plausible, and indeed compelling, to others as to oneself. It is, to repeat, the judgment that a moral goodness that exists as the agent's initial given nature, without ever having been chosen in the face of temptations to the contrary, is intrinsically less valuable than a moral goodness that has been built up over time through the agent's own responsible choices in the face of alternative possibilities.

If, then, God's purpose was to create finite persons embodying the most valuable kind of moral goodness, he (or she) would have to create them, not as already perfect beings but rather as imperfect creatures, who can then attain to the more valuable kind of goodness through their own free choices. In the course of their personal and social history new responses would prompt new insights, opening up new moral possibilities and providing a milieu in which the most valuable kind of moral nature can be developed.

We have thus far, then, the hypothesis that humanity is created at an epistemic distance from God in order to come freely to know and love their Maker; and that they are at the same time created as morally immature and imperfect beings in order to attain through freedom the most valuable quality of goodness. The end sought, according to this hypothesis, is the full realization of human potential in a spiritual and moral perfection within the divine kingdom. The question we have to ask is whether humans as we know them, and the world as we know it, fit the hypothesis.

Clearly we cannot expect to be able to deduce our actual world in its concrete character, and our actual human nature as part of it, from the general concept of spiritually and morally immature creatures developing ethically in an appropriate environment. No doubt an immense range of worlds is possible, any one of which, if actualized, would exemplify this concept. All that we can hope to do is to show that our actual world is one of these. And when we look at our human situation as part of the evolving life on this planet we can, I think, see that it fits this specification. As animal organisms, integral to the whole ecology of life, we are programmed for survival. In pursuit of survival, primitives not only killed other animals for food but fought other humans when their vital interests conflicted. The life of prehistoric persons must often have been a constant struggle to stay alive, prolonging an existence that was, in Hobbes's phrase, "poor, nasty, brutish and short." And in his basic animal self-regardingness, humankind was and is morally imperfect. In making this statement I am assuming that the essence of moral evil is selfishness, the sacrificing of others to one's own interests. It consists, in Kantian terminology, in treating others not as ends in themselves, but as means to one's own ends, as the survival instinct demands. Yet we are also capable of love, of self-giving in a common cause, of a conscience that responds to others in their needs and dangers. And with the development of civilization we see the growth of moral insight, the glimpsing and gradual assimilation of higher ideals, and tension between our animality and our ethical values. But that the human being has a lower as well as a higher nature, that one is an animal as well as a potential child of God, and that one's moral goodness is won through a struggle with innate selfishness, are inevitable given our continuity with the other forms of animal life. Further, the human animal is not responsible for having come into existence as an animal. The ultimate responsibility for humankind's existence, as a morally imperfect creature, can only rest with the Creator. We do not, in our degree of freedom and responsibility, choose our origin, but rather our destiny.

In brief outline, then, this line of thought is the Irenaean theodicy's answer to the question of the origin of moral evil: the general fact of humankind's basic self-regarding animality is an aspect of our creation as part of the realm of organic life, and this basic self-regardingness has been expressed over the centuries both in sins of individual selfishness and in the much more massive sins of corporate selfishness, institutionalized in slavery, exploitation, and all the many and complex forms of social injustice.

But nevertheless our sinful nature in an often harsh world is the matrix within which God is gradually creating children out of human animals. For as men and women freely respond to the claim of God upon their lives, transmuting their animal nature into that of children of God, the creation of humanity is taking place. In its concrete character this response consists in every form of moral goodness, from unselfish love in individual personal relationships to the dedicated and selfless striving to end exploitation and to create justice within and between societies.

But one cannot discuss moral evil without at the same time discussing the nonmoral evil of pain and suffering. (I propose to mean by "pain" physical pain, including the pains of hunger and thirst; and by "suffering" the mental and emotional pain of loneliness, anxiety, remorse, lack of love, fear, grief, envy, etc.) For what constitutes moral evil as evil is the fact that it causes pain and suffering. Conceiving of an instance of moral evil, or sin, that is not productive of pain or suffering to anyone at any time is impossible. But in addition to moral evil, another source of pain and suffering is present in the structure of the physical world, producing storms, earthquakes, and floods and afflicting the human body with diseases — cholera, epilepsy, cancer, malaria, arthritis, rickets, meningitis, AIDS, etc. — as well as with broken bones and other outcomes of physical accident. A great deal of both pain and suffering is humanly caused, not only by the inhumanity of man to man but also by the stresses of our individual and corporate lifestyles, causing many disorders — not only lung cancer and cirrhosis of the liver but many cases of heart disease, stomach and other ulcers, strokes, etc. But nevertheless, in the natural world itself, permanent causes of human pain and suffering remain. We have to ask why an unlimitedly good and unlimitedly powerful God should have created so dangerous a world, both in its purely natural hazards of earthquake and flood, for example, and in the liability of the human body to so many ills, both psychosomatic and purely somatic.

The answer offered by the Irenaean type of theodicy follows from and is indeed integrally bound up with its account of the origin of moral evil. We have the hypothesis of humankind being brought into being within the evolutionary process as a spiritually and morally immature creature, and then growing and developing through the exercise of freedom in this religiously ambiguous world. We can now ask what sort of a world would constitute an appropriate environment for this second stage of creation? The development of human personality — moral, spiritual, and intellectual — is a product of challenge and response that could not occur in a static situation demanding no exertion and no choices. So far as intellectual development is concerned, this well-established principle underlies the whole modern educational process, from preschool nurseries designed to provide a rich and stimulating environment to all forms of higher education designed to challenge the intellect. At a basic level the essential part played by the learner's own active response to environment was strikingly demonstrated by the Held and Heim experiment with kittens.[1] Of two littermate kittens in the same artificial environment, one was free to exercise its own freedom and intelligence in exploring the environment, while the other was suspended in a kind of gondola that moved whenever and wherever the free kitten moved. Thus, the second kitten had a similar succession of visual experiences as the first, but did not exert itself or make any choices in obtaining them. And whereas the first kitten learned in the normal way to conduct itself safely within its environment, the second did not. With no interaction with a challenging environment its capacities did not develop. I think we can safely say that the intellectual development of humanity has been due to interaction with an objective environment functioning in accordance with its own laws, an environment that we have to explore actively and cooperate with actively in order to escape its perils and exploit its benefits. In a world devoid both of dangers to be avoided and rewards to be won, we may assume that virtually no development of the human intellect and imagination would have taken place, and hence no development of the sciences, the arts, human civilization, or culture.

The presence of an objective world — within which

---

1. R. Held and A. Heim, "Movement-produced stimulation in the development of visually guided behavior," *Journal of Comparative and Physiological Psychology*, vol. 56 (1963), 872–876.

we have to learn to live on penalty of pain or death — is also basic to the development of our moral nature. For because the world is one in which men and women can suffer harm — by violence, disease, accident, starvation, etc. — our actions affecting one another have moral significance. A morally wrong act is, basically, one that harms some part of the human community, while a morally right action is, on the contrary, one that prevents or neutralizes harm or that preserves or increases human well-being.

We can imagine a paradise in which no one can ever come to any harm. Instead of having its own fixed structure, the world would be plastic to human wishes. Or perhaps the world would have a fixed structure, and hence the possibility of damage and pain, but a structure that is whenever necessary suspended or adjusted by special divine action to avoid human pain. Thus, for example, in such a miraculously pain-free world, one who falls accidentally off a high building would presumably float unharmed to the ground; bullets would become insubstantial when fired at a human body; poisons would cease to poison, water to drown, and so on. We can at least begin to imagine such a world. A good deal of the older discussion of the problem of evil — for example, in Part XI of Hume's *Dialogues Concerning Natural Religion* — assumed that it must be the intention of a limitlessly good and powerful Creator to make a pain-free environment for human creatures, so that the very existence of pain is evidence against the existence of God. But such an assumption overlooks the fact that a world in which there can be no pain or suffering would also be one without moral choices and hence no possibility of moral growth and development. For in a situation in which no one can ever suffer injury or be liable to pain or suffering, no distinction would exist between right and wrong action. No action would be morally wrong, because no action could ever have harmful consequences; likewise, no action would be morally right in contrast to wrong. Whatever the values of such a world, its structure would not serve the purpose of allowing its inhabitants to develop from self-regarding animality to self-giving love.

Thus, the hypothesis of a divine purpose in which finite persons are created at an epistemic distance from God, in order that they may gradually become children of God through their own moral and spiritual choices, requires that their environment, instead of being a pain-free and stress-free paradise, be broadly the kind of world of which we find ourselves to be a part, a world that provokes the theological problem of evil. Such a world requires an environment that offers challenges to be met, problems to be solved, and dangers to be faced, and which accordingly involves real possibilities of hardship, disaster, failure, defeat, and misery as well as of delight and happiness, success, triumph, and achievement. By grappling with the real problems of a real environment — in which a person is one form of life among many, and which is not designed to minister exclusively to our well-being — people can develop in intelligence and in such qualities as courage and determination. In relationships with one another, in the context of this struggle to survive and flourish, humans can develop the higher values of mutual love and care, self-sacrifice for others, and commitment to a common good.

However, this condition will not apply to the rest of the animal kingdom, whose members are not undergoing moral and spiritual development. From our human point of view the teeming multitude of lifeforms, each nourishing and nourished by others in a continuous recycling of life, constitutes the vast evolutionary process within which humanity has emerged; the fact that we are part of this ever-changing natural order is an aspect of our epistemic distance from God that we noted earlier. But if we ask why so many animals are carnivorous rather than vegetarian, killing and eating other species, no evident answer is available. We can note that the lower animals live almost entirely in the immediate present, unaware of their mortality, and without anxiety for the future or painful memories of the past — except, it would seem, for some individuals that have been in varying degrees adopted and domesticated by humans. But caution is in order. As the psychologists Eugene d'Aquili and Andrew Newberg say, "While it is difficult to determine with any certainty the emotions of animals, it seems that they must have some type of value response that tells them what to avoid and what to be drawn to. Whether these responses imply the emotions of fear and love as humans know them is, however, difficult to discern.... Suffice it to say that all animals must at least be able to derive an operational value from their experiences even if there is no emotional response similar in form to that of human beings."[2] Anthropomorphizing is easy here, and yet on the other hand it seems safer to risk erring on that side rather than the other; in any case the question mark about emotion does not lessen the immediately felt physical pain that takes place all the time. One can only say that pain is an aspect of the process of biological evolution as it has actually occurred, and is to us part of the same mysterious totality as earthquakes, volcanic eruptions, storms, hurricanes, and tidal waves. The very fact that it is mysterious may, however, itself have value. We shall come presently to the positive role of mystery, according to the Irenaean theodicy.

To summarize thus far:

1. The divine intention in relation to humankind, according to our hypothesis, is to create perfect finite personal beings in filial relationship with their Maker.

2. For humans to be created already in this perfect state is logically impossible, because in its spiritual aspect it involves coming freely to an uncoerced consciousness of God from a situation of epistemic distance, and in its moral aspect, freely choosing the good.

3. Accordingly, the human being was initially created through the evolutionary process, as a spiritually and morally immature creature, and as part of a religiously ambiguous and ethically demanding world.

4. Thus, that one is morally imperfect (i.e., that there is moral evil), and that the world is a challenging

and even dangerous environment (i.e., that there is natural evil), are necessary aspects of the present stage of the process through which God is gradually creating perfected finite persons.

In terms of this hypothesis, as we have developed it thus far, then, both the basic moral evil in the human heart and the natural evils of the world are compatible with the existence of a Creator who is unlimited in both goodness and power. But is the hypothesis plausible as well as possible? The principal threat to its plausibility comes, I think, from the sheer amount and intensity of both moral and natural evil. One can readily accept the principle that in order to arrive at a freely chosen goodness one must start out in a state of moral immaturity and imperfection. But are the depths of demonic malice and cruelty that each generation has experienced necessary, such as we have seen above all in the twentieth century in the Nazi attempt to exterminate the Jewish population of Europe? Can any future fulfillment be worth such horrors? Consider Dostoyevsky's haunting question: "Imagine that you are creating a fabric of human destiny with the object of making men happy in the end, giving them peace and rest at last, but that it was essential and inevitable to torture to death only one tiny creature — that baby beating its breast with its fist, for instance — and to found that edifice on its unavenged tears, would you consent to be the architect on those conditions?[3] The theistic answer is one that may be true but which takes so large a view that it baffles the imagination. Intellectually one may be able to see, but emotionally one cannot be expected to feel, its truth; and in that sense it cannot satisfy us. For the theistic answer is that if we take with full seriousness the value of human freedom and responsibility, as essential to the eventual creation of perfected children of God, then we cannot consistently want God to revoke that freedom when its wrong exercise becomes intolerable to us. From our vantage point within the historical

---

2. Eugene d'Aquili and Andrew Newberg, *The Mystical Mind: Probing the Biology of Mystical Experience* (Minneapolis: Fortress Press, 1999), 56–57.

3. Fyodor Dostoyevsky, *The Brothers Karamazov*, trans. Constance Garnett (New York: Modern Library, n.d.), bk. V, chap. 4, 254.

process, we may indeed cry out to God to revoke his gift of freedom, or to overrule it by some secret or open intervention. Such a cry must have come from millions caught in the Jewish Holocaust, and in the more recent laying waste of Korea, Vietnam, Rwanda, and Kosovo, and from the victims of racism in many parts of the world. And the thought that humankind's moral freedom is indivisible and can lead eventually to a consummation of limitless value which could never be attained without that freedom, and which is worth any finite suffering in the course of its creation, can be of no comfort to those who are now in the midst of that suffering. But while fully acknowledging this, I nevertheless want to insist that this eschatological answer may well be true. Expressed in religious language it tells us to trust in God even in the midst of deep suffering, for in the end we shall participate in the divine kingdom.

Again, we may grant that a world that is to be a person-making environment cannot be a pain-free paradise but must contain challenges and dangers, with real possibilities of many kinds of accident and disaster, and the pain and suffering which they bring. But need it contain the worst forms of disease and catastrophe? And need misfortune fall upon us with such heartbreaking indiscriminateness? Once again some answers may well be true, but truth in this area may nevertheless offer little in the way of pastoral balm.

We can see that a pain-free paradise would not constitute a person-making environment. But we cannot profess to see that the world's actual pains are just the amount needed and no more. However, at this point we meet the paradox that if we *could* see that, then the world would no longer serve a person-making purpose! For if we were right earlier in concluding that such a purpose requires a religiously ambiguous world, in which God is not evident, then God's purpose for the world must not be evident within it. That the world is as it is must be to us a mystery which, according to the Irenaean theodicy, is itself an essential aspect of its person-making character.

But one of the most daunting and even terrifying features of the world is that calamity strikes indiscriminately. In the incidence of disease, accident, disaster, and tragedy, no justice can be found. The righteous as well as the unrighteous are alike struck down by illness and afflicted by misfortune. There is no security in goodness, for the good are as likely as the wicked to suffer "the slings and arrows of outrageous fortune." From the time of Job this fact has set a glaring question mark against the goodness of God. But let us suppose that things were otherwise. Let us suppose that misfortune came upon humankind, not haphazardly and therefore unjustly, but justly and therefore not haphazardly. Let us suppose that, instead of coming without regard to moral considerations, misfortune was proportioned to desert, so that the sinner was punished and the virtuous rewarded. Would such a dispensation serve a person-making purpose? Surely not. For wrong deeds would obviously bring disaster upon the agent while good deeds would bring health and prosperity. In such a world truly moral action, action done because it is right, would be impossible. The fact that natural evil is not morally directed, but is a hazard that comes by chance, is thus an intrinsic feature of a person-making world.

In other words, the very mystery of natural evil, the very fact that disasters afflict human beings in contingent, undirected and haphazard ways, is itself a necessary feature of a world that calls forth mutual aid and builds up mutual caring and love. Thus on the one hand to say that God sends misfortune upon individuals, so that their death, maiming, starvation, or ruin is God's will for them would be completely wrong. But on the other hand God has set us in a world containing unpredictable contingencies and dangers — in which unexpected and undeserved calamities may occur to anyone — because only in such a world can mutual caring and love be elicited. As an abstract philosophical hypothesis, this may offer little comfort. But translated into religious language it tells us that God's good purpose enfolds the entire process of this world, with all its good and bad contingencies, and that even amidst tragic calamity and suffering we are still within the sphere of God's love and are moving towards the divine kingdom.

But there is one further all-important aspect of the Irenaean type of theodicy, without which all the foregoing would lose its plausibility. This is the eschatological aspect. Our hypothesis depicts persons as still in the course of creation towards an end-state of perfected personal community in the divine kingdom. This end-state is conceived of as one in which individual egoity has been transcended in communal unity before God. In the present phase of that creative process the naturally self-centered human animal has the opportunity freely to respond to God's noncoercive self-disclosures, through the work of prophets and saints, through the resulting religious traditions, and through the individual's religious experience. Such response always has an ethical aspect; the growing awareness of God is at the same time a growing awareness of the moral claim that God's presence makes upon the way in which we live.

This person-making process, leading eventually to perfect human community, is obviously not completed on this earth. It is not completed in the life of the individual — or at best only in the few who have attained sanctification, or *moksha,* or nirvana on this earth. Clearly the enormous majority of men and women die without reaching such levels. As Eric Fromm has said, "The tragedy in the life of most of us is that we die before we are fully born."[4] Therefore if we are ever to reach the full realization of the potentialities of our human nature, this fulfillment can only come in a continuation of our lives in another sphere of existence after bodily death. The perfect all-embracing human community, in which self-regarding concern has been transcended in mutual love, not only has evidently not been realized in this world, but never can be, since hundreds of generations of human beings have already lived and died and accordingly could not be part of any ideal community established at some future moment of earthly history. Thus if the unity of humankind in God's presence is ever to be realized it will have to be in some sphere of existence other than our earth. In short, the fulfillment of the divine purpose, as it is postulated in the Irenaean type of theodicy, presupposes each person's survival, in some form, of bodily death, and further living and growing towards that end-state. Without such an eschatological fulfillment, this theodicy would collapse.

A theodicy that presupposes and requires an eschatology will thereby be rendered implausible in the minds of many people today. The belief, however, in the reality of a limitlessly loving and powerful deity must incorporate some kind of eschatology according to which God holds in being the creatures whom he has made for fellowship with God, beyond bodily death, and brings them into the eternal fellowship that he has intended for them.[5] I have tried elsewhere to argue that such an eschatology is a necessary corollary

---

4. Eric Fromm, "Values, Psychology, and Human Existence," in *New Knowledge of Human Values,* ed. A. H. Maslow (New York: Harper, 1959), 156.

5. At this point I strongly agree with Marilyn Adams's insistence on the eschatological dimension of Christian theodicy when she argues that "the good of beatific, face-to-face intimacy with God is simply incommensurable with any merely non-transcendent goods or ills a person might experience. Thus, the good of face-to-face intimacy with God would *engulf* ... even the horrendous evils humans experience in this present life here below." ("Horrendous Evils and the Goodness of God" in Marilyn and Robert Adams, eds., *The Problem of Evil* [Oxford University Press, 1990], 218). I cannot, however, see her contention (in "Redemptive Suffering: A Christian Solution to the Problem of Evil" in Robert Audi and William Wainwright, eds., *Rationality, Religious Belief, and Moral Commitment,* [Ithaca, N.Y., and London: Cornell University Press, 1986]) that God is effectively dealing with the problem of evil in the cru-

cifixion of Jesus, by revealing God's love in becoming incarnate to suffer with us, as more than a valid insight within Christian pastoral theology. For those who accept her Christian premises, her vision can indeed be supportive, consoling, and potentially redemptive, and may be used with good effect in the pastoral work of the church. But if God is the God of the whole human race, and not only of its Christian minority, and indeed of those members of this minority who are wholeheartedly committed to the traditional belief-system, then God has not done enough to reconcile his human children to himself among the present realities of pain and suffering. For only that minority regard Jesus as God incarnate, and only for them can his martyrdom have the significance which Adams depicts. However, it is worth adding, that there could be a much broader, global, use of her insight into the redemptive power of a nonviolence which is willing to suffer, that does not require her exclusively Christian presuppositions.

of ethical monotheism; to argue for the realistic possibility of an after-life or lives, despite the philosophical and empirical arguments against this; and even to spell out some of the general features that human life after death may possibly have.[6] Since this task is very large, far exceeding the bounds of this paper, I shall not attempt to repeat it here but must refer the reader to my existing discussion of it. That extended discussion constitutes my answer to the question of whether an Irenaean theodicy, with its eschatology, is not as implausible as an Augustinian theodicy, with its human or angelic fall. (If the Irenaean theodicy is implausible, then the latter is doubly implausible; for it also involves an eschatology!)

One particular aspect of eschatology, however, must receive some treatment here, however brief and inadequate: the issue of "universal salvation" versus "heaven and hell" (or perhaps "annihilation" instead of "hell"). If the justification of evil within the creative process lies in the limitless and eternal good of the end-state to which it leads, then the completeness of the justification must depend upon the completeness, or universality, of the salvation achieved. Only if it includes the entire human race can it justify the sins and sufferings of the entire human race throughout all history. But, having given us cognitive freedom, which in turn makes moral freedom possible, can the Creator bring it about that in the end all will freely turn to him in love and trust? The issue is very difficult, but I believe that reconciling a full affirmation of human freedom with a belief in the ultimate universal success of God's creative work is in fact possible. We have to accept that creaturely freedom always occurs within the limits of a basic nature that we did not ourselves choose, as is entailed by the fact of having been created. If a real though limited freedom does not preclude our being endowed with a certain nature, it also does not preclude our being endowed with a basic Godward bias, so that, quoting from another side of St. Augustine's thought, "our hearts are restless until they find their rest in Thee."[7] If Augustine is correct, sooner or later, in our own time and in our own way, we shall all freely come to God; and universal salvation can be affirmed, not as a logical necessity but as the contingent but predictable outcome of the process of the universe, interpreted theistically. Once again, I have tried to present this argument more fully elsewhere, and to consider various objections to it.[8]

On this view the human, endowed with a real though limited freedom, is basically formed for relationship with God and destined ultimately to find the fulfillment of his or her nature in that relationship. This outlook does not seem to me excessively paradoxical. On the contrary, given the theistic postulate, this view seems to offer a very probable account of our human situation. If so, we can rejoice, for this situation gives meaning to our temporal existence as the long process through which we are being created, by our own free responses to life's mixture of good and evil, into "children of God" who "inherit eternal life."

6. John Hick, *Death and Eternal Life* (New York: Harper & Row, and London: Collins, 1976).

7. *The Confessions of St. Augustine*, trans. F. J. Sheed (New York: Sheed and Ward, 1942), bk. I, chaps. 1, 3.

8. Hick, *Death and Eternal Life*, chap. 13.

CHAPTER 46

Evil, Suffering, and Calvary

Peter Kreeft

"Not only do we only know God through Jesus Christ, but we only know ourselves through Jesus Christ; we only know life and death through Jesus Christ. Apart from Jesus Christ we cannot know the meaning of our life or our death, of God or of ourselves." Pascal

We Have Finally Come Home

This is the most important chapter in this book, for it is the answer, the only adequate answer, to our problem of man's suffering and God's silence. We are finally led not to the answer but to the Answerer. As in Job, God ends his silence and speaks his word. Christ is the Word of God, the answer of God. All the words of the prophets, philosophers, and poets are echoes of this Word. In him all the clues converge, like many pointing fingers, all pointing from different directions and distances to the same one.

The answer must be someone, not just something. For the problem (suffering) is about someone (God — why does he ... why doesn't he ...?) rather than just something. To question God's goodness is not just an intellectual experiment. It is rebellion or tears. It is a little child with tears in its eyes looking up at Daddy and weeping, "Why?" This is not merely the philosophers' "why?" Not only does it add the emotion of tears but also it is asked in the context of relationship. It is a question put to the Father, not a question asked in a vacuum.

The hurt child needs not so much explanations as reassurances. And that is what we get: the reassurance of the Father in the person of Jesus, "he who has seen me has seen the Father" (Jn 14:9).

The answer is not just a word but the Word; not an idea but a person. Clues are abstract, persons are concrete. Clues are signs; they signify something beyond themselves, something real. Our solution cannot be a mere idea, however true, profound, or useful, because that would be only another sign, another finger, another clue — like fingers pointing to other fingers, like having faith in faith, or hope in hope, or being in love with love. A hall of mirrors.

Besides being here, he is now. Besides being concretely real in our world, he, our answer, is also in our story, our history. Our story is also his-story. The answer is not a timeless truth but a once-for-all catastrophic event, as real as the stories in today's newspapers. God did not varnish over our sin and our suffering. He came into it, like a dentist or a surgeon, to get it all out. In fact, he became our garbage man. He touched and took away our garbage. God became a man; we touched him, we handled him. John the Evangelist begins his first letter in words that still tremble with awe at that fact:

> That which was from the beginning, which we have heard, which we have seen with our eyes, which we have looked upon and touched with our hands.... (1 Jn 1:1)

God's answer is simply the most incredible event in all of history. Eternity entered time. The mind of God, the word of life — timeless, eternal life — became as temporally alive, as jumpingly alive, as a lion.

We cannot help resisting the electric concreteness of this God: Men are reluctant to pass over from the notion of an abstract and negative deity to the living

God. I do not wonder. Here lies the deepest taproot of Pantheism and of the objection to traditional imagery. It was hated not, at bottom, because it pictured Him as man but because it pictured Him as king, or even as warrior. The Pantheist's God does nothing, demands nothing. He is there if you wish for Him, like a book on a shelf. He will not pursue you. There is no danger that at any time heaven and earth should flee away at His glance. If He were the truth, then we could really say that all the Christian images of kingship were a historical accident of which our religion ought to be cleansed. It is with a shock that we discover them to be indispensable. You have had a shock like that before, in connection with smaller matters — when the line pulls at your hand, when something breathes beside you in the darkness. So here; the shock comes at the precise moment when the thrill of *life* is communicated to us along the clue we have been following. It is always shocking to meet life where we thought we were alone. "Look out!" we cry, "it's *alive*." And therefore this is the very point at which so many draw back — I would have done so myself if I could — and proceed no further with Christianity. An "impersonal God" — well and good. A subjective God of beauty, truth and goodness, inside our own heads — better still. A formless life-force surging through us, a vast power which we can tap — best of all. But God Himself, alive, pulling at the other end of the cord, perhaps approaching at an infinite speed, the hunter, king, husband — that is quite another matter. There comes a moment when the children who have been playing at burglars hush suddenly: was that a *real* footstep in the hall? There comes a moment when people who have been dabbling in religion ("Man's search for God!") suddenly draw back. Supposing we really found Him? We never meant it to come to *that*! Worse still, supposing He had found us?

I hope the reader is not impatient with this long quotation. I think it is the greatest paragraph of the greatest Christian apologist of our century, C.S. Lewis, from his book *Miracles*. Only the paragraph at the end of his sermon "The Weight of Glory" rivals it.

The incarnation was the biggest shock in history. Even his own people, whom he had prepared for two thousand years for this event, could not digest it: "He came to his own home, and his own people received him not" (Jn 1:11). Even his own disciples could not understand him. It was the unthinkable, "the absolute paradox" (as Kierkegaard calls it) that the eternal God should have a beginning in time, that the maker of Mary's womb should be made in Mary's womb; that the first one became second, the independent one became dependent as a little baby, dependent for his very earthly existence — not on "the will of the flesh" but on the new Eve saying yes to the angel where the old Eve had said yes to the devil.

Even the devil did not expect this folly. That God should step right into Satan's trap, Satan's world, Satan's game, the jaws of death on the cross; that he should give Satan the opportunity to cherish forever, in dark, satanic glee, the terrible words from God to God, "My God, My God, why hast Thou forsaken Me?" — this was something "no eye has seen, nor ear heard, nor the heart of man conceived" (1 Cor 2:9). That God should take alienation away from man by inserting alienation into the very heart of God; that he should conquer evil by allowing it its supreme, unthinkable triumph, deicide, the introduction of death into the life of God, the God of life, the Immortal One; that he should destroy the power of evil by allowing it to destroy him — this is "the foolishness of God [that] is wiser than men, and the weakness of God [that] is stronger than men" (1 Cor 1:25).

Calvary is judo. The enemy's own power is used to defeat him. Satan's craftily orchestrated plot, rolled along according to plan by his agents Judas, Pilate, Herod, and Caiaphas, culminated in the death of God. And this very event, Satan's conclusion, was God's premise. Satan's end was God's means. It saved the world. Christians celebrate the greatest evil and the greatest tragedy of all time as Good Friday. In the symbolic language of Revelation, the meek little Lamb (*arnion*) defeats the great and terrible Beast (*therion*) in the last battle, the fight for the heavyweight championship of the universe, by shedding his own blood.

Satan's bloody plan became the means of his own despoilment. God won Satan's captives — us — back to himself by freely dying in our place.

It is, of course, the most familiar, the most often-told story in the world. Yet it is also the strangest, and it has never lost its strangeness, its awe, and will not even in eternity, where angels tremble to gaze at things we yawn at. And however strange, it is the only key that fits the lock of our tortured lives and needs. We needed a surgeon, and he came and reached into our wounds with bloody hands. He didn't give us a placebo or a pill or good advice. He gave us himself.

He came. He entered space and time and suffering. He came, like a lover. Love seeks above all intimacy, presence, togetherness. Not happiness. "Better unhappy with her than happy without her" — that is the word of a lover. He came. That is the salient fact, the towering truth, that alone keeps us from putting a bullet through our heads. He came. Job is satisfied even though the God who came gave him absolutely no answers at all to his thousand tortured questions. He did the most important thing and he gave the most important gift: himself. It is a lover's gift. Out of our tears, our waiting, our darkness, our agonized alone-ness, out of our weeping and wondering, out of our cry, "My God, my God, why hast Thou forsaken me?" he came, all the way, right into that cry.

In coming into our world he came also into our suffering. He sits beside us in the stalled car in the snowbank. Sometimes he starts the car for us, but even when he doesn't, he is there. That is the only thing that matters. Who cares about cars and success and miracles and long life when you have God sitting beside you? He sits beside us in the lowest places of our lives, like water. Are we broken? He is broken with us. Are we rejected? Do people despise us not for our evil but for our good, or attempted good? He was "despised and rejected of men." Do we weep? Is grief our familiar spirit, our horrifyingly familiar ghost? Do we ever say, "Oh, no, not again! I can't take any more!"? He was "a man of sorrows and acquainted with grief." Do people misunderstand us, turn away from us? They hid their faces from him as from an outcast, a leper. Is our love

betrayed? Are our tenderest relationships broken? He too loved and was betrayed by the ones he loved. "He came unto his own and his own received him not." Does it seem sometimes as if life has passed us by or cast us out, as if we are sinking into uselessness and oblivion? He sinks with us. He too is passed over by the world. His way of suffering love is rejected, his own followers often the most guilty of all; they have made his name a scandal, especially among his own chosen people. What Jew finds the road to him free from the broken weapons of bloody prejudice? We have made it nearly impossible for his own people to love him, to see him as he is, free from the smoke of battle and holocaust.

How does he look upon us now? With continual sorrow, but never with scorn. We add to his wounds. There are nineteen hundred nails in his cross. We, his beloved and longed for and passionately desired, are constantly cold and correct and distant to him. And still he keeps brooding over the world like a hen over an egg, like a mother who has had all of her beloved children turn against her. "Could a mother desert her young? Even so I could not desert you." He sits beside us not only in our sufferings but even in our sins. He does not turn his face from us, however much we turn our face from him. He endures our spiritual scabs and scars, our sneers and screams, our hatreds and haughtiness, just to be with us. Withness — that is the word of love.

Does he descend into all our hells? Yes. In the unforgettable line of Corrie ten Boom from the depths of a Nazi death camp, "No matter how deep our darkness, he is deeper still." Does he descend into violence? Yes, by suffering it and leaving us the solution that to this day only a few brave souls have dared to try, the most notable in this century not even a Christian but a Hindu. Does he descend into insanity? Yes, into that darkness too. Even into the insanity of suicide? Can he be there too? Yes, he can. "Even the darkness is not dark to him." He finds or makes light even there, in the darkness of the mind — perhaps not until the next world, until death's release.

For the darkest door of all has been shoved open

and light from beyond it has streamed into our world to light our way, since he has changed the meaning of death. It is not merely that he rose from the dead, but that he changed the meaning of death, and therefore also of all the little deaths, all the sufferings that anticipate death and make up parts of it. Death, like a cancer, seeps back into life. We lose little bits of life daily — our health, our strength, our youth, our hopes, our dreams, our friends, our children, our lives — all these dribble away like water through our desperate, shaking fingers. Nothing we can do, not our best efforts, holds our lives together. The only lives that don't spring leaks are the ones that are already all watery. The only hearts that do not break are the ones that are busily constructing little hells of loveless control, cocoons of safe, respectable selfishness to insulate themselves from the tidal wave of tears that comes sooner or later.

But he came into life and death, and he still comes. He is still here. "As you did it to one of the least of these my brethren, you did it to me" (Mt 25:40). He is here. He is in us and we are in him; we are his body. He is gassed in the ovens of Auschwitz. He is sneered at in Soweto. He is cut limb from limb in a thousand safe and legal death camps for the unborn strewn throughout our world, where he is too tiny for us to see or care about. He is the most forgotten soul in the world. He is the one we love to hate. He practices what he preaches: he turns his other cheek to our slaps. That is what love is, what love does, and what love receives.

Love is why he came. It's all love. The buzzing flies around the cross, the stroke of the Roman hammer as the nails tear into his screamingly soft flesh, the infinitely harder stroke of his own people's hammering hatred, hammering at his heart — why? For love. God is love, as the sun is fire and light, and he can no more stop loving than the sun can stop shining.

Henceforth, when we feel the hammers of life beating on our heads or on our hearts, we can know — we must know — that he is here with us, taking our blows. Every tear we shed becomes his tear. He may not yet wipe them away, but he makes them his. Would we rather have our own dry eyes, or his tear-filled ones?

He came. He is here. That is the salient fact. If he does not heal all our broken bones and loves and lives now, he comes into them and is broken, like bread, and we are nourished. And he shows us that we can henceforth use our very brokenness as nourishment for those we love. Since we are his body, we too are the bread that is broken for others. Our very failures help heal other lives; our very tears help wipe away tears; our being hated helps those we love. When those we love hang up on us, he keeps the lines open. His withness with us enables us to be with those who refuse to be with us.

Perhaps he is even in the sufferings of animals, if, as Scripture seems to say, we are somehow responsible for them and they suffer with us. He not only sees but suffers the fall of each sparrow.

All our sufferings are transformable into his work, our passion into his action. That is why he instituted prayer, says Pascal: to bestow on creatures the dignity of causality. We are really his body; the Church is Christ as my body is me. That is why Paul says his sufferings are making up in his own body what Christ has yet to endure in his body (Col 1:24).

Thus God's answer to the problem of suffering not only really happened 2,000 years ago, but it is still happening in our own lives. The solution to our suffering is our suffering! All our suffering can become part of his work, the greatest work ever done, the work of salvation, of helping to win for those we love eternal joy.

How? This can be done on one condition: that we believe. For faith is not just a mental choice within us; it is a transaction with him. "Behold, I stand at the door and knock; if anyone … opens the door, I will come in and eat with him" (Rev 3:20). To believe, according to John's Gospel, is to receive (Jn 1:12), to receive what God has already done. His part is finished ("It is finished," he said on the cross). Our part is to receive that work and let it work itself out in and through our lives, including our tears. We offer it up to him, and he really takes it and uses it in ways so powerful that we would be flattened with wonder if we knew them now.

You see, the Christian views suffering, as he views

everything, in a totally different way, a totally different context, than the unbeliever. He sees it and everything else as a *between,* as existing between God and himself, as a gift from God, an invitation from God, a challenge from God, something between God and himself. Everything is relativized. I do not relate to an object and keep God in the background somewhere; God is the object that I relate to. Everything is between us and God. Nature is no longer just nature, but creation, God's creation. Having children is pro-creation. My very I is his image, not my own but on loan.

What then is suffering to the Christian? It is Christ's invitation to us to follow him. Christ goes to the cross, and we are invited to follow to the same cross. Not because it is the cross, but because it is his. Suffering is blessed not because it is suffering but because it is his. Suffering is not the context that explains the cross; the cross is the context that explains suffering. The cross gives this new meaning to suffering; it is now not only between God and me but also between Father and Son. The first *between* is taken up into the Trinitarian exchanges of the second. Christ allows us to participate in his cross because that is his means of allowing us to participate in the exchanges of the Trinity, to share in the very inner life of God.

Freud says our two absolute needs are love and work. Both are now fulfilled by our greatest fear, suffering. Work, because our suffering now becomes *opus dei,* God's work, construction work on his kingdom. Love, because our suffering now becomes the work of love, the work of redemption, saving those we love.

True love, unlike popular sentimental substitutes, is willing to suffer. Love is not "luv." Love is the cross. Our problem at first, the sheer problem of suffering, was a cross without a Christ. We must never fall into the opposite and equal trap of a Christ without a cross.

Look at a crucifix. St. Bernard of Clairvaux says that whenever he does, Christ's five wounds appear to him as lips, speaking the words, "I love you."

In summary, Jesus did three things to solve the problem of suffering. First, he came. He suffered with us. He wept. Second, in becoming man he transformed the meaning of our suffering: it is now part of his work of redemption. Our death pangs become birth pangs for heaven, not only for ourselves but also for those we love. Third, he died and rose. Dying, he paid the price for sin and opened heaven to us; rising, he transformed death from a hole into a door, from an end into a beginning.

That third thing, now — resurrection. It makes more than all the difference in the world. Many condolences begin by saying something like this: "I know nothing can bring back your dear one again, but …" No matter what words follow, no matter what comforting psychology follows that "but," Christianity says something to the bereaved that makes all the rest trivial, something the bereaved longs infinitely more to hear: God can and will bring back your dear one again to life. There is resurrection.

What difference does it make? Simply the difference between infinite and eternal joy and infinite and eternal joylessness. Resurrection was so important to Christ's disciples that when Paul preached the good news in Athens, the inhabitants thought he was preaching two new gods, Jesus and resurrection (*anastasis*) (Acts 17). The same Paul said, "If Christ has not been raised, then our preaching is in vain and your faith is in vain.… If for this life only we have hoped in Christ, we are of all men most to be pitied" (1 Cor 15:14, 19).

Because of resurrection, when all our tears are over, we will, incredibly, look back at them and laugh, not in derision but in joy. We do a little of that even now, you know. After a great worry is lifted, a great problem solved, a great sickness healed, a great pain relieved, it all looks very different as past, to the eyes of retrospection, than it looked as future, as prospect, or as present, as experience. Remember St. Teresa's bold saying that from heaven the most miserable earthly life will look like one bad night in an inconvenient hotel!

If you find that hard to believe, too good to be true, know that even the atheist Ivan Karamazov understands that hope. He says,

I believe like a child that suffering will be healed

and made up for, that all the humiliating absurdity of human contradictions will vanish like a pitiful mirage, like the despicable fabrication of the impotent and infinitely small Euclidean mind of man, that in the world's finale, at the moment of eternal harmony, something so precious will come to pass that it will suffice for all hearts, for the comforting of all resentments, for the atonement of all the crimes of humanity, of all the blood that they've shed; that it will make it not only possible to forgive but to justify all that has happened.

Why then does Ivan remain an atheist? Because though he believes, he does not accept. He is not a doubter; he is a rebel. Like his own character the Grand Inquisitor, Ivan is angry at God for not being kinder. That is the deepest source of unbelief: not the intellect but the will.

The story I have retold in this chapter is the oldest and best known of stories. For it is the primal love story, the story we most love to tell. Tolkien says, "There is no tale ever told that men would rather find was true." It is suggested in the fairy tales, and it is why we find the fairy tales so strangely compelling. Kierkegaard retells it beautifully and profoundly in chapter two of *Philosophical Fragments*, in the story

of the king who loved and wooed the humble peasant maiden. It is told symbolically in the greatest of love poems, the Song of Songs, favorite book of the mystics. And the very loveliness of it is an argument for its truth. Indeed, how could this crazy idea, this crazy desire, ever have entered into the mind and heart of man? How could a creature without a digestive system learn to desire food? How could a creature without manhood desire a woman? How could a creature without a mind desire knowledge? And how could a creature with no capacity for God desire God?

Let's step back a bit. We began with the mystery, not just of suffering but of suffering in a world supposedly created by a loving God. How to get God off the hook? God's answer is Jesus. Jesus is not God off the hook but God on the hook. That's why the doctrine of the divinity of Christ is crucial: If that is not God there on the cross but only a good man, then God is not on the hook, on the cross, in our suffering. And if God is not on the hook, then God is not off the hook. How could he sit there in heaven and ignore our tears?

There is, as we saw, one good reason for not believing in God: evil. And God himself has answered this objection not in words but in deeds and in tears. Jesus is the tears of God.

CHAPTER 47

Horrendous Evil

Marilyn McCord Adams

1. Introduction

Over the past thirty years, analytic philosophers of religion have defined 'the problem of evil' in terms of the prima-facie difficulty in consistently maintaining

(1) God exists, and is omnipotent, omniscient, and perfectly good

and

(2) Evil exists.

In a crisp and classic article, 'Evil and Omnipotence',[1] J. L. Mackie emphasized that the problem is not that (1) and (2) are logically inconsistent by themselves, but that they together with quasi-logical rules formulating attribute-analyses — such as

(P1) A perfectly good being would always eliminate evil so far as it could,

and

(P2) There are *no limits* to what an omnipotent being can do — constitute an inconsistent premiss-set. He added, of course, that the inconsistency might be removed by substituting alternative and perhaps more subtle analyses, but cautioned that such replacements of (P1) and (P2) would save 'ordinary theism' from his charge of positive irrationality, only if true to its 'essential requirements'.[2]

In an earlier paper, 'Problems of Evil: More Advice to Christian Philosophers',[3] I underscored Mackie's point and took it a step further. In debates about whether the argument from evil can establish the irrationality of religious belief, care must be taken, both by the atheologians who deploy it and by the believers who defend against it, to ensure that the operative attribute-analyses accurately reflect that religion's understanding of divine power and goodness. It does the atheologian no good to argue for the falsity of Christianity on the ground that the existence of an omnipotent, omniscient, pleasure-maximizer is incompossible with a world such as ours, because Christians never believed God was a pleasure-maximizer anyway. But equally, the truth of Christianity would be inadequately defended by the observation that an omnipotent, omniscient egoist could have created a world with suffering creatures, because Christians insist that God loves other (created) persons than Himself. The extension of 'evil' in (2) is likewise important. Since Mackie and his successors are out to show that 'the several parts of the essential theological doctrine are inconsistent with *one another*',[4] they can accomplish their aim only if they circumscribe the extension of 'evil' as their religious opponents do. By the same token, it is not enough for Christian philosophers to explain how the power, knowledge, and goodness of God could coexist with some evils or other; a full account must exhibit the compossibility of divine perfection with evils in the amounts and of the kinds found in the actual world (and evaluated as such by Christian standards).

The moral of my earlier story might be summarized thus: where the internal coherence of a system

---

1. J. L. Mackie, 'Evil and Omnipotence', *Mind*, 64 (1955) . . . ; repr. in Nelson Pike (ed.), *God and Evil* (Englewood Cliffs, N.J.: Prentice-Hall, 1964), 46 – 60.

2. Ibid., 47.

3. Marilyn McCord Adams, 'Problems of Evil: More Advice to Christian Philosophers', *Faith and Philosophy* (Apr. 1988), 121 – 43.

4. Mackie, 'Evil and Omnipotence', pp. 46 – 47. (emphasis mine).

of religious beliefs is at stake, successful arguments for its inconsistency must draw on premises (explicitly or implicitly) internal to that system or obviously acceptable to its adherents; likewise for successful rebuttals or explanations of consistency. The thrust of my argument is to push both sides of the debate towards more detailed attention to and subtle understanding of the religious system in question.

As a Christian philosopher, I want to focus in this paper on the problem for the truth of Christianity raised by what I shall call 'horrendous' evils. Although our world is riddled with them, the biblical record punctuated by them, and one of them — namely, the passion of Christ; according to Christian belief, the judicial murder of God by the people of God — is memorialized by the Church on its most solemn holiday (Good Friday) and in its central sacrament (the Eucharist), the problem of horrendous evils is largely skirted by standard treatments for the good reason that they are intractable by them. After showing why, I will draw on other Christian materials to sketch ways of meeting this, the deepest of religious problems.

2. Defining the Category

For present purposes, I define 'horrendous evils' as 'evils the participation in (the doing or suffering of) which gives one reason prima facie to doubt whether one's life could (given their inclusion in it) be a great good to one on the whole'.[5] Such reasonable doubt arises because it is so difficult humanly to conceive how such evils could be overcome. Borrowing Chisholm's contrast between *balancing off* (which occurs when the opposing values of *mutually exclusive* parts of a whole partially or totally cancel each other out) and *defeat* (which cannot occur by the mere addition to the whole of a new part of opposing value, but involves some 'organic unity' among the values of parts and wholes, as when the positive aesthetic value of a whole painting defeats the ugliness of a small colour patch),[6] horrendous evils seem, prima facie, not only to balance off but to engulf the positive value of a participant's life. Nevertheless, that very horrendous proportion, by which they threaten to rob a person's life of positive meaning, cries out not only to be engulfed, but to be made meaningful through positive and decisive defeat.

I understand this criterion to be objective, but relative to individuals. The example of habitual complainers, who know how to make the worst of a good situation, shows individuals not to be incorrigible experts on what ills would defeat the positive value of their lives. Nevertheless, nature and experience endow people with different strengths; one bears easily what crushes another. And a major consideration in determining whether an individual's life is/has been a great good to him/her on the whole, is invariably and appropriately how it has seemed to him/her.[7]

I offer the following list of paradigmatic horrors: the rape of a woman and axing off of her arms, psychophysical torture whose ultimate goal is the disintegration of personality, betrayal of one's deepest loyalties, cannibalizing one's own offspring, child abuse of the sort described by Ivan Karamazov, child pornography, parental incest, slow death by starvation, participation in the Nazi death camps, the explosion of nuclear bombs over populated areas, having to choose which of one's children shall live and which be executed by terrorists, being the accidental and/or unwitting agent of the disfigurement or death of those one loves best. I regard these as *paradigmatic,* because I believe most people would find in the doing or suffering of them prima-facie reason to doubt the positive meaning of

---

5. Stewart Sutherland (in his comment 'Horrendous Evils and the Goodness of God — II', *Proceedings of the Aristotelian Society,* suppl. vol. 63 (1989), 311–23; esp. 311) takes my criterion to be somehow 'first-person'. This was not my intention. My definition may be made more explicit as follows: an evil *e* is horrendous if and only if participation in *e* by person *p* gives everyone prima-facie reason to doubt whether *p's* life can, given *p's* participation in *e,* be a great good to *p* on the whole.

6. Roderick M. Chisholm, 'The Defeat of Good and Evil', *Proceedings of the American Philosophical Association* 42 (1968–69), 21–38.

7. Cf. Malcolm's astonishment at Wittgenstein's dying exclamation that he had had a wonderful life, *Ludwig Wittgenstein: A Memoir* (London: Oxford University Press, 1962), 100.

their lives.[8] Christian belief counts the crucifixion of Christ another: on the one hand, death by crucifixion seemed to defeat Jesus' Messianic vocation; for according to Jewish law, death by hanging from a tree made its victim ritually accursed, definitively excluded from the compass of God's people, *a fortiori* disqualified from being the Messiah. On the other hand, it represented the defeat of its perpetrators' leadership vocations, as those who were to prepare the people of God for the Messiah's coming, killed and ritually accursed the true Messiah, according to later theological understanding, God Himself.

3. The Impotence of Standard Solutions

For better and worse, the by now standard strategies for 'solving' the problem of evil are powerless in the face of horrendous evils.

3.1. Seeking the Reason-Why

In his model article 'Hume on Evil',[9] Pike takes up Mackie's challenge, arguing that (P1) fails to reflect ordinary moral intuitions (more to the point, I would add, Christian beliefs), and traces the abiding sense of trouble to the hunch that an omnipotent, omniscient being could have no reason compatible with perfect goodness for permitting (bringing about) evils, because all legitimate excuses arise from ignorance or weakness. Solutions to the problem of evil have thus been sought in the form of counter-examples to this latter claim, i.e., logically possible reasons-why

that would excuse even an omnipotent, omniscient God! The putative logically possible reasons offered have tended to be *generic* and *global*: generic in so far as some *general* reason is sought to cover all sorts of evils; global in so far as they seize upon some feature of the world as a whole. For example, philosophers have alleged that the desire to make a world with one of the following properties — 'the best of all possible worlds',[10] 'a world a more perfect than which is impossible', 'a world exhibiting a perfect balance of retributive justice',[11] 'a world with as favorable a balance of (created) moral good over moral evil as God can weakly actualize'[12] — would constitute a reason compatible with perfect goodness for God's creating a world with evils in the amounts and of the kinds found in the actual world. Moreover, such general reasons are presented as so powerful as to do away with any need to catalogue types of evils one by one, and examine God's reason for permitting each in particular. Plantinga explicitly hopes that the problem of horrendous evils can thus be solved without being squarely confronted.[13]

3.2. The Insufficiency of Global Defeat

A pair of distinctions is in order here: (i) between two dimensions of divine goodness in relation to creation — namely, 'producer of global goods' and 'goodness to' or 'love of individual created persons'; and (ii) between the overbalance/defeat of evil by good on the global scale, and the overbalance/defeat of evil by good within the context of an individual

---

8. Once again, more explicitly, most people would agree that a person *p*'s doing or suffering of them constitutes prima-facie reason to doubt whether *p*'s life can be, given such participation, a great good to *p* on the whole.

9. 'Hume on Evil', *Philosophical Review*, 72 (1963), 180–97 ...; reprinted in Pike (ed.), *God and Evil*, p. 88.

10. Following Leibniz, Pike draws on this feature as part of what I have called his Epistemic Defence ('Problems of Evil: More Advice to Christian Philosopher's, pp. 124–25).

11. Augustine, *On Free Choice of Will*, iii. 93–102, implies that there is a maximum value for created worlds, and a plurality of worlds that meet it. All of these contain rational free creatures; evils are foreseen but unintended side-effects of their creation. No matter

what they choose, however, God can order their choices into a maximally perfect universe by establishing an order of retributive justice.

12. Plantinga takes this line in numerous discussions, in the course of answering Mackie's objection to the Free Will Defence, that God should have made sinless free creatures. Plantinga insists that, given incompatibilist freedom in creatures, God cannot strongly actualize any world He wants. It is logically possible that a world with evils in the amounts and of the kinds found in this world is the best that He could do, Plantinga argues, given His aim of getting some moral goodness in the world.

13. Alvin Plantinga, 'Self-Profile', in James E. Tomberlin and Peter van Inwagen (eds.), *Profiles: Alvin Plantinga* (Dordrecht; Boston, Mass.; and Lancaster, Pa.: Reidel, 1985), 38.

person's life.[14] Correspondingly, we may separate two problems of evil parallel to the two sorts of goodness mentioned in (i).

In effect, generic and global approaches are directed to the first problem: they defend divine goodness along the first (global) dimension by suggesting logically possible strategies for the global defeat of evils. But establishing God's excellence as a producer of global goods does not automatically solve the second problem, especially in a world containing horrendous evils. For God cannot be said to be good or loving to any created persons the positive meaning of whose lives He allows to be engulfed in and/or defeated by evils — that is, individuals within whose lives horrendous evils remain undefeated. Yet, the only way unsupplemented global and generic approaches could have to explain the latter, would be by applying their general reasons-why to particular cases of horrendous suffering.

Unfortunately, such an exercise fails to give satisfaction. Suppose for the sake of argument that horrendous evil could be included in maximally perfect world orders; its being partially constitutive of such an order would assign it that generic and global positive meaning. But would knowledge of such a fact defeat for a mother the prima-facie reason provided by her cannibalism of her own infant to wish that she had never been born? Again, the aim of perfect retributive balance confers meaning on evils imposed. But would knowledge that the torturer was being tortured give the victim who broke down and turned traitor under pressure any more reason to think his/her life worth while? Would it not merely multiply reasons for the torturer to doubt that his/her life could turn out to be a good to him/her on the whole? Could the truck-driver who accidentally runs over his beloved child find consolation in the idea that this middle-known[15]

but unintended side-effect was part of the price God accepted for a world with the best balance of moral good over moral evil he could get?

Not only does the application to horrors of such generic and global reasons for divine permission of evils fail to solve the second problem of evil; it makes it worse by adding *generic prima-facie* reasons to doubt whether human life would be a great good to individual human beings in possible worlds where such divine motives were operative. For, taken in isolation and made to bear the weight of the whole explanation, such reasons-why draw a picture of divine indifference or even hostility to the human plight. Would the fact that God permitted horrors because they were constitutive means to His end of global perfection, or that He tolerated them because He could obtain that global end anyway, make the participant's life more tolerable, more worth living for him/her? Given radical human vulnerability to horrendous evils, the ease with which humans participate in them, whether as victim or perpetrator, would not the thought that God visits horrors on anyone who caused them, simply because he/she deserves it, provide one more reason to expect human life to be a nightmare?

Those willing to split the two problems of evil apart might adopt a divide-and-conquer strategy, by simply denying divine goodness along the second dimension. For example, many Christians do not believe that God will ensure an overwhelmingly good life to each and every person He creates. Some say the decisive defeat of evil with good is promised only within the lives of the obedient, who enter by the narrow gate. Some speculate that the elect may be few. Many recognize that the sufferings of this present life are as nothing compared to the hell of eternal torment, designed to defeat goodness with horrors within the lives of the damned.

---

14. I owe the second of these distinctions to a remark by Keith De Rose in our Fall 1987 seminar on the problem of evil at UCLA.

15. Middle knowledge, or knowledge of what is 'in between' the actual and the possible, is the sort of knowledge of what a free creature *would do* in every situation in which that creature could possibly find himself. Following Luis de Molina and Francisco Suarez, Alvin Plantinga ascribes such knowledge to God, prior in the order

of explanation to God's decision about which free creatures to actualize (in *The Nature of Necessity* [Oxford: Clarendon Press, 1974], pp. 164–93). Robert Merrihew Adams challenges this idea in his article 'Middle Knowledge and the Problem of Evil', *American Philosophical Quarterly*, 14 (1977); repr. in *The Virtue of Faith* (New York: Oxford University Press, 1987), 77–93.

Such a road can be consistently travelled only at the heavy toll of admitting that human life in worlds such as ours is a bad bet. Imagine (adapting Rawls's device) persons in a pre-original position, considering possible worlds containing managers of differing power, wisdom, and character, and subjects of varying fates. The question they are to answer about each world is whether they would willingly enter it as a human being, from behind a veil of ignorance as to which position they would occupy. Reason would, I submit, dictate a negative verdict for worlds whose omniscient and omnipotent manager permits ante-mortem horrors that remain undefeated within the context of the human participant's life; *a fortiori*, for worlds in which some or most humans suffer eternal torment.

3.3. Inaccessible Reasons

So far, I have argued that generic and global solutions are at best incomplete: however well their account of divine motivating reasons deals with the first problem of evil, the attempt to extend it to the second fails by making it worse. This verdict might seem prima facie tolerable to standard generic and global approaches and indicative of only a minor modification in their strategy: let the above-mentioned generic and global reasons cover divine permission of non-horrendous evils, and find other *reasons* compatible with perfect goodness *why* even an omnipotent, omniscient God would permit horrors.

In my judgement, such an approach is hopeless. As Plantinga[16] points out, where horrendous evils are concerned, not only do we not know God's *actual* reason for permitting them; we cannot even *conceive* of any plausible candidate sort of reason consistent with worthwhile lives for human participants in them.

4. The How of God's Victory

Up to now, my discussion has given the reader cause to wonder whose side I am on anyway. For I have insisted, with rebels like Ivan Karamazov and John Stuart Mill, on spotlighting the problem horrendous evils pose. Yet, I have signaled my preference for a version of Christianity that insists on both dimensions of divine goodness, and maintains not only (a) that God will be good enough to created persons to make human life a good bet, but also (b) that each created person will have a life that is a great good to him/her on the whole. My critique of standard approaches to the problem of evil thus seems to reinforce atheologian Mackie's verdict of 'positive irrationality' for such a religious position.

4.1. Whys Versus Hows

The inaccessibility of reasons-why seems especially decisive. For surely an all-wise and all-powerful God, who loved each created person enough (a) to defeat any experienced horrors within the context of the participant's life, and (b) to give each created person a life that is a great good to him/her on the whole, would not permit such persons to suffer horrors for no reason.[17] Does not our inability even to conceive of plausible candidate reasons suffice to make belief in such a God positively irrational in a world containing horrors? In my judgement, it does not.

To be sure, motivating reasons come in several varieties relative to our conceptual grasp: There are (i) reasons of the sort we can readily understand when we are informed of them (e.g., the mother who permits her child to undergo painful heart surgery because it is the only humanly possible way to save its life). Moreover, there are (ii) reasons we would be cognitively, emotionally, and spiritually equipped to grasp if only we had a larger memory or wider attention span (analogy: I may be able to memorize small town street plans; memorizing the road networks of the entire country is a task requiring more of the same, in the way that proving Gödel's theorem is not). Some generic and global approaches insinuate that divine permission of evils has motivating reasons of this sort. Finally, there are (iii) reasons that we are cogni-

---

16. Alvin Plantinga, 'Self-Profile', pp. 34–35.

17. This point was made by William Fitzpatrick in our Fall 1987 seminar on the problem of evil at UCLA.

tively, emotionally, and/or spiritually too immature to fathom (the way a two-year-old child is incapable of understanding its mother's reasons for permitting the surgery). I agree with Plantinga that our ignorance of divine reasons for permitting horrendous evils is not of types (i) or (ii), but of type (iii).

Nevertheless, if there are varieties of ignorance, there are also varieties of reassurance.[18] The two-year-old heart patient is convinced of its mother's love, not by her cognitively inaccessible reasons, but by her intimate care and presence through its painful experience. The story of Job suggests something similar is true with human participation in horrendous suffering: God does not give Job His reasons-why, and implies that Job isn't smart enough to grasp them; rather Job is lectured on the extent of divine power, and sees God's goodness face to face! Likewise, I suggest, to exhibit the logical compossibility of both dimensions of divine goodness with horrendous suffering, it is not necessary to find logically possible reasons *why* God might permit them. It is enough to show *how* God can be good enough to created persons despite their participation in horrors — by defeating them within the context of the individual's life and by giving that individual a life that is a great good to him/her on the whole.

4.2. What Sort of Valuables?

In my opinion, the reasonableness of Christianity can be maintained in the face of horrendous evils only by drawing on resources of religious value theory. For one way for God to be *good to* created persons is by relating them appropriately to relevant and great goods. But philosophical and religious theories differ importantly on what valuables they admit into their ontology. Some maintain that 'what you see is what you get', but nevertheless admit a wide range of valuables, from sensory pleasures, the beauty of nature

and cultural artefacts, the joys of creativity, to loving personal intimacy. Others posit a transcendent good (e.g., the Form of the Good in Platonism, or God, the Supremely Valuable Object, in Christianity). In the spirit of Ivan Karamazov, I am convinced that the depth of horrific evil cannot be accurately estimated without recognizing it to be incommensurate with any package of merely non-transcendent goods and so unable to be balanced off, much less defeated, thereby.

Where the internal coherence of Christianity is the issue, however, it is fair to appeal to its own store of valuables. From a Christian point of view, God is a being a greater than which cannot be conceived, a good incommensurate with both created goods and temporal evils. Likewise, the good of beatific, face-to-face intimacy with God is simply incommensurate with any merely non-transcendent goods or ills a person might experience. Thus, the good of beatific face-to-face intimacy with God would *engulf* (in a sense analogous to Chisholmian balancing off) even the horrendous evils humans experience in this present life here below, and overcome any prima-facie reasons the individual had to doubt whether his/her life would or could be worth living.

4.3. Personal Meaning, Horrors Defeated

Engulfing personal horrors within the context of the participant's life would vouchsafe to that individual a life that was a great good to him/her on the whole. I am still inclined to think it would guarantee that immeasurable divine goodness to any person thus benefited. But there is good theological reason for Christians to believe that God would go further, beyond engulfment to defeat. For it is the nature of persons to look for meaning, both in their lives and in the world. Divine respect for and commitment to created personhood would drive God to make all those sufferings which

---

18. Contrary to what Sutherland suggests ('Horrendous Evils', pp. 314 – 15), so far as the compossibility problem is concerned, I intend no illicit shift from reason to emotion. My point is that intimacy with a loving other is a good, participation in which can

defeat evils, and so provide everyone with reason to think a person's life can be a great good to him/her on the whole, despite his/her participation in evils.

threaten to destroy the positive meaning of a person's life meaningful through positive defeat.[19]

How could God do it? So far as I can see, only by integrating participation in horrendous evils into a person's relationship with God. Possible dimensions of integration are charted by Christian soteriology. I pause here to sketch three:[20] (i) First, because God in Christ participated in horrendous evil through His passion and death, human experience of horrors can be a means of *identifying* with Christ, either through *sympathetic* identification (in which each person suffers his/her own pains, but their similarity enables each to know what it is like for the other) or through *mystical* identification (in which the created person is supposed literally to experience a share of Christ's pain[21]). (ii) Julian of Norwich's description of heavenly welcome suggests the possible defeat of horrendous evil through divine gratitude. According to Julian, before the elect have a chance to thank God for all He has done for them, God will say, 'Thank you for all your suffering, the suffering of your youth.' She says that the creature's experience of divine gratitude will bring such full and unending joy as could not be merited by the whole sea of human pain and suffering throughout the ages.[22] (iii) A third idea identifies temporal suffering itself with a vision into the inner life of God, and can be developed several ways. Perhaps, contrary to medieval theology, God is not impassible, but rather has matched capacities for joy and for suffering. Perhaps, as the Heidelberg Catechism suggests, God responds to human sin and the sufferings of Christ with an agony beyond human conception.[23] Alternatively, the inner life of God may be, strictly speaking and in and of itself, beyond both joy and sorrow. But, just as (according to Rudolf Otto) humans experience divine presence now as *tremendum* (with deep dread and anxiety), now as *fascinans* (with ineffable attraction), so perhaps our deepest suffering as much as our highest joys may themselves be direct visions into the inner life of God, imperfect but somehow less obscure in proportion to their intensity. And if a face-to-face vision of God is a good for humans incommensurate with any non-transcendent goods or ills, so any vision of God (including horrendous suffering) would have a good aspect in so far as it is a vision of God (even if it has an evil aspect in so far as it is horrendous suffering). For the most part, horrors are not recognized as experiences of God (any more than the city slicker recognizes his visual image of a brown patch as a vision of Beulah the cow in the distance). But, Christian mysticism might claim, at least from the post-mortem perspective of the beatific vision, such sufferings will be seen for what they were, and retrospectively no one will wish away any intimate encounters with God from his/her life-history in this world. The created person's experience of the beatific vision together

19. Note, once again, contrary to what Sutherland suggests ('Horrendous Evils', pp. 321–23) 'horrendous evil *e* is defeated' entails *none* of the following propositions: '*e* was not horrendous', '*e* was not unjust', '*e* was not so bad after all'. Nor does my suggestion that even horrendous evils can be defeated by a great enough (because incommensurate and uncreated) good, in any way impugn the reliability of our moral intuitions about injustice, cold-bloodedness, or horror. The judgement that participation in *e* constitutes prima-facie reason to believe that *p*'s life is ruined, stands and remains a daunting measure of *e*'s horror.

20. In my paper 'Redemptive Suffering: A Christian Solution to the Problem of Evil', in Robert Audi and William J. Wainwright (eds.), *Rationality, Religious Belief, and Moral Commitment: New Essays in Philosophy of Religion* (Cornell University Press, 1986), 248–67, I sketch how horrendous suffering can be meaningful by being made a vehicle of divine redemption for victim, perpetrator, and onlooker, and thus an occasion of the victim's collaboration with God. In 'Separation and Reversal in Luke-Acts', in Thomas Morris (ed.), *Philosophy and the Christian Faith* (Notre Dame, Ind.: Notre Dame University Press, 1988), 92–117, I attempted to chart the redemptive plot-line whereby horrendous sufferings are made meaningful by being woven into the divine redemptive plot. My considered opinion is that such collaboration would be too strenuous for the human condition were it not to be supplemented by a more explicit and beatific divine intimacy.

21. For example, Julian of Norwich tells us that she prayed for and received the latter (*Revelations of Divine Love,* ch. 17). Mother Teresa of Calcutta seems to construe Matthew 25:31–46 to mean that the poorest and the least are Christ, and that their sufferings are Christ's (Malcolm Muggeridge, *Something Beautiful for God* (New York: Harper & Row, 1960), 72–75).

22. *Revelations of Divine Love*, ch. 14. I am grateful to Houston Smit for recognizing this scenario of Julian's as a case of Chisholmian defeat.

23. Cf. Plantinga, 'Self-Profile', p. 36.

with his/her knowledge that intimate divine presence stretched back over his/her ante-mortem life and reached down into the depths of his/her worst suffering, would provide retrospective comfort independent of comprehension of the reasons-why akin to the two-year-old's assurance of its mother's love. Taking this third approach, Christians would not need to commit themselves about what in any event we do not know: namely, whether we will (like the two-year-old) ever grow up enough to understand the reasons why God permits our participation in horrendous evils. For by contrast with the best of earthly mothers, such divine intimacy is an incommensurate good and would cancel out for the creature any need to know why.

5. Conclusion

The worst evils demand to be defeated by the best goods. Horrendous evils can be overcome only by the goodness of God. Relative to human nature, participation in horrendous evils and loving intimacy with God are alike disproportionate: for the former threatens to engulf the good in an individual human life with evil, while the latter guarantees the reverse engulfment of evil by good. Relative to one another, there is also disproportion, because the good that God *is*, and intimate relationship with Him, is incommensurate with created goods and evils alike. Because intimacy with God so outscales relations (good or bad) with any creatures, integration into the human person's relationship with God confers significant meaning and positive value even on horrendous suffering. This result coheres with basic Christian intuition: that the powers of darkness are stronger than humans, but they are no match for God!

Standard generic and global solutions have for the most part tried to operate within the territory common to believer and unbeliever, within the confines of religion-neutral value theory. Many discussions reflect the hope that substitute attribute-analyses, candidate reasons-why, and/or defeaters could issue out of values shared by believers and unbelievers alike. And some virtually make this a requirement on an adequate solution. Mackie knew better how to distinguish the many charges that may be levelled against religion. Just as philosophers may or may not find the existence of God plausible, so they may be variously attracted or repelled by Christian values of grace and redemptive sacrifice. But agreement on truth-value is not necessary to consensus on internal consistency. My contention has been that it is not only legitimate, but, given horrendous evils, necessary for Christians to dip into their richer store of valuables to exhibit the consistency of (1) and (2).[24] I would go one step further: assuming the pragmatic and/or moral (I would prefer to say, broadly speaking, religious) importance of believing that (one's own) human life is worth living, the ability of Christianity to exhibit how this could be so despite human vulnerability to horrendous evil, constitutes a pragmatic/moral/religious consideration in its favour, relative to value schemes that do not.

To me, the most troublesome weakness in what I have said lies in the area of conceptual under-development. The contention that God suffered in Christ or that one person can experience another's pain requires detailed analysis and articulation in metaphysics and philosophy of mind. I have shouldered some of this burden elsewhere,[25] but its full discharge is well beyond the scope of this paper.

---

24. I develop this point at some length in 'Problems of Evil: More Advice to Christian Philosophers', pp. 127–35.

25. For example in 'The Metaphysics of the Incarnation in Some Fourteenth Century Franciscans', in William A. Frank and Girard J. Etzkorn (eds.), *Essays Honoring Allan B. Wolter* (St. Bonaventure, N.Y.: The Franciscan Institute, 1985), 21–57. In the development of these ideas, I am indebted to the members of our Fall 1987 seminar on the problem of evil at UCLA — especially to Robert Merrihew Adams (its co-leader) and to Keith De Rose, William Fitzpatrick, and Houston Smit. I am also grateful to the Very Revd. Jon Hart Olson for many conversations in mystical theology.

QUESTIONS AND FURTHER READINGS

Questions for Discussion

1. How would you describe Augustine's theodicy in your own words? What is your assessment of it as a theodicy?

2. Could an Augustinian theodicy and an Irenaean theodicy be combined, or are they mutually exclusive? Explain.

3. How does Plantinga's defense of free will address the logical problem of evil? Explain in your own words.

4. The concept of free will is, of course, central to the free will defense. For the defense to be successful in the way Professor Plantinga intends, must it include a *libertarian* notion of free will? Why? How might a theistic compatibilist respond to evil?

5. According to the free will defense it is possible that it is not within God's power to create a world containing moral good without creating one containing moral evil. Does it follow from this that God is not omnipotent? Why or why not?

6. What do you take to be the most significant objection to the free will defense? All things considered, which is more plausible: the defense or this objection to it? Explain your answer.

7. Using Kreeft's and Lewis's arguments, what would you say to a person who experienced a tragic loss due to a cataclysmic event such as the death of a child, genocide, rape, or some natural disaster?

8. Explain the soul-making theodicy. What are some of its strengths? What are some of its weaknesses?

9. Explain the difference between moral evil and natural evil. Does Professor Hick's theodicy adequately address both kinds of evil?

10. Is the soul-making theodicy generally congruent with orthodox Christian doctrine? Are there tensions between them? Explain.

11. How does Hick's eschatological view of the universal salvation of humankind relate to his soul-making theodicy?

12. How does Professor Adams' approach to the problem of evil differ from other theistic approaches, such as the one offered by Alvin Plantinga in this section? Can the various approaches be integrated? Explain.

13. What are horrendous evils, and how do they differ from non-horrendous evils? What makes horrendous evils more problematic, in terms of a response to the problem of evil?

Further Readings

Adams, Marilyn McCord (2006). *Christ and Horrors: The Coherence of Christology*. Cambridge: Cambridge University Press. (Develops her position from a theological point of view.)

Adams, Marilyn McCord (1999). *Horrendous Evils and the Goodness of God*. Ithaca, NY: Cornell University Press. (Elaborates on the position defended in Adams and Adams, *The Problem of Evil*, cited below.)

Adams, Marilyn McCord, and Robert Merrihew Adams, eds. (1990). *The Problem of Evil*. Oxford: Oxford University Press. (A scholarly collection of essays from a variety of perspectives; the essay in this section was taken from this book.)

Davis, Stephen T., ed. (1981). *Encountering Evil: Live Options in Theodicy*. Atlanta: John Knox Press. (Six Christian philosophers and theologians respond to intellectual and moral questions raised by the reality of evil; the selection by John Hick is taken from this volume.)

Geivett, R. Douglas (1993). *Evil and the Evidence for God: The Challenge of John Hick's Theodicy*. Philadelphia: Temple University Press. (Compares the Irenaean and Augustinian traditions in theodicy and offers a critique of John Hick's soul-making theodicy.)

Hick, John (2007). *Evil and the God of Love*. 3rd ed. New York: HarperSanFrancisco. (A modern classic on the problem of evil.)

Mackie, J. L. (1955). "Evil and Omnipotence." *Mind* 64:200 – 12. (Probably the most widely influential formulation of the atheological argument from evil.)

Peterson, Michael L. (1998). *God and Evil: An Introduction to the Issues*. Boulder, CO: Westview. (An accessible introduction to the problem of evil; includes a chapter on theodicy.)

Plantinga, Alvin (1977). *God, Freedom, and Evil*. Grand Rapids: Eerdmans. (A classic work on the problem of evil as well as an interesting formulation of the ontological argument; the selection above was taken from this book.)

Rowe, William L. (1979). "The Problem of Evil and Some Varieties of Atheism." *American Philosophical Quarterly* 16:335 – 41. (Presents a widely discussed version of the evidential problem of evil.)

Swinburne, Richard (1998). *Providence and the Problem of Evil*. Oxford: Oxford University Press. (Argues that God allows evil because God desires more for us than pleasure or escape from pain; God wants us to learn, to love, and to develop the right kind of character.)

Van Inwagen, Peter (1991). "The Problem of Evil, the Problem of Air, and the Problem of Silence." *Philosophical Perspectives* 5:135 – 65. (Provides a response to the evidential problem of evil.)

PART 10

CHRISTIANITY AND SCIENCE

In some ways, Christianity and science have been at odds for centuries. Whether referring to Copernicus and Galileo, who appealed to astronomical evidence for understanding the movements of the starry heavens, or to Charles Darwin, who sought natural explanations for the development of living organisms, many thinkers have sought after a *logos* (rational account) for explaining phenomena in the natural world. Some have argued that a proper *logos* excludes "religious" explanations. Stephen J. Gould, for example, argued that religion and science are "non-overlapping magisteria," whereby they are noncompeting domains: science deals with matters of fact; religion deals with matters of value.

Of course, there are also those who are not happy with explaining natural phenomena in purely naturalistic terms. Christians, and theists in general, affirm that in some sense God is responsible for many events in the natural world. But there are differences of opinion about how God is involved in the world and what divine action actually entails. So how should we approach the relationship between science and Christian faith? Does science contradict Christianity? The Bible? Perhaps an even more fundamental question is which worldview is most reasonable to affirm given what we know about the world.

In the first selection, John Polkinghorne begins by noting that in the West the two prominent views historically have been materialism and theism, and that each of these has certain foundational commitments. He then argues that the fundamental materialist commitment that nature is all there is is incomplete. The laws of nature, as understood by modern physics, require a deeper level of intelligibility; they point beyond themselves to a transcendent reality — an orderer, a designer, a creator.

Del Ratzsch, in the second essay, begins with a thought experiment — one based on the television program *Star Trek*. Suppose the doctor of the crew discovers miniature, complex subunits inside a person on the starship. Suppose further that these entities are self-contained and self-sustaining, with the design patterns of an inboard motor. In such a case, we would infer a designer of them. In fact, when we peer into the structure of living organisms, like human beings, this is precisely what we do find in such examples as E. coli bacteria. So doesn't science (microbiology in this case) lead us to infer a grand designer? Some scientists, including Michel Behe, argue that it does. Others, including Richard Dawkins, come to the opposite conclusion — that natural science demonstrates the absence of design in nature. So who is right? And how are we to decide? Ratzsch argues that there is a tendency on one side to overestimate the power of natural science and on the other side to underestimate nature. For him, while scientists themselves should have the most say on the subject, the question is currently an open one.

In the final selection, Kurt Wise begins by noting that most of the scientific community has accepted macroevolution, whereby life has continually branched to produce new organisms through nonintelligent natural processes. There are important reasons why many scholars and scientists affirm this view. Nonetheless, that is not the only game in town. He then argues that an intelligent Designer provides a better explanation of the evidence than macroevolution and that the claims of Scripture offer a model that provides an explanation of life's major features that is superior to the claims of evolution.

CHAPTER 48

God and Physics

John Polkinghorne

Every worldview involves a commitment to a foundational belief, which is not itself to be explained but which will provide the basis on which all subsequent forms of explanation will ultimately have to rest. No worldview can be free from such an initial commitment, for nothing comes of nothing.

In Western thinking about the nature of reality there have been two particularly influential traditions: materialism and theism. They are both still very active today, and they differ in what they treat as their assumed foundation. The unexplained brute fact of the former is the existence of matter; for the latter, the existence of a divine Creator. Which is to be chosen depends upon how intellectually satisfying its brute-fact assumption is found to be.

My contention will be that the materialist starting point is unsatisfying. The laws of nature, as modern physics has discovered them to be, have a character which is not self-contained but rather seems to point beyond them to the need for a further and deeper level of intelligibility.

The Universe Points beyond Itself

The universe that science explores has proved to be profoundly rationally transparent to our inquiry and endowed with a deep rational beauty. It is scarcely surprising that we are able to make good sense of the world at the level of everyday experience.

Evolutionary processes may be expected to have shaped our brains so that we can cope with survival necessities. If we could not figure out that it is a bad idea to step off the top of a high cliff, then life could prove short. That is one thing, but it is quite another

thing when someone like Isaac Newton comes along and, in an astonishing creative leap of the human imagination, is able to see that the same force that makes the cliff dangerous is also the force that holds the moon in its orbit around the earth and the earth in its orbit around the sun, and, by discovering the mathematically beautiful universal inverse-square law of gravity, can explain the behavior of the whole solar system. That goes far beyond anything that we need for our survival or what might be considered to be a happy spinoff from such a necessity. As Sherlock Holmes once remarked to a shocked Dr. Watson, it did not matter at all for his daily work as a detective whether the earth went round the sun or the sun went round the earth!

The insights of modern science carry us far beyond the macroscopic realm of everyday events, downward into the microscopic realm of quantum physics and upward into the cosmic realm of curved space-time. Understanding these regimes remote from mundane experience calls for counterintuitive ways of thinking quite different from those of everyday, but physicists have proved equal to the challenge. Thus the universe has proved to be deeply intelligible and profoundly transparent to scientific inquiry. This is surely a significant fact about the world, too remarkable to be accepted simply as a happy accident or a brute fact. Albert Einstein once said that the only mystery of the universe is that it is comprehensible.

Things are more mysterious than that, for it has proved time and again that mathematics provides the key to unlock the secrets of the cosmos. It is an actual technique of discovery in fundamental physics to seek theories that are expressed in terms of beautiful equations.[1] This quest for mathematical beauty is no aesthetic indulgence on the part of the physicists; it has repeatedly proved to be the case that the theories found in this way establish their claim to be describing true aspects of nature by the long-term fruitfulness of explanation that they provide. Einstein used this kind of mathematical insight to guide his formulation of general relativity. Paul Dirac, one of the founding figures of quantum theory, made his many discoveries by a lifelong and highly successful quest for beautiful equations. His most celebrated discovery made in this way was the relativistic equation of the electron (engraved on his memorial tablet in Westminster Abbey). It immediately provided an unanticipated explanation of why the magnetic properties of the electron are twice as strong as classical physics would have led one to expect. Two years later it led to the discovery of the existence of antimatter.

When the abstract subject of mathematics leads to important physical discoveries in this way, something remarkable is happening. Why is it the case that some of the most beautiful patterns that the mathematicians can dream up in their minds are found actually to occur in the structure of the physical world around us? What links together the reason within (mathematical thinking) and the reason without (the laws of physics)? Dirac's brother-in-law Eugene Wigner, who himself won a Nobel Prize for physics, put the matter epigrammatically: "Why is mathematics so unreasonably effective?"

It would be intolerably intellectually lazy just to shrug one's shoulders and say, "That's just the way it is — and a bit of good luck for those who are good at math." Science has found that the universe is profoundly rationally transparent and beautiful. The feeling of wonder at the marvelous order of the world is a fundamental experience in physics and a fitting reward for all the labor involved in research. In a word, one could say that physics explores a universe that is shot through with signs of mind. Thus the laws of physics seem to point beyond themselves, calling for an explanation of why they have this rational character. It is intellectually unsatisfying simply to treat them as brute fact.

The deep intelligibility of the cosmos can itself be made intelligible if behind its marvelous order is indeed the mind of its Creator. The theist can say that science is possible precisely because the universe is a creation and scientists are creatures made in the image of their Creator, the God whose role is not simply to initiate the big bang but continuously to hold in being a world endowed with wonderful rational structure. Materialism just does not explain enough.

A Finely Tuned Universe

The laws of physics have been found to point beyond themselves in another way as a result of an increasing understanding of the history of the cosmos. The observable universe started 13.7 billion years ago in an extremely simple form — just an almost uniform expanding ball of energy. Now it is very rich and varied, the home of saints and scientists. Cosmologists understand many of the processes by which this fertile evolution has occurred, and they have found that they were only possible because the laws of physics — the given physical fabric of the world — took a very precise, "finely tuned" form. Carbon-based life can evolve only in a universe that has a remarkably specific character. While life did not appear on the cosmic scene until the universe was about ten billion years old, fine-tuning meant that the cosmos was pregnant with the potentiality for life essentially from the big bang onward.

Many considerations have led to this conclusion; it is possible here to give only an illustrative sample of them. Let us start with the formation of the chemical elements essential for life. The very early universe, for the first three minutes of its life, was a kind of cosmic hydrogen bomb, sufficiently hot for nuclear reac-

---

1. Mathematical beauty involves qualities such as economy and elegance. Like all forms of beauty, it is easier to recognize than to describe, but mathematicians can agree about its presence, so that it is an intersubjectively recognized property.

tions to be taking place everywhere. When expansion cooled it below the relevant temperature, these reactions ceased, having made only the two simplest elements, hydrogen and helium. They have too boring a chemistry to be able to produce anything as interesting as life. For that many more elements are needed, including especially carbon, which is essential for the formation of the long chain molecules that are the biochemical basis of life.

After about a billion years, when the first stars had condensed, nuclear reactions started up again, now confined to hot stellar cores. These are the sites where carbon was made; every atom of carbon in every living being was once inside a star. We are people of stardust, made of the ashes of dead stars. The processes by which the heavier elements are made form a beautiful and delicate chain of nuclear reactions — essentially successively compounding a-particles (helium nuclei) step by step to form the sequence beryllium, carbon, oxygen.

There is a problem about the second step, however, since beryllium is very unstable and in the ordinary way would not survive long enough to enable the next reaction (forming carbon) to take place. This process is possible only because there is a very large enhancement effect (resonance) at precisely the right energy to enable the addition of the next a-particle to take place anomalously rapidly, catching the beryllium before it disappears. If the laws of nuclear physics were a little different, this resonance would either not be there at all or it would be at the wrong energy.

This chain of reactions inside the star cannot get beyond iron, the most stable of the nuclear species. Thus two problems remain: to make the elements beyond iron — some of which, such as zinc and iodine, are needed for life — and to get the elements already made out of the star and into the environment where eventually they can form part of a life-bearing planet. It turns out that with the nuclear forces in the form that they actually take in our universe, both of these problems are solved by some stars exploding as supernovae.

Another essential condition for a life-bearing universe is that it should neither expand too rapidly, becoming too dilute for fertile processes to take place, nor expand too slowly so that gravity causes it to collapse long before life can evolve. Avoiding these twin disasters requires an extremely fine balance between expansive and gravitational effects in the very early universe. Almost all cosmologists believe that this balance was achieved in our universe by a speculative but very plausible process called inflation, a kind of extremely rapid "boiling" of space which over a very short period had the effect of producing the necessary balance. This is a natural process, but it requires that the laws of physics take a particular form to enable it (technically, that they incorporate certain scalar fields called inflatons).

We have already seen how getting the right sort of stars is essential for a life-bearing universe. The character of stars depends very sensitively on the balance between two of the basic forces of nature: electromagnetism and gravity. If that balance were different to only a tiny degree in one direction or another, all stars would be either blue giants or red dwarfs. The blue giants would be short-lived in comparison with the timescales relevant to the evolution of life, and in any case, it is thought that they would be unlikely to form planets. The red dwarfs would probably be too feeble to support life on an encircling planet, and in any case, they would never explode as supernovae, an event whose indispensability we have already noted.

One final example of fine-tuning must suffice. It has recently been discovered that the expansion of the universe is accelerating, an effect which is attributed to a somewhat mysterious entity: dark energy, associated with space itself. Quantum physics can suggest a possible source of this energy: the vacuum is the lowest energy state of the system, but it is not an empty state in which nothing is happening. (Heisenberg's uncertainty principle does not permit a totally quiescent state in which one would know both what is happening — nothing — and where it is — here.) Instead there are continuous vacuum fluctuations in which entities appear and disappear in restless activity. This generates a vacuum energy that fills space.

A reasonable estimate of the magnitude of this vacuum energy yields an enormously high figure; the observed dark energy is $10-1^{20}$ smaller than this estimate. Were it not fine-tuned to this astonishing degree, the universe would have either blown apart or collapsed (depending upon the sign of the energy) with an incredible rapidity which would totally have eliminated any possibility of life forming.

Physicists agree that our universe is characterized by a precise quantitative specificity which has been necessary for its being able to evolve carbon-based life. This specificity refers to the physical fabric of the cosmos, the given ground rules which are the prior basis for the possibility of any actual events. The collection of insights on which this conclusion rests has often been given the name of the anthropic principle — a somewhat unfortunate term; the carbon principle would have been a better choice, since it is the potentiality for carbon-based life in general, rather than *homo sapiens* in particular, which is involved.

Fine-tuning came as a surprise to all physicists and as a shock to some. The inclination of scientists is toward the general rather than the particular. The natural prior expectation was that our universe would be just a typical specimen of what a universe might be like, with nothing too special about it. Fine-tuning seemed a counter-Copernican insight: humans do not live at the center of the universe, but the cosmos has been found to be intrinsically structured in a way that permits human presence within it. Of course, if that had not been the case, we would not be here to be astonished at fine-tuning. Yet the collection of anthropic insights seems altogether too remarkable and precise to be treated as just a happy accident. It seems to point beyond the brute fact of physical law and require to be set in a context of deeper intelligibility. Two metascientific possibilities have been extensively discussed.

The Multiverse

For the theist, the universe is not just "any old world." It is a creation which has no doubt been endowed by its Creator with just the finely tuned laws and circumstances which have enabled it to have the fruitful history which is the expression of the divine purpose.

Disliking the threat of theism, some scientists have sought an alternative explanation of apparent fine-tuning. This is provided by the conjecture of the multiverse, a grossly extended form of naturalism which supposes that this universe is just one member of a vast portfolio of separate worlds, each with its own different laws and circumstances. If this collection is sufficiently large and varied, it might be that one of these universes is fine-tuned for carbon-based life, and that is ours because we are carbon-based life. Our fertile universe is then simply a random winning ticket in some great multiversal lottery.

Of course, if this explanation is to have any force, there must be some independent reason for believing in the existence of the multiverse. Otherwise, any remarkable feature whatsoever could be explained away by incorporating it in some arbitrary assembly, a significant needle concealed in a meaningless haystack. The collateral arguments in support of the multi verse have relied mostly on speculative versions of quantum cosmology which may seem to suggest the generation of many different worlds. At present there is no fully worked out physical theory consistently combining quantum theory and gravity, but many believe that string theory represents the most promising candidate.

In evaluating this proposal, it is important to recognize how speculative much of contemporary fundamental physics has come to be, relying solely on mathematical possibility, without the complementary input of constraining empirical results. The string theorists purport to tell us how nature behaves on a scale sixteen orders of magnitude beyond anything of which we have direct knowledge. So great a change of scale would take one from the size of a town of a hundred thousand inhabitants to much less than the size of an atom, an immense extrapolation. For this reason, the multiverse must be classified as a metascientific approach to the issue of fine-tuning.

There are also many technical difficulties in evaluating the consistency and effectiveness of the multiverse theory as far as fine-tuning is concerned. For example, simply having an infinite collection of entities is no guarantee that it will contain one with any particular property. There are an infinite number of even integers, but one will never be found with the property of oddness. Materialism may be driven to the multiverse hypothesis in order to cope with fine-tuning, but theism finds an unforced explanation already available within its overall worldview.

God and Physics in the Twenty-First Century

The twentieth century saw a significant change in the character of the account that physics gives of the processes of the universe. Classical physics of the Newtonian type visualized individual hard atoms (possibly with hooks), interacting in a determinate manner in the container of absolute space and in the course of the unfolding of absolute time. This picture was not substantially changed when the discoveries of Michael Faraday and James Clerk Maxwell led in the nineteenth century to the formulation of field theories. Classical fields are strictly deterministic in their behavior and, though not directly visible, they are clearly perceptible from their effects, as when iron filings line up along the lines of force of a magnetic field. In a word, the physical world was still thought to be clear and determinate, mechanical in its character.

All this changed in the first quarter of the twentieth century with the discoveries of relativity theory and quantum theory. Space and time were found to be intimately interrelated and their description to be dependent on the motion of the observer, while subatomic processes were found to be cloudy and fitful in their character. Mere mechanism had died with the discovery of intrinsic unpredictabilities present in the processes of nature.

Later in the century, the discovery of chaos theory showed that even the classical Newtonian world was not free of intrinsic unpredictability, for there are many systems in it which are so exquisitely sensitive to the slightest disturbance from their environment that their future behavior is beyond the possibility of

detailed prediction. The word *intrinsic* is important here: these are not unpredictabilities that could be removed by more exact measurement or more precise calculation. Unpredictability is an epistemic property; it implies that we cannot know what future behavior will be. A fundamental problem in philosophy, and perhaps the central question in the philosophy of science, involves what connection there may be between epistemology (what we can know) and ontology (what is the case). The answer will not be determined by science alone, for it is a matter requiring metaphysical decision.

For example, quantum physics is certainly probabilistic, but does this feature arise from necessary ignorance of all the factors that actually fully determine what will happen, or is it due to an intrinsic indeterminacy in nature? In fact, it has turned out that, as far as science is concerned, either answer can be given. There are deterministic and indeterministic interpretations of quantum theory which lead to exactly the same empirical consequences. The choice between them has to be made on philosophical grounds, such as naturalness of explanation, rather than scientific criteria.

I claim that the same metaphysical options are open in the interpretation of chaotic unpredictabilities. The fact that mathematically chaos theory arose from studying the properties of deterministic nonlinear equations does not settle the issue, since these classical equations are known to be only approximations and not an exact and true account. Scientists are instinctively realists, believing that what we know is a reliable guide to what is the case — that is, that science is actually telling us what the world is like. For them it should be perfectly appropriate metaphysically to interpret the intrinsic unpredictabilities as signs of a degree of causal openness in nature. To do so is not to suppose that the future is some random lottery but that there are additional causal factors that bring it about, beyond the exchanges of energy between constituents that have been physics's traditional story.

Taking this view is encouraged further by a new development beginning to take place in science.

Instead of decomposing systems into their component parts, it has become possible to investigate the detailed behavior of modestly complex systems, treated in their totalities. It has been found time and again that dissipative systems, held far from thermal equilibrium by the exchange of energy and entropy with their environment, prove capable of spontaneously generating astonishing patterns of large-scale orderly behavior of a kind that is wholly unforeseeable in terms of constituent properties. As someone once said, "More is different"; the whole exceeds the sum of its parts.

A new kind of physics, complexity theory, seems to be on the scientific horizon, though it has not yet been properly formulated in any general kind of way. Its outline character, however, seems clear. It will be holistic rather than constituent, and its focus will be not on localized inputs of energy but on the overall patterns in which energy flows. The latter could be described by what one might appropriately call "information." It seems reasonable to expect that by the end of the twenty-first century some well-defined concept of information will have become as central in physics as energy has been for the last 150 years. The causal concept of active information, a top-down influence of the whole upon the parts, is a strong candidate for one of the extra principles that serve to determine the future. This prospect is made more attractive by the faint but suggestive analogy between active information and the exercise of agency, a fundamental experience of human persons, who have surely always known as well as they have known anything that they are not mechanical automata. The duality of energy-information is not wholly unlike the much more profound duality of matter-mind.

Physics has certainly not proved the causal closure of the world in its own reductionist terms. This conclusion is further supported by recognition of the patchiness of much of physics's account, with connections between different regimes not at all well understood. For example, it is not possible to combine quantum theory and chaos theory in a consistent synthesis, since quantum theory has an intrinsic scale, set by Planck's constant, while the fractal character of chaotic dynamics implies that it is scale free, appearing the same on whatever scale it is sampled. One may take physics with all the due seriousness that it deserves without being driven to deny our human capacity to act as intentional agents. And the theist cannot be forbidden to believe that God has chosen to interact providentially with unfolding history, within the open grain of cosmic process that modern science has discerned.

God, Evolution, and Quantum Theory

The potentiality present in the laws of nature has been turned into actuality in the course of the 13.7 billion years of cosmic history by a variety of evolutionary processes. While the biological evolution of life on earth is the most familiar of these scenarios, evolutionary process has also been of great significance for the physical structure of the universe. In the course of the first billion years of cosmic history, the initial almost uniform ball of matter-energy turned into a world that became grainy and lumpy with stars and galaxies. Where there had been a little more matter than average, there was an additional gravitational attraction, which then drew in further matter in a kind of snowballing process. In this way the initial small inhomogeneities were enhanced to produce ultimately a starry universe.

The essence of any evolutionary process is an interplay between contingent variations (in this case, small fluctuations of matter density in the early universe) and lawful regularity (in this case, the force of gravity). A slogan way of expressing this is to talk about chance and necessity. It is important to recognize that in this phrase "chance" is by no means a sign of meaninglessness but stands for the contingent particularity of what actually happens. Even in the course of 13.7 billion years, only a tiny fraction of what could have happened has actually taken place. The formation of stars and galaxies illustrates the general scientific insight that regimes in which true novelty emerges are always "at the edge of chaos," where order and openness, chance and necessity are interwoven. Too far on the orderly side of that frontier, and things are too rigid for the emergence of anything really novel to be possible; too far on the haphazard side of the frontier, and no novelty that does emerge will be able to persist.

The theist has no need to be worried by the widespread role of evolutionary process. God is the ordainer of nature, and God acts as much through natural processes as in any other way. Commenting on Charles Darwin's great discovery of biological evolution, his contemporary Charles Kingsley said that we had been shown that God had not made a ready-made world but had done something cleverer than that, making a world in which creatures "could make themselves." Chance is simply creation's shuffling exploration of divinely given fertility, by means of which potentiality is made actual. The theist will see the twin roles of chance and necessity as the gifts to creation of both independence and reliability, by a God who is both loving and faithful.

The physicist may well see this interweaving of order and openness reflected in the character of quantum physics and speculate that at the subatomic level this has been an important property in allowing the universe to be biofertile. While quantum physics is only capable of assigning probabilities for a number of possible results of a measurement, the range of these possibilities is also constrained by the actual character of the wave function describing the system. It is certainly not the case that anything might happen. The wave function itself evolves in time according to the Schrödinger equation, which is a deterministic differential equation. According to the widely accepted indeterministic interpretation of quantum theory, it is only when the definite form of the wave function is used to calculate the consequences of a measurement that probabilities enter the theory. Most physicists understand measurement to be the irreversible macroscopic registration of a state of affairs in the subatomic system, and it is not necessarily associated with the direct influence of a conscious observer. In other words, surely quantum processes had actual outcomes over the many billion years of cosmic history in which there were no observers present in the universe.

The interpretation of quantum theory is still a contentious issue, with a variety of incompatible points of view being advocated, but the notion of "observer-created reality" is very much a minority position. At most, "observer-influenced reality" (in laboratory experiments affected by choices of what measurements to make) is as much as should be said.

Quantum theory has also contributed to a growing recognition that nature is deeply relational and that atomism is only part of the picture. Once two quantum entities have interacted with each other, they can retain a power of mutual influence that is not diminished by spatial separation. Acting on one here will have an immediate effect on the other, even if it is now "beyond the moon," as we conventionally say. Einstein was the first to recognize the possibility of quantum entanglement, but he thought it was "too spooky" to be true. He considered that its prediction must show that there was something wrong with conventional quantum mechanics. However, experiments have abundantly confirmed the phenomenon. The instantaneous character of the influence conveyed does not contradict special relativity, since it turns out that it cannot be used to transmit information faster than the velocity of light. Nature, it seems, rebels against a crass reductionism: even the subatomic world cannot be treated atomistically. The theist who is a trinitarian thinker will not be surprised to learn that created reality is relational.

Finally, physicists can not only peer into the universe's past but also foresee aspects of its future. The timescales are very long, but in the end the prediction is that it will all end badly. As far as the earth is concerned, in about five billion years the sun will have consumed all its hydrogen fuel. It will then turn into a red giant, burning to a frazzle any life then left on the earth. By then life might well have migrated elsewhere in the galaxy; that, however, would only be a temporary reprieve. Over immensely long timescales, the universe itself will die, most probably by continuing to expand and becoming ever colder and more dilute. Carbon-based life will certainly prove to have been a transient episode in the history of the universe.

Eventual futility lies at the end of science's "horizontal" story, extrapolating physical process into the distant future. However, theism has a different, "vertical" story to tell, based on the everlasting faithfulness of God. For the religious believer, the last word lies not with death but with God. That is a conviction that goes beyond anything that physics can speak about, either for or against.

CHAPTER 49

Design and Science

Del Ratzsch

It could be a scene straight out of *Star Trek*. A doctor examining a crew member who has fallen mysteriously ill discovers something remarkable in samples taken from the patient. What she finds is a tiny, self-contained, self-sustaining unit tightly packed with even tinier subunits, which is controlled by what appear to be software and processors so compact and condensed that their components are specialized, complex individual molecules. Further, the doctor discovers, this microscopic entity contains a propulsion system driven by a nifty, minute, inboard electric rotary motor. The motor is attached to an outboard component which it rotates, thereby generating the propulsion. Although the entity is obviously not of human manufacture, the doctor recognizes an intelligently designed micro machine when she sees one. And though she does not yet know who designed it, what its purpose is or how it got into the crew member, she immediately issues a security alert.

That might have been a scene from *Star Trek*, but it is not. It is a story about *us*. Each of us has millions of these remarkable units in our own bodies — they are microorganisms called *E. coli*. Although *E. coli* are common parts of our natural internal and external environments, it is difficult not to be rather astonished by the existence of the microscopic electric rotary motors. In most contexts we (like the doctor) would take the existence of such a motor — complete with organic rotors, stators, bushings, driveshafts — as virtually conclusive evidence that some intelligent designer had been at work here. In fact, a number of scientists

(e.g., Michael Behe, author of *Darwin's Black Box*) have come to exactly that conclusion and maintain that we cannot have a complete *scientific* understanding of some parts of nature without incorporating the concept of *design*. However, other scientists have come to exactly the opposite conclusion. For example, the subtitle of *The Blind Watchmaker* by Richard Dawkins is "Why the evidence of evolution reveals a universe without design." Dawkins's position is not merely that we do not need the concept of design to properly explain nature (even including bacterial electric rotary motors) but that a correct scientific understanding of nature *establishes* the *absence* of deliberate design in nature.

Obviously the issue of whether or not there is genuine, scientific evidence of intelligent design in nature will have extremely important implications. So how should we think about this issue? Historically, most people (including scientists) have believed that there was an active mind (or minds) behind the visible face of nature and that some (or all) visible things and events were results of and thus evidence of the intentions and activity of that mind (minds). Nature, as most saw it, was deliberately *planned, directed* or *designed*. From that perspective, *reasons, ideas, plans, thoughts, patterns* and *design* would all factor into the causal history, structure and function of things, and thus any adequate scientific account of nature would have to involve reference to those factors. That perspective was visible in the new science of the sixteenth and seventeenth centuries[1] and was given explicit

---

1. It can be seen in the background and sometimes in the forefront of the scientific work of such majors figures as Newton, Boyle, Descartes and — later — Pasteur, Herschel, Faraday, Maxwell and others.

expression in the Natural Theology movement of the eighteenth and early nineteenth centuries.

The idea that science can uncover evidence of deliberate design in the cosmos, and especially the idea that *supernatural design* can figure in truly scientific accounts of natural phenomena, subsequently fell on hard times. Such ideas are now generally viewed as scientifically illegitimate or worse. In tracking some of the issues involved we will begin by examining the basic concept of design, look next at some of the reasons underlying the widespread scientific ban on the concept of supernatural design in science, then look briefly at a current attempt to reintroduce the concept into science.

Design: Concept Basics

1. Artifacts. Activities of human agents typically leave visible traces on the world — traces we are generally able to recognize as resulting from human activity. For instance, when we come across a diesel bulldozer, we recognize that humans had a hand in that machine's coming into existence. That recognition is based in part upon our knowing some things about nature's capabilities and our recognition that nature unaided by agent activity would not or could not have produced any such phenomenon. In the production and properties of diesel bulldozers, things or events involved have been pushed in a direction contrary to the normal flow of nature — they exhibit what I shall call *counterflow*. And since nature unaided by agency could not or would not have produced any such thing, agency (in this case, human agency) was obviously involved. Things that unaided nature could not or would not produce and in whose production finite agents (humans, aliens, whatever) played some role we classify as *artifacts*.

We often recognize artifactuality even if we have no idea who or what the agents involved were, what they had in mind, what (if anything) their purpose was or how they produced the phenomenon in question. We could do so in some cases even if (contrary to the diesel bulldozer example) we had previously neither seen any such object nor seen any such object produced. For example, if the first humans ever to set foot on Mars discovered a huge stainless steel exact replica of Stonehenge, they could tell from its counterflow characteristics that it was an undoubted *artifact*. And if they knew further that they were the first humans on Mars, they could also confidently conclude that it was an *alien* artifact. That would be a perfectly reasonable — even "scientific" — conclusion, even if the identity, intentions, purposes and methods of the alien agents involved were completely unknown.

Artifactual and *designed* are not, however, synonymous. Someone whittling idly on a stick and paying no mind whatever to what she was doing would still produce a recognizable artifact, but that artifact would not be in any strong sense designed since its key characteristics were not intentionally produced.

But although it comes close, *intentionally produced artifactuality* is not yet quite the same as designedness. An artist might deliberately and painstakingly produce an exact replica of a suburban garbage heap, perhaps as some sort of social commentary. Although both the original and the replica would be unmistakable artifacts exhibiting undeniable counterflow, and although the replica would be an intentionally produced artifact, neither of them would on its own exhibit any properties constituting any marks of design in any intuitive sense.[2] So exactly what is design?

2. Design. A design is an *intentionally produced (or exemplified) pattern*, where a *pattern* is an abstract structure that resonates, matches or meshes in certain ways with *mind*, with *cognition*. That structure can be exemplified in an object, an event, a sequence of events or other phenomena, either material or abstract. For instance, the SETI program (the Search for Extra-Terrestrial Intelligence) looks for electromagnetic

---

2. The replica garbage heap would be deliberately produced *in accord with an idea* and might be said in that sense to be designed. But the idea itself would not embody design in the more fundamental sense of resonating with mind. The isomorphisms (the match) between the original and the replica *would* exemplify such a resonance, and that is why the term *design* would be derivatively appropriate in this case. The Martian Stonehenge replica would exhibit designedness in *both* senses.

artifacts (alien microwave signals) representing deliberate alien attempts at communication — broadcasts of prime number sequences in binary code, for instance, as in the movie *Contact*.[3] Such a signal would clearly be a *designed* artifact — an intentionally produced pattern that nature on its own would not produce. And we would easily recognize it as such because of its very obvious *cognitive* character and content — its resonating with mind in a particularly evident way.[4]

There are several other possible categories of *resonating* as well. A hammer, for instance, is a designed artifact. In this case the resonating with mind consists in the correspondence between its actual artifactual characteristics and those required for fulfilling its intended purpose. A similar type of correspondence between the properties living organisms have and the properties they need in order to thrive in their environments — a matching typically referred to as the "adaptation of means to ends" — was frequently cited in the past as evidence of design in nature.

3. Agent activity. Since design involves the *deliberate* production of pattern, there is always agent activity somewhere in its history. Sometimes that activity is quite direct, sometimes not. Here is a simple analogy. Someone might carve a model wooden ship by hand *or* might construct some high-tech machine that would turn out carved model ships automatically. The agent, the person, must *do* something in both cases. But in the one case the activity is direct — and anyone watching the wood being turned into a model would see it. In the other case, with respect to the actual carving of the ship the agent activity is only indirect. Anyone watching the wood being turned into a model ship would see only the completely mechanical, law-driven, automatic operation of a purely physical machine. There would have to be direct agent activity *somewhere*, but in this case it would be directed toward the

making of the machine itself — or the machine that made the machine (or perhaps even further back).

4. Gaps. Whenever humans, aliens or other finite beings act to produce artifacts (or design), marks of that activity — counterflow marks — are left on the world somewhere or other. Since counterflow marks are exactly those that cannot or would not be produced by nature, counterflow is inescapably linked to gaps in the normal causal flow of nature. For instance, there is a substantial gap between the potential results of any and all unaided processes in nature and the existence of a diesel bulldozer — a gap that, when confronted by a diesel bulldozer, we bridge by appeal to human agency. Similarly there is a gap between what nature would or could do and the existence of a Martian stainless steel Stonehenge replica — a gap our explanations would bridge by appeal to the activity of aliens. We might call such inference to alien activity an *alien-of-the-gaps* argument. Gap-based inferences are foundational to our identification of artifacts as products of agent activity and in the case of human and alien activity are unproblematically legitimate. If there is something nature could not or would not produce unaided, yet there it is right in front of us, it follows that something else — a human, alien, or other agent — was involved in its production.

Recognizing Finite Designedness

Our recognition of finite designedness (design by finite agents) typically begins with a recognition of artifactuality, itself in turn based upon recognition of counterflow marks. Sometimes those marks are visible in the end product. For instance, we can identify a diesel bulldozer as a product of agent activity and design simply by examining the bulldozer itself. Sometimes such marks are completely absent from the end product, and identification of artifactuality and

---

3. That was the form of the initial alien communication in the movie *Contact*. SETI actually looks for signals of two sorts. Nearly any high-tech civilization is presumed to produce *unintentional* electromagnetic radiation (e.g., byproduct radiation from operation of electronic equipment, from communication systems, from manufacturing processes, etc.), and SETI looks for that kind of signal as well as for deliberately patterned signals. Either type of signal would

constitute an *artifact,* but the former would not represent *design.*

4. I am not suggesting that this sort of pattern is the only type relevant to designedness. Indeed, I think that there are several different, entire categories of pattern that are relevant. The present sort, involving obvious cognitive content, is simply the most intuitively easy to identify.

designedness can only be made from examination of the production processes. For instance, it might be impossible to determine that some molecule of some familiar protein has been synthesized merely from an examination of that molecule itself. That it had been artificially synthesized could, however, be determined if one could investigate the process of its production — that process involving all sorts of designed artifactuality, including labs, glassware and so forth.

In some cases, neither the end product nor even the processes once underway might reveal intentional, counterflow activity, but the initial conditions triggering the process out of which the end product is produced might be enormously and obviously artificial. Suppose that two mice (male and female) were produced by cloning and that they subsequently produced a litter in the usual mouse manner. Examination of the mice in that litter or of the processes of their conception and birth would not reveal anything out of the ordinary. Yet had it not been for the substantial, intentional intervention of human scientists involved in bringing about key necessary conditions for the eventual existence of that litter (i.e., the initial cloning of the parents), the litter would never have existed. Agent counterflow activity was crucially and obviously involved in the initial conditions.

In these and most other cases recognition of counterflow and artifactuality is the starting point toward recognition that something is designed. In some cases we may be able even to identify specifically what the design is. Sometimes the agents producing an artifact have had some particular purpose in producing it, and we are able to tell what that purpose was from investigation of the artifact. Archaeology provides various examples. Alien signals might provide possible cases as well. In the *Contact* binaryprime case, we could identify the thinking manifested in the pattern. Or we might be able to determine that the artifact has a key role in the production or preservation of some *value*.

In other cases while we might be unable to discover what the purpose actually was, we might nonetheless be able to tell that there *was* some purpose or other

and that the artifact in question was indeed intentionally generated. How might we tell that?

There are a variety of possible clues here. Suppose that (via, for example, counterflow marks) we know that we are dealing with an artifact — that the activity of some agent was involved in its production. If that artifact is enormously complex, or if we establish that its production would have taken significant care, attention or resources, then the conclusion that it is designed — whatever that design might actually be — is certainly a reasonable one. And we do as a matter of fact make such judgements. The Smithsonian reportedly has an entire collection of artifacts, obviously produced with some intention in mind, but the purposes of which have been completely lost. Still, we recognize that they were designed. Similarly if on first arriving upon Mars we came upon some wildly complex alien artifact or one that had clearly required enormous care and commitment of resources to produce, we would likely not put it into the "idly whittled-stick" category of alien artifact but would — probably correctly — conclude that it was intentionally produced and designed, even if we had no clue what it was for and even if we did not have the relevant (alien) concepts for properly describing it.

Of course, there is no guarantee that we can always identify design, always recognize designedness or always recognize artifactuality and counterflow. It is possible that we might confront cases where we were unable to tell whether we were dealing with a genuine artifact or some unusual natural phenomenon. Archaeologists trying to separate extremely primitive hand axes from stones chipped and formed by natural processes are frequently in that situation. Indeed, if there are technologically advanced aliens in our part of the cosmos, we might come upon things that are actually alien artifacts but that we mistakenly think are purely natural. There are a number of scientists who believe that life is not native to the earth and that the organisms we see around us descended from ancestors deliberately produced and transported here by advanced alien races. Were that true, then things we take to be completely natural — essentially everything that lives on earth — would actually be results of deliberate alien activity and design.[5]

Supernatural Design

The general conceptual structure outlined above would apply fairly well to some instances of design produced by supernatural agents as well. It is in principle possible for a supernatural being to bring about virtually any artifact that we humans (or aliens) can. In such cases the phenomenon produced would be as identifiably artifactual and designed (and on exactly the same evidence) as it would be were humans to have produced it. Of course, examining such an object might not tell us that the agent in question was supernatural — just as examining some unusual artifact on earth might not tell us whether it had been produced by humans or produced by covert aliens engaged in a counterfeit earth-souvenir ring for the market back home on Mars. In fact, in the supernatural case it might be that we could not even in principle discover that the agent in question was supernatural. Or perhaps we could never in principle have adequate evidence to conclude that the agent was supernatural. Or perhaps even if we could legitimately arrive at such conclusions, it might still be illegitimate to acknowledge it within a scientific context.[6] But whether or not any of those positions is correct, they are irrelevant to the possibility of our properly identifying the object in question as designed. Even had the Martian stainless steel Stonehenge replica been created by a supernatural agent, any human survey team that managed to overlook the fact that the object was designed would be inept indeed.

Counterflow means. A supernatural being would be able to employ a much wider range of means than would humans or other finite creatures (e.g., aliens). A supernatural being could, of course, employ exactly the same means and methods that we do in bringing about, say, a watch — could construct a factory employing the same principles we do, with the relevant sorts of machinery to form and assemble the parts. Of course, a supernatural agent might know of alternative (yet perfectly natural) means, employing principles of which we were unaware, or that we could not understand, or that we were for numerous reasons unable to employ. Or a supernatural agent might make a watch indistinguishable from some human watch by means involving breaking or suspending laws of nature. Or a supernatural being might simply create such a watch *ex nihilo*.

Precosmic initial conditions. The above different types of supernatural activity would all involve supernatural agent intervention into the course of history and would, like human activity, leave counterflow marks (whether we could recognize them — or even see them — or not). There is, however, one means available *only* to a supernatural *creating* agent and one involving no intervention in the course of nature at all.[7] A supernatural agent who *created* a cosmos could build design into the very structure and interrelationships among the fundamental laws governing that cosmos and/or into the created, initial empirical conditions of that cosmos upon which the created laws were to operate. In fact, those laws and conditions could be deliberately structured so that those laws operating upon those conditions would result

---

5. Of course, it can work the other way too. When Jocelyn Bell detected the first of what later came to be known as pulsars, there were no known or even suspected mechanisms by which nature could produce such pulsed signals, and the source was informally named "LGM – 1" — for Little Green Men 1.

6. This general sort of view with respect to creationism is explicitly endorsed by, for example, Douglas Futuyma, Michael Ruse and others.

7. I have been employing the concept of *intervention* here, but some Christians believe that the entire idea of intervention is a bit off target. For instance, it is possible that what we identify as statements of natural laws are actually just descriptions of God's free but

perfectly consistent activity, and that there simply are no independent "natural" regularities that those actions are interventions into or contraventions of. (For some technical exploration of that idea, see Del Ratzsch, "Nomo(theo)logical Necessity," in *Faith and Philosophy* 4 [1987]: 383 – 402.) Or it is possible that there are genuine background "natural" regularities but that God intervenes in various perfectly consistent, uniform ways in specific circumstances, so that at least *some* of the uniformities we identify as natural laws actually consist of specific supernatural activity. In the former case, and perhaps to some extent in the latter case, talk of "intervention" would be in some circumstances misdirected.

in preselected and intended patterns, phenomena or creatures being exemplified billions of years later. That is at least a *possibility* for such an agent. And it seems clear that any such eventuality would exemplify *design*.

But some unique aspects of designedness emerge here. In the above case since the results in question would arise from natural law operating upon ultimate, primordial initial conditions, no *further* specific supernatural action would be required. There would need be no *intervention* anywhere into cosmic causal history, there would be no gaps in nature, and the emergence of specific instances of design billions of years later would not involve any *counterflow* at all. So if a supernatural agent indirectly constructed life, for example, we could scientifically investigate the origin of life without seeing direct supernatural agent activity, seeing only the operating of natural laws and conditions constructing life.

Furthermore, part of creating a cosmos is choosing the laws and conditions of that cosmos — in other words, *specifying what nature itself will be.* Prior to the initial creating activity there simply would be no complete *nature* for anything to run counter to, and consequently there would be no counterflow either in the primordial initial conditions of the cosmos, nor in the selected laws themselves.

Those facts have two consequences for recognition of such designs. First, recall that recognition of designedness typically involves recognition of artifactuality that in turn rests upon recognition of counterflow. But in the present cases there will be no counterflow to provide that foundation. So what will recognition of design *in nature* rest upon? The usual answers are complexity of various sorts, improbability of various degrees, production paths of a certain precariousness, specific sorts of adaptation of means to ends and so on.

But the status of those answers is compl icated by a second consequence. Some things function best as clues to designedness in the context of identifiable artifactuality (that identifiability again resting typically upon counterflow). For instance, if we know that something is an artifact, then if that artifact is tre-

mendously complex we generally conclude that it was designed (or at least that it was intentionally made as it is). We typically do *not* think that such tremendous complexity was just an accidental result of "inattentive whittling."

But just bare complexity or bare high improbability seem not to have the same degree of evidential force. That you should be wearing just the ring you have on, containing specific atoms of some metal produced in the supernova of precisely the star that did it, occurring at just the right time and place and traveling on just the right path to end up in just the right place to be found by just the right miner to end up in just the right ring in just the right store for just the right person to buy for you — is *wildly* improbable. But it evidently happened. Yet we do not typically take that wild improbability alone as grounds for thinking that the entire sequence was *designed.*

The point is that a variety of factors, which *in the context of artifactuality* do seem to constitute evidence of design, do not seem *by themselves* to constitute evidence that is nearly as powerful. So the second consequence is this: reliance upon such factors in arguments for design in nature or upon analogical arguments based upon parallels to known human artifacts, may be a bit riskier than usually appreciated. The complexity *of en artifact* may indeed suggest design, but mere complexity alone may not. That is not to say that there is no evidence or no good argument for design in nature but only that the situation may be less straightforward than sometimes assumed.

It is widely held that the concept of supernatural design is illegitimate in science — that it must be barred from both scientific descriptions and scientific explanations. Those who advocate such prohibitions typically do not mean to ban the basic concept of design itself from science — only the concept of supernatural design.

Finite design and science. There is, as most such prohibitionists see it, absolutely nothing wrong with reference to *finite* design — whether human, alien or whatever — within science, because such design involves only beings which are in one very broad sense natural.[8] Archeology attempts to discover, identify and explain designedness and even specific design. The SETI program is aimed at discovering, identifying and understanding designed electromagnetic artifacts produced by aliens. And no one would object in principle to the identification by human explorers on other planets of some phenomenon as either artifact or designed by aliens.

It is even possible that we might — quite properly and scientifically — come to the conclusion that some things we had previously thought to be purely natural were actually results of alien design activity. For instance, as noted earlier, a few secular scientists have come to believe that life could not have originated on earth by natural processes and have concluded that life was deliberately designed and then seeded here by aliens.[9] Those scientists might be spectacularly wrong, but the view itself is not inherently unscientific. There is simply no a priori reason for thinking that science must conclude that life originated here on earth rather than somewhere else. Nor is there any a priori reason for thinking that if life did not originate here, science simply could never discover that truth on the basis of (among other things) revealing characteristics of living organisms on earth.

But if such a conclusion could even in principle be legitimately scientific and could be discovered from empirical investigation of organisms, then it follows that it is at least *in principle* possible that the organisms around us should carry evidences of having been designed. In any case, appeal to design produced by finite agents is perfectly legitimate in scientific contexts. Furthermore, there is nothing inherently unscientific even in claiming to identify evidences of design in living organisms (or in other phenomena within the "natural" realm). So if there are difficulties with the idea of genuinely scientific evidences of supernatural design in nature, the difficulties are rooted in the *supernatural* part of that equation. What might such difficulties be?

Supernatural design and science. It is important to distinguish between the possibility of identifying as designed something *that was in fact* (perhaps unknown to us) designed by a supernatural agent and the possibility of identifying something as having been designed by a supernatural agent. Suppose that our Martian stainless steel Stonehenge replica had been designed by a supernatural agent. We might not know that a supernatural agent had designed it. We might be completely unable to determine *that* fact, but there would be no serious question about the basic fact of its being designed. A Mars survey team would not be violating any canons of science in taking it to be designed. Anyone attempting to give a fully scientific explanation of that replica would not commit a scientific mistake in taking its designedness into account. Again that would be true even if the (unknown) fact of the matter was that a supernatural agent had designed it, made it, and placed it there. This indicates that any plausible prohibition on supernatural design within science cannot bar recognition and admission of the basic fact of designedness — no matter what the source. In other words, the identity of the designer need not be of crucial relevance to the proper identifiability of design.

Recall the earlier conclusion that there was no bar in principle to scientific recognition of any evidences of design even in what we would ordinarily identify as natural phenomena. We have just seen that there are no good grounds in principle for barring recognition of evidences of design even if the (perhaps unknown) fact of the matter is that the design is supernatural. Together, those suggest that *if nature or various things in nature are in fact designed, science cannot be forbidden to recognize that designedness even should the ultimate truth of the matter be that it was a supernatural being that did the designing.*

Some design prohibitionists might even accept that. So exactly what is the usual prohibition a prohibition *of*? The only prohibition even potentially

---

8. For instance, Eugenie Scott says: "To be dealt with scientifically, 'intelligence' must be natural because *all* science is natural … SETI is indeed a scientific project; it seeks *natural* intelligence."

NCSE Reports 10, no. 1 (January–February 1990): 16–18.

9. Among those holding all or part of that view are Fred Hoyle, Chandra Wickramesingh and the codiscoverer of DNA, Francis Crick.

plausible would be against recognizing (or claiming to recognize) within the scientific context *that the design is supernatural.*

What might be the grounds for that restriction?

Methodological Naturalism

The standard prohibition on the supernatural in science is generally referred to as *methodological naturalism.* The basic idea is that science must proceed as if philosophical naturalism is true (whether or not it is) — making no reference to supernatural design, causation or activity in its formal scientific descriptions, explanations and theories.[10]

Methodological naturalism is widely accepted — even by many Christians within science.[11] There are, I think, five primary reasons for that wide acceptance. They are (1) the belief that methodological naturalism is demanded by the very definition of *science,* (2) the belief that theories concerning the supernatural can have no stable, empirically testable .contents, (3) the belief that such theories have historically been complete scientific failures, (4) the belief that all such theories are versions of "God-of-the-gaps" theories and that such theories are scientifically unacceptable and (5) the belief that permitting use of design theories would erode science by fostering scientific laziness. None of those reasons, it seems to me, fares well under scrutiny. We will look very briefly at each in turn.

1. Definitions. The issue of what is or is not demanded in (or excluded from) science "by definition" is much less clear than it seemed prior to Kuhn. One of the lessons of Kuhn, recall, is that a variety of *metaphysical commitments* are utterly indispensable

to science itself. Establishing a definitional prohibition against supernatural design would thus require determining what sorts of "metaphysical" principles are or are not permissible in science, then showing that supernatural design falls on the wrong side of that boundary. That is vastly more difficult than merely emphatically pointing out that supernatural design involves the supernatural.

One factor making this definitional approach difficult is that, as we saw earlier in the book, there is no universally accepted *formal* definition of *science,* and proposed definitions almost invariably run into nasty difficulties sooner or later. That makes reliance upon a definition of science a bit "iffy." Furthermore, if we turn to some of the *informal* definitions suggested by scientists themselves, we find small comfort for prohibitionists. One such definition is that science is an attempt to get at the truth *no holds barred.* That is not likely to provide support for attempts to bar particular concepts. The scientific attitude has usually been characterized as a commitment to following the evidence wherever it leads. That does not look like promising ammunition for someone pushing an official policy of refusing to allow science to follow evidence to supernatural design no matter what the evidence turns out to be. Science has often been described as organized and formalized common sense. There might be some question about what actually constitutes common sense, but I suspect that most humans at most times in most cultures have considered it just good common sense that there is a supernatural realm and that supernatural activity is deeply linked to the structure,

---

10. Philosophical naturalism is basically the view that the natural realm is the only reality there is and that science is the only access we have to the fundamental structures and principles defining and governing that reality. There are some Christian advocates of methodological naturalism who object to the above characterization of *methodological naturalism* as "doing science as *if* philosophical naturalism were true." But their objections seem to me to be primarily that the definition makes no mention of God upholding all created things in such a way that were that support withdrawn all those things would collapse into nonexistence, no mention that the laws and character of created things are as they are because God

chose to make things that way, etc. — all things that many Christian methodological naturalists affirm. Those are indeed important differences from philosophical naturalism. Nonetheless, given what most methodological naturalists mean by "science," the expectation would be that a properly pursued methodological naturalist *science* and a properly pursued philosophical naturalist *science* would be identical — containing the same laws, principles, theories, data, methods and so forth. It is in that sense that the characterization I give of methodological naturalism is, I think, accurate.

11. Some early figures — for example, Leibniz — took this sort of position as *theologically* preferable to intervention views.

governance and history of the cosmos. Not much help for prohibitionists here either.

Some — especially some Christians — have argued that while there is indeed a supernatural realm that may impinge upon the natural realm, the natural realm has its own integral identity, character and operative principles, and the task of science is to trace the fabric of those natural structures in and on their own terms. There may be interventions (e.g., scriptural miracles), and such interventions may be of utterly crucial significance. But, it is argued, they have no bearing upon the character of the natural — which by this definition is what the created order would do and be in the absence of such interventions. Since the latter is the focus of science, science should properly proceed as if there were no interventions — at least, it should not formally take account of them.[12]

That may be a perfectly defensible position, but it certainly removes some of the starch from the claim that something is or is not scientific. It commits science to either having to deliberately ignore major (possibly even *observable)* features of the material realm or having to refrain from even considering the obvious and only workable explanation, should it turn out that those features clearly resulted from supernatural activity. Further, recall discussion from an earlier chapter indicating that any imposed policy of naturalism in science has the potential not only of eroding any self-correcting capability of science but of preventing science from reaching certain truths. Any imposed policy of methodological naturalism will have precisely the same potential consequences.

2. Empirical emptiness. It might be argued that although there may be no complete definition of *science,* we do know at least some of the essential components of any such definition. Among them is the requirement that any legitimately scientific theory or concept have some specifiable empirical content — that it have empirical implications, be empirically testable, empirically falsifiable and so forth. The problem with *supernatural design*, this line of thought continues, is that it has no stable empirical content. Indeed, it can be adapted to essentially anything in nature, or if the adaptation proves difficult it can simply be claimed that there really is some design or other, but that we just have not yet grasped it. But, the objection continues, in the face of such hyperflexibility the alleged empirical content of the concept simply evaporates.

That objection is not a frivolous one, and it does have some force. But two serious reservations are worth noting. First, recall from earlier discussion that no theory *just by itself* generates any empirical predictions or consequences at all. Theories predict only in conjunction with a variety of other things — bridge principles, initial conditions and so forth. And it is possible that the idea of supernatural design could, in conjunction with other principles, have empirical implications.[13]

The second reservation is that different parts of science operate in different ways, on different levels and must answer to different demands. Consider the principle of the uniformity of nature. Historically the underpinning of that principle is philosophical. It is not empirically testable — indeed, what test results might *mean* is itself determined in part in a context already defined by that very principle. The principle of uniformity is not at empirical risk — no matter what results are produced by what experiment, we would not decide that nature must have just changed the rules and abandon the principle of uniformity.

---

12. For instance, Dugald Stewart, in his 1792 *Elements of the Philosophy of the Human Mind* 1:52, says: "In the investigation of physical laws, it is well-known that our inquiries must always terminate in some general fact, of which no account can be given, but that such is the constitution of nature. After we have established, for example, from the astronomical phenomena, the universality of the law of gravitation, it may still be asked whether this law implies the constant agency of mind; and (upon the supposition that it does) whether it be probable that the Deity always operates immediately, or by means of subordinate instruments? But these questions, however curious, do not fall under the province of the natural philosopher [scientist]. It is sufficient for his purpose, if the universality of the fact be admitted."

13. Indeed, the apparent possibility of virtually *anything* having empirical consequences when conjoined with suitably constructed bridge principles posed difficulties for some key doctrines of positivism.

Indeed, we *protect* that principle, typically not even considering alternatives to it. Should what we took to be a uniformity begin to break down, we would simply conclude that we had misidentified what the *real* uniformity was. The principle of uniformity by itself makes no empirical predictions. It is involved in predictions only when we have specified some *respect* in which we take nature to be uniform. Otherwise, it says nothing whatever. It is unlimitedly flexible — no matter what turns up, we take uniformity to be consistent with it and able to accommodate it.

So uniformity makes no predictions, is untestable, is not at empirical risk, can be bent to accommodate anything, is preferentially protected and rests ultimately upon philosophical considerations. Yet the uniformity principle is not only legitimately scientific, it is utterly essential to science. Demands that it have evident empirical content, be testable, make predictions and so forth, are inappropriate to the type of principle it is, operating at the level in science on which it functions. But that suggests the possibility that depending upon how and where it operates in science, *supernatural design* might properly be no more subject to those demands than is the principle of uniformity. At the very least, since the charges leveled against *supernatural design* typically involve characteristics displayed by other perfectly legitimate concepts within science (e.g., uniformity), the conclusion that the mere having of those characteristics disqualifies *supernatural design* from science will require some additional — and perhaps difficult — work.

If either of the above two objections (definitions and empirical emptiness) were compelling, there would be difficulties *in principle* for introducing the idea of supernatural design into science. But objections have also been based upon more practical, pragmatic considerations. Let us look briefly at the three primary objections of that sort.

3. Historical track record. The claim here is that while *supernatural design* may not in principle be illegitimate in scientific contexts, it has been tried historically and has simply failed. Geocentric theories do not violate any normative principles of good scientific procedure and may have been scientifically useful in their time. But it would be extremely silly to try resuscitating them now. Similarly, it is argued, design theories might not violate any normative scientific principles, but they had their chance, ultimately failed, and it would be a waste of valuable scientific time and effort to turn back the clock and take them seriously again.

But plausible as that sounds, it is not just obvious that the concept of supernatural design was a historical failure. It has been often noted by historians of science that various theological themes (including specifically the doctrine of creation with its fundamental implications of design) played important roles in the rise and early career of modern science. In fact, some historians have argued that modern science as we know it would not have arisen as it did without that formative theological context. This suggests the possibility that concepts like the designedness of nature were essential to science's beginnings and may have generated some of the ongoing conceptual shapes of science that we, having forgotten their origins, now take as basic givens of the scientific outlook.

Of course, it might be argued that such concepts were both legitimate and even scientifically useful in getting science up and running but have long outlived any such usefulness. As an analogy, consider the construction of an arch in a medieval cathedral. While a wooden scaffolding might be essential for constructing such an arch, once the capstone is in place the scaffold is not only no longer needed but now constitutes an obstacle to those wishing to go through the arch. But the present case may not be quite so simple. In fact, some of the weightbearing members of science may still be remnants of early design concepts. Indeed, the physicist Paul Davies once remarked that "science began as an outgrowth of theology, and all scientists, whether atheists or theists ... accept an essentially theological worldview."[14] It may be that we sometimes

---

14. Paul Davies, *Are We Alone?* (New York: Basic, 1995), p. 138.

do not see the empirical ramifications of design simply because science as we now learn it is already immersed in empirical consequences of design that are parts of its very fabric. As Einstein once asked: What does a fish know of the water in which it swims all its life?

4. God of the gaps. Suppose that we come across some phenomenon for which we are unable to find a good, natural explanation. Were it scientifically permissible, there might be a strong temptation in such situations to conclude that there just *is not* any natural explanation — that the phenomenon in question has resulted from supernatural activity. Theories appealing to supernatural activity to account for various phenomena in nature are frequently termed *God-of-the-gaps* theories and are typically viewed as desperate, scientifically bogus attempts to cover our scientific ignorance with the appearance of an explanation. Such theories are generally seen as historically unfortunate for the cause of religion since, it is claimed, the gaps of ignorance in which such theories flourish have a tendency to disappear as science advances, leaving religion with little more in the scientific realm than a long, misguided trail of failure littered with shattered theories.

It is nearly unanimously charged that design theories are simply *God-of-the-gaps* theories and that such theories are automatically defective. Popular as that picture is, it is substantially skewed. First, *design theories need not involve gaps at all.* Suppose that a meteor swarm hit the moon, and after the dust settled it was discovered that the impacts had left thousands of small, uniformly sized meteor craters arranged in such a way that they constituted a really nifty proof of a previously unknown mathematical theorem that held the key to solving a bunch of global problems. Few would doubt that this episode exhibited design.

Suppose further that we fired up our new time machine, traced back the history of the meteor swarm and every individual meteor in it, and discovered that absolutely everything in that history back to the big bang was absolutely and completely natural — there were no gaps anywhere in the causal history of the entire sequence. We would not, I think, abandon our previous design conclusion — we would simply conclude that the design had been deliberately structured into the initiating event of the cosmos itself.

What our story indicates is that design and gaps are not necessarily linked and that the charge that design cases must of necessity be gap cases is mistaken. A *gap* has to do with the causal *history* of a phenomenon. *Design* has to do with whether or not the phenomenon has characteristics (however produced, whatever the immediate means of production) exemplifying a specific type of agent-dependent, mind-resonating pattern. Thus to claim that any design theory has to be a gap theory is simply to confuse two quite distinct issues.

Second, *many historical design theories did not involve gaps.* Some of the more popular design theories in the early nineteenth century were based upon the structure, inter-relationships and dovetailing of the basic laws of nature — not on gaps in nature's capabilities that required supernatural bridging.[15] It was widely held among design advocates — and can be found explicitly in the writings of, for example, Bacon and Boyle — that the deliberate achieving of some intended result through indirect means (involving the structure of laws and the initial conditions of the creation itself) demonstrated more impressive wisdom, foresight and planning than did activity within cosmic causal history — interventions to bridge gaps.[16] This was a common theme in the writing of Christian

15. Such arguments are contained in various of the *Bridgewater Treatises,* notably Whewell's and Chalmer's. Of course, some design arguments did rest quite explicitly upon gaps — see, for example, Bell's *Bridgewater Treatise.* A variety of non-gap arguments — all from scientists — can be found in Francis Mason, ed., *The Great Design* (1934; reprint, Freeport, N.Y.: Books for Libraries, 1972). Such arguments can also be found in works not usually associated with design cases — for example, Faraday's. See David Gooding,

"Metaphysics Versus Measurement: The Conversion and Conservation of Force in Faraday's Physics," *Annals of Science* 37 (1980): 29.

16. For instance, in *A Free Inquiry into the Vulgarly Received Notions of Nature* (1685–86), Boyle says: "It much more tends to the illustration of God's wisdom, to have framed things at first, that there can seldom or never need any extraordinary interposition of his power. And, as it more recommends the skill of an engineer to contrive an elaborate engine so, as that there should need nothing

scientists. Thus the claim that design theories historically were all gap theories is simply inaccurate.[17]

Third, as noted earlier, whatever its other defects, *gap cases* are at least *logically unproblematic*. If nature and chance cannot produce some phenomenon, yet there it inarguably is in front of us, it follows that something else did produce it — and agents of various sorts are essentially the only other alternative. And if we have good grounds for thinking that neither humans nor other finite creatures have the relevant capability, then supernatural agency is the only option left of course, those things may be difficult to *establish*, but that is irrelevant to the logical point.

Fourth, some design cases even involving gaps were *not based upon frustrated ignorance*. Our own postulation of a diesel-bulldozer gap is not driven by ignorance but by genuine knowledge of limitations on nature's capabilities. Similarly, historical design conclusions were often based upon characteristics that had a particularly mindresonant character and that were taken to be positive evidences of designedness because of that special character independent of any considerations of exactly how the characteristics were produced.[18]

5. Scientific laziness. Beginning at least as far back as the early seventeenth century and continuing to the present, some thinkers have expressed the fear that if supernatural explanations were allowed in science, then scientists would be tempted to appeal to supernatural activity as the explanation in scientifically difficult cases and might thus abandon too quickly scientific searches that otherwise might eventually turn up a correct, natural explanation. That is a legitimate concern, and it does provide a legitimate cautionary note.[19] But the fact that scientists might be tempted to adopt such theories too easily surely does not by itself imply that such theories should be forever placed off limits no matter what evidence might turn up. Some theorizers might too easily leap to alien explanations (for lights in the sky, crop circles, stalled cars, etc.). But that tendency would hardly justify a refusal even to consider explanatory reference to aliens if the first humans on Mars really did find a stainless steel replica of Stonehenge. So while care is called for, under some circumstances such a prohibition may screen science from seeing truth. That would not seem to be the most productive form of care.[20]

---

to reach his ends in it but the contrivance of parts devoid of understanding, than if it were necessary, that ever and anon, a discreet servant should be employed to concur notably to the operation of this or that part, or to hinder the engine from being out of order; so it more sets off the wisdom of God in the fabric of the universe that he can make so vast a machine perform all those many things, which he designed it should, by the mere contrivance of brute matter managed by certain laws of local motion and upheld by his ordinary and general concourse, than if he employed from time to time an intelligent overseer, such as nature is fancied to be, to regulate, and control the motions of the parts." (Marie Hall, ed., *Robert Boyle on Natural Philosophy* [Bloomington: Indiana University Press, 1965, 1966], pp. 150 – 51). Similar sentiments can be found in Boyle's *The Excellency of Theology, Compared with Natural Philosophy*, in Hall, *Robert Boyle on Natural Philosophy*, pp. 140 – 41.

17. And the common conception that historically the move among Christian scientists from locating design in gaps to locating design in laws was a desperate retreat in the face of Darwin is simply myth. That *type* of move long predated Darwin.

18. One additional interesting consideration is that although science may have an impressive record of closing gaps, it has a nearly equally distinguished record of opening new gaps. Every unsolved scientific puzzle represents a (perhaps very temporary) explanatory gap in our science — if it were not, it would not be a puzzle.

New theories that solve such puzzles — and thus close the gaps I question — typically open new lines of research. Indeed, some philosophers of science think that it is one criterion of a good theory that it suggest new research. But those new lines of research nearly invariably generate new puzzles. Thus scientific advances *themselves* frequently generate (or at least uncover) new gaps in our scientific understanding of the world. And every explanatory gap in our science is potentially a gap in the causal structure of the purely natural world. Historically science may have opened as many gaps as it has closed.

19. Of course, design arguments that do not involve gaps do not even in principle offer explanatory shortcuts, since in such cases there will still be a full immediate causal explanation of the production of the characteristics constituting evidence of design.

20. As Sir Oliver Lodge remarked: "If we have to postulate a spiritual world at all, we may as well utilize it throughout; not appealing to it unnecessarily. Seeking always a proximate explanation; holding on to physics as far as we possibly can, but being ready to abandon it whenever its methods are seen to be entirely incompetent" ("Design and Purpose in the Universe," in *The Great Design*, ed. Francis Mason [New York: Macmillan, 1934], p. 228). Later in the same paragraph Lodge explicitly includes design in nature in the relevant category.

Norms and Strategies

In light of the above it is not at all obvious that we have some rational or scientific obligation to adopt methodological naturalism in science. In fact, even were such justifications correct the last three would support at most the adoption of methodological naturalism as merely a pragmatic strategy. As a first approach to scientific problems, methodological naturalism may be a valuable — even the best — strategy. A search for natural explanations may virtually always be the best place to start. But if it becomes clear that limiting the search in that way hinders *understanding* of nature, if there are things in nature that constitute the natural equivalent of the stainless steel Stonehenge replica on Mars, then that limitation itself needs examination. And such examination is perfectly legitimate. However useful in practice, a pragmatically justified strategy does not constitute a norm that is inviolable no matter what the evidence.

The Intelligent Design Movement

As noted earlier, theories asserting the designedness of nature (or of various things in nature) have become increasingly prominent in the past few years. Suspicions that there was something about the fundamental structure of the cosmos that might require extraordinary explanation first surfaced seriously in physics around a quarter of a century ago and involved a cluster of issues including *anthropic cosmological* princi-

ples and *fine-tuning* arguments. Some of the proposed explanations were relatively tame, some involved design, and some were *really* extraordinary.[21]

More recently a number of (primarily) Christians in various disciplines have formed a loose coalition known as the *intelligent design* (or ID) movement. The ID movement exhibits a fair amount of diversity, but the center of gravity of the group is a rejection of methodological naturalism, at least as any sort of norm.[22] The fundamental contentions of the group are that design concepts can be given genuinely empirical content, cannot be ruled out of science *a priori* and that theories of design in nature should be given a fair scientific chance.[23] To charges that design theories were already given that chance historically and failed, design advocates respond that the evidential situation is now very different, that design theories can now be given much more sophisticated construction and content, and that design theories can be explanatorily competitive, especially in light of the extraordinary complexity and structures being uncovered in, for example, biochemistry.[24]

The design evidences cited by this group generally consist of either particular types of complexity, certain types of improbability in certain defined circumstances or considerations involving "information" in biological systems.[25] Given that design and gaps are separable issues, the evidences proposed as marks of design do not necessarily have to be linked to gaps. (In fact, even some of the more prominent design

---

21. Among the latter are strong anthropic principles, participatory anthropic principles and many worlds hypotheses.

22. The work of Phillip Johnson, who is the acknowledged leader of the ID group, constitutes the most visible statement of the ID movement on this issue.

23. Various people in this group do not explicitly identify the designer of the design in nature as God and have consequently been accused of disingenuousness. However, given the legitimate separability of issues of design, the character of design evidence, identification of designedness and so forth from questions concerning the identity of the designer in question, such accusations seem misguided. The former questions can in fact be investigated independently of the latter. It is true, however, that nearly every member of the movement does believe that design in nature would ultimately track back to God.

24. It is generally claimed both that biochemical data have undergone revolutionary changes making design vastly more plausible, and that alternative explanations (e.g., of origins of life, based on Miller-Urey results, etc.) have during the same time been increasingly exposed as unworkable.

25. The complexity in question is "irreducible" complexity, the probability involves "specification" of a certain sort, and the information in question is that of Shannon information theory. For complexity arguments see Michael Behe, *Darwin's Black Box* (New York: Free Press, 1996). For improbability arguments, see William A. Dembski, *The Design Inference* (New York: Cambridge University Press, 1998). Information arguments occur in quite a number of places, from for example, Thaxton, Bradley and Olson, to Wilder-Smith.

advocates have no serious quarrel with the possibility that all forms of life are descended from a common ancestor.) The majority of those within the movement, however, believe that there are gaps in nature, that the existence of various gaps can be *scientifically* substantiated and that evolution cannot close all such gaps. (That combination of views of course points to the occurrence of supernatural interventions in nature historically.)

Although the bulk of the ID movement rejects large-scale (macro) evolution, a few do accept some type of macroevolutionary history of life on earth. And some who reject macroevolution nonetheless admit that they could be wrong — that some form of macroevolution could turn out to be correct. However, given the biochemical and empirical evidence as they see it, nearly all within the ID movement take the odds of that to be quite small and would insist that even were some form of macroevolution correct, a *Darwinian* (chance-driven) evolution was empirically hopelessly inadequate. But even if life had an evolutionary history, that would not, on their view, change the fact that the biological realm exhibited evidences of deliberate design.[26]

There are other differences of opinion within the movement, but the general contention is that prohibitions on considering deliberate design as a scientific explanation of some aspects of nature are not legitimate and that a number of recent scientific discoveries may be best — or even only — made intelligible by reference to design.

Conclusion

What should we make of all this? If the foregoing is correct, there are no compelling grounds for ironclad prohibitions against genuinely scientific design theories, should any such theories arise.

Are there present prospects of such? Most people within the design movement believe that the answer is a clear yes, and most critics of the movement give an unequivocal no. Among factors underlying that disagreement there is on the one side a tendency to overestimate purely natural science and on the other side a tendency to underestimate nature. Overestimating science disposes one toward a belief that regardless of what explanatory puzzles confront us at the moment, human science unaided by any concepts beyond the purely natural, will ultimately conquer. Such a position could obviously induce scientists to pursue naturalistic hopes to unreasonable and even scientifically counterproductive lengths. At the other pole, underestimating nature may incline one to see gaps too readily and to not appreciate the enormous, remarkable capabilities nature in fact has.[27]

Ultimately, of course, scientists themselves will have the most say on this issue, but my own view is that for the moment the question is genuinely open. We are not in a position to say definitively that design concepts offer nothing that science will ever need or will ever find genuinely useful in its attempts to make sense of what we may discover within the cosmos. And nothing guarantees that we will never uncover a gap in nature itself that sober, rigorous scientific assessment will identify as being bridgeable only via agent activity. It is even possible that such a moment has already arrived. Contrary to some secular propaganda, there are fairly long stretches of empty space between any explicit chemical processes whose details we know and the structure of even simple forms of life. Unaided nature may be unable to navigate those stretches.[28] There may already be secular biologists who at around 3 a.m. find themselves just a *bit* anxious about the presumed natural origin of life or about electric rotary *E. coli* motors or about the fine-tuning of the cosmos.

On the other hand, it does not seem to me that our

26. Michael Behe, author of *Darwin's Black Box,* specifically denies any hostility toward common descent of all species.

27. Ironically, such underestimating of nature can also have roots in overestimations of science — for example, implicitly assuming that if *our science* cannot explain something, and thus tacitly

identifies it as a gap, then it really *is* a gap, and nature cannot have the requisite capabilities to bridge it.

28. There are a number of scientists — both Christian and non-Christian — who suspect that to be the case.

grasp of nature's capabilities is thorough enough and broad enough to permit us to simply dismiss the possibility of discovering that (perhaps presently unknown) natural processes can bridge what at the moment look, even to our best science, like gaps. We *may* be approaching such a moment in developments in, for example, "complexity theory."[29] Of course, given that evidences of design can be completely independent of gaps, it would still be possible to argue that specific phenomena exhibited evidences of design resulting from processes that, while natural, were themselves intentionally structured to produce just such design. But in that case, the cited phenomena would have to constitute evidence of design in and of themselves. Although they may be suggestive, some of the currently popular design evidences do not strike me as settling the issue *scientifically.*

We must be a bit cautious about underestimating nature's capabilities. During its history science has been surprised by nature pretty regularly, and it may happen again. And we must be equally wary of over-estimating science — particularly our own. During its history science has often been overestimated in various circles, and that is almost certain to happen again.

There are some parts of nature that when experienced uncritically seem to generate in us a deep sense of their createdness and design. Kant spoke of the "starry skies above" as affecting us like that, and Psalm 19:1 speaks of the heavens declaring God's glory. Furthermore, there are things in nature that even when (perhaps especially when) viewed *critically,* generate a nearly irresistible intuition of designedness. We find such things both in general structures in nature (e.g., cosmic fine-tuning) and in specifics (e.g., *E. coli* motors). I think that it is in principle possible for defensible design cases to be made, and such cases need not violate any fundamental requirements or conditions of science. But whatever the fate of *formal scientific* arguments in this area, we are violating no broad principles of *rationality* in thinking of the creation around us — perhaps inescapably — in terms of supernatural design.

---

29. The theories of, for example, Stuart Kauffman, Rupert Sheldrake and others constitute attempts to uncover the outlines of previously unsuspected capacities of nature.

CHAPTER 50

The Origin of Life's Major Groups

Kurt P. Wise

Anyone who reads whodunit mysteries is familiar with most of the basic principles involved in reconstructing the history of life. First of all, mysteries begin with a question or series of questions. What happened, in what order and when? We ask similar questions about living organisms (e.g., "What events occurred in what order and when to produce the incredible variety of organisms we see about us today?"). Second, since the events of interest occurred in the past and cannot now be observed, the sleuth in a mystery must diligently search for anything that might still remain from those events. Historical biologists also diligently search for any clues that might remain from the time when life's diversity came to be. Third, the sleuth and those of us tagging along begin to construct scenarios to explain the discovered clues; based on the new scenarios, the sleuths search for more clues. Likewise, biologists imagine scenarios to explain the evidence they find of the origin of life's diversity, then search for more evidence to evaluate each of these scenarios.

Invariably, as we follow a mystery several scenarios are imagined, tested and rejected before the solution presents itself. Ultimately, a given scenario is accepted over another because it explains more evidence. In this comparison the strength of any given piece of evidence is not terribly important — the key is how simply and satisfactorily a given scenario explains the *entire* package of evidence.

As scientists have studied the origin of life's diversity, many scenarios have been imagined, tested and rejected over the years. Currently, most of the scientific community has accepted the scenario of *macroevolution*. Under this scenario, life, starting with a single-celled organism, has changed and diverged along the path of an "evolutionary tree." Following nonintelligent natural law and process over many millions of years, life has repeatedly branched to produce new organisms and organismal groups. Today the many terminal twigs of the tree are present about us as living species.

Macroevolution seems to explain many clues thought to relate to the origin of life's diversity. Other scenarios do exist, however. I would like to suggest that at least one of these scenarios — that of an intelligent Designer — can explain more evidence better than macroevolution can.

Similarities

Similarities among brothers and sisters are due to their having inherited similar genetic material from their parents. Greater similarities are generally found between brothers and sisters than between first cousins, and between first cousins than second cousins. Similarities indicate relationship. Degree of similarity indicates degree of genetic relatedness. If carefully measured, similarities could be used to reconstruct trees of genetic relationship.

In like manner, the macroevolutionary claim that all organisms are related explains why all organisms share similarities (e.g., the presence of RNA). The degrees of similarity among organisms can then be used to reconstruct trees of genetic-relationship called *phylogenies*. Each tree of similarity can be used to construct a separate and apparently independent phylogeny. In this way one phylogeny can be developed from adult similarities (e.g., skeletal or muscular similarities), another from similarities in embryological development (e.g., similarities in order of organ development) and others from molecular similarities (e.g., similarities in amino acid sequences of cytochrome and blood plasma proteins). The trees produced from these different methods are generally very similar. This remarkable degree of concordance seems to be strong evidence in support of macroevolution. It is often offered as a defense of macroevolutionary theory and a challenge to other models to explain.[1]

On the other hand, similarities don't always denote genetic relatedness. First, even in macroevolutionary theory, some organismal similarities are not thought to be due to common descent. Squid eyes, for example, are often dissected in biology classes to help students understand the very similar eye of humans. Yet squid and human eyes are not thought to have been derived from a common ancestor. The same can be said of the origin of multicellularity in green, red and brown algae; the origin of wings in bats, pteranodons, birds and insects; the origin of the streamlined body form in fishes and whales; and countless other examples. This has led evolutionists to classify similarities into two categories — *homologies* (similarities due to genetic relationship) and *analogies* (similarities independently derived).

Analogies can be identified through the use of trees of similarity. Assuming the organisms in such a tree are related through a common ancestor, each tree then represents a possible phylogeny. From such phylogenies one can determine the order in which various features of the organisms would have come into existence if the groups had followed that evolutionary pathway. In this way it is possible to tell whether any given feature could have evolved just once or must have evolved more than once. With the assistance of computers, an increasing number of trees of similarity are being produced. One of the striking features of such trees is that analogies are being found to be a very common feature of life. Every tree that takes into account at least a couple dozen features and includes several major groups of organisms seems to encounter several noninherited similarities.[2]

Considering the fact that organisms are composed of millions or even billions of features, the true number of analogies is likely to be extremely high. Yet this does not seem to be consistent with evolutionary theory. In an evolutionary scenario, analogies are features formed independently in two different organismal groups. The pathway that evolution takes is thought to be so fraught with unpredictable events that the likelihood that two separate evolutionary pathways will end up at the same place is thought to be very low. This is the major theme of Stephen Jay Gould's book *Wonderful Life*.[3] If the evolutionary process were run over again, one would not expect to get the same organisms again. Only when a feature is extremely advantageous to the organism *and* easy to produce naturalistically can it be considered reasonable that it could have evolved more than once. Most features, however, are so very complex that it is not clear that any of them could be so easily produced as to make even one a probable event. In evolutionary theory analogies would be expected to be a very uncommon feature of life. If, on the other hand, the diversity of life is due to an intelligent Designer's creating a number of distinct organisms, analogies should be common, as is observed, and as will be more commonly recognized with time.

Second, organisms all share atomic and subatomic similarities to each other and to rocks on planetary surfaces and to gases in stellar atmospheres, but this does not indicate genetic relatedness. Nor does the degree of similarity indicate anything about the degree of relatedness.

Third, humans and other intelligences construct objects that possess similarities. The similarities in these cases do not indicate genetic relatedness, and the

1. W. D. Stansfield, *The Science of Evolution* (New York: Macmillan, 1977), pp. 103–29; T. M. Berra, *Evolution and the Myth of Creationism: A Basic Guide to the Facts in the Evolution Debate* (Stanford, Calif.: Stanford University Press, 1990), pp. 18–30.

2. See, for example, E. S. Gaffney, P. A. Meylan and A. R Wyss, "Computer Assisted Analysis of the Relationships of the Higher Categories of Turtles," *Cladistics* 7 (1991): 313–35; and other articles in this journal.

3. S. J. Gould, *Wonderful Life: The Burgess Shale and the Nature of History* (New York: Norton, 1989).

degree of similarity is not a measure of relatedness. Rather, the similarities are due to a combination of factors — common purpose (e.g., similarities among guns, among cars, among houses, among dishes), common materials (e.g., similarities among the products of glassblowers, among the products of carpenters, among the products of machinists) and common signature (e.g., the Impressionism of Monet, the columns of the Romans, the suspense of Poe).

If an intelligent Designer was responsible for the variety of life, we should expect similarities among organisms. It is also easy enough to see how that the more similar two adult organisms are, the more similar their molecules and embryology will be. If the intelligent Designer has a common purpose — the production of adult organisms — then embryonic forms and molecular structures were designed to produce the adult structures. Similarities in adults would be expected to be tied to similarities in embryology and molecules.

All organisms, for example, develop from a single cell. This means that any two organisms start out looking very similar. Two organisms that have similar adult forms *end* up looking very similar. The purpose of embryonic development is the same in each case — to efficiently produce an adult from an initial egg. Given that the starting points, the ending points, the purpose and producer of the process are similar or identical, one would expect similar development in organisms that are very similar as adults. In fact, one would expect the degree of adult similarity and the degree of developmental similarity to track each other quite well.

In like manner, similar adult forms would most likely involve construction by using similar materials. Thus one would expect degree of similarity of both molecules and development to track the degree of similarity among adults. This would explain the concordances in trees of similarity constructed from different types of data.

Besides the abundance of analogies, a second challenge to macroevolutionary theory are the *discordances* among trees of relationship. Identical methods of calculating similarity on different criteria of similarity produce similar but rarely identical trees of relationship. Since genetic relatedness might be expected to produce higher correspondence than would the actions of an intelligent Designer, the commonness of discordances seems to argue more in favor of a common Designer than in favor of macroevolution.

A third challenge comes from molecular similarities. Although a number of molecules show similarity across groups, other molecules do not. There appears to be evidence of many molecular discontinuities within the life of the earth. Those discontinuities appear to coincide with between-group gaps. If, for example, one looks at the blood serum protein similarities in turtles, one finds evidence of substantial drops in similarity across certain boundaries. Between the two primary types of turtles, cryptodires and pleurodires, for example, there is a substantial drop in serum similarity.[4] Serology studies such as this examine dozens of different proteins at the same time. At least some of the proteins must be very similar across the groups (for reasons considered above). Yet the similarity in some proteins does not cancel out the differences in the other molecules. This would suggest that many molecules are *very* different on opposite sides of the boundary. Many of the serum molecules are thus likely to indicate a molecular discontinuity between cryptodires and pleurodires. This discontinuity corresponds to the substantial gap in form that exists between the side-necked and vertical-necked turtles.

Further molecular studies, especially with individual molecules, are likely to demonstrate many more such discontinuities between major groups of life. A theory of intelligent design would predict that these discontinuities will correspond to gaps in form and reinforce the claim that major groups of life are not related by descent.

---

4. W. Frair, "Taxonomic Relations Among Chelydrid and Kinosternid Turtles Elucidated by Serological Tests," *Copeia* 1972, no. 1, pp. 97–108.

Embryological Recapitulation

One evidence of macroevolution popularly heralded in the later part of the nineteenth century was *embryological recapitulation*. According to this hypothesis, as organisms develop from a fertilized egg, they pass through stages very similar to the evolutionary stages of their ancestors. Each human, for example, starts as a single cell — as all life supposedly did — then develops through a wormlike stage, then a fishlike stage (complete with gill slits), then a froglike stage, then a stage in which there is a tail, and finally the stage of a human child.[5] In this way an organism's embryology (development) recapitulates (briefly repictures) its phylogeny (evolutionary history).

But recapitulation theory has fallen on hard times.[6] First, some organisms are thought to be a product of almost the opposite process. Some organisms are thought to have evolved by retaining juvenile characteristics into adulthood (paedomorphosis), such as by slowing down the development of all but the reproductive systems (neoteny). The axolotl, for example, is an example of a paedomorphic amphibian, retaining larval characteristics often to an advanced age. The human being is thought to be an example of neoteny, being an ape with an immature body but a mature reproductive system. The existence of such antirecapitulation transformations would indicate that recapitulation is not a general law of evolutionary development.

Second, if the theory is correct, it would seem to mean that organisms evolve by *adding* developmental stages to their ancestors' developmental process. Yet organisms that are thought to be more evolutionarily derived don't seem to have longer development. This might suggest that previous development was accelerated, but the genetic mechanism for this acceleration is unknown. Also, organisms do not seem to pass through earlier stages any faster than through later

stages, and DNA does not seem to be longer or more complicated in evolutionarily more derived forms (such as different vertebrates). Another suggestion might be that earlier stages are selectively lost, but again no genetic mechanism is known to account for this, and it makes the origin of a coherent developmental sequence even more difficult.

Third, although developmental stages appear to be *broadly* similar to earlier evolutionary stages, when examined closely the similarities break down. In human development, for example, the fertilized egg is a diploid eukaryotic cell with twenty-three chromosome pairs — not a haploid, prokaryotic cell with a single strand of DNA from which we supposedly evolved. In like manner, the similarity between human developmental stages and worms and frogs breaks down very quickly upon close examination. The so-called gill slits in human development are not gill slits, and the "tail" in human development is not actually a tail. These things only bear superficial resemblance to those structures.

Fourth, in many cases development runs through stages in "incorrect" order for phylogeny. In sum, embryological recapitulation suffers from too many difficulties to be considered a viable theory. It has been rejected by a number of evolutionary biologists and has even been expunged from textbooks over the years.[7]

Yet embryological recapitulation theory is not dead. The general similarities between embryology and phylogeny are so compelling that they demand an explanation. Some feel that only macroevolutionary theory can provide that explanation.[8] I would suggest that an intelligent Designer hypothesis provides yet another explanation. In this hypothesis, as claimed above, the optimally designed transformation of an organism from a single cell is its *embryology*. Evolutionary biologists have also designed what they feel is

5. C. Sagan and A. Druyan, "Is It Possible to Be Pro-life and Pro-choice?" *Parade Magazine,* April 22, 1990.

6. See the extended discussion in S. J. Gould, *Ontogeny and Phylogeny* (Cambridge, Mass.: Belknap, 1977).

7. Ibid.; Stansfield, *Science of Evolution,* pp. 103 – 13; R. Milner,

The Encyclopedia of Evolution: Humanity's Search for Its Origins (New York: Facts on File, 1990), p. 44.

8. Sagan and Druyan, "Is It Possible"; L. W. Swan, "The Concordance of Ontogeny with Phylogeny," *Bioscience* 40, no. 5 (1990): 376 – 84.

the most efficient series of transformations connecting the ancestral cell with a given organism of today. The adult embodiment of the stages in this process makes up the organism's *phylogeny*. The general similarities between embryology and phylogeny are due to similar endpoints demanding similar pathways and broadly similar designs resulting from a higher-order similarity in intelligences. The differences in detail are simply the result of the lower-order differences between the intelligence that designed life and the intelligences that designed evolutionary phylogenies. In this sense intelligent design provides a *better* explanation for embryological recapitulation than does evolutionary theory.

Nested Hierarchy of Form

Given that a set of objects have different degrees of similarity, there are still many ways that such similarities could suggest groupings or classifications of the objects. Let's say we are considering two characteristics of some objects — their length and their color. Each characteristic has a linear spectrum of possibilities, and their combination has an areal "spectrum" of possibilities. We can lay down two axes perpendicular to each other, where the rectangle described by the two axes represents all possible combinations of length and color (figure 6.la).

Let's now consider a few of many possible ways the objects could be distributed in our length-color character space. First it could be that objects occupy the space randomly (figure 6.1b). In this case no one classification of objects suggests itself — all seem equally arbitrary. Another possibility is that all the objects are evenly spaced in our length-color plane (figure 6.1c). Once again, any classification seems arbitrary. Unlike the random distribution of points, however, the orderly arrangement here leads one to believe that there is cause for the pattern. Yet another possibility is shown in figure 6.1 d. As in the previous figure, there appears to be a pattern to be explained, but here a way of classifying the objects appears evident (figure 6.1e).

It seems that the similarities group some objects together, distinct from other objects (groups a through h), yet even some of these lower-level groupings can be grouped, or nested, into distinct higher-level groups (groups 1, 2 and 3). This "nested hierarchy" of form not only allows for a way to classify the objects, but also begs for an explanation. We could imagine that as we considered a third characteristic of the objects, figure 6.1's examples could each be placed into three-dimensional character space. As we added more and more characters, the same could be said about the distribution of objects in *n*-dimensional character space.

When we study organisms, we measure many characteristics. We can then plot our organisms in *n*- dimensional character space (sometimes called *morphospace*) and see how organisms are distributed. When we do, we find that they are distributed as in figure 6.1d — in a nested hierarchy of form. This has permitted the hierarchical classification of organisms — of species within genera, genera within families, families within orders, orders within classes, classes within phyla, and phyla within kingdoms. It also begs for an explanation. Why are organisms in a nested hierarchy of form?

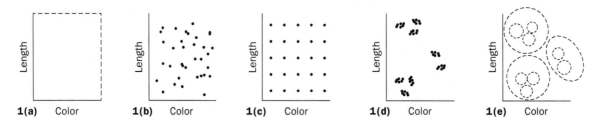

Figure 6.1. (a) 2-dimensional character space; (b) a random scatter of objects; (c) a regular pattern; (d) a nested hierarchy pattern; and (e) the classification of the pattern in d.

Macroevolutionists maintain that nested hierarchy is the result of macroevolution — and some claim it can *only* be due to that.[9] After all, evolutionary change is to have followed the path of an "evolutionary tree" — a trunk that branched into large limbs, which in turn branched into smaller limbs, which branched into smaller branches, which branched into even smaller branches, which finally branched into twigs. The twigs are species that can be grouped together into genera (small branches) and then into families (larger branches) and so on.

But the analogy of the evolutionary tree as an explanation for the nested hierarchy of biological form meets up with a few difficulties. If it is a "tree," then it is a very unusual tree indeed. First, the twigs of a real tree (analogous to modern species) tend to occupy most of the space available to them. This is because the twigs can proliferate more quickly than the large limbs, and the large limbs cannot diverge more rapidly than one twig at a time. The twigs thus tend to fill in the gaps. *As* a result, the twigs (when you ignore the branches to which they are connected) tend to fill space more or less randomly (as in figure 6.1b). This is unlike modern species, which are distributed much more like figure 6.1d. Most of morphospace is unfilled.

It would appear that (1) on the average, species do not proliferate as rapidly as larger groups are produced, and/or (2) large groups are produced in larger steps than species-by-species, and/or (3) species have a *much* higher extinction rate than higher groups. The first two possibilities run counter to gradualist theory and would demand an explanation for the rapid and/or hugestep origin of major groups. Although such proposals have been made, no suitable mechanism for such an origin has been found. Although the last possibility has an element of truth in it, it does not seem capable of explaining the distribution of species. Since higher groups become extinct only when every species in the group becomes extinct, species have a higher probability of becoming extinct than higher groups. Studies in the fossil record indicate, however, that most extinctions are more or less indiscriminate or random.[10] If that is the case, then a random extinction among organisms distributed randomly in morphospace would simply produce another random distribution of organisms — just rarer. That in fact happens in a real tree, for twigs are more susceptible to death than larger branches, and still they are distributed more like a random pattern than a nested hierarchical pattern. In order to produce the pattern in figure 6.1d by extinction, one needs to be selective in extinction — selectively preserving species most similar to their ancestors. It is unclear that any currently proposed macroevolutionary process could truly produce a nested hierarchy of form.

Second, in the tree analogy, as one travels from the tree's base to its twigs, one is going forward through time. As one does, the trunk gradually diverges into branches, the large branches diverge into smaller branches and so on. By this we see that trees grow by gradual divergence. If the analogy is to hold, organismal groups should have arisen by gradual divergence. Yet the gaps in form between living groups also exist in the fossil record. *As* one goes back in time, organismal groups tend not to converge in morphology, but remain distinct. Most major groups remain identifiable by modern characters and distinct from their supposed ancestors all the way back to their oldest fossil representatives. This would seem to imply that the branching event of one major group from another never did occur.

Third, in a real tree the connection between branches and their sub-branches is clearly seen. In the fossil record, on the other hand, transitions between major groups are rarely evidenced. Interspecific transitional forms seem to be rare to absent in the fossil record,[11] and transitional series between major groups are conspicuously rare to absent.

9. Stansfield, *Science of Evolution*, pp. 98–103; M. Ruse, *Darwinism Defended: A Guide to the Evolution Controversies* (Reading, Mass.: Addison-Wesley, 1982), p. 40.

10. D. M. Raup, "Extinction: Bad Luck or Bad Genes?" *Acta Geologica Hispanica* 16 (1981): 25–33.

11. S. J. Gould and N. Eldredge, "Punctuated Equilibria: The Tempo and Mode of Evolution Reconsidered," *Paleobiology* 3, no. 2 (1977): 115–51.

Fourth, in the tree analogy, the number of major branches increases through time. The branches arise due to the proliferation of twigs, so the number of twigs increases faster than numbers of branches. In the fossil record, however, such a "cone of increasing diversity" is not observed. Instead, the number of major groups we have today was achieved early in earth history, when species diversity was low. In fact, the number of classes of arthropods and echinoderms at the time of the first appearance of each of these groups was actually *higher* than it is at present.[12] This would argue — as do the distribution of species, higher group stasis and the paucity of intermediates — that major groups do not arise due to a proliferation of species. Yet no evolutionary mechanism for how this transformation *did* occur has yet been found.

Another possible explanation for the nested hierarchy of biological form is in an intelligent Designer. Think of it this way: Humans have designed a large number of different types of teaspoons. Some are made of stainless steel, others of silver. Some have monograms on them, others do not. Some have artistic designs engraved on their handles, others do not. Yet they are all classifiable as teaspoons. And though there are many types of tablespoons, many types of soup spoons and many types of serving spoons, all these types of spoons can be classified together as spoons. The wide variety of spoons can be classified with the wide variety of forks and the wide variety of knives as silverware; and the silverware can be classified with plates, bowls and cups as tableware. Tableware can be classified with furniture and appliances as housewares, and so on. Humans, without so intending, create objects that are distributed in character space in a nested hierarchy of form.

If life is the result of an intelligence analogous to humankind's, then a nested hierarchy of life forms would be the expected result. Furthermore, an origin by intelligent design allows the possibility that organisms originated at times and or places where fossilization did not occur. It also allows for the possibility that no transitional forms were involved at all. Either way, the lack of transitional forms, higher group stasis, and the inverted cone of diversity would be explained. And if the gaps between major groups were so large that speciation has had insufficient time to bridge them, the general stasis of major groups and the marked nested hierarchy of biological form through time would be an expected result. In this sense intelligent design is more successful at explaining the nested hierarchy of biological form than is modern evolutionary theory.

Suboptimal Improvisations

Near-optimum form is often thought to be equally predictable from the always-perfecting process of natural selection and the optimum design of an intelligent Creator. Stephen Jay Gould, on the other hand, has suggested that the theories are distinguishable by *imperfections*.[13] As he reasons, the evolutionary process, being blind to purpose, limited in resources and constrained by history, might be expected to produce less-than-optimal designs. These "suboptimal improvisations" of evolution would be expected in an evolutionary process, but not in the design of an intelligent Creator. Gould's showcase example is the panda, which, because of the constraints of being descended from five-fingered bears, lacks an opposable thumb. Yet the inefficient, blind process of evolution provided the panda with a "second-best" solution: an extension of the radial sesamoid bone in the wrist which can function as an immovable "thumb." This thumb is used by the panda to strip leaves off bamboo shoots for food. Such a less-than-optimal design is evidence, Gould claims, for evolution and not intelligent design.

There are at least two reasons to doubt that suboptimal improvisations are truly suboptimal. First of all, we are far from understanding the complexity of individual organisms, let alone the entire ecosystem in which that organism lives. What appears to be less than optimal design to us with our limited knowledge

---

12. Gould, *Wonderful Life.*

13. S.J. Gould, *The Panda's Thumb: More Reflections on Natural History* (New York: Norton, 1980), pp. 19–26.

may actually be an optimal design when the entire system is considered. Consider the thickness of armor plating on the side of a warship. Since the purpose of such plating is to protect the ship from the puncture of an incoming warhead, it is advantageous to make the plating as thick as possible. Yet the plating on actual warships is much thinner than it could be made. The reason is, of course, that an increase in plating thickness makes the ship heavier, and thus slower. A less mobile ship is more likely to get hit more often and less likely to get to where it is needed when it is needed. The actual thickness of the armor on a warship is a tradeoff—not so thin as to make the ship too easily sinkable, and not so thick as to make the ship too slow. We know too little about the complexity of organisms and the environment in which they live to conclude that any one particular feature is actually less than optimal.

In the case of the panda, it's not clear that an opposable thumb would be any better design than its current wrist-bone extension. My sixth-grade career in basketball was cut short by a pass made to me when my wonderfully designed opposable thumb was oriented in such a way so as to receive the full force of the ball along its main axis. At that moment I would have preferred that my thumb had been an extension of a bone in my wrist than a dexterous digit with two well-designed hinge joints. So it's not at all clear that an immovable stub would be any less desirable to a panda than a relatively fragile, hinged, opposable thumb.

Second, all claimed suboptimal improvisations seem to work efficiently enough. The thumb of the panda, for example, seems quite efficient at stripping bamboo leaves. In fact, according to evolutionary history, the panda's thumb has probably provided food for the panda for millions of years. The fact that the panda is now endangered seems to be due to dwindling food reserves and the encroachment of human beings—neither of which is likely to have been prevented if the panda had had an opposable thumb.

Vestigial Organs

According to macroevolutionary theory, not only do species, genera and higher groups of organisms come and go, but so do organismal structures. Species will linger in dwindling populations (e.g., endangered species) for long periods of time before submitting to extinction. In like manner, organismal structures probably linger with reduced function for long periods of time before finally disappearing. These organs with reduced or no function are called *vestigial.*

Although many organs once thought vestigial have been found to have function, others are sure to have at least a reduced function from the past (e.g., hip bones that appear briefly in the embryology of sperm whales and small appendage bones that are found in some snakes). These then are less-than-optimal organs that would seem to be evidence of evolution rather than intelligent design.[14]

A serious problem with this argument for evolution is that whereas vestigial organs are known, nascent organs are not. If evolution were true, one would expect to see not just organs "going out" but also organs "coming in." These new organs would be called *nascent* organs. The absence of such organs would seem to argue that although we have evidence of degeneration from an earlier, more optimal design, we lack evidence of a move toward a new optimal design. It would seem that if an intelligent Designer created optimal designs *in the past* and life's history has been a move away from that optimum, the presence of vestigial organs and the absence of nascent organs would be better explained by intelligent design than by evolutionary theory.

Macrobiogeography

The last major class of evidences in support of evolution from the living world includes those in the field of biogeography. There are two sorts of biogeographical evidences. One type of claim is that very similar species are often found near to one another, as if they

---

14. Berra, *Evolution and the Myth.*

evolved from one another. This type of biogeography, which I call *microbiogeography,* has many supporting examples. Microbiogeography is evidence for microevolution (the evolution of populations) and the origin of species — however, *not* for macroevolution and the origin of major groups. What I call *microbiogeography* is the claim that major types of organisms tend to be associated with one another.

There are very few examples of macrobiogeographical evidences for macroevolution, and none of them is very strong. The best-known claim is the concentration of marsupials in Australia. But there are several reasons that marsupials in Australia are actually a poor example. First, all marsupials are not in Australia. The Virginia opossum of North America, for example, is a marsupial. It is thought to have come from South America, not Australia. Thus not all similar organisms *are* in the same area. Second, in the fossil record marsupials are known from every continent.[15] Third, marsupials are the oldest fossil mammals known from Africa, Antarctica and Australia — in that order.[16] The fossil record seems to show a migration of marsupials from somewhere around the intersection of the Eurasian and African continents and then a survival in only the continents farthest from their point of origin (South America and Australia). The same major groups of marsupials (opossums) are found in both South America and Australia. Macroevolutionists claim that these major groups of marsupials are together because they evolved from a common ancestor, but the evidence can be at least as well explained as similar organisms (fit for similar environments and with similar capabilities) traveling more or less together to similar environments.

Fossil Order

If one were able to see the history of life in accelerated playback, macroevolution should show up as major changes in life on earth. It turns out that we can, in a way, see life in this accelerated mode. It is generally thought that the geologic column of rocks was formed over the course of most of earth history. Every once in a while those rocks preserved a sample of that life — an occasional motion-picture frame in earth history. As a result, a review of the fossils (picture frames) from the deepest (oldest) rocks to the present should provide an accelerated playback of earth history. It's only reasonable that evolutionary theorists should turn to the fossil record for evidence of macroevolutionary theory. Three types of evidences for evolution are found in the *order* of the fossils.

First, if evolution were true, the fossil record "playback" should show an ever-changing set of organisms. This would allow researchers to identify where one is in the geologic column (and time) by the set of fossils known in that section of the column. And truly such a wholesale change in fossils is seen through the fossil record, and an order has been found that allows relative dating by the suites of fossils that are known from particular rocks.

Second, if evolution were an ongoing process, species should be coming and going. At any given time there should be species that have just recently come to be (young species), species that have been around for a long time and are about ready to go extinct (old species), and species in between (middle-aged species). And as one moves above and below that group of fossils, one should see suites of species that gradually show less and less similarity with the original group. This is exactly what is seen in the fossil record. In the Cenozoic (the uppermost deposits), for example, the frequency of species that are known to be alive today gradually drops to zero as one travels lower — or further into the past.

Third, if macroevolution were true and we knew the evolutionary phylogeny of an organism or group of organisms, then one would expect to see the members of that pathway appearing in the order predicted by the phylogeny. Such a correspondence between first-appearance order and phylogeny *is* seen in

---

15. D. E. Savage and D. E. Russell, *Mammalian Paleofaunas of the World* (Reading, Mass.: Addison-Wesley, 1983).

16. Ibid.

the fossil record. In the phylogeny of humankind, for example, the following are the steps (with the radiometric time of first appearance of each step in parentheses, in millions of years before the present): bacteria (3500[17]); protists (1500 – 1800[18]); invertebrate animals (590 – 570[19]), jawless fish (517 – 510[20]), jawed fish (424 – 409[21]), bony lobe-finned fish (408[22]), amphibians (377 – 363[23]), reptiles (323 – 311[24]), mammals (210 – 208[25]), primates (70 – 65[26]), apes (22[27]), hominid (5.5[28]), *Homo* (1.8? – 1.6[29]), *H. sapiens* (0.1[30]), art (0.05), civilization (0.01). Within this list is recorded the general correspondence between the first appearance of vertebrate classes and their phylogeny. Similarly, arthropod classes tend to appear in phylogenetic order. Finally, in a most remarkable manner, the plant phyla appear in the order predicted by their phylogeny.[31]

Although at first glance the order of fossils seems to be good evidence for macroevolutionary theory, it does present a couple of difficulties. The first concerns the issue of polarity. Although macroevolutionary theory predicts major changes over the course of time, it is incapable of predicting ahead of time what the direction or nature of change will be. For example, parasites have limited internal complexity, but macroevolutionists generally do not know whether they were derived from simpler animals without internal complexity or whether they were derived from more complex organisms but have since lost internal complexity due in some part to disuse. Green algae are thought to be related to land plants because of similar photosynthetic chemistry, but without the fossil record it might have been impossible to determine whether land plants evolved from algae or algae from plants. Similarly, without the fossil record it might have been difficult to determine whether marine mammals evolved from or into land mammals. As a result, to use the fossil record to verify the "predictions" of phylogeny may in some cases (or all?) be assuming the order of fossils to prove it. The details of this relationship need to be studied in detail to determine how this affects the use of fossil-record order to evidence evolution.

Second, the correspondence between phylogeny and the fossil record is not as strong as it might first seem. When the order of *all* kingdoms, phyla and classes is compared with the most reasonable phylogenies, over 95 percent of all the lines are not consistent with the order in the fossil record.[32] The only statistically significant exceptions are the orders of first appearances of the phyla of plants and the classes of vertebrates and arthropods. Yet these three lineages also order organismal groups from sea-dwellers to land-dwellers. The land-plant phyla, for example, are in a simple sequence from plants that need standing water to survive (e.g., algae and bryophytes) to those that can survive extreme desiccation (e.g., the cacti).

17. A. H. Knoll and J. H. Lipps, "Evolutionary History of Prokaryotes and Protists," in *Fossil Prokaryotes and Protists,* ed. J. H. Lipps (Boston: Blackwell, 1993).

18. Ibid.

19. W. B. Harland et al., *A Geologic Time Scale* (New York: Cambridge University Press, 1989), pp. 28 – 30.

20. R. L. Carroll, *Vertebrate Paleontology and Evolution* (New York: Freeman, 1988); Harland et al., *Geologic Time Scale.*

21. Carroll, *Vertebrate Paleontology*; Harland et al., *Geologic Time Scale.*

22. Carroll, *Vertebrate Paleontology*; Harland et al., *Geologic Time Scale.*

23. Carroll, *Vertebrate Paleontology*; Harland et al., *Geologic Time Scale.*

24. Carroll, *Vertebrate Paleontology*; Harland et al., *Geologic Time Scale.*

25. J. A. Lillegraven, Z. Kielan-Jaworowska and W. A. Clemens, *Mesozoic Mammals: The First Two-Thirds of Mammalian History*

(Berkeley: University of California Press, 1977); Harland et al., *Geologic Time Scale.*

26. Lillegraven, Kielan-Jaworoska and Clemens, *Mesozoic Mammals*; Harland et al., *Geologic Time Scale.*

27. Savage and Russell, *Mammalian Paleofaunas*; Harland et al., *Geologic Time Scale.*

28. T. W. Phenice and N. J. Sauer, *Hominid Fossils: An Illustrated Key,* 2nd ed. (Dubuque, Iowa: Brown, 1977); F. H. Smith and F. Spencer, *The Origins of Modern Humans: A World Survey of the Fossil Evidence* (New York: Liss, 1984).

29. Phenice and Sauer, *Hominid Fossils*; Smith and Spencer, *Origins of Modern Humans.*

30. Phenice and Sauer, *Hominid Fossils*; Smith and Spencer, *Origins of Modern Humans.*

31. K. P. Wise, "First Fossil Appearances of Higher Taxa: A Preliminary Study of Order in the Fossil Record," unpublished paper.

32. Ibid.

The vertebrate classes go from sea-dwellers (fish) to land/sea creatures (amphibians) to land creatures (reptiles, mammals), to flying creatures (birds). The arthropod classes go from sea-dwellers (e.g., trilobites, crustaceans) to land-dwellers (e.g., insects). So it's not clear that macroevolution is truly a good explanation for the order of fossil-first appearances of major groups of life. Such a radical idea as a global flood, for example, which gradually overcame first the sea and then the land, actually explains the primary order of major groups in the fossil record (sea to land) better than macroevolutionary theory.[33]

The general features of the fossil record that *are* explained by evolutionary theory are at least as well explained by other theories. The existence of a Creator who introduced organisms on the earth in a particular order could explain the general change in organisms through the record, but so could the effects of a global flood as it successively sampled from a biogeographic ally zoned distribution of organisms. The general change in organisms through time can be predicted by anyone and all of these three theories (macroevolution, progressive creation, global deluge). On the other hand, the rarity or absence of evidence for transitions between major groups and the fact the major groups do not converge on one another as one goes back in the fossil record seem to argue that major groups were introduced in the fossil record only *after* they were fully formed. This is more consistent with creative order and global deluge theories than with macroevolutionary theory. As for the linear relationship of species similarity above and below a particular level in the geologic column, this can be just as well explained by global deluge theory or progressive creation theory as it is by macroevolution. In deluge theory, different species are found in different preflood environments and get mixed with species from adjacent environments, providing the species similarity relationship. Continual introduction of species whether by evolution or creation would produce the same relation-ship. In short, all fossil-record order can be at least as well explained by order of creation decided by creative fiat or ocean-to-land burial of organisms in a diverse world overcome by global deluge as it is by macroevolution.

Fossil Transitions

If macroevolution is true, then organisms have made many substantial transformations in the course of history. The preservation of these transformations might be expected in the fossil record. Series of fossil species like the horse series, the elephant series, the camel series, the mammal-like reptile series, the early birds and early whales all seem to be strong evidence of evolution. Another class of fossil evidence comes in individual *stratomorphic intermediates*. These are fossils that stand intermediate between the group from which they are descendent and the one to which they are ancestral — both in stratigraphic position and in morphology. They have a structure that stands between the structure of their ancestors and that of their descendants. However, they are also found in the fossil record as younger than the oldest fossils of the ancestral group and older than the oldest fossils of the descendent group.

Stratomorphic intermediate species and organis-mal groups should be a common feature of the fossil record. And examples of stratomorphic intermediates do exist. Mammal-like reptiles stand between reptiles and mammals, both in the position of their fossils and in the structure of their bones. The same can be said of the anthracosaurs, which stand between amphibians and reptiles, and the phenacodontids, which stand between the horses and their claimed ancestors. In like manner, some fossil genera are stratomorphic intermediates in the group in which they are classified. They are the oldest fossils known in the group and most similar to the group from which they are supposedly descendent. Examples include *Pikaia* among the chordates, *Archaeopteryx* among the birds,

33. K. P. Wise, "Ecological Zonation and the First Appearances of Higher Taxa," unpublished paper.

Baragwanathia among lycopods, *Ichthyostega* among the amphibians, *Purgatorius* among the primates, *Pakicetus* among the whales and *Proconsul* among the hominoids.

Once again, the existence of stratomorphic intermediate groups and species seems to be good evidence for evolution. However, the stratomorphic intermediate evidences are not without difficulty for evolutionary theory. First, none of the stratomorphic intermediates have intermediate structures. Although the entire organism is intermediate in structure, it's the *combination* of structures that is intermediate, not the nature of the structures themselves. Each of these organisms appears to be a fully functional organism full of fully functional structures. *Archaeopteryx,* for example, is thought to be intermediate between reptiles and birds because it has bird structures (e.g., feathers) and reptile structures (e.g., teeth, forelimb claws). Yet the teeth, the claws, the feathers and all other known structures of *Archaeopteryx* appear to be fully functional. The teeth seem fully functional as teeth, the claws as claws, and the feathers as any flight feathers of modern birds. It is merely the *combination* of structures that is intermediate, not the structures themselves. Stephen Jay Gould calls the resultant organisms "mosaic forms"[34] or "chimeras." As such they are really no more intermediate than any other member of their group. In fact, there are *many* such "chimeras" that live today (e.g., the platypus, which lays eggs like a reptile and has hair and produces milk like a mammal). Yet these are not considered transitional forms by evolutionists because they are not found as intermediates in stratigraphic position.

As a result, the total list of claimed transitional forms is very small (the above list is very nearly complete) compared to the total number of mosaic forms. The frequency seems intuitively too low for evolutionary theory. The very low frequency of stratomorphic intermediates may be nothing more than the low percentage of mosaic forms that happen to fall in the correct stratigraphic position by chance — perhaps because of random introduction of species by a Creator or the somewhat randomized burial of organisms in a global deluge.

Second, stratomorphic intermediates tend to be found in groups that we have already seen show a fossil-record order consistent with evolutionary order — that is, vertebrates and plants. They are absent among the groups of invertebrates. In some cases a series of intermediates cannot even be imagined. More often the imagined intermediates cannot have survived. Transitions from one major group of organisms to another are challenges to the ingenuity of even the most capable macroevolutionists.

Just as the more general order may be due to a pattern of a Creator's introduction or of the advance of a global flood, these few stratomorphic intermediates may be explainable in the same way. If, for example, the general order of the fossil record is due to introduction of organisms, then one might occasionally expect stratomorphic intermediates to have been created in the sequence between the two groups. Likewise, on an earth that is zoned biologically, fully functional, structurally intermediate organisms are likely to be geographically located between the two groups they lie between structurally. An advancing global flood would then tend to land structural intermediates between the other two groups in the fossil record. Thus, whereas the mosaic nature of claimed "transitional forms" presents a challenge to evolutionary theory, that and the existence of stratomorphic intermediates *are* consistent with progressive creation and global deluge theories.

Evidence That Evolution Leaves Unexplained

Complexity. Anyone who has taken college biochemistry has been impressed with the extraordinary complexity of replication, transcription, the Krebs cycle and other features of living things. For those who did

---

34. Gould and Eldredge, "Punctuated Equilibria."

not take such a course, these are a few of the many chemical processes that occur within anyone of your trillions of body cells at any given moment. Photosynthesis, as an example of a subcellular process, is thought to involve as many as five hundred chemical steps — of which we "fully" understand only a few. Yet a number of these kinds of processes occur spontaneously within individual cells.

At a higher level, introductory biology classes often require the biology student to understand the general structure and function of Golgi bodies, smooth and rough endoplasmic reticulum, microbodies, lysosomes, mitochondria, nucleus, chromosomes and the cell membrane. These are some of the fascinating and complex structures found *within* cells of our body. At an even higher level, in advanced biology we learn the classes of cardiac, smooth muscle, striated muscle, epidermal and other tissues. These are special associations of specialized cells that make up larger structures of our body.

At an even higher level, we learn early in our education of human organs: the heart, lungs, liver, gall bladder, kidney, gonads, brain and the like. There are many such complex working elements within each of our bodies. Science education has also told us about systems in our bodies-circulatory, respiratory, urinary, digestive, nervous, skeletal, muscular and so on. Each of these systems challenges our powers of memorization and understanding.

At a higher level still, there are countless fascinating and complex interrelationships between one organism and others. For example, living in our intestines there is a diverse set of microorganisms from which we benefit almost as much as they benefit from us. These organisms break down molecules we cannot break down, providing us with food we would otherwise lack. In return, they are provided with a comfortable home (to them!) and a constant supply of food. Similar cases of mutual symbiosis exist throughout our world (e.g., cellulose-lignin-digesting microorganisms in the guts of termites; sulfur-reducing bacteria in ocean-vent tubeworms; algae and fungi in lichens; photosynthetic microorganisms in corals).

At a higher level again, communities of organisms are made up of a complex arrangement of a large number of organisms — herbivores and carnivores; pollinators and flowering plants; decomposers; under-story and upper-story plants, and so on.

Higher than these, the earth and its living organisms exist together in a great network of complex interactions — oxygen used by animals must be produced by photo synthesizers, and carbon dioxide used by plants must be released by animals. The complex interaction of the earth and its life can be seen in how the earth and its life have responded to the changes that humankind has made (such as the interaction of fossil-fuel burning and global climate, the interaction of aerosol sprays and ozone).

On a level even above this, the earth exists in a complex arrangement of planets, asteroids, moons, stars and galaxies in such a way as to allow life on earth to exist and persist.

Each of these levels features a complexity that is staggering to the human mind — a complexity greater than any that in our experience can be produced by nonintelligent natural cause. If we follow the principle of appealing only to principles that are reasonable in our experience, then the complexity of any one of these levels seems to require an appeal to an intelligent cause. However, the *total* complexity is at least the sum of the complexities of each level. If the complexity of each level suggests an intelligent cause, the total complexity screams for an intelligent cause. Macro-evolutionary theory has never successfully explained the acquisition of any level of this complexity, let alone the total complexity.

Integration. As if the basic complexity of things were not enough, the integration of that complexity is truly astounding. Not only do subcellular chemical processes involve a large number of complex molecules and chemical steps, but those items and events are connected in a well-balanced and well-timed series of items and steps to produce a well-integrated process. Similarly, the workings of subcellular organelles, cells in tissues, tissues in organs, organs in systems, systems in bodies, organisms with other organisms, organisms in communities, and communities in the biosphere all show staggering integration. As with the complexity of these items and events on any given level, such a level of integration has never been observed to arise from nonintelligent natural law and process. Integration seems to argue for intelligent cause.

In addition, the integration that is so striking *within* levels is even more striking *between* levels. Not only do subcellular organelle systems and chemical processes show integration, but the chemical and organelle systems are themselves linked together, and must be for the cell to survive. Even more impressive, a similar integration exists between all levels. Once again, this level of integration is unexplained by evolutionary theory but is addressable by intelligent cause theory.

Another interesting point here concerns the observed structure of integration. Chemical processes lie within subcellular organelles, subcellular organelles within cells, cells within tissues. There is a nested hierarchy of complexity and integration of life on earth. This nested hierarchy of complexity might be expected if it came about by means of the same intelligent cause that brought about the nested hierarchy of classification of biological form. It is not expected by macroevolutionary theory.

Aesthetics. One striking characteristic of life unexplained by evolution is its aesthetic nature. Mathematicians often find aesthetic beauty in elegant proofs. The remarkable integration of organismal complexity strikes mathematicians as another example of profound beauty. Artists see beauty in life's symmetry and its vast array of color. The countless pieces of fine and performing art sparked by the symmetry and colors of life testify to the level of beauty perceived by artists worldwide through all of earth history.

This magnificent beauty, observed across a variety of levels among living organisms, cannot be explained by macroevolutionary theory. It is, however, consistent with an intelligent cause for life — a Designer whose tastes and predilections human beings may share.

Conclusion

Macroevolutionary theory explains a large number of seemingly independent categories of evidence (see table 6.1). The many *corresponding similarities* among adults, embryologies and molecules of organisms are explained as characters shared by reason of common descent. The *nested hierarchy of form* is explained as due to the successive branching pattern of evolutionary transformation. *Suboptimal improvisations* are explained as structures that are suboptimal because of the transformation of organisms by purposeless, infinitely myopic process of evolution. *Vestigial organs* are explained as organs that have fallen into disuse because of organic change. The *biogeographic distribution* of Australian marsupials is explained as due to

Macroevolution	Intelligent Creator
Adult similarities	Adult similarities
Embryological similarities	Embryological similarities
Molecular similarities	Molecular similarities
Correspondence of similarities	Correspondence of similarities Abundant analogies Discordances in phylogenies
Embryological recapitulation Evidences?	Embryological recapitulation Evidences Counter evidences
Nested hierarchy of life	Nested hierarchy of life Nested hierarchy of complexity Large morphological gaps Molecular discontinuities Higher group stasis
Stratomorphic intermediates	Stratomorphic intermediates? Mosaic/chimera nature of Rarity of Inverted cone of diversity
Suboptimal improvisations	Suboptimal improvisations
Vestigial organs	Vestigial organs? Absence of nascent organs
Macrobiogeographic evidences	Macrobiogeographic evidences?
Water-to-land fossil order	Water-to-land fossil order Nonevolutionary order of first appearances Organismal complexity Integration of complexity Aesthetics of life

Table 6.1. Types of data explained by theories of macroevolution and intelligent creator. "?" indicates possible or partial explanation.

the origin and diversification of Australian marsupials solely in Australia. The *change in fossils* through the fossil record is explained as due to the continuous change of organisms through time. The *orders of first appearance* of plant phyla, vertebrate classes, arthropod classes and organisms in the phylogeny of humankind are explained by major evolutionary transformations being preserved in the fossil record. *Fossil series* and *stratomorphic intermediates* are explained as specially preserved steps in the evolutionary process. Macroevolution is a powerful theory of explanation for a wide variety of physical data.

But macroevolution is not the only theory capable of explaining such a wide variety of data. I would maintain that the claims of Scripture provide us with a model that can give a better explanation of far more of the major features of life than evolution (again, see table 6.1). According to the Bible, God is an all-knowing, intelligent being with immeasurable beauty and glory. According to Scripture, he created all things, including life on the earth, in such a way that they reflect his very nature (including his intelligence and his beauty). We infer from the nature of other things he created that he fashioned all things in a mature form in a hierarchical pattern. In the case of life, we are told that he created a number of distinct kinds of organisms. These organisms have been allowed to change since the time of introduction. And we are told that God created humankind in his own image, to reflect him in unique ways (e.g., to reason in similar ways, to appreciate aesthetics in similar ways and to produce hierarchical pattern in similar ways). We are also told that sometime after the creation God judged the earth with a global deluge.

A single wise Designer creating a variety of organisms to construct a fully integrated biosphere explains the *corresponding similarities* among adults, embryologies and molecules which are traditionally used to evidence evolution. It also explains the high frequency of *analogies*, the *discordances in trees of relationship* and possibly *molecular discontinuities* that evolution cannot explain. A wise Designer might well produce embryologies that are generally similar and specifi-

cally different from phylogenies engineered by human minds — thus explaining both *embryological recapitulation evidences* and the *counterevidences* that are challenges to current evolutionary theory. A wise Designer who creates in nested hierarchy of form explains the *nested hierarchy of life* explained by evolutionary theory and the *nested hierarchy of complexity* that is not explained by evolutionary theory. Distinct kinds of organisms' being created in the recent past explains the *large gaps* between major groups of organisms, *higher group stasis*, the *mosaic/chimera nature and rarity of stratomorphic intermediates* and the *inverted cone of diversity*, which are not explained by evolutionary theory. *Suboptimal improvisations*, thought to be confirmations of evolutionary theory, may turn out to be optimal designs when the entire ecosystem is considered. Environmental changes and genetic errors introduced since the creation can explain *vestigial organs*, traditionally explained in the context of evolutionary theory.

If intelligent design were the only source of biological complexity and innovation, then the *absence of nascent organs* would be explained, as it is not in evolutionary theory. Similar organisms' migrating together into similar environments and postcreation diversification within created groups may explain *biogeographic evidences for macroevolution*. A global deluge that gradually buried organisms already filling a well-integrated biosphere explains the *general water-to-land fossil order* as well as *stratomorphic intermediates* among the plants and vertebrates, often used as evidence for evolution. At the same time, it explains the *general nonevolutionary order of higher group appearance*, the *rarity of stratomorphic intermediates* and *higher group stasis*, which are not explained by evolutionary theory. The high level of intelligence of the Creator explains the high level of life's *complexity* and *integration of complexity*, unexplained by evolutionary theory. Finally, the aesthetic nature of the Creator explains the *strong aesthetic components* of life, which again cannot be explained by evolutionary theory.

A hypothesis of divine Designer and Judge based on biblical claims is much more successful at explaining the major features of life than is macroevolutionary theory. However, the matter need not be left here. In the next chapter we will investigate human language and linguistic capacity. We will see that these features of human beings are utterly unlike the various abilities of other species, and that they could not have evolved in the way Darwin and his followers have thought.

Bibliography

Committee for Integrity in Science Education. *Teaching Science in a Climate of Controversy: A View from the American Scientific Affiliation.* Ipswich, MA: American Scientific Affiliation, 1988.

Davis, Percival, and Dean H. Kenyon. *Of Pandas and People.* 2nd ed. Dallas: Haughton, 1993.

Denton, Michael. *A Theory in Crisis.* Bethesda, MD: Adler, 1986.

Frair, Wayne, and Percival Davis. *A Case for Creation.* 3rd ed. Chicago: Moody Press, 1983.

Gould, Stephen Jay. *Wonderful Life: The Burgess Shale and the Nature of History.* New York: Norton, 1989.

QUESTIONS AND FURTHER READINGS

Questions for Discussion

1. Evolution and creationism are often considered to be diametrically opposed beliefs about the existence and development of flora and fauna. Do you believe they can be reconciled? If so, how? If not, why not?

2. Should religion be studied scientifically? What are some benefits of a natural science of religion? What are some risks or concerns?

3. What are some obstacles to the scientific study of religion?

4. If a naturalist believes that false beliefs are not adaptive, what could she say about the widespread human belief in the supernatural?

5. Should reason be used to justify or validate faith? Why or why not?

6. According to nonevidential views of faith and reason, there are times when we need to choose to believe even if there is insufficient evidence for the belief. But can we simply choose to believe anything directly? If we cannot choose beliefs directly, how might we end up having beliefs — in particular religious ones?

7. John Polkinghorne argues that the fundamental materialist commitment about nature is incomplete. What is his argument?

8. Can natural science include notions of intelligent design? Explain your view.

9. In a paragraph, explicate Del Ratzsch's position on the role science should play in one's faith.

10. What is your own view of how science and faith should be integrated, if at all?

Further Readings

Barbour, Ian (1990). *Religion in an Age of Science: The Gifford Lectures.* Vol. 1. San Francisco: Harper & Row. (A highly influential and insightful work on the integration of science and religion.)

Dembski, William A. (1998). *The Design Inference: Eliminating Chance through Small Probabilities.* Cambridge: Cambridge University Press. (Using probability and information theory, Dembski argues for the design inference — a method for detecting intelligent causes. Fairly technical.)

Dembski, William A., and Michael Ruse, eds. (2004). *Debating Design: From Darwin to DNA.* Cambridge: Cambridge University Press. (A fine collection of essays for and against intelligent design.)

Evans, C. Stephen (1998). *Faith beyond Reason: A Kierkegaardian Account.* Grand Rapids,: Eerdmans. (Explains and defends a Kierkegaardian view of fideism.)

Harris, Sam (2004). *The End of Faith: Religion, Terror, and the Future of Reason.* New York: Norton. (Argues that religious faith is based on irrational thinking and is dangerous and harmful, and that a rational, scientific view should replace a religious one.)

Kuhn, Thomas (1970). *The Structure of Scientific Revolutions.* Chicago: University of Chicago Press. (Often hailed as one of the most influential books of the twentieth century; presents an understanding of scientific progress as consisting of various paradigm shifts that include social and psychological factors.)

McGrath, Alister (1998). *The Foundations of Dialogue in Science and Religion.* Oxford: Blackwell. (Explores the relation between science and faith at the level of method; utilizes Christianity as a case study.)

Miller, Kenneth R. (2000). *Finding Darwin's God: A Scientist's Search for Common Ground between God and Evolution*. New York: Harper Perennial. (A defense of theistic evolution by a professor of biology.)

Moreland, J. P. (1999). *Christianity and the Nature of Science*. Grand Rapids: Baker. (A helpful contribution to the integration of Christianity and science.)

Morris, Henry, ed. (1985). *Scientific Creationism*. El Cajon, CA: Master Books, 1985. (This is the classic defense of "young-earth" creationism. Clear and articulate.)

Peacocke, Arthur (1984). *Intimations of Reality: Critical Realism in Science and Religion*. Notre Dame, IN: University of Notre Dame Press. (A renowned biochemist and theologian argues for a critical realist approach to understanding the relation between science and religion.)

Plantinga, Alvin, and Nicholas Wolterstorff, eds. (1983). *Faith and Rationality*. Notre Dame, IN: University of Notre Dame Press. (A collection of important essays on faith and reason by seven leading Reformed epistemologists.)

Polkinghorne, John (2000). *Faith, Science and Understanding*. New Haven, CT: Yale University Press. (Explores the interaction of science and religion and focuses on what science can say about the processes of a universe in which God is active.)

Ruse, Michael (2000). *Can a Darwinian Be a Christian? The Relationship between Science and Religion*. Cambridge: Cambridge University Press. (A Darwinian philosopher of science argues that one can be a Christian and a Darwinian, but it is no easy task.)

Swinburne, Richard (2005). *Faith and Reason*. 2nd ed. Oxford: Clarendon. (Argues that one should practice that religion which has the best goals and is more probably true; proposes criteria for analyzing the probabilities of different religious creeds being true.)

Taliaferro, Charles (2005). *Evidence and Faith: Philosophy and Religion since the Seventeenth Century*. Cambridge: Cambridge University Press. (An excellent and accessible overview of philosophy of religion from the modern period to the present; focuses on developing views of faith and evidence.)

Trigg, Roger (1998). *Rationality and Religion: Does Faith Need Reason?* Oxford: Blackwell. (Examines the question of whether religious faith needs reason; considers the question in a pluralistic society.)

Ward, Keith (2006). *Pascal's Fire: Scientific Faith and Religious Understanding*. Oxford: Oneworld. (Utilizing the latest scientific research and discussions about religion and morality, Ward delves into the science and religion debate and provides a unique and original perspective.)

PART 11

CHRISTIANITY AND THE WORLD

Jesus' closing words to his disciples in the book of Matthew are these: "Therefore go and make disciples of all nations, baptizing them in the name of the Father and of the Son and of the Holy Spirit, and teaching them to obey everything I have commanded you. And surely I am with you always, to the very end of the age" (Matt 28:19 – 20). The call here is to engage the world — to transform the world in word and deed through the power of the Holy Spirit and the redeeming message of the risen Christ. But how are we to do this? How should we engage the world?

In every age since the founding of the church, Christians have been confronted with the reality of what Augustine referred to as two cities: the city of man (the material earthly city) and the city of God (a spiritual city, which on earth is basically the church). Christians are, for now, to dwell in a world in which there are competing religions and philosophies and political regimes; they are to work with God to transform it. But how are they to reach out to the world — to reach the world? Furthermore, does the city of God impact the city of man? Is Christianity truly good for the world, and if so, how so? These are some of the questions and challenges addressed in this final section of the book.

The first selection, the *Epistle to Diognetus* (sometimes called the *Epistle of Mathetes to Diognetus* — *mathetes* meaning "disciple"), is one of the earliest examples of Christian apologetics — dating to the late second century, or perhaps earlier. The Diognetus to whom it is addressed is unknown, though some scholars believe it is a reference to a teacher of Marcus Aurelius. In any case, he is unlikely to be the actual recipient, or even the assumed recipient, of this anonymous work. In a manner similar to most of the early Christian apologies, it begins by emphasizing the foolishness of worshiping idols and the inadequacy of the Jewish religion. It then offers a sketch of Christian faith, lauds Christian character, and elaborates on the benefits that it provides to those who convert to the faith. Regarding the world, the author says that Christians "dwell in their own countries, but only as sojourners.... Their existence is on earth, but their citizenship is in heaven."

In the next essay, taken from Augustine's classic, *The City of God*, he begins by noting that the two cities mentioned above — the city of God and the city of man — are inter-mingled in this life. This will continue until the final judgment, at which time they will be separated forever. In Augustine's day, the Western Roman Empire was for all intents and purposes the "city of man," and he demonstrates how following the one true God will benefit this city and following false gods will harm this city. While there are certain kinds of "goods" in this city, being devoted to them will ultimately end in misery. The best things are of the heavenly city, and by following them we will ultimately enter that promised kingdom, where its citizens will reign in peace with their Prince — the "King of the ages."

In the next essay, Francis Schaeffer argues that there has been a shift in Western culture from a Christian worldview to a humanistic one (humanism understood here as mankind being the measure of all things). There are many symptoms of this change, but we would err if we see the symptoms as the root problem. The reason for the breakdown in values in our culture is a worldview problem — one in which ultimate reality is only matter or energy shaped by pure chance. Speaking prophetically in the piece (written in the latter half of the twentieth century), Schaeffer predicts that without a cultural shift in which God is the foundation and Jesus is Lord, relativism, abortion, and loss of freedoms will permeate the landscape. The answer to our cultural waywardness, he maintains, is "true spirituality," which he defines as having Christ be Lord of all of life. His call is just as timely today as when it was penned.

In the final selection, Joseph Cardinal Ratzinger — Pope Benedict XVI — reflects on Christianity and the world over the last several decades. He notes that at a crucial moment in world history — 1989, when the socialist regimes in Europe occurred — Christianity failed at making its message heard as an epoch-making alternative to the Marxist "redemption of humankind." Christian consciousness, to a great extent, acquiesced to the belief that faith in God is purely subjective — something belonging only in the private realm. But for faith to truly be transformative in life and culture, it must come out of the ghetto and be brought into the public arena. Furthermore, he notes, faith was relativized and, as such, was radically changed in two fundamental ways relevant to its message. First, the person of Christ has been perceived by many in a new way. Instead of being the God-man, he has become simply another man who has *experienced* God in a special way. Second, the concept of God has been fundamentally altered. For many, God has become the "Absolute-Other," and so God's personal nature is no longer relevant. But on this changed view of God, Pope Benedict argues, we lose the possibility of personal communion with God, and we are ultimately deprived of the grounding of moral values. What is needed, he argues, is a renewal of the personal nature of God and a Christology that has the courage to see Christ in all his greatness, as he is presented in the Gospels.

CHAPTER 51

Christians and the World: The Epistle to Diognetus

Author unknown

CHAPTER 1
Occasion of the epistle

Since I see you, most excellent Diognetus, exceedingly desirous to learn the mode of worshipping God prevalent among the Christians, and inquiring very carefully and earnestly concerning them, what God they trust in, and what form of religion they observe, so as all to look down upon the world itself, and despise death, while they neither esteem those to be gods that are reckoned such by the Greeks, nor hold to the superstition of the Jews; and what is the affection which they cherish among themselves; and finally, why this new kind or practice [of piety] has only now entered into the world, and not long ago; I cordially welcome this your desire, and I implore God, who enables us both to speak and to hear, to grant to me so to speak, that, above all, I may hear you have been edified, and to you so to hear, that I who speak may have no cause of regret for having done so.

CHAPTER 2
The vanity of idols

Come, then, after you have freed yourself from all prejudices possessing your mind, and laid aside what you have been accustomed to, as something apt to deceive you, and being made, as if from the beginning, a new man, inasmuch as, according to your own confession, you are to be the hearer of a new [system of] doctrine; come and contemplate, not with your eyes only, but with your understanding, the substance and the form of those whom you declare and deem to be gods.

Is not one of them a stone similar to that on which we tread? Is not a second brass, in no way superior to those vessels which are constructed for our ordinary use? Is not a third wood, and that already rotten? Is not a fourth silver, which needs a man to watch it, lest it be stolen? Is not a fifth iron, consumed by rust? Is not a sixth earthenware, in no degree more valuable than that which is formed for the humblest purposes?

Are not all these of corruptible matter? Are they not fabricated by means of iron and fire? Did not the sculptor fashion one of them, the brazier a second, the silversmith a third, and the potter a fourth? Was not every one of them, before they were formed by the arts of these [workmen] into the shape of these [gods], each in its own way subject to change? Would not those things which are now vessels, formed of the same materials, become like to such, if they met with the same artificers? Might not these, which are now worshipped by you, again be made by men vessels similar to others? Are they not all deaf? Are they not blind? Are they not without life? Are they not destitute of feeling? Are they not incapable of motion? Are they not all liable to rot? Are they not all corruptible?

These things you call gods; these you serve; these you worship; and you become altogether like them. For this reason you hate the Christians, because they do not deem *these* to be gods. But do not you yourselves, who now think and suppose [such to be gods], much more cast contempt upon them than they [the Christians do]? Do you not much more mock and insult them, when you worship those that are made of stone and earthenware, without appointing any persons to guard them; but those made of silver and gold you shut up by night, and appoint watchers to look after them by day, lest they be stolen? And by those gifts which you mean to present to them, do you not, if they are possessed of sense, rather punish [than honour] them? But if, on the other hand, they are destitute of sense, you convict them of this fact, while you worship them with blood and the smoke of sacrifices. Let any one of you suffer such indignities! Let any one of you endure to have such things done to himself! But not a single human being will, unless compelled to it, endure such treatment, since he is endowed with sense and reason. A stone, however, readily bears it, seeing it is insensible. Certainly you do not show [by your conduct] that he [your God] is possessed of sense. And as to the fact that Christians are not accustomed to serve such gods, I might easily find many other things to say; but if even what has been said does not seem to any one sufficient, I deem it idle to say anything further.

CHAPTER 3
Superstitions of the Jews

And next, I imagine that you are most desirous of hearing something on this point, that the Christians do not observe the same forms of divine worship as do the Jews. The Jews, then, if they abstain from the kind of service above described, and deem it proper to worship one God as being Lord of all, [are right]; but if they offer Him worship in the way which we have described, they greatly err. For while the Gentiles, by offering such things to those that are destitute of sense and hearing, furnish an example of madness; they, on the other hand by thinking to offer these things to God as if He needed them, might justly reckon it rather an act of folly than of divine worship. For He that made heaven and earth, and all that is therein, and gives to us all the things of which we stand in need, certainly requires none of those things which He Himself bestows on such as think of furnishing them to Him. But those who imagine that, by means of blood, and the smoke of sacrifices and burnt-offerings, they offer sacrifices [acceptable] to Him, and that by such honours they show Him respect — these, by supposing that they can give anything to Him who stands in need of nothing, appear to me in no respect to differ from those who studiously confer the same honour

on things destitute of sense, and which therefore are unable to enjoy such honours.

CHAPTER 4
The other observances of the Jews

But as to their scrupulosity concerning meats, and their superstition as respects the Sabbaths, and their boasting about circumcision, and their fancies about fasting and the new moons, which are utterly ridiculous and unworthy of notice — I do not think that you require to learn anything from me. For, to accept some of those things which have been formed by God for the use of men as properly formed, and to reject others as useless and redundant — how can this be lawful? And to speak falsely of God, as if He forbade us to do what is good on the Sabbath-days — how is not this impious? And to glory in the circumcision of the flesh as a proof of election, and as if, on account of it, they were specially beloved by God — how is it not a subject of ridicule? And as to their observing months and days, as if waiting upon the stars and the moon, and their distributing, according to their own tendencies, the appointments of God, and the vicissitudes of the seasons, some for festivities, and others for mourning — who would deem this a part of divine worship, and not much rather a manifestation of folly? I suppose, then, you are sufficiently convinced that the Christians properly abstain from the vanity and error common [to both Jews and Gentiles], and from the busybody spirit and vain boasting of the Jews; but you must not hope to learn the mystery of their peculiar mode of worshipping God from any mortal.

CHAPTER 5
The manners of the Christians

For the Christians are distinguished from other men neither by country, nor language, nor the customs which they observe. For they neither inhabit cities of their own, nor employ a peculiar form of speech, nor lead a life which is marked out by any singularity. The course of conduct which they follow has not been devised by any speculation or deliberation of inquisitive men; nor do they, like some, proclaim themselves the advocates of any merely human doctrines. But, inhabiting Greek as well as barbarian cities, according as the lot of each of them has determined, and following the customs of the natives in respect to clothing, food, and the rest of their ordinary conduct, they display to us their wonderful and confessedly striking method of life. They dwell in their own countries, but simply as sojourners. As citizens, they share in all things with others, and yet endure all things as if foreigners. Every foreign land is to them as their native country, and every land of their birth as a land of strangers. They marry, as do all [others]; they beget children; but they do not destroy their offspring. They have a common table, but not a common bed. They are in the flesh, but they do not live after the flesh. They pass their days on earth, but they are citizens of heaven. They obey the prescribed laws, and at the same time surpass the laws by their lives. They love all men, and are persecuted by all. They are unknown and condemned; they are put to death, and restored to life. They are poor, yet make many rich; they are in lack of all things, and yet abound in all; they are dishonoured, and yet in their very dishonour are glorified. They are evil spoken of, and yet are justified; they are reviled, and bless; they are insulted, and repay the insult with honour; they do good, yet are punished as evil-doers. When punished, they rejoice as if quickened into life; they are assailed by the Jews as foreigners, and are persecuted by the Greeks; yet those who hate them are unable to assign any reason for their hatred.

CHAPTER 6
The relation of Christians
to the world

To sum up all in one word — what the soul is in the body, Christians are in the world. The soul is dispersed through all the members of the body, and Christians are scattered through all the cities of the world. The soul dwells in the body, yet is not of the body; and Christians dwell in the world, yet are not of the world. The invisible soul is guarded by the visible body, and Christians are known indeed to be in the world, but their godliness remains invisible. The flesh hates the soul, and wars against it, though itself suffering no injury, because it is prevented from enjoying pleasures; the world also hates the Christians, though in nowise injured, because they abjure pleasures. The soul loves the flesh that hates it, and [loves also] the members; Christians likewise love those that hate them. The soul is imprisoned in the body, yet preserves that very body; and Christians are confined in the world as in a prison, and yet they are the preservers of the world. The immortal soul dwells in a mortal tabernacle; and Christians dwell as sojourners in corruptible [bodies], looking for an incorruptible dwelling in the heavens. The soul, when but ill-provided with food and drink, becomes better; in like manner, the Christians, though subjected day by day to punishment, increase the more in number. God has assigned them this illustrious position, which it were unlawful for them to forsake.

CHAPTER 7
The manifestation of Christ

For, as I said, this was no mere earthly invention which was delivered to them, nor is it a mere human system of opinion, which they judge it right to preserve so carefully, nor has a dispensation of mere human mysteries been committed to them, but truly God Himself, who is almighty, the Creator of all things, and invisible, has sent from heaven, and placed among men, [Him who is] the truth, and the holy and incomprehensible Word, and has firmly established Him in their hearts. He did not, as one might have imagined, send to men any servant, or angel, or ruler, or any one of those who bear sway over earthly things, or one of those to whom the government of things in the heavens has been entrusted, but the very Creator and Fashioner of all things — by whom He made the heavens — by whom he enclosed the sea within its proper bounds — whose ordinances all the stars faithfully observe — from whom the sun has received the measure of his daily course to be observed — whom the moon obeys, being commanded to shine in the night, and whom the stars also obey, following the moon in her course; by whom all things have been arranged, and placed within their proper limits, and to whom all are subject — the heavens and the things that are therein, the earth and the things that are therein, the sea and the things that are therein — fire, air, and the abyss — the things which are in the heights, the things which are in the depths, and the things which lie between. This [messenger] He sent to them. Was it then, as one might conceive, for the purpose of exercising tyranny, or of inspiring fear and terror? By no means, but under the influence of clemency and meekness. As a king sends his son, who is also a king, so sent He Him; as God He sent Him; as to men He sent Him; as a Saviour He sent Him, and as seeking to persuade, not to compel us; for violence has no place in the character of God. As calling us He sent Him, not as vengefully pursuing us; as loving us He sent Him, not as judging us. For He will yet send Him to judge us, and who shall endure His appearing?... Do you not see them exposed to wild beasts, that they may be persuaded to deny the Lord, and yet not overcome? Do you not see that the more of them are punished, the greater becomes the number of the rest? This does not seem to be the work of man: this is the power of God; these are the evidences of His manifestation.

CHAPTER 8
The miserable state of men before the coming of the Word

For, who of men at all understood before His coming what God is? Do you accept of the vain and silly doctrines of those who are deemed trustworthy philosophers? Of whom some said that fire was God, calling that God to which they themselves were by and by to come; and some water; and others some other of the elements formed by God. But if any one of these theories be worthy of approbation, every one of the rest of created things might also be declared to be God. But such declarations are simply the startling and erroneous utterances of deceivers; and no man has either seen Him, or made Him known, but He has revealed Himself. And He has manifested Himself through faith, to which alone it is given to behold God. For God, the Lord and Fashioner of all things, who made all things, and assigned them their several positions,

proved Himself not merely a friend of mankind, but also long-suffering [in His dealings with them]. Yea, He was always of such a character, and still is, and will ever be, kind and good, and free from wrath, and true, and the only one who is [absolutely] good; and He formed in His mind a great and unspeakable conception, which He communicated to His Son alone. As long, then, as He held and preserved His own wise counsel in concealment, He appeared to neglect us, and to have no care over us. But after He revealed and laid open, through His beloved Son, the things which had been prepared from the beginning, He conferred every blessing all at once upon us, so that we should both share in His benefits, and see and be active [in His service]. Who of us would ever have expected these things? He was aware, then, of all things in His own mind, along with His Son, according to the relation subsisting between them.

CHAPTER 9
Why the Son was sent so late

As long then as the former time endured, He permitted us to be borne along by unruly impulses, being drawn away by the desire of pleasure and various lusts. This was not that He at all delighted in our sins, but that He simply endured them; nor that He approved the time of working iniquity which then was, but that He sought to form a mind conscious of righteousness, so that being convinced in that time of our unworthiness of attaining life through our own works, it should now, through the kindness of God, be vouchsafed to us; and having made it manifest that in ourselves we were unable to enter into the kingdom of God, we might through the power of God be made able. But when our wickedness had reached its height, and it had been clearly shown that its reward, punishment and death was impending over us; and when the time had come which God had before appointed for manifesting His own kindness and power, how the one love of God, through exceeding regard for men, did not regard us with hatred, nor thrust us away, nor remember our iniquity against us, but showed great long-suffering, and bore with us, He Himself took on

Him the burden of our iniquities, He gave His own Son as a ransom for us, the holy One for transgressors, the blameless One for the wicked, the righteous One for the unrighteous, the incorruptible One for the corruptible, the immortal One for those who are mortal. For what other thing was capable of covering our sins than His righteousness? By what other one was it possible that we, the wicked and ungodly, could be justified, than by the only Son of God? O sweet exchange! O unsearchable operation! O benefits surpassing all expectation! That the wickedness of many should be hid in a single righteous One, and that the righteousness of One should justify many transgressors! Having therefore convinced us in the former time that our nature was unable to attain to life, and having now revealed the Saviour who is able to save even those things which it was [formerly] impossible to save, by both these facts He desired to lead us to trust in His kindness, to esteem Him our Nourisher, Father, Teacher, Counsellor, Healer, our Wisdom, Light, Honour, Glory, Power, and Life, so that we should not be anxious concerning clothing and food.

CHAPTER 10
The blessings that will flow from faith

If you also desire [to possess] this faith, you likewise shall receive first of all the knowledge of the Father. For God has loved mankind, on whose account He made the world, to whom He rendered subject all the things that are in it, to whom He gave reason and understanding, to whom alone He imparted the privilege of looking upwards to Himself, whom He formed after His own image, to whom He sent His only-begotten Son, to whom He has promised a kingdom in heaven, and will give it to those who have loved Him. And when you have attained this knowledge, with what joy do you think you will be filled? Or, how will you love Him who has first so loved you? And if you love Him, you will be an imitator of His kindness. And do not wonder that a man may become an imitator of God. He can, if he is willing. For it is not by ruling over his neighbours, or by seeking to hold the supremacy over

those that are weaker, or by being rich, and showing violence towards those that are inferior, that happiness is found; nor can any one by these things become an imitator of God. But these things do not at all constitute His majesty. On the contrary he who takes upon himself the burden of his neighbour; he who, in whatsoever respect he may be superior, is ready to benefit another who is deficient; he who, whatsoever things he has received from God, by distributing these to the needy, becomes a god to those who receive [his benefits]: he is an imitator of God. Then you shall see, while still on earth, that God in the heavens rules over [the universe]; then you shall begin to speak the mysteries of God; then shall you both love and admire those that suffer punishment because they will not deny God; then shall you condemn the deceit and error of the world when you shall know what it is to live truly in heaven, when you shall despise that which is here esteemed to be death, when you shall fear what is truly death, which is reserved for those who shall be condemned to the eternal fire, which shall afflict those even to the end that are committed to it. Then shall you admire those who for righteousness' sake endure the fire that is but for a moment, and shall count them happy when you shall know [the nature of] that fire.

CHAPTER 11
These things are worthy to be known and believed

I do not speak of things strange to me, nor do I aim at anything inconsistent with right reason; but having been a disciple of the Apostles, I have become a teacher of the Gentiles. I minister the things delivered to me to those that are disciples worthy of the truth. For who that is rightly taught and begotten by the loving Word, would not seek to learn accurately the things which have been clearly shown by the Word to His disciples, to whom the Word being manifested has revealed them, speaking plainly [to them], not understood indeed by the unbelieving, but conversing with the disciples, who, being esteemed faithful by Him, acquired a knowledge of the mysteries of the Father? For which reason He sent the Word, that He might be manifested to the world; and He, being despised by the people [of the Jews], was, when preached by the Apostles, believed on by the Gentiles. This is He who was from the beginning, who appeared as if new, and was found old, and yet who is ever born afresh in the hearts of the saints. This is He who, being from everlasting, is today called the Son; through whom the Church is enriched, and grace, widely spread, increases in the saints, furnishing understanding, revealing mysteries, announcing times, rejoicing over the faithful, giving to those that seek, by whom the limits of faith are not broken through, nor the boundaries set by the fathers passed over. Then the fear of the law is chanted, and the grace of the prophets is known, and the faith of the gospels is established, and the tradition of the Apostles is preserved, and the grace of the Church exults; which grace if you grieve not, you shall know those things which the Word teaches, by whom He wills, and when He pleases. For whatever things we are moved to utter by the will of the Word commanding us, we communicate to you with pains, and from a love of the things that have been revealed to us.

CHAPTER 12
The importance of knowledge to true spiritual life

When you have read and carefully listened to these things, you shall know what God bestows on such as rightly love Him, being made [as you are] a paradise of delight, presenting in yourselves a tree bearing all kinds of produce and flourishing well, being adorned with various fruits. For in this place the tree of knowledge and the tree of life have been planted; but it is not the tree of knowledge that destroys — it is disobedience that proves destructive. Nor truly are those words without significance which are written, how God from the beginning planted the tree of life in the midst of paradise, revealing through knowledge the way to life, and when those who were first formed did not use this [knowledge] properly, they were, through the fraud of the Serpent, stripped naked. For neither can life exist without knowledge, nor is knowledge secure without life. Wherefore both were planted close together. The Apostle, perceiving the force [of this conjunction], and blaming that knowledge which, without true doctrine, is admitted to influence life, declares, Knowledge puffs up, but love edifies. For he who thinks he knows anything without true knowledge, and such as is witnessed to by life, knows nothing, but is deceived by the Serpent, as not loving life. But he who combines knowledge with fear, and seeks after life, plants in hope, looking for fruit. Let your heart be your wisdom; and let your life be true knowledge inwardly received. Bearing this tree and displaying its fruit, you shall always gather in those things which are desired by God, which the Serpent cannot reach, and to which deception does not approach; nor is Eve then corrupted, but is trusted as a virgin; and salvation is manifested, and the Apostles are filled with understanding, and the Passover of the Lord advances, and the choirs are gathered together, and are arranged in proper order, and the Word rejoices in teaching the saints — by whom the Father is glorified: to whom be glory for ever. Amen.

CHAPTER 52

The City of God

Augustine

BOOK 1

CHAPTER 35
Of the Sons of the Church Who Are Hidden among the Wicked, and of False Christians within the Church

Let these and similar answers (if any fuller and fitter answers can be found) be given to their enemies by the redeemed family of the Lord Christ, and by the pilgrim city of King Christ. But let this city bear in mind, that among her enemies lie hid those who are destined to be fellow-citizens, that she may not think it a fruitless labor to bear what they inflict as enemies until they become confessors of the faith. So, too, as long as she is a stranger in the world, the city of God has in her communion, and bound to her by the sacraments, some who shall not eternally dwell in the lot of the saints. Of these, some are not now recognized; others declare themselves, and do not hesitate to make common cause with our enemies in murmuring against God, whose sacramental badge they wear. These men you may today see thronging the churches with us, to-morrow crowding the theatres with the godless. But we have the less reason to despair of the reclamation even of such persons, if among our most declared enemies there are now some, unknown to themselves, who are destined to become our friends. In truth, these two cities are entangled together in this world, and intermixed until the last judgment effects their separation. I now proceed to speak, as God shall help me, of the rise, progress, and end of these two cities; and what I write, I write for the glory of the city of God, that, being placed in comparison with the other, it may shine with a brighter lustre.

CHAPTER 36
What Subjects Are to Be Handled in the Following Discourse

But I have still some things to say in confutation of those who refer the disasters of the Roman republic to our religion, because it prohibits the offering of sacrifices to the gods. For this end I must recount all, or as many as may seem sufficient, of the disasters which befell that city and its subject provinces, before these sacrifices were prohibited; for all these disasters they would doubtless have attributed to us, if at that time our religion had shed its light upon them, and had prohibited their sacrifices. I must then go on to show what social well-being the true God, in whose hand are all kingdoms, vouchsafed to grant to them that their empire might increase. I must show why He did so, and how their false gods, instead of at all aiding them, greatly injured them by guile and deceit. And, lastly, I must meet those who, when on this point convinced and confuted by irrefragable proofs, endeavor to maintain that they worship the gods, not hoping for the present advantages of this life, but for those which are to be enjoyed after death. And this, if I am not mistaken, will be the most difficult part of my task, and will be worthy of the loftiest argument; for we must then enter the lists with the philosophers, not the mere common herd of philosophers, but the most renowned, who in many points agree with ourselves, as regarding the immortality of the soul, and that the true God created the world, and by His providence rules all He has created. But as they differ from us on other points, we must not shrink from the task of exposing their errors, that, having refuted the gainsaying of the wicked with such ability as God may vouchsafe, we may assert the city of God, and true piety, and the worship of God, to which alone the promise of true and everlasting felicity is attached. Here, then, let us conclude, that we may enter on these subjects in a fresh book.

BOOK 15

CHAPTER 1
Of the Two Lines of the Human Race Which from First to Last Divide It

Of the bliss of Paradise, of Paradise itself, and of the life of our first parents there, and of their sin and punishment, many have thought much, spoken much, written much. We ourselves, too, have spoken of these things in the foregoing books, and have written either what we read in the Holy Scriptures, or what we could reasonably deduce from them. And were we to enter into a more detailed investigation of these matters, an endless number of endless questions would arise, which would involve us in a larger work than the present occasion admits. We cannot be expected to find room for replying to every question that may be started by unoccupied and captious men, who are ever more ready to ask questions than capable of understanding the answer. Yet I trust we have already done justice to these great and difficult questions regarding the beginning of the world, or of the soul, or of the human race itself. This race we have distributed into two parts, the one consisting of those who live according to man, the other of those who live according to God. And these we also mystically call the two cities, or the two communities of men, of which the one is predestined to reign eternally with God, and the other to suffer eternal punishment with the devil. This, however, is their end, and of it we are to speak afterwards. At present, as we have said enough about their origin, whether among the angels, whose numbers we know not, or in the two first human beings, it seems suitable to attempt an account of their career,

from the time when our two first parents began to propagate the race until all human generation shall cease. For this whole time or world-age, in which the dying give place and those who are born succeed, is the career of these two cities concerning which we treat. Of these two first parents of the human race, then, Cain was the first-born, and he belonged to the city of men; after him was born Abel, who belonged to the city of God. For as in the individual the truth of the apostle's statement is discerned, "that is not first which is spiritual, but that which is natural, and afterward that which is spiritual,"[1] whence it comes to pass that each man, being derived from a condemned stock, is first of all born of Adam evil and carnal, and becomes good and spiritual only afterwards, when he is grafted into Christ by regeneration: so was it in the human race as a whole. When these two cities began to run their course by a series of deaths and births, the citizen of this world was the first-born, and after him the stranger in this world, the citizen of the city of God, predestinated by grace, elected by grace, by grace a stranger below, and by grace a citizen above. By grace — for so far as regards himself he is sprung from the same mass, all of which is condemned in its origin; but God, like a potter (for this comparison is introduced by the apostle judiciously, and not without thought), of the same lump made one vessel to honor, another to dishonor.[2] But first the vessel to dishonor was made, and after it another to honor. For in each individual, as I have already said, there is first of all that which is reprobate, that from which we must begin, but in which we need not necessarily remain; afterwards is that which is well-approved, to which we may by advancing attain, and in which, when we have reached it we may abide. Not, indeed, that every wicked man shall be good, but that no one will be good who was not first of all wicked; but the sooner any one becomes a good man, the more speedily does he receive this title, and abolish the old name in the new. Accordingly, it is recorded of Cain that he built a city,[3] but

---

1. 1 Cor. xv. 46
2. Rom. ix. 21.

3. Gen. iv. 17.

Abel, being a sojourner, built none. For the city of the saints is above, although here below it begets citizens, in whom it sojourns till the time of its reign arrives, when it shall gather together all in the day of the resurrection; and then shall the promised kingdom be given to them, in which they shall reign with their Prince, the King of the ages, time without end.

CHAPTER 2
Of the Children of the Flesh and the Children of the Promise

There was indeed on earth, so long as it was needed, a symbol and foreshadowing image of this city, which served the purpose of reminding men that such a city was to be rather than of making it present; and this image was itself called the holy city, as a symbol of the future city, though not itself the reality. Of this city which served as an image, and of that free city it typified, Paul writes to the Galatians in these terms: "Tell me, ye that desire to be under the law, do ye not hear the law? For it is written, that Abraham had two sons, the one by a bond maid, the other by a free woman. But he who was of the bond woman was born after the flesh, but he of the free woman was by promise. Which things are an allegory:[4] for these are the two covenants; the one from the mount Sinai, which gendereth to bondage, which is Agar. For this Agar is mount Sinai in Arabia, and answereth to Jerusalem which now is, and is in bondage with her children. But Jerusalem which is above is free, which is the mother of us all. For it is written, Rejoice, thou barren that bearest not; break forth and cry, thou that travailest not, for the desolate hath many more children than she which hath an husband. Now we, brethren, as Isaac was, are the children of promise. But as then he that was born after the flesh persecuted him that was born after the Spirit, even so it is now. Nevertheless, what saith the Scripture? Cast out the bond woman and her son: for the son of the bond woman shall not be heir with the son of the free woman. And we, brethren, are not children of the bond woman, but of the free, in the liberty wherewith Christ hath made us free."[5] This interpretation of the passage, handed down to us with apostolic authority, shows how we ought to understand the Scriptures of the two covenants — the old and the new. One portion of the earthly city became an image of the heavenly city, not having a significance of its own, but signifying another city, and therefore serving, or "being in bondage." For it was founded not for its own sake, but to prefigure another city; and this shadow of a city was also itself foreshadowed by another preceding figure. For Sarah's handmaid Agar, and her son, were an image of this image. And as the shadows were to pass away when the full light came, Sarah, the free woman, who prefigured the free city (which again was also prefigured in another way by that shadow of a city Jerusalem), therefore said, "Cast out the bond woman and her son; for the son of the bond woman shall not be heir with my son Isaac," or, as the apostle says, "with the son of the free woman." In the earthly city, then, we find two things — its own obvious presence, and its symbolic presentation of the heavenly city. Now citizens are begotten to the earthly city by nature vitiated by sin, but to the heavenly city by grace freeing nature from sin; whence the former are called "vessels of wrath," the latter "vessels of mercy."[6] And this was typified in the two sons of Abraham — Ishmael, the son of Agar the handmaid, being born according to the flesh, while Isaac was born of the free woman Sarah, according to the promise. Both, indeed, were of Abraham's seed; but the one was begotten by natural law, the other was given by gracious promise. In the one birth, human action is revealed; in the other, a divine kindness comes to light.

CHAPTER 3
That Sarah's Barrenness Was Made Productive by God's Grace

Sarah, in fact, was barren; and, despairing of offspring, and being resolved that she would have at least

---

4. Comp. De Trin. xv. c. 15.
5. Gal. iv. 21 – 31.

6. Rom. ix. 22, 23.

through her handmaid that blessing she saw she could not in her own person procure, she gave her handmaid to her husband, to whom she herself had been unable to bear children. From him she required this conjugal duty, exercising her own right in another's womb. And thus Ishmael was born according to the common law of human generation, by sexual intercourse. Therefore it is said that he was born "according to the flesh" — not because such births are not the gifts of God, nor His handiwork, whose creative wisdom "reaches," as it is written, "from one end to another mightily, and sweetly doth she order all things,"[7] but because, in a case in which the gift of God, which was not due to men and was the gratuitous largess of grace, was to be conspicuous, it was requisite that a son be given in a way which no effort of nature could compass. Nature denies children to persons of the age which Abraham and Sarah had now reached; besides that, in Sarah's case, she was barren even in her prime. This nature, so constituted that offspring could not be looked for, symbolized the nature of the human race vitiated by sin and by just consequence condemned, which deserves no future felicity. Fitly, therefore, does Isaac, the child of promise, typify the children of grace, the citizens of the free city, who dwell together in everlasting peace, in which self-love and self-will have no place, but a ministering love that rejoices in the common joy of all, of many hearts makes one, that is to say, secures a perfect concord.

CHAPTER 4
Of the Conflict and Peace
of the Earthly City

But the earthly city, which shall not be everlasting (for it will no longer be a city when it has been committed to the extreme penalty), has its good in this world, and rejoices in it with such joy as such things can afford. But as this is not a good which can discharge its devotees of all distresses, this city is often divided against itself by litigations, wars, quarrels, and such victories as are either life-destroying or short-lived. For each part of it that arms against another part of it seeks to triumph over the nations through itself in bondage to vice. If, when it has conquered, it is inflated with pride, its victory is life-destroying; but if it turns its thoughts upon the common casualties of our mortal condition, and is rather anxious concerning the disasters that may befall it than elated with the successes already achieved, this victory, though of a higher kind, is still only short-lived; for it cannot abidingly rule over those whom it has victoriously subjugated. But the things which this city desires cannot justly be said to be evil, for it is itself, in its own kind, better than all other human good. For it desires earthly peace for the sake of enjoying earthly goods, and it makes war in order to attain to this peace; since, if it has conquered, and there remains no one to resist it, it enjoys a peace which it had not while there were opposing parties who contested for the enjoyment of those things which were too small to satisfy both. This peace is purchased by toilsome wars; it is obtained by what they style a glorious victory. Now, when victory remains with the party which had the juster cause, who hesitates to congratulate the victor, and style it a desirable peace? These things, then, are good things, and without doubt the gifts of God. But if they neglect the better things of the heavenly city, which are secured by eternal victory and peace neverending, and so inordinately covet these present good things that they believe them to be the only desirable things, or love them better than those things which are believed to be better — if this be so, then it is necessary that misery follow and ever increase.

CHAPTER 5
Of the Fratricidal Act
of the Founder of the Earthly City,
and the Corresponding Crime
of the Founder of Rome

Thus the founder of the earthly city was a fratricide. Overcome with envy, he slew his own brother, a citizen of the eternal city, and a sojourner on earth. So that

---

7. Wisdom viii. 1.

we cannot be surprised that this first specimen, or, as the Greeks say, archetype of crime, should, long afterwards, find a corresponding crime at the foundation of that city which was destined to reign over so many nations, and be the head of this earthly city of which we speak. For of that city also, as one of their poets has mentioned, "the first walls were stained with a brother's blood,"[8] or, as Roman history records, Remus was slain by his brother Romulus. And thus there is no difference between the foundation of this city and of the earthly city, unless it be that Romulus and Remus were both citizens of the earthly city. Both desired to have the glory of founding the Roman republic, but both could not have as much glory as if one only claimed it; for he who wished to have the glory of ruling would certainly rule less if his power were shared by a living consort. In order, therefore, that the whole glory might be enjoyed by one, his consort was removed; and by this crime the empire was made larger indeed, but inferior, while otherwise it would have been less, but better. Now these brothers, Cain and Abel, were not both animated by the same earthly desires, nor did the murderer envy the other because he feared that, by both ruling, his own dominion would be curtailed — for Abel was not solicitous to rule in that city which his brother built — he was moved by that diabolical, envious hatred with which the evil regard the good, for no other reason than because they are good while themselves are evil. For the possession of goodness is by no means diminished by being shared with a partner either permanent or temporarily assumed; on the contrary, the possession of goodness is increased in proportion to the concord and charity of each of those who share it. In short, he who is unwilling to share this possession cannot have it; and he who is most willing to admit others to a share of it will have the greatest abundance to himself. The quarrel, then, between Romulus and Remus shows how the earthly city is divided against itself; that which fell out between Cain and Abel illustrated the hatred that subsists between the two cities, that of God and that of men. The wicked war with the wicked; the good also war with the wicked. But with the good, good men, or at least perfectly good men, cannot war; though, while only going on towards perfection, they war to this extent, that every good man resists others in those points in which he resists himself. And in each individual "the flesh lusteth against the spirit, and the spirit against the flesh."[9] This spiritual lusting, therefore, can be at war with the carnal lust of another man; or carnal lust may be at war with the spiritual desires of another, in some such way as good and wicked men are at war; or, still more certainly, the carnal lusts of two men, good but not yet perfect, contend together, just as the wicked contend with the wicked, until the health of those who are under the treatment of grace attains final victory.

CHAPTER 6
Of the Weaknesses Which Even the Citizens of the City of God Suffer During This Earthly Pilgrimage in Punishment of Sin, and of Which They Are Healed by God's Care

This sickliness — that is to say, that disobedience of which we spoke in the fourteenth book — is the punishment of the first disobedience. It is therefore not nature, but vice; and therefore it is said to the good who are growing in grace, and living in this pilgrimage by faith, "Bear ye one another's burdens, and so fulfill the law of Christ."[10] In like manner it is said elsewhere, "Warn them that are unruly, comfort the feeble-minded, support the weak, be patient toward all men. See that none render evil for evil unto any man."[11] And in another place, "If a man be overtaken in a fault, ye which are spiritual restore such an one in the spirit of meekness; considering thyself, lest thou also be tempted."[12] And elsewhere, "Let not the sun go down upon your wrath."[13] And in the Gospel, "If thy brother shall trespass against thee, go and tell him

8. Lucan, Phar. i. 95.
9. Gal. v. 17.
10. Gal. vi. 2.
11. 1 Thess. v. 14, 15.
12. Gal. vi. 1.
13. Eph. iv. 26.

his fault between thee and him alone."[14] So too of sins which may create scandal the apostle says, "Them that sin rebuke before all, that others also may fear."[15] For this purpose, and that we may keep that peace without which no man can see the Lord,[16]many precepts are given which carefully inculcate mutual forgiveness; among which we may number that terrible word in which the servant is ordered to pay his formerly remitted debt of ten thousand talents, because he did not remit to his fellow-servant his debt of two hundred pence. To which parable the Lord Jesus added the words, "So likewise shall my heavenly Father do also unto you, if ye from your hearts forgive not everyone his brother."[17] It is thus the citizens of the city of God are healed while still they sojourn in this earth and sigh for the peace of their heavenly country. The Holy Spirit, too, works within, that the medicine externally applied may have some good result. Otherwise, even though God Himself make use of the creatures that are subject to Him, and in some human form address our human senses, whether we receive those impressions in sleep or in some external appearance, still, if He does not by His own inward grace sway and act upon the mind, no preaching of the truth is of any avail. But this God does, distinguishing between the vessels of wrath and the vessels of mercy, by His own very secret but very just providence. When He Himself aids the soul in His own hidden and wonderful ways, and the sin which dwells in our members, and is, as the apostle teaches, rather the punishment of sin, does not reign in our mortal body to obey the lusts of it, and when we no longer yield our members as instruments of unrighteousness,[18] then the soul is converted from its own evil and selfish desires, and, God possessing it, it possesses itself in peace even in this life, and afterwards, with perfected health and endowed with immortality, will reign without sin in peace everlasting.

---

14. Matt. xviii. 15
15. 1 Tim. v. 20.
16. Heb. xii. 14.
17. Matt. xviii. 35.
18. Rom. vi. 12, 13.

CHAPTER 53

A Christian Manifesto

Francis A. Schaeffer

Christians, in the last 80 years or so, have only been seeing things as bits and pieces which have gradually begun to trouble them and others, instead of understanding that they are the natural outcome of a change from a Christian World View to a Humanistic one; things such as overpermissiveness, pornography, the problem of the public schools, the breakdown of the family, abortion, infanticide (the killing of newborn babies), increased emphasis upon the euthanasia of the old and many, many other things.[1]

All of these things and many more are only the results. We may be troubled with the individual thing, but in reality we are missing the *whole* thing if we do not see each of these things and many more as only symptoms of the deeper problem. And that is the change in our society, a change in our country, a change in the Western world from a Judeo-Christian consensus to a Humanistic one. That is, instead of the final reality that exists being the infinite creator God; instead of that which is the basis of all reality being such a creator God, now largely, all else is seen as only material or energy which has existed forever in some form, shaped into its present complex form only by pure chance.

I want to say to you, those of you who are Christians or even if you are not a Christian and you are troubled about the direction that our society is going in, that we must not concentrate merely on the bits and pieces. But we must understand that all of these dilemmas come on the basis of moving from the Judeo-Christian world view — that the final reality is an infinite creator God — over into this other reality which is that the final reality is only energy or material in some mixture or form which has existed forever and which has taken its present shape by pure chance.

The word Humanism should be carefully defined. We should not just use it as a flag, or what younger people might call a "buzz" word. We must understand what we are talking about when we use the word Humanism. Humanism means that *man is the measure of all things.* Man is the measure of all things. If this other final reality of material or energy shaped by pure chance is the final reality, it gives no meaning to life. It gives no value system. It gives no basis for law, and therefore, in this case, man must be the measure of all things. So, Humanism properly defined, in contrast, let us say, to the humanities or humanitarianism, (which is something entirely different and which Christians should be in favor of) being the measure of all things, comes naturally, mathematically, inevitably, certainly. If indeed the final reality is silent about these values, then man must generate them from himself.

So, Humanism is the absolute certain result, if we choose this other final reality and say that is what it is. You must realize that when we speak of man being the measure of all things under the Humanist label, the first thing is that man has only knowledge from himself. That he, being finite, limited, very faulty in his observation of many things, yet nevertheless, has no possible source of knowledge except what man, beginning from himself, can find out from his own observation. Specifically, in this view, there is no place for any knowledge from God.

1. This address was delivered by the late Dr. Schaeffer in 1982 at the Coral Ridge Presbyterian Church, Fort Lauderdale, Florida. It is based on one of his books, which bears the same title.

But it is not only that man must start from himself in the area of knowledge and learning, but any value system must come arbitrarily from man himself by arbitrary choice. More frightening still, in our country, at our own moment of history, is the fact that any basis of law then becomes arbitrary — merely certain people making decisions as to what is for the good of society at the given moment.

Now this is the real reason for the breakdown in morals in our country. It's the real reason for the breakdown in values in our country, and it is the reason that our Supreme Court now functions so thoroughly upon the fact of arbitrary law. They have no basis for law that is fixed; therefore, like the young person who decides to live hedonistically upon their own chosen arbitrary values, society is now doing the same thing legally. Certain few people come together and decide what they arbitrarily believe is for the good of society at the given moment, and that becomes law.

The world view that the final reality is only material or energy shaped by pure chance, inevitably, (that's the next word I would bring to you) mathematically — with mathematical certainty — brings forth all these other results which are in our country and in our society which have led to the breakdown in the country — in society — and which are its present sorrows. So, if you hold this other world view, you must realize that it is inevitable that we will come to the very sorrows of relativity and all these other things that are so represented in our country at this moment of history.

It should be noticed that this new dominant world view is a view which is exactly opposite from that of the founding fathers of this country. Now, not all the founding fathers were individually, personally, Christians. That certainly is true. But, nevertheless, they founded the country on the base that there is a God who is the Creator (now I come to the next central phrase) *who gave the inalienable rights.*

We must understand something very thoroughly. If society — if the state gives the rights, it can take them away — they're not inalienable. If the states give the rights, they can change them and manipulate them. But this was not the view of the founding fathers of this country. They believed, although not all of them were individual Christians, that there was a Creator and that this Creator gave the inalienable rights — this upon which our country was founded and which has given us the freedoms which we still have — even the freedoms which are being used now to destroy the freedoms.

The reason that these freedoms were there is because they believed there was somebody who gave the inalienable rights. But if we have the view that the final reality is material or energy which has existed forever in some form, we must understand that this view never, never, never would have given the rights which we now know and which, unhappily, I say to you (those of you who are Christians) that too often you take all too much for granted. You forget that the freedoms which we have in northern Europe after the Reformation (and the United States is an extension of that, as would be Australia or Canada, New Zealand, etc.) are absolutely unique in the world.

Occasionally, some of you who have gone to universities have been taught that these freedoms are rooted in the Greek city-states. That is not the truth. All you have to do is read Plato's *Republic* and you understand that the Greek city-states never had any concept of the freedoms that we have. Go back into history. The freedoms which we have (the form / freedom balance of government) are unique in history and they are also unique in the world at this day.

A fairly recent poll of the 150 some countries that now constitute the world shows that only 25 of these countries have any freedoms at all. What we have, and take so poorly for granted, is unique. It was brought forth by a specific world view and that specific world view was the Judeo-Christian world view especially as it was refined in the Reformation, putting the authority indeed at a central point — not in the Church and the state and the Word of God, but rather the Word of God alone. All the benefits which we know — I would repeat — which we have taken so easily and so much for granted, are unique. They have been grounded on the certain world view that there was a Creator there to give inalienable rights. And this other view over here, which has become increasingly dominant, of the material-energy final world view (shaped by pure chance) never would have, could not, has, no basis of values, in order to give such a balance of freedom that we have known so easily and which we unhappily, if we are not careful, take so for granted.

We are now losing those freedoms and we can expect to continue to lose them if this other world view continues to take increased force and power in our county. We can be sure of this. I would say it again — inevitably, mathematically, all of these things will come forth. There is no possible way to heal the relativistic thinking of our own day, if indeed all there is is a universe out there that is silent about any values. None, whatsoever! It is not possible. It is a loss of values and it is a loss of freedom which we may be sure will continually grow.

A good illustration is in the public schools. This view is taught in our public schools exclusively — by law. There is no other view that can be taught. I'll mention it a bit later, but by law there is no other view that can be taught. By law, in the public schools, the United States of America in 1982, legally there is only one view of reality that can be taught. I'll mention it a bit later, but there is only one view of reality that can be taught, and that is that the final reality is only material or energy shaped by pure chance.

It is the same with the television programs. Public television gives us many things that many of us like culturally, but is also completely committed to a propaganda position that the last reality is only material / energy shaped by pure chance. Clark's *Civilization*, Brunowski, *The Ascent of Man*, Carl Sagan's *Cosmos* — they all say it. There is only one final view of reality that's possible and that is that the final reality is material or energy shaped by pure chance.

It is about us on every side, and especially the government and the courts have become the vehicle to force this anti-God view on the total population. It's exactly where we are.

The abortion ruling is a very clear one. The abortion ruling, of course, is also a natural result of this other world view because with this other world view,

human life — your individual life — has no intrinsic value. You are a wart upon the face of an absolutely impersonal universe. Your aspirations have no fulfillment in the "what-isness" of what is. Your aspirations damn you. Many of the young people who come to us understand this very well because their aspirations as Humanists have no fulfillment, if indeed the final reality is only material or energy shaped by pure chance.

The universe cannot fulfill anything that you say when you say, "It is beautiful"; "I love"; "It is right"; "It is wrong." These words are meaningless words against the backdrop of this other world view. So what we find is that the abortion case should not have been a surprise because it boiled up out of, quite naturally, (I would use the word again) mathematically, this other world view. In this case, human life has no distinct value whatsoever, and we find this Supreme Court in one ruling overthrew the abortion laws of all 50 states, and they made this form of killing human life (because that's what it is) the law. The law declared that this form of killing human life was to be accepted, and for many people, because they had no set ethic, when the Supreme Court said that it was legal, in the intervening years, it has become ethical.

The courts of this country have forced this view and its results on the total population. What we find is that as the courts have done this, without any longer that which the founding fathers comprehended of law (A man like Blackstone, with his *Commentaries*, understood, and the other lawgivers in this country in the beginning): That there is a law of God which gives foundation. It becomes quite natural then, that they would also cut themselves loose from a strict constructionism concerning the Constitution.

Everything is relative. So as you cut yourself loose from the Law of God, in any concept whatsoever, you also soon are cutting yourself loose from a strict constructionism and each ruling is to be seen as an arbitrary choice by a group of people as to what they may honestly think is for the sociological good of the community, of the country, for the given moment.

Now, along with that is the fact that the courts are increasingly making law and thus we find that the legislatures' powers are increasingly diminished in relationship to the power of the courts. Now the pro-abortion people have been very wise about this in the last, say, 10 years, and Christians very silly. I wonder sometimes where we've been because the pro-abortion people have used the courts for their end rather than the legislatures — because the courts are not subject to the people's thinking, nor their will, either by election nor by a re-election. Consequently, the courts have been the vehicle used to bring this whole view and to force it on our total population. It has not been largely the legislatures. It has been rather, the courts.

The result is a relativistic value system. A lack of a final meaning to life — that's first. Why does human life have any value at all, if that is all that reality is? Not only are you going to die individually, but the whole human race is going to die, someday. It may not take the falling of the atom bombs, but someday the world will grow too hot, too cold. That's what we are told on this other final reality, and someday all you people not only will be individually dead, but the whole conscious life on this world will be dead, and nobody will see the birds fly. And there's no meaning to life.

As you know, I don't speak academically, shut off in some scholastic cubicle, as it were. I have lots of young people and older ones come to us from the ends of the earth. And as they come to us, they have gone to the end of this logically and they are not living in a romantic setting. They realize what the situation is. They can't find any meaning to life. It's the meaning to the black poetry. It's the meaning of the black plays. It's the meaning of all this. It's the meaning of the words "punk rock." And I must say, that on the basis of what they are being taught in school, that the final reality is only this material thing, they are not wrong. They're right! On this other basis there is no meaning to life and not only is there no meaning to life, but there is no value system that is fixed, and we find that the law is based then only on a relativistic basis and that law becomes purely arbitrary.

And this is brought to bear, specifically, and perhaps most clearly, in the public schools (I'll come to that now) in this country. In the courts of this country,

they are saying that it's absolutely illegal, from the lowest grades up through university, for the public schools of this country to teach any other world view except this world view of final material or energy. Now this is done, no matter what the parents may wish. This is done regardless of what those who pay the taxes for their schools may wish. I'm giving you an illustration, as well as making a point. The way the courts force their view, and this false view of reality on the total population, no matter what the total population wants.

We find that in the January 18 — just recently — *Time* magazine, there was an article that said there was a poll that pointed out that about 76% of the people in this country thought it would be a good idea to have both creation and evolution taught in the public schools. I don't know if the poll was accurate, but assuming that the poll was accurate, what does it mean? It means that your public schools are told by the courts that they cannot teach this, even though 76% of the people in the United States want it taught. *I'll give you a word. It's TYRANNY. There is no other word that fits at such a point.*

And at the same time we find the medical profession has radically changed. Dr. Koop, in our seminars for *Whatever Happened to the Human Race*, often said that (speaking for himself), "When I graduated from medical school, the idea was 'how can I save this life?' But for a great number of the medical students now, it's not, 'How can I save this life?', but 'Should I save this life?' "

Believe me, it's everywhere. It isn't just abortion. It's infanticide. It's allowing the babies to starve to death after they are born. If they do not come up to some doctor's concept of a quality of life worth living. I'll just say in passing — and never forget it — it takes about 15 days, often, for these babies to starve to death. And I'd say something else that we haven't stressed enough. In abortion itself, *there is no abortion method that is not painful to the child* — just as painful that month before birth as the baby you see a month after birth in one of these cribs down here that I passed — just as painful.

So what we find then, is that the medical profession has largely changed — not all doctors. I'm sure there are doctors here in the audience who feel very, very differently, who feel indeed that human life is important and you wouldn't take it, easily, wantonly. But, in general, we must say (and all you have to do is look at the TV programs), all you have to do is hear about the increased talk about allowing the Mongoloid child — the child with Down's Syndrome — to starve to death if it's born this way. Increasingly, we find on every side the medical profession has changed its views. The view now is, "Is this life worth saving?"

I look at you … You're an older congregation than I am usually used to speaking to. You'd better think, *because — this — means — you!* It does not stop with abortion and infanticide. It stops at the question, "What about the old person? Is he worth hanging on to?" Should we, as they are doing in England in this awful organization, EXIT, teach older people to commit suicide? Should we help them get rid of them because they are an economic burden, a nuisance? I want to tell you, once you begin chipping away the medical profession … The intrinsic value of the human life is founded upon the Judeo-Christian concept that man is unique because he is made in the image of God, and not because he is well, strong, a consumer, a sex object or any other thing. That is where whatever compassion this country has is, and certainly it is far from perfect and has never been perfect. Nor out of the Reformation has there been a Golden Age, but whatever compassion there has ever been, it is rooted in the fact that our culture knows that man is unique, is made in the image of God. Take it away, and I just say gently, the stopper is out of the bathtub for all human life.

The January 11 *Newsweek* has an article about the baby in the womb. The first 5 or 6 pages are marvelous. If you haven't seen it, you should see if you can get that issue. It's January 11 and about the first 5 or 6 pages show conclusively what every biologist has known all along, and that is that human life begins at conception. There is no other time for human life to begin, except at conception. Monkey life begins at conception. Donkey life begins at conception. And human life begins at conception. Biologically, there is

no discussion — never should have been — from a scientific viewpoint. I am not speaking of religion now. And this 5 or 6 pages very carefully goes into the fact that human life begins at conception. But you flip the page and there is this big black headline, "But is it a person?" And I'll read the last sentence, "The problem is not determining when actual human life begins, but when the value of that life begins to outweigh other considerations, such as the health or even the happiness of the mother."

We are not just talking about the health of the mother (it's a propaganda line), or even the happiness of the mother. Listen! Spell that out! It means that the mother, for her own hedonistic happiness — selfish happiness — can take human life by her choice, by law. Do you understand what I have said? By law, on the basis of her individual choice of what makes her happy. She can take what has been declared to be, in the first five pages [of the article], without any question, human life. In other words, they acknowledge that human life is there, but it is an open question as to whether it is not right to kill that human life if it makes the mother happy.

And basically that is no different than Stalin, Mao, or Hitler, killing who they killed for what they conceived to be the good of society. There is absolutely no line between the two statements — no absolute line, whatsoever. One follows along: Once that it is acknowledged that it is human life that is involved (and as I said, this issue of *Newsweek* shows conclusively that it is) the acceptance of death of human life in babies born or unborn, opens the door to the arbitrary taking of *any* human life. From then on, it's purely arbitrary.

It was this view that opened the door to all that followed in Germany prior to Hitler. It's an interesting fact here that the only Supreme Court in the Western World that has ruled against easy abortion is the West German Court. The reason they did it is because they knew, and it's clear history, that this view of human life in the medical profession and the legal profession combined, before Hitler came on the scene, is what opened the way for everything that happened in

Hitler's Germany. And so, the German Supreme Court has voted against easy abortion because they know — they know very well where it leads.

I want to say something tonight. Not many of you are black in this audience. I can't tell if you are Puerto Rican. But if I were in the minority group in this country, tonight, I would be afraid. I've had big gorgeous blacks stand up in our seminars and ask, "Sir, do you think there is a racial twist to all this?" And I have to say, "Right on! You've hit it right on the head!" Once this door is opened, there is something to be afraid of. Christians should be deeply concerned, and I cannot understand why the liberal lawyer of the Civil Liberties Union is not scared to death by this open door towards human life. Everyone ought to be frightened who knows anything about history — anything about the history of law, anything about the history of medicine. This is a terrifying door that is open.

Abortion itself would be worth spending much of our lifetimes to fight against, because it is the killing of human life, but it's only a symptom of the total. What we are facing is Humanism: Man, the measure of all things — viewing final reality being only material or energy shaped by chance — therefore, human life having no intrinsic value — therefore, the keeping of any individual life or any groups of human life, being purely an arbitrary choice by society at the given moment.

The flood doors are wide open. I fear both they, and too often the Christians, do not have just relativistic values (because, unhappily, Christians can live with relativistic values) but, I fear, that often such people as the liberal lawyers of the Civil Liberties Union and Christians, are just plain stupid in regard to the lessons of history. Nobody who knows his history could fail to be shaken at the corner we have turned in our culture. Remember why: because of the shift in the concept of the basic reality!

Now, we cannot be at all surprised when the liberal theologians support these things, because liberal theology is only Humanism using theological terms, and that's all it ever was, all the way back into Germany right after the Enlightenment. So when they come down on the side of easy abortion and infanticide, as some of these liberal denominations as well as theologians are doing, we shouldn't be surprised. It follows as night after day.

I have a question to ask you, and that is: Where have the Bible-believing Christians been in the last 40 years? All of this that I am talking about has only come in the last 80 years (I'm 70 ... I just had my birthday, so just 10 years older than I am). None of this was true in the United States. None of it! And the climax has all come within the last 40 years, which falls within the intelligent scope of many of you sitting in this room. Where have the Bible-believing Christians been? We shouldn't be surprised the liberal theologians have been no help — but where have we been as we have changed to this other consensus and all the horrors and stupidity of the present moment has come down on our culture? We must recognize that this country is close to being lost. Not, first of all, because of the Humanist conspiracy — I believe that there are those who conspire, but that is not the reason this country is almost lost. This country is almost lost because the Bible-believing Christians, in the last 40 years, who have said that they know that the final reality is this infinite-personal God who is the Creator and all the rest, have done nothing about it as the consensus has changed. There has been a vast silence!

Christians of this country have simply been silent. Much of the Evangelical leadership has not raised a voice. As a matter of fact, it was almost like sticking pins into the Evangelical constituency in most places to get them interested in the issue of human life while Dr. Koop and Franky and I worked on *Whatever Happened to the Human Race*, a vast, vast silence.

I wonder what God has to say to us? All these freedoms we have. All the secondary blessings we've had out of the preaching of the Gospel and we have let it slip through our fingers in the lifetime of most of you here. Not a hundred years ago — it has been in our lifetime in the last 40 years that these things have happened.

It's not only the Christian leaders. Where have the Christian lawyers been? Why haven't they been challenging this change in the view of what the First Amendment means, which I'll deal with in a second. Where have the Christian doctors been — speaking out against the rise of the abortion clinics and all the other things? Where have the Christian business-men been — to put their lives and their work on the line concerning these things which they would say as Christians are central to them? Where have the Christian educators been — as we have lost our educational system? Where have we been? Where have each of you been? What's happened in the last 40 years?

This country was founded on a Christian base with all its freedom for everybody. Let me stress that. This country was founded on a Christian base with all its freedom for everybody, not just Christians, but all its freedom for everyone. And now, this is being largely lost. We live not ten years from now, but tonight, in a Humanistic culture and we are rapidly moving at express train speed into a *totally* Humanistic culture. We're close to it. We are in a Humanistic culture, as I point out in the public schools and these other things, but we are moving toward a TOTALLY Humanistic culture and moving very quickly.

I would repeat at this place about our public schools because it's worth saying. Most people don't realize something. Communism, you know, is not basically an economic theory. It's *materialistic* communism, which means that at the very heart of the Marx, Engels, Lenin kind of communism (because you have to put all three together to really understand) is the materialistic con-cept of the final reality. That is the base for all that occurs in the communist countries.

I am wearing a Solidarity pin — in case you won-der what this is on my lapel. We had two young men from L'Abri take in an 8 ton truck of food into Poland — very bad weather — they almost were killed on the roads. They got in just three days before the crack-down. We, of L'Abri, have taken care of small numbers of each successive wave of Europeans who have been persecuted in the communist nations, the Hungarians, Czechoslovakians, now the Poles. A dear wonderful Christian schoolteacher that we love very much (she's a wonderful, wonderful Christian young woman, bril-

liant as brilliant, and she studied at L'Abri for a long time and she was one of the contact points for the des-tination of the food) — thought that the crackdown might come. So she sent me out this Solidarity pin. This wasn't made in Newark! This came from Poland. I have a hope. I hope I can wear it until I can hand it back to her and she can wear it again in Poland. That's my hope! But all the oppression you have ever heard of in Mao's China, Stalin's day, Poland, Czechoslova-kia — any place that you can name it — Afghanistan — *all the oppression is the automatic, the mechanical certainty, that comes from having this other world view of the final reality only being material or energy shaped by pure chance.* That's where it comes from.

And what about our schools? I think I should stress again! *By law*, you are no more allowed to teach reli-gious values and religious views in our public schools than you are in the schools of Russia tonight. We don't teach Marxism over here in most of our schools, but as far as all religious teaching (except the religion of Humanism, which is a different kind of a thing) it is just as banned by law from our schools, and our schools are just as secular as the schools in Soviet Rus-sia — just exactly! Not ten years from now. Tonight!

Congress opens with prayer. Why? Because Con-gress always is opened with prayer. Back there, the founding fathers didn't consider the 13 provincial congresses that sent representatives to form our coun-try in Philadelphia really open until there was prayer. The Congress in Washington, where Edith and I have just been, speaking to various men in political areas and circles — *that* Congress is not open until there is prayer. It's illegal, in many places, for youngsters to merely meet and pray on the geographical loca-tion of the public schools. I would repeat, we are not only immoral, we're stupid. I mean that. I don't know which is the worst: being immoral or stupid on such an issue. We are not only immoral, we are stupid for the place we have allowed ourselves to come to with-out noticing.

I would now repeat again the word I used before. There is no other word we can use for our present situ-ation that I have just been describing, except the word

TYRANNY! TYRANNY! That's what we face! We face a world view which never would have given us our freedoms. It has been forced upon us by the courts and the government — the men holding this other world view, whether we want it or not, even though it's destroying the very freedoms which give the freedoms for the excesses and for the things which are wrong.

We, who are Christians, and others who love liberty, should be acting in our day as the founding fathers acted in their day. Those who founded this country believed that they were facing tyranny. All you have to do is read their writings. That's why the war was fought. That's why this country was founded. They believed that God never, never, never wanted people to be under tyrannical governments. They did it not as a pragmatic or economic thing, though that was involved too, I guess, but for principle. They were against tyranny, and if the founding fathers stood against tyranny, we ought to recognize, in this year 1982, if they were back here and one of them was standing right here, he would say the same thing — what you are facing is tyranny. The very kind of tyranny we fought, he would say, in order that we might escape.

And we face a very hidden censorship. Every once in a while, as soon as we begin to talk about the need of re-entering Christian values into the discussion, someone shouts "Khomeni." Someone says that what you are after is theocracy. Absolutely not! We must make absolutely plain, we are not in favor of theocracy, in name or in fact. But, having said that, nevertheless, we must realize that we already face a hidden censorship — a hidden censorship in which it is impossible to get the other world view presented in something like public television. It's absolutely impossible.

I could give you a couple of examples. I'll give you one because it's so close to me. And that is, that after we made *Whatever Happened to the Human Race*, Franky made an 80 minute cutting for TV of the first 3 episodes (and people who know television say that it's one of the best television films they have ever seen technically, so that's not a problem). Their representative presented it to a director of public television, and

as soon as she heard (It happened to be a woman. I'm sure that's incidental.) that it was against abortion, she said, "We can't show that. We only show things that give both sides." And, at exactly the same time, they were showing that abominable *Hard Choices*, which is just straight propaganda *for* abortion. As I point out, the study guide that went with it (as I quote it in *Christian Manifesto* [the book] with a long quote) was even worse. It was saying that the only possible view of reality was this material thing — this material reality. They spelled it out in that study guide more clearly than I have tonight as to what the issue is. They said, "that's it!" What do you call that? That's hidden censorship.

Dr. Koop, one of the great surgeons of the world, when he was nominated as Surgeon General, much of the press (printed) great swelling things against him — a lot of them not true, a lot of them twisted. Certainly though, lots of space was made for trying to not get his nomination accepted. When it was accepted though, I looked like mad in some of the papers, and in most of them what I found was about one inch on the third page that said that Dr. Koop had been accepted. What do you call that? Just one thing: hidden censorship.

You must realize that this other view is totally intolerant. It is totally intolerant. I do not think we are going to get another opportunity if we do not take it now in this country. I would repeat, we are a long way down the road. I do not think we are going to get another opportunity. If the Christians, specifically, but others also, who love liberty, do not do something about it now, I don't believe your grandchildren are going to get a chance. In the present so-called conservative swing in the last election, we have an opportunity, but we must remember this, and I would really brand this into your thinking: *A conservative Humanism is no better than a liberal Humanism. It's the Humanism that is wrong, not merely the coloration.* And therefore, at the present moment, what we must insist on, to people in our government who represent us, is that we do not just end with words. We must see, at the present opportunity, if it continues, a real change. We mustn't allow it to just drift off into mere words.

Now I want to say something with great force, right

here. What I have been talking about, whether you know it or not, is true spirituality. This is true spirituality. Spirituality, after you are a Christian and have accepted Christ as your Savior, means that Christ is the Lord of ALL your life — not just your religious life, and if you make a dichotomy in these things, you are denying your Lord His proper place. I don't care how many butterflies you have in your stomach, you are poor spiritually. True spirituality means that the Lord Jesus Christ is the Lord of all of life, and except for the things that He has specifically told us in the Bible are sinful and we've set them aside — all of life is spiritual and all of life is equally spiritual. That includes (as our forefathers did) standing for these things of freedom and standing for these things of human life and all these other matters that are so crucial, if indeed, this living God does exist as we know that He does exist.

We have forgotten our heritage. A lot of the evangelical complex like to talk about the old revivals and they tell us we ought to have another revival. We need another revival — you and I need revival. We need another revival in our hearts. But they have forgotten something. Most of the Christians have forgotten and most of the pastors have forgotten something. That is the factor that every single revival that has ever been a real revival, whether it was the great awakening before the American Revolution; whether it was the great revivals of Scandinavia; whether it was Wesley and Whitefield; wherever you have found a great revival, it's always had three parts. First, it has called for the individual to accept Christ as Savior, and thankfully, in all of these that I have named, thousands have been saved. Then, it has called upon the Christians to bow their hearts to God and really let the Holy Spirit have His place in fullness in their life. But there has always been, in every revival, a third element. *It has always brought SOCIAL CHANGE!*

Cambridge historians who aren't Christians would tell you that if it wasn't for the Wesley revival and the social change that Wesley's revival had brought, England would have had its own form of the French Revolution. It was Wesley saying people must be treated correctly and dealing down into the social needs of

the day that made it possible for England to have its bloodless revolution in contrast to France's bloody revolution.

The *Wall Street Journal*, not too long ago, and I quote it again in *A Christian Manifesto*, pointed out that it was the Great Awakening, that great revival prior to the founding of the United States, that opened the way and prepared for the founding of the United States. Every one of the great revivals had tremendous social implications. What I am saying is, that I am afraid that we have forgotten our heritage, and we must go on even when the cost is high.

I think the Church has failed to meet its obligation in these last 40 years for two specific reasons. The first is this false, truncated view of spirituality that doesn't see true spirituality touching all of life. The other thing is that too many Christians, whether they are doctors, lawyers, pastors, evangelists — whatever they are — too many of them are afraid to really speak out because they did not want to rock the boat for their own project. I am convinced that these two reasons, both of which are a tragedy and really horrible for the Christian, are an explanation of why we have walked the road we have walked in the last 40 years.

We must understand, it's going to cost you to take a stand on these things. There are doctors who are going to get kicked out of hospitals because they refuse to perform abortions; there are nurses that see a little sign on a crib that says, "Do not feed," and they feed and they are fired. There's a cost, but I'd ask you, what is loyalty to Christ worth to you? How much do you believe this is true? Why are you a Christian? Are you a Christian for some lesser reason, or are you a Christian because you know that this is the truth of reality? And then, how much do you love the Lord Jesus Christ? How much are you willing to pay the price for loyalty to the Lord Jesus?

We must absolutely set out to smash the lie of the new and novel concept of the separation of religion from the state which most people now hold and which Christians have just bought a bill of goods. This is new and this is novel. It has no relationship to the meaning of the First Amendment. The First Amendment was that the state would never interfere with religion. THAT'S ALL THE MEANING THERE WAS TO THE FIRST AMENDMENT. Just read Madison and the *Spectator Papers* if you don't think so. That's all it was!

Now we have turned it over and we have put it on its head and what we must do is absolutely insist that we return to what the First Amendment meant in the first place — not that religion can't have an influence into society and into the state — not that. But we must insist that there's a freedom that the First Amendment really gave. Now with this we must emphasize, and I said it, but let me say it again, we do not want a theocracy! I personally am opposed to a theocracy. On this side of the New Testament I do not believe there is a place for a theocracy till Jesus the King comes back. But that's a very different thing while saying clearly we are not in favor of a theocracy in name or in fact, from where we are now, where all religious influence is shut out of the processes of the state and the public schools. We are only asking for one thing. We are asking for the freedom that the First Amendment guaranteed. That's what we should be standing for.

All we ask for is what the founding fathers of this country stood and fought and died for, and at the same time, very crucial in all this is standing absolutely for a high view of human life against the snowballing low view of human life of which I have been talking. This thing has been presented under the hypocritical name of choice. What does choice equal? Choice, as I have already shown, means the right to kill for your own selfish desires. To kill human life! That's what the choice is that we're being presented with on this other basis.

Now, I come toward the close, and that is that we must recognize something from the Scriptures, and that's why I had that Scripture read that I had read tonight. When the government negates the law of God, it abrogates its authority. God has given certain offices to restrain chaos in this fallen world, but it does not mean that these offices are autonomous, and when a government commands that which is contrary to the Law of God, it abrogates its authority.

Throughout the whole history of the Christian

Church, (and again I wish people knew their history. In *A Christian Manifesto* I stress what happened in the Reformation in reference to all this) at a certain point, it is not only the privilege but it is the duty of the Christian to disobey the government. Now that's what the founding fathers did when they founded this country. That's what the early Church did. That's what Peter said. You heard it from the Scripture: "Should we obey man? ... rather than God?" That's what the early Christians did.

Occasionally — no, often, people say to me, "But the early Church didn't practice civil disobedience." Didn't they? You don't know your history again. When those Christians that we all talk about so much allowed themselves to be thrown into the arena, when they did that, from their view it was a religious thing. They would not worship anything except the living God. But you must recognize from the side of the Roman state, there was nothing religious about it at all — it was purely civil. The Roman Empire had disintegrated until the only unity it had was its worship of Caesar. You could be an atheist; you could worship the Zoroastrian religion ... You could do anything. They didn't care. It was a civil matter, and when those Christians stood up there and refused to worship Caesar, from the side of the state, they were rebels. They were in civil disobedience and they were thrown to the beasts. They were involved in civil disobedience, as much as your brothers and sisters in the Soviet Union are. When the Soviet Union says that, by law, they cannot tell their children, even in their home about Jesus Christ, they must disobey and they get sent off to the mental ward or to Siberia. It's exactly the same kind of civil disobedience that's represented in a very real way by the thing I am wearing on my lapel tonight.

Every appropriate legal and political governmental means must be used. "The final bottom line" — I have invented this term in *A Christian Manifesto. I hope the Christians across this country and across the world will really understand what the Bible truly teaches: The final bottom line!* The early Christians, every one of the reformers (and again, I'll say in *A Christian Manifesto* I go through country after country and show that there was not a single place with the possible exception of England, where the Reformation was successful, where there wasn't civil disobedience and disobedience to the state), the people of the Reformation, the founding fathers of this country, faced and acted in the realization that if there is no place for disobeying the government, that government has been put in the place of the living God. In such a case, the government has been made a false god. If there is no place for disobeying a human government, that government has been made GOD.

Caesar, under some name, thinking of the early Church, has been put upon the final throne. The Bible's answer is NO! Caesar is not to be put in the place of God and we as Christians, in the name of the Lordship of Christ, and all of life, must so think and act on the appropriate level. It should always be on the appropriate level. We have lots of room to move yet with our court cases, with the people we elect — all the things that we can do in this country. If, unhappily, we come to that place, the appropriate level must also include a disobedience to the state.

If you are not doing that, you haven't thought it through. Jesus is not really on the throne. God is not central. You have made a false god central. Christ must be the final Lord and not society and not Caesar.

May I repeat the final sentence again? *Christ must be the final Lord and not Caesar and not society.*

CHAPTER 54

Christianity: Yesterday, Today, and Tomorrow

Joseph Ratzinger (Pope Benedict XVI)

*"If God has truly assumed manhood then he participates,
as man, in the presence of God, which embraces all ages."*

Since this work was first published, more than thirty years have passed, in which world history has moved along at a brisk pace. In retrospect, two years seem to be particularly important milestones in the final decades of the millennium that has just come to an end: 1968 and 1989. The year 1968 marked the rebellion of a new generation, which not only considered post-war reconstruction in Europe as inadequate, full of injustice, full of selfishness and greed, but also viewed the entire course of history since the triumph of Christianity as a mistake and a failure. These young people wanted to improve things at last, to bring about freedom, equality, and justice, and they were convinced that they had found the way to this better world in the mainstream of Marxist thought. The year 1989 brought the surprising collapse of the socialist regimes in Europe, which left behind a sorry legacy of ruined land and ruined souls. Anyone who expected that the hour had come again for the Christian message was disappointed. Although the number of believing Christians throughout the world is not small, Christianity failed at that historical moment to make itself heard as an epoch-making alternative. Basically, the Marxist doctrine of salvation (in several differently orchestrated variations, of course) had taken a stand as the sole ethically motivated guide to the future that was at the same time consistent with a scientific worldview. Therefore, even after the shock of 1989, it did not simply abdicate. We need only to recall how little was said about the horrors of the Communist gulag, how isolated Solzhenitsyn's voice remained:

no one speaks about any of that. A sort of shame forbids it; even Pol Pot's murderous regime is mentioned only occasionally in passing. But there were still disappointment and a deep-seated perplexity. People no longer trust grand moral promises, and after all, that is what Marxism had understood itself to be. It was about justice for all, about peace, about doing away with unfair master-servant relationships, and so on. Marxism believed that it had to dispense with ethical principles for the time being and that it was allowed to use terror as a beneficial means to these noble ends. Once the resulting human devastation became visible, even for a moment, the former ideologues preferred to retreat to a pragmatic position or else declared quite openly their contempt for ethics. We can observe a tragic example of this in Colombia, where a campaign was started, under the Marxist banner at first, to liberate the small farmers who had been downtrodden by the wealthy financiers. Today, instead, a rebel republic has developed, beyond governmental control, which quite openly depends on drug trafficking and no longer seeks any moral justification for this, especially since it thereby satisfies a demand in wealthy nations and at the same time gives bread to people who would otherwise not be able to expect much of anything from the world economy. In such a perplexing situation, shouldn't Christianity try very seriously to rediscover its voice, so as to "introduce" the new millennium to its message, and to make it comprehensible as a general guide for the future?

Anyway, where was the voice of the Christian faith

at that time? In 1967, when the book was being written, the fermentation of the early post-conciliar period was in full swing. This is precisely what the Second Vatican Council had intended: to endow Christianity once more with the power to shape history. The nineteenth century had seen the formulation of the opinion that religion belonged to the subjective, private realm and should have its place there. But precisely because it was to be categorized as something subjective, it could not be a determining factor in the overall course of history and in the epochal decisions that must be made as part of it. Now, following the council, it was supposed to become evident again that the faith of Christians embraces all of life, that it stands in the midst of history and in time and has relevance beyond the realm of subjective notions. Christianity — at least from the viewpoint of the Catholic Church — was trying to emerge again from the ghetto to which it had been relegated since the nineteenth century and to become involved once more in the world at large. We do not need to discuss here the intra-ecclesiastical disputes and frictions that arose over the interpretation and assimilation of the council. The main thing affecting the status of Christianity in that period was the idea of a new relationship between the Church and the world. Although Romano Guardini in the 1930s had coined the expression, *"Unterscheidung des Christlichen"* [distinguishing what is Christian] — something that was extremely necessary then — such distinctions now no longer seemed to be important; on the contrary, the spirit of the age called for crossing boundaries, reaching out to the world, and becoming involved in it. It was already demonstrated upon the Parisian barricades in 1968 how quickly these ideas could emerge from the academic discussions of churchmen and find a very practical application: a revolutionary Eucharist was celebrated there, thus putting into practice a new fusion of the Church and the world under the banner of the revolution that was supposed to bring, at last, the dawn of a better age. The leading role played by Catholic and Protestant student groups in the revolutionary upheavals at universities, both in Europe and beyond, confirmed this trend.

This new translation of ideas into practice, this new fusion of the Christian impulse with secular and political action, was like a lightning bolt; the real fires that it set, however, were in Latin America. The theology of liberation seemed for more than a decade to point the way by which the faith might again shape the world, because it was making common cause with the findings and worldly wisdom of the hour. No one could dispute the fact that there was in Latin America, to a horrifying extent, oppression, unjust rule, the concentration of property and power in the hands of a few, and the exploitation of the poor, and there was no disputing either that something had to be done. And since it was a question of countries with a Catholic majority, there could be no doubt that the Church bore the responsibility here and that the faith had to prove itself as a force for justice. But how? Now Marx appeared to be the great guidebook. He was said to be playing now the role that had fallen to Aristotle in the thirteenth century; the latter's pre-Christian (that is, "pagan") philosophy had to be baptized, in order to bring faith and reason into the proper relation to one another. But anyone who accepts Marx (in whatever neo-Marxist variation he may choose) as the representative of worldly reason, not only accepts a philosophy, a vision of the origin and meaning of existence, but also and especially adopts a practical program. For this "philosophy" is essentially a "praxis," which does not presuppose a "truth" but rather creates one. Anyone who makes Marx the philosopher of theology adopts the primacy of politics and economics, which now become the real powers that can bring about salvation (and, if misused, can wreak havoc). The redemption of mankind, to this way of thinking, occurs through politics and economics, in which the form of the future is determined. This primacy of praxis and politics meant, above all, that God could not be categorized as something "practical." The "reality" in which one had to get involved now was solely the material reality of given historical circumstances, which were to be viewed critically and reformed, redirected to the right goals by using the appropriate means, among which violence was indispensable. From this perspective, speaking about God belongs neither to the realm of the practical nor to that of reality. If it was to be indulged in at all, it would have to be postponed until the more important work had been done. What remained was the figure of Jesus, who of course no longer appeared now as the Christ, but rather as the embodiment of all the suffering and oppressed and as their spokesman, who calls us to rise up, to change society. What was new in all this was that the program of changing the world, which in Marx was intended to be not only atheistic but also anti-religious, was now filled with religious passion and was based on religious principles: a new reading of the Bible (especially of the Old Testament) and a liturgy that was celebrated as a symbolic fulfillment of the revolution and as a preparation for it.

It must be admitted: by means of this remarkable synthesis, Christianity had stepped once more onto the world stage and had become an "epoch-making" message. It is no surprise that the socialist states took a stand in favor of this movement. More noteworthy is the fact that, even in the "capitalist" countries, liberation theology was the darling of public opinion; to contradict it was viewed positively as a sin against humanity and mankind, even though no one, naturally, wanted to see the practical measures applied in their own situation, because they of course had already arrived at a just social order. Now it cannot be denied that in the various liberation theologies there really were some worthwhile insights as well. All of these plans for an epoch-making synthesis of Christianity and the world had to step aside, however, the moment that that faith in politics as a salvific force collapsed. Man is, indeed, as Aristotle says, a "political being," but he cannot be reduced to politics and economics. I see the real and most profound problem with the liberation theologies in their effective omission of the idea of God, which of course also changed the figure of Christ fundamentally (as we have indicated). Not as though God had been denied — not on your life! It's just that he was not needed in regard to the "reality" that mankind had to deal with. God had nothing to do.

One is struck by this point and suddenly wonders: Was that the case only in liberation theology? Or was this theory able to arrive at such an assessment of the question about God — that the question was not a practical one for the long-overdue business of changing the world — only because the Christian world thought much the same thing, or rather, lived in much the same way, without reflecting on it or noticing it? Hasn't Christian consciousness acquiesced to a great extent — without being aware of it — in the attitude that faith in God is something subjective, which belongs in the private realm and not in the common activities of public life where, in order to be able to get along, we all have to behave now *"etsi Deus non daretur"* ("as if there were no God")? Wasn't it necessary to find a way that would be valid, in case it turned out that God doesn't exist? And, indeed it happened automatically that, when the faith stepped out of the inner sanctum of ecclesiastical matters into the general public, it had nothing for God to do and left him where he was: in the private realm, in the intimate sphere that doesn't concern anyone else. It didn't take any particular negligence, and certainly not a deliberate denial, to leave God as a God with nothing to do, especially since his Name had been misused so often. But the faith would really have come out of the ghetto only if it had brought its most distinctive feature with it into the public arena: the God who judges and suffers, the God who sets limits and standards for us; the God from whom we come and to whom we are going. But as it was, it really remained in the ghetto, having by now absolutely nothing to do.

Yet God is "practical" and not just some theoretical conclusion of a consoling worldview that one may adhere to or simply disregard. We see that today in every place where the deliberate denial of him has become a matter of principle and where his absence is no longer mitigated at all. For at first, when God is left out of the picture, everything apparently goes on as before. Mature decisions and the basic structures of life remain in place, even though they have lost their foundations. But, as Nietzsche describes it, once the news really reaches people that "God is dead," and they take it to heart, then everything changes. This is demonstrated today, on the one hand, in the way that science treats human life: man is becoming a technological object while vanishing to an ever-greater degree as a human subject, and he has only himself to blame. When human embryos are artificially "cultivated" so as to have "research material" and to obtain a supply of organs, which then are supposed to benefit other human beings, there is scarcely an outcry, because so few are horrified any more. Progress demands all this, and they really are noble goals: improving the quality of life — at least for those who can afford to have recourse to such services. But if man, in his origin and at his very roots, is only an object to himself, if he is "produced" and comes off the production line with selected features and accessories, what on earth is man then supposed to think of man? How should he act toward him? What will be man's attitude toward man, when he can no longer find anything of the divine mystery in the other, but only his own know-how? What is happening in the "high-tech" areas of science is reflected wherever the culture, broadly speaking, has managed to tear God out of men's hearts. Today there are places where trafficking in human beings goes on quite openly: a cynical consumption of humanity while society looks on helplessly. For example, organized crime constantly brings women out of Albania on various pretexts and delivers them to the mainland across the sea as prostitutes, and because there are enough cynics there waiting for such "wares," organized crime becomes more powerful, and those who try to put a stop to it discover that the Hydra of evil keeps growing new heads, no matter how many they may cut off. And do we not see everywhere around us, in seemingly orderly neighborhoods, an increase in violence, which is taken more and more for granted and is becoming more and more reckless? I do not want to extend this horror-scenario any further. But we ought to wonder whether God might not in fact be the genuine reality, the basic prerequisite for any "realism," so that, without him, nothing is safe.

Let us return to the course of historical developments since 1967. The year 1989, as I was saying,

brought with it no new answers, but rather deepened the general perplexity and nourished skepticism about great ideals. But something did happen. Religion became modern again. Its disappearance is no longer anticipated; on the contrary, various new forms of it are growing luxuriantly. In the leaden loneliness of a God-forsaken world, in its interior boredom, the search for mysticism, for any sort of contact with the divine, has sprung up anew. Everywhere there is talk about visions and messages from the other world, and wherever there is a report of an apparition, thousands travel there, in order to discover, perhaps, a crack in the world, through which heaven might look down on them and send them consolation. Some complain that this new search for religion, to a great extent, is passing the traditional Christian churches by. An institution is inconvenient, and dogma is bothersome. What is sought is an experience, an encounter with the Absolutely Other. I cannot say that I am in unqualified agreement with this complaint. At the World Youth Days, such as the one recently in Paris, faith becomes experience and provides the joy of fellowship. Something of an ecstasy, in the good sense, is communicated. The dismal and destructive ecstasy of drugs, of hammering rhythms, noise, and drunkenness is confronted with a bright ecstasy of light, of joyful encounter in God's sunshine. Let it not be said that this is only a momentary thing. Often it is so, no doubt. But it can also be a moment that brings about a lasting change and begins a journey. Similar things happen in the many lay movements that have sprung up in the last few decades. Here, too, faith becomes a form of lived experience, the joy of setting out on a journey and of participating in the mystery of the leaven that permeates the whole mass from within and renews it. Eventually, provided that the root is sound, even apparition sites can be incentives to go again in search of God in a sober way. Anyone who expected that Christianity would now become a mass movement was, of course, disappointed. But mass movements are not the ones that bear the promise of the future within them. The future is made wherever people find their way to one another in life-shaping convictions. And a good future grows wherever these convictions come from the truth and lead to it.

The rediscovery of religion, however, has another side to it. We have already seen that this trend looks for religion as an experience, that the "mystical" aspect of religion is an important part of it: religion that offers me contact with the Absolutely Other. In our historical situation, this means that the mystical religions of Asia (parts of Hinduism and of Buddhism), with their renunciation of dogma and their minimal degree of institutionalization, appear to be more suitable for enlightened humanity than dogmatically determined and institutionally structured Christianity. In general, however, the result is that individual religions are relativized; for all the differences and, yes, the contradictions among these various sorts of belief, the only thing that matters, ultimately, is the inside of all these different forms, the contact with the ineffable, with the hidden mystery. And to a great extent people agree that this mystery is not completely manifested in any one form of revelation, that it is always glimpsed in random and fragmentary ways and yet is always sought as one and the same thing. That we cannot know God himself, that everything which can be stated and described can only be a symbol: this is nothing short of a fundamental certainty for modern man, which he also understands somehow as his humility in the presence of the infinite. Associated with this relativizing is the notion of a great peace among religions, which recognize each other as different ways of reflecting the One Eternal Being and which should leave up to the individual the path he will grope along to find the One who nevertheless unites them all. Through such a relativizing process, the Christian faith is radically changed, especially at two fundamental places in its essential message:

1. The figure of Christ is interpreted in a completely new way, not only in reference to dogma, but also and precisely with regard to the Gospels. The belief that Christ *is* the only Son of God, that God really dwells among us as man in him, and that the man Jesus is eternally in God, is God himself, and therefore is not a figure in which God appears, but rather the sole and irreplaceable God — this belief is thereby excluded. Instead of being the man who *is* God, Christ becomes the one who has *experienced* God in a special way. He is an enlightened one and therein is no longer fundamentally different from other enlightened individuals, for instance, Buddha. But in such an interpretation the figure of Jesus loses its inner logic. It is torn out of the historical setting in which it is anchored and forced into a scheme of things which is alien to it.

Buddha — and in this he is comparable to Socrates — directs the attention of his disciples away from himself: his own person doesn't matter, but only the path that he has pointed out. Someone who finds the way can forget Buddha. But with Jesus, what matters is precisely his Person, Christ himself. When he says, "I am he," we hear the tones of the "I AM" on Mount Horeb. The way consists precisely in following him, for "*I* am the way, the truth and the life" (Jn 14:6). He himself is the way, and there is no way that is independent of him, on which he would no longer matter. Since the real message that he brings is not a doctrine but his very person, we must of course add that this "I" of Jesus refers absolutely to the "Thou" of the Father and is not self-sufficient, but rather is indeed truly a "way." "My teaching is not mine" (Jn 7:16). "I seek not my own will, but the will of him who sent me" (Jn 5:30). The "I" is important, because it draws us completely into the dynamic of mission, because it leads to the surpassing of self and to union with him unto whom we have been created. If the figure of Jesus is taken out of this inevitably scandalous dimension, if it is separated from his Godhead, then it becomes self-contradictory. All that is left are shreds that leave us perplexed or else become excuses for self-affirmation.

2. The concept of God is fundamentally changed. The question as to whether God should be thought of as a person or impersonally now seems to be of secondary importance; no longer can an essential difference be noted between theistic and nontheistic forms of religion. This view is spreading with astonishing rapidity. Even believing and theologically trained Catholics, who want to share in the responsibilities of the Church's life, will ask the question (as though

the answer were self-evident): "Can it really be that important, whether someone understands God as a person or impersonally?" After all, we should be broad-minded — so goes the opinion — since the mystery of God is in any case beyond all concepts and images. But such concessions strike at the heart of the biblical faith. The *shema*, the "Hear, O Israel" from Deuteronomy 6:4–9, was and still is the real core of the believer's identity, not only for Israel, but also for Christianity. The believing Jew dies reciting this profession; the Jewish martyrs breathed their last declaring it and gave their lives for it: "Hear, O Israel. He is our God. He is one." The fact that this God now shows us his face in Jesus Christ (Jn 14:9) — a face that Moses was not allowed to see (Ex 33:20) — does not alter this profession in the least and changes nothing essential in this identity. Of course, the Bible does not use the term "person" to say that God is personal, but the divine personality is apparent nevertheless, inasmuch as there is a Name of God. A name implies the ability to be called on, to speak, to hear, to answer. This is essential for the biblical God, and if this is taken away, the faith of the Bible has been abandoned. It cannot be disputed that there have been and there are false, superficial ways of understanding God as personal. Precisely when we apply the concept of person to God, the difference between our idea of person and the reality of God — as the Fourth Lateran Council says about all speech concerning God — is always infinitely greater than what they have in common. False applications of the concept of person are sure to be present, whenever God is monopolized for one's own human interests and thus his Name is sullied. It is not by chance that the Second Commandment, which is supposed to protect the Name of God, follows directly after the First, which teaches us to adore him. In this respect we can always learn something new from the way in which the "mystical" religions, with their purely negative theology, speak about God, and in this respect there are avenues for dialogue. But with the disappearance of what is meant by "the Name of God," that is, God's personal nature, his Name is no longer protected and honored, but abandoned outright instead.

But what is actually meant, then, by God's Name, by his being personal? Precisely this: not only that we can experience him, beyond all [earthly] experience, but also that he can express and communicate himself. When God is understood in a completely impersonal way, for instance in Buddhism, as sheer negation with respect to everything that appears real to us, then there is no positive relationship between "God" and the world. Then the world has to be overcome as a source of suffering, but it no longer can be shaped. Religion then points out ways to overcome the world, to free people from the burden of its seeming, but it offers no standards by which we can live in the world, no forms of societal responsibility within it. The situation is somewhat different in Hinduism. The essential thing there is the experience of identity: At bottom I am one with the hidden ground of reality itself — the famous *tat tvam asi* of the Upanishads. Salvation consists in liberation from individuality, from being-a-person, in overcoming the differentiation from all other beings that is rooted in being-a-person: the deception of the self concerning itself must be put aside. The problem with this view of being has come very much to the fore in Neo-Hinduism. Where there is no uniqueness of persons, the inviolable dignity of each individual person has no foundation, either. In order to bring about the reforms that are now underway (the abolition of caste laws and of immolating widows, etc.), it was specifically necessary to break with this fundamental understanding and to introduce into the overall system of Indian thought the concept of person, as it has developed in the Christian faith out of the encounter with the personal God. The search for the correct "praxis," for right action, in this case has begun to correct the "theory": We can see to some extent how "practical" the Christian belief in God is, and how unfair it is to brush these disputed but important distinctions aside as being ultimately irrelevant.

With these considerations we have reached the point from which an "Introduction to Christianity" must set out today. Before I attempt to extend a bit farther the line of argument that I have suggested, another reference to the present status of faith in God and in Christ is called for. There is a fear of Christian "imperialism," a nostalgia for the beautiful multiplicity of religions and their supposedly primordial cheerfulness and freedom. Colonialism is said to be essentially bound up with historical Christianity, which was unwilling to accept the other in his otherness and tried to bring everything under its own protection. Thus, according to this view, the religions and cultures of South America were trodden down and stamped out and violence was done to the soul of the native peoples, who could not find themselves in the new order and were forcibly deprived of the old. Now there are milder and harsher variants of this opinion. The milder version says that we should finally grant to these lost cultures the right of domicile within the Christian faith and allow them to devise for themselves an aboriginal form of Christianity. The more radical view regards Christianity in its entirety as a sort of alienation, from which the native peoples must be liberated. The demand for an aboriginal Christianity, properly understood, should be taken as an extremely important task. All great cultures are open to one another and to the truth. They all have something to contribute to the Bride's "many-colored robes" mentioned in Psalm 45:14, which patristic writers applied to the Church. To be sure, many opportunities have been missed and new ones present themselves. Let us not forget, however, that those native peoples, to a notable extent, have already found their own expression of the Christian faith in popular devotions. That the suffering God and the kindly Mother in particular have become for them the central images of the faith, which have given them access to the God of the Bible, has something to say to us, too, today. But of course, much still remains to be done.

Let us return to the question about God and about Christ as the centerpiece of an introduction to the Christian faith. One thing has already become evident: the mystical dimension of the concept of God, which the Asian religions bring with them as a challenge to us, must clearly be decisive for our thinking, too, and

for our faith. God has become quite concrete in Christ, but in this way his mystery has also become still greater. God is always infinitely greater than all our concepts and all our images and names. The fact that we now acknowledge him to be triune does not mean that we have meanwhile learned everything about him. On the contrary: he is only showing us how little we know about him and how little we can comprehend him or even begin to take his measure. Today, after the horrors of the [twentieth-century] totalitarian regimes (I remind the reader of the memorial at Auschwitz), the problem of theodicy urgently and mightily [*mit brennender Gewalt*] demands the attention of us all; this is just one more indication of how little we are capable of defining God, much less fathoming him. After all, God's answer to Job explains nothing, but rather sets boundaries to our mania for judging everything and being able to say the final word on a subject, and reminds us of our limitations. It admonishes us to trust the mystery of God in its incomprehensibility.

Having said this, we must still emphasize the brightness of God, too, along with the darkness. Ever since the Prologue to the Gospel of John, the concept of Logos has been at the very center of our Christian faith in God. Logos signifies reason, meaning, or even "word" — a meaning, therefore, which is Word, which is relationship, which is creative. The God who is Logos guarantees the intelligibility of the world, the intelligibility of our existence, reason's accord with God, and God's accord with reason, even though his understanding infinitely surpasses ours and to us may so often appear to be darkness. The world comes from reason and this reason is a Person, is Love — this is what our biblical faith tells us about God. Reason can speak about God, it must speak about God, or else it cuts itself short. Included in this is the concept of creation. The world is not just *maya*, appearance, which we must ultimately leave behind. It is not merely the endless wheel of sufferings, from which we must try to escape. It is something positive. It is good, despite all the evil in it and despite all the sorrow, and it is good to live in it. God, who is the creator and declares himself in his creation, also gives direction and measure to human action. We are living today in a crisis of moral values [*Ethos*], which by now is no longer merely an academic question about the ultimate foundations of ethical theories, but rather an entirely practical matter. The news is getting around that moral values cannot be grounded in something else, and the consequences of this view are working themselves out. The published works on the theme of moral values are stacked high and almost toppling over, which on the one hand indicates the urgency of the question, but on the other hand also suggests the prevailing perplexity. Kolakowski, in his line of thinking, has very emphatically pointed out that deleting faith in God, however one may try to spin or turn it, ultimately deprives moral values of their grounding. If the world and man do not come from a creative intelligence, which stores within itself their measure and plots the path of human existence, then all that is left are traffic rules for human behavior, which can be discarded or maintained according to their usefulness. All that remains is the calculus of consequences — what is called teleological ethics or proportionalism. But who can really make a judgment beyond the consequences of the present moment? Won't a new ruling class, then, take hold of the keys to human existence and become the managers of mankind? When dealing with a calculus of consequences, the inviolability of human dignity no longer exists, because nothing is good or bad in itself any more. The problem of moral values is back on the table today, and it is an item of great urgency. Faith in the Logos, the Word who is in the beginning, understands moral values as *responsibility*, as a response to the Word, and thus gives them their intelligibility as well as their essential orientation. Connected with this also is the task of searching for a common understanding of responsibility, together with all honest, rational inquiry and with the great religious traditions. In this endeavor there is not only the intrinsic proximity of the three great monotheistic religions, but also significant lines of convergence with the other strand of Asian religiosity we encounter in Confucianism and Taoism.

If it is true that the term Logos — the Word in the beginning, creative reason, and love — is decisive for the Christian image of God, and if the concept of Logos simultaneously forms the core of Christology, of faith in Christ, then the indivisibility of faith in God and faith in his incarnate Son Jesus Christ is only confirmed once more. We will not understand Jesus any better or come any closer to him, if we bracket off faith in his divinity. The fear that belief in his divinity might alienate him from us is widespread today. It is not only for the sake of the other religions that some would like to de-emphasize this faith as much as possible. It is first and foremost a question of our own Western fears. All of this seems incompatible with our modern worldview. It must just be a question of mythological interpretations, which were then transformed by the Greek mentality into metaphysics. But when we separate Christ and God, behind this effort there is also a doubt as to whether God is at all capable of being so close to us, whether he is allowed to bow down so low. The fact that we don't want this appears to be humility. But Romano Guardini correctly pointed out that the higher form of humility consists in allowing God to do precisely what appears to us to be unfitting, and to bow down to what he does, not to what we contrive about him and for him. A notion of God's remoteness from the world is behind our apparently humble realism, and therefore a loss of God's presence is also connected with it. If God is not in Christ, then he retreats into an immeasurable distance, and if God is no longer a God-with-us, then he is plainly an absent God and thus no God at all: a god who cannot work is not God. As for the fear that Jesus moves us too far away if we believe in his Divine Sonship, precisely the opposite is true: were he only a man, then he has retreated irrevocably into the past, and only a distant recollection can perceive him more or less clearly. But if God has truly assumed manhood and thus is at the same time true man and true God in Jesus, then he participates, as man, in the presence of God, which embraces all ages. Then, and only then, is he not just something that happened yesterday, but is present among us, our contemporary in our today. That is why I am firmly convinced that a renewal of Christology must have the courage to see Christ in all of his greatness, as he is presented by the four Gospels together in the many tensions of their unity.

If I had this *Introduction to Christianity* to write over again today, all of the experiences of the last thirty years would have to go into the text, which would then also have to include the context of interreligious discussions to a much greater degree than seemed fitting at the time. But I believe that I was not mistaken as to the fundamental approach, in that I put the question of God and the question about Christ in the very center, which then leads to a "narrative Christology" and demonstrates that the place for faith is in the Church. This basic orientation, I think, was correct. That is why I venture to place this book once more in the hands of the reader today.

QUESTIONS AND FURTHER READINGS

Questions for Discussion

1. The essay entitled *The Epistle to Diognetus* is one of the earliest works of Christian apologetics. What are some points that can be learned from it and applied to your own culture and context?

2. In following Augustine's direction, how might you demonstrate today that following the one true God will benefit the "city of man" and following false gods (and whatever that might mean in your cultural milieu) will harm this city?

3. What are some of your thoughts about how the "city of God" and the "city of man" should interact? Is their value in the "holy huddle," whereby Christian communities separate from the world (e.g., Amish, Hutterites, etc.)? What involvement should Christians have in politics, and why?

4. Should Christians be engaged in issues in the "culture wars" such as abortion, gay marriage, stem cell research, etc.? Explain and defend your views.

5. What are some ways that religious relativism is impacting Christian faith today? How would you respond to it?

6. How would you respond to someone who claims that Christianity has not been good for the world?

7. Pope Benedict XVI states that toward the end of the twentieth century much of Christian consciousness acquiesced to the belief that faith in God is a subjective matter, and he argues that this has been a problem. Do you agree? What is the problem?

8. Should Christianity be morally transformative in the lives of people? Should we be able to see moral differences between Christian communities and non-Christian communities? Do we? Why or why not?

9. What are some ways that Christians are not engaging very well with the world today? What are some ways of improving this engagement?

10. What are some ways in which Christians can engage in interreligious dialogue? Does apologetics entail the denial of all truth in other religions? Are there truths in other religions in which common ground can be built? Explain your view.

Further Readings

Harris, Sam (2004). *The End of Faith: Religion, Terror, and the Future of Reason*. New York: Norton. (One of the leading "new atheists" argues against all religion.)

Hitchens, Christopher (2007). *God Is Not Great: How Religion Poisons Everything*. New York: Twelve. (Another leading "new atheist" argues that, as the title says, religion poisons everything.)

Hitchens, Christopher, and Douglas Wilson (2008). *Is Christianity Good for the World?* Moscow, ID: Canon. (Hitchens and Wilson elaborate on some of the points raised in the essay in this section.)

Marty, Martin, with Jonathan Moore (2000). *Politics, Religion, and the Common Good: Advancing a Distinctly American Conversation about Religion's Role in Our Shared Life*. San Francisco: Jossey-Bass. (Marty argues that while religion can be dangerous, it can also contribute to the common good and is key to the well-being of a nation.)

Mittelberg, Mark (2008). *Choosing Your Faith: In a World of Spiritual Options* Carol Stream, IL: Tyndale. (In a world of spiritual options, this book presents a solid, reasonable strategy for choosing faith.)

Schmidt, Alvin J. (2004). *How Christianity Changed the World* Grand Rapids: Zondervan (A survey of the various ways whereby Christianity has impacted the world, making the world a better place and enriching our everyday living.)

Stark, Rodney (2003). *For the Glory of God: How Monotheism Led to Reformations, Science, Witch-hunts, and the End of Slavery*. Princeton, NJ: Princeton University Press. (Argues that in acting for the glory of God, people have formed modern Western culture.)

Strobel, Lee (2000). *The Case for Faith: A Journalist Investigates the Toughest Objections to Christianity*. Grand Rapids: Zondervan. (This award-winning investigative reporter turned apologist addresses the primary objections to Christianity in our world today.)

Ward, Keith (2006). *Is Religion Dangerous?* Oxford: Lion. (Argues that religion is not a force for evil but rather a powerful force for good and the best rational basis for morality.)

Willard, Dallas (2009). *Knowing Christ Today: Why We Can Trust Spiritual Knowledge*. New York: HarperCollins. (Argues that Christian thought is true knowledge; also offers a response to pluralism.)

Willard, Dallas (2006). *The Great Omission: Reclaiming Jesus's Essential Teachings on Discipleship*. New York: HarperCollins. (A must-read for Christians interested in living as disciples of Jesus in our world today.)

Scripture Index

Subject Index

Name Index

Printed in the USA
CPSIA information can be obtained
at www.ICGtesting.com
JSHW052254160624
64899JS00001B/1